Hungarian Émigrés in the
American Civil War

Hungarian Émigrés in the American Civil War

A History and Biographical Dictionary

István Kornél Vida

McFarland & Company, Inc., Publishers
Jefferson, North Carolina, and London

LIBRARY OF CONGRESS CATALOGUING-IN-PUBLICATION DATA

Vida, István Kornél, 1977–
    Hungarian émigrés in the American Civil War : a history and biographical dictionary / István Kornél Vida.
    p.   cm.
    Includes bibliographical references and index.

    ISBN 978-0-7864-6562-0
    softcover : acid free paper ∞

    1. United States — History — Civil War, 1861–1865 — Participation, Hungarian. 2. United States — History — Civil War, 1861–1865 — Registers. 3. Political refugees — Hungary — History — 19th century. 4. Hungarians — United States — History — 19th century. 5. Hungary — Emigration and immigration — History — 19th century. I. Title
E540.H6V53 2012
973.7089'4511 — dc22   2011043491

BRITISH LIBRARY CATALOGUING DATA ARE AVAILABLE

© 2012 István Kornél Vida. All rights reserved

No part of this book may be reproduced or transmitted in any form or by any means, electronic or mechanical, including photocopying or recording, or by any information storage and retrieval system, without permission in writing from the publisher.

On the cover: *The Charge of the "Frémont Bodyguard" in Springfield, Missouri*, October 24, 1861 (in *Harper's Weekly*, Vol. 5, No. 255, November 16, 1861).

Manufactured in the United States of America

McFarland & Company, Inc., Publishers
  Box 611, Jefferson, North Carolina 28640
  www.mcfarlandpub.com

To Irene and Mickey Schubert
for their support and decade-long friendship.

Table of Contents

Acknowledgments ... ix

Preface ... 1

Introduction: Martyrs of Freedom ... 5

Part I: History

Chapter One. "To These Shores I Was Driven by Tyranny": Hungarian Emigration to the United States in the 1850s ... 15

Chapter Two. "Extra Hungariam Non Est Vita, Si Est Vita, Non Est Ita": Kossuth Émigrés in the United States ... 29

Chapter Three. "To See This Great Country United Again": Hungarians' Motivations to Enlist in the Union and Confederate Armies ... 50

Chapter Four. Taking Up Arms in the Civil War ... 63

Chapter Five. The Triumvirate: the Civil War Careers of Asboth, Stahel and Zagonyi ... 79

Chapter Six. An International Fraud: Colonel Béla Estván ... 100

Chapter Seven. "'Furreners,' Yankees, and 'Nigger Lovers'": Slavery and Hungarians in the Colored Regiments ... 110

Chapter Eight. The Aftermath: Kossuth Émigrés in the Post–Civil War Years ... 120

Part II: Biographical Dictionary ... 131

*Appendix: Misspellings and Anglicized Versions of Hungarian
    Names in American Sources*   211

Notes   213

Bibliography   238

Index   253

Acknowledgments

This book is the result of continuing research over nearly ten years and this means that I owe my thanks to a lot of people without whom I would have never been able to accomplish this task.

I am indebted to Tibor Glant, head of the North American Department at IEAS at the University of Debrecen, who taught me first the history of the United States, and supervised my work with the conference paper. He not only offered me a full-time position at his department, but he has helped me both with useful material and encouragement. Similarly to him, I am grateful for the help of Csaba Lévai, whose classes were the first in-depth analyses I encountered as an undergrad, and who supervised all my work since then, including my dissertation. I am indebted for his insightful comments and grasp of the subject, and, also, for inviting me to the wonderful community of Cliohres.net. My colleagues also helped me a lot, many of them not even knowingly, by their devotion to their fields of study. My thanks go to the associates of the Institute Office for taking much of the burden of administrative matters off me when I badly needed time, and arranging the most suitable schedule of classes for me, so that — in the complete lack of sabbaticals — I could work on my dissertation.

I could not be more indebted to some institutions and foundations for their generosity in financing my research — without them I simply would not have been able to accomplish this task. The Fulbright Commission provided me with a six-month research grant at the University of Maryland, College Park, which made it possible to do the bulk of archival research. I am greatly indebted to Professor Leslie Rowland at Maryland for her academic supervision during my stay there in 2003–2004. In 2006, I was awarded a research grant by the European Association for American Studies which enabled me to finish the investigation of major primary sources accessible in the United States. The John F. Kennedy Institute of the Freie Universität in Berlin, Germany, awarded me a one-month research grant two times (2002, 2006), which is a great privilege indeed. I am grateful for all their generous support. Some research concerning the Forty-Eighters in the United States was carried out as part of my two-year postdoctoral fellowship: my heartfelt thanks go to the Alexander von Humboldt Foundation for the generous support as well as the Department of History of the John F. Kennedy Institute of the Freie Universität for their hospitality. I am particularly indebted to my supervisor, Prof. Andreas Etges, and Catya de Laczkovich for making my research stay in Berlin as smooth and fruitful as possible.

Many individuals helped me through this long academic journey in one way or another. I owe heartfelt thanks to Irene and Mickey Schubert, who have shown so many signs of friendship and generosity that it would be hard to mention all. Mickey not only sent me about a dozen books which were otherwise not available and shared his knowledge of history as well as of the historian's profession with me, but offered to read my manuscript and comment on it. Furthermore, they provided hospitality, kept me fed and entertained, and even provided my one and only bicycle in the United States. For all this I am indebted, but especially for what I consider most important: they represent everything that I adore in America, and I am able to overlook many of its deficiencies, because I know that there are such people living there as Irene and Mickey.

I could not be more indebted to Stephen Beszedits, who has been studying the Hungarians' involvement in the American Civil War for decades, and who taught me a great deal about academic humility and precision. Although no historian by formal education, he has achieved much more than all professionals in the field, and through our decade-long correspondence I learned a lot. He was generous enough to share not only his insights, but many results of his research as well. I hope that my work will raise so many questions in him that he will finally find the time and incentive to write his own interpretation of the subject.

I also wish to express thanks to Murry Nelson, professor of education and American studies at Pennsylvania State University, for offering to read my typescript and for his insightful comments and suggestions for improvement. I learned a lot from him during his one-year stay at the University of Debrecen as a Fulbright visiting lecturer and Országh chair.

Of course, without the help of a multitude of librarians and archivists, I could not have written this book. I owe thanks to the associates of the following institutions: the Library of the University of Debrecen; the National Archives in Budapest; Mária Kórász, affiliated with the Vasváry Collection at Somogyi Library in Szeged, Hungary; the National Archives and the Library of Congress in Washington, D.C.; the McKeldin Library of the University of Maryland at College Park, MD; the numerous libraries of Indiana University at Bloomington, IN; the archival collection of the Chicago Historical Society; and the library of the John F. Kennedy Institute of the Freie Universität in Berlin, Germany.

I wish to express my gratitude to some individuals as well. Catherine Catalfamo was kind enough to shed light on several aspects of the regimental history of the Garibaldi Guard. Mr. Roy Gustrowski provided crucial bits and pieces of information on the life and career of Joseph Vandor. I am also indebted to Janet Kozlay for setting a wonderful example of academic zeal and devotion, proving that genealogy can indeed be of great help for historians. She let me participate in the translation and transcription of the German and Hungarian letters of her ancestor, Hungarian Civil War participant Eugene Kozlay. She also shared with me documents which enabled me to illustrate some points I intended to make in my dissertation. I am indebted to Dr. William A. Dobak, from the U.S. Army Center of Military History, who found the time to read my chapter on Hungarians in the colored regiments and commented on it. For his assistance in the exhausting processing of the census data I am indebted to István Rózsa, who happens to be my best friend, too.

This work would not have been possible without the love and support of my family. Both my grandmothers kept nagging me to continue with my work, encouragement I frankly needed sometimes. I owe thanks to Dr. György Póta for designing a map for this book, and for not driving me away whenever I needed assistance with computer-related issues or just insightful advice. And last, but by far not the least, my heartfelt thanks go to my wife, Bori, who put up with my long hours in front of the computer, read the manuscript and had sharp eyes for incoherence. Without her love my life would not be complete.

Preface

This book is the result of a research project I started as an undergraduate student. In the past 10 years, its various forms went through several stages (master of arts thesis, Hungarian National Students' Conference competition paper, doctoral dissertation), each taking it to a higher level of complexity in order to contribute to the insufficient and out-of-date literature of the field. So far three book-length studies of the Hungarian involvement in the American Civil War have been published: Eugene Pivány's *Hungarians in the American Civil War* (1913), Edmund Vasváry's *Lincoln's Hungarian Heroes* (1939) and Tivadar Ács's *Magyarok az észak-amerikai polgárháborúban, 1861–65* (*Hungarians in the American Civil War*) (1964). All three are riddled with errors, obviously out of date, and lack correct referencing, which makes them suspect in the eyes of anyone looking for scholarly discussions of the subject. What is more, all three authors were inclined towards myth- and hero-making, by no means a rarity in works written about the contributions of ethnic groups *by* ethnic authors, yet hardly compatible with scholarly history writing. The most serious mistake they committed, however, was that they had taken this short episode of the Hungarian refugees' lives out of the context of antebellum immigration to America, ignoring most of their experience as immigrants who had carried their heavy "cultural baggage" with them all the way from Hungary.[1]

Surprisingly enough, not a single comprehensive monograph has been published on the so-called Kossuth emigration (the term used in this volume as an umbrella term for Hungarian refugees who left their fatherland following the failed revolution and war of independence in 1848–49) on either side of the Atlantic. The existing literature on this subject consists of several primary source-collections, diaries, autobiographies, and memoirs (the majority are available in Hungarian only), which obviously did not venture to do systematic analysis. This necessitated that, in the process of archival research in the United States, Hungary as well as Germany, I venture into new fields of study that no Hungarian historian had yet attempted to do concerning this specific historical phenomenon: immigration history, historical geography, diaspora and community studies, and genealogy, among many others.

Due to the amateurish mythologizing efforts of the Hungarian-American authors of previous works and the general lack of authoritative scholarship on Hungarian forty-eighters in general, I often had to start from scratch. Throughout my work, I laid special emphasis on the utilization of the results of modern Civil War studies, military history, migration and ethnic studies, and historical memory. The use of these sources represents perhaps the most significant contribution of this work to the specific study of Hungarian-American links and contacts, as well as to the often ignored subject of the involvement of foreigners in the Civil War.

This book fills a conspicuous gap in the Civil War literature which treated the foreigners' participation in the conflict as a stepchild for long decades. Of course, among the most important authors, Ella Lonn has to be mentioned, whose pioneering *Foreigners in the Confederacy* (1940) and *Foreigners in the Union Army and Navy* (1951) are still valuable sources of information. Unfortunately, but not surprisingly, Lonn's works contain many inaccuracies concerning Hungarians, mainly due to her reliance on the works of the earlier-mentioned Hungarian-American authors, particularly Vasváry. Other influential works of comprehensive nature are William Burton's *Melting Pot Soldiers: The Union's Ethnic Regiments* (1998) as well as Dean B. Mahin's *The Blessed Place of Freedom: Europeans in Civil War America* (2002). Although it is more specific, I was influenced greatly by the approach Martin W. Öfele used in his *German-Speaking Officers in the U.S. Colored Troops* (2004), one of the most excellent works in the field. I was particularly reassured by his observation that "the Hungarians' participation in the American Civil War has so far received only scarce attention in historical literature," and his emphasis on the need for a work of academic quality.[2]

In my book the Kossuth emigration is placed within the wider context of the Old Immigration in general, and that of the émigrés of the European revolutionary wave of 1848–1849 in particular. Low as their numbers were, compared to, for instance, the German or the Irish, Kossuth and his followers were in the forefront of attention of the American public in 1850 and 1851 and by today's standards Kossuth was a celebrity of the day. He decided not to settle in America, unlike Frederick Hecker and Carl Schurz, the iconic Forty-Eighters from Germany, and the book discusses how and why many of his followers selected the United States as their adopted country, offering the first quantitative and qualitative analysis of this wave of Hungarian emigration.

In the focus of this analysis is the participation of Hungarian-born soldiers in the American Civil War. I deemed it essential to point out that Hungarians had volunteered both in the Union and Confederate armies, although this was almost entirely ignored in all earlier works (Edmund Vasváry even gave the title *Lincoln's Hungarian Heroes* to his book, suggesting that no soldiers of Hungarian origin wore the gray uniform of the Confederacy). My primary aim was, learning from the mistakes of my predecessors, to avoid the pitfalls of ethnic history writing and present the story of the Hungarian emigrants by offering an objective picture of the role they played in the Civil War, void of biases and myth-making tendencies. Taking a measure of the Civil War careers of the most celebrated Hungarian-born officers creates an excellent opportunity to investigate the hero-making mechanisms of the Hungarian-American authors, which definitely corresponds to the similar tendencies of historians of other ethnicities.

In contrast to the previous discussions of the topic, I considered the Civil War service as inseparable from the overall immigrant experience, therefore, I laid special emphasis on studying the post–Civil War careers of the Hungarian soldiers seeking the answer to the question whether or not their — and any other foreigners'— military service meant a leap forward in the process of integration into American society and assimilation.

The second part of the book offers a comprehensive biographical list of Hungarian-born Civil War participants, a long-needed contribution to Civil War genealogy, where extensive referencing makes it possible to identify and trace back the various stages of the immigrants' "journey" in Hungary, the Ottoman Empire, Britain, and the United States. As the overwhelming majority of the Hungarians served as officers, their personal stories do intertwine with those of their regiments, so I hope that genealogists as well as historians studying specific military units will find this book useful.

Hungarian names are more often than not hopelessly misspelled in American sources. Due to the intended audience of this book, I decided to use the most frequent English spellings of the names; however, the Appendix provides a list of the individuals' names and their most frequent "Anglo-Saxonized" variations. As for those whose first names had no English versions mentioned in the literature, I used their Hungarian names.

For about 40 years, under the communist regime in Hungary, only a few privileged scholars were allowed to do research in the United States and many of them had no opportunity to organize their students into workgroups. Unfortunately, not even Julianna Puskás, the sole founder of Hungarian migration studies, whose *Ties That Bind, Ties That Divide* (2000) is the most Hungary can offer in the field as yet, was able to create a school of young migration historians around her and pass on her knowledge. This necessarily meant that after the "Peaceful Revolution" of 1989, the new generation of scholars often had no other option but to start from scratch. In many respects the region's migration studies are lagging three generations behind Northern Europe, Western Europe or the United States. This applies to the subject of my book: because of the inadequacies of earlier literature, it represents the beginning in modern pre–1870 Hungarian transatlantic migration studies, and it is my sincere hope that this volume will raise many questions, opening the stage for academic discussion by giving the long-needed momentum to the scholarly study of Hungarian emigration in the context of world migration patterns.[3]

Introduction: Martyrs of Freedom

Martyrs of Freedom, your sympathies blending,
Whom here I invoke from the lone Danube's shore,
'Tho vanquished the cause of my country defending,
My spirit, unconquered, soars free as before! (1850)[1]

On August 17, 1849, a middle-aged British merchant arrived at the Hungarian-Ottoman border crossing point in Orsova, a port city on the River Danube located in present-day Romania, and applied for admission into the Ottoman Empire. James Bloomfield, a beardless, short-moustached, balding man, was received with solemn hospitality by the Ottoman border patrol commander who greeted him, "I know who you are. Luck has been hard on you. Under the protection of the padisah you will now have the chance to take some rest. I welcome you in the name of Allah."

Not all foreign traveling merchants were received with such hospitality. The Ottoman commander had already heard it through the grapevine that a prominent Hungarian politician was to request admission that day, and it was not difficult for him to figure out the true identity of the man, and was in fact well aware that he greeted the disguised Hungarian ex-governor Lajos Kossuth, who was literally running for his life to escape Habsburg retaliation following the surrender of the remnants of the Hungarian armed forces to the Russian Army. When Kossuth crossed the border and bade farewell, he probably had similar feelings as actor Gábor Egressy, who wrote in his diary, "Farewell to you, Good Motherland, who gave birth to me, My ragged country, Let me kneel down in front of you one last time.... Farewell to you, my orphaned family, far away in the heart of the country, You are an inseparable part of my Soul, in the depth of my bosom I will take you with me as eternal longing and suffering."[2]

Kossuth (1802–1894), the son of a lesser nobleman, studied law and pursued legal practice until he became involved in national politics in 1832. During the next 17 years, his name would become inseparable from the history of the Hungarian Reform Age: a comprehensive set of reforms initiated partly by the nobility, the members of which gave up some of their privileges so that Hungary could pull up with Europe and the foundations of the Hungarian bourgeoisie could be laid. Settling the conditions of the serfs in bondage, the creation of the independent, modern Hungarian industry, and the birth of the national anthem symbolizing the unity of the Hungarian nation were just some of the numerous social, economic, cultural attainments signaling a new phase in the history of Hungary. Kossuth played a pivotal role in securing publicity for the reform movement. He was imprisoned by the Habsburg authorities for his activity as editor of the parliamentary gazette (*Országgyűlési Tudósítások*). While imprisoned, he studied economics and learned English. When he was released, already a national icon, he started the newspaper *Pesti Hírlap*, which discussed the most urgent political, social, and economic problems of the country, thus laying the foundations of modern journalism in Hungary.

In 1847 he was elected to the new diet, and he soon found himself in the midst of the whirlwind of the European revolutionary wave reaching Hungary in March 1848. He demanded a parliamentary government for Hungary and got involved in high politics as secretary of finance in the first responsible government of Hungary. In what historian István Deák called a "legitimate revolution," the Hungarian diet managed to codify most achievements of the revolution in March, legalizing its power and even securing the loyalty of the conservatives. This made the Hungarian revolution unique in the revolutionary wave of 1848, as these laws (collectively referred to as April Statutes) secured a legal governmental position for the liberals. The statutes promoted social transformation, secured political rights, created a modern parliamentary system, and controlled Hungary's links to the Habsburg Empire.[3]

Kossuth directed the arming of the Hungarian self-defense against the Croats and Serbs, manipulated by Vienna against the Hungarian uprising. Kossuth did an almost superhuman job rousing the people in defense of the country and created the so-called "honvéd" force, the corps of homeland defenders. Due to his growing popularity he managed to gain control of the whole government, yet proved incapable of controlling his generals, especially Artúr Görgei, who were unwilling to accept his interference with military matters, since he possessed no military training. Kossuth readily recognized the military talent of Görgei, but their conflict did cast its shadow on the second half of the Hungarian War of Independence.

In December 1848, the Hungarian government had to flee the capital, which was threatened by General Alfred von Windischgrätz and his 70,000 imperial troopers. Kossuth, took King St. Stephen's Holy Crown, the sacred emblem of Hungarian nationhood, with him to Debrecen. There he set up his headquarters and managed to give a new momentum to the Hungarian freedom fight. He re-organized the Hungarian troops, enabling his generals to carry out a series of highly successful campaigns in the spring of 1849, recapturing Buda and pushing back the Austrian forces.

On April 14, 1849, Kossuth issued the Declaration of Hungarian Independence, obviously on the model of the American Declaration of Independence of 1776. Kossuth, who drafted the document, followed both the structure and the logic of this American original, and it is not by chance that President Zachary Taylor was among the first ones receiving a copy of the Hungarian version from Kossuth in May 1849. On the very same day the Hungarian independence was declared, Lajos Kossuth was appointed governor of Hungary.[4]

It was about then that Habsburg Emperor Francis Joseph realized that Austria was incapable of putting down the Hungarian freedom struggle on its own and requested "The Gendarme of Europe," Russian Czar Nicholas I, to intervene in the conflict. He was more than willing to help, and in June 1849, 200,000 Russian troops under the command of Ivan Fyodorovich Paskevich crossed the Hungarian border. The Austrian-Russian coalition forces outnumbered Görgei's troops 2.5 to 1, sealing the fate of the Hungarian freedom fight.

After several futile attempts to convince France, Britain and the United States to intervene in support of the cause of the Hungarian independence, Kossuth handed in his resignation on August 11, 1849. He was convinced that only a military leader could save the nation, so he gave over his power to Görgei. It turned out to be too late, however. On August 13, 1849, Görgei saw no other option but to capitulate to the Russians at Világos. Kossuth never forgave him for this and held him responsible for the collapse of the Hungarian cause. He himself had to flee and that is how he wound up on the Ottoman border disguised as a British merchant.

The Austrian reprisal started immediately after the unconditional surrender of the Hungarian army. Julius Freiherr von Haynau, who was appointed governor of Hungary, ordered the execution of 13 commanders of the Hungarian army. On October 6, 1849, not only they were put to death in Arad, but Prime Minister Lajos Batthyány was executed in Pest, as well. Altogether more than 100 people were sentenced to death, and some 1,200 officers were imprisoned. Lower-ranking *honvéd*s, who were promised no reprisal, were impressed into the Imperial Army for several years. This fate awaited some 40,000 to 50,000 Hungarian soldiers.

Revenge was undoubtedly the primary motivation of the court. The Austrian Council of Ministers seriously considered asking the czar for territories in Siberia where concentration camps would be set up and 10,000 Hungarians who were considered the most dangerous would be interned. Austrian Prime Minister Felix Schwarzenberg cynically remarked that "before granting pardons they would do a little hanging," which clearly shows that the Habsburgs' goal was the physical annihilation of the Hungarian political and military elite.

There is no doubt that the same fate would have awaited Kossuth, had he not fled the country. He and hundreds of his followers found refuge in the Ottoman Empire. The news of the mass executions spread like wildfire in Europe, and the resulting public outrage impelled the British and French governments to counterbalance Austrian pressure on Turkey to extradite Kossuth and the Hungarian political refugees. The so-called Kossuth émigrés, this relatively small group of Hungarian expatriates — politicians, soldiers, followers of Kossuth — had no other option but to flee Hungary, leaving the country in the stranglehold of Habsburg retaliation and restoration. Although the freshly-acquired constitutional system, national self-determination, the unity and independence of Hungary were all lost, not everything the Forty-Eighters had fought for perished. The economic and social order of feudalism would never be restored, and under the circumstances, emigrating offered a way to continue the struggle, this time in the field of politics instead of battlefields.

For the time being, Kossuth was in "salutary isolation," into which he was forced by being the prime target of the Habsburgs' campaign of revenge. Being the guest of the padisah served his own personal safety, as frequent rumors could be heard that the court hired assassins to murder him, and, in the meanwhile, Austrian diplomats were trying everything from promises to threats to get the Ottoman Empire to surrender their desired trophy. However, the publicity of the bloody reprisals in Hungary all over Europe would have made any such decision extremely unpopular, so the padisah consistently refused referring to the usual diplomatic practice that political refugees — unlike criminals — were not extradited. Austria and Russia eventually backed down and reluctantly made do with the porte's decision that Kossuth and the Hungarian fugitives would be removed from Vidin to Shumla, and eventually interned to Kütahya in Asia Minor. Those who adopted Islam, among them József Bem, the legendary Polish general of the Hungarian War of Independence, were moved to Aleppo, in present-day Syria.

Kossuth had to spend one and a half years in Kütahya, in the "comfortable captivity of the good Turks," as he put it. He was celebrated as the champion of freedom, and his figure captured the imagination of people worldwide. Many Americans, for instance, were convinced that he had fought for the very same principles that their own revolutionary fathers had struggled for. Rev. Franklin Tefft, a Methodist Episcopal minister, suggested that Kossuth should be invited to America as the "Nation's Guest," and the popular demand found support among the legislators. In February 1851 the Congress endorsed a resolution calling upon President Millard Fillmore to obtain Kossuth's release and to transport him to America onboard a U.S. Navy vessel.

The porte consented, and on September 10, 1851, Kossuth, accompanied by his family members and some three dozen refugees, stepped out of his two-year-long isolation and boarded the USS *Mississippi*. As he was eager to make contact with both the French and British political elite as well as the public, he decided to interrupt his transatlantic voyage. He visited Marseille (although the authorities did not allow him to land in the city, the enthusiastic demonstrators rowed out in boats to greet him) and Gibraltar, where he boarded the steamer *Madrid* and traveled to Britain. He was anxious to finally break out of isolation and meet the British political elite, the general public as well as members of the Hungarian emigrant community, who had eagerly waited for this reunion for long months. He had elaborate plans regarding his visit both to Britain and the United States: "Upon my release sympathies towards Hungary steps into a new phase in which we can channel them into a practical direction. There are two destinations: England and America. In the former I hope to get money, while in the latter to start agitation built on the principle of non-intervention."[5]

Kossuth set foot on British soil in Southampton. As German fellow Forty-Eighter Carl Schurz reminisced: "His entry was like that of a national hero returning from a victorious campaign. The multitudes crowding the streets were immense. He appeared in his picturesque Hungarian garb, standing upright in his carriage, with his saber at his side, and surrounded by an equally picturesque retinue. But when he began to speak, and his voice, with its resonant and at the same time mellow sound, poured forth its harmony over the heads of throngs in classic English, deriving a peculiar charm from the soft tinge of foreign accent, then the enthusiasm of the listeners mocked all description." His listeners, as researcher Stephen Beszedits points out, "sat enraptured, almost mesmerized by the flow of words."[6]

Kossuth stayed only a month in Britain, but his tour remained indeed a memorable one. On November 24, 1851, he boarded the steamer *Humboldt* and headed for the United States with high expectations. He arrived at New York on December 4, and no foreigner had ever seen such a reception as he did, save for the French champion of freedom Marquis de La Fayette. In front of the cheering crowd of 200,000 people at the Battery in Lower Manhattan, Kossuth delivered his first speech in the United States, in which he immediately started campaigning: "If the doctrine of non-intervention is understood as you state, then the generous and efficient aid of the United States to my country's sovereign independence is gained. We will have fair play in the struggle which we will have yet to fight, and that is all which the people of Hungary want."[7]

Grand reception of Kossuth, "the Champion of Hungarian Independence," at the City Hall, New York, December 6, 1851 (courtesy Library of Congress Prints and Photographs Division).

Kossuth was the distinguished guest of a multitude of public receptions, dinners and fundraisers. He was highly successful in winning support for the cause of Hungarian freedom; the meeting in Henry Ward Beecher's Plymouth Church alone raised $12,000. Kossuth was very popular among abolitionists and foreigners, particularly German-Americans, but there were several other groups who could easily associate with him or the cause he represented. Native American chief George Copway of the Ojibwa tribe welcomed him by drawing a close parallel between the fate of Native Americans and the Hungarian nation and expressed his gratitude for Kossuth's teaching the "Anglo Saxon race the word 'liberty.'"[8]

In the following months, Kossuth started a tour during which he delivered some six hundred speeches and visited the most significant cities in the United States. What he sought to achieve can be best described as intervention for non-intervention: he tried to obtain American financial and military support in case a new freedom fight started, to make sure that the Russian troops would not get the chance to interfere this time. Concerning the Washingtonian heritage of neutrality in American foreign policy, he concluded, "The principle of neutrality does not involve the principle of indifferentism to the violation of the laws of nations, which are a common property to all nations. Indiffer-

"One of the people's saints for the calendar of liberty, 1852." Kossuth, armed with the sword of Eloquence and the shield of Truth, comes to the aid of Liberty (fallen, at left) against the three-headed monster; the heads representing the Vatican, Austria and Russia. The hero is cheered on by representatives of various nations, waving their respective flags: an American, an Italian, and a Frenchman, who carries a flag of the revolution of 1793 (courtesy Library of Congress Prints and Photographs Division).

ence to these violations is rather contrary to the principle of neutrality; as, indeed, it is a fallacy to believe that you are neutral." He, however, turned out to have misread this. Abraham Lincoln, just to mention one example, in his "Resolutions in Behalf of Hungarian Freedom" of January 9, 1852, wrote that Louis Kossuth was to be recognized as "the most worthy and distinguished representative of the cause of civil and religious liberty on the continent of Europe," but also pointed out that it was "the duty of our government to neither foment, nor assist, such revolutions in other governments," and made it clear "we may not legally or warrantably interfere abroad, to aid, so no other government may interfere abroad."

On December 31, Kossuth was invited to the White House, but only as a private citizen. Secretary of State Daniel Webster was reluctant to meet the Hungarian or attend the congressional dinner planned in his honor, as he felt that Kossuth, in his open appeal for American support, went beyond the limits of acceptable international behavior. Indeed, at the White House, Kossuth again failed to resist the temptation to make a statement in behalf of his Hungarian cause. President Fillmore responded with a mild rebuke and reminded Kossuth that the United States had no intention of getting involved in Europe's internal affairs. At the White House dinner, Kossuth did not even try to conceal his anger. At the Congress' festive dinner for Kossuth, Webster said, "We shall rejoice to see our American model upon the Lower Danube and on the mountains of Hungary," but also pointed out that the obligation to establish that model belonged solely to the Hungarian patriots.[9]

Kossuth's strategy was to avoid getting involved in domestic issues of the United States, which, however, soon made him suspect in the eyes of many. The abolitionists were disappointed with him, feeling that he let them down. In an open letter, the American Anti-Slavery Society accused him of hypocrisy for showing indifference towards the slaves' fate: "You have eyes, but see not; you have ears, but hear not — except what you suppose is in accordance with popular sentiment, and will be sure to further your own designs." William Lloyd Garrison also attacked Kossuth for refusing to openly condemn slavery as an evil institution. William Ellery Channing, the foremost Unitarian preacher, in his poem *The American Slave to Kossuth*, urged the Hungarian ex-governor:

> Strike, then, for us, with thought and prayer,
> God give thee power, most noble heart!
> Nor waste thy words on empty air,
> But, flying slave, take the slave's part![10]

Frederick Douglass, an ex-slave himself and one of the leaders of the anti-slavery movement, became a bitter enemy of Kossuth for his aloofness towards the fate of millions of slaves. He concluded, "the eloquence with which Kossuth speaks ... delight the ear, and then pass away."[11]

Kossuth also became the target of anti-foreigner sentiment. One of the leading figures of Know-Nothingism, Samuel Clagett Busey, in his *Immigration: Its Evils and Consequences* (1856) lashed out against foreigners "whose education, training, the associations of his youth have impressed upon his mind the pecularities of his race and his country," as he put it. In his book's third chapter, "Kossuth Mania," he accused Kossuth of arrogance: "For what purpose did he come? Did he come to live amongst us and to become identified with a republican government? No. Did he come to this land of constitutional liberty to share with us in the enjoyment of its privileges and blessings? No. He came with the arrogance of a conqueror, though an exile. He came not as a pupil, but as a teacher.[12]

He also blamed Kossuth, and Hungarians in general, for seeking allies among other foreigners in the United States in support of their goal to secure the military intervention of the United States in case of a coming Hungarian freedom fight. Busey also claimed that Kossuth was an ardent foe of slavery, therefore, was calling for the "destruction of American institutions."[13]

Slave owners also associated Kossuth with abolitionism and feared that he would speak up against human bondage in the United States and even instigate a slave rebellion. No wonder that he failed to win the sympathy of Dixie; except for New Orleans, none of the Southern cities invited him and the attitude towards him approached open hostility.[14]

Kossuth was deeply disappointed with his failure to achieve the major goal of his trip: diplomatic and military support for a new Hungarian freedom fight that he hoped would come in the not very distant future. His advocacy probably alienated the majority of the American public from him, which was made even worse by embezzlement charges.

On July 14, 1852, an embittered Kossuth left America for Britain aboard the liner *Africa*. On June 9, 1852, *The New York Times* summarized the essence of the Kossuth phenomenon: "We have heard the grandest of orators; our view of the National duty and destiny has been enlarged ... and the warmth of our patriotism and humanity tested by the sure gauge of a practical appeal." The author bade farewell by naming him the "Epaminondas, the last Greek of European annals."[15]

Most accounts of this early chapter of Hungarian-American historical links finish the discussion at this point, more or less ignoring the fact that between the end of 1849 and Kossuth's visit to America, several thousand political refugees, usually referred to as Kossuth émigrés, arrived in the United States, forming the first major influx of immigrants from Hungary. Despite its importance in creating the first Hungarian diaspora overseas, this influx was dwarfed numerically both by the millions of Old Immigrants arriving in the antebellum era and the approximately 700,000 "new immigrants" from Hungary who arrived between the 1870s and World War One, lured to America by the promise of financial security and pushed away from their homeland by land shortages and the inability to provide for their families.

Part I

History

CHAPTER ONE

"To These Shores I Was Driven by Tyranny": Hungarian Emigration to the United States in the 1850s

The decade between 1845 and 1855 saw a spectacular increase in immigration in the United States. The approximately three million immigrants who entered the country represented one half of those who sought refuge or a better life in the United States between the 1810s and the Civil War. The majority of them were pushed away from Europe by economic hardships, such as land shortages, labor surpluses, and the potato blight in Ireland, but after the revolutions of 1848 and 1849 politically motivated immigration became considerable for the first time. In the history of Hungarian migration to the United States, the "Kossuth emigration," which started after the defeat of the Hungarian War of Independence against the Habsburg rule and peaked around Lajos Kossuth's trip to America in 1851–1852, can be considered as the first noteworthy wave. Prior to 1848, only sporadic contacts had existed between Hungary and the United States; it was more or less limited to travelers and adventurers, entrepreneurs, craftsmen and missionaries. According to the National Archives' passenger arrival lists, some fifty Hungarians visited America in the period between 1828 and 1848. This does not mean, however, that these years did not have any significance in the history of Hungarian-American links; the first accounts of America and its people reached a relatively wide audience in Hungary, which played a major role in forming public opinion about the United States and sowing the seeds of America's image as the "Land of the Free."[1]

Many Hungarian political and military leaders, having clashed with the Habsburgs in 1848–49, sought refuge from retaliation following the defeat of the cause of Hungarian freedom. In the first 2 or 3 years following 1849, Hungarian expatriates were scattered about in various countries, only to realize how awfully difficult it was for them to make a living. When the internment of the Kossuth émigrés in Turkey concluded, the overwhelming majority of them left for Britain, forming the largest Hungarian immigrant community of the time in London. However, they soon realized that there was a shortage of employment opportunities, particularly as most of them did not have command of English at all. Furthermore, they were embarrassed by the fact that the British government failed to provide them the financial support they had hoped they would be granted. That was the main reason why many of them started to contemplate leaving Albion for the New World. The British Parliament also supported this solution for the problem of Hungarian political refugees, and voted £1,000 for financing the expenses of their transatlantic voyage. But what gave a real impetus to Hungarian emigration to the United States was the visit of Lajos Kossuth himself in America, as the "Nation's Guest" between December 1851 and July 1852, and the immense enthusiasm with which Americans greeted the Hungarian "Champion of Freedom."

However, it would be a mistake to suggest that only external forces turned the Hungarians' attention towards America. Although it is true that the connections between the two countries had been limited prior to 1848, there were definitely sources upon which the Hungarian public could base a picture of the United States.

Despite the sporadic nature of the links between the two countries, the Hungarian press quite regularly published articles on various social issues in America. Special emphasis, of course, was given to the institution of slavery, which was abhorred by most of the Hungarian public, and to the situation of Native Americans. Although only a very small number of Hungarians lived in America in the period between 1810 and 1848, every now and then, first-hand accounts appeared in Hungarian journals. The ones penned not by travelers but those who actually settled down overseas went beyond a superficial analysis of certain aspects of American social relations or simply praising the high level of technological advancement as compared to Hungary, but they were able to give well-founded comparisons between what they had experienced in their homeland and how they lived in America.

Freedom is a recurrent theme in most of the accounts. Mrs. Gáspár Princz, for instance, wrote from Baltimore, Maryland, in 1818, "This is a free country, we have no king here, but a president. Everyone can do whatever they wish here in order to make a living. Nobody is nobler than the others, all of us are nobles. People don't greet each other by raising their hats — the poor is as good here as the wealthy." Her final remark makes it clear that she did not have second thoughts about staying in the United States: "Our country is a free republic."[2]

Similar ideas were expressed by ship captain Károly Gy., who said in a letter written in 1834: "Everybody is free to think, write, and speak as they wish — others might attempt to contradict, but the government does not get involved in any of these debates." He described the America as a very peaceful nation, since "even in a huge city like New York, not a single soldier is to be seen, as there is no need for them."[3]

Lőrinc Tóth, in his article entitled "The Old and The New World" published in 1837, wrote that "despite some of its imperfections, America is still promising, a Soul, an energetic Youth, as compared to the crippled institutions of the Old World." His conclusion was: "Although the Americans are only at the dawn of their existence, they understand the science of Truth and Reality way better than we do."[4]

In 1893, one of the Hungarian Civil War participants, Cornelius Fornet, recalled his knowledge of America prior to his emigration in 1849 as follows:

> Forty-four years ago there were very few who were familiar with the social and intellectual conditions of this great, distant western continent — not just in Hungary, but in Europe in general. I myself could infer to the conditions in the New World from accounts which were hard to access and were very often distorted, and from Cooper's novels. However, I knew much about the history of the glorious and successful War of Independence which brought about the founding of this giant republic.[5]

Those who had belonged to the social layer of peasantry back in Hungary could not but applaud the lack of oppression and feeling of social inferiority. All of these accounts necessarily had great influence on everyone who read them in Hungary, which was groaning under the adverse effects of her union with Austria as well as of the negative legacy of long centuries of feudalism.

Probably the most important of all the accounts of the United States in this period was Sándor Farkas Bölöni's *Journey in North America,* which appeared in 1834. Bölöni, one of the preeminent intellectuals from Transylvania, was granted permission by Vienna to travel to the United States. Moreover, his book escaped the attention of the Habsburg authorities, and he managed to publish his travelogue without censorship. His three-month stay in the United States resulted in much more than a simple travelogue. Bölöni gave a very thorough analysis of the working of American democracy, and his observations regarding the social framework were also wise. No wonder the intellectual elite of Hungary heartily welcomed his *Journey in North America.* István Széchenyi, prominent Hungarian liberal thinker and reformer of the time, wrote the following in his letter addressed to Bölöni, "How unexpressably pleasant moments I experienced by reading your book I can hardly explain. If only they had been hours and days! When I took it in hand I was not able to put it aside! I thank the Almighty for the birth of this book; its beneficial effect on our country can not be estimated." The opinion of Miklós

Wesselényi, another leading figure of the Hungarian reform movement of the 1830s-1840s, was not less enthusiastic about the book. He expressed his "scholarly envy," for Bölöni could see "the young giant of human rights and freedom" with his own eyes, while he himself was continuously denied permission by Vienna no matter how eager he was to travel to the U.S. In his opinion, the three major achievements of the American system were civic equality, the political system and the pleasant social conditions. He considers the ideas of Bölöni's books as "seeds which would soon begin to sprout and will grow into a giant tree in Hungarian soil."

Besides Bölöni's book, many read Alexis de Tocqueville's *Democracy in America*, and historian Stephen Béla Várdy is probably right when writing that the influence of Bölöni's book in Hungary was very similar to that of Tocqueville in Western Europe. These books created a strikingly attractive picture of America among Hungarians. It is no wonder, therefore, that after the defeat of the War of Independence, many opted to try their luck overseas.[6]

Another highly intriguing account was written by Ágoston Haraszthy, who visited America some ten years later than Bölöni, and spent considerably more time overseas. During his almost two-year visit, he focused more on the economic opportunities offered by America, and in this fact lies the influence of his work published in 1844, also under the title *Utazás Éjszakamerikában* (Journey in North America). What is more, Haraszthy himself left Hungary for good and settled down in America along with this family. His career was a typical series of ups and downs for an entrepreneur; he is reputed to be the father of vine culture in California; however, he was very often on the verge of bankruptcy. Even his death cannot be considered banal: he was probably killed by alligators on his own estate in Nicaragua in 1869.[7]

All these works played major roles in popularizing America and creating an image of it in Hungary as a land where individuals are not denied the freedoms of speech, religion, press, or assembly by the government, and where there is an immense variety of opportunity for everyone to get along. As the lack of these in Hungary were among the hardest of all the grievances in the Reform Age, their very existence in America made it an appealing place for many émigrés.

The first immigrants in this wave of Hungarian revolutionaries, soldiers and political refugees arrived as early as 1849, about two years prior to Kossuth's visit to America. Usually we consider László (Ladislaus) Újházy, János (John) Prágay and the above-mentioned Kornél (Cornelius) Fornet as the first Kossuth émigrés; they set foot on American soil on December 9, 1849. Nevertheless, the analysis of the passenger lists shows that they were by no means the only Hungarians winding up in the United States as early as 1849. In 1847 the official records name only two persons of Hungarian origin arriving in America, whereas in 1849 there are forty of them, which was a twentyfold increase. Until 1851, the year when Kossuth himself traveled to America, the number of Hungarian arrivals doubled each year.

Just as the attention of the Hungarian revolutionary leader turned away from the United States after 1852, the number of Hungarians immigrating to America decreased considerably, as well, and showed constant shrinking in the subsequent years with the exception of 1857, when the number of arrivals peaked again, rather unexpectedly. Although some might jump to the conclusion that this had to do with the end of the Crimean War, which could have resulted in the inflow of veterans seeking opportunities in America, when we take a closer look at the sample it becomes evident that most of the people arriving during 1857 were men taking their families with them: spouses and often 4 or 5 children. Earlier this had been rather unusual; the typical emigrant from Hungary in that period was single, male, and in his late twenties or thirties.

Immigration records indicate that by 1858 the inflow of Hungarians descended almost to the level of pre–1848 immigration and hit rock bottom in 1861. Although the Civil War years saw a fresh increase, this cannot be

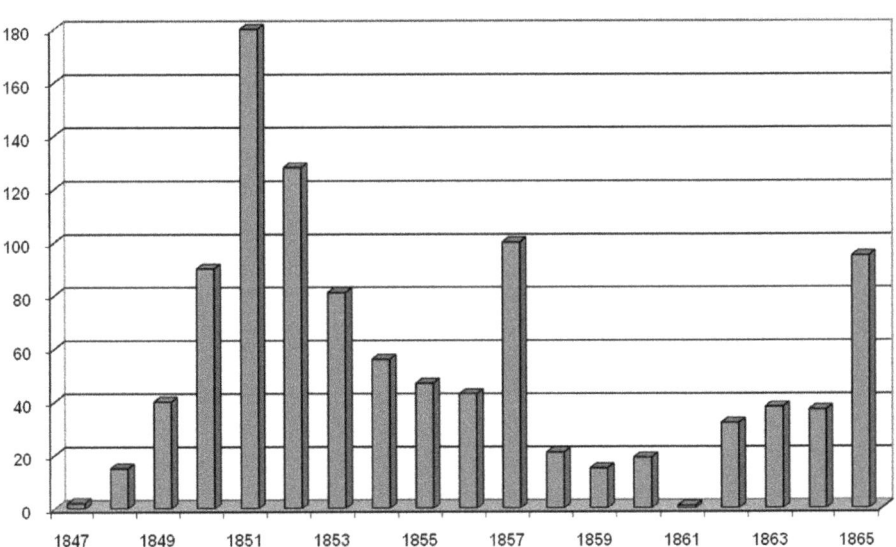

Hungarians in the Ship Passenger List (1847–1865)

Data compiled from records of the U.S. Customs Service, Record Group 36, Passenger Arrival Lists, M334, National Archives, Washington, D.C.

assigned exclusively to the conflict being a pull-factor. The composition of the immigrants in the period between 1861 and 1865 was rather heterogeneous. Still, it can be safely stated that the earlier works were wrong in claiming that, after the hopes of a new Hungarian freedom fight had come to nothing with the peace treaty of Villafranca in 1859. Several hundred disappointed soldiers had retired from service in the Hungarian Legion in Italy and had moved to the United States, many of them actually entering the service of the Union Army. In reality, as the chapter on the biographical information of Civil War participants demonstrates, hardly any Hungarians went to the United States for the purpose of performing military service during the years of the Civil War. (A notable exception is Joseph Pulitzer). Many had not reached military age, or were arriving with their families (being quite unlikely fresh volunteers), and by collating the list of immigrants with that of Civil War service records, it can be easily seen that there is basically no overlap between the two groups.

A study of the ports of departure for emigrants of Hungarian origin immediately reveals a major transition. In 1848 the German ports of Bremen and Hamburg were still the locations from which more than sixty percent of the emigrants embarked. In 1849, however, half of the passengers set off from Liverpool, Southampton, Glasgow or London, indicating that by then a considerable number of Hungarians had moved to the British Isles. In 1850 this rate was eighty percent, and the proportion of those Hungarians leaving for America from Britain did not shrink below 50 percent in the subsequent years either, although it seems that Kossuth's visit attracted basically every member of the Hungarian refugee community who contemplated emigrating to America. Starting in 1854, there was a steady shift back toward the port of Bremen, and by 1857 more than ten times as many Hungarians sailed from Germany to America as from Britain. This tendency seemed to come to a halt around the coming of the Civil War, and British ports managed to get back some of their passengers. In 1865 exactly half of the Hungarian passengers embarked in Liverpool or London.

Immigrating to the United States was a major undertaking at the time, although making preparations was not too complicated for most Hungarians. As refugees, very few of them had any belongings with them. However, purchasing their tickets was indeed an obstacle. The fare was rather high; according to estimates about one third of a laborer's annual income was required to buy passage for an average-sized family. Many Hungarians, unable to find employment in Britain, could hardly make ends meet. To save them from starvation and find a way to get rid of the unwanted refugees quickly, as well as to comply with the diplomatic pressure of Austria, the British Parliament voted to take on the cost of the voyage to America. In his letter on the transportation of Hungarians to America, Miklós Kiss reported to Kossuth that everyone received £12 from the British government: £5 for transportation, £3 to pay off their debts, £2 after embarkation, and £2 upon their arrival in America. Kiss informed the Hungarian ex-governor that the British authorities had warned them that they could not expect any further help, and were advised to leave. Altogether 76 Hungarians made use of this opportunity and immigrated to America between April 2 and August 21, 1852.[8]

The contemporary Hungarian saying went, "Those who sail, learn to pray." Indeed, we can be certain that the majority of emigrants of the age did not look back on their ship with fond memories. Although there were more and more steamers in service, the tickets for sailing ships were considerably cheaper, which is why many refugees opted for the latter. Crossing the Atlantic Ocean onboard a sailing ship lasted on average 43 days, whereas a steamship could usually make it in 12 to 14 days. No wonder that for most passengers the voyage onboard sailing ships seemed to last for eternity. What is more, they had to face a variety of hardships, including sea sickness, inadequate food, lack of privacy, and frequent illnesses. Most Hungarians had never been on an ocean-going vessel, and seasickness gave many of them a hard time. Lajos Dancs recalls a fellow Hungarian named Almády who was a real giant on land, but aboard ship went down with sea-sickness immediately. He did not even get out of bed throughout the 31 days of their voyage to New York. Dancs slyly remarked that Almády became a giant again as soon as he felt solid land under his feet.[9]

The one-and-a-half month sea voyage gave plenty of time for the passengers to linger about onboard—if the weather was calm—and puzzle over their situation and prospects. Some lamented leaving their homeland, but the great majority looked forward to catching sight of the American coastline— which would not only mean the end of their maritime ordeals, but the beginning of their new lives. Ladislaus Újházy, one of the key figures of Hungarian immigration to the United States in this period, summarized his major motivation for moving to America: "To these shores I was driven by tyranny."[10]

Positive thinking sometimes gave place to feelings of homesickness and sorrow over not knowing whether they would ever be able to return to Hungary. Emigration itself was indeed a very intense experience. Having spent a few months in America, Eugene Kozlay penned the following long poem about it around 1852:

> Let you emigrate...
> When the heart is not feeling, as it ponders upon
> this word,—when you love
> your country only when it gives you pleasure and
> glory, and not when it is
> bitter,—when the one who is leaving doesn't hear in

his soul: "stay,
stay" — when you are convinced after your calculations that you can't use
anything anymore at home, — when your secret hopes are quenched in your
heart, — when you don't love anyone anymore, or anything that you leave here, —
then, — let you emigrate.

But then, what is the home? Land, what is given freely elsewhere, — here the
green grass is grown on the blood of your ancestors, but there it is still
richer; here you find national memories at every step you take, gladness or
sorrow, glory or grief; one hill — one field of victory — one ruin, or
grave — what do you see? There are views elsewhere too, and for those who
passed away it is no matter whether someone remembers them or not.

Be cool. What is the merit of this nation, for you to love her, for you to
belong to her? Other nations also have their history, maybe greater than
ours — all of their future is more shining, all of them are richer.

And what is patriotism all about? Weakness of the soul, poetic ardour,
childish instinct. When some secret emotion is asking in you: do you see
those familiar hills, whose flowers you know by name? Isn't your memory
dreaming of the threshold of that house where you played your childhood
years, aren't you hearing those familiar sounds that are rising with the
flowers of the field, don't you see in your dreams the faces of those whom
you loved, don't you sleep quietly knowing your head is leaning on the heart
of your fatherland, don't the boastings fly in your heart when you think of
the past, doesn't it swell when you look into the future? Can you bring them
with you? The plain of mirages, the familiar dwelling place, the sweet

melody, the kind faces, the memory and hope that are bound to the life of
the nation? Banish the emotion from your heart, and make yourself believe
that the world is big enough, that the people are equal everywhere, that it
doesn't matter for humankind whether there is a Hungarian nation or not.

Let you emigrate! Let you sell your land to whoever is willing to pay the
best price, let a stranger nation come in to your place, and let stay to be
Hungarian only those who are fools, and are in love with the land, and the
poor who have to love it. Let us tell to each other that now is the time
when the nation should be divided, to spread into the east and into the
west. Let him not live there where his ancestors have died, and he die where
he was born.

Let you emigrate, who doesn't feel else than the changing of seasons, who
can look back from the border without wet eyes, who doesn't have a burden
other than his luggage, who doesn't want to turn with a bold face toward the
dark times, and who is looking for sunshine only. He is a happy man, and he
is smart if he leaves us here, we who are determined to bear all things, to
be tired always, and keep the old heart forever.[11]

Kozlay cannot be considered a typical emigrant in the sense that he was not looking backward, but was confident that emigration would eventually mean their fate turning for the better.

Most accounts of the sea voyages recalled clearly the moment of the first glimpse of American land. József Madarász wrote about his feelings at this moment: "I caught sight in a quarter-of-an-hour distance the outlines of the state of New Jersey.... We were eager to take a look at the Free Land, America with sacred reverence. I greeted the sacred shelter of the long-persecuted with the blessings of my homeland, my blood and my beloved ones."[12] Another emigrant, Salamon Neumann, gave the following advice to everyone following his footsteps: "Everyone setting foot on the soil of the United States should erase from their memories what they were, what they were accustomed to, what their ranks used to be in their homelands, because here they will get right into the midst of a whirlpool the waves of which will suffuse them at once."[13]

Based on federal immigration records, we can see that the overwhelming majority of the Kossuth emigrants landed at the port of New York City. At the end of the 1840s some arrived in Boston or New Orleans, but their proportion remained under 10 percent. Starting in 1850, data show that Hungarians almost exclusively landed in the city of New York. In this, of course, there might be some discrepancies, as the passenger lists for some harbors and for some years are rather scant, nevertheless the extant records clearly indicate the trend.

There are two clearly distinguishable periods in Hungarians' arrival in America. Starting in 1849, and ending with Kossuth's leaving for Britain disappointed and rather ignored, Hungarians enjoyed immense popularity in the United States. The American public had been following the events of the Hungarian War of Independence with elevated interest — it is not at all an exaggeration to state that this event placed Hungary on the world map for Americans. In Henry J. Raymond's *New York Times* alone nearly 1,000 articles appeared on Kossuth or his followers during 1851 and 1852. The huge demand for information about Hungary led the renowned philanthropist Charles Loring Brace to visit the country in 1851 and to summarize his impressions in a book entitled *Hungary in 1851: With an Experience of the Austrian Police* (the title refers to his not-so-pleasant experience when he was arrested by the Austrian authorities and briefly imprisoned in Nagyvárad). His book was published at the time of Kossuth's visit in America and became a bestseller right away.[14]

The American press was full of outbursts of sympathy. On November 18, 1851, the *New York Times* wrote about the Hungarian refugees: "In exile, without home — friendless, penniless, and every feeling of their sad hearts and every thought of their minds imprisoned by our unknown language, they are among us, either knowing not what to do, or else wringing from most unsuitable labors a precarious and scanty subsistence."[15]

The first refugees to arrive were received with utmost cordiality. President Zachary Taylor in his letter to Ladislaus Újházy, who was considered to be the leader of the Hungarian immigrants by both the Hungarians themselves and the Americans, wrote: "I am sure that I speak the universal sentiment of my countrymen in bidding you and your associates a cordial welcome to our soil, the natural asylum of the oppressed from every clime. We offer you protection and a free participation in the benefits of our institutions and our laws, and trust that you may find in America a second home." Hamilton Fish, governor of New York, also offered an asylum for the "unsuccessful defenders of liberty and the rights of man." The euphoria definitely peaked in December 1851, when Lajos Kossuth set foot on American soil. Two hundred thousand people awaited him at the Battery in Lower Manhattan. Kossuth's speeches were listened to with great eagerness, and he was hailed as the champion of liberty. Probably the Hungarian refugees benefited most from his popularity. They were introduced into the social life in New York City, and became the distinguished guests of countless meetings, banquets and rallies. Numerous Associations of Friends of Hungary were founded all over the country, with the exception of the Southern states, of course. The Americans also proved to be great donors: the total amount of money collected was $84,000, as indicated by Kossuth's treasurer, Pál Hajnik, in his report. People of Hungarian origin enjoyed such popularity in the United States those days that many immigrants of other nationalities actually pretended to be Hungarians. One of the finest examples was Col. Béla Estván, who we now know was neither Hungarian by birth (he was born in Vienna, his original name was Peter Heinrich) nor a colonel in the Hungarian Army, as he claimed. (See the chapter on him.) There are several references in the correspondence of Hungarian refugees to impostors pretending to be Hungarians. *The New York Times* published a number of articles on Dr. Naphegyi, who claimed to be a Hungarian physician. He was, however, exposed as a swindler by Ujházi, who revealed that he did not even speak Hungarian.[16]

As most Hungarians came to realize very quickly, American enthusiasm proved to be short lived. The Kossuth craze suddenly died down, so much so, that soon William Henry Seward complained upon the return of Kossuth in Washington, D.C., "Hungary and Kossuth have passed from the memory of all men here but myself." One of the Kossuth sympathizers wrote to him in June 1852:

> I am sad and almost discouraged when I reflect upon the fact that we cannot give solid and substantial proofs of the sympathy we profess and which many really feel.... As I told you I sent out hundreds of letters appealing to our friends to form associations and send us funds.... I have received only four answers and only one of the four contained money.... The wealthy men of the State are all conservative and opposed to your projects.... You electrified our people and from a multitude of small contributions obtained a much larger sum than I supposed to be possible.[17]

Very similar news reached Kossuth from Pittsburgh; a Mrs. Eliot lamented to Kossuth that "she was not willing to believe [the interest in the Hungarian cause] has all vanished as the distance between [him] and this community has increased."[18]

Kossuth left the United States soon afterward, so the real losers as American interest diminished were the subsequent waves of emigrants from Hungary. Lajos Dancs, who arrived some two years after the very first emigrants under the leadership of Újházy, summarized his group's reception in New York City:

> We arrived at the Promised Land. No one was waiting for us, we were not received with such an ovation as Újházy and those who had capitulated at Komárom were, and who were welcomed so enthusiastically. They were even granted land by Congress in the state of Iowa, where they founded the city of New Buda.... Hardly two years elapsed since the arrival of Újházy, but this time was enough for the Americans to completely forget everything what had happened in Hungary. No one asked who we were, where we were heading for and how we were to make a living. We had to take care of everything by ourselves.[19]

Sándor Lukács, who made a brief, 10-day-long trip to New York City in 1850, came to the very same conclusion. In his letter published in the Hungarian daily *Pesti Napló,* he pointed out, "It is typical of the American people that they are very enthusiastic about every novelty, they gaze at it, but when they are finished watching ... they just throw it away just like used clothing."[20]

By the time Kossuth left the United States several hundred Hungarians had arrived. Although their original intention had been to use the hospitality of the American people and prepare for a new freedom fight in Hungary, they soon realized that no opportunity seemed available. They had no other option but to settle down and get along in the United States. The so-called Kossuth emigration lost its political nature with lightning speed, as several of its members were often forced to do even most menial jobs to make ends meet. How the majority of Hungarians living in America experienced the period which started in 1852 and lasted up to the beginning of the Civil War was probably best described by József Majthényi in a letter written to his wife, "If a man emigrates to America ... all he needs are strong hands and the will to work."[21]

CHAPTER TWO

"Extra Hungariam Non Est Vita, Si Est Vita, Non Est Ita"[1]: Kossuth Émigrés in the United States

For most Kossuth emigrants, it became obvious very soon after their arrival that they would have to prepare for a longer stay in the United States, as the situation of Hungary was not likely to improve in the short run. Ladislaus Újházy, the key figure of this first phase of the Hungarians' inflow into the country, was convinced that the Hungarians in America should try to stick together, settle down and form a coherent community prepared for any opportunity to start a new freedom fight in Hungary. Right after his landing in America in December 1849, he wrote to Ferenc Pulszky: "My hobbyhorse theory is that all Hungarian expatriates and the remnants of our Revolution should concentrate here, because we could not organize ourselves strongly in order to be able to do something for the sake of the rebirth of our homeland elsewhere, but in this free country, where all our activities are free."[2]

At first not everyone agreed with Újházy. As long as the Americans' enthusiasm towards Kossuth and the Hungarians lasted, it was relatively easy for the refugees to make a living, in spite of the fact that very few of them spoke English. However, as soon as they had nothing much to expect from the Americans anymore, they were to learn probably the hardest lesson of all: the American work ethic.

Most of the Kossuth émigrés knew no trade, and they had no experience regarding manual labor. Without this and the knowledge of English they were soon to realize that they faced no chance whatsoever on the labor market, and, unfortunately enough, many of them were very slow to understand this. Having been politicians, intellectuals and soldiers back in Hungary, they had no qualification or expertise they could have utilized in America. Lajos Dancs, who arrived in America in the summer of 1851, recalled: "We were out to look for jobs, but when we were asked what trade we knew, they were highly surprised at us responding, 'none.' "How can you live without a business?" We replied that we were well up in making war, fencing, riding. We were almost laughed at: "What is the point in all that?" ... It was to no avail us saying that we were willing to learn anything, we were determined and had talent, they were just shaking their heads and no one would give us work."[3]

The Kossuth emigrants, although they had fought under the flag of social change in Hungary, carried along with them the social conceptions of their homeland, where the nobility was exempt from work, and manual labor was considered degrading. Francis Pulszky summarized what he had come across in America:

> But now after having seen more than half of the states I must confess I feel the greatest respect for this nation of workers.... Idleness is not the distinctive feature of gentlemanship but even if blended with a great fortune, it is always despised. *Otium cum dignitate*, this great aim of the Europeans is here entirely impossible. A rentier who lives to spend and to enjoy, not to work, would be turned out from every society, and every work is regarded as honorable. It is a new feature in mankind's history.[4]

József Majthényi had very similar impressions about this aspect of life in America. He wrote to his wife in 1851: "I have seen neither a beggar nor any poor looking person, because the flourishing industry and extensive trade provide an honest livelihood for everybody unless he prefers to remain lazy. Work is a virtue here, and by it one can acquire not only the daily bread, but even, within a few years, a little capital." The first warning newcomers usually received from those who had spent some time in America was similar to the one István Kinizsi got from Gedeon Ács: "My friend, here you have to work, otherwise you will not only be starving, but become excluded from the higher society."[5]

The next crucial, and often painful, realization was summarized by the very same Gedeon Ács: "I know no trade, I am ignorant as regards arts, I am not skillful and strong enough to do even hoeing or cutting wood. I studied Caesar's wars against the Gauls, the points of the Treaty of Utrecht, the way noble estates are inherited ... but nothing that could earn me a living, if Fate happens to cast me among foreigners." Lázár Mészáros, former secretary of war in Hungary, also pointed out: "Those who have positive professions, trades will find work everywhere, and if they are skillful, persevering and industrious enough, will do just fine and will later probably get rich. Those, however, who are cultivated, have knowledge only of literature and other arts, will starve here, unless they get some hard and difficult work."[6]

The accounts of Hungarian immigrants reveal much about their prospects regarding finding employment. Some had qualifications that made them suitable for certain professions. Alexander Asboth, who had obtained a degree as a civil engineer from the Institutum Geometricum in the Hungarian capital, was able to find employment as a civil engineer, and he even worked for the renowned landscape architect Fredick Law Olmsted. Similarly, John Fiala had been a civil engineer in Hungary and had no problem getting a job as a topographer. Anton Gerster, another Hungarian civil engineer, was a colleague of John Augustus Roebling, the foremost suspension bridge builder of the time. There were several Hungarians with medical degrees and they without exception managed to start their practices in the United States, as well.

The overwhelming majority of the Hungarians were not this lucky. Those who had no marketable qualifications soon found themselves looking for jobs among the unskilled or semi-skilled workforce. In New York City they could rely on large manufacturing plants hiring cheap immigrant labor; particularly the factory system in the skyrocketing clothing industry provided employment for many who could bear the dull routine for long hours at low wages. The Hungarians soon found themselves in rivalry with other immigrant groups, especially with the Irish, who were "envious of others, rude, hated laborers of any other nationality and could not become reconciled until they crowded them out," as Károly László put it.[7]

The rather fragmented federal census records of 1850 reveal occupations of only 245 out of the 452 Hungarians living in the United States. About one third of the Hungarians worked as skilled craftsmen, particularly in the garment industry, and as metal or construction workers. There were also numerous Hungarians with low-skilled employment such as cigar makers and painters. This seems to prove that in this early stage in the Hungarian emigration toward the United States, the expatriates mostly made use of their qualification and job experience from their homeland. None of them worked as skilled workers in the fast-growing industrial sector, in which Hungary lagged far behind America. Hungarians had no experience as machinists, steamboatmen, or mechanics.

The second largest group was white-collar workers. The most represented occupations in this category were merchants and clerks. As far as the first groups were concerned, it is quite likely that the majority of them had come to the United States prior to 1848, as obviously a longer time was required to build up their business connections. For the latter group, English proficiency was a precondition of being hired.

Eighteen percent of the Hungarians whose professions are indicated in the population records worked in agriculture as either farmers or agricultural laborers. Every tenth Hungarian living in the United States held a professional position, such as doctor, civil engineer, clergyman, or lawyer. In contrast, relatively few Hungarians found employment in the service industry and

Professions of Hungarian (1850)

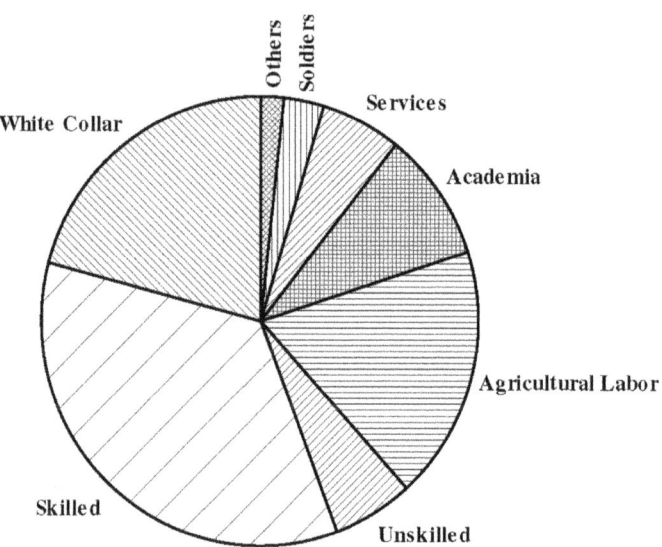

Statistical data compiled from records of the Bureau of the Census, Record Group 29, Census of 1850 M432, National Archives, Washington, D.C.

worked as salesmen, barbers, and confectioners. The fact that there were two who indicated their professions as gentleman or nobleman reflected the persistence of Hungarian social views in the American setting.

Altogether, we do not know the professions of 45 percent of the Hungarians either because they were not indicated in the census or because these people did not have employment. The New York state census of 1855 gives some idea of Hungarian unemployment (and of Bohemian, as they were not separately indicated in the records) living in New York City. Out of the total of 331 residents, only 85 (26 percent) were gainfully employed, which was considerably lower than the proportion of the foreign-born with employment in general (43 percent). As compared to employment statistics derived from the federal census records of 1850, it becomes apparent right away that white collar jobs as well as skilled industrial jobs were fields in which Hungarians found employment in higher proportions (32.4 percent and 41 percent respectively, compared to 20 and 33 percent, respectively).[8]

The shockingly high rate of unemployment among Hungarians living in New York explains why so many of the Kossuth emigrants moved to the West seeking new opportunities. Therefore, at this point it definitely makes sense to take a look at the regional distribution of Hungarians in the 1850s, mainly through the federal censuses of 1850 and 1860.

In 1850, 452 people of Hungarian origin lived in the United States. Almost half (206) of them chose to settle down in the Mid-Atlantic states, with the overwhelming majority living in New York City (180). New England did not prove to be so receptive towards immigrants; only one out of ten Hungarians lived in these states. Although an approximately equal number of Hungarian refugees settled down in the Southern and Midwestern states (81–80), the latter states showed a considerably higher level of concentration. In the South, New Orleans, Louisiana, was the single center of immigration for Hungarians, whereas the Midwestern states appear to have been more balanced. Comparatively few Hungarians got as far as the Western coast, and most of them were attracted to California by the Gold Rush. For instance, József Majthényi wrote his wife on August 4, 1850: "It is my utmost intention to travel to California and there get down to gold digging, and I intend to do it until I can acquire such a fortune which can found a basis for your common future."[9]

Throughout the decade between the censuses of 1850 and 1860, a major transformation took place in the geographical distribution of Hungarians living in the United States. New York City still remained the "gateway to America" for most of them, but the proportion of those who actually settled down in the city decreased from 40 percent to only 22.7 percent. (The total number of the Hungarian-born population in the United States in 1860 was 2,710.) The very same tendency occurred in the Mid-Atlantic states in general, and New England: in the case of the former, the decrease was only 8 percent (from 45 to 37 percent), but the proportion of the Hungarians choosing any of the New England states shrank to less than half of the level of 1850 (from 10.3 to 4.5 percent). A considerable fall took place in the representation of Southern states as a place to settle down (from 17 percent to 10). As opposed to the apparent decrease in the proportion of Hungarian-born inhabitants, the Hungarian population of the Midwestern states, particularly Illinois, Iowa, Missouri and Ohio, skyrocketed in this period. In 1850 less than 20 percent of the Hungarians tried their luck in the Midwest, but by 1860 more than 41 percent lived there. This more than twofold increase well indicates a tangible change in how the Hungarians saw their opportunities and prospects in America.

As already noted, Kossuth émigrés experienced hard times in New York and the big cities of the East Coast. Without the command of English and marketable qualifications or trades, the fading away of Americans' enthusiasm towards them and the cause of Hungary's freedom seemed frightening and pushed many of them to the verge of poverty.

There were two main responses to this challenge. Firstly, some individuals tried to adapt their talents to the American environment and make a living one way or another. One of the very first of these attempts was the formation of a singing group called *Magyar Dalárda* (Hungarian Vocalists).

The group was founded on August 17, 1851, by 11 members, none of them trained singers. Lajos Dancs, a member, quite straightforwardly stated in his book that their sole purpose was to earn enough to make a living, and they did not give too much thought to popularizing Hungarian culture overseas. Their very first performance at Castle Garden proved to be the last one as well, and it was such a huge failure that, according to Dancs, "they were glad they were not pummeled." The group soon dissolved and the members were out looking for manual labor. There were other attempts to start enterprises and earn an independent living. János Kalapsza founded a riding school at No. 103 13th Street in South Boston (American Horse Care of Captain J. N. Kalapsza), where fellow Hungarian Charles Zagonyi was employed as assistant instructor and István Kinizsi as a riding master. The institution was opened on October 1, 1852, and enjoyed relative success during the subsequent years, as it was supported by the elite of Boston, some of them still enthusiastic supporters of Kossuth.[10] Former hussar captain Lajos Török founded a pub named *A Három Magyarhoz* (To the Three Hungarians), which did not particularly flourish, yet served as an important meeting place for the Hungarian expatriates in New York. Lajos Kossuth got involved in creating employment for several fellow Hungarians when he instructed Alexander Asboth to organize a belt factory in Weaverton, New York, and Gustav Wagner to establish an ammunition factory in Morningville, although his primary aim was to produce weapons and military equipment for the purposes of a future freedom fight in Hungary by making use of the sums flowing in from the Americans' donations. Most of these enterprises proved to be short lived and soon many of the Hungarians started to have doubts about staying in New York. This was the time when the Kossuth emigration lost its political nature, and soon became scattered all over the country.

Bertalan Szemere, former Hungarian prime minister, described the miserable condition of the Hungarian community as follows: "The refugees don't formulate an association, there is no organizing, no mutual responsibilities, no political directions. The Hungarian émigrés were scattered about, and there was nobody who would have taken care of saving the banner or replacing the lost one. Everyone seemed to save themselves only, and nobody thought of preserving the intellectual and moral treasures, not even those who could have done so."[11]

Szemere was not entirely right in claiming that there were no Hungarian associations formed in the United States in this period. One attempt to bring the Kossuth emigrants together was the founding of the first Hungarian Protestant Church by Gedeon Ács, who became its preacher. Services were held at the side chapel of the Dutch Reformed Church in Fulton Street every Sunday morning from 10 A.M. to noon. Later he recalled what he felt about the importance of this group: "Even I felt often touched when I glanced at the small congregation, the first Hungarian congregation in America. We were expatriates without a country, and the church linked us together fraternally when we met once a week."[12]

The Hungarian preacher soon saw the congregation tailing away, shrinking along with New York's Hungarian population. He continued working, although he became most disappointed with the American lifestyle, and he is a perfect example of the unsuccessful immigrant who criticizes everything that is different from what he was used. He was not alone with his delusions, as he himself put it: "They assumed that it was easy to make a living in America, and the roast pigeon might not fly directly in their mouths, but at least it flies pretty close to them.... These dreamers ... were all bitterly disappointed.... They would not have thought that they might not be able to get an easy, yet well-paying job."[13]

More and more, stories spread among the Kossuth emigrants about fellow Hungarians starving and living in immense poverty. Ács became the major proponent of the founding of a Hungarian mutual aid society, motivated after an incident in which, as he said, "A friend of ours went down with a contagious disease and his landlord drove him away because of this. The poor Hungarian died in the street."[14]

Another possible device to bring the dispersed members of the Hungarian community together was an almost one-person enterprise. Károly Kornis, aided by Lajos Dancs and Xavér Gorszky, started a newspaper targeting specifically the Hungarian speakers living in the United States in general and in New York City in particular. The first issue of the *Magyar Száműzöttek Lapja* (*Hungarian Exiles' Newspaper*) appeared on October 15, 1853. The subscription fee was one dollar a month and they managed to collect 117 subscribers. Several Hungarians contributed to the paper, including ex-secretary of war Lázár Mészáros and General Antal Vetter. The first four-page issue was printed in 100 copies. However, they soon turned out to be short of subscribers, and the third issue came out only with a week delay, and the fourth one was only 2 pages long. Due to financial problems, the editors discontinued the paper after November 30. Altogether, the *Magyar Száműzöttek Lapja* was a noble effort, but the fact that it was an all-Hungarian paper limited the readership to the small Hungarian community, the members of which were not very well off either. What is more, unlike other ethnic papers, it failed to serve either as a mirror of immigrant life in the United States or as a vehicle for adjustment. The insufficient number of subscribers not only reflected the exodus of the Hungarians from New York, but also the lack of unity within the Hungarian community, which was not a new phenomenon among the immigrants. Mészáros wrote sarcastically about this in his letter to Sebő Vukovics, former secretary of justice: "Hungarians here [in New York] are just like over there, in London: they love each other." Therefore, we cannot but agree with historian Géza Kende, who concluded the paper "was choked to death by the lack of unity among Hungarians, by jealousy and insults."[15]

The news of the coming of the Crimean War seemed an excellent opportunity for the Hungarian community to re-activate its members again and for the entire group to re-gain its political character. On November 10, 1853, they organized a meeting in New York to mobilize Hungarians and demonstrate their readiness to protect their homeland. Soon the so-called *Amerikai Magyar Emigrációs Bizottmány* (American Hungarian Emigrational Committee) was formed to collect signatures and drum up Hungarians willing to serve in the Crimean War. However, their efforts failed to raise the interest of Hungarians, causing many to become disappointed with politics once and for all. Lázár Mészáros, who had been the chairman of the committee, allegedly said that his pistol would respond to anyone trying to get him involved in politics again.[16]

One more occasion brought the Kossuth emigrants out of their isolation. The news of the outbreak of the war between the coalition forces of France and Piedmont against Austria in 1859 was heartening for the Hungarian expatriates, as they felt that this could pave the way for a new Hungarian freedom fight as well. No wonder that many of them seemed to be eager to give up their existence in the United States and cross the Atlantic to join the already-existing Hungarian Legion in Italy. However, many of them did not have enough money to finance their trip, and both Kossuth and Alexander Asboth warned them to wait for the right opportunity. For the time being, they contented themselves with forming committees in New York and Chicago expressing their sympathies with the Italians. Julian Kuné, president of the Hungarian North Western Central Committee, summarized their major goals, "We are ready now and hereafter to support the cause of universal liberty against all enemies, and pledge ourselves to assist morally and physically the true cause of freedom wherever our services are required."[17]

Despite its increasing activity, the Hungarian-American community still lacked effective leadership, and this resulted in inadequate communication between the various Hungarian groups scattered all over the country. Hungarians bombarded the editors of the *Chicago Press and Tribune* inquiring if there indeed had been Hungarians who had already sold their properties and were preparing to return to Hungary. They also asked if there was any sign that a revolution would start soon in their homeland. In response, The *Chicago Press and Tribune* published György Klapka's proclamation written to Hungarian soldiers serving in Austrian ranks in which he called on them to desert the Imperial Army. He also urged them, "Let us form in Italy a Hungarian army, with which, after fighting on alien ground, we may return to our own country, to take part also in the war of independence, and save the honor of the Magyar nation." Klapka referred to 300 Hungarians who had already left America to join the Hungarian Legion in Italy, but no historical sources confirm the existence of these reinforcements. Lajos Kossuth warned the members of the Hungarian-American community that they should be patient and wait for the perfect moment, which was probably as discouraging for many as the lack of money to finance their crossing the Atlantic Ocean.

There were associations, such as the Central Committee of American Citizens under the influence of Shepherd Knapp, president of the Mechanics Bank in New York, which acted on behalf the Hungarians, accepting contributions to arm them and finance their voyage. It proved quite difficult, however, to rally Americans behind the Hungarian cause, particularly as the organizers had very short time to make arrangements. The French made peace rather unexpectedly, giving a final blow to all Hungarian hopes of starting over the war of independence against Austria, and sinking the Kossuth émigrés living in America back to their non-political routine almost entirely void of the prospect of ever living to see Hungary free.[18]

With the gradual loss of every hope of returning to their homeland, and at the same time, facing grave financial problems, more and more Hungarians made up their minds to leave New York and the major cities in the East Coast and venture to the Midwest or beyond. The first major group of Hungarian refugees to leave New York, led by Ladislaus Újházy, did so as early as April 1851. He failed to convince the American Congress to grant them land for a Hungarian settlement. So they set out to claim the federal lands on the frontier, which had already been surveyed. After four months of tiresome travel, they finally arrived in the Southern part of Iowa, close to the Thompson River. At that point Újházy had a wait-and-see attitude concerning the future of the Hungarian settlement: "We won't stand entirely on our feet as long as Kossuth is not here, and he either joins us, or, if he wishes to found a bigger settlement elsewhere, we can move there with him." Although Kossuth had neither the intention to join the Hungarians in New Buda nor the desire to stay in the United States, there were more and more arriving at the small settlement, which was named after the capital of Hungary.

A correspondent for *The New York Times* visited the small frontier village in the summer of 1851 and gave a description of it:

> The aspect of the country presents ridges of elevation, narrow ravines, and occasionally wide spread vallies, all covered with a rich soil, varying from one to 3 feet deep, which displays its fruitfulness in the abundant production of grass, of

fruit and flowers. The Thompson River about 50 yards in width, but too shallow for navigable purposes, winds slowly through Decatur county.... Its course is lined by a heavy body of timber, from 1 to 3 miles wide, consisting chiefly of sugarmaple, black walnut, white oak and elm.[19]

This was the place where Újházy intended to form a settlement of Hungarians, still hoping that Lajos Kossuth might join them soon. However, when he had the chance to meet Kossuth on March 9, 1852, in St. Louis, Missouri, the Hungarian ex-governor made it clear that he did not have specific plans concerning New Buda, and he considered Újházy's plan to found a Hungarian settlement out on the American frontier a serious mistake. His major argument was that they would become hopelessly isolated there with no prospect of doing anything for the cause of Hungarian freedom.

Left on their own, Kossuth's followers were indeed trying hard. In spite of the fact that the population of the village was increasing for some time, the inhabitants became doubly isolated: they hardly had any contact with the leaders of the Hungarian emigration, New Buda being some 800 miles away from Pittsburgh without any railroad connection at the time; what is more, the tiny frontier settlement mainly attracted Hungarians and Germans, so they did not have much contact with the "Jankók" (Johnies) either, as Hungarians generally nicknamed the Yankees.[20]

Most of the immigrants realized very soon that in order to get along they needed to learn a trade and to master the English language. As for the former, there were several articles published in Hungarian dailies in the second half of the 1850s warning those who were thinking about emigrating to America to have some kind of profession, otherwise they might have a hard time finding employment. In 1859, the Hungarian weekly *Vasárnapi Újság* published an article introducing two artisans of Hungarian origin who succeeded in making a career overseas. As the writer, István Cserépy, put it, "By sticking to their principle 'The enduring will pioneer all path,' they reached a position and respect all Hungarians can be proud of. They must be grateful, however, to their Good Fate for being artisans, they were the masters of a trade." The examples of carpenter Anton Gerster and saddler Mihály Mohor showed, Cserépy pointed out, that "all those who dare to sail to America without any qualification or not being used to hard work, will face a future full of hardship and misery."[21]

Concerning the professions of the Kossuth emigrants in the latter half of the 1850s, the major source at our disposal is the federal census of 1860. The higher number of people of Hungarian origin living in America and the more complete data provided by the census make it possible to assemble a clearer picture of the Hungarians' lives in the United States prior to the Civil War. Out of the 2,710 Hungarians living in the United States, based on the federal census records, the professions of 914 were indicated. On the one hand, this offers a much larger sample to work with than the census data taken a decade earlier; on the other hand, one might jump to the conclusion that this number would result in a less representative sample, as this is only 33.7 percent of the total Hungarian-born population in the United States. However, it is crucial to point out that the census of 1860 was the first one in which not only household-heads, but Hungarian spouses and children, were also listed. Of course, the great majority of those having professions were household-heads, so we must analyze the number of employees in their proportion to the total number of household-heads, which was 1,125. This finally gives us a definitely more representative sample (81.2 percent).

Statistical data from the censuses of 1850 and 1860 shows that no radical changes took place in the distribution of jobs throughout this decade. The proportion of Hungarians with white-collar work shrank by 5 percent to 15 percent, whereas the rate of skilled craftsmen basically remained unchanged (34.3 percent to 35 percent). The proportion of those with agricultural jobs increased to 23 percent, which shows that there was a major movement of Hungarians towards the frontier areas where they either claimed moderate parcels of land and were engaged in farming, or they worked for other farmers as agricultural laborers. Interestingly, the rate of those serving in the armed

Professions of Hungarians (1860)

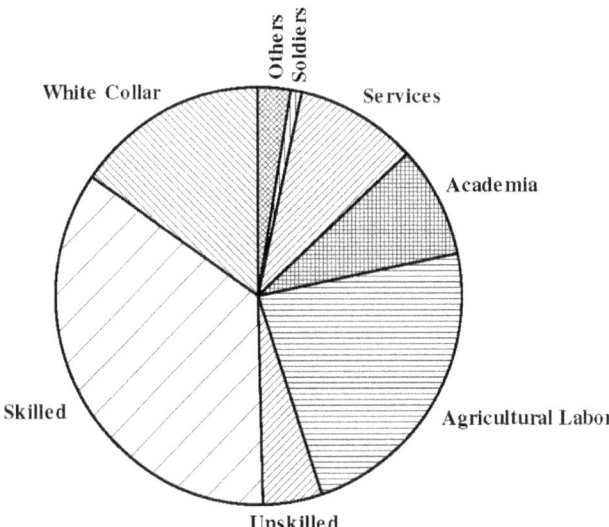

Statistical data compiled from records of the Bureau of the Census, Record Group 29, Census of 1860 M653, National Archives, Washington, D.C.

forces decreased by 3 percent, whereas the proportion of Hungarians in the services sector increased by the very same rate, which shows at least some restructuring of the occupation patterns of the urban population.

New Buda was more like a group of independent farms than a single town. All that connected these small farms was the fact that the majority of their owners were Hungarians. Still, the number of inhabitants of Hungarian origin never exceeded 30 or 40. By the time of the Census of 1860, this number had shrunk to 13. There were several reasons for this. First, the vanishing hope for its becoming a center of Hungarians in America surely turned many away from it. The hardships of frontier life also proved to be unbearable for those unaccustomed to physical labor. The geographical location of the settlement was far less promising than it had seemed at the beginning of the 1850s, as it became clear that no railroad line was going to reach it, causing many prospective settlers as well as investors to re-consider moving there. Furthermore, the climate turned out to be cooler than ideal for farming, which forced several Hungarians to leave and move farther to the south. New Buda was the brainchild of Ladislaus Újházy, but he was among the first ones to leave it. For some time, he had had second thoughts about moving to the South, as he pointed out in his letter written to Ödön Beöthy, "My present habitation is not as warm as I hoped it would be, but I cannot move further to the South, as then I would have to live in a slave state, which is against my principles." However, in March 1853, about two years after the death of his wife, he moved to Texas where he founded yet another Hungarian settlement which he named Sírmező (Grave Site), which very well reflects how desperate and bitter this old man was. He even took the coffin of his wife with him and reburied it there.[22]

By the 1870s only a handful remained at New Buda. During his travel to the United States, Pál Liptay visited there in 1870 and summarized the divergence between his expectations and what he found: "I imagined it as a great flourishing settlement, but I was mistaken—I saw flourishing farms, although spread out away from each other. The name New Buda will be kept alive by our fellow Hungarians living there, but after their time even it may disappear from the map of America, just like many other settlements did." He was right about the future of the small settlement, although it is not quite clear when the last Hungarian left it for good, but it seems safe to conclude that by the end of the 1880s, it ceased to exist.[23]

Károly Rácz-Rónay, one of the forgotten chroniclers of the Hungarian-American past, published a series of articles about the major Hungarian settlements which constitute an excellent starting point for the discussion of the geographical distribution of Kossuth émigrés in the antebellum era. He listed New Buda, along with New York, Chicago, New Orleans, Philadelphia, St.

Louis, Haraszthyfalva, Bridgeport, and Cleveland as locations where most Hungarians concentrated. Rácz-Rónay worked mostly with the papers of Hungarian immigrants, so we have to take a look at the federal census records and locate the geographical centers of Hungarians based on them.

According to the census data from 1860, New York still had the largest Hungarian community with 458 people living there. This meant a 2.5 fold increase in the decade between 1850 and 1860, but it was by no means the most considerable one. The Hungarian population of Philadelphia accrued to 129, almost six times as large as a decade earlier. In the East Coast no other significant Hungarian community remained by 1860, and — as we have seen earlier — there was a major influx of Hungarians in the Midwestern states. The most significant centers were St. Louis, Chicago and Detroit. Most of the Hungarians had left New Buda by this time, and it had given way to Davenport in Scott County as the most thriving Hungarian community in Iowa. In the South, New Orleans remained the most important center of immigrants, and basically it was the only place where Hungarians concentrated in relatively higher numbers. In the West, San Francisco had the highest Hungarian population, consisting of people lured by the Gold Rush, adventurers as well as entrepreneurs.

The analysis of the distribution of Hungarian populations in the United States confirms that although there were some centers, they were not significant (with the sole exception of New York) and they provided no real basis for the members of the Hungarian-American community to keep in touch, cooperate, and form associations capable of acting on behalf the whole group.

The overwhelming majority (2,452) of the 2,710 Hungarians then living in the United States settled in what shortly became the Union, as opposed to only 258 who lived in one of the future Confederate states.

It is not by chance that the Hungarian immigrant experience is almost entirely reconstructed based on various

Rank	City	Hungarian Population
1.	New York, NY	458
2.	Philadelphia, PA	129
3.	St. Louis, MO	82
4.	San Francisco, CA	62
5.	Chicago, IL	59
6.	New Orleans, LA	57
7.	Detroit, MI	48
8.	Davenport, IA	45
9.	Cincinnati, OH	40
10.	Cleveland, OH	38

Statistical data compiled from records of the Bureau of the Census, Record Group 29, Census of 1860 M653, National Archives, Washington, D.C.

Proportion of Women in Hungarian Passenger Arrivals in the U.S. (1850–1860)

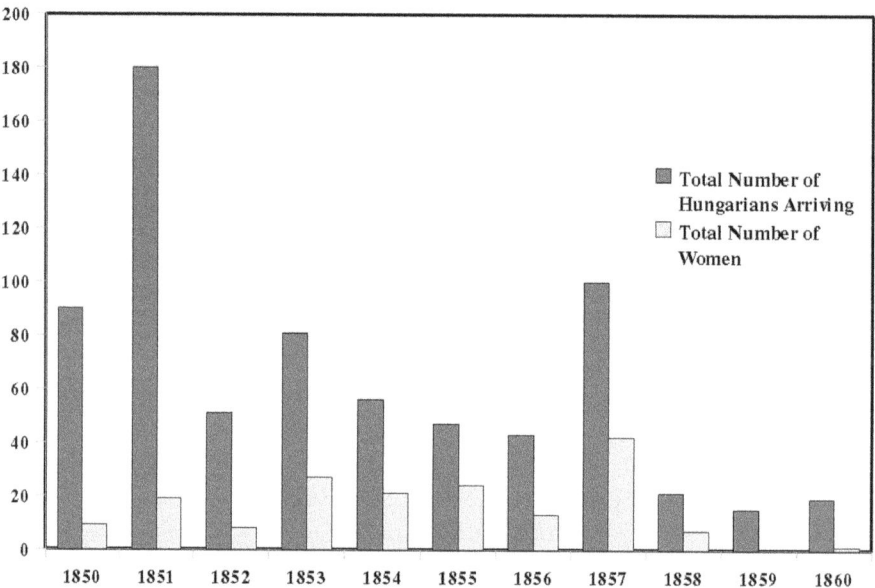

Data compiled from records of the U.S. Customs Service, Record Group 36, Passenger Arrival Lists, M334, National Archives, Washington, D.C.

sources written by males. The analysis of immigration statistics reveals that women were disproportionately underrepresented in this early Hungarian-American community. When the Census of 1850 was taken, only 5.5 percent of all the Hungarian-born household heads were female, and their proportion barely increased throughout the decade before the Civil War: in 1860, 8.5 percent of the Hungarian household heads were women. Whereas approximately 30 percent of the male household heads were married in 1850 (about one third of them had Hungarian wives), a decade later the proportion of married household heads reached 50 percent, and the rate of Hungarian spouses increased to 40 percent. József Majthényi, in a letter to his wife, wrote on December 4, 1851, from New Buda, "The young maid here gets married right away, as the several Hungarians here or on their way here, are almost exclusively bachelors," and suggested that his wife "should bring an old maid." Calculations based on the two censuses show that the total number of women of Hungarian origin in 1850 was only 45 (female household heads and wives together), that is 10 percent of the total Hungarian population in the United States, whereas their proportion slightly increased to 12.9 percent by 1860.

The fact that the rate of adults in the sample dropped from 73.9 percent in 1850 to 50.9 percent in 1860 proves that by the second half of the 1850s it was more and more typical that the Kossuth émigrés got married and were raising children, and this increase in the rate of female immigrants of Hungarian origin was reflected in the passenger arrival lists of the mid–1850s, as well.[24]

No matter how steadily the number of Hungarian women increased in the United States, their prospects of employment were very limited. Most of the women were housewives, and those who were independent household heads had a poor choice of jobs: out of the only 29 women whose jobs we have information about, 14 worked as servants, 3 as housekeepers, 3 as dressmakers, 1 as French teacher and 1 as music teacher. Furthermore, 3 of them were nuns.

Despite the hardships of life in the United States of America, leaving the country and returning to Hungary was not even an option for the Kossuth emigrants at least until 1867, when the compromise between Hungary and the Habsburgs resulted in a general amnesty to those who had taken up arms against the Habsburg monarchy in 1848–49. Therefore, the majority of the Kossuth émigrés stayed in America, and Hungarian return-migration remained negligible throughout the 1850s and the Civil War years. As far as general statistics go for this period, the rate of those who returned to their homelands was an estimated 6.6 percent, based on passenger arrival numbers via Hamburg (most of whom were Germans).[25]

With the prospect of returning to their homelands in the near future ruled out, a unique duality characterized the life of Hungarian emigrants. Having been involved in Hungary's fight for freedom only to see it fail, most of them were fervently attached to it. Their everyday life was often made miserable by homesickness; it is a recurrent topic in their correspondence, and some of them even penned poems reflecting such sentiments. Roderick Rombauer published his own verse in his autobiography:

> And I am man, though in loving heart
> My fatherland's saint [holy] shrine may higher rise,
> And for its sufferings my soul keener smart.
> The world's my home.[26]

John Xantus, who was among those returning to Hungary after the Civil War, established, "There is only one place for us in this great world: 'Home,' which may not be great, magnificent or famous, and though poor, is still the most potent magnet for its wandering sons." Ladislaus Újházy, who was frequently overcome by homesickness, concluded, "Displaced people, you are the truly awful image of unhappiness." The Hungarian exiles often quoted a popular saying in Latin at the time: "*Extra Hungariam non est vita, si est vita, non est ita.*" Gedeon Ács, yet another emigrant apparently unable to accept his situation, wrote: "He [the emigrant] is grabbed by the neck by the two old feelings you cannot get rid of: Grief and Homesickness, and he is doing his best to get them drunk."[27]

Not all members of the Kossuth emigration shared their views, though. Some seemed to appreciate what the United States offered to them; Ferenc Varga, one of the inhabitants of New Buda, formulated it this way: "I became separated from my adored homeland, but the Almighty blessed me with a family in which I found compensation." Another immigrant from Hungary, Dániel Kászonyi, had very different impressions about living in America:

> Was I so happy in that country? Was there any capital in the world in which I would not have wished to live less than in that of Hungary, Pest? I saw myself losing my entire estate there. It was Hungarians who deceived my mother, and took away all her wealth.... Or should I love the landscape and the country, because I do not know anything more beautiful? Oh, no, I had already known then England, Scotland and Italy—they are all much more beautiful than Hungary. England surpasses Hungary in all respects.[28]

Many of the Hungarians decided to apply for American citizenship. Due to the sporadic state of naturalization records, we can only rely on estimates, but it is safe to conclude that the majority of them did go through naturalization some time during the 1850s or the Civil War. Although a number of them failed to realize their individual "American Dreams," they still looked upon the United States as the place where they possessed all the freedoms for which they had been fighting in vain in their homeland. Ladislaus Újházy explained, "In America I have found the protection of a caring homeland that I have grown to love and respect, where I achieved freedom for myself among a noble kind, unlike the other side of the ocean, in Europe." A parallel between the freedom fight of Hungary and that of the Americans back in 1775–1783 was frequently drawn by Americans as well as Hungarians. Dr. A. Sidney Doane, health officer of New York port, in his speech welcoming Lajos Kossuth in New York City expressed, "The great struggle which you have begun in Hungary—the blow which you have struck for Hungarian nationality, is so like the struggle of our fathers, so like the blow they struck, ... and we have looked upon ... you, sir, and your compatriots, as sons of the same liberty." Acceptance and giving citizenship by naturalization can be seen, therefore, as a reciprocal gift and was definitely encouraged by the American government. The Congress—due to the several supporters of the Hungarians both in the House and the Senate, including future Secretary of State William H. Seward—passed a bill granting land to "the refugees who took part in the support of the struggles for liberty and independence in Hungary."[29]

Sources reveal that Hungarians who did apply for American citizenship outnumbered those who were hesitant to do so in the first half of the 1850s. In the years following the Kansas–Nebraska Act in 1854 and especially the Supreme Court's infamous Dred Scott decision in 1857, they got more and more confused and had a hard time making something out of the unraveling sectional strife in the United States. Most of them abhorred the institution of slavery and were deeply disappointed that it might be on its way to territorial expansion. Gedeon Ács wrote in his diary in the fall of 1858: "From this very day on, I could be an American citizen if I wished. How fantastic this prospect had seemed to me once, when I did not know what despicable character the people living in the Southern states have.... I could be a citizen now, if I wanted to, but I feel ashamed to do so." Still, a couple of weeks later he made the following entry, "Today I have become an American citizen.... I thought it would be better than remaining what I had been for nine years — homeless pilgrim."[30]

Naturalization was an uncomplicated process at that time. The immigrants had to declare their intention to become full members of the American society. After living in the country for five years, they were required to pledge allegiance to the Constitution of the United States of America. The text of the oath went as follows: "I hereby solemnly take the oath and declare that it is my bona-fide intention to become a citizen of the United States of America and that I am ready to denounce my allegiance to any foreign prince, potentate, state or sovereignty, especially to the Kaiser of Austria, as King of Hungary for ever...."[31]

By becoming American citizens the Hungarian refugees hoped to obtain all the rights of a free citizen they had been denied in the Austrian Empire. This definitely accounts for their leaving Hungary (which became even more oppressed by Austria after 1849) and their intention to become American citizens. Charles Loring Brace, who spent some time in Hungary in 1851 and wrote a book entitled *Hungary in 1851*, documented the attraction of American freedom to Hungarians. A Hungarian merchant in the capital told him, "We are all like just slaves! If I can only sell my stock I shall go over at once to America!" Similarly, he writes about another encounter: "The next morning ... a very old [Hungarian] man came in just to shake hands with me, and see an American before he died. 'Ah! You are happy,' said he, 'You are free! But we....'"[32]

Apparently, the United States had great appeal as far as both individual freedoms and economic opportunities were concerned. But were Hungarians indeed doing so well financially overseas in the 1850s? In order to be able to place them in the contemporary American social spectrum, we have to study carefully statistical evidence of their financial situation. Data from 1860 offer insight into the economic conditions of families in 31 states and territories, and they reveal that Hungarians had personal property worth more than the average in only 14 of the states. In California, Ohio and Tennessee, Hungarians

Personal Property of Hungarian Families (1860)

State	Personal Property (Hungarians) (USD/Family Unit)	Personal Property (General) (USD/Family Unit)
Alabama	3,814	5,763
Arkansas	204	338
California	1,224	1,156
Connecticut	864	1,593
Florida	133	411
Georgia	333	450
Illinois	1,416	740
Indiana	335	119
Iowa	806	579
Kansas	163	98
Kentucky	121	297
Louisiana	930	3,709
Maryland	183	250
Massachusetts	92	261
Michigan	532	608
Minnesota	579	427
Mississippi	No Data	642
Missouri	537	1,356
Nebraska	No Data	167
New Jersey	519	232
New York	447	187
North Carolina	3,402	2,961
Ohio	207	133
Oregon	430	308
Pennsylvania	317	174
Rhode Island	125	231
South Carolina	25	7,209
Tennessee	478	401
Texas	839	3,412
Virginia	110	368
Wisconsin	270	92

Statistical data compiled from records of the Bureau of the Census, Record Group 29, Census of 1860 M653, National Archives, Washington, D.C.

owned slightly above average personal property. In Illinois there seems to be a considerable difference between the Hungarians and the mean personal property, however, a Hungarian-born fur trader, A. Hertsack (maybe Herczeg?) alone owned property worth 80,000 dollars, which must be considered as an exception by all means. Excluding him, we can establish that Hungarians on average owned only $458, well below the average level of $740. The same applies to North Carolina, where there were only 5 family units with Hungarian-born household heads. Physician J. Schonwald from Wilmington, N.C., had personal property worth $15,000, which was some seven times as much as that of all the other families combined. This is, therefore, no basis for conclusions.

Another crucial factor in wealth accumulation was real estate ownership. This is much more difficult to determine, as the only source available is the federal censuses. These pieces of information were self-reported, similarly to occupations, and, unfortunately, they are very sporadic, which might not be surprising considering the fact that 1860 was the first time they were included in the census. The real estate property of only 210 out of the altogether 1,125 Hungarian household units is known (18.6 percent), strongly limiting our ability to generalize.

The examination of the Hungarians' territorial distribution in the United States in 1860 revealed that by then there were more and more Hungarians living in the frontier states, such as Wisconsin, Iowa, Minnesota, California, or territories like Kansas. The prospect of acquiring riches was naturally among the most important pull-factors for Hungarian as well as other immigrants, and indeed, three of the top five states with the highest average of Hungarian-owned real estate property were frontier states: Iowa, Wisconsin, and California. (What is more, in these states there is a relatively high proportion of known real estate property holdings, unlike, for instance, Alabama and Connecticut, where the real wealth of only a fragment of Hungarian household heads is known.) In three-fourths of the states, however, Hungarians owned real estate valued at less than $400. Joseph P. Ferrie's excellent study "Migration to the Frontier in Mid-Nineteenth Century America: A Re-examination of Turner's Safety Valve" pointed out that the average real property holding in the more settled states was worth $2,770, whereas on the frontier it was $508 in 1860. It is easy to see that Hungarians both on the frontier and elsewhere had below-average real estate wealth. However, their example seems to support Ferrie's conclusion that "migration to the frontier conferred benefits on those at the bottom of the ability distribution and provided an important alternative means to economic success."[33]

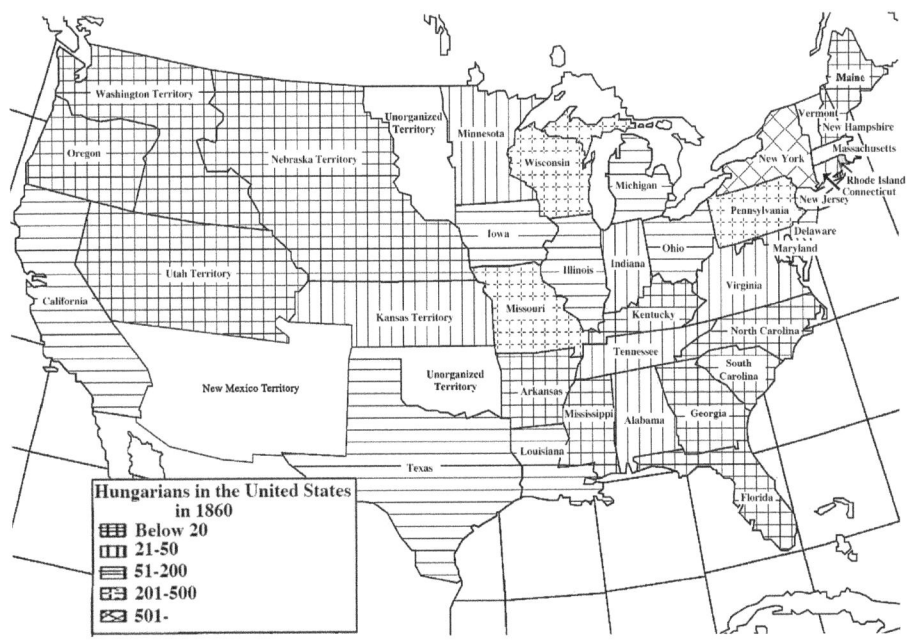

Territorial distribution of Hungarians in the United States in 1860.

Proportion of Hungarians with Real Estate Property by State (1860)

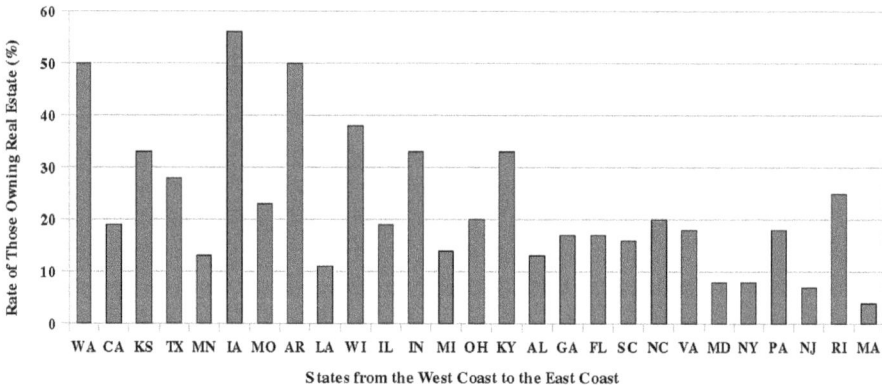

Statistical data compiled from records of the Bureau of the Census, Record Group 29, Census of 1860 M653, National Archives, Washington, D.C.

According to many of the personal accounts, a large number of Hungarians living in any of the bigger cities on the East Coast had grave financial problems, and census data reveal that in New York, for instance, hardly any of the Hungarians reported real wealth. This was definitely among the major factors which pushed Hungarian immigrants towards the frontier. Indeed, the analysis of census records confirms that the rate of Hungarian families owning real estate was considerably higher in the Midwest or even farther to the West than in any part of the Eastern Seaboard. In some of the Midwestern states (Iowa, Wisconsin) more than half of the Hungarian household units had real estate properties to report, whereas in the states of Massachusetts, New Jersey or even New York, it did not exceed 10 percent.

Although the very presence of real estate property might be a sign of relative economic advantages of the frontier over East Coast territories, the level of real wealth is an even more significant factor. From this perspective, one might conclude that Hungarians' wealth accumulation on the frontier was considerable only when compared to that of those who remained in the East Coast. Ladislaus Újházy, when he decided to leave New Buda for Texas, sold his farm for $800 in the fall of 1852. Taking this as a point of reference, we can learn from population statistics that in 34 out of 36 states and territories, the mean value of real estate owned by Hungarian families did not exceed this level.

The farther Hungarians moved to the West, the more likely they were to accumulate more wealth. A comparison of mean real wealth of Hungarians in Iowa, where the Hungarians' mean real wealth was the highest, with general state statistics, making use of data collected and published by David W. Galenson and Clayne L. Pope, brings to light a number of interesting results. It becomes apparent that Hungarian-born household heads had slightly above-the-average real wealth in Iowa ($1,147 in contrast to the mean $1,131 in Galenson's random samples in 1860). However, the same cannot be established regarding personal wealth; the mean personal wealth in the 1860 Iowa random sample was $468, whereas the Hungarians' personal wealth was lower, $359 per household head.[34]

All in all, Hungarians moved to the frontier seeking improved economic opportunities, and in total numbers they managed to accumulate wealth, as compared to their previous status. However, relative to the national level of wealth, their financial situation was below average more or less regardless of their actual place of residence. Especially those who had had to escape the retaliation of the Habsburgs back in 1849 had difficulty finding employment, as they had no marketable qualifications, since the majority of them were soldiers and knew no other trade. No wonder that when the Civil War came, several members of the Kossuth emigration proved to be more than willing to utilize their martial expertise and rallied to either the Union or, in smaller numbers, to the Confederate ranks in the fraternal war between North and South.

Mean Value of Real Estate Owned by Hungarian Families by State (1860)

State	Hungarian Household Heads	Mean Real Wealth
Iowa	24	$1,147
Wisconsin	28	964
Connecticut	2	778
Alabama	2	667
California	18	577
Texas	8	533
Rhode Island	1	500
Missouri	23	424
North Carolina	1	400
Michigan	4	369
Louisiana	4	368
Pennsylvania	18	348
Illinois	16	336
Ohio	10	330
Indiana	8	312
Kentucky	2	283
Arkansas	3	200
D.C.	1	187
New York	20	156
Maryland	1	154
New Jersey	2	134
Kansas	5	107
Minnesota	2	87
Florida	1	83
Virginia	2	73
Georgia	1	67
South Carolina	1	50
Massachusetts	1	36
Washington	1	0

Statistical data compiled from records of the Bureau of the Census, Record Group 29, Census of 1860 M653, National Archives, Washington, D.C.

CHAPTER THREE

"To See This Great Country United Again": Hungarians' Motivations to Enlist in the Union and Confederate Armies

The fact that Hungarians opted for settling down in the frontier states in great numbers did not mean that they failed to pay attention to the sectional strife between North and South that dominated American domestic politics in most of the 1850s. On the contrary, since some of the worst manifestations of the conflict were acted out for instance in Kansas, those who settled in the West might have even been more tuned to this issue than others. It can be established from the correspondence of some of the Kossuth émigrés that they had a clear conception of what was happening on the national level. In general, it is safe to conclude that the vast majority of them allied with the Republican Party, since they frowned on the very idea of the territorial expansion of slavery, which they considered to be an evil institution. Some of the Hungarians even took an active part in political rallies. Miklós (Nicholas) Perczel argued in Davenport in Iowa at the turn of 1860–1861:

> We pointed out that the Union is a constitutional law of the land, the cornerstone of the entire organization of the nation, the disturbance of which is politically unsound and should not go unpunished, because it would result not only in the dissolution of the country, but also threaten the very existence of the republican form of government since the aristocratically inclined citizens of the pro-secession states would soon seek to establish a monarchy to ensure the security of their institutions and the fruition of their grandiose plans.

He also warned that "from political as well as economic considerations the breakup of the Union would not only be harmful to the United States but fatal."[1]

Right after the election of the Republican presidential candidate, Abraham Lincoln, on November 30, 1860, Gedeon Ács devoted a long entry in his diary to popular sovereignty, perhaps the most hotly-debated contemporary issue, and he complained about the prospect of the territorial expansion of the "peculiar institution." Nevertheless, he came to the conclusion that "the above-mentioned causes will [not] prompt the cotton-growing states to secede," in which he turned out to be mistaken very soon.[2]

After the first shots had been fired at Fort Sumter and the long and bloody Civil War commenced, Hungarians responded quickly and rallied to the Union ranks in the first months of the conflict. Discussions of their motivations for doing so abound with misconceptions and errors. One of the most-frequently appearing explanations for the Hungarians' enthusiastic support of the Union cause was that they were eager to fight for the liberation of slaves, in order to do away with the anachronistic institution which they considered to be the major blemish on the American system of democracy. Hungarian-American historian Emil Lengyel, for instance, in his book *Americans from Hungary*, promoted the idea that the Kossuth émigrés volunteered in the Union Army to fight "the tyrant of slavery, and they offered their arms to strike it down." Although not as one-sidedly as Lengyel, Edmund Vasváry also suggested that "all of them joined voluntarily," as "they believed in the supreme aims of this struggle." Vasváry did not even take notice of the fact that there were Hungarians supporting the Confederate cause, and gave the title *Lincoln's Hungarian Heroes* to his 1939 book. Tivadar Ács, in the epilogue of his *Magyarok az észak-amerikai polgárháborúban*, wrote that the Hungarian soldiers "fought on a distant part of the world, and sacrificed their lives for the Grand Cause of the emancipation of slaves." However, when one takes a closer look at the possible motives of foreign soldiers in general, and Hungarians in particular, to support either the North or the South, it becomes clear that the issue was much more complex than that.[3]

Actually none of the Hungarian Civil War participants said that they had been motivated to fight for the emancipation of slaves. Compared with any of the ethnic groups' representatives, or even native-born Americans, they rarely indicated this as a major driving force to enter military service. All three of the Hungarian authors, Pivány, Vasváry and Ács, ignored the fact that in the first two years of the conflict liberation of the slaves was nowhere to be found among the official goals of the Lincoln administration.

Rather than abolition, the most important motivating force to fight for the Union was definitely the affection of the Kossuth émigrés — similarly to other Forty-Eighters — for the American model of democracy. Many of them had already become naturalized citizens of the United States by the beginning of the war, and they considered America as their adopted country. Alexander Asboth, the most prominent figure of the Kossuth emigration in the city of

New York, addressed the Hungarians living in America on the pages of the *New York Times* on May 3, 1861, as follows:

> We see with deep sorrow the glorious Republic of the United States, our adopted Country, upon the verge of dissolution, the realization of which would be a triumph for all despots and the doom of self-government.
>
> In this distracted state of the country, it behooves us Hungarians to remember that we belong to that nation which struggled gallantly, but unsuccessfully, for the same liberty, which crowned the efforts of Washington, it beheaves [sic] us to remember, that when after the disastrous termination of our national struggle, at the demand of Austria and Russia, Gov. Kossuth, our Chief, with others of us now here, were detained by the Sultan in Asia Minor, the generous intervention by the United States set us free, and the national steam-frigate *Mississippi*, under the glorious flag of Stars and Stripes, brought us safely from a gloomy prison to the free shores of America.
>
> The sympathy and assistance thus bestewed upon down-trodden Hungary and its scattered exiled sons moved me with a feeling of everlasting gratitude, and ten years of citizenship of this country, by virtue of which I have enjoyed the blessings of its institutions, render me deeply impressed with all its duties and obligations, as deeply and earnestly as if I was native of the soil.
>
> Thus actuated, I have already offered my military services to the government. Many of you have done the same, and I feel confident that you all share my sense of indebtedness to the United States, and would feel equally gratified with myself in attesting it by substantial service.
>
> You all know the value of the Union as it was, and will stand by it faithful and true, and defend it at all hazards, with that same firmness and gallantry displayed so emphatically in the defence of our native land, the rights and Constitution of Hungary. To embody these sentiments in a practical form, we Hungarians in New York and its vicinity must meet, unite and organize.[4]

Asboth called a meeting of Hungarians in New York for May 4, which was followed by another one on July 18, 1861. At the latter the possibilities of organizing an all-Hungarian regiment were discussed and those present even appointed Major Stephen Kovács as prospective colonel of the would-be regiment. Regimental surgeon Dr. Attila Kelemen and Emanuel Lulley were commissioned to find supporters to raise the necessary funds to equip the regiment. Although this particular attempt to found a Hungarian regiment came to nothing, just like all the others, soldiers of Hungarian origin were enthusiastic about joining multi-ethnic units such as the "Garibaldi Guard," the 39th New York Volunteers, or the Lincoln Riflemen, 24th Illinois Volunteer Regiment.[5]

Among the reasons for enlisting most often mentioned in the correspondence of ethnic soldiers, the preservation of the Union and maintaining "the best government on Earth" were the most prevalent, and several of the soldiers expressed that they felt it was their duty to serve their adopted country. Albert

Ruttkay, one of Lajos Kossuth's nephews, who served in the Third Colored Heavy Artillery, said the following about his motivations for volunteering, "I joined the service out of pure motives of patriotism, at a time when our country justly demanded the firm support."[6]

In this respect Hungarians were not at all different from other foreign-born soldiers. However, particular parallels can be observed between them and the German Forty-Eighters. Partly because they had fought for the very same cause in their homelands, their military qualifications, the circumstances among which they wound up in the United States of America, and their appreciation of the opportunities they came across in America, they found a common cause. Their unity was further strengthened by the fact that both ethnic groups spoke German, then the official language of occupied Hungary and familiar to those Hungarians who had served in the Imperial Army prior to 1848–49. In the United States they very often served in common regiments, so much so that Hungarians were often taken for Germans by the American public. József Madarász recalls a conversation of his in the United States with an Englishman which well illustrates contemporary misconceptions in the Anglo-Saxon countries:

> Sir, are you a foreigner?
> Yes, Sir.
> Are you German?
> No, Sir, I am Hungarian.
> Hungarian, Hungarian, but Hungarians are also Germans.
> No, Sir, Hungarians are not Germans.
> And what are Hungarians, if not Germans?
> Hungarians are totally different from Germans in their language, customs and characteristics. Magyar is Hungarian in English, whereas we call the Germans German or Dutch.
> And Sir, are the Austrians German?
> Yes, the Austrians are German.
> And isn't Hungary part of the Austrian Empire?
> Sir, Hungary is indeed governed by the Austrians despite its Constitution, it's true, still Hungary is a distinct nation, and it is not German, unlike Austria.
> But if Hungary is part of the Austrian Empire and the Austrians are German, consequently, Hungarians also must be German.[7]

Hungarian-born Major General Julius H. Stahel had very strong connections with the leading figures of the German-American community, including Carl Schurz and Franz Sigel, and this probably strengthened similar misconceptions. Even President Lincoln misspelled his name as Stahl and his lines written to Secretary of War Edwin M. Stanton suggest that Stahel's promotion was a likely gesture towards German-Americans in exchange for their supporting Lincoln at the 1860 election: "I intended proposing you ... that

Schurz and Stahl should both be Maj. Genls. They together with Sigel, are our sincere friends." It comes as no surprise, therefore, that in numerous instances the Germans enumerated very similar reasons for taking up arms. An anonymous German soldier wrote in the *Louisville Journal* on June 11, 1861, "We all left our fatherland because we desired to rid our necks of the heel of the tyrant that trampled upon our rights. The proud spirit of our race will never submit to the yoke of bondage with [which] Jeff. Davis and his followers are striving to fasten upon us." Marquis Adolphe Chambrun, a French diplomat visiting America to investigate the progress of the Civil War, found it paradoxical that "professed enemies of order and established institutions in Prussia or Austria, here they are ... readily giving their intelligence, activity, and even their blood in the service of a new country." What Chambrun failed to understand was the fact that the Forty-Eighters were not avowed enemies of constitutional law and order, but hoped to support the one which to them represented the safeguard of democratic ideals they had in vain fought for in their homelands. Their support of democracy in Europe and in America became linked to each other, and although indirectly, the failure of the revolutions in Europe in 1848–49 influenced their views and positions regarding Civil War volunteering as well.[8]

Újházy sent the following proclamation to the Hungarian soldiers serving in the Union Army on December 1, 1861, upon his leaving for Italy as consul of United States to Ancona:

> The miserable Hungarian exiles became dispersed on the entire globe, and still: we have come together here in such great numbers! One might ask: "How come?" The main reason is that whereever the bugle-call of freedom blares, Hungarians leave all of their properties behind no matter how cherished they had been to them, and they rush to the battle field where honor and valor can triumph against villainy and tyranny. You have gathered in defense of the sacred cause of freedom, helping to defend the government of this republic, which was attacked by an evil and pretentious aristocracy — such an aristocracy that not only forces other human beings to serve them, but degrades them to the level of animals.... As long as we don't get the chance to fight for our constitutional existence against the blood-sucking Austrians, let us fight here, for our adopted country. And once the day of the triumph comes, and not only the old glory of the Republic will be restored, but it will become an even shinier example for other nations to follow, we will be able to stand out with our arms toughened in fight to the battlefield where we have to take revenge for our many martyred fellow countrymen.[9]

In his diary, Col. Emeric Szabad summarized his major motivations for volunteering in the Northern Army, "I came to America to fight for the Union, the destruction of which would cause joy to none but tyrants and despots." Charles Zagonyi, another Hungarian participant of the Civil War, expressed similar sentiments to those of Asboth, Újházy and Szabad. In his testimony before the Joint Committee on the Conduct of War he declared, "I took service in the United States army only for the reason that I wanted to see this great country united again, and put down the rebellion, and not to divide it more and more. I am not a fortune hunter." However, it was not by chance that he was defending himself from insinuations suggesting that he was seeking the advancement of his own economic status, similarly to other foreign-born officers in the Civil War. In the Civil War South, there was a firm belief that the North hired foreign mercenaries who would do the fighting instead of them, and were interested in nothing else but money. For instance, Michael Egan, captain of 15th West Virginia, quotes in his recollections entitled *The Flying, Gray-Haired Yank* the common Southern sentiment at the time, that The Union "had sent 'the off-scourings' of Europe ... to invade our homes and firesides in an effort to overthrow constitutional right and rob us of our property." All this suggested that many of the foreigners were attracted to the ranks of the Union army by "the offer of 13 dollars a month and rations" which many saw as "the only chance to provide for themselves and their families," as German regional historian Michael Loeffler concluded.[10]

But was this the case with the members of the Kossuth emigration as well? Mary Chesnut in her famous diary placed the Hungarians in the category of mercenaries, "an appalling list of foreigners in the Yankee army," she wrote in October 1861, "these newspapers tell of the Hungarians, Russians, Prussians...." It was certainly true that the majority of Hungarians in the United States had problems finding employment, and their economic conditions were worse than the average in most parts of the country. This was particularly the case with the Kossuth émigrés, so it is hardly surprising that they were among the first to volunteer their services in the military. The prospect of financial advancement was definitely a factor for many of them, although it must be said that in the first phase of the war the pay was rather poor and unreliable; the large enlistment bounties were exceptional. For the Hungarians it was important that they had marketable skills as seasoned veterans who knew considerably more about warfare than the immense majority of the American volunteers. Col. Gustave Waagner, chief of artillery under General John C. Frémont, once complained about his inexperienced fellow soldiers, "It is most astonishing how ignorant they are; there is not one of these men who can trace a regular work. Of West Point I speak not, but of the people about here, and they will not learn of me — from me who know [*sic*]."

Their experience was badly needed by both the Union and the Confederate Armies in the initial phase of the conflict, which was described by historian James M. McPherson as one in which "amateurs went to war." As we will see later, Hungarians indeed served in the most urgently-needed positions which required considerable expertise such as military engineers, topographers, cavalry and artillery officers, and surgeons. Beyond the regular monthly payment, which came in handy for many of them, it must have been a great relief for them to feel that they were finally useful members of the community and they could use their skills and experience.[11]

Some allegations of mercenary motives are hard to repudiate. One of the most famous cases was General György Klapka, renowned Hungarian commander of the Hungarian War of Independence. In response to the attempts of the American consul in Torino to recruit experienced officers to join the Union Army, Klapka sent a letter to General George B. McClellan, commander of the Army of Potomac, in which he expressed his willingness to go to the United States for an unashamedly-high $100,000 bonus and $25,000 per annum salary. McClellan was even more outraged by Klapka's stated intention of becoming commander-in-chief as soon as he mastered the English language, and this incident further deepened his, and many others,' distrust in foreign soldiers.[12]

For many, however, the prospect of a higher bounty was not as attractive as the military challenge of the Civil War. Especially those who were serving in the Hungarian Legion in Italy felt that the "treacherous" peace of Villafranca in 1859 deprived them of all hope for a new freedom fight in Hungary, and many started seeking new opportunities. Although statistics show that there was no mass migration of Hungarian veterans from Italy to the United States throughout the Civil War, some did go to serve in the Union Army, among them Nicholai Dunka and Philip Figyelmessy, and several others contemplated the idea of taking their sabers overseas. Nándor Éber, former brigadier general under Garibaldi, wrote to his comrade, István Türr: "The American struggle is very interesting: hundreds of thousands of people facing each other, this is not to be seen every day." Still, eventually he gave up the idea of moving to America.[13]

Military service had a certain appeal to many young men who often volunteered seeking adventure and were convinced that the war would last for only a couple of months. Most Kossuth émigrés, on the other hand, were well aware of the real nature of war, and serving in the army was an utterly different kind of magnet for them than for the majority of inexperienced Americans. The Hungarians had been accustomed to the prestige of being a soldier either in their homeland or in Italy, and they were hoping for similar recognition in the United States. The enlistment of Eugene Kozlay, for instance, had nothing to do with the abolition of slavery, which he definitely opposed. Moreover, his involvement in the trading business in New York which had gained much of its profit from cotton prior to the Civil War led him to sympathize with the South. Nevertheless, he joined the Union Army and by the end of the conflict, he rose to the rank of brigadier general by brevet. Military service for him, and for many other Hungarian emigrants, provided an avenue for respect, in some cases even for glory. Janet Kozlay, Eugene's descendant, ardent genealogist and researcher of her family's past, attributes his enlistment to his "huge ego," and concludes, "being called a general (in fact brigadier general by brevet) must have been a huge satisfaction for him." Similarly to him, young Joseph Pulitzer also dreamed of becoming a soldier, although due to his frail health he was turned away by the Austrian Army as well as the French Foreign Legion. He could enlist in the Union cavalry just to become miserably disappointed with the military career he had anticipated to be glorious.[14]

Except for Hungarians who either joined one of the ethnic regiments with Hungarian companies or were invited to serve on the staff of General John Charles Frémont, the majority of Kossuth emigrants enlisted in local regiments, usually closest to their actual place of residence. Another major motive to do so was, therefore, maintaining not only their own freedom, but that of their neighbors and the members of the local community. (Here I do not necessarily mean physical freedom, but maintaining the existence of a free government against an expansionist South — that was how many interpreted the impact of the Kansas-Nebraska Act and the Dred Scott Decision as well as the armed conflict between North and South.) This seemed the best way for them to demonstrate their loyalty to their adopted country and also to enhance their integration and acceptance within these communities.

What is even more intriguing is why foreigners in general, and Hungarians in particular, made up their minds to support the Confederate cause with their arms. Although almost entirely ignored in the Hungarian-American historical literature, there were indeed Hungarians who not only settled down in what later became Confederate states, but joined the ranks of the Southern army, as well. Due to the small number of Hungarians serving in the Confederate army, and to the fragmented nature and insufficient number of sources, the reconstruction of their motivations is a trying endeavor.

The definitive work for information on volunteering in the Confederate army is still Ella Lonn's *Foreigners in the Confederacy*, in which she established, "Sometimes voluntary enlistments came from men so out of sympathy with the [Southern] cause that their presence in the Confederate States army can be only explained by the phrase 'drifting along with the tide.'" Lonn cites a Hungarian, Col. Béla Estván, who turned out to be neither colonel nor Hungarian, and whose real name was Peter Heinrich, as an example for this. Estván, in his *War Pictures from the South*, wrote the following about the reasons for his enlistment, "Circumstances led me to take service in the Confederate army — my long residence in the Southern States being, however, the main inducement thereto." Elsewhere he added, "It was now 13 years that I had been away from my native home and now, drawn into the whirlpool of events, I found myself, almost against my will, serving in the ranks of a foreign army, and fighting for a cause, with which neither my head nor my heart could thoroughly sympathize." However, a careful analysis of Estván's career reveals that — despite his self-styled reluctance — he wrote at least two letters to Confederate President Jefferson Davis, offering his services to him, and outlining a plan to form two foreign regiments, an infantry and a cavalry unit, from the states of Virginia, Kentucky and Tennessee. These, of course, do not suggest any reluctance to participate in the conflict, yet it would be a mistake to think that Estván was a committed supporter of the cause of the Confederacy either. In light of his entire career, one cannot but agree with historian Robert W. Frazer, who remarked that Estván really wished to serve only himself. A reviewer of Estván's book, rather maliciously, remarked, "[He] gazes on the battlefield with the calm indifference of the woman who witnessed the conflict between her husband and a bear," which is the "correct temperament of a soldier, but it is also the characteristics of a mercenary."[15]

Other Hungarians serving in the Confederate Army were not immune to charges of seeking only personal financial gains through their volunteering either. Another well-known case was that of another Hungarian, Col. Adolphus Adler, who was engineer-in-chief in the Wise Brigade, and was arrested by the Richmond authorities; the charges, however, are not quite clear. Some attributed it to the fact that he brought suspicion against himself by openly criticizing his superiors, but there were many who said that he himself was not satisfied with the opportunities offered to him, as a foreigner, in Confederate service. William Harris, who met Adler in the prison, directly questioned his commitment: "He would have turned Turk, Secesh, and Unionist alternately, in order to escape his portending doom."[16]

Although he saw no military service in the Civil War, Anthony Vallas, a Hungarian-born professor of mathematics and philosophy at Louisiana State Seminary of Learning and Military Academy, also became the target of criticism for his lack of enthusiasm for the Confederate cause. William Tecumseh Sherman, then superintendent of the institution, described him as a "foreigner who doesn't care [too much about] the Confederacy, but will follow his immediate self-interests," and referred to him as a "hypocritical foreigner who would serve the Devil for his pay."[17]

In the Confederate states there was public hostility to foreigners, which was further exacerbated by the common belief that actually it was the despised foreign mercenaries who did the bulk of fighting in the North. These sentiments appeared in legislation as well. In August 1861, the Confederate president signed an act which said, "Conferred upon every noncitizen in the military service protection during the war and the rights of a citizen, together with the right to become naturalized and entitled to all the rights of citizenship upon taking an oath to support the Constitution and indicating which one of the Confederate States he intended to become a citizen." In the winter of 1861–62, however, the Confederate Congress enacted a bill that was to bar any foreign-born person from becoming a citizen of the Confederacy. Jefferson Davis vetoed it, saying that it would impose a "legislative stigma" on aliens serving in the army and "on those of our fellow-citizens who are of foreign birth." The Confederate Conscription Act passed on April 16, 1862, ordered that "foreigners who are not citizens of the Confederate States and who shall not have acquired a domicile shall not be subject to military duty" and if enlisted "shall be discharged at the expiration of their original term of enlistment." Furthermore, General Order No. 82 issued by the Adjutant-General's Office contained the following regulations: "Foreigners not domiciled in the Confederate States are not liable to conscription.... Long residence, of itself, does not constitute domicile. A person may acquire domicile in less than one year, and he may not acquire it in twenty years.... The principal evidences of intention to remain are the declarations of the party, the exercise of rights of citizenship, marriage and the acquisition of real estate."[18]

We can be sure that both Adler and Estván volunteered to promote their own social and financial status, and it soon became obvious that promotion for the foreign-born was not easy in the Confederate Army. "Our service offers but little inducement to the soldiers of fortune, but a great deal to the men of principle," said President Davis to a visitor at Charleston. Indeed, Estván, who hardly fit in the latter category, as we will later see, soon started to search for other opportunities and left the service, which resulted in the *Richmond Examiner* writing about him, "In these war times, they [the deserters] are plentiful under the uniform of military officers. Estván, the soi-disant count, who ran to the North after playing out his calls here, was one of a particular class."[19]

Not all foreign soldiers were attracted by the hope of individual financial gains. Another major motivation was what William Watson called "sympathy with other loyal, law-abiding people who felt contempt for the federal government's failure to afford loyal Southerners aid and support." It is highly interesting that Hungarian-born Southerners — similarly to those living in the North — found parallels between the cause for which they jumped to arms in their homeland and in their adopted country: between the struggle for states' rights and Hungary's efforts to break free from the tyranny of the Habsburgs. At first this might sound farfetched; however, they were not alone in doing so. A native-born Confederate captain explained to Emeric Szabad, a Hungarian prisoner-of-war, that "he found it incomprehensible how a Hungarian could fight with the damned Yankees against the Southern people who were fighting for what Hungarians had fought for in 1848." Similarly, in 1866 the *Old Guard* referred to a not-yet-identified Hungarian surgeon who had served in the Confederate Army telling a [Southern] lady not to complain: "I know that you suffer for I have been through it before in my own country."[20]

It can also be taken for granted that many people of foreign birth enlisted so that they would not be regarded as cowards by their neighbors, and also to avoid suspicions that they might sympathize with the Union, which could very easily result in severe persecution. The renowned Irish reporter and war correspondent to *The Times* William H. Russell took note in his diary, "Persons found guilty ... of stating their belief that the Northerners will be successful are sent to prison for six months. The accused are generally foreigners." In Richmond alone more than 350 Germans were arrested without stated charges, but evidently due to the Confederate authorities' distrust of their loyalty. In Texas atrocities againts the foreigners — especially Germans — were not at all rare, as many of them were unwilling to accept conscription into the Confederate Army even if it meant risking the confiscation of their properties. Some of the Germans decided to flee to Mexico; on August 10, 1862, Col. Duff's cavalrymen found a group of some 60 Germans on the Nueces River killing and wounding about half of them. It was no wonder, consequently, that many Germans were among the first to surrender to the advancing Union troops in the South.[21]

In San Antonio, Texas, four sons of a Hungarian-born saddler, Ben Varga, volunteered in the Confederate Army. It is highly probable that the appreciation of the local community and the hope to integrate more easily played major roles in prompting the boys to volunteer and serve throughout the Civil War.

The love of adventure was also certainly present in the heart of all young men, regardless of which country they were born in, attracting many to join the Southern Army. Nevertheless, the grave realities of fighting in the Civil War soon discouraged many from enlisting or re-enlisting upon the expiration of their terms of service.

Although the Hungarians who served in the Confederate Army were volunteers, on April 9, 1862 the first draft law went into effect applying to all males between the ages of 18 and 35, later to be followed by similar laws further expanding the circle of those obliged to perform military service (in February 1864, 17–50 years of age). These laws were very unpopular among the foreigners, as they associated the passing of similar pieces of legislation with despotic regimes.[22]

Chroniclers of the presence of Hungarians in the United States did not really know what to make out of the Hungarians supporting the Confederacy, mainly due to the existence of the peculiar institution which they considered as a disgrace that went counter to all the democratic ideals they believed the United States represented. This was the main reason why all of them left more or less uncommented the fact that there were Hungarians serving in the army of the South. Of course, we know very well that there were. But what was their attitude towards the institution of slavery?

The vast majority of the foreigners in the states of the Confederacy had little or no connection at all with the plantation system, and had hardly any contact with slaves. It seems safe to state that most of them felt very similar to William Watson, who wrote about his own stance regarding slavery, "I had no interest in it, or connection with it, but was rather opposed to it," and he added that a large number in the South were opposed to it, although on quite different principles from the New England political abolitionists. Similarly to the foreign-born in the ranks of the Union army who — with the exception of the few ardent abolitionists — were not fighting *against* the institution of slavery, it seems that foreigners in Confederate service were not fighting *for* it. In this respect, there was no considerable difference between their positions in the two armies, just as there was a similarity between the native-born and the immigrants in the South, as well. James M. McPherson said to a Civil War newsgroup in August 1996, "In fighting for their home and country, Southern soldiers took slavery for granted as the basis of the society and the country for which they fought."[23] Slavery was, therefore, not of particular importance for the vast majority of Southern soldiers, with the single exception being the so-called 'white trash' layer of society, who had no wealth or property, the color of their skin and the privileges that went along with this being basically the only things differentiating them from the slaves. No wonder, consequently, that they were trying to preserve their superiority, valuing "the one dignity belonging to them, as white people, in a slave country." Having no interest in the peculiar institution, for most foreigners — Hungarians included — defending their homes, families, and their adopted country was a major motive for volunteering.

McPherson devoted an entire book, *For Cause and Comrades: Why Men Fought in the Civil War*, to the analysis of the causes which moved soldiers — Northerners and Southerners alike — to enlist, and identified as many as fourteen possible key motivations ranging from the defense of homeland through adventure to the pursuit of promotion. However, his research proved that Confederate and Union soldiers gave similar reasons, except, as one would expect, on the subject of slavery. The sheer number of possible motivations suggests that volunteering in the Civil War was a complex issue which was definitely further complicated by the specific influencing factors in the case of the foreign-born. The analysis of the motivations which prompted Hungarians to take up arms in the conflict seems to support this. Although there were individual variants, we can conclude overall that the members of the Kossuth emigration mostly enlisted in order to utilize their military talents and prove their loyalty towards their adopted country. Earlier assumptions that they primarily took arms to help bring about the emancipation of slaves are not sustainable, although they cannot be entirely ruled out.[24]

CHAPTER FOUR

Taking Up Arms in the Civil War

Hungarian-born authors have overstated the number of Hungarians in the war between North and South. Just to mention one example, Eugene Pivány in his *Hungarians in the American Civil War* (1913), which broke new ground despite its many factual errors, suggested that the number of Hungarians living in the United States in 1860 exceeded 4,000, and even estimated that approximately 800 of them (a whopping 1 out of 5) served in the Civil War. Tivadar Ács went even further, claiming that no fewer than 5,000 Hungarian-born soldiers saw service in the war. No wonder that many of the works dealing with various aspects of Hungarian-American historical links and contacts took pride in stating that the Hungarians were the most over-represented ethnic group serving in the war in proportion to their overall number.[1]

These exaggerations were not confined to Hungarian authors. In his *The Blessed Place of Freedom*, a recent work scrutinizing immigrant involvement in the American Civil War, Dean B. Mahin concludes, "Estimates of the number of volunteers from each major immigrant group have been inflated by ethnic authors eager to prove that their group had made an important contribution to the ultimate Union victory." These tendencies went hand in hand with the common Southern exaggeration of the role of "foreign mercenaries," who they said served in such great numbers in the Northern armed forces that they turned the scales in favor of the Union. General Robert E. Lee allegedly said, "Take the Dutch out of the Union Army and we could whip the Yankees easily."[2]

Modern Civil War research has shown that the proportion of foreigners in the Union Army was below 20 percent. So immigrants were hardly a decisive element in terms of numbers. The Union had a great advantage in manpower anyway. Moreover, about 10 percent of the Northern population as a whole volunteered in the Union army, so the proportion of volunteers coming from many ethnic groups was inevitably higher than the national rate.

Overall, the rate of volunteers in proportion to the total population of the specific ethnic group was close to 10 percent in most cases. In some groups the proportion of volunteers approached 15 percent.

It is difficult to determine the exact number of Hungarians serving in the ranks of either army. Recruiting officers rarely indicated the volunteers' nationality or place of birth, so Civil War service records have to be complemented with population statistics and pension records. Even the combined use of these types of sources does not guarantee the identification of the nationality of individuals. All three above-mentioned Hungarian authors attached a list of alleged Hungarian-born soldiers in the Civil War, but the number of names in these lists did not even approach their overall estimates. Pivány, Vasváry and Ács did not take into account the fact that many of those they identified as Hungarians were in reality of other nationality, and in some cases they even lied about having served in the war. With this in mind, the current study names only those whose nationality is clearly identifiable as Hungarian.

The Biographical List section of this work includes eighty-seven Hungarian soldiers in the Union Army and twelve who joined the Confederate Army. This list is not complete, and probably never will be. However, there is little likelihood that future research will significantly expand this total number of known Hungarian soldiers. Of the total number of identified Hungarian-born Civil War soldiers on the list, almost nine of every ten joined the Union army, closely corresponding with the distribution of Hungarians north and south in the general population. (According to the population statistics taken from the federal census of 1860, 993 (88 percent) out of the total number of 1,125 Hungarian family heads in the United States settled down in Northern states.) Enlistment rates on both sides were also similar: in the Union Army their proportion was 8.7 percent; in contrast, in the Confederate Army it was slightly higher, 9 percent. This definitely proves that Hungarian-Americans were by no means exceptional regard-

Ethnic Group	Total Number in the North	Total Number of Civil War Participants	Percentage (%)
Germans	1,229,144	180,000	13.8
Irish	1,526,541	150,000	9.3
Britons	563,186	50,000	8.8
Belgians	9,072	500	5.5

Data taken from Dean B. Mahin, *The Blessed Place of Freedom* (Washington, D.C.: Brassey's, 2002), 1–3, 15, 29, 43–49.

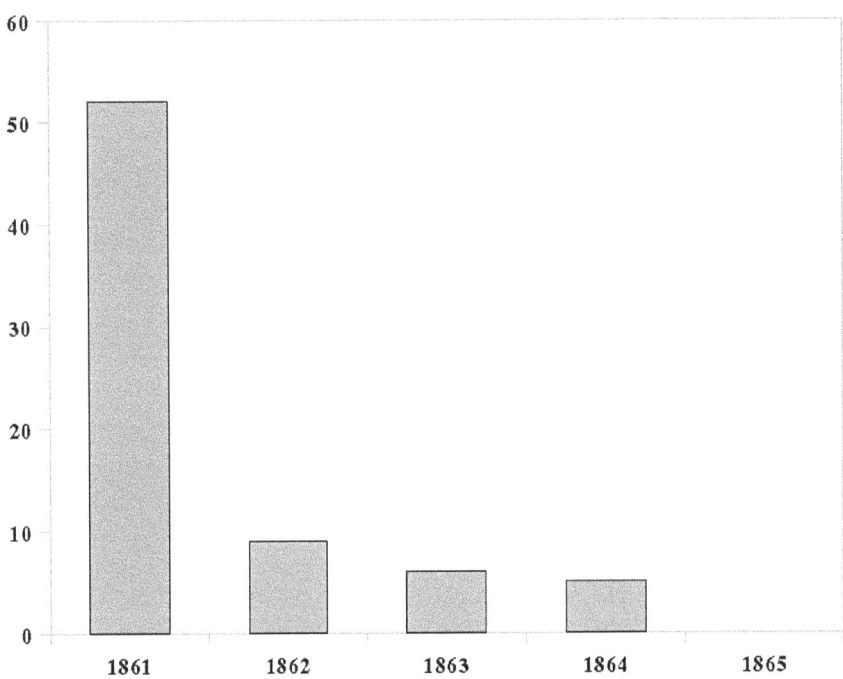

Data compiled from the records of the Adjutant General's Office, 1780s–1917, Record Group 94, Compiled Military Records, National Archives, Washington, D.C.

ing their willingness to volunteer in the Civil War. Fifty-two of the total of 72 Hungarians, whose exact date of enlistment is known, volunteered in the very first year of the conflict, most of them during the very first month, as service records show. This enthusiasm faded in the subsequent years, and in 1865 we have no data of Hungarians entering the service of the Union.

Two-thirds of the Hungarians who were mustered in the various volunteer regiments were commissioned as officers. Many had experience from the Hungarian freedom fight and were mostly mustered in as 1st lieutenants or captains. Some even received commissions as commanders of regiments with the rank of colonel, or more rarely obtained the rank of brigadier general. Their enlistment was beneficial for them and for the Union Army: they were able to utilize their military talents, which were badly needed in the first phase of the conflict when the Union army was short of seasoned veterans.

By the time individuals were mustered out in the Union Army, most of

Muster-In Ranks of Hungarians in the Union Army

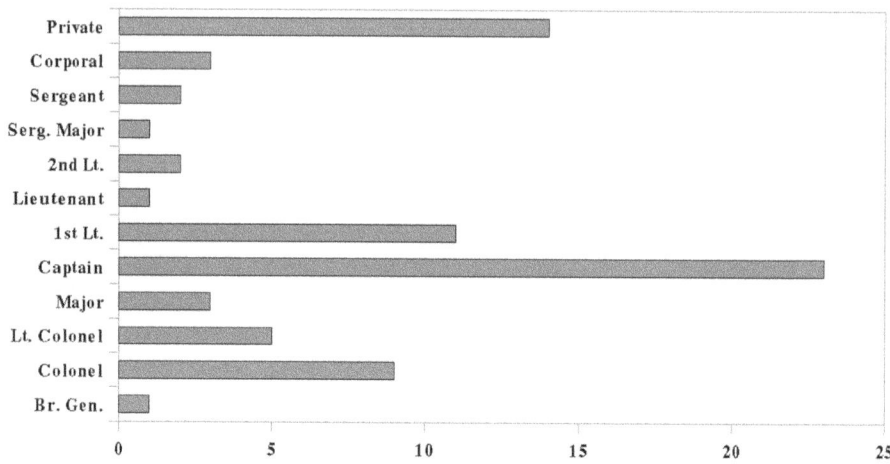

Data compiled from the records of the Adjutant General's Office, 1780s–1917, Record Group 94, Compiled Military Records, National Archives, Washington, D.C.

Muster-Out Ranks of Hungarians in the Union Army

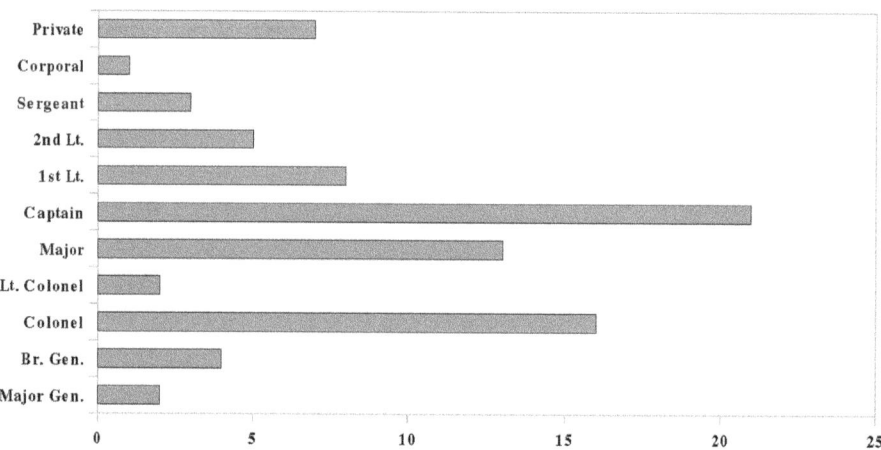

Data compiled from the records of the Adjutant General's Office, 1780s–1917, Record Group 94, Compiled Military Records, National Archives, Washington, D.C.

Branches of Arms Hungarians Volunteered In (Union Army)

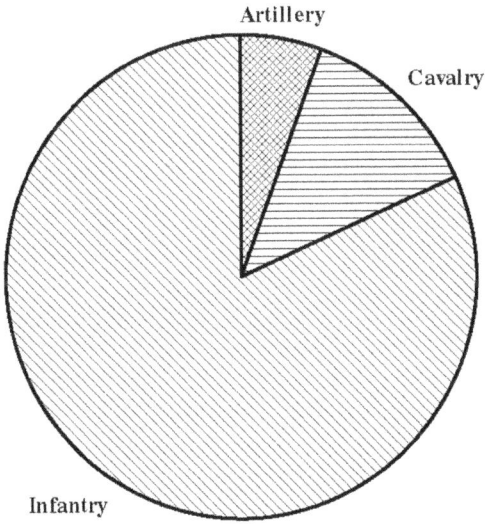

Data compiled from the records of the Adjutant General's Office, 1780s–1917, Record Group 94, Compiled Military Records, National Archives, Washington, D.C.

them had risen significantly in rank. While 75 percent had mustered in as officers, 87 percent finished their service with commissions. Two of the Hungarians rose to the rank of major general, and four obtained the rank of brigadier general. The number of Hungarian colonels commanding regiments more than doubled, and majors rose at an even more remarkable rate (more than a fourfold increase). Those joining in the latter half of the Civil War with no military experience were mustered in as privates, and they had little opportunity to get promoted. These included Joseph Pulitzer, who enlisted in the 1st New York (Lincoln) Cavalry as a private.[3]

The distribution of Hungarians among the various branches of arms more or less reflected the general composition of the Union Army. About 80 percent of the units were infantry regiments. Out of the estimated 2.5 million soldiers serving in the Northern Armed forces, about 326,000 were in the 272 cavalry regiments, which was about 13 percent of the total manpower of the North. The proportion of Hungarian-born soldiers in the Union's cavalry was similar.[4]

Thirty-five percent of Hungarian soldiers joined in New York, twenty-seven percent in Missouri, and twelve percent in both Illinois and Iowa.

Although no all-Hungarian regiments were formed in the Civil War, some military units in these states showed a high concentration of the foreign-born, and Hungarians in particular.

New York and the "Melting Pot Soldiers"

In the Hungarian-American literature, the 39th New York Volunteer Infantry Regiment, known usually as the 'Garibaldi Guard,' was often designated as a Hungarian unit. However, only 10 verifiable Hungarians served in this regiment. Confusion about the ethnicity of the members may be due to the fact that Hungarian Frederick George D'Utassy raised and commanded the regiment. Furthermore, this truly multi-ethnic unit, which had French, French Canadian, Spanish, Portuguese, Swiss and German ethnic companies also had three companies that were referred to as 'Hungarian.' Probably this caused Anthony Tihamer Komjathy, among others, to conclude that "half of the rank and file of the Garibaldi Guard were Hungarians." Careful analysis of the rosters of the regiment does not support these claims; despite the lack of standardized muster rolls indicating the soldiers' country of birth, we can safely assert that there were not several hundred Hungarians serving in the regiment.[5]

Nevertheless, the importance of "Hungarianness" was not due to the actual number of Hungarians; rather it stood for the common cause of Italians, Hungarians or Germans who had fought in 1848–49 in their home countries. When the regiment was mustered in on May 23, 1861, in New York on LaFayette Place, an American, a Hungarian and an Italian flag were presented to the soldiers. In the white stripe of the Hungarian flag a wreath of laurel and oak leaves surrounded the inscription: "Vincere vele mori" with the translation on the reverse, "Conquer or die." Across the flag, in letters of green and gold, was inscribed: "Garibaldi Guard." Attached to the staff, which was surmounted by a silver battle-axe, was a red, white and blue pennant, with the motto, "Brethren before, brethren again." The symbolism was clear.[6]

The regiment was built on a mixture of European traditions. To start with, they wore an Italian-style uniform similar to that of Italian Bersaglieri (Sharpshooters), with broad flat hats adorned with feathers. Furthermore, there were several so-called "Vivandières" or "Cantinières" with them: women who traveled with the soldiers for little or no pay as sutlers, mascots or nurses. Some even fought alongside their male counterparts, although the majority was sent home near the end of 1861 when the regiment began to see real fighting.[7]

The most controversial figure of the regiment was Colonel Frederick

George D'Utassy. A veteran of the Hungarian War of Independence with considerable political support in New York, he raised the regiment and became its colonel. However, many officers and men resisted his primary goal of Americanizing the regiment as much as possible. This played a major role in generating accusations against him of fraud and falsification of regimental documents as early as the fall of 1861. For the time being he managed to prove his innocence. Nevertheless, his strict disciplinary style turned several of his soldiers against him, including some fellow Hungarians. Captain Francis Takats got into a disagreement with D'Utassy and on July 8, 1861, he wrote a petition demanding the resignation of the colonel. Several officers of the regiment also signed it. Two days later they went as far as refusing to drill, and two companies marched to Washington, D.C., where they were arrested.

Captain Takats was court-martialed and discharged in November 1861. D'Utassy was cleared, but frequent rumors linked him with corrupt practices, particularly diverting government funds to his personal purposes. Moreover, his rather extravagant taste and lifestyle alienated many of his soldiers. He was arrested in March 1863 and was charged with 25 criminal specifications. The court-martial found him guilty and sent him to prison for one year.[8]

Alfred R. Waud, "Surrender of the revolting Garibaldi Guard to the U.S. Cavalry," with Capt. Francis Takats in the middle of the picture. Source: *New York Illustrated News*, July 22 1861 (Library of Congress, DRWG/US, Waud, No. 17).

All of the confusion surrounding the regiment turned many soldiers, including Hungarians, away from the unit (all the Hungarians who are known to have served here volunteered in 1861), but those who did see service with the 39th New York were eager to prove themselves. Hugo Hillebrandt, another veteran of the Hungarian War of Independence, rose from sergeant major to major within a year. He was involved in the battle of Harper's Ferry on September 13, 1862, which was probably the darkest day in the history of the regiment, as on the Maryland Heights 3,000 Union soldiers surrendered to the Confederates. The subsequent investigations found that Hillebrandt was one of the few officers of the Garibaldi Guard who did their best to avoid the fiasco. Later, on the second day of the battle of Gettysburg he led four companies and re-took Watson's Battery from the 21st Mississippi. For his gallantry, he was brevetted colonel by President Andrew Johnson in 1869. Anthony Weekey also progressed quickly in rank, from 1st lieutenant to major within less than a year. However, he fell victim to some unidentified disease in the spring of 1862.

Hungarians living in New York as well as other parts of the country had very strong links with the German-American community. Eugene Kozlay organized the 54th New York Volunteer Infantry, which was named 'Schwarze Jaeger,' and its soldiers were recruited mainly from among German-Americans in Brooklyn. The regiment was named after the volunteer force of Ludwig Adolf Wilhelm, Baron von Lützow in the Napoleonic Wars. The overwhelming majority of the soldiers were of German origin, but Kozlay was not the only Hungarian, as another Kossuth emigrant, Stephen Kovats, was his major. Julius H. Stahel assisted Col. Louis Blenker in raising the 8th New York Volunteer regiment, and became the lieutenant-colonel of the unit. Kossuth émigrés served in some ten other New York regiments that did not have noticeable concentrations of Hungarians.

Frémont's Hungarians in Missouri

The state of Missouri played a crucial role in the Civil War. Not only did the nation's major lines of westward travel and communication pass through the state, but its relatively large population made it an excellent source of manpower. A high proportion of the population was foreign-born, mostly German, who were instrumental in keeping the slave state in the Union after the secession crisis of 1860. In fact, about four-fifths of the population of St. Louis were foreigners, mostly Germans, who supported the Union. In contrast, more than two-thirds of the white population in Missouri were of Southern stock.

St. Louis was also the residence of the third largest Hungarian community in the United States. Similarly to New York, Kossuth émigrés were strongly attached to the local German community, and, starting in 1861, they shared in organizing pro-Union forces into effective home guard units in the city. Probably the most prominent of all of them were the four Rombauer brothers: Roderick, Robert, Roland and Raphael, who had all settled down in St. Louis and were deeply involved in the public life of the city. All four of them volunteered in Missouri regiments, and greatly contributed to the final victory of the Union forces in the state. They were not the only ones, though. Anton Gerster organized a company of St. Louis volunteers in 1861 which was called Gerster's Independent Company of Pioneers. In the later phase of the Civil War, he became captain of the 5th Missouri Infantry and the 27th Missouri Infantry. In both units, he was responsible for building and repairing fortifications and bridges, utilizing his qualification as a civil engineer.

However, another factor beyond German-American unionism attracted the finest, most experienced Hungarian officers into the state. John Charles Frémont was a real romantic hero in the eyes of many in America: the Pathfinder who played a major role both in the exploration of the West and the conquest of California. His ardent opposition to the territorial expansion of slavery resulted in his nomination as the Republican presidential candidate in the election of 1856. His loss to James Buchanan forestalled disunion for another four years, as the Southern states threatened to secede if Frémont was elected. At the outbreak of the Civil War, his political connections secured him a major generalship, although the "political general" had never commanded larger armies before. Lincoln appointed him to command the rather precarious Department of the West, which had its headquarters in St. Louis, Missouri. This appointment, however, was not what one would call rewarding. Missouri was a border-state hotbed of secessionist sentiments with the population being badly divided: 100,000 of the state's citizens volunteered in the Union Army, while 50,000 in the ranks of the Confederacy. The special convention of Missouri on secession voted decisively for remaining in the Union, but the state's pro-Confederate governor, Claiborne F. Jackson, ordered the mobilization of several hundred state militia troops. However, Union General Nathaniel Lyon quickly encircled their camp and forced their surrender. This did not end the clashes between pro-slavery and anti-slavery forces in Missouri, though. The latter continued to wage a guerrilla-type of warfare against the Union troops, enjoying the support of many in the state, and even in St. Louis, where Frémont established his headquarters.[9]

These were the major challenges John Charles Frémont was supposed to face. However, he encountered immense difficulties in establishing his command. Headstrong and independent, Frémont deeply distrusted regular officers and West Pointers. He surrounded himself mainly with European officers—all of them veterans of either the revolutionary wars of 1848–49 or the Crimean War. Frémont particularly favored Hungarians; no wonder his Department Headquarters soon contained a major concentration of Kossuth émigrés ready to take up arms in defense of the Union.[10]

Frémont did not care much about military regulations and procedures. He often appointed officers without asking authorization from anyone, and often fabricated commissions which did not even exist. Brigadier General Samuel R. Curtis, in his letter written to Lincoln on October 12, 1861, complained, "What has particularly surprised me, is the general's mode of calling, organizing and officering and supplying his Army—Law and rank, and usage, are apparently lost sight of." He also concluded, "In my opinion Gen Fremont lacks the intelligence, the experience, the sagacity necessary to his command." It was not only Curtis, but most of the ignored West Pointers, among them John Pope and Samuel D. Sturgis, who complained about his extensive employment of foreigners, and the forming of such irregular units as the Benton Hussars or the Frémont Hussars.[11]

Frémont made one of the most experienced as well as respected members of the Kossuth emigration, Alexander Asboth, his chief-of staff. The Hungarian played a preeminent role in organizing the Department of the West into an effective fighting unit. Stephen Beszedits quotes Alan Nevins in his "Hungarians with General John C. Frémont in the American Civil War," who wrote about Asboth, "He was highly efficient in seeing that the new regiments drilled hard, steadily and with growing precision."[12]

Another Hungarian, Albert Anselm, was selected as Asboth's adjutant on Frémont's staff. Anselm had played a major role in organizing Home Guard units in St. Louis. John Fiala became Frémont's chief topographical engineer, and contributed greatly to the completion of the fortifications around the city of St. Louis. What is more, he was one of the proponents of establishing a river flotilla of gunboats. Nevertheless, he did not escape anti-foreigner sentiments that surrounded the Hungarian officers on Frémont's staff: Br. General Curtis complained that Frémont "makes a German by the name of Col. Fiala, 'Chief of Engineers and Inspector General' and gives him entire control of the forts now nearly finished in this city [Benton Barracks, near St. Louis, MO]."[13]

Probably the most famous of all Hungarian officers serving under the command of General Frémont was Charles Zagonyi, who organized a special cavalry unit named Frémont Bodyguard primarily to provide him personal protection. Later the troopers were more widely used, and participated in Frémont's efforts to push back the Confederates in Missouri. The peak of Zagonyi's career and the existence of the bodyguard was undoubtedly their

"Death Ride" at Springfield, Missouri, on October 25, 1861, when they managed to re-capture the small city for a couple of hours from an enemy force well outnumbering Zagonyi's own troopers. Zagonyi became well known and his deeds were widely publicized.

Several other Hungarian-born officers offered their services to Frémont and served in his Western Department. Gustave Waagner was appointed chief of artillery in Cairo, Illinois, and his adjutant was a fellow Hungarian, Lt. Raphael Guido Rombauer. Unlike Frémont, however, they felt distrust not towards regular officers and West Pointers, but other American volunteers who they felt were hopelessly inexperienced.

Frémont, who was very much concerned about the activity of the Confederate intelligence service in Missouri and highly desired confidentiality, used the Hungarian language as a kind of encryption in his telegraph communication with Washington, D.C., or Cairo, Illinois, which in a way anticipates the use of Navajo code-talkers in the Pacific campaign of World War II.

Alexander Asboth sent the telegrams to the Post Office Department, where a Hungarian clerk, Albert De Zeyk, translated and delivered them to Lincoln. Similarly, in Cairo, General Grant used the services of Lt. Rombauer in processing and translating the messages coming from Frémont's headquarters.[14]

Frémont faced many difficulties as the commander of the Western Department. Numerous secessionist guerrillas and bushwhackers gave him and the Union Army a hard time, and his political enemies accused him of

Frémont's telegram in Hungarian to De Zeyk, September 4, 1861 (Abraham Lincoln Papers, Library of Congress, Series I, General Correspondence, 1833–1916, No. 1485).

reckless expenditures and misappropriation. His promotion to major general created jealousy in many regular army officers, and the long-time lack of Union military success in Missouri added fuel to the fire. Frémont's most controversial decision concerned his proclamation of August 31, 1861, in which he established martial law in the entire state of Missouri. In this document, he also declared, "The property, real and personal, of all persons in the State of Missouri who shall take up arms against the United States, and who shall be directly proven to have taken an active part with their enemies in the field, is declared to be confiscated to the public use; and their slaves, if any they have, are hereby declared free. "Although Frémont immediately became the celebrated hero of the Radical Republicans, Lincoln, who was anxious to keep the slaveholding border states within the Union, ordered Frémont to rescind the proclamation. Frémont, whose error "was to act the brave man's part, without the statesman's tact," as John Greenleaf Whittier put it, was nevertheless convinced that he had made the right decision and refused to carry out Lincoln's order. Eventually the president issued an order modifying the general's proclamation, and on October 24, 1861, relieved him of command.[15]

Many of the foreign officers, among them Hungarians, were removed with Frémont. Their services were declared unwanted because that they were claimed to have been commissioned illegally by Frémont, but their loyalty to him had much to do with their dismissal. Zagonyi, the commander of the Frémont Bodyguard, was placed on the inactive list; he returned to service for a short period of time only when Frémont was appointed commander of the Mountain Department in early 1862. After a couple of months, in June 1862, both of them resigned. Zagonyi never saw service in the Civil War again and sank into complete oblivion. Along with him, Anselm Albert and John Fiala were also shelved. Alexander Asboth was the only one among the Hungarian officers on Frémont's staff who remained in active service after the housecleaning.[16]

The Midwest: Hungarians Enlisting in Illinois, Indiana and Iowa

Chicago had the fifth largest Hungarian community in the United States in 1860, and Hungarians were actively involved in forming associations in the city. For instance, the Hungarian North Western Central Committee was established in 1859 with the primary aim of keeping touch with the European Central Committee, and preparing for the Hungarians' mobilization in the War of 1859 in Italy. There was also a Chicago Hungarian Benevolent Association, and, like in St. Louis or New York, they had very strong links with the local German-American community. When the Civil War came, several Kossuth émigrés responded to Asboth's call to enlist in the Union Army, and they followed a very similar pattern in volunteering to that of Hungarians in New York. Despite the claims of Vasváry or Ács, there were no all-Hungarian regiments in Chicago either. Nevertheless, Hungarians did play a significant role in organizing foreign elements into fighting units.

One of them, Géza Mihalotzy, a former captain in the Hungarian War of Independence, asked fellow-Hungarian Julian Kuné, who was involved in the political activity of the Republican Party and personally knew Abraham Lincoln, to take a request to the newly-elected president to allow them to organize a militia unit "composed of men of Hungarian, Bohemian and Slavonian origin" and name it "Lincoln Riflemen." Kuné observed that "many of the naturalized citizens who had served in European armies, began to organize companies, and drilled them night after night." Kuné talked highly of Mihalotzy, "who stands in front rank as a patriotic and far-seeing naturalized citizen." He apparently managed to convince Lincoln who scribbled at the bottom of the page, "I cheerfully grant the request above made." Accordingly, the militia unit was organized with Mihalotzy as colonel, and another Hungarian, Augustus Kovats as lieutenant. The soldiers of the "Lincoln Riflemen" enlisted for three months and were assigned to General George B. McClellan.[17]

Kuné himself contemplated forming a regiment of foreigners. Therefore, when the Civil War broke out, he asked McClellan to relieve both the Riflemen and the all-German Union Cadets, whose three-month service was about to expire anyway, and let them be incorporated into the newly-organized 24th Illinois Volunteer Infantry regiment. Again, Kuné secured Lincoln's approval, and the 24th Illinois was formed. However, he was bitterly disappointed when he learned that Friedrich Hecker was elected colonel, Mihalotzy lieutenant-colonel, and he became only major of the regiment. He resigned shortly afterward. In December 1861 Hecker also left, to be substituted by Mihalotzy as colonel and commander of the Lincoln Riflemen. Mihalotzy was fatally wounded in 1864, and battle wounds also forced Augustus Kovats to resign. The 24th Illinois contained some other Hungarian-born soldiers, but not in significant positions. Alexander Jekelfalussy rose to the rank of captain, whereas Francis Langenfeld served as a 1st lieutenant.

The state of Illinois and Chicago were not the only centers of Hungarians in the 1850s. About ten percent of the Hungarians lived in Ohio, Indiana and Iowa. The main centers of Hungarians were the small settlement of Davenport in Iowa, as well as Cleveland and Cincinnati in Ohio. The urge of the community to volunteer was definitely strong here, and many of the foreigners joined the ranks of the Union Army. However, in the regiments formed in these Midwestern states, there was no such concentration of Hungarians as in the Garibaldi Guard or in the 24th Illinois Volunteers. Nicholas Perczel organized the 10th Iowa Infantry and became its colonel, but this attracted basically no Hungarians to this regiment. It seems that in the Midwest ethnic origin was less important than the place of residence as motivation for mobilization. Accordingly, several foreigners, including Hungarians, took part in organizing militia units with the primary purpose of self-defense. The Radnich brothers, Emeric and Stephen, for example, both volunteered to serve in an Iowa Home Guards unit. All this did not mean, however, that volunteering in Midwestern regiments did not hold the promise of promotion and a successful military career: Frederick Knefler, for instance, was commissioned as 1st lieutenant and in 1865 was mustered out as brigadier-general by brevet, thus becoming the highest-ranking Jewish soldier in the Civil War.

Hungarians in Confederate Ranks

The symmetrical treatment of the Hungarians' service in the Union and the Confederate armies requires that the latter group is discussed here, although it is essential to point out that the sporadic nature of the sources concerning Kossuth émigrés taking up arms in the Confederate army hardly enables us to draw far-reaching conclusions.

As mentioned earlier, approximately 12 percent of all soldiers of confirmed Hungarian origin enlisted in the Confederate army. Statistically this barely qualifies as representative sample, enabling us to step beyond the level of individuals and make some generalizations. All that can be known is that the rate of Hungarian volunteers in proportion to the number of the Hungarian-born in Union and Confederate territory corresponded (8.7 percent and 9 percent, respectively), although in the latter the population was considerably lower.

As far as the date of enlistment is concerned, Hungarians were as fast to respond to the Confederate call as those volunteering in the Union Army; about 70 percent of the enlistments in both armies took place in the very first year of the Civil War. We have no data of Hungarian soldiers enlisting in the Confederate army in 1864 and 1865.

We have seen that a whopping 75 percent of the Hungarians were mustered in the Union Army as officer, and an even higher proportion (87 percent) of them left service as one. Interestingly, this tendency was the direct opposite in the Confederate army: more than 60 percent of the Hungarian-born never elevated to ranks of officer; as a matter of fact, 50 percent of them remained in the rank of private throughout the conflict.[18]

A lower proportion of Hungarians served in the infantry in the Confederate army than in the Union army (66 percent as compared to 81 percent), but, again, due to the considerably smaller sample, this does not necessarily reveal significant differences between enlistment patterns in North and South. Hungarian enlistment concentrated in only four states of the Confederacy: Virginia, Tennessee, Louisiana and Texas. These four states were among the five Southern states with the most numerous Hungarian population. Texas and Louisiana happened to be the ones with the highest number of foreigners in general.

The two highest-ranking officers in the Confederate Army, Col. Béla Estván and Col. Adolphus Adler, were among the most controversial Hungarian participants. Both of them enlisted in Virginia and served (if they did) for a brief period only.

The group of Hungarians joining the Confederate army in Texas concentrated in or around San Antonio and the small yet thriving settlement of Galveston. Four of the five sons of the Hungarian saddle maker Benjamin Varga volunteered in various Texas regiments, and, although none of them elevated beyond the rank of private, they served throughout the conflict.

Branches of Arms Hungarians Served In (C.S.A.)

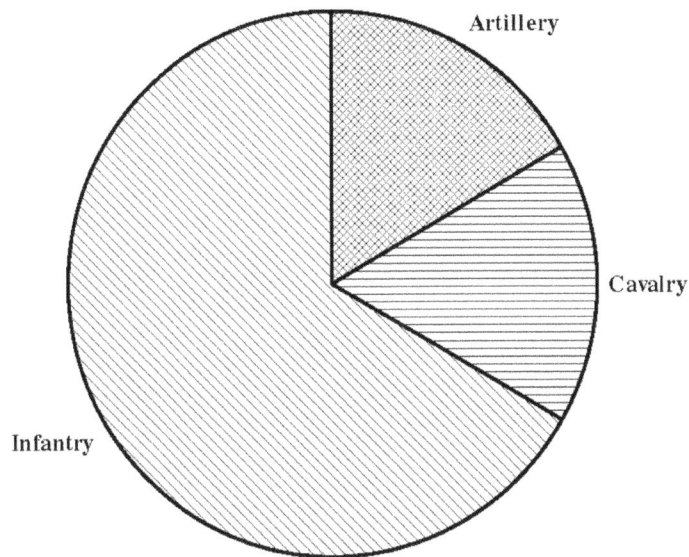

Data compiled from the records of the Adjutant General's Office, 1780s–1917, Record Group 94, Compiled Military Records, National Archives, Washington, D.C.

State	Number of Hungarian born (1860)	In proportion to the total population of Hungarians in the Confederacy (258)
Louisiana	88	34.1%
Texas	53	20.5%
Alabama	28	10.8%
Virginia	23	8.9%
Tennessee	21	8.1%

Statistical data compiled from records of the Bureau of the Census, Record Group 29, Census of 1860 M653, National Archives, Washington, D.C.

(They were not the only Hungarian sibligs to do so: both the four Rombauer and Zulavsky brothers enlisted in the Union army.) Along with them, four other Hungarians joined the Confederate army in Texas, and one served in Louisiana.

As it can be seen, we have only deficient information regarding Hungarians supporting the Southern cause. There are a few Confederate soldiers whose Hungarian origin can be suspected (based on names, bits and pieces of personal information, references in first-hand accounts), but the verification is yet to be carried out. However, on the basis of statistical data concerning soldiers of other ethnicities, and general enlistment tendencies, at this point we have no reason to expect that future works of research will be able to identify a much higher number of Hungarians who served in Confederate regiments.

Chapter Five

The Triumvirate: The Civil War Careers of Asboth, Stahel and Zagonyi

What all works scrutinizing any aspect of the Hungarians' involvement in the American Civil War have in common is that they give special prominence to three Hungarian soldiers: Alexander Asboth, Julius H. Stahel and Charles Zagonyi. Although they played very different roles in the military events of the Civil War, the formation of the heroic freedom-fighter image of Hungarians in the United States could be mainly assigned to their careers, according to Pivány, Vasváry, as well as Ács. Similarly to other students of ethnic participation, they felt that the more heroes they can line up who fought for the preservation of the Union, the more justified their presence in America was. (This was particularly crucial at the times of both world wars, when Hungary was at war with the United States, and it was of vital importance for Hungarian-Americans to prove their loyalty towards their adopted country.) This resulted in their being immensely biased towards the achievements of Hungarians in the conflict. All Hungarians were considered to be military heroes, and most details which could have shaken this assertion were simply ignored. The importance of their military achievements were hopelessly exaggerated; Pivány, for example, called Zagonyi's cavalry charge at Springfield, Missouri, on October 25, 1861, "one of the most heroic deeds recorded in the annals of warfare," and added, "it gave tone and spirit to the western army, instilled courage and a feeling of safety into the hearts of the loyal population of Missouri, and had a much-needed bracing effect all the country over." Vasváry agreed that Zagonyi was unquestionably "the greatest Hungarian hero of the Civil War" and his victory was "a real boost to the Northern morale." Ács also celebrated this event, although the way he describes it can rather be regarded more as pure fiction than a work of any historical value.[1]

These were the major factors which provided enough motivation for me to include a chapter in this work with the primary aim to investigate the historical validity of the hero-making mechanism of Hungarian-American historians, and to try and offer an objective, historically accurate analysis of the careers and achievements of these three key figures among the Civil War participants of Hungarian origin.

Alexander Asboth

Alexander Asboth was one of the most renowned members of the Kossuth emigration and probably the most respected soldier of Hungarian origin in the Civil War. His military achievements were appreciated not only by the Hungarian-American community, but Americans also talked highly of him. Upon his retirement in 1864, *The New York Times* bade farewell to him in an article of appraisal in which he was called "a man of high character and of very marked ability ... one of the few in that contest who brought practical military knowledge and experience to the aid of the cause.... He has won the respect and friendship of all who knew him by the sterling qualities of his character, and by the modest manliness of his demeanor."[2]

Asboth was born on December 18, 1811, in Keszthely. He acquired an engineer's degree in Pest from the Institutum Geometricum. As a civil engineer he took part in a number of canal-building projects. He left his profession and joined the Hungarian army in the 1848–49 War of Liberation and reached the rank of lieutenant-colonel. He became one of the most loyal adherents of Lajos Kossuth, and accompanied him to exile after the collapse of the Hungarian cause. He was interned in Turkey until they got the chance to travel to the United States aboard the *USS Mississippi*. In the United States he continued working as an engineer: first he was head engineer in the railroad-building projects of the Syracuse–New York and New York–Binghampton lines. Later he was employed by famous landscape architect Fredick Law Olmsted, and he participated in surveying Central Park and the Upper West Side of Manhattan.[3]

At the outbreak of the Civil War, General John Charles Frémont, freshly appointed commander of the Western Department, made Asboth his chief-of-staff. Being quite in the focus of attention of the press, a number of articles appeared about the Hungarians on Frémont's staff. *The New York Times* wrote about Asboth on September 3, 1861:

> Gen. Asboth goes to work quietly and firmly. His penetrating glance at once judges what position the applicant is fit for, or if for none at all, and a few questions will speedily testify the correctness of his judgment. And in spite of his

martial appearance, so kind is his heart and manner, that all who come in contact with him love him. The extent of his labors, comprising all the duties devolving upon the Chief of the Staff of the General [Frémont] commanding the Western Department, is enormous, and requires a superhuman energy to surmount. At midnight Gen. Asboth leaves his office, and at 5 o'clock in the morning, while his clerks are still in 'slumber's quiet arms' you can find him already at his desk.[4]

Gen. Alexander Asboth (ca. 1863) (Hungarian National Museum, Historical Photographs Division).

Most of his contemporaries agreed that he did an excellent job in organizing and drilling the regiments under his command.

Asboth remained in the Army of the Southwest even after the resignation of Frémont. He participated in the Pea Ridge campaign in Arkansas. On March 7, 1862, in the battle of Pea Ridge a musket ball passed through his right arm, fracturing the humerus. However, he was back in saddle the following day. Although the surgeons reported it healed by May, Asboth suffered from a considerable pain because of the injured bone and that he did not rest it.[5]

On March 21, 1862, he was promoted to the rank of brigadier general. On November 9, 1863, he assumed command of the District of Pensacola (District of West Florida), thus he became in charge of a number of colored regiments. He managed to collect several fellow Hungarian expatriate officers around him, including Kossuth's nephews, Ladislaus and Emile Zulavsky, and Albert Ruttkay. Some of these officers commanded colored troops. As one can imagine, Asboth was not too popular among the local population. Historian William Watson Davis commented on this as follows: "He and his fellow Hungarians were hated, dreaded, and condemned by the country people of that section on the triple charge of being 'furreners,' Yankees, and 'nigger lovers.'"[6]

Asboth was severely wounded at Marianna, Florida, on September 27,

"General Asboth and his staff at the Battle of Pea Ridge, Ark (March 6–8, 1862) (Frank Leslie, *Famous Leaders and Battle Scenes of the Civil War*, New York: Mrs. Frank Leslie, 1896, 119).

1864. One of the bullets hit him in the left cheek and the other broke his left arm in two places. One of the eyewitnesses described the incident as follows, "It was the women that did all the fighting, for they fired out of the windows and every by-place they met us. One woman walked right into the street with a pistol, and aimed at the general. She fired and shot him in the left arm, breaking it between the shoulder and elbow." He was taken to a private house, his wounds were dressed, but he could not return to service. On November 16 he was admitted to St. Louis Army General Hospital in New Orleans. It took several months before the bones started to unite, but his wounds rendered his arm more or less useless. Moreover, the surgeons could not locate and remove the bullet which lodged upon the palatine bone, so Asboth had to put up with the pain in his head for the rest of his life.[7]

These wounds forced him to resign his commission. Of how popular a commander Asboth was, the following lines published in *The New York Times* on November 26, 1864 are most revealing: "We see that Gen. Asboth has been compelled by the severity of his wounds to retire for the present from active service and go to New Orleans for medical attendance. He is succeeded by Gen. Bailey. Gen. Asboth is one of the oldest and most meritous of the foreign officers who entered our service when the rebellion broke out."[8] Despite the severity of his wounds and the fact that he was very feeble, weighing only 140 pounds, Asboth resumed command. On March 13, 1865, he was brevetted major-general.

After the Civil War, in August 1865 he was appointed United States minister to Argentina and Urugay. He did his best to bring about a cease-fire in the devastating armed conflict between Paraguay and the Triple Alliance of Argentina, Brazil and Urugay (1864–1870.) Despite the best efforts of his doctors, suppuration and exfoliation on account of his head wound continued, and he died on January 21, 1868, in Buenos Aires. His remains were taken back to the United States in 1990 and were reinterred in Arlington National Cemetery.[9]

Julius H. Stahel

Unlike Brigadier General Asboth, Julius H. Stahel did not reach real prominence in the Hungarian War of Independence in 1848–49, and he cannot be considered a Kossuth emigrant proper either, as he did not leave the country following the fall of the Hungarian cause in order to flee economic and political persecution of the Austrian government. Nevertheless, his name probably sounds the most familiar in the United States as well, since he was the only officer of Hungarian origin in the Civil War awarded the highest military decoration of the United States, the Congressional Medal of Honor. Moreover, he also attained the highest rank among the Hungarians, as he obtained a major-generalship in 1863.

He was born Gyula Számwald in Szeged on November 5, 1825. He had classical education in his hometown and Pest. Some sources claim that he served in the Imperial Army as private and deserted at the coming of the Hungarian revolution in 1848. However, this is not supported by the sources at our disposal, but it is known that he moved to Buda, the Hungarian capital, and in 1846 he was employed by Gusztáv Emich, a leading printer, publisher and bookseller.[10]

That was where he got acquainted with the poet laureate of the Hungarian freedom struggle of 1848–49, Sándor Petőfi. The poet even wrote a highly ironic poem to Számwald, which went as follows:

> **"Into a Bookseller's Memorial Book"**
> The goal of life is happiness, but before,
> You have to make efforts to reach this goal.
> Nobody can get hold of it free of charge,
> Lots of various things are needed for it:
> Never straggle from Honor
> Neither out of temper, nor for reward,
> Love truly your fellow human beings,
> Do not draw up the bridge between you and others.
> The name of the homeland. The precious sacred homeland
> Close into the purest depth of your heart.
> And worship God, but above all,
> Sell my poems vigorously.[11]

Like hundreds of thousands of young men in Hungary, Számwald got involved in the events of the War of Liberation in 1848. He joined patriotic organizations, including the Committee of Public Safety, created in order to maintain law and order, and later he volunteered in the Hungarian Revolutionary Army. He rose to the rank of lieutenant and served as adjutant on the staff of General Richard Guyon.

After the surrender of the Hungarian troops to the Austro-Russian forces, Stahel fled the country. However, he was lucky enough to have influential friends who managed to arrange that he could return to Hungary without having to fear any retaliation. First he became Emrich's silent partner, then he set off his own publishing enterprise, which, however, soon went bankrupt. It is likely that his financial failure forced him to leave his homeland and try his luck somewhere else. (Ferenc Agárdi suggests in his article that he had got married, but his young wife died in childbirth. The pain-stricken Számwald left Hungary, as it turn out, for good. Agárdi's claims are difficult to support with documents as well as those of Károly Rácz-Rónay, who stated that Számwald left Hungary because he was wanted for cheating and forgery, leaving behind his 20-year-old wife and their half-year old baby.)[12]

This was the time when he changed his name to Julius Stahel, which was probably the name of his ancestors, and in 1856 he immigrated to the United States. He settled down in New York City and took employment as an assistant editor for the *New York Illustrated News*. He wrote articles for the German-American press and won the recognition of the entire German-American community within a very short time.[13]

At the commencement of the Civil War, he helped another German emigrant, Louis Blenker, organize the 8th New York Volunteer Infantry regiment, with Stahel as its lieutenant-colonel and Blenker its colonel. Both of them played important roles in organizing and drilling the regiment, which became a model unit. Soon they got the chance to prove themselves: although they did not participate in the battle of Bull Run on July 20, 1861, they provided cover for the retreat of the remnants of the defeated Union Army to Washington, D.C. For their meritous conduct, both Blenker and Stahel were promoted: the former obtained a brigadier generalship, whereas the latter became colonel of the 8th New York. He was then promoted to brigadier general on November 12, 1861.[14]

In 1862 his regiment was assigned under the command of General Fremont's Mountain Department. The men of the 8th New York found themselves in the thick of fighting at the battle of Cross Keys on June 8, 1862, in Rockingham County, Virginia. The regiment served as a spearhead for the Union attack and faced the deadly volley of the Confederate forces marching across a clover field. One of the soldiers of the 21st Georgia regiment recalled this: "The Germans came marching across the clover field in beautiful line, carrying their guns at 'support arms' The Col. walked backwards in front of them ... as though they were simply drilling." When the Confederates pulled the triggers, "the Germans fell across each other in piles" and "the whole regiment was annihilated at a single fire." Fifty-three soldiers were killed on the spot, 27 later, and 100 men were wounded. The Southern troops took 74 prisoners of war.[15]

H. Stahel (Library of Congress Prints and Photographs Division, Washington, D.C., LC-DIG-cwpb-05220).

There were some who laid the blame on Stahel for the bloodshed, but the Northern press focused on the bravery of the Northern men. *The New York Times* wrote about Stahel, "The part taken by Gen. Stahel and his Brigade of Germans, is the theme of general commendation. He has won the popular favor among American as well as foreign officers for his ... soldierly qualities. He is brave, enthusiastic, and was seen during the day in the thickest of the fight, encouraging and urging his men."[16]

Most people who got acquainted with Stahel were impressed by his military bearing and gentlemanly qualities. One of his officers, Alexander Hamilton, described him in his letter to H. W. Halleck: "From many months' intimacy with Stahel both in private life and in the field I have every confidence in assuring you that he will be a great acquisition to you. His quiet, gentlemanlike demeanour has endeared him to officers of all ranks and his thorough military knowledge and accomplishments have secured the confidence and respect of both officers and men." Even General McClellan, who had the reputation of not being fond of soldiers of foreign origin, wrote about him, "Of his [Blenker's] subordinate officers the best was Gen. Stahl [sic], a Hungarian, who had served with distinction under Georgei. His real name, I believe, was Count Serbiani."[17]

He participated in the second battle of Bull Run on August 29–30, 1862 and his bravery was praised by General Pope. In the absence of Sigel he was named commander of the 11th Corps temporarily, then named to the command in January 1863. He was assigned to command of cavalry in the newly formed Grand Reserve Division under Sigel (Special Order No. 29.)[18]

On March 8, 1863, John Singleton Mosby with 30 men slipped through the Union defense and captured Brig. Gen. Edwin H. Stoughton, 2 other officers, 30 enlisted men and 60 horses. Abraham Lincoln personally ordered Stahel to take command of cavalry in defense of Washington, D.C., as there were rumors that the raiders were actually planning attacks on the federal capital. On March 14, 1863, the Hungarian officer was promoted to the rank of major general. He spent the next months chasing Mosby, nicknamed the Gray Ghost, managing to check him, but failing to capture him.

In the days before the battle of Gettysburg, Stahel and his division performed reconnaissance duty. Brigadier General Alfred Pleasonton, commander of the cavalry Corps of the Army of the Potomac, in his letter written to John Farnsworth on June 23, 1863, wanted Stahel to be removed from the field and his division added to the Army of the Potomac. He argued that Stahel was lacking the energy and good sense required from a cavalry commander and even implied that Stahel was unfit because of his foreign origins. Stahel was indeed relieved of command, but was soon pressed into service to supplement Pleasonton's forces. Nevertheless, not everyone accepted Stahel with similar reservations. Alexander Hays from Centerville, Virginia, wrote about his encounter with the Hungarian, "Yesterday we had a visit from Gen. Stahel and staff, who were passing through with 1,600 cavalry and several pieces of artillery. They had been down to Warrenton Junction. I was pleased with the general. He is small, not very handsome, but looks as if he could fight, is the most unassuming Dutchman I have met."[19]

In the following months, Stahel was staying in the Union capital and participated in the social life of Washington, D.C., which was vibrant despite the war. Stahel escorted President Lincoln to Gettysburg when, on November 19, 1863, he delivered his famous address at the establishment of the military cemetery where the battle had been fought.[20]

On March 13, 1864, Stahel was assigned to the Department of West Virginia, where he became General Sigel's chief of cavalry and chief of staff. After the debacle at New Market on May 15, 1864, Sigel was relieved and replaced by General Hunter. Hunter had very serious doubts about Stahel: "He has but little experience as a cavalry officer in this country, nor I am aware that he has any experience with cavalry elsewhere," he wrote. During Hunter's Shenandoah Valley campaign, however, Stahel played a crucial role, particularly in the battle of Piedmont on June 5, 1864. In the engagement Stahel personally led his unmounted troopers in the battlefield when he was hit by a bullet in the left shoulder. He left his command only for a short period during which the surgeons dressed his wounds and returned to service in spite of the fact that he was unable to mount his horse without assistance. Under his leadership their charge routed the Confederates. He was awarded the Congressional Medal of Honor on November 4, 1893, "for distinguished gallantry at the battle of Piedmont, West Virginia on June 5, 1864 in accordance with the act of Congress approved on March 3, 1863." Even General Hunter acknowledged his performance. "It is but justice to Maj. Gen. Stahel to state that in the recent engagement he displayed excellent qualities of coolness and gallantry, and that for the final happy result the country is much indebted to his services," he wrote to Major General Halleck.[21]

While he was recuperating, he was relieved of command on July 16 and returned to duty only in August. He was soon transferred to the Middle Department and served as president of court-martial in Baltimore, Maryland. Nevertheless, his health remained very fragile; he had large internal and external hemorrhoids which caused him such pain and suffering that he eventually resigned his commission on February 8, 1865. Just two days following his resignation, he received a letter from Franz Sigel in which he expressed his appreciation for Stahel's "faithful and excellent assistance." His finishing lines went as follows[22]: "I had good opportunity to become aware of your excellent qualities as a commander, while your incessant labors on long and fatiguing marches, your success in organizing, drilling and disciplining troops, as well as your bravery in battle, will be and are duly acknowledged by the many thousands, who have been under your command."[23]

Stahel's outstanding military service and excellent connections secured him a nomination by President Andrew Johnson to consulship at Yokohama, Japan, on May 9, 1866. He remained in diplomatic service in Japan until 1884. He subsequently served as consul to Osaka and Hiogo. For an additional year he was consul of the United States in Shanghai, China. Stahel performed diplomatic duty in the Far East along with John Singleton Mosby, his former Civil War adversary, and they became best friends.

In 1885 he returned to New York City. He worked as an executive for Equitable Life Assurance Society. He was actively involved in the life of the Hungarian-American community; his name can be found among the founders of First Hungarian Association for Self Culture of Philadelphia. He was, among others, Companion of the First Class of the Military Order of the Loyal Legion of the U.S.[24]

For about a quarter of a century, the Hungarian veteran of two wars resided in the Hoffman House where he was known as "The General." Julius H. Stahel died of angina pectoris on December 4, 1912, in New York City. He was buried at Arlington National Cemetery.

Charles Zagonyi

> Let the Crown-Poet paid
> Sing of the "Light Brigade"
> And "The wild charge they made"
> When "Some one had blundered;"
> Following the British Bard,
> I sing of the Body-Guard —
> The Heroes that fought so hard —
> Where nobody blundered.
> Hail, brave Zagonyi — hail!
> All hail, the Body-Guard! —
> The glorious —
> The victorious —
> The invincible Three Hundred.[25]

The excerpt above is taken from Henford Lennox Gordon's poem entitled "Charge of Fremont's Body-Guard." The author's aim was to commemorate one of the first Union successes of the Civil War: the cavalry charge at Springfield, Missouri, on October 25, 1861, which is generally remembered as Zagonyi's Death Ride, named after Hungarian Major Charles Zagonyi. His figure stood in the focus of all works dealing with the Hungarians' involvement in the American Civil War, and none of the authors seemed to care that there was an apparent contradiction between the hero-cult they created and the fact that most comprehensive Civil War histories do not even mention this particular event or the name of the Hungarian who was leading the Union troopers. What follows here is a short biography of Charles Zagonyi, and also an attempt will be made to take objective measure of him and his famous charge.

There are lots of uncertain details concerning Zagonyi's life. Even the place and exact date of his birth is not clear. Some sources say that he was born in Szatmár County in 1826, whereas others claim that he was born in Szinérváralja on October 19, 1822. All we know for sure is that he was drawn into the whirlpool of events in 1848–49 and took part in the Hungarian struggle for freedom against the Austro-Russian coalition forces. He served under legendary Polish General Josef Bem as first lieutenant and commanded a select cavalry unit. After the surrender of the Hungarian forces, he followed his commander to Turkey and he was interned for almost two years along with Bem. Later he left for Britain and eventually decided to emigrate to the United States. He set foot on American soil on July 2, 1851. Soon he found himself in the very same situation as other Hungarian exiles who had military experience but knew no trade. Zagonyi tried his luck in the already-mentioned group called Hungarian Vocalists, which dissolved very quickly. Zagonyi was in search of any kind of employment, and worked as a house painter in New York City and Philadelphia. In fall of 1852 he was lucky enough to be invited to a newly-founded riding school in Boston, Massachusetts, as a riding master. The institution itself was founded by a Hungarian, Stephen Thoult, and there were some other Hungarians employed, including István Kinizsi and John Kalapsza.[26]

Zagonyi got acquainted with Amanda Schweiger, from a German immigrant family, and after a short period of courting, married her in 1854. There are several references to her in the letters and diaries of Hungarian émigrés. Károly László, for instance, described her as a "pleasant-mannered, nice-faced and figured American lady from a German family who does not keep away from work and is very industrious." László met the couple in 1859 and noted that Zagonyi and his wife both worked as tailors.[27]

When the Civil War came, Zagonyi obviously felt that it was the right time to make use of his military experience. His service in the Union Army was due to General Frémont, who offered him a commission at his Western Department and appointed him "chief of cavalry" with the rank of captain. The Hungarian later summarized his motivations for joining the ranks of the Union army as follows[28]: "I took service in the United States army only for the reason that I wanted to see this great country united again, and put down the rebellion, and not to divide it more and more. I am not a fortune hunter.... I had made up my mind that I would fight for no country but my own. But later, being called to serve under General Frémont whom I had never seen in my life, but for who I had a high esteem, I offered my services and was accepted."[29]

Frémont, who seemed to be more interested in the pomp of war than the actual waging of it, authorized Zagonyi to organize a company of horsemen which was to serve as his bodyguard. The idea itself probably came from the Hungarian who convinced Frémont that this was customary in Europe and such a unit could both serve as a police force and a training school for further cavalry companies. There was no shortage in volunteers. Within five days there were enough recruits for two companies, and very soon two more. Zagonyi was personally responsible for training and drilling, soon turning the civilians into a well-trained cavalry force. He made sure that his soldiers were armed with quality sabres and modern revolvers, and ordered their saddles and equipment from a company in Chicago.

It did not take long until Frémont and his bodyguard unit grew very unpopular in St. Louis. Many civilians thought that the unit and its outfit was too pompous and the very idea of having a bodyguard unit was more fitting to an emperor than an American general. Zagonyi's rather arrogant behavior and thick accent did not help too much either. Soon the Hungarian and his troopers were nicknamed "Frémont's Pets" and the "Kid Glove Brigade" and were targets of much ridicule, as they had not seen any action since the forming of the unit.

This is not to suggest that other units under Frémont's command which actually saw action had so much to boast of. On August 10, 1861, Brigadier General Nathaniel Lyon's army was defeated by the Confederates at Wilson's Creek, Missouri (Lyon himself was killed in the battle). On September 20, 1861, the small Union fortress of Lexington, Missouri, fell and 3,000 Union troops surrendered. Frémont badly needed a military victory. He worked out a grandiose plan to fight his way to New Orleans.

Frémont started out from St. Louis and went to Jefferson City, then encamped his troops near Warsaw, Missouri. That was where he received news of 300 or 400 poorly-armed Confederates in the city of Springfield, Missouri, just 55 miles away.

Zagonyi and the bodyguard were eager to prove themselves. Jay Monaghan wrote that "his men were eager to belie their reputation as 'parlor pets' in fancy uniforms and kid gloves. Even their glossy horses had been pointed out as toys." Fremont granted the permission for him to start with an expeditionary force and try to capture the city, but only on the condition that they were not overpowered by the Confederates.[30]

Zagonyi and the bodyguard set off at 8 P.M. on October 24, when the 21-year-old Major White had already been on his way with his squadron, the so-called Prairie Scouts with 154 troopers to perform scouting duty. Zagonyi's unit soon caught up with them and the Hungarian officer took over command of the entire force, above all because White was ill and was able to follow his men only in a carriage. They agreed that White would stay and have a rest in a nearby farmhouse and follow only later. Zagonyi pushed on towards

Charles Zagonyi (Library of Congress, Prints and Photographs Division Washington, D.C., LC-DIG-ppmsca-08367).

Springfield, and a 2-hour march away from the city he was informed by a Union farmer that there were about 2,000 rebels stationing there. Furthermore, any chance of a surprise attack faded away, as they surprised a Confederate foraging party and managed to capture all of them but one, who rode back to the city and evidently alerted the city.

Zagonyi sent a message to Fremont informing him of the circumstances and asked for reinforcement. He was, however, determined to continue with his mission, although he did not have authorization to do so. He made up his mind to leave the Bolivar Road leading directly to the city and a pro-Union farmer led him on a circuitous road to the east on the Mount Vernon Road in order to get into the rear of the Confederate positions. However, while haphazardly, yet probably wisely, changing his original plans, he forgot to inform the left-behind Major White about all this. The major, when he somewhat recuperated, tried to catch up with Zagonyi and his men, but he was captured by men from the Missouri State Militia. He was relieved of his belongings, but his life was spared.[31]

According to accounts of the battle, Zagonyi ordered his men to gather around him and told them that anyone who wished could leave before the battle, which Captain Foley called "a queer proposition for a foreign-born officer to make an American soldier under arms in defence of his country!" According to another account Zagonyi addressed his soldiers in an elevated speech, which is, however, quite unlikely due to the fact that the Hungarian spoke only broken English. Anyway, what he said, if he did, went as follows[32]:

> Fellow soldiers, comrades, brothers! This is your first battle. For our three hundred, the enemy are two thousand. If any of you are sick, or tired by the long march, or if any think the number is too great, now is the time to turn back. We must not retreat. Our honor, the honor of our General and our country, tell us to go on. I will lead you. We have been called holiday soldiers for the pavements of St. Louis; today we will show that we are soldiers for the battle. Your watchword shall be, "The Union and Fremont" Draw saber! By the right flank, quick trot, march![33]

The Confederates formed near the fairground on the open slope of the hill backed by the dense stand of oak trees — both their flanks and rear were protected. The approaching Union cavalry was received with a murderous fire; Zagonyi found that he lost about one fourth of his men within seconds. However, he ordered an all-out attack against the Confederates, although a stout rail fence confined them into a narrow lane. Captain Foley and the Kentuckians, adhering to their initial orders, tried to outflank the enemy, in spite of the fact that their lines were confused, as some of them joined Zagonyi instead. Nevertheless, it is quite likely that it was due to them that Zagonyi's force escaped total annihilation. Their surprise attack gave enough time for

Five. The Triumvirate 93

the bodyguard to re-form under the shelter of the hill and the cavalry, under the command of Captain Majthenyi, another Hungarian officer, charged right against the center of the rebels and made them flee. Particularly the State Militia broke fast, but the infantry did not hold much longer either. What followed was the bodyguard pursuing the rebels and sabering many of them. The Union cavalry fought its way to the city, without much opposition, and raised the Union banner on the courthouse pole. According to J. Winston's account of the battle, "As [Zagonyi] approaches a barn, a man steps from behind the door and lowers his rifle; but, before it has reached a level, Zagonyi's saber point descends upon his head and his life-blood leaps to the very top of the huge barn door."[34]

As the fighting in the city was over, they could reckon up their casualties which were rather heavy on both sides. No official state report has ever been made on the number of killed and wounded. Zagonyi reported that 15 Union soldiers were killed, 27 were wounded and 10 were missing in action, whereas he estimated the number of killed Confederate soldiers to be 106. According to *The Medical and Surgical History of the Civil War*, 18 Union troopers were killed, 37 were wounded, and 30 missing in action. Zagonyi's estimates regarding the number of fatalities in the Confederate lines are accepted by this work, and no reliable data is given for the number of Confederate wounded. How-

The Charge of the "Frémont Bodyguard" in Springfield, Missouri, October 24, 1861 (in *Harper's Weekly*, Vol. 5, No. 255, November 16, 1861, page 728).

ever, it is worth pointing out that Zagonyi reported that the soldiers of the bodyguard buried only 23 enemy soldiers, the rest of the Confederate casualties are just estimations.³⁵

Anyway, it seemed clear that they were not able to hold the city for a long time, as the rebels were expected to return. Zagonyi, therefore, having released the imprisoned Union sympathizers, decided to leave some soldiers behind to guard the Union wounded and left the city as early as 9 P.M., taking with him about $4,000 from the local bank. Major White, who was held captive a couple of miles away from the city, was freed by Union soldiers.

Zagonyi sent a report of the victory to Frémont, who arrived with the main army and re-captured Springfield a couple of days later after having sent jubilant dispatches of the victory to President Lincoln.

Zagonyi's victory was indeed something the Northern public opinion had desired for a long time. However, it soon turned out that it was not such a victory as it could be assumed on the basis of the initial reports, and Zagonyi could definitely not claim all the recognition for the action. In his report he stated that both the Prairie Scouts and the Irish Dragoons fled and left the bodyguard on its own. When the ladies of Springfield offered to present the bodyguard and Major White's Prairie Scouts alike a flag in recognition of their heroism, an indignant Zagonyi turned down the offer, explaining that "it would be idle to affect ignorance of the fact that the same distinction has been conferred upon a body of men who, though placed under my command upon the occasion to which your partially [*sic*] obliges me to refer, deserted me at the very moment of the conflict, and exposed the officers and men of the bodyguard to a fate which the hand of Providence alone could avert." Fremont convened a court of inquiry which established that Zagonyi's report contained inaccuracies. The major general awarded Major White a pair of silver spurs engraved with the names Springfield and Lexington. Zagonyi, however, was not willing to accept the court's finding.³⁶

The news of the charge, however, received positive reaction throughout the Union which shows how badly the Northerners needed a military victory in this first phase of the Civil War. Poems were written to the Hungarian officer to commemorate the role he played in the charge. One of these was written by George H. Boker and published in *Littel's Living Age* for the first time, then re-published in a number of journals.

"Zagonyi"

    Bold captain of the Body Guard
    I'll troll a stave to thee.
    My voice is somewhat harsh and hard,
    And rough my minstrelsy.
    I've cheered until my throat is sore

> For how our boys at Beaufort bore;
> Yet here's a cheer for thee!
>
> I hear the jingling spurs and reins,
> Thy sabres at thy knee;
> The blood runs lighter through my veins,
> As I before me see
> Thy hundred men, with thrusts and blows,
> Ride down a thousand stubborn foes,
> The foremost led by thee.
>
> With pistol snap and rifle crack,-
> Mere salvos fired to honor thee-
> Ye plunge, and stamp, and shoot, and hack,
> The way your sword make free;
> Then back again- the path is wide
> This time- ye gods! It was a ride,
> The ride they took with thee!
>
> No guardsmen of the whole command
> Halts, quails, or turns to flee;
> With bloody spur and steady hand
> They gallop where they see.
> Thy leading plume stream out ahead,
> O'er flying, wounded, dying, dead;
> They can but follow thee.
>
> So, captain of the Body Guard,
> I pledge a health to thee!
> I hope to see thy shoulders starred,
> My Paladin; and we
> Shall laugh at fortune in the fray,
> Whene'er you lead your well-known way
> To death or victory.[37]

It was not only civilians but military experts as well who set Zagonyi and his troopers' charge as an example "to illustrate what can be accomplished by a few cavalry, with but little training and no experience, when enthusiastic in a noble cause," just as James A. Congdon did in his *Cavalry Compendium* published in 1864.[38]

Despite all these examples of acknowledgment and recognition, the success of Zagonyi and Frémont was short-lived. The latter was soon relieved by Abraham Lincoln and replaced by General David Hunter on November 2, 1861. The investigations found that many of the appointments by Frémont were actually illegal and the majority of the soldiers brought into the volunteer army by him were improperly mustered in. That is why, when Zagonyi and the bodyguard returned to St. Louis, they were refused rations, forage for their horses, uniforms and pay. The bodyguard was dissolved, and an embittered Zagonyi testified: "They have been discharged; dismissed with disgrace, really, not discharged. They were dismissed with disgrace. I saw a telegraphic despatch from Washington, which stated that we used some expressions at Springfield for which our further service in the United States army is doubtful expediency. So there was a reason why we should be dismissed from the service of the United States." Edmund Vasváry went as far as to suggest that the bodyguard was dissolved because "President Lincoln felt jealousy towards Major General Frémont and sticked too much to the supreme command of the armed forces."[39]

As time passed, however, there were more and more questions concerning the validity of some of Zagonyi's claims and more doubts about the overall importance of the Death Ride, what is more, it became a political issue as well. Missouri Congressman Frank Blair, an ally of Lincoln and enemy of Frémont, delivered a speech to the House of Representatives claiming that "the charge of Zagonyi was in no sense a victory. Zagonyi and the men under him made a gallant charge; they came in and went out very much worsted, and fell back twenty-five miles." In this case, military perspective obviously fell victim to political considerations, but this did not mean that the charge and its importance was not re-considered from a military point of view.

One of the strongest critics of Zagonyi was Confederate Colonel William Preston Johnston, who wrote some two decades after the Civil War that "Zagonyi's rhodomontade was merely a cloak for disaster. He was ambuscaded by militia, not more numerous than his own command, and severely handled, with the loss of only two or three of his opponents." There are some apparent distortions of truth in his arguments, but there were many who came to a similar conclusion. *The Sentinel*, in an article published in 1898, concluded, "Military Fustian Zagonyi's chasseurs [Fremont Bodyguard] made one dashing charge on the enemy, and then passed away into history. Such a charge was duplicated, more fiercely and decisively, fully forty times by Sherman's bummers on the march to the sea and history will never record them." Somewhat unfairly, in its article dealing with foreign military talent, *The Oregonian* established that "Zagonyi and Asboth were daring troopers, fit to lead a reckless charge and fit for nothing else."[40]

Robert E. Miller published an article about Zagonyi in the *Missouri Historical Review* in 1982, which is probably the first attempt to provide an objective evaluation of the Hungarian's role in the Civil War. He pointed out that "Zagonyi's charge appears to have been a rash act, given the lack of information concerning the strength and disposition of the Confederate forces," as "General Fremont had given permission for the charge under the assumption that the enemy camp contained only 300 soldiers." He also called attention to the inaccuracies of Zagonyi's report in which he tried to avoid giving acknowledgement to the Prairie Scouts as if they had not deserved it, and quoted Captain Naughton, of the Irish Dragoons, who charged Zagonyi with "deliberately withholding all credit so that the public might conclude that his company ... was not in the fight." Ten years after Miller's article, Judy Yandoh published an article entitled "Taking Off the Kid's Gloves" in *America's Civil War* in which she concluded that the sole importance of the battle of Springfield lay in the Northern public's hunger for victory, and the picture she offered of Zagonyi was not a very sympathetic one either.[41]

Zagonyi's fate is very much different from those of Asboth and Stahel. He remained loyal to Frémont even after his being relieved of command and was on inactive list himself for a longer period of time, which was very difficult for him in all probability. It was then that he met Ralph Waldo Emerson when he paid a visit to the Frémonts. The famous essayist and poet wrote about his encounter with him in his diary: "She [Mrs. Frémont] introduced me to Major Zagyoni [sic], the captain of Fremont's Bodyguard, the hero of Springfield, Mo., a soldierly figure, who said, that he was as well as his inactive life permitted." Zagonyi returned to active service for a brief period, when Frémont was appointed commander of the Mountain Department in early 1862, serving as his chief of cavalry with the rank of colonel. In June 1862, however, Frémont resigned and the Hungarian officer followed his example never to return to active service.[42]

In 1865 the *Lowell Daily Citizen and News* reported that Frémont and Zágonyi had taken out a patent for expelling sap that produces rot in the wood and inserting sulphate of iron and other substances that render it incorruptible. This procedure promised that the wood could be prepared very cheaply and the writer of the article predicted that "it will be a fortune to the owners of the patent."[43]

It seems that this was not the case, however. The only reference to his possible fate comes from a fellow-expatriate Lajos Dancs, who did return to Hungary:

> Later, in the mid–1860s I received a letter from him [Zagonyi] in which he asked me to look for an appropriate estate here, in Szőllős, because he intends to come home and settle down.... In this letter he notified me that he had become wealthy, and invested his money in a railroad company, and even become a member of the board of directors.... At the beginning of 1867 he wrote that he was coming home in the middle of that year, but [later] he let me know that the company had gone bankrupt and he had lost all his wealth. He did not intend to come home until he accumulated wealth again. It has been 23 years now that I have not heard anything from him: he is probably not alive now.[44]

Unfortunately, we do not have any reliable information concerning Zagonyi's fate. An article published in the *Tuscumbia Osage Valley Sentinel* stated that Zagonyi kept a cigar shop in Pest in 1871. However, there is no proof that Zagonyi indeed returned to Hungary. The *Daily Bulletin Supplement* of San Francisco wrote in 1880 that Zagonyi disappeared mysteriously in 1870. Hungarian-American historian Károly Rácz-Rónay wrote in a letter to Sándor Márki in 1921 that Zagonyi had starved to death in the United States. Anyhow, what we know for sure is that according to the federal census of 1870 his wife, Amanda Zagonyi, married someone in 1870 in Manhattan, New York, which means that Zagonyi had either died between 1865 and 1870, or they got divorced and he returned to Hungary; however, the former case seems to be the most plausible.[45]

The overall military importance of Zagonyi's Death Ride is arguable, but there is no denying that it has been of special importance from the perspective of the Hungarian-American community and its local significance is obvious as well. In 1931 the University Club erected its Historical Marker No. 17 commemorating the event. In Springfield a 10-acre park was named after Zagonyi.[46]

What connects the three Hungarian soldiers discussed in this chapter is the role they played in the process of self-justification of Hungarian-Americans. What can be argued is whether their military careers were as outstanding as they are presented in the sometimes very much biased works written by the chroniclers of ethnic Hungarian past. Asboth and Zagonyi were both brought into the machine of the Union volunteer army by Major General Frémont amid highly controversial circumstances. Zagonyi obviously fell victim to the political intrigues that surrounded Frémont's command, and perhaps to his own excessive loyalty towards him. Asboth was in a very similar situation; however, being a renowned high-ranking officer back in Hungary, he was very much respected in America, as well. His excellent military career secured him a foreign service appointment after the Civil War. At the same time, Julius Stahel was relatively unknown at the beginning of the Civil War, and his connections with other Kossuth émigrés were rather loose as compared to those of Zagonyi and Asboth. Actually, he seemed to have much closer links to German-Americans in New York, so much so that some suggested his promotion to the rank of major general was a gesture towards German-Americans by President Abraham Lincoln. This is, of course, not to suggest that Stahel was a political general, as his achievements are beyond dispute, yet his connections with the German community are not to be denied. In 1861 *The Chicago Tribune*, for instance, referred to him as "The German Brigadier." Nevertheless, he was the only Hungarian officer who received the Congressional Medal of Honor, and this raises him well above his contemporary critics.[47]

In conclusion, it has to be emphasized that all three of these Hungarian officers had outstanding careers in the Civil War: they rose to high ranks, and were acknowledged. Asboth and Stahel played significant roles on a national level, but Zagonyi seems to be the odd one out here, as his Death Ride at Springfield, Missouri, was of local importance only and there might be justification for questioning whether attacking the Confederates there made sense from a strategic point of view at all. What is more, although the Union cavalry was outnumbered by the rebels, it was not taken into consideration in the historical literature that most of the Southern forces belonged to home guard units, and were inexperienced and poorly-armed.

Nevertheless, the careers of Asboth, Stahel as well as Zagonyi all seem to support the words of Franklin Delano Roosevelt, who in his letter wrote to Edmund Vasváry on the occasion of the publishing of his book, *Lincoln's Hungarian Heroes*: "Men of Hungarian blood — many of them exiles from their fatherland — rendered valiant service to the cause of the Union." However, and this is my main argument in this chapter, significant differentiations are necessary to be made in the evaluation of the historical role these individuals played. Due to the hero-making activity of Hungarian-American historians, Asboth, Stahel and Zagonyi, similarly to numerous other ethnic heroes, acquired special historical importance: their actions had significant effect on ethnic collective memory. Their contribution to the war effort of the Union guaranteed the success of the Hungarian-American community in the postwar United States as well as its visibility in American society. This is what all three above-mentioned Hungarian officers share: negligible as the effect of Zagonyi's Death Ride may seem from a military point of view, its historical significance was great for the Hungarian-American community in creating group-cohesion, similarly to the undeniably heroic Civil War careers of Asboth and Stahel.[48]

CHAPTER SIX

An International Fraud: Colonel Béla Estván[1]

Béla Estván is one of the most often quoted participants of Hungarian origin in the American Civil War, in spite of the fact that hardly anything was known about him either by the scholars studying Hungarian-American historical links and contacts, or by his contemporaries in the United States. His book *War Pictures from the South*, however, became a real bestseller of the Civil War years, and made Estván's name familiar to many. Because no other book by a Hungarian enjoyed such popularity in the period, Pivány, Vasváry and Ács accepted everything he wrote about himself or his wartime experience. However, careful research shows that Estván was not only a notorious liar, but was not even Hungarian! Estván's example shows that Hungarians were so popular at the beginning of the 1850s in the United States that some non-Hungarians even pretended to be Hungarians. Estván's popularity did not carry over into the community of real Hungarians. No fellow Hungarian emigrant wrote about him or reacted to his book. There was no trace of him in works about the Hungarian War of Liberation either. In fact, the absence of Hungarian interest in his exploits provided the first clues that he had fabricated his persona.[2]

In spite of Estván's claim to have served in the ranks of the Confederate Army, in 1961 the Kossuth Foundation commemorated the centennial of the outbreak of the Civil War by highlighting his exploits. The foundation published a booklet by András Pogány entitled *Béla Estván: Hungarian Cavalry Colonel in the Confederate Army*. It did not matter to them that Estván apparently fought for secession and slavery, as they took for granted Estván's own words about his enlistment: "It was now 13 years that I had been away from my native home and now, drawn into the whirlpool of events, I found myself, almost against my will, serving in the ranks of a foreign army, and fighting for a cause, with which neither my head nor my heart could thoroughly sympathize." The author, Pogány, did not spend too much time researching Estván's life, except for some vague attempts which led him to false assumptions concerning the genealogy of Estván. The scope of his book, therefore, is very limited, and the thin volume is not only riddled with errors, but it hardly goes beyond summarizing Estván's *War Pictures*.[3]

Edmund Vasváry, the ardent student of the history of the Hungarian-American community and author of *Lincoln's Hungarian Heroes*, also mentioned Estván among the Hungarians who supported the South in the War Between the States in his articles published serially in the monthly of the William Penn Fraternal Association between 1961 and 1964. Yet, he himself called for further research, which, he indicated, "would be able to discover some favorable testimony about the life of this mysterious and elusive individual." Nevertheless, it is hard to tell how he came to the conclusion that "in his paper, Pogány writes about Estván with academic thoroughness." So it may be useful to summarize what the most recent investigations revealed about Estván.[4]

Little is known about Estván's early life. According to Pogány, he was born in 1827, although in the Census of 1860 the date of birth he gave was 1815. Pogány managed to identify a family of lesser nobility in Hungary named Estván, but could not prove any connection with that particular family. Béla became an officer of the Imperial Army of Austria-Hungary and later he wrote that he had "served the king of Hungary for fourteen years." He marched in Italy under Radetzky as captain of cavalry and participated in the Italian campaign of 1848. Having heard of the outbreak of the Hungarian revolution, he returned to Hungary and Governor Kossuth appointed him colonel of cavalry.[5]

After the Hungarian forces laid down their arms at Világos in 1849, Estván had to leave the country in order to escape Habsburg retribution and, like many of his comrades, sought refuge in England. The exact date of his departure for the United States is not known, but it is highly probable that he sailed for the "Land of the Free" in 1850–51, right before or during Kossuth's tour of the country. None of the sources mention him as a member of Kossuth's retinue, and the reasons why he wound up in Richmond, Virginia, are not clear either. That notwithstanding, in his letter to Confederate President Jefferson Davis in 1861 he wrote that he had been the citizen of the city for eight years, i.e., since 1853.[6]

These are the details concerning Estván's early life as reconstructed by András Pogány and Ella Lonn. Yet sources make it clear that Estván lied about his past and he was indeed an adventurer, a real Münchausen figure. It turned out that Béla Estván was only an assumed name and his real name was Peter Heinrich. He was born in Vienna on July 12, 1827. And, most importantly, he was Austrian by birth. It seems likely that later he only claimed to be Hungarian to win the sympathy and support of the Americans who were enthusiastic about the Hungarian freedom fight of 1848–49. According to Károly Rácz-Rónay, he followed the footsteps of his father, and learned the trade of a painter.[7]

The most mysterious part of Estvàn's adventurous career was yet to come. In his book he boasted of having participated in the Crimean War and called himself the Hero of Sebastopol. No sources support these statements. As a matter of fact, Hungarian refugees in the United States were organizing an expeditionary force which was to sail over to Europe and help the Turks against the Russians. There is no evidence to prove that organized Hungarian units participated in the Crimean war, although there were some individuals who did. None of them, however, sided with the Russians, except for Col. Estvàn, assuming his claims can be trusted. Nevertheless, one clue shows that at least some credit could be given to Estvàn's words. The would-be Union commander-in-chief, Gen. George B. McClellan, was present in the Crimean War as a military observer and it is possible that he met the Hungarian adventurer there. It is known that McClellan had shown great interest in the Hungarian fight for freedom against the Habsburgs back in 1849 and had asked to be sent to Hungary as a military observer. However, because of the victory of the joint Austrian and Russian forces, his plan came to naught. He may have met Estvàn in the Crimea and this might provide an explanation to the surprising fact that, when his *War Pictures* was first published in Britain in 1863, Estvàn dedicated it to McClellan, in spite of the fact that the Hungarian colonel had served in the Confederate Army. (The 1864 edition was dedicated to the soldiers of both armies.)[8]

After the Crimean War, Estvàn claimed to have returned to the United States and settled down in Richmond. There is only sporadic reference to his pre–Civil War years. Hermann Schuricht, in his significant book on the Germans living in Virginia, writes the following not too flattering lines about Estvàn: "He (the so-called Count) lived there (in Richmond) upon the earnings of his two ladies, his wife and his sister-in-law, who gave lessons.... He himself was a very good-looking jovial man and knew how to play the part of an upright Austrian country nobleman to perfection." The first mention of Estvàn in the American press is dated to 1854, when the *National Intelligencer* reported the concert of Count Estvàn and Countess Maria De Estvàn at Carusi's Saloon in Washington, D.C.[9]

The census of 1860 supports Schuricht's claims. One can find two ladies living in Estvàn's household: Marie Estvàn, 25, and Laura Lacey, 22, both of whom made their living as teachers of French. Béla and Marie had a two-year-old daughter, Mary.[10]

Ella Lonn, one of the foremost scholars of the field, states that Estván reached prominence in the Virginia militia and, mainly due to his experience gained in European battlefields, obtained a colonelcy by the time of John Brown's raid on Harper's Ferry in 1859, and, according to Pogány, Estván also took part in the suppression of Brown's rebellion.[11]

There is a 5-page sheet musical composition titled *Chicora, the Original Name of Carolina; Chicora, the Indian name of Carolina* from 1861 in the Rare Book, Manuscript and Special Collections Library of the Duke University in Durham, North Carolina, on which the name of C. B. Estván is specified as the publisher. It is dedicated to the patriotic ladies of the Southern Confederated States of North America, suggesting that Estván enthusiastically supported the Confederate cause. The outbreak of the Civil War found him in Richmond, the future capital of the newly-born Confederate States of America. Estván states in his book that he served as a commander of cavalry in the Confederate Army, and participated in a number of engagements including the first battle at Bull Run and Fair Oaks. He belonged to General Longstreet's staff in the battle of Seven Pines and Gaines' Mill and claimed that he was the one who changed the outcome of the latter engagement. A glorious military career. The only problem is that no evidence can be found to validate his statements. No Confederate commander ever bothered mentioning his name in either his memoirs or letters, and there is no trace of him in the *Official Records of the War of the Rebellion*. Considering this fact, no words will be wasted here upon the military deeds of which he boasts in his book. Instead, it is more worthwhile to take a look at the documents at the archives and try to take the measure of Estván on that basis.[12]

In writing about his motives for joining the Confederate army, Estván made it seem as if he had been almost forced into it: "Circumstances led me to take service in the confederate army—my long residence in the Southern States being, however, the main inducement thereto."[13] Nevertheless, on June 22, 1861, he wrote the following letter to Confederate President Jefferson Davis:

To His Excellency

The undersigned most respectfully begs have to [sic] offer his services to his Excellency the President of the Southern Confederated States.

I served the king of Hungary for fourteen years as a captain of cavalry and fought the victories in Italy under Radetzki.

Governor Kossuth of Hungary appointed me afterwards to Colonel of cavalry and served him in that capacity for two years. For the last eight years I have been a citizen of Richmond Virginia.

Being widely known amongst my countrymen and hoping to meet with ultimate success, I should be highly flattered if his Excellency would give me the

> permission to furnish me with the necessary means to establish a foreign Legion. I refer to Hon. Porcher Miles of Charleston.
>
> I have the honor to remain Your Excellency's most obedient servant:
> C. B. Estván[14]

These lines suggest that Estván was more than willing to offer his services to the Confederate cause. But even so, barely a fortnight after the first letter, Estván wrote another one to Davis:

> His Excellency, President Jefferson Davis.
>
> I, the undersigned most respectfully submit to your Excellency the following plan which if it should meet your approbation will be carried into execution as soon as I am furnished with the necessary permission.
>
> I propose to raise in the states of Virginia, Tennessee and Kentucky recruits for two foreign regiments: one of cavalry and one of infantry which if formed will be subject to the command of Brigadier General Wise.
>
> The two regiments would be mustered in for the duration of the war;—the soldiers to be allowed to elect their officers captains included.
>
> In [illegible] you will please allow me to give some details of my military life:
>
> I have served fourteen years as captain of cavalry in the Austrian army and afterwards as colonel under Gov. Kossuth in Hungary.
>
> For the last eight years I have been a citizen of Richmond Virginia.
>
> I have the honor to remain
>
> Your Excellency's most obedient servant: B. Estván[15]

Davis passed both letters on to Confederate Secretary of War Leroy P. Walker, who inquired of opinions of Robert E. Lee and other military leaders in Richmond.

These two letters are the only documents which reveal some direct connection between Estván and the military apparatus of the Confederate States. It cannot be confirmed whether or not Estván had been commissioned, as his name cannot be found in any of the rosters of regiments. A post–Civil War Texas newspaper wrote that Estván had claimed to be General Wise's chief, authorized to collect hospital and other stores, and added that the ladies of Wilmington, North Carolina, would in all likelihood recollect him as they had entrusted to his care several thousand dollars worth of clothing, wine and supplies for the soldiers which he had disposed of for his own benefit.[16]

Considering all this, it is clear that all of Estván's statements in *War Pictures* must be treated with extreme caution, especially the parts about his own role. Even his contemporaries could not agree on how much his analyses of the events of the Civil War can be taken for granted. *The New York Herald*, for example, wrote that Estván had started a military school in Richmond, so he undisputedly was a military expert. On the contrary, his reviewer in *The New York Times* wrote that Estván was "unimportant as a historian and probably insignificant as a commander" and "his claims as a military critic are not likely to be accepted by either side."[17]

Another documented aspect of Estván's career definitely links his name to the Confederate war effort, although it is neither directly related to military heroism nor, as far as the outcome is concerned, particularly glorious. In 1861, along with Louis Froehlich, Estván started a business that made cavalry sabers and bayonets in Wilmington, North Carolina. As early as January 20, 1861, their firm of Froehlich and Estván or C.S. Arms Factory had a contract with the state of North Carolina and made 61 cavalry sabers and 133 saber bayonets, and this was followed three days later by an order for another 35 cavalry sabers and 97 saber bayonets; the two orders combined were worth $5,267. Between January 20, 1861, and March 1, 1862, the firm produced 479 cavalry sabers, 1054 saber bayonets and a couple of artillery bayonets. In 1862 cavalry sabers cost $24.50 apiece, whereas for the saber bayonets the Ordnance Office of North Carolina at Raleigh paid $10.50 apiece. However, there were more and more complaints regarding the quality of the weapons produced by Estván and his partner. For instance, Confederate Secretary of War J. P. Benjamin received a letter dated March 11, 1862, from Henry T. Clark writing on behalf of the Nineteenth North Carolina Cavalry Volunteer Regiment from Raleigh, N.C., in which he complained that the regiment was just partly armed and was "yet without sabers, although we spared neither effort nor money. We engaged from the Eastvan & Froelich [sic] sword factory at Wilmington, and paid high prices, but three-fourths of the swords proved worthless."[18]

About that time the firm started to face grave financial difficulties. On April 23, 1862, *The Weekly Standard* of Raleigh published a short notice seeking people who had claims against Froehlich and Estván or C.S. Arms Factory. Although the exact date is not known, it seems very probable that Estván quit very soon thereafter; the Richmond papers reported that the partnership was being dissolved. Ella Lonn confirmed this by stating that Louis Froehlich continued making swords alone at Kenansville, N.C., after his unsuccessful venture with Estván. Froehlich employed about 15 or 20 hands in his manufactory, which was eventually closed down in 1864.[19]

The documents do not verify any other details of Estván's Civil War career. In his *War Pictures* he states that after 18 months of campaigning with the Confederate Army he contracted yellow fever and resigned his commission. In the eyes of Ella Lonn his resignation was rather due to the fact that promotion was hard to come by for the foreign-born in the Confederate Army. She wrote that "probably this slowness of recognition had much to do with Estván's disgruntled attitude toward the Confederacy and ultimate departure in the midst of the war."

Hermann Schuricht, however, offered an entirely different explanation for Estván's leaving the Southern states: "When the Civil War commenced, he pretended to have recruited in North Carolina a regiment of Lancers and was authorized to draw from the Ordnance Department the necessary equipage" which he took to North Carolina and sold there. He also said that Estván tried to gain popularity in the North by claiming that he had deserted, going to Washington, D.C., in full Confederate uniform and even obtaining an audience with President Lincoln. Although no records support any of these claims, there is a striking similarity between this part of the stories of Estván and another Hungarian in Confederate service, Col Adolphus Adler, as both of them claimed to have been forced into the ranks of the Confederate army, and they acted as if they had been in possession of military information of vital importance, which they were, of course, more than willing to share with the federal authorities. Whatever Estván's real reasons for leaving the Confederate States might have been, on September 13, 1862, he applied for a passport to the authorities in Washington and left America for Britain soon after.[20]

Once in England, Estván wrote his *War Pictures from the South*, which saw three editions within slightly more than a year. This shows its considerable success, although even the contemporary American press was divided over the book — Northern and Southern alike. Of course, the Confederate press treated him as a deserter and a foreign mercenary. The *Daily Richmond Examiner* described him in these words, "In these war times, they [the deserters] are plentiful under the uniform of military officers. Estván, the soi-disant count, who ran to the North after playing out his calls here, was one of a particular class." *The New York Times* reviewer of his book was similarly critical, claiming that Col. Estván belongs to the large class of warriors who can "be sharked up for any enterprise that hath a stomach in't.... We should prefer that he stood up more manfully either for the North or the South." In contrast, it was Estván's impartiality that was particularly emphasized by *The North American Review*. That reviewer concludes, "His book seems to us eminently wise in its judgments and opinions, is in its tone friendly to the people of the North."[21]

This is the point where most sources finish Estván's story. Schuricht suggests that he revisited his old fatherland, Austria, and he was arrested and prosecuted as a criminal in Vienna. In the summer of 1864 the Emperor Maximilian of Austria's Habsburg-Lorraine family arrived in Mexico with the intention to create a new imperial order in the country. He enjoyed the military and financial support of Napoleon III, but he soon started to face grave financial difficulties, as the French emperor lost interest and gradually withdrew his support. He also found an avowed enemy in the person of President Andrew Johnson, who wanted to get rid of the French as soon as the Civil War in the United States was over. The Monroe Doctrine became a subject for public discussion and the American public demanded its enforcement.[22]

Maximilian decided to meet this challenge by counter-propaganda. He sought recognition and he did not think that he was playing a losing game. He established an agency in New York which served as the center for imperial intrigue and propaganda. In 1865 the emperor appointed Luis de Arroyo consul general for the Mexican empire. His primary — and improbable — task was to secure recognition by the United States.[23]

Arroyo was visited in his New York office a number of times by Béla Estván. Arroyo recalled that "he gave the impression that he was a man of some consequence, and spoke encouragingly of the imperial prospects of recognition." Estván told him that he had been the special correspondent for the *New York Herald*, and was sent to Mexico by James Gordon Bennett in October 1865. (It is worth mentioning here that on March 10, 1866, the *New York Herald* published a short notice reporting that Col. Estván had lately visited Mexico as the special correspondent of the *Herald* and disclaiming any connection between the paper and Estván.) He managed to secure an audience with the emperor and later he summed up his motivations: "Despite my seventeen years of absence from my homeland I still preserved a deep affection for the imperial Family of the House of Habsburg, I took the opportunity with vivid interest to indirectly serve an imperial Prince, thus redeeming the political debt which I still had to pay to the Austrian House from previous years." More accurately, perhaps, historian Robert W. Frazer observed that "it was doubtful that he desired to serve an imperial prince as much as he wished to serve Béla Estván."[24]

Nevertheless, Estván's plan of subsidizing the American press was backed both by Maximilian and Arroyo. The emperor retained Estván for two years at $5,000 a year. In addition, the Hungarian was provided a whopping $40,000 a year for expenses, which was still only half of what Estván had hoped for. Estván returned to New York, where his task was to prepare the material furnished by others for publication. He had to account for his expenditures at the end of each month, which displeased him very much. Whatever his feelings about these restrictions, he got down to opening offices in Washington and New York at once and employed several assistants. He overspent the $40,000 during the first year. In addition, his budget called for an additional $35,000, well above the sum provided for that year.[25]

Both Louis Borg, head of the Mexican consulate, and Maximilian's agent, Mariano Degollado, were amazed at Estván's budget. They hesitated to provide the Hungarian with the additional sum he requested. Finally they agreed to give him $7,500, but refused to give him a cent more.

Estván made extensive use of propaganda in New York, whereas in Washington he was more interested in developing personal contacts and planning petty intrigues. According to his own account, he managed to bribe — among others — three New York newspapers and paid $750 each to the *Herald, Tribune* and *Times*. However, none of the three dailies published articles favorable to the empire, except some sporadic ones in the *Tribune* which may have been rather due to Horace Greeley's opposition to the administration. Therefore, it is not at all unlikely that Estván pocketed the subsidies himself.[26]

The "Hungarian" spent most of his time in the capital trying to form acquaintances. For example, he met with the leaders of the Fenian movement and soon boasted that he had won almost a million voters for the empire.[27]

Estván fought vigorously for a free hand as far as the expenditure of money was concerned, but his pleas were rejected. When one of his installments failed to arrive, he turned to George Francis Train, one of his Fenian acquaintances and a candidate for the U.S. Senate from Nebraska, from whom he received a loan of $15,000; in return he gave Train a bill of exchange on the imperial government. Estván's drafts, however, returned unpaid and he could not turn Maximilian's order into cash either.[28]

Arroyo was not satisfied with the output of Estván's bureau. A number of articles treating the Mexican question appeared in the press, but most of them were partisan in nature (the Republicans were for the peaceful settlement of the question, whereas the Democratic press favored measures against the empire), and not the product of the Estván and his assistants. In April 1866, Arroyo finally decided not to provide Estván additional funds. Estván was forbidden to call himself an employee of the imperial government or to make offers and concessions concerning Mexico. The documents regarding his activities were sent to the imperial foreign office, and the press campaign was terminated. He followed Castillo, who was in Europe with the Empress Charlotte, to Paris and Rome, but he could not achieve anything. He returned to New York, but his part in Maximilian's propaganda activities had ended. Meanwhile, the emperor's days in Mexico were numbered. In May 1867 he was captured by the soldiers of Juarez and — despite the objections of European diplomacy — he was executed on June 19.[29]

Soon thereafter, on July 6, *The New York Times* published an open letter to the editor written by Béla Estván, who titled himself as director of the Imperial Bureau of Mexico in the United States. In this letter, Estván accused the United States government of a "reprehensible and self-dishonoring hesitation" and questioned why the United States failed to defend the life of Maximilian. Referring to the Monroe Doctrine, he asserted that it was the United States that forced France and other European powers to leave Mexico and that the U.S. should have had "the moral power, supported by an invincible military force, to protect, in the interest of our modern civilization, the life of a Christian Prince, from whom it had taken the means of self-protection and even of escape." Estván called it the last act of his official duty to the murdered emperor to give this solemn protest to the American people.[30]

Not much is known about his life thereafter. At the end of 1867 he wrote a letter to Cassius Marcellus Clay, the American ambassador to Russia, from London. This indicates that soon after the tragic end of Maximilian he returned to Europe. It is not clear how well Clay and Estván knew each other, but the informal parts of the letter show that they had been acquainted for some time. It is not clear either what Estván was doing in St. Petersburg, Berlin and London.[31]

Estván returned to his Austrian homeland in 1872. He published a memorandum to Emperor Francis Joseph in which he demanded that he be paid 80,000 dollars that the deceased Maximilian had owed him. According to Vasváry, he elicited a considerable amount of money when he founded a mining company. Finally he was arrested and during his trial his own brother, who was living in Vienna, gave him up. Peter Heinrich, this Austrian swindler, was sentenced to 6 years of imprisonment on April 6, 1872. One of the contemporary papers described him as a "tall, dry man, with short neck, big head, high forehead, thinning hair and grey beard.... Very pleasant, engaging personality." We do not have any further information concerning the later stage of his life.[32]

So there are still a number of uncertainties concerning the life and career of Béla Estván, although several hitherto unknown documents shed light on many aspects of his personality and prove that Béla Estván was indeed a soldier of fortune, an adventurer whose primary aim was to make personal profit of every possible situation. It can be also be declared safely that he was not Hungarian, but was an international swindler. Nevertheless, his book became a real bestseller of the day; every now and then, excerpts from his book are republished in books and magazines even today, and his *War Pictures* is really a thrilling book to read — even if its credibility at many points is definitely questionable.[33]

CHAPTER SEVEN

"'Furreners,' Yankees, and 'Nigger Lovers'": Slavery and Hungarians in the Colored Regiments[1]

> You have officers who have faith in your manhood. They have left their homes and come among you, knowing they are liable of being hung by the rebel gov[ernment] should they be taken prisoners. [A]nd why? Because they instruct you to be soldiers.[2]

As mentioned earlier, it is essential to re-evaluate claims that Hungarians volunteered in the Union army because they were primarily motivated by abolitionist sentiment, and intended to fight for the liberation of slaves. In spite of the fact that virtually none of the Hungarian-born soldiers in the Civil War expressed abolitionist ideals, it cannot be entirely ruled out as a possible motivation, particularly because a number of them applied for commissions in colored regiments. Of course, the question can be raised whether they were motivated by their desire for emancipation, or by some additional factors.[3]

To evaluate the Kossuth émigrés' approach to the peculiar institution, we have to explain briefly how slavery was perceived by the Hungarian public, that is, what "cultural baggage" the Hungarian emigrants of the era carried to America, and how their attitude changed, if it did change at all, after they had gained first-hand experience regarding human bondage.

Hungarians in the Reform Age (the period in Hungarian history roughly between 1820 and 1848) saw a unique duality in the United States. On the one hand, they considered it the "Young Giant of Democracy" which epitomized everything they had been fighting for first on the political stage and later on the battlefields. On the other hand, they could not quite understand how such a dark, evil institution as slavery could flourish in "the Land of the Free." Not many Hungarians had the chance to actually travel to America and collect first-hand experience, and perhaps this was one of the main reasons why Sándor Farkas Bölöni's travelogue *My Journey to North America* became a real bestseller in Hungary. He related his first encounter with slavery:

> I felt as if an icy hand touched my heart when I read this [a newspaper ad about a slave auction]. So, we arrived in the land of slavery. I sighed in sorrow.... Having observed the unprecedented freedom stemming from the Constitution of this great country, with all its principles based on natural law and its institutions devoted to the advancement of mankind — the monstrous variance between the magnificent theory and this shameful practice was always incomprehensible to me.[4]

Most Hungarians, of course, were aware of this nature of the United States as well, but when many of them had to flee their homeland after the collapse of the rebellion in 1849, no Kossuth émigrés refused to migrate to America because of aversion to slavery. This does not mean that they failed to express their revulsion. József Madarász, who visited the United States briefly, wrote in his diary upon his landfall: "I gave a hearty welcome to America from onboard the ship, and I wished flourishing of this country, the institutions of which are so humane with a single exception. With one single exception! Yes, the existence of slavery in you, America, is antagonistic to the spirit of your institutions; it is the shame of your greatness, and a blemish on your freedom.... If you wish to take your proper position, you have to do away with this blemish."[5]

Later, as he traveled by train, he saw a plantation owner with his slaves, and he burst out: "My sense of humanity was exasperated! Such a humiliation of people because of the difference in the color of their skin in a free country! My face was flushed! My soul became disgusted, I was ashamed of these chains in the Land of the Free. Why can't I just make these poor creatures just tear the chains apart, why aren't those humiliated who themselves humiliate others this way."[6]

Hungarian settlers in America tended to avoid slave states where they would have to encounter the physical presence of the institution of slavery or the plantation system daily. This was the main reason why Ladislaus Újházy put off moving to one of the Southern states, even though the climate there was far more suitable for agriculture. Similarly, only a handful of Hungarians wound up in the Southern states; altogether less than ten percent of the Hungarian-born population in the United States lived in one of the states that would soon secede. This can only partly be attributed to their own decision, for the society of the South was considerably less receptive towards immigrants than that of the North.[7]

Nevertheless, Hungarian immigrants thought about, and acted toward, slavery in a variety of ways during the 1850s. The 38-year-old Hungarian-born Sigismund Brock owned a 240-acre plantation in Lawrence County, Alabama, and twelve slaves (six adults and six children). This meant that he possessed a little bit above average slave property, and quite typically, it represented most of his capital. So far, only one more Hungarian slave owner has been identified. Ladislaus Újházy in one of his letters denounced Martin Koszta, who had prompted grave diplomatic crisis between the United States and Austria in 1853: "He owns a female black slave.... I feel ashamed that there are Hungarians who hold slaves. How fast some people degenerate." Hungarians typically did not sympathize with the system.

Hungarian traveler Béla Széchenyi sought a solution to the problem of slavery that was less radical than those offered by the abolitionists: "There are a lot of people — including me — who are in favor of transitionary periods, and would prefer a bloodless revolution to ... a rebellion destroying everything. The same could be applied to the emancipation of slaves." He also agreed that "modern times cannot put up with such a blight," but, according to him, the elevation of slaves had to precede their liberation, because they "stood on a very low level of civilization." Széchenyi accused the North of hypocrisy, where — although they claimed that the Confederacy was racist — free blacks were also discriminated against, and were denied full civil rights. He thought conditions as depicted in Harriet Beecher Stowe's *Uncle Tom's Cabin* were atypical, and that a paternalistic presentation of the plantations would be much more accurate. Furthermore, he believed that liberation of slaves would unjustly deprive slaveowners of their "miserable property," and concluded that the South "standing on its own feet" would surely solve the problem, which was its internal affair anyway.[8]

Nevertheless, some Hungarians in America were not content with temporary, gradual changes, but demanded immediate abolition, and sometimes even advocated violence. One of them, as the *Chicago Daily Tribune* reported, incited a slave cook to put arsenic into her masters' food at a feast in Augusta, Georgia. Six people died, and thirty-one became ill. The cook was burnt alive, and similar fate awaited the Hungarian radical abolitionist, whose name was Coskina, according to the account.[9]

Violence also seemed acceptable to another Hungarian, Ferenc Kaiser, who joined the anti-slavery forces in Kansas during the armed conflicts there over the territorial expansion of slavery. He participated in the battle of Black Jack on June 2, 1856, was captured by pro-slavery troops in the battle of Osawatomie, and then shot in the head by F. N. Coleman. His name appears on the monument of the casualties of the battle.[10]

Not all Hungarians held such extreme views about the future of slavery. Perhaps the most interesting representative of this group was Eugene Kozlay, whose career is unusually well documented from the time he left Hungary after the defeat of the 1848 revolt. Kozlay wrote prolifically in his diaries, correspondence and literary works. All of them — first in Hungarian and German, and from the mid–1850s increasingly in English — reveal much about his opinion about slavery and blacks.[11]

The liberal ideals of the Hungarian War of Independence in 1848–49 were apparent in Kozlay's long German poem, written during his crossing of the Atlantic. He found parallels between the oppression of Hungarians and Native Americans, and his works gave special importance to the topics of discrimination and racism. While living in New Orleans for a year, he wrote an article entitled "The Slave Market" in which he thoroughly evaluated the institution of slavery. He described the process of selling and buying slaves, and concluded, "In a free country it is terrible to do such a thing." By the end of the 1850s Kozlay's opinion seemed to have changed concerning blacks. In 1857 *The United States Democratic Review* serialized his novel under the title *Secrets of the Past: A Romance of the South* in which the black characters appeared stupid and naive.[12]

An equally interesting insight into Kozlay's opinion about emancipation can be found in his wartime diary. Well before the Emancipation Proclamation, on July 14, 1862, he wrote:

> There are great many who will resign, because they say and with justice that they don't fight for the niggers and the Emancipation policy of the Abolitionist. That Congress had no right to pass law to abolish slavery anywhere is, and that this war is only for that purpose instituted by the fanatics. I agree in many things with this Genls who are high officers and influential; and if Congress, the President or their fanatical Abolitionist General will institute measures for the emancipation of the slaves, against the wishes of the majority and the wishes of the Eastern & Western states, then I will myself withdraw from the field. I came here to reestablish the Union as it was, but not to robe [rob] and subjugate any people. Let the South to be paid as they deserve for their fooly [folly]. Let every men die who works to destroy this land of liberty; but never steal their property, as the Abolitionist desire to do with the Southern men, and their slaves.[13]

On other occasions he complained about blacks, as well. In the same diary entry he wrote, "Some of them who followed our army — left us again and returned to their masters, to their prior capacity. So [is] this the class of people the fanatics desire to free?" Considering his opinion, it is hardly surprising that he did not agree with organizing colored regiments, and employing them in the Union war effort. He did not think that blacks were suitable for organized fighting, or amenable to military discipline. He complained several times that soldiers of the colored regiments were looting. Besides, he doubted their ability: "These last two nights, I had an alarm. The colored men are coming in by dozens and report the rebels 600 strong. I was prepared to receive them, but as I expected, they would not come. These colored men if they see a dozen rebels, they generally set their number at 500."[14]

Kozlay was also suspected of turning a blind eye to his soldiers' occasional acts of cruelty against emancipated slaves. James C. Beecher, brother of Harriet Beecher Stowe, commander of the 35th Colored Regiment, stated that Kozlay asserted in front of witnesses that a lieutenant of the 54th New York regiment (Kozlay's unit) "settled all freedmen cases quickly — by tying the complainant by the thumbs."[15]

This does not suggest that Kozlay was unusually racist. He distrusted blacks, but he was by no means the only one in the North to do so. More than anything, he merely assimilated to the society of his adopted country's characteristic Negrophobia. Just to offer an ethnic analogy, Martin Öfele concluded about German-Americans that they "internalized the existing racial conceptions about societal hierarchies and had to establish their position ... as distinctly above that of African Americans."[16]

Several Kossuth émigrés, however, expressed their sympathy with the oppressed. Among the Hungarian soldiers who served in the American Civil War, ten Hungarian soldiers applied for commissions in colored regiments, which for a long time was considered to be obvious evidence of their abolitionist sentiments in the literature. Similarly to the Hungarians' motivations for volunteering in the Civil War in general, the motives of these soldiers should be investigated to see whether their friendship to the Negro race really attracted them to the colored regiments.

The decision to recruit blacks and organize them into regiments dates back to May 22, 1863, when the War Department issued its General Order No. 143, which established a bureau in the Adjutant General's Office for this purpose. It was generally agreed on, however, that white officers should command these units, which was an obvious sign that Negrophobia had not been erased from the society of the North overnight, and many were still convinced that the Negro was an inferior race characterized by irresponsibility, laziness, childishness, and it was immensely difficult to keep them in line.[17]

The applicants were evaluated by committees who were looking for real vocation in them. What were the major motivations for applying for these positions? Some applicants sympathized with the colored people, and earnestly believed that they can help improve their conditions; they considered serving in a colored regiment as a mission. Others, in contrast, thought that these regiments would be pivotal in breaking the resistance of the Confederacy, therefore, the better organized they were, the sooner the Union would win. Commissions in the United States Colored Troops meant higher wages as well, which was very attractive for many. An applicant from Illinois with a wage of 13 dollars a month remarked, "I would drill a company of alligators for a hundred and twenty a month."[18]

A commission as a commander or an officer, even in a colored regiment, definitely held prestige, and it was an important opportunity to step forward, particularly for the foreign-born, as volunteer regiments usually elected their own officers, and they — lacking connections and not being known by many — had no chance to become commanders. (It is worth pointing out, however, that in ethnic regiments, usually ethnic officers were elected, which was very typical, for instance, of the Germans.) Anyway, foreign officers, very often veterans of one or more European wars, enjoyed a relative advantage over Americans, although some of them had problems with acquiring the necessary level of proficiency in the English language.

The application procedure was simple: a letter had to be sent in along with a recommendation from the candidate's commanding officer. Applications were judged on a competitive basis, and the final decision was made following a thorough oral examination. The four-member panel tested the applicant's expertise in tactics, military regulations, general military knowledge, arithmetic, history and geography.

Rumors of the difficulty of the entrance examination spread very quickly, and soon an enterprise was started offering preparation for the exam. The Free Military School for Applicants for Commands of Colored Troops proved to be so successful that by the beginning of 1864 they had had 170 applicants registered each week. Ninety-six percent of those who completed their training were classified fit for service in colored regiments, whereas less than half of other applicants were admitted.[19]

On the basis of available sources, there were eleven Hungarians who applied for commission at colored regiments, and ten of them did actually serve in such units. Dr. Rudolph Tauszky served as assistant surgeon in a volunteer regiment. Seeking promotion, he applied for a commission as a regimental surgeon. When he was offered a position of assistant surgeon of the 1st Colored Regiment, however, he rejected it without hesitation. This might suggest that he considered it inferior to serve in a colored unit, but it merely shows that he was not willing to move without a promotion, particularly as travel took a lot of trouble. After the Civil War, Tauszky became a prominent physician in New York City. However, on January 3, 1885, he took his gun and shot his wife and then attempted to commit suicide. Both of them survived, but Tauszky spent the rest of his life at Bloomingdale mental asylum. He died in 1889.[20]

Not all Hungarian immigrants had second thoughts about commissions in colored regiments. Alexander Asboth received an order from General Lorenzo Thomas to organize the recruitment of blacks in Florida. As commander of the District of West Florida, Asboth had enough influence to help some fellow Hungarians get commissions in colored regiments. Peter Paul Dobozy became his aide-de-camp and later organized the 2nd Tennessee Heavy Artillery in the rank of major.

Later he was promoted to lieutenant colonel, when the 2nd Tennessee Heavy Artillery became the Fourth Colored Heavy Artillery. Dobozy did a very good job in organizing and drilling the regiment of black soldiers, yet, similarly to many foreigners in the Union Army, he was target of suspicion on the part of Americans. His ability to lead a regiment was questioned, but the inspection commission found that Dobozy was "a perfect gentleman in every respect; a very energetic, and good officer." They even considered his proficiency in English satisfactory, although this was one of the major complaints of his accusers against him. What is more, Acting Medical Inspector John Rush reported about Dobozy's regiment that both medical and line officers "took much interest in procuring the comfort and well-being of the men," and he also emphasized the good morale appearance, which he attributed to the officers' high commitment.[21]

Probably the most renowned Hungarian officer serving in the colored regiments was Ladislaus Zulavsky, one of Lajos Kossuth's nephews. He already held the rank of lieutenant-colonel at the age of twenty-seven in the Union Army and his bravery was widely praised, and not only by Hungarian-Americans. Still, he also had his enemies who harshly criticized him as a commander, since he laid much larger emphasis on the moral education of black soldiers, and often pushed military training into the background. Lt. Col. Isaac S. Bangs, for instance, was convinced that "Zulavsky especially lacked the persistent discipline required in such an organization as the USC." In December 1864 the Hungarian-born officer faced court-martial for negligence of duty, because it turned out that he had never instructed his regiment in battalion drill. Although Zulavsky himself often declared that he was not competent enough to command a regiment, the jury found him not guilty, and confirmed his rank and position. In spite of the fact that his further Civil War service was not entirely void of criticism either, Zulavsky did a good job leading his regiment. Brig. Gen. William A. Pile mentioned the 82nd in his report on the battle of Fort Blakely (April 9, 1865): "Although in reserve and consequently late in starting on the charge, preserved their regimental organization throughout, the officers exhibiting both skill and bravery."[22]

Contemporary sources mentioned another Hungarian officer, Ignatz Kappner, as a person in whose eyes blacks were on equal footing. In his obituary published by the Military Order of the Loyal Legion of the United States, Kappner's service at a colored regiment gained special importance: "There was no thought on the part of Col. Kappner that, in organizing and commanding a regiment of such troops, he was doing an action unworthy of the highest type of a soldier." He was armed, similarly to Zulavksy, with the moral principles he brought along with him from Hungary. He tolerated no lies and plundering in his regiment. What made him particularly suitable for leading a colored regiment was his empathy with which he approached blacks. Once, when his superiors were planning to remove the contraband camp outside Fort Pickering where the relatives of most soldiers lived, he communicated their protests to the Bureau of Colored Troops, "The men seem to be seriously allarmed [sic] and I would respectfully request to be informed what to tell them, and whether it would not be best to endeavour to have such families left here."[23]

Another Hungarian officer, Captain Joseph Csermelyi, had participated in the ill-fated filibustering expedition of Narciso Lopez in 1851. During the Civil War, he was among the Hungarians who gathered around Brigadier General Asboth when he assumed command of the Department of West Florida, and Csermelyi became captain in the 82nd Colored Regiment. He was breveted major on March 13, 1865.

Not all of the Hungarians managed to cope with the difficulties they were supposed to face as officers serving in colored regiments. First Lieutenant Alexander Toplanyi had to stand in front of an examining board in April 1863, which pointed out that he was deficient in artillery and infantry tactics and had little or no knowledge of guard duty and other workings of a company. The board heavily criticized him for not showing "the disposition to learn his duties" and for being meddlesome and troublesome." Although the board ruled that he was unqualified to hold the rank of 1st lieutenant in the Union Army, Toplanyi refused to accept the decision and asked for another examination. Interestingly enough, this time Brigadier General Barry, chairman of the board, found that Toplanyi was an able if not superior artillery officer. Col. William Birney of the 22nd U.S. Colored Troops proposed that he be added to the list of captains." Toplanyi soon rose to the rank of captain in the 3rd Colored Infantry Regiment.[24]

In February 1865, however, he was court-martialed for assaulting one of his black soldiers. Pvt. John Banks testified that while he was on guard duty, Toplanyi, drunk, approached him and charged him with sleeping on the post. When Banks requested that witnesses be called, Toplanyi started beating him. Toplanyi said that he had felt insulted by the soldier's lack of discipline and morale. All his officers substantiated that Toplanyi rejected corporal punishment and supported him, but the court obviously wanted to set a precedent. Furthermore, the incident revealed the most serious defect of Toplanyi's character: alcoholism. He had already had bouts of drinking in his former unit, and this seemed to be the gravest problem this time as well, more than his being racist, as some of his contemporaries suggested. To the contrary, he seems to have been very effective in organizing the regiment. Brigadier General E.P. Scammon wrote to him that he managed to transform "a company of untaught Negroes into a highly disciplined and most efficient company of

Artillery." In any case, the court found Toplanyi guilty and dismissed him, but his corps commander, Major Gen. Quincy A. Gillmore, intervened, and Toplanyi managed to obtain a pardon and retain his reputation.[25]

Emile and Sigismund Zulavsky, along with their brother Ladislaus, and Albert Ruttkay also saw service in colored regiments in the Civil War, and it was probably their and Asboth's support which more or less saved them from the attacks of anti-foreigner nature. There were others, however, who were not that fortunate; it was not his black men but other white officers who gave Louis Voneky, captain at the 68th Colored Infantry regiment in 1864, later major of the 51st Missouri Infantry regiment, a hard time, so much so that eventually he resigned. "I am so unfortunate as to be a Dutchman; that I never do anything by halves and cannot conform myself to do business in a lackadaisical style, but follow up my purposes and duties without regard to persons or showing favor or affection to anyone," he grumbled about his difficulties as a foreigner.[26]

It can be concluded that, on the basis of available sources, earlier assumptions claiming that the majority of Hungarians volunteered in the Union Army because they intended to fight for the liberation of slaves can be refuted.

The names of Ladislaus and Sigismund Zulavsky on the base of the African American Civil War Memorial. Ladislaus' name is misspelled and appears twice on the monument, in all likelihood in place of his brother, Emile, whose name is absent from the list (photograph by the author).

Undoubtedly, there were some who were concerned about the fate and emancipation of slaves so much so that they joined the United States Colored Troops. Unfortunately, this can be supported with evidence only in the case of Ladislaus Zulavsky. However, through analogies with other ethnic groups, we have every reason to suspect that Hungarian officers volunteered to be able to use their military talents and the experience they had gained on European battlefields, and were also seeking promotion and higher payment.

On July 18, 1998, a statue by black sculptor Ed Hamilton was unveiled in Washington, D.C., which was named the African American Civil War Memorial. It commemorates soldiers who contributed to bringing about the emancipation of slaves. The monument bears the names not only of black soldiers but of white officers, as well. Among them are the names of Albert Ruttkay, Ladislaus and Sigismund Zulavsky, Alexander Toplanyi, and Joseph Csermelyi.

CHAPTER EIGHT

The Aftermath: Kossuth Émigrés in the Post–Civil War Years

On April 9, 1865, at about one o'clock in the afternoon General Robert E. Lee arrived at the home of Wilmer and Virginia McLean in the small town of Appomattox Court House, Virginia. A half hour later Union Lieutenant General Ulysses S. Grant joined him. After a meeting lasting no longer than ninety minutes, Lee accepted Grant's rather generous terms for surrender, thus putting an end to the bloody fraternal struggle. Lee reportedly said to Grant before signing the document, "This will have a very happy effect on my army."[1]

It did have a very happy effect on the entire war-weary nation, which had suffered more than 630,000 fatalities. There were hardly any families nationwide which were not affected by the war: dead or crippled fathers, husbands, and sons and ruined families marked the slaughter that had been raging for four years.

The Civil War also took a heavy toll on the Hungarians who had been caught up in it. Captain Nicolai Dunka, Frémont's Hungarian aide-de-camp, was shot dead while forwarding a message to a distant part of the battlefield at the engagement of Cross Keys on June 8, 1862. Captain George Grechenek of the 72nd New York Volunteers was so severely wounded in the battle of Williamsburg, Virginia, on May 5, 1862, that his leg had to be amputated. Still, gangrene attacked the stump and he passed away on May 16. Another former officer of Kossuth, Captain Hugo Hollan of the 119th Illinois Infantry, was killed in combat on April 1, 1863, at Jackson, Tennessee. Similar fate awaited Colonel Géza Mihalotzy of the 24th Illinois Infantry Regiment, who died on March 11, 1864, of the gunshot wound he sustained on February 24, 1864. Major Anthony Weekey of the 39th New York Volunteers died of a disease contracted in the vicinity of Washington, D.C., on April 28, 1862, while Sigismund Zulavsky fell victim to typhoid fever in Louisiana at Port Hudson on September 16, 1863.[2]

In addition, several of them were discharged due to battlefield wounds or diseases contracted during the campaigns. This is one of the reasons why only about 30 percent of the total number of Hungarian soldiers were still in service at the end of the Civil War. (The other reason is that the majority of them volunteered in the very first months of the Civil War.) Among the wounded, quite a few never recovered from wartime injury. Colonel Gabriel De Korponay and his son Stephen both received disability discharges from their Pennsylvania regiments and died within a couple months of each other in 1865–66. Sixteen-year-old Nicholas Fejervary was so severely wounded in what was probably his very first battle that he was taken home to his father's estate in Iowa only to die. At Marianna, Florida, Brigadier General Alexander Asboth was hit by two bullets on September 27, 1864: one hit him in the left cheek and the other broke his left arm. The surgeons could never locate the former one and it gave him immense pain for the rest of his life. Asboth was appointed U.S. minister to Argentina and Urugay, but he died of his head wound in 1868. Colonel Philip Figyelmessy suffered a serious riding accident in 1864 and was unable to return to field service; he headed the court-martial in Baltimore, Maryland, for the rest of the Civil War.[3]

Despite the casualties, about 87 percent of the Hungarians participating in the American Civil War were mustered out as officers, and — as it has been pointed out earlier — most of them advanced considerably in rank in the course of the war. Two of them, the already-mentioned Alexander Asboth and Julius H. Stahel, rose to the rank of major general; furthermore, the latter was awarded the Congressional Medal of Honor in 1893 for his heroic conduct at the battle of Piedmont, Virginia, on January 5, 1864. He was the only Hungarian-born officer in the Civil War so honored. Frederick Knefler, Eugene Kozlay, Charles Mundee and Albin Schoepf were all breveted brigadier for their service.[4]

Considering all this, it can be established that the overwhelming majority of Hungarians who volunteered in the Civil War did actually benefit from their military service; having had problems integrating into American society and making a living in their adopted country (not unrelated to each other), they could utilize their military talent — very badly needed in the Union Army in the initial phase of the war — and their service earned them the well-deserved respect of their communities. This acceptance, and the fact that the majority of the Kossuth émigrés had applied for American citizenship prior to the Civil War and in fact had become U.S. citizens by the beginning of the Civil War, explains why the proportion of Hungarians deciding to return to their mother country in relation to their number in the United States remained relatively low.

On June 8, 1867, as part of the Austro-Hungarian Compromise establishing the dual monarchy of Austria-Hungary, Austrian Emperor Francis Joseph was crowned king of Hungary and he gave general amnesty to Hungarians who had fought in the War of Independence in 1848–49. This practically meant that after 1867 each member of the so-called Kossuth emigration could have returned to Hungary. Yet the statistics show that only 11 Hungarian Civil War veterans made up their minds to leave the United States for Hungary, which is only ten percent of the total number of Hungarian-born in the conflict. John Xantus, one of them, gave the following explanation for his decision: "Believe me, my friends, the Hungarian can never become American, for his heart and soul can never become as hard as the metal from which the dollar is minted. There is only one place for us in this great world: 'Home,' which may not be great, magnificent or famous, and though poor, is still the most potent magnet for its wandering sons."[5]

Xantus was among those who proved unable to find their places in America. Nevertheless, after his brief visit to Hungary in 1861 brought him the honorary presidency of Budapest Zoo and membership in the Hungarian Academy of Sciences but no employment, he returned to the United States and tried his luck in the American Civil War. However, most of his attempts to get settled failed, and rather disappointed, he left the country.

Cornelius Fornet also returned to Hungary and, like Ignátz Debreczeny, found employment as a minor government official. Joseph Kemenyffy also decided to bid farewell to America and re-settled in Hungary, working as a lawyer. Physician Ignatz Langner gave up his rather profitable practice to start over again after returning to Hungary. Nicholas Perczel, who back in 1851 had been sentenced to death by the Habsburgs along with his brother Mór, legendary general of the Hungarian War of Liberation, was also allowed to set foot on Hungarian soil again in 1868, and held important administrative positions in the next decades. Emeric Radnich, a civil engineer in the United States before the Civil War, returned to his homeland, and had a prominent career, eventually becoming director of the Győr-Sopron-Ebenfurt railway. On the other hand, Theodore Majthenyi, one of the heroes of Zagonyi's Death Ride at Springfield, Missouri, gave up his commission in the U.S. Army in 1868 and took his family back to Hungary. He was commissioned in the Hungarian Army as a major, but soon he resigned and returned to the United States, never to see his homeland again.

Approximately nine out of ten Hungarian Civil War participants remained in their adopted country even after they could have returned to Hungary without having to worry about Habsburg retaliation. We have already seen that financially most of them had not done particularly well before the Civil War, so it is worth taking a look at how much the financial situation improved and position them on the contemporary American social ladder.

In 2007 The United States Department of State published a booklet entitled *The United States & Hungary: Paths of Diplomacy, 1848–2006,* which quoted three Kossuth émigrés who entered service in the American diplomatic corps after the Civil War. Actually as many as seven Hungarian veterans served as consuls and ministers in various parts of the world from Tahiti through Argentina to Russia, and an eighth member of the Kossuth emigration was also appointed to a similar position.[6]

It was rather typical that the loyal service of high-ranking officers was awarded with foreign service posts, among them these Hungarians. Two of the "triumvirate" of the most renowned Hungarian-born soldiers, Alexander Asboth and Julius Stahel, were almost immediately offered positions in the American foreign service after the Civil War. In August 1865, Asboth became minister to Argentina and Uruguay. He was focused on bringing about a ceasefire in the so-called War of the Triple Alliance between Paraguay and the alliance many Argentina, Brazil and Urugay in 1864–1870. However, the Hungarian veteran of two wars suffered immensely from his Civil War wounds and died on January 21, 1868. Julius H. Stahel was appointed by President Andrew Johnson as consul at Yokohama, Japan, on May 9, 1866. He remained in diplomatic service in Japan until 1884, and he subsequently served as consul to Osaka and Hiogo. He was consul of the United States in Shanghai, China, for an additional year and eventually returned to New York City in 1885.

Approximately at the same time as Stahel, another Hungarian Civil War veteran was appointed to a consulship by President Johnson: Brevet Brigadier General George Pomutz became U.S. consul to Russia in 1866 and served in this capacity in St. Petersburg until 1870. He played an instrumental role in the purchase of Alaska in 1867. He was appointed consul general, also in St. Petersburg, in 1874, and he remained in that post until President Rutherford B. Hayes called him back. However, he remained in Russia and died in 1882.

Philip Figyelmessy was a veteran of three wars. He had served in the Hungarian War of Liberation as well as in the Hungarian Legion in Italy before participating in the American Civil War, in which he rose to the rank of colonel but received a disability discharge at the end of 1864. He had rather influential friends, shown by the fact that on January 3, 1865, President Lincoln wrote the following letter to Secretary of State Seward, "A Hungarian by the name of Foegelmeisy [sic] was on Gen Stahl's [sic] staff, and by his going out of active service is thrown out. Some of our Pennsylvania friends are desirous to get him a Consulship. Can you find one for him? If you can, I will ascertain the christian name." Seward could find a consulship for Figyelmessy, and he was appointed American consul at Demerara in British Guyana the next month. He became an American citizen the very same month.

He remained in his post for no less than twenty-two years, as he was reappointed by the Cleveland government in 1887.[7]

Colonel Joseph Vandor, organizer and commander of the 7th Wisconsin Infantry regiment, was mustered out due to his wounds. He was appointed consul to Tahiti by Abraham Lincoln in 1862 and served in this position for six years. Particularly in the first phase of his consulship, he was frequently criticized for not being effective enough in attracting business interests to Tahiti. He himself complained quite extensively that his salary was $1,000, which was barely enough to support his family. In 1868 President Andrew Johnson recalled him and he returned to the United States.[8]

Albert De Zeyk never actually performed military service in the Civil War, but still played a key role in the Hungarian-language communication between Frémont's Western Department and the Post Office Department in Washington, D.C. He personally knew both President Lincoln and Secretary of State Seward, but when he applied for a consulship, it was probably the support of the influential fellow-Hungarian László Újházy which mattered most. Újházy's son Farkas wrote to Francis Pulszky, "Did not you meet an Albert Zeyk in Paris who was on his way to Italy? He has become a consul in Taranto. My father recommended him to Seward." Indeed, De Zeyk became American consul to Taranto, and was later actively involved in the American diplomatic corps. He worked at the embassy in Paris and later at the consulate in Lyon. His subsequent posts included Frankfurt, Cairo and St. Gallen. In 1882 he was transferred to Lisbon, and the following year to Turin, where he was American vice-consul until 1885, when he returned to Hungary.[9]

Colonel-by-brevet Hugo Hillebrandt was appointed United States consul at Candia, on the island of Crete, in 1869. There he met the daughter of the Austrian consul and married her. He and his wife remained at his post until 1874.[10]

John Xantus, who was one of the most controversial figures in the whole Kossuth emigration, made use of his influential connections and secured an appointment as United States consul at Manzanillo in Mexico in December 1862. However, his term in office proved to be short-lived: when he recognized one of the Mexican rebel chiefs, not only he was removed, but the State Department closed the consulate as well.[11]

Other Kossuth emigrants who saw no service in the American Civil War also received consular appointments in the Reconstruction Era. One of them, Louis Czapkay, who — despite Vasváry's claims — did not serve in the conflict, was a prominent citizen of the city of San Francisco. He represented the United States Department of Agriculture at the international exposition in Prussia in 1865 (Lincoln wrote a letter of recommendation for him) and after his return, Andrew Johnson appointed him U.S. consul in Romania and Serbia. No matter how successful a physician and landed capitalist he was, he died poor and forgotten in a room at the Clarendon Hotel in Portland, Oregon, in 1882.[12]

Ladislaus Újházy, one of the key figures of the Kossuth emigration, was also appointed consul to Ancona, Italy, on December 23, 1861, and served until 1864, when he resigned. Some sources say he was still in office when he took part in the battle of Aspromonte in support of Garibaldi, and was captured by the royal troops. He was released after the intervention of Green Clay, the American ambassador.[13]

These appointments in the American diplomatic corps reflect the appreciation of their adopted country for armed service in defense of its institutions and democratic ideals, and shows that they were readily accepted as full-fledged citizens of the United States. Actually, most of them had been naturalized by the end of the Civil War, which shows the mutual willingness to consider the temporary phase of their staying in America concluded.

Hungarian-born Civil War veterans seem to have found their place in the United States. Even those who eventually left America to settle down in Hungary carried permanent reminders of their years overseas. In his *Recollections*, Charles W. Marsh gave an account of his encounter with Baron Baróthy in Nagyvárad, who returned to Hungary after 1867, and praised the United States and its institutions after having been treated so well he became a citizen.[14]

Those who stayed in America found employment without exception. Those who served as assistant or regimental surgeons utilized their wartime experience and all of them started successful practices. Some of them became prominent in American medical circles. Dr. Lazarus Schoney, who spent three years right after the Civil War in Paris and Berlin continuing his studies, became a distinguished professor of pathology and clinical microscopy at the New York Eclectic Medical College and a fellow of the New York Academy of Sciences. Dr. Rudolph Tauszky was also a celebrated expert in his field, mental illnesses, until he himself went insane and finished his life in a mental asylum after trying to shoot his wife and commit suicide. Another Hungarian, Dr. Arthur Wadgymar, who had served as a 2nd lieutenant in the C.S. Laboratory in Nashville, TN, became professor of chemistry and botany at Humboldt Medical College, 1866–67, and he published several articles in medical journals.

Several other examples can be mentioned from other walks of life. Louis Solyom, the extraordinarily talented linguist, who was fluent in more than twenty languages and could make himself understood in twelve others, worked for the Library of Congress for 45 years. Raphael Rombauer made a fortune through his mining enterprise, whereas his brother, Roderick, graduate of the Dane Law School of Harvard University, made a name for himself as a lawyer and judge in St. Louis, Missouri. And of course, the name of Joseph Pulitzer cannot be omitted here; despite his failure to prove himself as a Union trooper in the Civil War, he carved out an extraordinary career in journalism, becoming one of the most influential tycoons of his age.

Quite a few Kossuth emigrants learned a trade and found employment as artisans or took up in farming in the West. Most of them were respected members of local communities, with many known to be public-spirited citizens. Colonel Peter Paul Dobozy farmed in Western Arkansas and later in Missouri, and was referred to as "something of a local miracle," since besides English and Hungarian, he also spoke Turkish, German and Italian. He was a founding member of the First Baptist Church of West Plains, Missouri. Robert Rombauer, who was editor of the St. Louis daily *New World*, was a whole-hearted proponent of cultural improvement in the city: the St. Louis Public Library was his brainchild. He was also president of the board of assessors and a member of the board of education. Nicholas Fejervary, father of Nicholas, Jr., who had died in the Civil War, left part of his fortune to the city of Davenport and opened an old folks' home.[15]

It is essential to emphasize that no distinctions have to be made here: Hungarians who had served in the ranks of the Confederate army also prospered, and none of them left the place where they had been living prior to the Civil War, indicating their strong local attachments. The four sons of Ben Varga, a Hungarian saddler in San Antonio, Texas, all returned to the state after they had been paroled at the end of the war; three of them worked as saddlers in San Antonio, while the youngest brother, Paul, became a farmer. Charles Vidor, also from Texas, became very active in the bustling business life of the Lone Star State after the end of the Civil War. Not only did he have his own firm (in partnership with others), but he was a charter member of the Galveston Cotton Exchange, too. What is more, he was one of the founding members of the city's very first volunteer firefighting company organized in 1868, which also shows his commitment to the interests of the people living in Galveston, Texas.[16]

Brevet Brigadier General Frederick Knefler, founder and long-time commander of the 79th Indiana Volunteers, became a respected member of Indianapolis society, and the Hungarian lawyer worked very hard to represent the interests of Civil War veterans and pensioners. His pet project was erection of the Soldiers' and Sailors' Monument in Indianapolis, which was finished in 1902. Knefler himself did not live to see it unveiled, as he died the previous year.[17]

"In Everlasting Remembrance"

The treatment of Hungarian involvement in the American Civil War by historians, professional as well as self-appointed, reveals the limited influence of scholarship on public memory. Historical accuracy very often falls victim to attempts to commemorate ethnic heroes by their own ethnic communities. Yet they are the ones to most often produce tangible results in the form of monuments, statues, plaques, or even documentaries.

In spite of the fact that the Hungarians' involvement in the War of the Rebellion attracted the attention of Hungarian-Americans, it has not been commemorated in general. In 1939, at the seventy-fifth anniversary of the battle of Piedmont, a Hungarian delegation visited the grave of Major General Julius H. Stahel, the only Hungarian Civil War participant to be awarded the Congressional Medal of Honor. President Franklin Delano Roosevelt sent a letter to Edmund Vasváry commemorating this and the anniversary of the Hungarian War of Independence of 1848–1849. Roosevelt wrote, "Men of Hungarian blood — many of them exiles from their fatherland — rendered valiant service to the cause of the Union. Their deeds of sacrifice and bravery deserve to be held in everlasting remembrance." More than half a century later, on June 6, 1992, the Hungarians in the U.S. Armed Forces Commemorative Plaque was unveiled in the American-Hungarian Heritage Center in New Brunswick, New Jersey.[18]

On the other hand, individual Hungarians' contributions and heroic conduct have been recognized. One of the best-known Hungarian participants was Charles Zagonyi. Two principle factors made his "Death Ride" at Springfield, Missouri, and his name familiar. In 1861 the army of the Union was so short of victories, particularly in the state of Missouri, that much more importance was attached to Zagonyi's short-lived victory than it actually deserved. Hungarian-American authors played on this, and further exaggerated its importance. The result of these tendencies, abetted by local historians, was erection of a historical marker in Springfield, Missouri in 1931, commemorating "one of the most daring and brilliant cavalry charges of the Civil War."[19]

Alexander Asboth died in 1868

The bust of George Pomutz in Gyula (courtesy Sándor Bak).

in Buenos Aires. His grave was long neglected until his remains were re-interred at Arlington National Cemetery in Washington, D.C., on October 23, 1990, in an imposing tomb, complying with his last wish to be buried in American soil. His homeland, however, was much slower in recognizing him than his adopted country: one of the high schools in his native city, Keszthely, was named after him only on June 22, 2001. In December 2010 a conference commemorated the 200th anniversary of his birth in Keszthely.[20]

In contrast, George Pomutz was in a much more fortunate situation as far as his fatherland is concerned. What developed was a real competition between the Hungarian and Romanian ethnic groups in the United States, both of them claiming Pomutz as their own. (He was born in the Hungarian city of Gyula, in a Romanian family.) In 2004 a statue was unveiled at the Falling Asleep of the Ever-Virgin Mary Cathedral in Cleveland, OH, by the local Romanian-American community, which was followed by another one commemorating Pomutz in Gyula.

After Pomutz died in Russia, the Congress issued a joint resolution (No. 775) in 1913 in which it proposed that his remains be taken back to the United States and re-buried at Arlington. However, when World War I came, the whole initiative was forgotten. Nevertheless, a Colonel Pomutz obelisk was erected at Arlington. Furthermore, in 1944 a Liberty ship was named after him: the *S.S. George Pomutz* was launched on October 1944 and remained in service until 1970.

Although not due to his achievements in the Civil War in particular, or, as a matter of fact, in the United States in general, Dr. Bernard Bettelheim remains definitely one of the most recognized of all Kossuth emigrants. As a missionary

Bettelheim's monument in Ryu Kyu (courtesy LordAmeth).

in the Liu Ch'iu (Loo Choo) islands, belonging to Ryu Kyu, he compiled the first grammar and dictionary of the Ryukyuan language and translated the gospels of John and Luke and the books of the Acts and Romans into Ryukyu, which was republished by the Japan Bible Society in 1977. As a recognition of his efforts, a statue commemorating him was erected in Ryu Kyu in 1926. Although it was destroyed in the battle of Okinawa in 1945, it was restored in 1954 in honor of the 100th year anniversary of his arrival on Okinawa.

Probably nothing indicates more clearly the respect and reverence of a group than naming a settlement, a place or an institution after an individual, and there are plenty of places in the United States which bear names of members of the Kossuth emigration. No fewer than four cities in the United States are named Kossuth (in Pennsylvania, Indiana, Mississippi and Ohio), and there is a Kossuthville in Florida and a Kossuth County in Iowa. The city of Rombauer in Butler County, Missouri, was named after Roderick Rombauer, presiding judge of the St. Louis Court of Appeals for nine years, whereas Vidor in the state of Texas was named after Charles Vidor, charter member of the Galveston Cotton Exchange. Koszta, Iowa, bears the name of yet another Kossuth émigré, Martin Koszta. One of the wealthiest of all the Kossuth emigrants, Nicholas Fejervary left part of his fortune to the city of Davenport, Iowa, in 1895, including vast portions of his estate, on which a city park was created, named Fejervary Park. Similarly, one of the parks in Springfield, Missouri, was named after Charles Zagonyi.

Hungarian Civil War participants did contribute to the Civil War literature, as well. Col. Béla Estván's bogus *War Pictures from the South* became a bestseller and appeared in three editions in as many years — in Britain, the United States and Germany. Less familiar but more reliable was Robert J. Rombauer's *The Union Cause in St. Louis: A Historical Sketch*, which is considered to be the definitive source about the pro-Union movement in St. Louis in 1861. Emeric Szabad, who rose to a colonelcy in the Civil War and was a prolific writer, produced a Libby Prison diary (published by Stephen Beszedits) and a book called *Modern War: Its Theory and Practice,* published in 1863, as well as several other books in English and French as well as Hungarian.[21]

Numerous Kossuth émigrés penned their memoirs, some of them in English, others in their native tongue. Most of them reveal little about the Civil War proper, but there are exceptions. Julian Kuné wrote quite extensively about his role in the organization of the Lincoln Riflemen in Chicago in his recollections entitled *Reminiscences of an Octogenarian Hungarian Exile.*

Literary depictions of the subject do not abound. Hungarian playwright Pál Békés devoted a play entitled *New Buda* to it, in which he drew a rather grotesque picture of the Kossuth émigrés: Hungarian noblemen realizing their equality in America with their former servants, featuring a very human (as opposed to his image as the hero of universal freedom and champion of liberty) and often seasick Kossuth, and László Madarász, former minister of interior, spending the anniversary of the revolution on March 15 drinking and playing cards with Keokuk, a Sauk chief. The grand subject of tragedies of immigrant life (death of Mrs. Újházy, the young poet Frigyes Kerényi committing suicide, the feeling of isolation and hopelessness) is sometimes mocked by manifestations of human fallibility counterbalancing it.[22]

Péter Bogáti was inspired by the subject of Hungarians' participation in the American Civil War and wrote two historical novels for young adults: one about Zagonyi, *Őrnagy úr, keressen magának ellenséget* (*Major, Search for an Enemy*) and another one about New Buda: *Flamingók Új-Budán* (*Flamingos in New Buda*). His *Édes Pólim* (*My sweet Póli*) is based on the correspondence between Ladislaus Újházy and his daughter, and *A mahagóni ember* (*The Mahogany Man*) is the biographical novel of Károly László.[23]

Only a single movie depicts any aspect of the American "adventure" of the Kossuth emigration. Director Gábor Bódy's movie *Amerikai Anzix* (*American Torso*) (1975) is based on John Fiala's diary, and structurewise it follows Ambrose Bierce's short story "George Thurston." Bódy won the grand prize at the film festival in Mannheim, Germany. In its approach it is somewhat similar to Békés's play, and what makes it really unique is its cinematographic devices: Bódy applied a self-invented special editing process called "light-editing" making the image torn, aged and over-exposed in order to resemble a silent film from the late 19th century, successfully creating the impression that the film was a documentary. No actual documentaries have been made so far on the Hungarians' involvement in the American Civil War.[24]

As it becomes apparent from this chapter, the study of the historical memory of the Hungarians' involvement in the American Civil War is in its infant stage. As this is not the main focus of my work, I offer only a collage of ways how this event impacted literature, film and how its memory is preserved in the United States and in Hungary. What one finds is hardly surprising: the forty years of the communist regime left its imprint on historical memory, too. Therefore, I am convinced that several interpretations of the cultural meaning of the Kossuth émigrés' taking up arms in the Civil War are yet to follow, as its cultural legacy on the Hungarian-American community is unquestionable, and there are a number of so-far unexplored cultural materials to study.[25]

Part II

Biographical Dictionary

(of Hungarian Participants in the American Civil War)

This complete biographical list of Hungarians who took part in the American Civil War is the result of seven years of research. Several soldiers in this list have appeared in earlier works, but, unfortunately, none of the authors studying the Hungarians' involvement in the conflict indicated their sources; therefore, I have paid special attention to proper documentation here. The list is by no means complete, but it contains all the soldiers whose Hungarian origin can be substantiated, and whose service in either the Union or the Confederate army can be proved. The list is in alphabetical order; the affiliation of each soldier is indicated.

Adler, Adolphus

Many contemporary accounts state that Adolphus Adler was born in Hungary, but little can be found out concerning his career prior to his moving to the United States. He claimed to have been a civil and military engineer by profession, and he allegedly participated in the Hungarian War of Independence in 1848–49. His name cannot be found in any of the Hungarian archival files. He was reputedly wounded in the battle of Szolnok and was captured and imprisoned by the Austrians. He managed to escape and fled to Germany and France. He claimed to have served under Garibaldi in Italy in 1859, and he was wounded in the neck at Varese. However, passenger lists show that he arrived in New York on September 13, 1848, along with his two brothers, Jacob and Maurice. He was 19 at the time.[1]

Once in the United States, he decided to settle down in Virginia. Adler, a Jew, faced the distrust of Southern society even at the outbreak of the Civil War. When the *Richmond Examiner* editorialized that Jews and foreigners were hesitant about offering their services and compared them to vultures, the outraged Adler (in the tradition of Southern gentlemen as well as Hungarian officer) challenged the editor to a duel. The *Examiner* published a retraction right away. In 1861 he was, as he put it, "so situated that no other alternative presented itself than to take service in the rebel army." He obtained a colonelcy in the brigade of Gen. Henry A. Wise, who assigned him to the position of engineer-in-chief. The general wrote the following about Adler in his report on the skirmish at Scary Creek: "[For] locat[ing] the sites and plan the constructions of works for defence ... I have employed Col. Adler — a Hungarian — a man of consummate ability, science and bravery."[2]

Adler soon became suspect in the eyes of his superior officers, particularly Wise. It is not clear what exactly happened, but in August 1861 he was arrested and imprisoned. Some sources state that this was due to his disloyalty towards the Southern cause. We have a rare opportunity to approach this story from a number of perspectives, because quite a few Northern officers who shared a cell with him in various Richmond prisons, including Castle Goodwin, mentioned him in their personal recollections. According to some, he was imprisoned because he openly questioned the military talents of General Wise, who he "persisted in styling 'no soljare, no soljare.'" Others ascribed his imprisonment to his refusal to obey Wise's orders.[3]

The *Weekly Raleigh Register* also gave an account of Adler's story. According to the article, Adler was distrusted in Wise's brigade, so he left it and tried his luck in Richmond. After having failed in all his plans, he attempted to return to the troops. However, he turned out to be an impostor who did not have any official documents confirming his military service in the Southern army. That was the reason why Adler was put behind bars, and he apparently became so much obsessed with the idea that he was going to be executed that on August 31, 1861, he tried to cut his own throat with a razor or sword, yet he survived. He soon recovered enough and due to the lack of prisons, he was confined in the same cell as Union officers. One of the Northern men in the prison was Alfred Ely, Republican Congressman, who had driven up to watch the battle of Bull Run and was captured by the Southerners. In his journal, Ely gave an account of Adler's sad story and, along with all Union officers in the jail, felt sympathy towards him. He concluded that Adler "was a better officer and a better man than Wise and was indeed the 'noblest Roman of them all.'"[4]

Adler was kept imprisoned until August 1862. It is not quite clear whether he was released and expelled from the Confederate States or he managed to escape. *The New York Times* covered the rather adventurous story of his escape based entirely on his own account. Adler posed as if he had resigned his commission while he was dissatisfied with the Confederate service and this cast suspicion on him, which resulted in his arrest. This, along with other details of his extraordinary heroism. how he presented them, make his narrative rather dubious.[5]

According to *The New York Times* he was about to offer his services to the Union army, but no information has surfaced so far about his life after that point.

Albert, Anselm

Anselm Albert was born Ignatz Albert in 1819 in Pest. He had an excellent education in the military schools of Graz and Vienna. He was a lieutenant in the Austrian army until 1845, when he resigned. He volunteered in the Hungarian War of Independence — he was mustered in as a lieutenant, he served on General Perczel's staff, and by May 1849 he was elevated to the rank of major. After the surrender of the Hungarian forces, he had to flee. He was taken prisoner by Romanian insurgents, but he was freed by General Bem's troops. He stayed with Bem and accompanied him to Turkey and Aleppo. For a short period of time he served in the Ottoman army, as well.[6]

He migrated to the United States in 1852. He tried his luck in several places, including Louisiana, Nebraska and Davenport, Iowa, which was populated by many Hungarians. In St. Louis, Missouri, he played a preeminent role in organizing the pro–Union Home Guard units in 1861. He enlisted on April 24, 1861, in St. Louis as a captain. In June he got transferred to the staff. As lieutenant colonel of the 3rd

Missouri Infantry Regiment, the Hungarian officer was wounded and taken prisoner at the battle of Wilson's Creek on August 10, 1861. He was released ten days later and discharged on September 24, 1861.[7]

Albert was assigned as aide-de-camp of General John Charles Frémont on March 31, 1862. Frémont relied heavily on the services of foreign officers both as the commander of the Western Department and that of the Mountain Department. In his report written after the battle of Cross Keys, June 8, 1862, Frémont praised the services of Albert, whose "uncommon professional ability, joined to previous long experience in the field, rendered [his] services of the greatest value throughout a very laborious and hazardous campaign."[8]

After Frémont was forced to resign, Albert, who was loyal to him, was placed on the inactive list and did not see service until he finally resigned on June 8, 1864. Jessie Benton Frémont, wife of the general, wrote about Albert to Indiana Congressman George Julian: "Col. Albert has been twelve years in America.... He has steadily done good duty until shelved in with the general. He speaks as good English as we do and is thorough in French and German — is a Hungarian and a trained officer."[9]

After the Civil War he became the president of the Metropolitan Bank of St. Louis and was a highly respected citizen. Although he managed to accumulate considerable wealth, he soon lost much of it. He became assistant editor of the German-language newspaper *Amerika* and was also employed as district assessor. Anselm Albert died on November 20, 1893, in St. Louis.[10]

Asboth, Alexander

For a detailed biography see Chapter Five, "The Triumvirate"

Baróthy, Charles

Charles Baróthy was born in Nagyvárad in 1846. His father served in the Hungarian War of Independence, and rose to the rank of major in General Joseph Bem's army. As for his post–1849 career, there are some discrepancies in the sources, but it seems certain that by 1855 Baróthy had moved to America along with his family. They settled down in Omaha, Nebraska, and were engaged in farming. When the Civil War broke out, young Charles could hardly wait to come of age: in 1864, at the age of 18, he was mustered in as a private at Company B, 1st Battalion Cavalry, then Company G at the 1st Nebraska Cavalry Regiment. He was mustered out as a private, too.[11]

According to some sources, after the Civil War he was involved in the Indian wars. Later he was engaged in different business pursuits, but remained in Omaha until the end of his life. His father returned to Hungary after the amnesty that went with the Compromise of 1867. Charles W. Marsh, who visited Nagyvárad at the turn of the century, met him and remarked, "He had become an American citizen, and, apparently, had been so fortunate or so well treated while in the U.S. that he was enthusiastic in his praises of our country and its institutions." One of Charles' brothers, Árpád, became a well-known physician in Chicago.[12]

In 1938, at the age of 92, Charles Baróthy took part in the anniversary celebrations of the battle of Gettysburg, being one of the oldest Civil War veterans present, and definitely the oldest Hungarian survivor of the conflict. He died in 1944 in Omaha.

Bettelheim, Bernard

Bernard Bettelheim was born in a Jewish family in Pozsony in 1811. He attended a rabbinical school, later studied in Nagyvárad and at Debrecen Reformed College. As a result of his thorough education he mastered several languages at a young age: German, Slovakian, Hebrew, Latin, Greek, French, Spanish and Hungarian. He studied to become a doctor in Pest, Vienna and Padua. He obtained his medical degree in 1836. He authored a number of articles mainly on the treatment of patients falling sick with cholera. Some sources assert that he served in the Egyptian navy and he was the head surgeon of the Turkish army.[13]

He was converted to Christianity some time in the late thirties and became a British subject. A British naval missionary society sent him to the Liu Ch'iu (Loo Choo) islands, belonging to Ryu Kyu. Bettelheim took his family with him, and his son, Bernard Jr., was actually born onboard the British vessel *William Jardine* transporting the family to Ryu Kyu. They arrived in Liu Ch'iu on May 1, 1846, and 8 years of living in want started. Although his activities were officially tolerated by the Japanese authorities, the Hungarian missionary had to face constant opposition. He was beaten several times while he was preaching outdoors and one of the members of William Perry's expedition, Edward Yorke McCauley, noted in his diary after meeting Bettelheim: "[He] made one convert who on acknowledging it in public was immediately stoned to death." Despite all the hardships, the missionary developed cow-pox vaccine, and secretly trained local doctors to Western medicine. He compiled the first grammar book and dictionary of the Ryukyuan language and translated the gospels of John and Luke and the books of the Acts and Romans into Ryukyu, which was republished by the Japan Bible Society in 1977. As a recognition of all his efforts, a statue commemorating him was erected in Ryu Kyu in 1926. His journal and official correspondence were published in 2005.[14]

Bettelheim finally left the island on February 8, 1854, and he served as Commodore Perry's interpreter. Coincidentally, Perry's flagship, the USS *Mississippi*, was the very same vessel that had carried Kossuth from Turkey to England in 1850. The Bettelheims finally settled down in Illinois.

In the Civil War he enlisted as a surgeon at 106th Illinois Infantry Regiment on April 16, 1863, holding a rank of major. He resigned on June 9, 1864.[15]

After the Civil War he returned to his profession as a physician. He died on February 9, 1870, in Brookfield, Missouri.

Botsay, Alexander

Alexander Botsay was born in 1828 in Hungary. We have no details concerning his life prior to the outbreak of the Civil War. He settled down in New Orleans and he volunteered in the Confederate Army as a private in the 3rd Regiment European Brigade (Garde Francaise), Louisiana Militia.[16]

After the war, he returned to New Orleans and found employment as a carpenter. He married a Bavarian woman and they had five children. According to a city directory he was working as a box maker and box manufacturer in 1890. He died on December 22, 1913.[17]

Csermelyi, Joseph

Joseph Csermelyi was born in 1830. According to Vasváry he had been a student of philosophy prior to 1848, when he got involved in the War of Liberation. He served as a lieutenant in the 33rd Hussar Regiment. After the downfall in 1849, he left the country and 1851 found him in America. He was one of the few Hungarians who took part in the ill-fated Cuban expedition led by Narciso Lopez in 1851. The Spanish captured him and he was sentenced to imprisonment and hard labor in the lead mines of Ceuta, on the Mediterranean coast of North Africa. After about 15 months, he was released and he returned to the United States.[18]

In the Civil War he was mustered in as 1st lieutenant of Company K, 45th New York Volunteer Infantry. In June 1862 he was promoted to captain, but was discharged on October 3, 1862. He was among the Hungarians who gathered around Brigadier General Asboth when the latter was assigned commander of the Department of Western Florida, and Csermelyi became captain in the 82nd U.S. Colored Infantry Regiment. He was brevetted major for his extraordinary heroism at the battle of Fort Blakely (April 2–9, 1865).[19]

After the War of the Rebellion he became actively involved in the life of the Hungarian-American community and was elected president of the Hungarian Society in New York. He died in 1878 in New York.

Debreczeny, Ignatz

Debreczeny was born in 1822 in Szeged. He finished only a single year at the Piarist high school, then quit. He became a tailor's apprentice, and when the Hungarian War of Independence came, he joined the ranks of the *honvéd*s immediately. He served as a lieutenant in the 13th Honvéd Battalion until January 1849, when he transferred to the 48th Battalion. He distinguished himself at the siege of Buda on May 22, 1849, and received the 3rd Class Medal for his heroism. After he regained his strength, he returned to active service, and was transferred to the 93rd Battalion in the rank of 1st lieutenant. He served in V Corps in the Bánság district up to the end of the conflict.[20]

After the surrender of the Hungarian troops, he fled the country. According to Edmund Vasváry, he had a personal reason to do so, as he shot his sweetheart to death. He emigrated to America, settled down in New York and found employment as a tailor. Gedeon Ács, Hungarian Protestant preacher, described him as "a man who bragged of his taciturnity, although he was prattling all the time, never keeping his mouth shut."[21]

He participated in the Civil War, but no particulars have been found out about his career so far. He returned to Hungary after 1867. He worked as a supervisor for the Alföld Railroad Company in Szeged. He died there in 1913.[22]

De Korponay, Gabriel

Gabriel De Korponay was one of the very few Hungarians who had migrated to the United States well before the defeat of the Hungarian War of Independence in 1848–49. He set foot on American soil in New York on May 14, 1844. He made his first appearance as dancer virtuoso in the United States that year. *The New York Herald* described him as "a very possessive figure" who was able to perform "very daring, complicating steps in his solo." Most sources agree that Korponay, along with Mademoiselle Desjardins, introduced the polka dance in the United States, which gained immense popularity. The two of them started a dance school, and later Korponay taught fencing in the military school of Major Dorm as well. One of his favorite students was Dashiell Bayard, later a Civil War general, who was mortally wounded in the battle of Fredericksburg. According to Bayard's biographer, he acquired the military spirit from Korponay, so much so that he sought admission to West Point.[23]

Korponay enlisted in the Mexican war and he was mustered in on May 21, 1847, as captain. In October 1847 and in the beginning of 1848, Korponay was on permanent recruiting duty in the United States. In July 1848 he and a company of cavalry recruits were attacked by a band of Comanches on the Santa Fe trail, but his soldiers routed the Indians in an engagement which was later called "Gabriel's Barbecue" and was part of the larger battles of the Cimarron River (July 10 and 20, 1848). Korponay was finally mustered out on October 13, 1848, in Independence, Missouri. Some sources refer to Korponay as recruiting volunteers for the British at the time of the Crimean War.[24]

In the Civil War he was mustered in as lieutenant-colonel in the 28th Pennsylvania Volunteer Regiment on June 28, 1861. On December 19, 1861, he commanded his regiment in the skirmish at Point of Rocks, Maryland, in which he managed to drive back the enemy. He was promoted to colonel on April 25, 1862, when he took over the command of the regiment from Brigadier General John W. Geary. The same year he was in command of Camp Banks, near Alexandria, Virginia, and was responsible for the exchange of paroled soldiers. His efforts, which earned praise, included setting up a camp theater and organizing team sports for the inmates. He was ordered back to his command in March 1863 and received a disability discharge on March 26, 1863.[25]

He died in Philadelphia, PA, on February 10, 1866. He barely outlived his son, Stephen, who also served in a Pennsylvania regiment.[26]

De Korponay, Stephen

He was the son of Colonel Gabriel De Korponay of the 28th Pennsylvania Infantry Regiment. He was born in Paris, France, on February 15, 1841. He was three years old when his parents migrated to the United States. Not much is known about his life, beyond the fact that he volunteered in the Civil War and was mustered in as a private on July 9, 1863, at Company C, 52nd Pennsylvania Infantry Regiment. After a very brief service, during which he was promoted to corporal, he was mustered out on September 1, 1863. He died on 20 June, 1865.[27]

De Zeyk, Albert J.

Albert J. De Zeyk was born in 1828 in Kolozsvár. He studied law and was admitted to the bar in 1847. Along with his brother, he volunteered in the Hungarian War of Liberation in 1848, and by February 12, 1849, he was elevated to the rank of lieutenant in the 73rd Honvéd Battalion. In July he was promoted to captain and transferred to the 3rd Ferdinand Hussar regiment.[28]

In 1849 he escaped Austrian retaliation and fled first to France and then to Britain. He studied chemistry and engineering. On July 9, 1852, he left Falmouth for Rio De Janeiro onboard the ship *Teriot*, and he worked in Brazil, Urugay and Paraguay as an engineer at river regulation projects. In 1853 he was shipwrecked on the river La Plata and was saved by a U.S. vessel. He sailed to the United States, joined the navy and was involved in coast surveying. Károly László mentioned him in his memoirs, saying that later he tried to get a job as a drawing engineer. In 1857 he was working together with fellow Hungarian exile George Grechenek as land agent, civil engineer and land surveyor in the vicinity of Webster City, Iowa. They played an important role in the development of the small frontier settlement. Before moving to the west, on March 10, 1857, he married Elizabeth M. Whittlesey at Rock Creek Church in Washington, D.C. Two years later they had a daughter, Ilka, who was born in Iowa. Around 1859 he returned to Washington, D.C., and was employed part-time in the drawing division of the United States Coast Survey as a draughtsman.[29]

De Zeyk did not take arms in the Civil War, but after returning to the capital, he worked as a 2nd class clerk in the Post Office Department from May 11 to December 31, 1861. On November 5, he and his two partners were granted a patent on military fatigue hats, but based on the sources this business enterprise did not last long. He is included in this list of Hungarian participants in the Civil War because General Frémont, being somewhat obsessed with coding his telegrams so that the rebels could not learn any important details concerning the plans of the Western Department, chose to send telegrams to Washington in the Hungarian language. Having surrounded himself by Hungarian officers on his staff, this was rather easy to accomplish, and De Zeyk translated all dispatches in the Post Office Department and delivered them to the War Department or personally to Lincoln.[30]

Albert De Zeyk (*Vasárnapi Újság*, July 19, 1885, 461).

It was probably due to this acquaintance with Lincoln that when Ladislaus Újházy recommended him to Secretary of State William Henry Seward, De Zeyk was nominated to the consul of the United States in Taranto, Italy, on December 10, 1861.[31]

He was involved in diplomacy in the second half of the 1860s as well. He was fluent in French, English, Spanish, Italian, German and, of course, Hungarian. He was working at the embassy in Paris, then at the consulate in Lyon. His further posts included Frankfurt, Cairo and St. Gallen. In 1882 he was transferred to Lisboa, and the following year to Turin, where he was American vice-consul until 1885. It was then that he was visited by his niece, 17-year-old Sarolta Zeyk, who got acquainted with Kossuth, the exiled Hungarian icon, and started a very controversial correspondence with him, which was the source of rumors about a romantic relationship between the aging politician and the teenaged girl.[32]

In 1885 he returned to Hungary and was employed by the Hungarian government as a councilor at the Regency of Fiume. Later he worked for the Adria Shipping Company. He died in 1896 in Czéczke.

Dobozy, Emeric

He was born on April 10, 1827, in Debrecen. He learned the trade of shoemaker. In the Hungarian War of Liberation he volunteered and served as a private. In 1849 he migrated to America and settled down in the small Hungarian settlement of New Buda, Iowa, where he continued working as a shoemaker. According to the Census of 1860, he was of rather modest means and lived alone. In the Civil War he enlisted in Company D of the 10th Iowa Cavalry in September 1861, and he remained a private throughout the conflict. Apparently, he was not wounded, although he saw active service throughout the war.[33]

After being mustered out in 1865, he returned to New Buda and opened a shoemaker's shop. He proved to be an excellent workman, yet in 1876 he purchased a small farm, and started farming as well. On September 2, 1867, he married nineteen-year-old Maria Sanders, a native of Germany. They had nine children. He passed away on July 6, 1885. His widow applied for his Civil War pension in 1890.[34]

Dobozy, Peter Paul

Peter Paul Dobozy was born on April 17, 1833, in Szombathely. His original occupation was butcher. He took part in the Hungarian War of Independence, then he escaped to Turkey. He joined the Hungarian Legion in Italy and served as a lieutenant from August 1860 to 1862. He was wounded in the head on April 4, 1862, while fighting with the infamous Italian outlaw Carmine Crocco Donatelli (1830–1905) near Venosa. Based on the 1910 census data, he migrated to the United States in 1862. In the American Civil War, first he became Brig. Gen. Asboth's aide-de-camp with the rank of captain, and he so much respected Asboth that he declined a promotion to major in order to stay under his command. In June 1863 Asboth ordered him to organize the 2nd Tennessee Heavy Artillery Regiment, and he soon became major of the newly-formed unit. Later he was lieutenant-colonel of the Fourth Colored Heavy Artillery.[35]

Dobozy did an excellent job in organizing black soldiers into an effective fighting unit. Like fellow Hungarian Ladislaus Zulavsky, he also had to face charges questioning his capability to command a regiment. Eventually, however, the reviewing commission concluded that Dobozy was a perfect soldier and good officer.[36]

After the Civil War, he first moved to the Ozark Mountains of western Arkansas and worked as a farmer and land surveyor for the railroad. Later he moved on to Howell, Missouri, where he pursued farming. According to both the censuses of 1870 and 1880, he was living there. He married Malinda Frances McHan on January 11, 1874. They brought up several children and Dobozy played a crucial role in the life of the community. He was founding member of the First Baptist Church of West Plains, Missouri. He died there in 1919. His name is commemorated on the African American Civil War Memorial in Washington, D.C.[37]

Dunka, Nicolai

He was born in Moldavia, in a family of Romanian origin. In the Hungarian War of Independence he served as a *honvéd*. Later, in July 1860, he became captain of the division of hussars in the Hungarian Legion in Italy. According to Philip Figyelmessy's memoirs, he was a restless man who always got involved in rivalries between officers, and he had a number of duels. Figyelmessy ascribed his dismissal from the Legion to this fact and refers to him as "the Volcano." Anyway, they left Turin, Italy, together in November 1861 first for Britain then for the United States. Dunka set his foot on American soil in New York on December 4, 1861.[38]

He was made additional aide-de-camp on Frémont's staff with the rank of a captain. He did not fail to provoke some of his fellow officers even in the Civil War, although, luckily, none of the incidents ended in a duel. The "Crazy Vlach," as Figyelmessy sometimes called him, spent most of his life in various armies, but he first saw actual fighting in the battle of Cross Keys on June 8, 1862.[39]

Dunka's death in this fight is very well documented. His task was to take orders from Frémont to Stahel throughout the battle. Figyelmessy found his dead body in the evening: his pockets had been obviously searched, his sword was missing and he had two deep wounds on his stomach. He had been shot by Private John Long of Company B of the 21st Georgia. "Long performed a historical service to posterity when he took from the captain's body a copy of Fremont's order of march that morning," historian Robert K. Krick concluded, as "Gen. Trimble took the document with his report and it reached print; Federal copies did not survive." Frémont also mentioned the death of Dunka in his official report of the battle: "One of my aides-de-camp, Cpt. Nicolai Dunka, a capable and brave officer, was killed by a musketball while carrying an order to this part of the field." Dunka was buried at Union Church Graveyard in Cross Keys, Virginia.[40]

D'Utassy, Anthony

One of the three D'Utassy brothers serving in the American Civil War. He was born around 1831, according to Michael Bacarella, in "Temensai," which is probably an awkwardly misspelled version of Temesvár.[41]

In the Civil War he was mustered in on September 1, 1861. He became 1st lieutenant of Company F at 39th New York Infantry Regiment, also known as the Garibaldi Guard. His brother, Col. Frederick George D'Utassy, was the commander of the regiment.[42]

On September 22, 1862, he was transferred to Company E and was promoted to the rank of captain. There are no records of him subsequent to May in 1863. As far as we can judge from the sources, he was not involved in Frederick's fraud scandal.[43]

D'Utassy, Carl

Brother of Anthony and Frederick D'Utassy. Along with them, he volunteered in New York City for 3 years. He also served in the 39th New York Volunteer regiment; on June 1, 1862, he was 2nd lieutenant in Company C. He was promoted to 1st lieutenant on September 22, 1862, and was mustered out on May 31, 1863.[44]

D'Utassy, Frederick George

According to his own testimony, he was born in 1827 in Nagykanizsa in a relatively well-off Jewish family with long military traditions. He attended a military academy in Austria and entered Austrian service as a cadet in 1845. By 1848 he reached the rank of 2nd lieutenant, but he deserted and volunteered in the Hungarian army in the War of Liberation. That was when he changed his name to Utasi, later to Utassy and D'Utassy. He claimed that he was a major in the 127th Honvéd Battalion. However, based on Gábor Bona's book studying the lieutenants of the Hungarian War of Independence, he volunteered as a sergeant and became a lieutenant in the 67th Honvéd Battalion. Later he served in the 31st Battalion and on March 25 he was promoted to 1st lieutenant.

As he related it, he was wounded several times, and even captured in the battle of Temesvár. He was sentenced to death for desertion, but he managed to escape to Turkey. However, all we know for sure is that he was forced into the Austrian Army in the 3rd Infantry Regiment as a private. He was released on April 5, 1851, and that was when he left the country. He instructed the Ottoman cavalry, and later was appointed private secretary to the high commissioner of the Ionian Islands, and he traveled extensively in the East and Italy. There are some documents which mention him as a veteran of the Hungarian Legion in Italy, although there is no trace of him in that capacity in the archival sources.[45]

There are at least as many uncertainties concerning the further phase of his pre–Civil War career. There are assertions that he served in the Crimean War, but his name could not be located in the official records. Some sources claim that in 1855 he went to England, became secretary to the governor of Nova Scotia, Gaspar Le Marchand, and he was the person who secured for him an appointment at Dalhousie College in Nova Scotia, Canada, as a professor of languages. This is, however, quite unlikely, as this particular college was basically inactive in the period between 1843 and 1863. Other contemporaries claim that he was a dance and fencing instructor and a language master. He probably moved to New York City around 1860.[46]

Catherine Catalfamo, in her Ph.D. dissertation entitled "The Thorny Rose: The Americanization of an Urban, Immigrant, Working Class Regiment in the Civil War. A Social History of the 39th New York Volunteer Infantry" describes D'Utassy as a master of many languages who spoke Hungarian, Spanish, German, French, and Italian, and "an accomplished, articulate, even poetic writer in the English language, [whose] penmanship [was] perfect."[47]

His winning personality and many letters of recommendation secured him enough support to raise a regiment. He enlisted on May 17, 1861, in New York and set out to organize the 39th New York Infantry Regiment, of which he became the colonel.

The 39th New York Infantry, usually called the Garibaldi Guard, was indeed a multiethnic unit, which started out as an all-Italian regiment. Later some companies comprised of other ethnic groups were added including Germans, Hungarians, Swiss, Spanish, and Portuguese. D'Utassy's primary aim was to Americanize his regiment, matching his personal goal of a transfer to an American regular unit. In 1861 he applied for American citizenship as well. However, many around the Guard did not sympathize with his efforts, leading to attacks in the press (a newspaper editor accused him of being an impostor and manufacturing his previous record of military service), and in a number of letters written to his superiors. He had to face diatribes which focused on him as a foreigner as well as ones which had anti–Semite overtones.

A very good description of him is offered by Cornelia McDonald, wife of a Virginia slave-owner, who actually met D'Utassy, and did not hesitate to give voice to her opinion that the Yankees hired Dutchmen (Germans) to do their fighting. Hers is probably the most vivid description of the appearance and temperament of the Hungarian:

> June 12, 1862 — This afternoon I was called on by an officer, very short in stature, very gorgeously arrayed and very red in the face. He walked up to me quickly as I appeared in the hall and presented his card, Col. D'Utassy.
> I bowed and then he held before my eyes a paper, so close that I could see the writing with difficulty, and asked if that was my handwriting, speaking in very broken English.... [I] said, 'Yes' that it was my handwriting. He stood still for a moment, his face glowing with gathering wrath, and at last gasped out in his anger, 'You call my men Dutchmen.' His rage and his broken English excited my risibility so that I burst out laughing. His anger then knew no bounds, and almost dancing with excitement, he averred that they were no Dutchmen, adding a great deal that I did not understand. I said nothing till he had finished and then politely asked, 'Of what nationality are you, Col. D'Utassy? I could see at a glance that you are no Dutchman. I should have taken you for a Hungarian.' This was said at a venture, but it had a wonderfully modifying effect. His face instantly changed; a bland smile took possession of his little grey eyes, smoothed his forehead and puffed out his fat cheeks. 'Dat ish me, Hungary is my country.'[48]

In the fall of 1861 he was accused of fraud: drawing rations for 900 soldiers, although he had only 700. D'Utassy, however, managed to prove his regimental figures.

His military record in charge of the Guard was spotless. He defended the Shenandoah Valley town of Romney with just 300 men, and at the battle of Cross Keys he led his regiment with extraordinary heroism in a daring assault against the enemy to the utmost satisfaction of his superior, General Frémont.

During the Maryland Campaign, D'Utassy also got involved in the Harper's Ferry debacle, when the Union troops evacuated Maryland Heights on September 13, 1862, destroyed their arms, and about 3,000 soldiers walked under parole to Frederick, Maryland. The investigations, however, found that it was D'Utassy who tried to impede the surrender, and during the trial many officers from this command testified in favor of him. Col. Daniel Cameron said about D'Utassy: "I deem it but justice to Col. D'Utassy to say that during the time I was in his brigade he acted uniformly the part of a brave, energetic, and good officer. I saw nothing like cowardice, or anything approximating to it, in anything he did. I believe he would have been pleased to have gone out with us."[49]

D'Utassy was known as a strict disciplinarian, who was an ardent foe of drinking. He encouraged his men to send home most of their pay to their families. Soon, however, when the federal government started a series of investigations in order to stop fraud and corruption, D'Utassy got into the crossfire of charges. He was well known for his extravagant tastes, and his love of women, and rumors could be heard that he spent governmental money for his own purposes. In March 1863 he was arrested and charged with 25 different criminal specifications.[50]

There were three major charges against him: 1. Advising and persuading a soldier to desert 2. Unlawfully selling and disposing of government horses for his own personal benefit 3. Conduct prejudicial to good order and military discipline. The court found him not guilty of the first charge and also acquitted him in the charge of horse theft; however, he was convicted of converting the proceeds of the sale of government horses for his own use. The most serious of all was the third charge, with 19 different specifications of acts of graft and fraud. The court found that D'Utassy was selling sutler businesses, and was also guilty of selling a commission to Cpt. Charles Wiegand of Company A for $180. He allowed the members of the regimental band to draw privates' pay, and was also found responsible for defrauding the government of $3,265.40 in illegal vouchers for expenses incurred in raising the regiment. Ultimately, he was not convicted of knowingly defrauding the government or profiting from his actions, but as a colonel he was responsible.

The court-martial sentenced D'Utassy to a one-year confinement at hard labor at Sing Sing, and ordered that he may not hold any rank, office, or employment in the service of the United States. The Hungarian officer requested a presidential pardon from Abraham Lincoln, arguing that he was only following European practices, and explaining most of the charges as fabrications of his enemies, yet Lincoln approved the sentence on May 27, 1863.[51]

Catherine Catalfamo claims that after D'Utassy served his term, he owned a photo studio in New York City (1865–67), and worked as an importer in a store at 41 Maiden Street. Later he was involved in the insurance business.[52]

He died on May 2, 1892, in Wilmington, Delaware, the circumstances of which were widely discussed in the contemporary press. *The Democratic Standard* wrote that he "died of the congestion of the brain, the result of inhaling illuminating gas. Hanging his umbrella on the gas bracket on retiring at a hotel in Wilmington, the supposition is that the inside blinds of the window swung back, and, striking the umbrella, the gas was turned on." He did not regain consciousness. It has been suggested by some that he might have committed suicide, but it remained a mere supposition.[53]

Estván, Béla (Heinrich, Peter)

For a detailed biography see, Chapter Six, "An International Fraud."

Fejérváry, Nicholas, Jr.

He was the only son of Nicholas Fejérváry (1811–1895), parliamentary deputy during the Hungarian War of Liberation of 1848–49. He was a wealthy man who managed to take most of his wealth out of the country when he emigrated. He arrived in the United States in 1852 and he found his new home in Davenport, Iowa. There he

Col. Frederick D'Utassy (Library of Congress Prints and Photographs Division LC-B813–2184 A)

even managed to increase his wealth through real estate transactions to such an extent that on the basis of the Census of 1860 the value of his real estate wealth could be estimated around $70,000, which definitely made him the most well-to-do of all the Kossuth émigrés. He built a huge mansion and designed a giant park around it, which was presented to the city of Davenport after his death by his daughter, Celestine. The city opened a public park on the site which holds the name of Fejervary. Nicholas Fejérváry also founded a home for the aged and homeless in 1892, which was named after him as well.[54]

Nicholas, Jr., was born in 1846 in Hont County. He was six years old when his parents emigrated to America. As his father was rich, Nicholas had an excellent education. He had a private tutor, who had been the student of education reformer Johann Heinrich Pestalozzi (1746–1827), and he also had his father's huge library at his disposal. At the age of 15 he entered the local Griswald College, where he intended to continue his studies.[55]

Hardly any details are known about his Civil War career. All we know is that he volunteered in 1862, when he was still only 16 (he must have lied about his date of birth to the recruiting officer). He was probably so seriously wounded in the first months of 1863 that he was taken home to Davenport. He died on March 13, 1863, and was buried at Oakdale Cemetery, Davenport, Iowa.[56]

Fekete, Alexander, Dr.

Alexander Fekete was born on December 2, 1827, in Pest-Buda. His early education took place under Jesuit instruction. In 1845 he was admitted to the medical faculty at the University of Vienna. He got involved in the events of the Hungarian War of Liberation in 1848, volunteered in the Hungarian Army and served for 18 months. He was wounded at the battle of Nagyszeben and was captured by the Austrians. After 3 months of imprisonment he managed to escape to Turkey. In 1850 he moved to Britain, and some time around Kossuth's visit to America, he himself crossed the Atlantic Ocean.[57]

In the United States he went to live in St. Louis, Missouri, and worked as a drug clerk in 1852. He got the chance to finish his studies and graduated from St. Louis Medical College. He moved to Aviston, Illinois, where he met the young Catherine Fisher and soon married her. They settled down in Marinetown, Illinois, where Fekete soon became a prominent physician. In 1860 they were of modest means, and they had two children.[58]

In the Civil War, Dr. Fekete served as an assistant surgeon in the 5th Regiment Cavalry, Missouri State Militia, and was discharged on April 13, 1865.[59]

Right after the Civil War he was arrested in New Orleans and held in lieu of $5,000 bail for causing the death of a little girl and boy who were suffering from chills and fever; both died two hours after taking a medicine he had prescribed. He must have been acquitted in the malpractice suit that followed, as he moved to East St. Louis, Illinois, where he settled and re-started his practice. He became a prominent citizen of the community who was elected, among other public duties, postmaster in East St. Louis and coroner of St. Clair County in 1880. He had two children, Ida and Thomas. His son was a successful businessman in East St. Louis. Dr. Fekete probably died there; the exact date of his death is not known.[60]

Fiala, John A.

John A. Fiala was born on January 26, 1822, in Temesvár in a wealthy civic family. He attended military school in Graz, then served in the 39th Infantry Regiment from 1836 to 1842. Later he was transferred to the headquarters of the Bánság District in Temesvár, but he soon left the military and found employment as a civil engineer. At the outbreak of the Hungarian War of Independence in 1848, he immediately volunteered in the Hungarian army. In January 1849 he was captain of the 9th Honvéd Battalion and was awarded the Military Medal 3rd Class for his bravery in the April campaign. In May he was promoted to major. In the last phase he belonged to the Southern army, and he claimed that he had been promoted to the rank of lieutenant colonel, but it cannot be substantiated.[61]

After the collapse of the Hungarian cause, he fled to Turkey and joined General Bem in Aleppo. Then, like many other Hungarian exiles, he chose to emigrate to America. After his arrival in America, he spent some time in New Orleans, worked at the Pacific Railroad, then he found employment in Missouri as a topographer. He settled down in St. Louis. Making use of his knowledge of military engineering gained at the Graz military school, he became an excellent topographer and surveyor.

He was employed at the surveyor-general's office and he prepared the first large sectional and topographical map of Missouri, and also of the territories between the Mississippi and the Pacific Ocean. He married the daughter of Theodore Rombauer, Ida, and they had 7 children born between 1855 and 1871.[62]

At the coming of the Civil War, he assisted Albert Anselm in organizing the pro–Union forces of St. Louis into effective fighting units. General Frémont appointed him to the position of chief of engineers and inspector general, and he played a preeminent role in the construction of fortresses around the city of St. Louis. *The New York Times* wrote about him: "The range of his talents extends to every military subject, and his minute knowledge of the topography of Missouri makes his services especially valuable. To plan fortifications and arrange military dispositions of the troops, he brings a genius of which the present war will offer many chances to develop the resources."[63]

Fiala was responsible for raising a river flotilla of gunboats for Frémont. Although he — similarly to other foreigners, including fellow Hungarian officers — was attacked by many because he was favored by Frémont, he was promoted to colonel on July 17, 1862. He continued to serve under Frémont during his command at the Mountain Department as a chief of topographical engineers. When Frémont resigned from command, Fiala was also put on the inactive list and did not see active service again.[64]

After the Civil War the Fiala family continued to live in St. Louis, but in the beginning of the 1870s they moved to California. In San Francisco he was employed as a draughtsman, while Ida worked in a fancy goods store. John Fiala died on December 8, 1911, in San Francisco. His memoirs were published by Tivadar Ács in 1943 with the title *A száműzöttek. Fiala János emlékiratai (The Outcast. The Memoirs of John Fiala)*.[65]

Figyelmessy, Philip

He was born on January 1, 1822, in Pest in a wealthy bourgeois family. His father owned a slaughterhouse and large parcels of land. Philip attended the prestigious military academy in Wiener Neustadt (1832–1840), and served in the 6th Hussar Regiment from 1841 to 1843.[66]

In September 1848 he became lieutenant of the Pest mounted militia, and on January 6, 1849, was transferred to the 17th Bocskai hussar regiment. On April 1, 1849, he was promoted to 1st lieutenant. Toward the end of the conflict, he served in the fortress of Komárom in the rank of captain.[67]

After the surrender of the Hungarian forces, as a result of the compromise between the Austrians and the defenders of Komárom, he received a safe-conduct from the Austrians, but he was involved in helping Hungarian political refugees to escape, therefore, he soon became the focus of attention of the authorities and he himself had to escape. He followed Kossuth to Turkey. Soon he became one of the most important secret agents of the Hungarian ex-governor, who promoted him to major. He was responsible for stirring up Transylvania, as the initial idea was to continue the struggle from there. Figyelmessy, at the order of Joseph Mack, the leader of this undertaking, illegally went to Hungary at least three times. Unfortunately, one of their companions betrayed them and soon they had to flee Austrian retaliation again.[68]

Figyelmessy went to London in 1853 and stayed there until 1859. At the end of 1853 he was ready to travel to Turkey and participate in the organization of Hungarian troops in the Crimean War, but these plans came to nothing. In order to make a living, he became the assistant to fellow Hungarian-in-exile Dr. Károly Dombory, who was involved in the very popular practice of day, mesmerism. Following some apparently successful cures, the wealthy thronged to his office. When he left for the Near East to head a British military hospital in the Crimean War, Figyelmessy took over his practice. According to Dániel Kászonyi's memoirs, in the summer of 1856, he got an offer to move to Aberdeen, Scotland, by a Sir Michael Bruce and continue his profitable practice in mesmerism there for full board and a payment of 5 guineas per week. At the rumors of the coming of the War of 1859, he went to Piedmont as Kossuth's adjutant. There were rumors that he had had eight pairs of boots made in expectation of a prolonged military conflict. After the sudden disheartening end of the war, he spent some time in London, but in 1860 he asked Kossuth to present him a letter of recommendation and on June 27, 1860, left London for Italy again to join the Hungarian Legion there. On July 27, 1860, he became the commander of the hussar squadron in the rank of lieutenant colonel. He was one of the leading figures of the open mutiny among the officers on April 23, 1861, when they demanded the removal of Major General Antal Vetter, commander of the Hungarian Legion. Figyelmessy went so far that he physically abused his commander in order to force him to resign, which he finally did, and was replaced by Dániel Ihász. However, Figyelmessy himself had to leave the legion. Moreover, he was sentenced to six months in prison, which was later reduced to two months. He served his time in Alessandria.[69]

The American consul to Turin was trying to recruit experienced cavalry officers for the Union Army and this opportunity came in the nick of time for Figyelmessy. He was given a letter of recommendation to Secretary of State William Henry Seward by Kossuth, and together with Nicolai Dunka and George Sárpy he crossed the Atlantic and arrived in New York on December 4, 1861. Based on his account of the events, he was offered a colonelcy of a volunteer regiment, but he, having spent most of his career as a regular soldier, was highly mistrustful towards volunteers, and declined the offer. First he was inspector general at Wheeling, West Virginia, then he was given a commission as assistant of fellow-Hungarian, Col. Charles Zagonyi, chief of cavalry, under Frémont at the Mountain Department, in the rank of lieutenant colonel. He distinguished himself in the night charge at Strasburg, Virginia, on June 1, 1862. He was promoted to colonel and officially confirmed by Congress on July 17, 1862. After the resignation of Frémont, he was also dismissed. After a couple of months, however, he managed to secure a position on the staff of another fellow Hungarian, Gen. Julius Stahel. Figyelmessy was injured seriously after falling from his horse near Harrisburg on February 22, 1864, and he could not return to active service in the Civil War. When he recuperated, however, he became head of the court martial in Baltimore, MD, and remained in this position until December 1864.[70]

His influential friends secured him a consular appointment, and in February

1865 he became American consul at Demerara in British Guyana, the very same month he was naturalized and became an American citizen. According to most sources, he did excellent work in the foreign service, but the tropical climate and the tropical diseases such as yellow fever and malaria proved problematic. His wife, Clara, fell sick very often, and Philip asked for a different service. In 1872 he was transferred to Mainz, in Hessen-Darmstadt. But it was too late: on September 7, 1872, his wife died, at the age of 42.[71]

He remained in Georgetown in British Guyana. In 1875 he paid a visit to the United States and married Eliza J. Haldemann from Pennsylvania. They returned to Guyana together and in 1877 Eliza gave birth to a son, Louis, who was named after Louis Kossuth. In 1880 their second son, Julius was born, who got his name after Brigadier-General Julius H. Stahel, who agreed happily to be the godfather of the boy.[72]

In 1887 the Cleveland government recalled Figyelmessy, who, after a 22-year consulship, returned to the United States. That was when a tragic event happened in the family: the 12-year-old Louis drowned in the Susquehanna River. Both parents were devastated and decided to travel to Europe to try to forget.[73]

They got to Turin and Figyelmessy finally met Kossuth after a long time. They decided to settle down in Switzerland for some time, and that is how Figyelmessy had the opportunity to be by Kossuth's side when the Great Hungarian patriot died in Turin on March 20, 1894. The Figyelmessy family returned to the United States in 1900, and settled down in Philadelphia, PA. Philip passed away there on July 25, 1907. He is buried at Marrietta Cemetery in Lancaster City, PA.[74]

Philip Figyelmessy is commemorated in Jenő Szekula's short novel entitled *Az emberiség lovagja* (*The Knight of Mankind*). His second wife, Eliza, published a children's' book: *Two Boys in the Tropics* (New York, Macmillan, 1910), which is based on the family's experience in British Guyana. During his consulship, Figyelmessy donated exotic wild animal species to the Hungarian National Museum.

Finto, John

Finto was born in 1831. He arrived in America in 1854 and settled in Texas. At the commencement of the Civil War, he enlisted in San Antonio as private at Company D, 5th Texas Infantry Regiment. He participated in the 1862 New Mexico campaign, during which he got wounded. He was left in a hospital in Santa Fe and was captured by Union troops. He was sent to Camp Douglas in Illinois and exchanged at Vicksburg in September 1862. He was finally paroled at San Antonio.[75]

After the Civil War he returned to Texas and was engaged in farming apparently for the rest of his life. He had a wife and six children. He passed away in 1905.[76]

Fornet, Cornelius

He was born in a family of French origin on August 10, 1818, in Strázsa, Szepes County, Hungary. He attended the Protestant college in Lőcse, then he went on to study engineering at the University of Pest. He graduated in 1843 and entered state service as a mining engineer in Délegyháza.[77]

He enlisted right away in the Hungarian War of Liberation in 1848 and he became an engineer officer in a sapper battalion. He was promoted to captain for his heroism in the battle of Nagysarló (April 19, 1849). He organized the 4th Sapper Battalion, and he became major of the new military unit.[78]

Around the time of the defeat of the Hungarian Army, he was among the first ones who set off and left the country. He said farewell to his homeland on September 20, 1849, and arrived in Boston on December 9. Thus, he and his companion, John Prágay, had first-hand experience of the utmost sympathy of the Americans towards the Hungarian freedom fighters. In Boston a special committee welcomed them, and they were housed in the Tremont Hotel as distinguished guests. Later he and Prágay moved on to New York City and wrote *The Hungarian Revolution*, the first book on the Hungarian War of Liberation in English, published by Putnam in 1850.[79]

The gold rush attracted him to California in 1850 and he founded a furnace and mint through which he accumulated a nice profit. With fellow Hungarians Samu Wass, Géza Molitor, Ede Damburghy and István Uznay, he purchased a quartz and gold mine, which they sold for a great profit in less than two years, while even retaining some shares. In April 1852 he met Kossuth in Boston, and in June he returned to Europe for a few weeks. On August 7, 1852, he married Adél Szépréthy at the American Embassy in Paris, then returned to New York onboard the *Atlantic* with his wife on October 3, 1852.[80]

The couple settled down in New Jersey and Fornet was engaged in farming. Lázár Mészáros, Hungarian secretary of war during 1848–49, who settled down very close to Fornet, wrote about him, "A Hungarian friend of mine, Fornet Kornél, accumulated enough wealth and now owns a farm of 40 holds [57.8 acres]: he has 50 hotbeds under glass, which ... costs him 120 dollars ..., but makes him 150-dollar pure profit." Soon he managed to increase the amount of land he owned to 240 acres. Besides, he was working as a civil engineer as well.[81]

When the Civil War came, he became military engineer in Frémont's Western Department in a rank of major. In October 1861 he was severely wounded in an accident and he was temporarily relieved of service. After his recovery, nevertheless, he took part in the battle of Antietam (September 17, 1862), and he took an active part in organizing the 22nd New Jersey Infantry Regiment. Although he was appointed commander and colonel of the newly-formed regiment, due to the internal strife within the unit and the fact that the men of the regiment and the citizens of Bergen County, NJ, objected to him, he was not willing to accept the appointment and serve. His appointment was revoked on January 26, 1863, and his second-in-command, Abraham G. Demarest, was appointed commander. Fornet retired from service.[82]

Soon after the Civil War, following the Compromise of 1867 in Hungary which secured general amnesty to the participants of the War of Liberation, Fornet returned to his homeland. He settled down near Mohács, and worked as a minor government official at a salt store. He died in Vác on March 10, 1894, and was buried at Kerepesi Street Cemetery in Budapest. In 1946, one of his descendants, László Fornet, published a small volume about his life entitled *Fornet Kornél, 1848-as őrnagy, amerikai ezredes élete—The Life of G.C. Fornet Colonel of Lincoln's Army. Adatok az amerikai magyar emigráció életéhez* (*Particulars on the Life of Hungarian-American Emigration*).[83]

Gaal, Alexander

He was born in 1831 and was a corporal in the Imperial Army until 1848, when he deserted and probably took part in the Hungarian War of Liberation. After the collapse of the Hungarian cause, he escaped, but hardly any information can be found on his career. According to some sources he served in the Hungarian Legion in Italy as a 1st lieutenant. If so, he must have resigned some time in 1862–64 and migrated to the United States.[84]

On October 10, 1864, he volunteered in the American Civil War and was mustered in as a captain at Company F, 1st Florida Cavalry Regiment. He was probably severely wounded in one of the engagements, as he was mustered out of service on November 27, 1864.[85]

After the Civil War he settled down in Louisiana. From the New Orleans directories it can be established that he worked as a lottery agent in the city in 1890–1891. He died at the age of 79 on February 29, 1912. He is buried at Chalmette National Cemetery in Louisiana.[86]

Gallfy (Gallik), Andrew

He was born in 1818 in Berzéte, in Gömör and Kishont County. He was first employed as a store clerk, but soon became an independent store owner in Kassa. In the Hungarian War of Independence he served as a 1st lieutenant at the National Guards, he was wounded, and after he recuperated he was transferred to the 8th Battalion. After the surrender of the Hungarian troops, he fled to Paris, then crossed the Atlantic and tried his luck overseas. He worked as a woodcutter and a laborer in a box factory, and had a number of other menial jobs. He settled down in Dayton, Ohio, then roved over much of the Midwest as a peddler, but he returned to Dayton broke. The Hungarian adventurer did not despair, but decided to travel to Australia and try his luck in digging gold. However, no fortunes awaited him there either, so he worked in a brick factory, then as a shepherd.[87]

He returned to the United States right away when he heard about the outbreak of the Civil War. He was mustered in as a captain on October 2, 1861, at Company A, 58th Ohio. His regiment participated in the campaign along the Yazoo River in the last days of 1862, and in one of the engagements at Chicksaw Bayou on December 29 Gallfy was captured by the Confederates. He was paroled in March 1863.[88]

He was detached from his regiment on May 22, 1863, and he served on the ironclad river gunboat *Mound City* until August 1, 1863. Then he returned to the 58th Ohio and was promoted to major on October 20, 1864. During the fights, Gallfy contracted yellow fever, and was finally mustered out on January 14, 1865, at Vicksburg.[89]

After the Civil War he went to Boston and studied medicine. For some time he worked as a physician in Cincinnati, Ohio, then he started a veterinary practice in Kansas City, Missouri, and opened a hospital for animals. In 1881, he returned to Hungary. He died in Kassa in 1885.[90]

Gerster, Anton

Anton Gerster was born on June 7, 1825, in Kassa. He attended the Technical University in Vienna and graduated as an engineer. When the Hungarian War of Independence broke out, he volunteered and served in the 1st Battalion of Engineers first as a lieutenant, then 1st lieutenant. After the Austrian and Russian armies crushed the Hungarian freedom fight, he escaped and emigrated to the United States.[91]

He was lucky enough to get employment in his profession, and he worked for the German-American John Augustus Roebling (1806–1869), one of the most renowned architects and foremost suspension bridge-builder of the time. He started the building of the Brooklyn Bridge, which was finished by his son, Washington Augustus Roebling, in 1883.[92]

In August 1861 he volunteered and became commander of a company called Gerster's Independent Company of Pioneers, organized in St. Louis. Later on he became captain of Sappers and Miners 5th Regiment Missouri Home Guard. As captain of the 5th Missouri Infantry and later the 27th Missouri Infantry, he was responsible for building and repairing fortifications and bridges. As engineer of the District of the Frontier, he supervised the construction of the forts around Fort Smith in Arkansas in April 1864 and at Fort Davidson in Missouri in August 1864. His terms of service expired on September 9, 1864, and he was mustered out.[93]

After the Civil War he lived in Brooklyn, New York, for quite a long time. He was uncle of Dr. Árpád Gerster, renowned surgeon of the time, and Etelka Gerster, the famous soprano. Anton Gerster died in San Jose, CA, on June 2, 1897.[94]

Grechenek, George

George Grechenek was born in either 1825 or 1826. He attended the agricultural school in Keszthely, and after graduation he was employed by the Count Károlyi family as an estate overseer.[95]

In the fall of 1848, he volunteered in the militia of Szatmár County and participated in the fights in Transylvania. In April 1849 he was promoted to lieutenant of the 88th Honvéd Battalion, and by the end of the War of Liberation he obtained the rank of 1st lieutenant.[96]

In 1850 he escaped from Hungary, and — like many fellow exiles — stayed in Turkey for some time. He belonged to the very close circle of Kossuth, and formed, along with Dániel Ihász, István Kinizsi, and János Kalapsza, the bodyguard for the ex-governor. He escorted Kossuth on his voyage to Britain, then to the United States.[97]

He stayed in America after Kossuth left the country in 1852. He was sharing rooms with Károly László, who quite frequently mentioned him in his memoirs. He gave account of the fact that Grechenek did all kinds of menial work at projects such as canal building in New York state and the construction of the railroad line between New York and Syracuse, but he could hardly make ends meet. In 1857 he was working as a land agent and county surveyor with fellow exile Albert De Zeyk in Hamilton County, Iowa.[98]

He volunteered on May 22, 1861, and became captain of Company H of the 72nd New York Volunteers on June 1, 1861. In the battle of Williamsburg, Virginia, he was severely wounded on May 5, 1862. His file is available in the *Medical and Surgical History of the Civil War*, so based on the report of his surgeon, R.B. Bontecou, we have a clear picture of what happened to the Hungarian officer in a hospital in Washington, D.C., where he was taken: "Gunshot wound of the right popliteal space. A minie ball transfixed the thigh between the hamstrings and condyles of the femur, grooving that bone slightly at the attachments of the gastrocnemius muscles and injuring the artery and nerve." His foot became gangrenous, the lower third of the thigh had to be amputated. However, the gangrene attacked the stump on the 15th and he died on the 16th May, 1862. He was buried at the National Cemetery across from Soldiers' Home in Washington, D.C.[99]

Grossinger, Charles

Charles Grossinger was born in 1825 or 1826 in Pest. According to Gábor Bona, he was a student as the time of the outbreak of the Hungarian freedom fight in 1848. In September 1848 he served as a sergeant at 14th Honvéd Battalion in Pest. On June 27, 1849 he was promoted to lieutenant.[100]

After the defeat of the Hungarian War of Independence, he left Hungary. There is some confusion in the sources, as Lajos Dancs mentions him as one of the exiles in Turkey in 1850–1851. On the other hand, Bona writes that he was captured by the Austrians and on February 1, 1850, he was forced to enter the 30th Infantry Regiment in the Imperial Army. If Bona is not mistaken, Grossinger deserted on March 14, 1851, then sought refuge in London.[101]

He decided to migrate to America and he arrived in New York on August 2, 1851, aboard the vessel *Davonshire*. Similarly to many other recently-arrived immigrants, he was hardly able to make a living. Along with 10 fellow Hungarians, including Dancs and Zagonyi, he formed a group with the name Hungarian Vocalists (Magyar Dalárda) on August 17, 1851, but it failed and he turned to some kind of manual labor.[102]

In the 1850s he was involved in importing Hungarian wines. The company, named Grossinger and Freund, was located at 170 Water Street in New York. They seem to have had occasional financial difficulties, so much so that in October 1860 their entire stock was sold at auction. By then, Grossinger was living in North Bergen, New Jersey, with his 19-year-old wife, Sarah. In 1860 he was one of the pall bearers of Emilie Zulavsky Kossuth (1817–1860), sister of Louis Kossuth. He was also a member of the Universal Masonic Lodge.[103]

He volunteered in the Civil War and was mustered in as 1st lieutenant on May 22, 1861. He got a commission in Company A of the 72nd New York Volunteer Infantry. After the death of fellow Hungarian George Grechenek, he was promoted to captain on May 18, 1862. He was discharged on June 23, 1862. His son, Charles, was born in New Jersey in 1863.[104]

In 1870 he lived with his family in New Jersey and worked as a lighthouse keeper. His wife, Sarah, applied for his Civil War pension as a widow in 1877, so it is safe to assume that he died sometime in 1876 or 1877.[105]

Haraszthy, Gaza

He was born Géza Haraszthy on December 27, 1833, in Puszta Kútas. He was the eldest son of Ágoston Haraszthy, who deservedly became renowned as the father of California viticulture. They arrived in New York City on September 28, 1842. They chose to settle down in Wisconsin. It was then that Géza changed his name to Gaza. His father was one of the wealthiest Hungarians in America at the time: according to the Census of 1860 he had real estate worth $200,000. His son, however, was more interested in the navy and was preparing for the entrance examination at the U.S. Naval Academy at Annapolis, Maryland.[106]

On June 28, 1863, he was mustered in as a captain at Company B, 18th New York Cavalry. His baptism of fire took place in New York during the July riots prompted by the National Conscription Act. The regiment then went to Washington, D.C., where it performed scouting duty until February 1864. On February 16, the 18th New York Cavalry was ordered to the Department of the Gulf. On March 7, 1864, it was placed under the command of Major Gen. Nathaniel Banks and transferred to the Gulf of Mexico as part of the 5th Cavalry Brigade, pushing north towards the Mississippi River. On May 17–18, 1864, it was engaged in a two-day battle at Yellow Bayou, Louisiana, which was the end of Gen. Banks's ill-fated Red River Expedition. Although the battle was a strategic Union victory which ensured their retreat, Gaza's company was captured by Confederate troops led by Gen. John Bankhead Magruder. He was imprisoned at Tyler, Texas, and was released only on May 25, 1865, in a prisoner exchange. Despite the hardships of the long detention, he re-joined his regiment and took part in the campaigns in Western Mississippi and Texas. After the Civil War, on December 5, 1865, he was promoted to major and was mustered out with his company on May 31, 1866, in Victoria, Texas.[107]

After his father, Ágoston Haraszthy, went bankrupt in California from his venture in the Buena Vista Winery in California, he moved to Nicaragua in 1868. He was about to build a distillery, but in 1869 he died while exploring the interior territories; evidence suggests that he either drowned or was killed by alligators. Gaza stayed at the family estate in Nicaragua and died on December 17, 1878.[108]

Hillebrandt, Hugo

There are several versions of his date of birth, but his own statement that he had been a soldier since his fourteenth year, in 1843, seems the most reliable. So, he was probably born in 1829. An obituary in the *New York Times* (April 7, 1896) gives his birthplace as southeastern Hungary in a wealthy but not noble family. He attended a military academy, but left it immediately when the Hungarian War of Liberation broke out in 1848. He served as a lieutenant in the Hungarian Revolutionary Army (he was commissioned on May 14, 1849) "showing military genius and cool courage." After the Austrian-Russian coalition crushed the Hungarian army, he fled to Turkey, where he spent several months, but — unlike some of his fellow exiles — refused to join the Turkish Army. Louis Kossuth's visit to America attracted him to America as well, but he had a hard time finding employment. He worked for the U.S. Coast Survey Service, but he was too restless to stay there.

Around 1859 he left the United States for Italy, where he joined Garibaldi and stayed in his army until the Army of Liberation entered Rome. In 1860 he returned to America and soon volunteered in the American Civil War.[109]

He enlisted in New York and was mustered in as sergeant major on May 9, 1861. On June 6, 1861, he was commissioned at 39th New York Infantry, nicknamed the Garibaldi Guard, commanded by fellow Hungarian, Col. Frederick George D'Utassy. On September 14, 1861, he was appointed adjutant and promoted to captain on January 27, 1862. He rose to the rank of major on July 18, 1862, and was involved in the evacuation of Maryland Heights in an engagement on September 13, 1862, after which about 3,000 Union soldiers surrendered and were paroled. The investigations found that Hillebrandt was not responsible. Actually he did his best to stop the flight of his mostly green soldiers.[110]

Hillebrandt commanded four companies at the Battle of Gettysburg. On July 2, 1863, the Guard managed to protect the flank of Willard's charge and re-take the guns of Watson's Battery from the 21st Mississippi. Next day he was wounded in the thick of the fight, but recuperated relatively quickly, so he could take part in the Mine Run campaign in November 1863. However, due to the diseases contracted during this particular campaign and his earlier wounds, he was mustered out on December 10, 1863.[111]

On February 2, 1864, he was commissioned captain in the 12th Veteran Reserve Corps, then in the 16th Veteran Reserve Corps, which were organized to retain in service those who had been unfit for active service. They were employed at bureaus, guarding stores or on court-martial duty. Hillebrandt was stationed in Washington, D.C., in 1864–65. In 1866 he was ordered to the Freedmen's Bureau in North Carolina until January 1868, first as officer, later as agent. On March 1, 1869, he was brevetted colonel by President Andrew Johnson for his "gallant service at the battle of Cross Keys ... and Harper's Ferry."[112]

President U.S. Grant appointed him consul at Candia, Island of Crete, in 1869. There he got acquainted with the daughter of the Austrian consul and married her. He and his wife remained at his post until 1874.

In the years that followed, Hillebrandt settled down in Brooklyn and found employment as a clerk. He died on April 4, 1896, at the New York home of his long-time friend Gen. Robert Avery.[113]

Hollan, Hugo

A son of a physician, he was born in a bourgeois family on March 14, 1819, in Szombathely. He became a professional soldier in the Imperial Army in 1838, and by 1845 was a lieutenant. On August 1, 1848, he was promoted to 1st lieutenant at the 12th Hussar Regiment stationed in Bohemia.[114]

When he heard about the outbreak of the Hungarian revolution, which soon reached the proportions of a full-fledged war of independence in 1848, he deserted, taking the 7th and 8th companies of his regiment with him on October 21, and joined the Hungarian cause. By November he reached the rank of vice-captain, and in April 1849 he was promoted to full captain in the Upper-Danube Division.[115]

After the collapse, he followed General Bem to Aleppo, Turkey, where he even served in the Ottoman Army for a brief period. In the spring of 1852 he decided to emigrate to the United States.

He settled down in Quincy, Illinois. On August 17, 1852, he married Regina Butze from Prussia, who gave birth to their first child, a girl, two years later. (Hollan had two sons from his previous marriage who were born in 1844 and 1846, and who followed their father to America.) He tried his luck in several enterprises, and in 1860 he was working as a tea dealer.[116]

When the Civil War came, Hollan, a former professional soldier, saw a golden opportunity to make use of his experience and volunteered right away. He was mustered in as a corporal at Company A, 10th Illinois Infantry Regiment, on April 20, 1861, and upon the expiration of his three-month term of service, was mustered out on July 29, 1861, in Cairo, Illinois.[117]

He did not stay out of service for long: he became commander of the 1st Battalion Reserve Corps, Missouri Cavalry, which was often referred to as Hollan Horse. His men soon got involved in pillaging, looting and even violence against civilians, which was not rare for them. Brigadier General Schofield complained about Hollan and his unit, "These men had preceded me only a few days but they had already murdered one of the best Union men in that vicinity and committed numerous depredations upon the property of peaceful citizens. Since that time their conduct has been absolutely barbarous — a burning disgrace to the Army and the Union cause." Schofield arrested 5 of the robbers as well as Hollan and one of his captains. The Hungarian officer was court-martialed and he lost command of his battalion.[118]

Nevertheless, on October 7, 1862, he managed to re-enlist and became captain of Company A, 119th Illinois Infantry Regiment. He died in combat on April 1, 1863, at Jackson, Tennessee. The *Daily Whig Republican* in Quincy, Illinois, covered the news of his death and concluded, "The loss of so worthy a man and so capable a soldier, will excite universal regret wherever he was known." He was buried at Quincy, Illinois, on April 9, 1863.[119]

Holmy, Johann Rudolph

In some sources he is referred to as Halmy. All we know about him is that he was born around 1839, probably in Hungary. At the time when the federal census of 1850 was taken, he was living in Westmoreland, Pennsylvania. Later he moved on and he worked as a farmer in Victoria County, Texas, in the second half of the 1850s. He volunteered and was mustered in as 1st sergeant on October 5, 1861, at Company B, 8th Texas Infantry. The only thing the recruiting officer noted about him is that he was 5 feet, 6 inches tall. In July 1863 he obtained the rank of 2nd lieutenant, and was assigned with his unit to defend Galveston, Texas. In 1865 he was appointed post quartermaster and acting adjutant, and remained at the post of Battery Green. He was paroled, and no further information is available about him.[120]

Jekelfalussy, Alexander

He was born at Körmöcbánya on May 16, 1833. He was a student at the outbreak of the Hungarian War of Liberation, but he volunteered in Kassa and served at the 9th Honvéd Battalion. He was soon promoted to lieutenant and by the time of the Hungarian capitulation in August 1849, he was 1st lieutenant.[121]

On August 27, 1849, he was forced into Austrian service as a private, deserted at Altona on March 1, 1850, and escaped to the United States. He settled down in Peoria, Illinois, and when the Civil War came, he volunteered in Chicago. He was mustered in as 1st lieutenant at Company F at 24th Illinois Infantry Regiment, also known as Lincoln Riflemen on July 8, 1861, and later he was promoted to captain. He was mustered out on August 6, 1864.[122]

After the Civil War he settled down in Manitowoc, Wisconsin. He worked as a cigar manufacturer for several decades. He married Susanna, who was born in 1845, and emigrated to the United States from Prussia. They had two children: Magdalena was born in 1867, and Alex in 1872. Based on Gábor Bona's information, Alexander Jekelfalussy died in Milwaukee, Wisconsin, on November 28, 1905. He is buried at Evergreen Cemetery in Manitowoc.[123]

Kappner, Ignatz

Martin Öfele refers to Kappner in his *German-Speaking Officers in the U.S. Colored Troops, 1863–1867* as a Hungarian officer in the American Civil War. He is mentioned in Károly László's diary as a Hungarian captain. However, the naturalization records show him to have been born in Austria. (This might or might not mean that he was not Hungarian. Practically, Hungarian citizenship did not exist at the time, as Hungarians were also Austrian subjects. Notwithstanding, proud and patriotic Hungarians would rarely give their nationality as Austrian.)[124]

According to Öfele, Kappner was born in Sopron in 1826. Unfortunately, there is only sporadic information available concerning his pre–Civil War career. It is quite likely that in 1848–49 he served in the Hungarian army and rose to the rank of captain. After the surrender of the Hungarian army, he followed Kossuth to his exile in Turkey, and Károly László in the above-mentioned section of his diary gives his position as maître d'hôtel around the ex-governor.[125]

He probably immigrated to the United States during or after Kossuth's visit to America. He was naturalized in 1860, so he had appealed for American citizenship five years prior to that. At the outbreak of the Civil War he was living on 4th Avenue in New York City.[126]

He volunteered right away and was mustered in as a private in the 7th New York State Militia. After the expiration of his 30-day service, he was mustered out, but he re-enlisted quite soon and became lieutenant of the Engineer Regiment of the West Missouri Volunteers.[127]

For the third time he enlisted on April 15, 1863, in Memphis, Tennessee, and organized the 1st Tennessee Heavy Artillery of African Descent, which soon became one of the constituents of the 3rd U.S. Colored Heavy Artillery. He became commander of Fort Pickering, and on September 3, 1863, Kappner was promoted to colonel and was commanding the regiment.[128]

Most sources agree that he was a typical military professional, fought earnestly, and needed no political strings to pull for promotion. Major General Quincy Gillmore, inspector general of fortifications, praised Kappner's courteous attention and efficient aid during his stay at Memphis, and also "took pleasure in commending his zeal, intelligence, and ability" to the notice of his superiors. Kappner did an excellent job in organizing the untrained blacks into an effective fighting unit, and contemporary military experts found the 3rd U.S. Colored Heavy Artillery one of the best drilled regiments in the Civil War. His obituary published by the Military Order of the Loyal Legion of the United States emphasized Kappner's service in a colored regiment: "There was no thought on the part of Col. Kappner that, in organizing and commanding a regiment of such troops, he was doing an action unworthy of the highest type of a soldier." He tried to fight whites' Negrophobia and challenged traditional norms of blacks' behavior. For instance, he urged his soldiers to participate in the celebrations organized by the Sons of Ham, a black fraternal association on August 1, 1865, while making sure that officers escorted them constantly.[129]

He tried hard to keep his unit in service, but he lacked the necessary political connections, so along with his regiment, he was mustered out on April 30, 1866.

After the Civil War, he moved to St. Louis and became partner of fellow Hungarian and skyrocketing journalist mogul Joseph Pulitzer, co-editor of *St. Louis Post-Dispatch*. Later he was business manager of the paper, as well. He died on October 20, 1891.[130]

As a commander of a colored regiment, he certainly deserved commemoration by the African American community: his name is engraved on the African American Civil War Memorial in Washington, D.C.[131]

Keményffy, Joseph

Keményffy was born Hartmann in a Jewish family in Szentistvánbaksa in 1812 or 1814. He is one of the "mystery men" of the Hungarian Civil War participants, as we have hardly any information about his life. Based on Gábor Bona's work, he served as a sergeant in the 60th Infantry Regiment between 1831 and 1840. Then he studied pedagogy in Vienna, and found employment as a tutor in Kassa.[132]

In 1848 he entered Hungarian military service as 1st lieutenant in a Home Guard regiment. He changed his name to Keményffy then. In September he was promoted to captain, and in November, being immensely popular among students, became an instructor at the military school of the University of Pest, and was responsible for drilling. He was appointed commander of the University Legion in Pest, and later commanded the 90th Honvéd Battalion. On March 22, 1849, Keményffy badly whipped the Serbs at Kiszombor.[133]

After the defeat of the Hungarian forces, he was captured by the Austrians, and forced into military service as a private in the Imperial Army. In 1851, he was released, or based on Dancs's account, he escaped, and emigrated to America. Dancs's book, the only source at our disposal, states that he served in the Civil War as a captain.[134]

After the conflict he returned to Hungary, settled down in Zilah and worked as a lawyer, and an archivist after 1887. He died on November 24, 1895.[135]

Kiss, Anthony

Most of the information about Anthony Kiss can only be inferred from the census data and his military profile. He was born in 1826 or 1827. All we know for sure about him is that in 1860 he was living in Philadelphia, PA. He was single and was working as a shoemaker.[136]

In the Civil War he was mustered in as a private in Company F of the 39th New York Volunteers, or Garibaldi Guard, which was organized and later commanded by Col. D'Utassy. Kiss was promoted to sergeant and was mustered out on October 1, 1862.[137]

He re-enlisted in Battery C, 1st New Jersey Light Artillery, and was mustered in as a private on November 9, 1863. He was severely wounded and was taken to Lincoln U.S. Army General Hospital in Washington, D.C., and was discharged on December 17, 1864 due to disability. He later lived at the National Military Home in Montgomery, Ohio. The date of his death has not yet been identified.[138]

Knefler, Frederick

Frederick Knefler was the highest-ranking Jewish officer in the American Civil War. He was born on April 12, 1834, in Arad. The original name of the family was Knoepfler. His father, Nathan Knefler, was a physician who was one of the key figures of the local Jewish community as well as the city of Arad. This prosperous middle-class family background made it possible for young Frederick to acquire an excellent education.[139]

He was barely 15 years old when the Hungarian War of Liberation broke out. With his father in charge of a military hospital in Arad, and later chief surgeon of the 101st and 102nd battalions with a rank of captain, the young boy was also attracted to the Hungarian freedom fight and enlisted. When the Hungarian cause collapsed, the whole family had to flee abroad, and they wound up in the United States. Having spent some time in New York, where young Frederick learned the trade of carpenter, they moved to the West and settled down in Indianapolis, Indiana.[140]

The Kneflers were one of the very first Jewish families in Indianapolis and Nathan Knefler was among the two dozen founders of Indianapolis Hebrew Congregation, the city's first synagogue, established on November 2, 1856. Fred was working as a carpenter and studied law. He mastered English by reading Shakespeare and daily papers. He gained experience as deputy to the clerk of Marion County. In 1856 he was admitted to the bar, where he met Lew Wallace, lawyer, and future writer of *Ben Hur*. Wallace and Knefler became life-long friends.[141]

When the Civil War broke out, Lew Wallace was appointed state adjutant-general by Indiana Governor Oliver P. Morton and his primary task was to raise the volunteer regiments needed to fill the state quota. He chose Knefler as his assistant. When Wallace was made commander of one of the newly-formed regiments, the 11th Indiana Volunteer Infantry Regiment, Knefler followed him and was commissioned 1st lieutenant. On August 31, 1861, he was elevated to the rank of captain, and on September 8, 1861, he was promoted to full captain. This took place when

Wallace left the regiment to become brigadier-general and Knefler became his assistant adjutant-general. On May 16, 1862, he was promoted to the rank of major, and at Wallace's side participated in the capture of Forts Donelson and Henry, and took part in the battle of Shiloh (April 6–7, 1862), one of the bloodiest engagements of the Civil War. Shiloh's more than 23,000 casualties exceeded the casualties of the War of Independence, the war of 1812 and the Mexican war combined. No wonder that the Union commander, U.S. Grant, was heavily criticized for his performance, and for the fact that he let himself be surprised by the enemy, and Grant, in order to share at least part of the responsibility, made a scapegoat out of Brig. Gen. Wallace, who — according to him — was way too slow in marching to the battlefield, and thus endangered the entire Union army. Wallace argued that he did not have the faintest idea of the situation, and Captain Baxter, who handed him the dispatch of Grant's scribbled on a small piece of paper, failed to inform him how grave the situation was. Knefler actually recalled that "Baxter brought cheering news." Unfortunately, we will probably never know who is correct in his statement, as the small note was entrusted to the care of Knefler, who simply tucked it under his sword belt and, as it turned out, lost it. Anyway, Wallace was removed from active duty for a while, and although reinstated, never again was entrusted with a battlefield command.[142]

On August 27, 1862, Knefler was promoted to colonel and assigned to command the newly-organized 79th Indiana Volunteer Infantry regiment. He proved to be a very strict disciplinarian (like most officers who saw service in any of the European regular armies), and so quite unpopular among his men, but he soon gained their respect on the battlefield. The newly-formed regiment was immediately assigned under the command of Gen. Buell, in the Army of the Ohio in Louisville, Kentucky. The 79th Indiana participated in the battles of Perryville (October 7, 1862) and Stone's River (December 31, 1862 to January 2, 1863). Knefler reported about the latter engagement, "The regiment went into action on December 31 with 341, rank and file, and lost during both engagements fully one-third of its available force, including more than half the commissioned officers in killed and wounded; but very few men are missing or taken prisoners." The 79th also took part in the battle of Chickamauga (September 18–20, 1863), and as a recognition of Knefler and his regiment, the state of Indiana erected a monument on the site of the battle.[143]

The battle of Chattanooga (November 23–25, 1863) brought even more success for Knefler and his regiment. The 79th Indiana captured Missionary Ridge, a formidable position heavily defended by the Confederates. Colonel George F. Dick, commander of the 86th Indiana Volunteers, wrote in his official report, "While it is out of place, and I feel a delicacy in presuming to dictate as a junior officer, yet I must say that Col. Fred Knefler, Seventy-ninth Indiana Volunteers, well deserves and richly merits a commission as a brigadier-general, for his gallantry displayed in the charging and taking of Missionary Ridge."[144]

Knefler took part in the Atlanta campaign, and his regiment was present at the siege of Atlanta. They were among the troops marching into the city.

As a recognition of his gallant service throughout these months leading the 79th Indiana Volunteers, he was brevetted brigadier general on March 13, 1865. He was mustered out on June 7, 1865.[145]

After the Civil War he remained in Indianapolis and entered into a law partnership with former U.S. District Attorney John Hanna: Hanna and Knefler. In 1882 Hanna died and Knefler's new partnership was Knefler and Berryhill. He was commissioner of pensions between 1877 and 1885 and he worked extremely hard to rationalize the working of the system. He became president of the board of regents in charge of the erection of the Soldiers and Sailors Monument in Indianapolis, which was finished in 1902. Knefler died on June 14, 1901. His last wish was to be buried in the plainest coffin available without any service, as he said, "I have never believed in wasting on dead bodies that which can benefit the living."[146]

Kovács, Stephen

It is not easy to reconstruct the details of the life and career of Stephen Kovács. According to his Civil War muster roll he was born in 1823, but other sources indicate 1817 (Gábor Bona), 1830 (Census of 1870) and 1833 (Census of 1880.) Bona gives Szeged as his place of birth. All that seems to be sure about his early career is that he was a preacher and volunteered in the Hungarian War of Liberation in 1848. In the war he elevated to the rank of major, and towards the end of it, he served on the staff of General Guyon, commander of the Fourth (Bácska) Division.[147]

After the collapse of the Hungarian cause, he left the country for Turkey, taking his fiancée, Fáni Ottoványi, with him. They got married at Christmas in 1849 in Sumla, Turkey.[148]

They arrived in the United States onboard the USS *Mississippi* in 1851. While in New York City, Kovács desperately sought employment. The renowned hat maker and entrepreneur John N. Genin (1819–1878), who made huge fortunes out of the Hungarian exiles, selling Kossuth hats — black felt hats adorned with a black feather — offered him a job as a shop clerk in December 1851. He struggled for further opportunities for work in the U.S., but finally tried his luck in the frontier settlement of New Buda in Iowa in 1853, where it proved hard to make ends meet. The family returned to New York, and Kovács played an important role in the life of the Hungarian community there. His son, Cornelius, was born in 1853 and in 1858 Fanny gave birth to a baby girl, baptized as Anna. Kovács pondered going to Italy in 1859 to fight against Austria but stayed.[149]

In 1861 he was among the Hungarians organizing an all-Hungarian regiment in New York. The meeting of July 18, 1861, elected him as acting colonel of the future regiment, which, however, never materialized. He volunteered and was mustered in as a captain on September 7, 1861, in the 54th New York Volunteer regiment, also referred to as Barney Rifles. This regiment was organized by fellow Hungarian Eugene Kozlay, who became colonel of the unit. Kovács started his service at Company K on September 23, 1861, and was transferred to Company E on October 16. He was promoted to captain on January 4, 1862, and on June 3, 1862, he was elevated to the rank of major. He participated in the battle of Gettysburg (July 1–3, 1863) where his regiment was part of the Eleventh Army Corps. In the battle he was taken prisoner, and was sent to the infamous Libby Prison in Richmond. He was imprisoned there until March 11, 1864, when he was paroled. At Libby he joined fellow Hungarian exile and Civil War participant Emeric Szabad, who wrote of his experience in his Libby Prison Diary.[150]

Many sources praise Kovács's Civil War career, but a unique primary source, Col. Kozlay's regimental journal, gives a highly critical description of Kovács:

> My Major Kovacs, he should like to retain his position by all means in this regiment. But I am sure that if I go, he will not be able to hold himself up. He is a good fellow, but a very useless soldier. If the regiment is veteran, the best he does will be, go home. I have no help, but not the least in him; the men do not respect him, he does not understand how to drill them. He knows tolerable well the command, but whether it is executed right or wrong, there he has no judgment or knowledge to decide.[151]

He also writes about getting an official notification that Kovács would be promoted to lieutenant-colonel. His immediate reaction to this was as follows: "What a folly? To appoint a man for that position who is totally unfit. I cannot understand the folly of this appointment. How was it done? Who recommended him? I did not. I am sorry for poor Kovacs because he loses even his former position by this mad act of his to accept such appointment for which he is unfit."[152]

In the end Kovács was not promoted, and was discharged on June 2, 1865. However, he was mustered in again as a major on June 20, 1865, and eventually mustered out with his regiment on April 14, 1866, in Charleston, SC.[153]

After the Civil War he lived in New York City. According to the federal census of 1880, he worked as a cigar maker. He died in 1884 at the residence of his longtime friend, fellow Hungarian Dr. Attila Kelemen. (Some sources erroneously claimed that Kovacs perished at Libby Prison.)[154]

Kováts, Augustus

He was born on August 22, 1830, in Pécel. He attended military school, and in 1848 volunteered right away for the Hungarian revolutionary army. He served in Pest with the 1st Honvéd Battalion, then, already a sergeant, he was transferred to the 99th Battalion. By the end of the conflict he had elevated to the rank of lieutenant, and was one of the defenders of the fortress in Komárom.[155]

After the Austrian-Russian coalition forces crushed the Hungarian troops, he was arrested and forced into Austrian service as a private in the 42nd Infantry Regiment. He managed to desert in Schleswig-Holstein, and fled to London in 1850. Soon he emigrated to the United States of America.

In 1851, he set off organizing a force to assist Narciso Lopez's filibuster expedition to Cuba, but had only gotten as far as Savannah by the time Lopez was captured by the Spanish. Although his party was dissolved, he remained in the South and made a living by giving fencing lessons. Soon, however, he returned to the North, largely because of the tangible secessionist sentiments in the South. He tried his luck in the small settlement of New Buda in Iowa, but later moved on and settled in Cincinnati, Ohio, and ran a grocery store. In 1852 he married

Martha A. Wallace. In 1856 they moved to Chicago and Kováts had various occupations.[156]

On June 22, 1861, he volunteered in the Union Army and was mustered in as a captain of the 24th Illinois Infantry regiment. By then he had already assisted Géza Mihalotzy, fellow Hungarian expatriate, in organizing the militia unit called the Lincoln Riflemen. He was so severely wounded at an engagement at Jasper, Tennessee on June 21, 1862, that he had to resign on January 19, 1863. His property was almost entirely destroyed by fire at Camp Butler, Illinois, on December 2, 1865, for which he desperately sought compensation from the Committee of Claims. As a recognition of his meritous service, he was brevetted major and was mustered into the 7th Regiment Veteran Reserve Corps, and after the actual end of the Civil War served in the 2nd Battalion Veteran Reserve Corps. He was honorably discharged on June 30, 1866.[157]

After the Civil War he returned to civilian life in Chicago. First he worked as an inspector of customs, then he became justice of the peace until 1870. Later he moved to Jefferson, Illinois, where he was also justice of the peace and was involved in the real estate business. He died on November 7, 1886, in Jefferson. Ács and Bona claim that Kováts returned to Hungary in 1870, settled down in Gyula, and died in 1874. However, the available American sources suggest that both are mistaken.[158]

Kozlay, Eugene

He was born János Kecskés or János Kozik in 1825 in Jászladány and baptized in Jászkisér. He spent some of his childhood years in the small town of Acsa, then attended high school in Aszód between 1837–1839. He enrolled at the institution under the name of János Kozik. His further education is not clear, but he probably attended a military school. According to his diary, he received his military education under the Austrians and became an officer while still a teenager. Following that he was admitted to the University of Pest, where he studied law. It was probably around that time that he changed his name to Jenő Kozlay.[159]

He volunteered in the Hungarian War of Liberation in 1848, and he was a lieutenant in the 12th (Asboth) Division organized in Balmazújváros. Later he was transferred to II Corps. On September 22, 1849, he was a 1st lieutenant in the 25th Honvéd Battalion stationed at Komárom, responsible for the provisioning of soldiers.[160]

After the fall of the Hungarian cause the Austrian government granted the defenders of Komárom a safe-conduct and Kozlay emigrated to the United States, where he arrived in 1850. At that time he changed his name from Jenő Kozlay to Eugene A. Kozlay. He moved to New Orleans where he worked strenuously to learn English as quickly as possible, while employed by an exporter of cotton and sugar. The next year he returned to New York and resumed working in the export business hoping the some day he would be able to start his own business, which apparently never happened. He applied for American citizenship and received it in 1855. He continued his legal studies and he was admitted to the bar, although he never actually practiced law. In the second half of the 1850s, he was employed at the New

York Customhouse as withdrawal entry clerk. His English improved remarkably throughout the decade and he wrote a mediocre English novel entitled *Secrets of the Past: A Romance of the South*, which was serialized in the *United States Democratic Review* between September 1857 and June 1858.[161]

Kozlay received authority from the War Department on August 30, 1861, to recruit a regiment of infantry in New York City. He recruited mainly from among the German-Americans in Brooklyn, and the unit became the 54th New York Infantry Volunteers on October 15, 1861. The regiment was named after Lutzow's 'Black Rifles' or 'Schwarze Jaeger,' and wore a black-silver uniform. Another name for the regiment, Barney Rifles, came from Kozlay's boss at the customhouse, Hiram Barney. The winter of 1861–62 was spent perfecting the men in drill and in April 1862 they were ordered to West Virginia to join the Mountain Department. While crossing the Shenandoah River, swollen by the melting snow, each man in one of the companies drowned in front of the horror-stricken eyes of their comrades, who were unable to help. They participated in a number of battles under the command of Col. Kozlay, including the battle of Cross Keys (June 8, 1862), and 2nd Bull Run (August 29–31, 1862), where heavy casualties were suffered. At the battle of Chancellorsville on May 1–3, 1863, the 54th New York held the extreme right of the 11th Corps. They had the very similar assignment in the battle of Gettysburg (July 1–3, 1863). At the end of the first day, they were forced to retreat and having run out of ammunition, quite a number, including four officers, were taken prisoners. Among the officers captured was Hungarian Major Stephen Kovacs.[162]

After the battle of Gettysburg, the regiment was assigned to the Department of South and arrived at Folly Island in front of Charleston on August 9, 1863. They took part at the siege of Fort Wagner, and later built fortifications, patrolled, and reconnoitered the surrounding islands. On March 13, 1865, Kozlay was breveted brigadier general for his gallant leadership. In March 1865, the Fifty-fourth entered Charleston, S.C., after which it was detailed in detachments for duty in the Freedmen's Bureau throughout South Carolina, with headquarters at Orangeburg. Kozlay, along with his regiment, was mustered out on April 14, 1866.[163]

After the war, he returned to his previous job and worked at the New York Customhouse until 1869. Then he found employment in Brooklyn as a draftsman, surveyor and mapmaker and that is where he was working when the Census of 1880 was taken. He was sacked that very year due to cost-cutting measures. He became the chief engineer of the Coney Island Transit Company, and then joined the Brooklyn Elevated Railroad, which built the first above-ground railroad in Brooklyn, although Kozlay did not live to see it completed.[164]

Eugene Kozlay died on April 1, 1886, in New York, and he was buried at Evergreen Cemetery. His son, Charles Meeker Kozlay, was a successful publisher and printer, patron of writer Bret Harte.[165]

Kuné, Julian

Julian Kuné conveniently provided a narrative of his own life in his 1911 autobiography entitled *Reminiscences of an Octogenarian Hungarian Exile*.[166]

Kuné was born in Belényes, in Bihar County in 1831. He was barely 17 years old, when, freshly out of college, he joined the Hungarian revolutionary army, and fought throughout the whole conflict.[167]

After the collapse in 1849, he followed Kossuth to exile in Turkey, and later he was transported to Aleppo, Syria. According to his own account, he was employed as the Hungarian aide-de-camp to the governor general of Syria. Soon, however, more and more Hungarian exiles decided to emigrate to the United States, and Kuné joined a group who left for New York City onboard the *Cornelius Grinnel* and set foot on American soil on May 1, 1852.[168]

Like many immigrants he faced difficulty getting employment. He worked at a clock factory in Bristol, Connecticut, and later moved on to Hartford to teach German and French. Kuné became acquainted with Rev. Samuel W. Longfellow — Henry W. Longfellow's brother — who allegedly gave him the manuscript of "Psalm of Life." He must have read its lines very carefully, as he was "up and doing, With a heart for any fate; Still achieving, still pursuing." He learned to labor and to wait, but by 1855, however, he realized that he could not make a living from teaching and made up his mind to try his luck in the West. His original plan was to move to St. Louis, but he eventually settled down in Chicago.[169]

In 1855 Kuné got a position in the law office of Jonathan Young Scammon, who was very much interested in Hungarian exiles. Scammon's son had a Hungarian tutor, a Prof. Beck. Later Scammon offered Kuné a job at Marine Bank, which clearly meant better prospects for him. Meanwhile, Kuné instructed Scammon's daughter in French. He got very actively involved in political life in Chicago and built very good connections with the leaders of the local German-American community. He supported the Republican Party, and, according to his own account, he took part at the Republican National Party Convention in Chicago. He first supported the nomination of Simon Cameron, but after Abraham Lincoln's nomination, he worked extremely hard in Lincoln's election campaign. He even insisted on going to Southern Illinois, where the Republicans seemed to have no support at all, and announced his determination "to stand up for his constitutional right to speak and preach Republicanism wherever he chooses," reported the *Chicago Press and Tribune* in October 1860. He even had a private interview with Lincoln in his Springfield office, and gave the following account of his conversation with the future president: "I was prevented from speaking freely my sentiments regarding the extension of slavery beyond its present limits and ... I was one of the Hungarian exiles. [Lincoln said] "No man has the right to keep his fellowman in bondage, be he black or white; and the time will come, and must come, when there will not be a single slave within the borders of this country."[170]

When the Civil War came, he tried to make use of his political connections to acquire permission to organize a regiment of foreigners in Chicago. He had an interview with the secretary of war, then with Lincoln himself, displaying the enthusiasm with which volunteers thronged to the Union Army with twice as many offers for organizing regiments as the actual state quotas. Kuné himself had presented a letter written by fellow Hungarian Géza Mihalótzy to Lincoln and induced him to consent to forming a militia unit comprised mainly of foreigners, one that would bear his name, the Lincoln Riflemen. Kuné managed to convince Lincoln of the necessity of organizing an entire regiment of foreigners, and he was granted the permission to do so by the president personally. He also obtained the permission of Gen. George B. McClellan, whom he knew from his years back at Marine Bank, to release the militia unit and incorporate it, along with another one, the Union Cadets, into the newly-formed regiment, which was enumerated as 24th Illinois Infantry Regiment, soon to be called Lincoln Riflemen.[171]

When Kuné returned from Washington, D.C., much to his surprise he learned that Mihalótzy was elected lieutenant colonel of the regiment, and Friedrich Hecker was elected colonel, while he himself became the major of the unit. He was obviously very disappointed and thought it to be the work of Hecker. He wrote a letter to Illinois Governor Yates seeking to be relieved from his duty at the 24th Illinois to organize a new regiment. His request was declined.[172]

He was mustered in as a major on June 17, 1861, but due to his personal grievances and continuous conflicts with Col. Hecker, he resigned. In his reminiscences, he wrote that he was relieved of duty on account of his state of health by Hecker, although no medical examinations were actually carried out. Kuné rather saw the source of their conflict in his unwillingness to take part in "Hecker's periodical drinking orgies." However it might be, Kuné resigned on October 31, 1861.[173]

After leaving the army, he got involved in various business activities. He was a member of the Chicago Board of Trade, and later he was a grain broker. He edited the musical column of the *Chicago Evening Journal*, and he even played a part in founding the Chicago Historical Society. After the Compromise of 1867, he paid several visits to Hungary. In 1869 he met Ármin Vámbéry, Francis Pulszky and Joseph Pulitzer. He covered the Franco–Prussion War for the *Chicago Tribune*. He was in Vienna when he heard news of the great Chicago fire: he organized a musical performance for the benefit of the sufferers of the fire. He died in Chicago in 1914.[174]

Lang, Henry

Hardly anything is known about this Hungarian participant in the American Civil War. We do know for sure that he was born in Hungary, and probably served in the Hungarian War of Liberation of 1848–49. After the Austrian-Russian coalition forces had crushed the Hungarian freedom fight, he fled to Turkey and wound up in Bucharest. After staying one and a half years there, he left the city on May 25, 1851, and moved to Giurgiu. He spent a short period of time in the Near East, then emigrated to the United States around 1854.

According to his own account, he worked hard to learn the language, which is why he boarded with a natural-born American family, and when the Civil War came, he volunteered for an all-American regiment. He served in Company C of the 48th New York Volunteer Infantry Regiment as a private. He got quite badly wounded in an engagement in early 1864 and was captured by the Confederates — he was a prisoner of war for nine months at the infamous prisoner of war camp at Andersonville, Georgia, then was exchanged. After the Civil War he directed a factory, then returned to Hungary. He published a number of articles in Hungarian newspapers on various aspects of everyday life in America. His widow applied for his Civil War pension in 1908, which means that he must have died prior to that.[175]

Langenfeld, Francis

We do not have much information about Francis Langenfeld either. Based on the federal census of 1880, he was born in 1827. He arrived in the United States in 1855 and settled down in Chicago. In the Civil War, he joined the 24th Illinois Volunteers, the regiment organized by fellow Hungarians Col. Mihalotzy and Maj. Kuné in Chicago. He was mustered in as a sergeant, but rose to the rank of 1st lieutenant. On February 22, 1863, he was discharged.[176]

After the conflict, he continued living in the Windy City and worked as a merchant. His wife, Sophie, gave birth to three children: Wilhelm (born in 1858), Fred (1863) and Martha (1862). His name appears in the Chicago voter registration records in 1892, so he was alive then. The exact date of his death is not known.

Langer, Ignatz, M.D.

Dr. Ignatz Langer was born in Arad in a Jewish family and attended medical university in Hungary. He volunteered in the Hungarian Army in 1848–49 and served as a honvéd staff surgeon. Subsequent to the collapse of the Hungarian cause, he emigrated and was one of the Hungarian pioneers on the American frontier. He tried his luck in Davenport, Iowa, and John Fiala recalled him as a person who

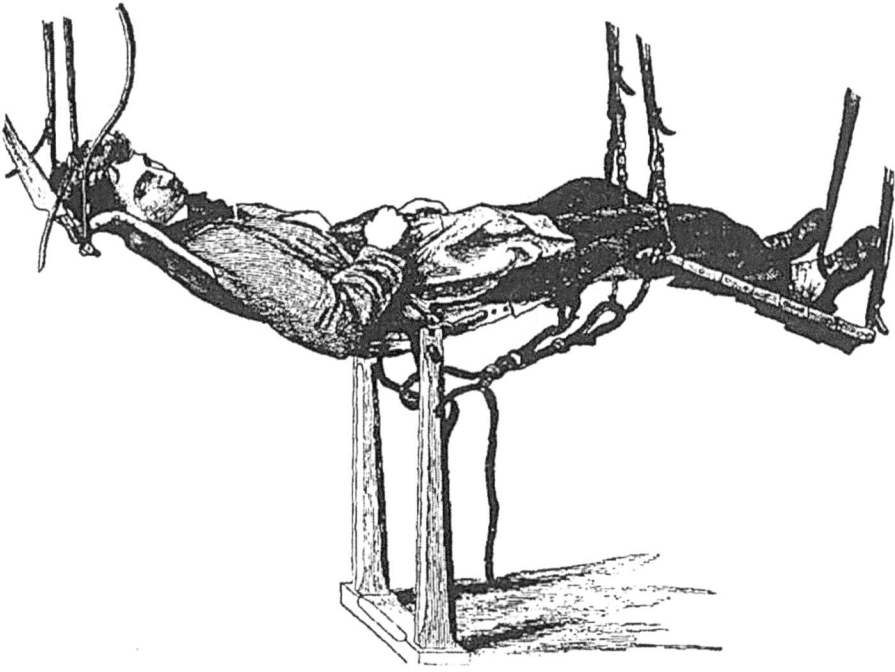

Dr. Langer's combined splint and fraction bed (*Medical and Surgical History of the Civil War*, Broadfoot Publishing Co., Wilmington, N.C., 1991, Vol. XI, 349).

helped Hungarian émigrés with important bits and pieces of advice on how to find employment, and he himself was offered board in Langer's house. Otherwise, Langer farmed and practiced his profession in the small rural community.[177]

In the Civil War he volunteered and was mustered in as a surgeon in the Union Army. His name is mostly linked to his invention for easing the sufferings of hundreds of wounded soldiers in the Civil War: a combined splint and fracture bed (1865).

Surgeon W. L. Faxon, 32nd Massachusetts, who was assigned to try out the invention in practice, wrote the following about it in his report: "I consider Dr. Langer's combined splint and fracture bed as I have seen it in operation at this hospital as the best appliance I have used, or seen used in the army. The patient can always be made comfortable; he seldom requires opiates to procure sleep...; the patients can always be kept clean; ... one nurse can take care of as many cases as of simple wounds."[178]

Dr. Faxon concluded his report by requesting fifty of the new beds for his hospital. Moreover, Dr. Langer submitted the plan of an army wagon, claiming:

> This change of the army wagon would not interfere with its design of conveying forage or other articles to and from a camp; that when the wagon is used for carrying forage the twelve beds are packed under a movable bottom, and the railing supporting them is stowed away on the sides, so that the capacity of the wagon box is not impaired; that in ten minutes after the wagon is unloaded it is changed into an ambulance wagon with all the equipments for transport — six patients in a sitting posture, six in a lying, two of which, if necessary, suspended on fracture beds of Dr. Langer's pattern; that there is room for all the equipments of the patients, for a water-keg, and for boxes with provisions and bandages, and that the wagon can be loaded from the front as well as the rear.[179]

Despite its obvious superiority over ones already used, Langer's wagon never entered service.

After the Civil War, Dr. Langer returned to Hungary and died on April 2, 1879, in Arad.

Lederer, Emanuel

He was born in Buda-Pest in 1841. He emigrated to the United States some time in the 1850s. When the Civil War broke out, he volunteered and was mustered in on May 17, 1861, as a private in Company G, 39th NY Infantry Regiment, organized by another Hungarian, Col. Frederick George D'Utassy. He was promoted to corporal on October 1, 1861, and sergeant on November 1, 1862. He was transferred to Company B on May 31, 1863, elevated to the rank of 2nd lieutenant on November 13, 1863. *The New York Times* mentioned him as captain in his obituary, however, his service records show that he was discharged due to disability on March 21, 1864, while still a 2nd lieutenant.[180]

After the Civil War he worked as a newspaper man and ran a cigar shop in Chicago. Later he became interested in the theater: he did some acting and was a manager both in the U.S. and Germany. Later he moved to New York and got involved in importing foreign plays. He had a close working relationship with Augustine Daily (1838–1899), one of the most renowned American theater managers and directors in the 19th century.[181]

Lederer died on August 21, 1917, at his home at 150 E. 74 Street in New York of heart disease. One of his sons, W.J. Lederer, became a well-known physician in New York City.

Lulley, Charles

Son of Emanuel Lulley, also participant of the Civil War. He was born in 1845, in a Jewish family. Along with his parents and four siblings, he was among the passengers of the USS *Mississippi*. In the United States they could barely make a living, so he was sort of adopted by the well-known ethnologist Henry Rowe Schoolcraft and his wife. He was very young when the Civil War started and he is the only Hungarian to serve in the Union Navy during the Civil War. However, he was wounded and was honorably discharged for disability in 1863. He died at the age of 22 in a tragic fire in Washington, D.C., on March 8, 1867. Mrs. Schoolcraft wrote a tribute to him.[182]

Lulley, Emanuel

Emanuel Lulley was born in an Israelite family in Baja in 1807. He was one of the most important spies employed by Kossuth during the Hungarian War of Independence of 1848–49. After the end of the conflict he escaped to Turkey and remained with Kossuth, although many of the Hungarian émigrés looked at him with suspicion.[183]

He arrived in the United States onboard the U.S. steamer *Mississippi* with his wife and five children. They lived in grave poverty during most of the 1850s. They settled down in the federal capital in 1855. Károly László mentioned him in his diary, describing him as a Hungarian Jew "who could hardly speak Hungarian" and was involved in dealing with second-hand furniture.[184]

At the commencement of the War Between the States, Lulley was among those planning to organize an all-Hungarian regiment. The meeting held on July 18, 1861, elected him to adjutant, and his responsibility would have been equipping the soldiers, obviously on account of his business skills. The plan, however, failed. Lulley took part in the Civil War as an agent of the Department of Justice in the rank of major.[185]

After the Civil War he returned to Washington, D.C., and worked as a tobacconist. Some sources claim that he was employed by the Secret Service at the Department of Justice. He died in 1895 in Washington, D.C.

Majthenyi, Theodore

Son of Joseph Majthenyi, prominent politician and former member and secretary of the Upper House of Hungary, Theodore was born in 1838, and was only 13 years old when he followed his father into exile. They settled down in New Buda,

Iowa, where the young boy got accustomed to the hardships of frontier life, but they soon moved on to Davenport, which seemed to be more civilized.[186]

When the Civil War came, Theodore volunteered for the 2nd Iowa Infantry Regiment, where he held the rank of sergeant. While stationed in St. Louis, Missouri, he was transferred to the Frémont Body Guard, which had been organized by another Hungarian, Major Charles Zagonyi. He was promoted very quickly: he became a 2nd lieutenant and adjutant within a month. Besides Zagonyi, he was the only Hungarian to participate in the famous cavalry charge at Springfield, Missouri, on October 25, 1861. His heroism was praised by Zagonyi in his official report of the battle.[187]

When Frémont was removed from the Department of the West, Majthényi managed to obtain a commission as a captain at Company K, 1st Indiana Cavalry Regiment, on April 17, 1862. He served in that regiment until he was mustered out on December 13, 1864.[188]

Majthényi was among the few Hungarian Civil War participants who remained in service after the end of the conflict. He was appointed 2nd lieutenant at the 6th U.S. Cavalry in February 1866. He rose to the rank of first lieutenant on October 20, 1866. After a bit more than two years of service, on December 23, 1868, he resigned from the army.[189]

Most sources agree that he subsequently returned to Hungary with his wife and their son. He took part in the forming of the Hungarian national army and rose to the rank of major. Later, however, he resigned and returned to the United States. We have no further information about him, except for the date and location of his death, which, according to Lillian May Wilson, was November 6, 1909, at Good Hope, Missouri.[190]

Menyhart, John G.

John Menyhart was born in 1829 or 1830 in Arad. At the commencement of the Hungarian War of Liberation, he volunteered and was mustered in as sergeant in the 7th Honvéd Battalion in Szombathely. He was later transformed to the Honvéd HQ to Buda-Pest. In January 1849 he was promoted to lieutenant and served in the 50th Hunyadi Battalion.

After the defeat of the Hungarian forces, he was captured and forced into Austrian service at the 42nd Infantry Regiment. He managed to flee, however, in Altona and emigrated to the United States.[191]

He settled down in New York City and, similarly to other Hungarians, was having a hard time finding employment. He joined a singing group formed entirely of Kossuth émigrés, named Magyar Dalárda (Hungarian Vocalists). According to Dancs's book, the primary purpose of the group, formed on August 17, 1851, was to try to make a living. Their first and last performance at Castle Garden was a huge failure; the group was dissolved and Menyhart sought manual labor. Károly László also mentioned having met him in New York.[192]

In the Civil War he volunteered in the 45th New York Volunteer regiment and was mustered in as a captain on October 6, 1861. He resigned on June 14, 1862, for reasons which are not quite clear.[193]

After the Civil War he returned to New York. In the following few decades he worked as a silver plater in Brooklyn. He married a German woman, Emma, and they had 5 children. He applied for a Civil War pension in 1892. According to Bona, he died in 1904 in New York.[194]

Mészáros, Emeric

Based on the information gained from the federal census of 1880, Mészáros was born in 1824. He studied law and was admitted to the bar in the beginning of the 1840s. At the commencement of the Hungarian War of Liberation in 1848, he became a captain in one of the militia regiments, and later he was mustered in as a sergeant of the 39th Honvéd Battalion in Győr. On November 15, 1848, he was promoted to lieutenant. He rose in rank very quickly; in April 1849 he became 1st lieutenant, and at the time of the surrender of the Hungarian armed forces, he was captain.[195]

He fled to Turkey first, then he was among those — including Zagonyi and Grossinger — who left Constantinople for Britain. He was one of the cadets at the Hungarian Officers' School in London organized by Hungarian exiles. Eventually he made use of the opportunity offered them by the British government from which they received 12 pounds for transportation, for paying off their debts, and for expenses, and set sail for New York on June 26, 1851. He lived in New York City in June 1852. István Kinizsi mentions him as his co-worker and foreman at Freund's marble factory that year, so it seems that Mészáros may have done a variety of menial jobs to make a living.[196]

When the Civil War started, Mészáros volunteered for the Frémont Hussars. In February 1862, the unit, along with three companies of the Hollan Horse, was consolidated into 4th Missouri Cavalry in February 1862 and the Hungarian officer became captain, and soon after major of the regiment. He took part in the Battle of Pea Ridge, Arkansas (March 6–8, 1862), and he managed to defeat a smaller Confederate detachment and capture 17 enemy of soldiers, including a captain and a lieutenant. Lt. William S. Burns of the regiment heavily criticized Mészáros for his cowardly behavior, while he ordered an unnecessary retreat and disappeared from the scene at critical moments in the battle. Burns and other officers of the regiment attempted to have Major Mészáros court-martialed, but while he was arrested and found guilty of disobedience, he was not found guilty of cowardice. The major resigned from the 4th Missouri Cavalry in July 1862.[197]

He got another commission in Company C, 1st Florida Cavalry Regiment, but he had to make do with the rank of captain that time. He was mustered out after the end of the Civil War, on November 17, 1865, in Tallahassee, Florida.[198]

Subsequently, he decided to settle down in Florida. In 1875 he purchased 160 acres of land in Tallahassee, and according to the federal census of 1880, he was engaged in orange growing. He lived alone, without a wife or children. He probably died there, but the exact date of his death is unknown.[199]

Mihalótzy, Geza

He was born on April 21, 1825, in Nagyvárad. His father was a major in the Imperial Army, but resigned and joined the Hungarian Army in 1848 and rose to lieutenant colonelcy in a militia regiment.

Géza followed his father's footsteps and attended the military academy at Wiener Neustadt between 1831 and 1841, and later saw service in the 9th Infantry Regiment.

The outbreak of the Hungarian War of Independence prompted him to join his father in the Hungarian Army, and he served in the militia unit of Óbuda. By September he rose to the rank of lieutenant, and in February 1849 he was promoted to 1st lieutenant and transferred to the 14th Honvéd Battalion in the Upper-Danube Region. In June he became a captain in VII Corps.[200]

After the defeat of the Hungarian armed forces, Mihalótzy emigrated. He tried his luck in London. Dániel Kászonyi, who knew him very well, wrote that he was working in the book binding shop owned by a Zahnsdorf, but could barely make a living. Several sources gave an account of Mihalótzy's conflict with Francis Pulszky which almost ended in a duel. Pulszky insulted the Hungarian officer, but refused to stand up and fight him; eventually he was slapped in the face twice by him. Most of the authors describe Mihalótzy as a restless, quarrelsome and very proud person.[201]

Finally his financial difficulties forced him to emigrate to the United States. He resided in Chicago, as reported by the spies of the Austrian Court.[202]

In February 1861, Mihalotzy asked fellow Hungarian Julian Kuné, who had gotten acquainted with Abraham Lincoln, the freshly-elected, not yet inaugurated president, to forward his letter to him. The letter read as follows:

> We have organized a company of Militia in this city [Chicago] composed of men of Hungarian, Bohemian and Sclavonic [sic] origin. Being the first company in the United States of said nationalities, we respectfully ask leave of your Excellency to entitle ourselves 'Lincoln Riflemen' of Sclavonic origin.
>
> If you will kindly sanction our use of your name, we will endeavor to do honor to it, whenever we may be called to perform active service.[203]

This letter is now in the custody of the Chicago Historical Society, and on the bottom of the page one can read in Lincoln's handwriting, "I cheerfully grant the request above made." Accordingly, the Lincoln Riflemen was formed as a militia unit with Mihalótzy as colonel and fellow Hungarian Augustus Kovats as lieutenant. They, along with the all-German unit called Union Cadets, belonged to the command of George B. McClellan. Later Mihalótzy expressed his wish that his militia unit be incorporated into the newly-formed 24th Illinois Infantry Regiment, which eventually happened. He was elected lieutenant colonel of the regiment, with Friedrich Hecker as colonel, and his friend Julian Kuné as major.[204]

The regiment saw its first combat duty in Missouri, then was ordered to Kentucky on September 29, 1861, and later to Tennessee and Alabama. On December 13, 1861, Hecker resigned and Mihalótzy was assigned to replace him as colonel and commander. During the Alabama campaign, on May 2, 1862, soldiers of the 24th participated in the sacking of the small town of Athens, Alabama, which further intensified anti-foreigner feelings among Americans in the North and South alike. The Union Army started an investigation and — although not court-martialed — Mihalótzy was reprimanded for having "behaved rudely and coarsely to the ladies" of Athens.[205]

The 24th Illinois fought its first considerable battle at Perryville on October 8, 1862, and suffered heavy casualties: 28 killed and 79 wounded. Colonel Mihalótzy did not participate in the battle as he was left behind in Louisville, severely sick. In the battle of Chickamauga (September 19–20, 1863), at the engagement at Lookout Mountain, he was shot through the hand, but was not seriously wounded. However, he was severely wounded in the clashes at Buzzard's Roost Gap on February 24, 1864, when he was hit by a stray Confederate shell. He was taken to the military hospital at Lookout Mountain, where Surgeon L.D. Harlow made the following diagnosis, "Deep gunshot flesh wound of the right arm above the elbow, Haemorrhage, amounting to 16 ounces, from the anastomatica magna, took place on March 2nd." A solution of perchloride of iron was applied, but Mihalótzy died on March 11, 1864, "probably from pyaemia which succeeded the haemorrhage." According to General Order No. 63 by the Headquarters of the Department of Cumberland, one of the forts in the defenses of Chattanooga "on the spur of Cameron Hill, immediately south of the gap and of the summit of the hill, will be called Fort Mihalotzy, in honor of Col. Geza Mihalotzy."[206]

Mundee, Charles

Charles Mundee is one of the most mysterious Hungarian-born participants of the Civil War, but there seems to be enough evidence suggesting that he was indeed Hungarian. However, his identity is very difficult to trace back. According to Gábor Bona, his original name was Károly Mandl, and he was born in Nagybecskerek in 1817 in a Jewish family. (Most American sources, however, agree that he was born in 1826, whereas in the federal census of 1860, his date of birth was indicated as 1830.) He served as a corporal in the Imperial Army between 1835 and 1845, then joined the Hungarian Army in the War of Liberation of 1848–49. He became a lieutenant in the honvéd artillery. Bona claims that Mandl escaped to Turkey on September 11, 1849, and later became an officer in the Turkish Army with the name Ahmed Effendi. Later he was employed as a railroad engineer in Constantinople.[207]

By 1850 he lived in Leavenworth, Kansas. On May 5, 1851, he married Alice Ryan in Missouri. They continued living in Leavenworth, and Alice gave birth to their first-born son in 1854, who was later followed by 5 more children.

Charles Mundee (Brady Civil War Photograph Collection, Library of Congress, Call Number: LC-B813-1524).

Mundee got involved in the public life of the city very soon, and became, for example, secretary of the Leavenworth Association. On the basis of the federal census of 1860, by then Mundee was a notary public in Leavenworth.[208]

In the Civil War, Mundee served in the rank of major in the Army of Potomac in Smith's Division from August 1861 to January 11, 1862, and was promoted to colonel by brevet. On January 17, 1862, he had to go on sick-leave, but recuperated soon. He resumed his service, but was wounded again a couple of times. At the battle of Wilderness he got shot in the right thigh, then later in the shoulder, and a portion of his left ear was also shot off.[209]

He showed extraordinary courage at the capture of Petersburg and Brevet Major M. Barber praised him in his official report:

> Command was turned over to Bvt. Col. Charles Mundee, assistant adjutant-general of the division, who led it in person with most conspicuous gallantry throughout all the subsequent movements. With perfect confidence that the troops under his command would follow wherever he would lead the way, he pressed forward in front of the line of battle with a perfect disregard of all danger, and by his example, as well as by the skill with which he handled the command, contributed in a very great degree to the glorious achievements that day performed by the Vermont brigade.[210]

On April 20, 1865, upon the recommendation of Brevet Major General Getty, 2nd Division, 6 Corps, Mundee was promoted to Brigadier General by brevet "for gallantry and meritorious services in the assault on the enemy's line."[211]

After the Civil War, Mundee returned to the civilian life, and the family moved to Tallahassee, Florida. He regularly participated in the activities of veterans' associations.[212]

His death took place under strange circumstances. In June 1871 he was on his way back to Florida from a reunion of the Army of the Potomac in Boston, when he stopped in New York. Nobody really knows why, but for $250 he purchased an interest in a low drinking saloon at No. 110 West Street, and was later arrested on a charge of cheating a customer. He was taken to the Tombs, the central prison in New York City. On the night of June 4, 1871, he died in his cell.[213]

Nagy, Alexander

Alexander Nagy was born in 1827. No information is available about his life and career in Hungary. He probably took part in the Hungarian War of Liberation, as he emigrated right after the collapse of the Hungarian cause. He stayed in Britain for some time, but, took the opportunity when the British government offered to finance the voyage of the Hungarian émigrés and on April 2, 1852, left London for New York onboard the *Cornelius Grinnell*.[214]

Once in the United States, he moved to the West and did all sorts of menial jobs. In 1860 he was employed as a day laborer in San Jose, California. He married an Austrian woman and their first child, Alex, was born in 1860.[215]

At the commencement of the Civil War, Nagy did not jump to arms right away. He volunteered in the Union Army and was mustered in as private in Company B, 2nd California Infantry, on March 30, 1864. He rose to the rank of sergeant, and was mustered out at Presidio, California, on May 10, 1866. Of his post–Civil War career we do not have any information.[216]

Nemett, Joseph

Joseph Nemett was born in 1816 in Losonc. According to Géza Závodszky, he was a professional soldier in the 4th Cavalry Regiment in the Imperial Army with the rank of 1st lieutenant. When learning the news of the outbreak of the Hungarian War of Independence, he deserted along with some 500 hussars and returned to Hungary from Polish Galicia, where they were stationed at the time.[217]

He volunteered in one of the militia regiments and was mustered in as 1st lieutenant. Later he was promoted to captain in the 62nd Honvéd Battalion. He participated in more than two dozen engagements and was wounded several times; finally he was discharged on July 14, 1849.[218]

After the surrender of the Hungarian revolutionary forces, he fled to Turkey, where he remained in the closest circle of Kossuth. First he was the stableman of the governor, but after the death of Károly Mertai, he became Kossuth's cook and served in this position throughout their stay in Turkey.[219]

Nemett arrived in the United States of America on the steamer USS *Mississippi* on November 10, 1851, and settled in New York for some time. His signature can be found among those Hungarians living in New York who let their voices be heard in defense of Kossuth after the assaults against him in the *Courier and Inquirer* on May 7, 1852.[220]

Nemett faced almost constant unemployment in New York, so some time after 1853 he decided to try his luck on the frontier and moved to St. Louis. He made excellent use of his experience with horses, and started a practice as surgeon and horse doctor. He married a German woman from Hessen-Darmstadt and they had two children. Their younger daughter, Gisella, died when she was 11 months old in 1860.[221]

At the commencement of the Civil War, Nemett enlisted in the 5th Missouri Infantry Regiment as 1st lieutenant and adjutant, and was mustered out in August 1861 at the termination of his three-month contract. However, he re-enlisted as a major in the battalion named Benton Hussars and served as its commander until the whole unit became incorporated into 5th Missouri Cavalry on February 14, 1862. He was appointed colonel and the commander of the entire regiment. The regiment took part in the battle of Pea Ridge under his command on March 6–8, 1862. He was discharged in November 1862, when the 5th Missouri Cavalry merged with the 4th Missouri Cavalry regiment.[222]

According to Géza Závodszky he settled down in Georgia after the Civil War and was involved in viticulture: he created a wine culture he named 'Buda.' In fact, Nemett settled down in Chicago after the Civil War and continued his practice as a veterinary surgeon at least until 1880. One of his daughters became the first female special examiner at the request of federal court; based on an article published in the *Daily Inter Ocean* while she was living with her mother at No. 151 Goethe Street in Chicago in 1895. Mrs. Nemett applied for her husband's Civil War veteran pension in 1881, so it is likely that Joseph Nemett died in 1880 or 1881 in Chicago.[223]

Perczel, Nicholas

Nicholas Perczel was born in Bonyhád on December 15, 1812, in a noble family. His father, Sándor, a veteran of the Napoleonic Wars, had 21 children. Among the nine boys were Nicholas, and his elder brother, Mór, one of the most renowned Hungarian generals in 1848–49. They were very close to each other, and there is no denying that the more dominant Mór had great influence on Nicholas. "With Móric we had been inseparable since our childhood. We fought side by side through all the hardships of private and political life. I took my share in his struggles and victories, I was his faithful companion and follower," Nicholas wrote about his brother in his diary. They were both students of one of the greatest Hungarian poets, Mihály Vörösmarty, and Nicholas studied law at the University of Pest. After his graduation in 1832, he became a government official in Baranya and Tolna counties. He got involved in the political movement of the Reform Age and was elected representative in the Parliament of 1848.[224]

At the outbreak of the War of Liberation, he became major of the militia of Tolna County, and participated in the fights in Bácska as commander of a militia battalion. In December 1848 he joined Mór and commanded one of the battalions in his corps. He was promoted to lieutenant colonel on April 5, 1849. Between April and July 1849, he was the commander of the fortress at Pétervárad. On July 9, 1849, he was elevated to the rank of colonel, and Kossuth appointed him to the command of the fort in Arad. However, he got into a disagreement with Major General János Damjanich, supervisor of Arad, who even locked him up for a short period. After his release, he joined his brother again and took part in the battle of Temesvár (August 9, 1849).[225]

Like other high-ranking revolutionary officers, he fled to Turkey and remained with Kossuth throughout their internment. (He was sentenced to death and executed in effigy in 1851 by the Austrian authorities.) He left the Ottoman Empire onboard the USS *Mississippi* and arrived in New York City on November 10, 1851.[226]

As one of the most prominent and highest ranking of the Hungarian exiles in the United States, he was introduced to the finest of the social circles of New York City. He made the best possible impression on whoever he met: Catharine M. Sedgwick, daughter of Theodore Segwick, leading lawyer in New York, who was a distinguished author herself, wrote about Perczel in a letter to her niece, Mrs. K.S. Minot: "We were all charmed by Colonel Perczel. He is about forty-five — a fine person, ... having a certain tone expressing purity, refinement, manliness, health, and giving to beautiful and harmonious features just the ground they want.... His manners, too, have a high-bred quality, kindly and gentle, with a certain reserve of delicacy, and not hauteur."[227]

Realizing that the initial enthusiasm Americans felt for the Hungarian cause faded away, he let himself be convinced by his major American patron, Rev. Henry Ward Beecher, brother of Harriet Beecher Stowe, to start a language school where he taught German and French to a select group of upper-class New Yorkers including "3 Protestant preachers, two married women and a young lady." However, being hardly able to make a living from teaching, he decided to move to the West. Together with Nicholas Fejérváry, he went to Davenport, Iowa, where he purchased a considerable portion of land in September 1852 and joined the small Hungarian community there in the spring of 1853.[228]

He hoped that the events foreshadowing the Crimean War in 1854 might bring some progress for the Hungarian cause, so he sold his farm and was about to move to Europe. Finally the family wound up on the Island of Jersey, where his brother, Mór lived. One of his neighbors was the famous writer Victor Hugo. They spent there five years, and due to his disappointment in the treaty ending the War of 1859, in which he felt the Hungarian Cause was disgracefully let down, he returned to Iowa.[229]

He actively participated in the political debates preceding the Civil War and spoke at several political meetings expressing his sympathies with the Republican party. He believed that the Southern states did not have the Constitutional right to secede from the Union, and he pointed out the grave economic consequences of a possible break-up of the republic.[230]

At the start of the War Between the States, Governor Samuel J. Kirkwood of Iowa asked Perczel to organize a volunteer infantry regiment. Nearly fifty years old, he was hesitant, but finally he agreed and raised the 10th Iowa Infantry Regiment.[231]

He was commissioned on September 1, 1861, as colonel and commander of the regiment. They took part in the skirmishes in Eastern Missouri, then participated in the capture of New Madrid and Island No. 10. They performed particularly well in the battle of Iuka, Mississippi (September 19, 1862): second-lieutenant L.D. Immel wrote to his superior about the Hungarian colonel and his unit, "I call your attention to the great bravery of Col. Perczel, his officers and men, the gallant manner in which they fought, supported the artillery, and repulsed the enemy with great loss."[232]

There seemed some chance that Perczel would be promoted to brigadier general, but it came to nothing. What is even worse, his continuous bouts with malaria finally left him no other option but to resign on November 1, 1862.[233]

After the Civil War, he waited eagerly for the general amnesty to all participants of the Hungarian War of Liberation, which eventually followed the Great Compromise of 1867. In 1868 he returned to Hungary and spent the rest of his life holding important administrative positions in his home county. He also participated in the veterans' movements, and was member of the Honvéd Association in Tolna County. He died on March 4, 1904.[234]

An edited and somewhat abridged version of Nicholas Perczel's diary was published in Hungarian in two volumes in 1977 and 1979, entitled *Naplóm az emigrációból* (*My Diary from the Emigration*), and is one of the most important primary sources available on the history of the Kossuth emigration.

Pomutz, George

Pomutz provides an excellent case study of the use of a prominent historical figure by competing ethnic groups in the United States in attempts to legitimize their presence in America and strengthen internal group cohesion. The ethnicity of George Pomutz is debated by Romanians and Hungarians, although his life is actually quite well documented. He was born on May 31, 1818, in Gyula, Békés

County, in Hungary, but in an ethnic Romanian family. Maria Berenyi, in her article published in the *Transylvanian Review*, refers to him as a Romanian from Gyula, disregarding the fact that none of the Hungarian emigrants ever referred to Pomutz as a Romanian person. Ladislaus Újházy, in his letter written on November 27, 1850, gave an account of the newly-arrived Pomutz in Iowa, "Of our Hungarians four more have arrived," including Pomutz among them. On the other hand, in a letter to Francis Pulszky, Pomutz wrote as follows about himself, "I have been member of Orthodox Church and I know the language of those people, I am acquainted with their religious needs.... I understand the operation of our [Hungarian] institutions for two decades and my commitment towards them have been proved by my determinate deeds." In the Census of 1860 he gave his nationality as Hungarian in spite of the fact that officially it did not exist, and he might have as well indicated it as Romanian. In any case, his memory is cherished by both Hungarians and Romanians.[235]

The young Pomutz probably grew up in Somogy County, as many fellow exiles remembered him as having lived there. Berenyi claims that he became a prosecutor and opened an attorney's office. At the outbreak of the Hungarian War of Independence, he became lieutenant in a militia unit around Gyula and played an important role in organizing the volunteers. During the conflict he was elevated to the rank of captain and was appointed police chief of the fortress of Komárom. He was, therefore, among those granted a safe-conduct from the Austrian authorities on condition that they leave the country. He was elected road marshal by his comrades and they founded an Emigration Society, and it seems that they set off with a colonization scheme even at this early stage.[236]

Pomutz arrived in New York City in February 1850 and soon decided to move on to the West. Along with other Hungarian emigrants, he followed Ladislaus Újházy to Iowa, where they founded a Hungarian settlement they named New Buda. Pomutz, "tall blond with full beard and mustachios and light wavy hair," as Lillian May Wilson described him, was immensely popular among the local Hungarians. John Xantus, who also spent some time in New Buda, wrote about Pomutz: "Of all the newcomers, none knew how to till the land, and, losing patience, they were all desperate. Pomutz Gyuri realized that this would break up the colony. As one of its founders, he left his own place and helped the others.... When his own bones were freezing, he covered and warmed up the others, when he had no boots, he gave boots to the others. This is what [he] was like and this settlement is only due to his noble soul and spirit of sacrifice."[237]

Like many others, he applied for American citizenship and was naturalized in 1855, five years after his arrival in the country.

At the commencement of the Civil War, he enlisted as 1st lieutenant on December 23, 1861, and was mustered into Company S, 15th Iowa Infantry Regiment. On April 6, 1862, he was wounded in the shoulder in the battle of Shiloh, but recuperated relatively quickly. He steadily rose through the ranks: on April 22, 1863, he was promoted to major, on August 18, 1864, to lieutenant colonel, after he had commanded the 15th Iowa at the siege of Atlanta. He was brevetted colonel, and on March 13, 1865, for his gallant and meritorious services during the war, he became brigadier general by brevet. Pomutz was mustered out on July 24, 1865, along with his regiment, in Louisville, Kentucky.[238]

After the war, President Andrew Johnson appointed him consul in St. Petersburg, Russia, on February 16, 1866. He served in that capacity until September 30, 1870. He played an important role in American-Russian negotiations for the Alaska Purchase. On June 17, 1874, he was appointed consul general, also in St. Petersburg, and he remained in that post until President Rutherford B. Hayes called him back. It is not known why Pomutz decided to stay in Russia after this, but he did, although he was hardly able to make ends meet; he died poor on October 12, 1882, and was possibly buried in Smolensk.[239]

In 1913 Congress issued a joint resolution (No. 775) in which it was proposed that his remains be brought back to the United States and re-buried at Arlington. However, World War I came, and the initiative was forgotten. In 1944 a Liberty ship was named after him: the SS *George Pomutz* was launched on October 1944 and served until 1970.

As I have already pointed out, Pomutz is remembered by both Hungarians and Romanians. In his hometown, Gyula, a street was named after him and in 2006 the city and its Romanian ethnic community erected a statue together in commemoration of him. In 2004 another statue was unveiled outside the St. Mary Cathedral in Cleveland, OH, by the local Romanian-American community.[240]

Pulitzer, Joseph

Pulitzer is definitely the most famous of all the Civil War participants of Hungarian origin, but this is due to neither his military career nor his Hungarian birth. He became one of the greatest newspapers editors and moguls in the history of the United States and his name today is remembered through his sponsoring the founding of Columbia Graduate School of Journalism, the most prestigious institution of its kind in the world, and the Pulitzer Prize "as an incentive to excellence," as he put it in his will.

Joseph Pulitzer was born in a Jewish family in Makó on April 10, 1847. His father, Philip, was a merchant in the city; his mother, Elize Berger, also came from a merchant family. Her younger brother, Vilmos, was an officer in a hussar regiment, and soon became a role model for young Pulitzer.[241]

His early childhood was spent in a carefree manner — his father was one of the leaders of the local Jewish community and his trading business prospered. Even the coming of the War of Liberation in 1848 brought about further opportunities for him: he made a contract on provisioning the Hungarian troops in Southern Hungary with the revolutionary government. After the fall of the Hungarian cause, he continued his business, yet this time he made a contract with the Imperial Army. However, the memory of 1848–49 had great influence on Joseph, who developed great interest in the military and talked highly of Kossuth and the Hungarian freedom fighters all through his life.

In 1855 his father moved to Pest seeking better business opportunities. Pulitzer was educated by private tutors until his father fell sick with tuberculosis and died in 1858. (The shadow of death was constantly hanging over the Pulitzers: out of the nine children only Joseph and his younger brother Albert lived to adulthood.) Philip Pulitzer's enterprise quickly went bankrupt and his widow had a hard time trying to provide for her family. Joseph attended a prestigious trading school in Pest, but it turned out that he did not have much interest in this profession.[242]

Instead, he tried to volunteer in Maximilian's expeditionary force preparing for Mexico in the spring of 1864, but, as he had not seen military service, was turned away. (His uncle William Berger was a member of the contingent.) Being very persistent, he traveled to France to become a legionnaire, but he was turned down there too. He moved to London, but it seems that he ran out of money, so finally he set sail for the United States, probably at the encouragement of a Union recruiting agent. He arrived in New York City broke, so volunteering in the Civil War meant not only the realization of his dreams to become a cavalry soldier, but pretty much the only means of survival, as the young man spoke no English at all. He enlisted in the 1st New York (Lincoln) Cavalry, the reasons for which he summarized: "I wanted to ride a horse, to be a horse-soldier. I did not like to walk. In Europe we knew the regiments by names of celebrities. They were named for kings or princes. We had in Austria a regiment, Maria Theresa, named after the great empress. So I inquired for the names of some of the regiments of horsemen, and was told of one called Lincoln. I knew who he was and so went to that regiment. I did not have any idea what it was like."[243]

Many of the soldiers of the regiment were German, so Pulitzer did not have problems communicating, but his English proficiency did not develop at all during the Civil War. The frail, shortsighted young man was constantly teased and hazed by his fellow troopers, so it is little wonder that he was pleased when his regiment was mustered out on June 24, 1865, in Alexandria, Virginia. He remained a private throughout the Civil War. He was paid off on July 7, 1865, in New York City, and he was about to search for employment: he had no trade, hardly spoke English and had 13 dollars in his pocket. For a time he was homeless, and did all sorts of menial jobs, but his physique did not enable him to do hard physical labor. Later he recalled the nights he spent outdoors at Madison Square: "That is where I also slept many a night. I had no bed when I first came to this city; I had no roof over my head. Every pleasant night until I found employment I slept upon that bench, and my summons to breakfast was frequently the rap of a policeman's club." That was the main reason why he decided to move to St. Louis, which was called the capital of German-Americans at the time, hoping for an easier integration there.[244]

He started out with blue-collar work in Missouri, as well, but soon got employment as a freelance journalist at the St. Louis German paper, *Westliche Post*. In the meantime, he studied law, acquired his license, but failed to start a thriving practice.

He became interested in political life and joined the Republican Party. Moreover, he was elected to the Missouri State Assembly in 1869. Still interested in journalism, in 1872 he bought the *Westliche Post* for 3,000 dollars. He broke with the Republican Party and he was elected to the State Assembly as member of the Democratic Party. In 1879 he purchased the *St. Louis Dispatch*, and merged the two papers into *St. Louis Post-Dispatch* which still exists today. Pulitzer had a deep interest in the common man, which remained the main focus of his exposés.[245]

In 1882 he purchased the *New York World*, which was burdened with debt at the time. By shifting his emphasis to scandal and sensationalism, he managed to increase the *World*'s circulation from 15,000 to 600,000, making it the largest daily newspaper in the United States. His famous circulation war with William Randolph Hearst, owner of the rival *New York Journal* at the time of the Spanish-American War, inseparably linked Pulitzer's name with yellow journalism.

He married the niece of Jefferson Davis, Miss Kate Davis of Washington, D.C., in 1877, and they had five children.[246]

Joseph Pulitzer died aboard his yacht in the harbor of Charleston, South Carolina, on October 29, 1911. Hearst, his greatest rival, called him "the founder and foremost exemplar of modern journalism — the great originator and exponent of the journalism of action and achievement," and concluded that "in his death journalism has lost a leader, the people a champion, the nation a valuable citizen."[247]

Radnich, Emeric

Brother of another Hungarian participant of the Civil War, Stephen Radnich, Emeric was born in 1824. Gábor Bona claims that he was a railroad engineer in Pest prior to 1848, but when the Hungarian War of Independence started, he enlisted as lieutenant first in the 3rd, then the 2nd, Sapper Battalion. In July he was promoted to 1st lieutenant and in August he was not only transferred to the Sapper Battalion of Komárom, but further elevated to the rank of captain.[248]

After the collapse of the Hungarian cause, according to its promise to the defenders of the fortress of Komárom, the Austrian government granted him a safe conduct and he escaped first to Hamburg, then to Britain. Along with the Újházy family he soon set sail for America onboard the *Hermann* and arrived in New York City on December 17, 1849, as one of the very first Kossuth emigrants in the country.[249]

The Census of 1850 found him in Prairie, Arkansas, where he was farming. Soon he decided to join Narciso Lopez's filibustering expedition to Cuba, together with other Hungarians, Lopez's chief of staff, for instance, was Col. John Prágay. The enterprise turned out to be a huge fiasco: the Spanish defeated the small army, killing or imprisoning many of the participants. (Col. Prágay committed suicide to avoid falling into the hands of the Spanish.) Radnich belonged to the latter group and was sentenced to imprisonment and hard labor at Ceuta in North Africa. He spent one and a half years there, although he tried his best to get out of the prison. On May 2, 1852, he wrote to Kossuth asking for money which could have opened the prison doors; Radnich complained that the Austrians applied pressure on the Spanish to keep the 8 Hungarians imprisoned. Finally his brother John turned to D.M. Barringer at the legation of the United States in Madrid asking for his intervention by calling his attention to the fact that Emeric had already applied for U.S. citizenship. Finally, on January 28, 1853, Barringer could send the following letter to Emeric Radnich:

> I have the satisfaction informing you that yourself and your seven Hungarian companions in prison have been pardoned at my solicitation, by Her Majesty, the Queen of Spain, and that the necessary orders for your release will be issued ASAP. If it is still your wish to return to the US, you will put yourself in commu-

nication with Mr. H.J. Sprague, Consul of our Gov. at Gibraltar, to whom I have written on the subject and who will extend to you all proper protection while making your arrangements to return to your adopted country.[250]

Radnich, indeed, returned to the United States, and settled down in New Buda, Iowa, joining the small Hungarian community there. László Károly mentions meeting him in 1859 when he was working as an engineer. In 1860 he was one of the pallbearers of Emilie Zulavsky Kossuth (1817–1860), sister of Louis Kossuth.[251]

At the commencement of the Civil War he volunteered in one of the Iowa Home Guards regiments, but nothing specific is known about his career. After the Compromise of 1867 he returned to Hungary and had a prominent career. He became inspector of the Hungarian State Railways and then director of the Győr-Sopron-Ebenfurt Railway. He died on January 25, 1903, in Kálóz, Fejér County. His remains were later exhumed and transported to the cemetery of Zsámbék.[252]

Radnich, Stephen

According to his obituary, he was born in Egra, Toker, but Stephen Beszedits is right when he states that this is probably confused with Egres in Fejer County. His date of birth is July 24, 1828. Basically nothing is known about his life back in Hungary except that he took part in the Hungarian War of Independence; some sources claim that he served in a cavalry unit under General Bem, whereas others refer to him as an artillery lieutenant.[253]

After the surrender of the revolutionary army, he left the country. First he moved to Britain, and even wound up in Scotland, but finally emigrated to the United States. He set foot on American soil in New York City on February 25, 1850, accompanied by one of his brothers, John. (His older brother, Emeric, arrived some two months earlier.) Many sources claim that he stayed in New York for a longer time learning the trade of carpentry, but when the Census of 1850 was taken, he was already in Prairie, Arkansas. There are some indications that he spent longer time in New Orleans as well, but it is sure that in 1856 he settled in Decatur County, Iowa. He soon became a model farmer and he was acknowledged as an excellent carpenter. (He built the old school building in New Buda.)[254]

When the Civil War came, Radnich followed many of the Hungarians and volunteered in the Iowa Home Guards protecting local citizens from outlaws and guerrillas.[255]

After the Civil War he purchased a farm adjoining Davis City, and soon married Laura Hainer, the daughter of fellow Hungarian exile Ignatz Hainer. His wife died in 1871 (she allegedly committed suicide), and Radnich remarried. Some sources claim that he married his former housekeeper, Sarah Boldwan, but census data reveal that his wife's name was Dallas. They had altogether eight living children; Dallas well outlived her husband: she died in 1934. Stephen was a member of the Davis City School Board for more than thirty years and worked extremely hard to promote the importance of education. He became actively involved in political life as a radical Republican. Later he became president of the Farmer's Bank in Davis City. He visited his home country in 1896, but, unlike his brothers, Emeric and

John, never seriously considered returning to Hungary. He died in Davis City on September 13, 1912.[256]

Rombauer, Raphael

The youngest of the Rombauer brothers, Raphael was born in 1838 in Munkács. He was taken to America by his family and he followed his older brothers' footsteps when he volunteered in the Civil War. He also sought service at the 1st Missouri Infantry Regiment, in which he served as sergeant. After the termination of his three months he became a lieutenant and adjutant to fellow Hungarian Colonel Gustav Wagner, chief of Artillery at Cairo, Illinois. They served under General Ulysses Grant, commander of the District of Southeast Missouri, which reported to Gen. Frémont's Western Department. Frémont laid special emphasis on secrecy, so much of his communication was conducted in Hungarian. Raphael did the translations from Hungarian to English for Grant. Later he became captain of the 1st Illinois Light Artillery Regiment. On August 21, he took part in the attack on Memphis, Tennessee, and received special mention from Lt. Col. William B. Bell in his report. On October 26, 1864, he was elevated to the rank of major. On February 11, 1865, he became chief of artillery at Memphis and stayed in that position until he was mustered out on August 18, 1865.[257]

After the war, he married a woman named Emma from Kentucky, and they had five children. He was involved with the expanding railroad business, and later he established his own company, Rombauer Coal Co., in Missouri. The beginnings were not easy for the company, they opened only one mine called Rombauer No. 1, but as it became increasingly prosperous, Rombauer leased lands further up the Davis Creek Valley and three more mines were opened. At this stage, a rival company offered Rombauer $30,000 for his mines and holding, but he turned down the offer. The company continued to work very successfully until his death on September 15, 1912, in Kirksville, Missouri.[258]

Rombauer, Robert Julius

He was born in Szelestó, Bereg County, in 1832. At the time of the Hungarian War of Liberation he was a student in Pest. He joined the revolutionary army without hesitation. He became an artilleryman, and on February 24, 1849, he was promoted to lieutenant. By the end of the war, he was a 1st lieutenant.

Along with many who were captured by the Austrians, Robert was impressed into the 39th Infantry Regiment in the Imperial Army on September 9, 1849, but was lucky enough to be discharged in 1850.[259]

He joined his father and brothers in the United States and settled first in Iowa, then in St. Louis, Missouri. He became a prominent member of the German community, but this does not mean that he was not planning to return to Hungary. In 1859 he wrote a letter to Francis Pulszky in which he asked him to inform him "when the time comes, and Hungary will need the arms of her children within its borders." The quick termination of the War of 1859, however, meant that their hopes vanished.[260]

In 1861 he played a major role in rallying the pro–Union elements in St. Louis and became lieutenant colonel of the 1st Regiment U.S. Reserve Corps in Missouri. Later as colonel he commanded the 1st Missouri Infantry. Towards the end of his Civil War career he was the commander of the 5th Regiment City Guard in St. Louis, which was organized in September 1864 to protect the city during Major General Sterling Price's invasion of Missouri.[261]

At the end of the Civil War, he returned to civil life in St. Louis and edited the local paper, the *New World*. Robert was highly interested in education and was one of the most devoted proponents of the founding of the St. Louis Public Library, which opened to the public in 1874. Rombauer was even president of the library for some time, but also president of the board of assessors and a member of the board of education. He wrote one of the best histories of the Union movement in St. Louis at the outbreak of the Civil War: *The Union Cause in St. Louis in 1861: An Historical Sketch*, published in 1909. In 1922 his autobiography was released with the title *Biographical Notes of Robert J. Rombauer, 1917*.[262]

His wife was Emilie Dembinsky (they married on May 2, 1857) and the couple had three sons. Robert Rombauer died on September 25, 1925, in St. Louis and is buried at the local Bellefontaine Cemetery.[263]

Rombauer, Roderick E.

One of four brothers offering their arms for the Union cause in the Civil War, Roderick Rombauer was born on May 9, 1833 in Szelestó, in Bereg County, Upper Hungary. His father, Tivadar Rombauer, was a metallurgical engineer by profession who played a crucial role in the development of metal industry in Hungary. He was founder of the iron works at Rimamurány-Salgótarján. Roderick was educated by private tutors from the age of four. The family moved to Munkács, where he attended a private elementary school. His father became director of the local styptic works there, and in 1845 he was director of an iron works in Gömör County.[264]

When the Hungarian War of Liberation broke out in 1848, he was offered a position in the Department of Agriculture, Industry and Commerce by Secretary Gábor Klauzál, which he accepted and moved to Pest. He became director of the National Weapon Factory, thus was responsible for the production of most of the war material in Hungary. Roderick attended military academy in Pest, and his father considered sending him to Switzerland to the military academy of Thun. In January 1849 he followed his father to Oradea.[265]

At the end of the fights, Rombauer had to escape. He arrived in New Buda, Iowa, on December 16, 1851. The entire family was engaged in farming, which proved unsuccessful, so they first moved to Davenport, Iowa, then to St. Louis, Missouri. Roderick got a job as a railroad surveyor for the Pacific Railroad, then for the Northern Cross Railroad between Quincy and Galesburg in Illinois. Meanwhile, in 1855, his father died in New Buda, which led to increased homesickness. He even wrote poems about his sufferings caused by his longing for Hungary: "And I am man, though in loving heart/ My fatherland's saint shrine may higher rise/ And for its sufferings my soul keener smart/ The world's my home."[266]

Roderick studied law in Quincy, Illinois, at the office of Williams and

Lawrence, and later attended Dane Law School of Harvard University. He had almost no money, so he had to give German and fencing lessons. He obtained his bachelor of law degree in 1858, and having been admitted to the bar, started his practice in St. Louis. For some time he lived in his office, but his practice started to prosper and he was able to pay back his debts within two years.[267]

When the Civil War approached, the Rombauer brothers did their best to organize the pro–Union forces in St. Louis into effective Home Guards units. Roderick became captain of the 1st Regiment U.S. Reserve Corps in Missouri, the very same three-month unit in which his brother, Robert, served first as lieutenant-colonel, and later as colonel. After the expiration of their three-month term, he helped organize a Home Guards unit and was involved in the fightings in Southeast Missouri as captain. According to his memoirs, he contracted a violent fever of typhoid character and was bedridden for several months. Once he recuperated, he joined General Frémont and served on his staff in the Mountain Department.[268]

After the war, Rombauer eagerly returned to his legal practice and had a very successful career. He was judge of the circuit court of St. Louis County from 1867 to 1870. Between 1884 and 1896, he served on the bench of the St. Louis Court of Appeals, being presiding judge for nine years. According to the Harvard University Alumni Directory, he still practiced law in 1913, at the age of 80. After a long and successful life, he passed away on March 26, 1924, in St. Louis. He had six children with his wife, Augusta Koerner, whom he married on December 28, 1865.[269]

There is actually a city named after Roderick E. Rombauer in Butler County about 120 miles south of St. Louis. The directory of place names of Butler County told the following story behind the origin of the name of the city: "Some of the citizens wanted to name it for George Spangler, who gave the town site and right-of-way for the road, but a vote was taken for Judge Rombauer of St. Louis. A story is told that Judge Rombauer was on the train with the first inspection group. When they came to this place, all the members of the party got off except him, and someone remarked they should name the place for him."[270]

Rombauer, Roland

Roland Rombauer was born in 1837 in Munkács. He was still a young child when the Hungarian War of Liberation was raging, and he was taken to the United States by his mother, following the head of the family, Tivadar Rombauer. Roland arrived in New York aboard the Hamburg vessel *Copernicus* on September 6, 1851, at the age of 14. Not much is known about his teenage years, but we have information that he volunteered in the Civil War.[271]

Like his brothers, Robert and Roderick, he enlisted in Company A, 1st Missouri Infantry Regiment, as a private for a term of three months. After the expiration of his term of service, he served as sergeant in Company A of the 1st Missouri Light Artillery regiment. Later he joined the 1st Florida Cavalry as captain (he was promoted on August 27, 1864) and first became assistant provost marshal of the District of West Florida, which belonged under the command of Brig. Gen. Alexander Asboth, and later provost marshal. He was mustered out on November 15, 1865, along with his regiment.[272]

Subsequent to the Civil War, he first settled down in St. Louis and worked as a cashier in a bank. Later he moved farther west and started a mining enterprise in Montana, and later was an official in the forestry service. His sudden death on November 20, 1898, was probably caused by a heart attack, as his brother, Roderick recalls it, "on a solitary path in the wilderness near Missoula, Montana." Roland Rombauer was buried near Philipsburg, Montana.[273]

Rozsafy, Matthias

Born in a family owning a small tobacco shop in Komárom, Matthias Rozsafy (his original name was Ruzicska) was born on November 29, 1828. He turned out to be a very bright student, so his parents intended to educate him for the clergy. He was indeed sent to study at Pazmaneum, a theological seminary in Vienna. However, as József Szinnyei, Sr., a fellow student recalled, "He made his little circles around the girls, just like we did. I noticed this, and it came to my mind that our friend, Matthias, would not make a good clergyman."[274]

At the outbreak of the Hungarian War of Independence, he indeed quit the order, and volunteered in the revolutionary army. He was sent to the fortress of Komárom, where he was involved in editing a newspaper entitled *Komáromi Értesítő*, which played a major role in buoying up the defenders during the Austrians' siege.[275]

After the surrender of the Hungarian troops, he followed Kossuth to Turkey in his internment. Along with Joseph Mack he became one of the key secret agents of Kossuth and in disguise returned to Hungary and Transylvania several times on various missions. He was even captured by the Austrians, but managed to escape. He left for London and joined the Hungarian exiles there. He was one of the students of the short-lived Hungarian Military Academy organized in the British capital. Still in Britain, in 1854, he got married. Eventually he wound up in the United States of America — according to Edmund Vasváry he set foot on American soil in 1858. Vasváry claims that he settled down in Wilmington, North Carolina, and was engaged in farming.[276]

When the Civil War came, however, Matthias Rozsafy moved to the North and enlisted in the Union Army. (In the U.S. he used the name Ernest M. Rosafy.) He was mustered into the 1st West Virginia Light Artillery as captain and later he became ordnance officer.[277]

After the Civil War, he returned to North Carolina and farmed there until 1874, when he took his family to Washington, D.C. First he worked as a government official, then he became a clerk at the patent office.[278]

He was actively involved in the life of the Hungarian-American community. Among his biggest plans, special priority was given to bringing together the dispersed Hungarian-American community. In 1891 he was one of the founders of the weekly entitled *Szabadság* in Cleveland. He was hindered by his sickness due to which he almost went blind, but he somewhat regained his eyesight after surgery. He was planning to visit his mother country one last time, but he never managed to go. János Vadona mentioned him as one of the two Hungarian veterans living at Soldiers' Home at the very end of the 1880s. He died in Washington, D.C., on May 6, 1893.[279]

Ruttkay, Albert

Like the four Zulavsky boys, Kossuth's seventh nephew (he had two elder brothers), Albert Ruttkay also saw service in the Civil War. The son of Joseph Ruttkay and Louise Kossuth, Albert saw service in the Hungarian War of Liberation. He volunteered in the Fifth Honvéd Battalion and rose to the rank of lieutenant by October 1848. On February 9, 1849, he was captured by the enemy at Piski and was impressed into the 19th Infantry Regiment of the Imperial Army stationed in Italy. He managed to flee in April 1849 and emigrated to the United States.[280]

When the Civil War came, he volunteered. He wrote about his motivations: "[I] joined the service out of pure motives of patriotism, at a time when our Country justly demanded the firm support." His military career started in Tennessee, and he became captain of the 1st Battalion, 3rd U.S. Colored Heavy Artillery at Fort Quinby, Columbus, KY. In March 1864, at the age of 22, he was promoted to major of the 1st Regiment, Colored Florida Cavalry at Barrancas, Florida, where he served under the command of General Asboth. In September 1864 he was appointed assistant acting adjutant general at the HQ of the District of West-Florida, and in April 1865 he was made aide-de-camp to Major Gen. Nathaniel P. Banks. He resigned on May 31, 1865.[281]

After the Civil War, he became involved in the cotton business in Texas. He founded his own company, Ruttkay and Co., from the money he inherited, and apparently he was rather successful. The exact date of his death is not known; his wife, Laura, filed for his Civil War pension in 1899.[282]

Schoepf, Albin

Many controversies surround the nationality of Albin Schoepf. In most sources, including census data and biographies, he is referred to as Hungarian, although he was born on March 1, 1822, in Podgorze, Poland. His father was Polish by birth, while it seems that his mother was of Hungarian origin.[283]

Schoepf, like many of his countrymen, supported the Hungarian freedom fight in 1848–49 and he was allegedly a major in the Polish Legion. After the War of Liberation ended, he fled to Turkey and there were rumors among his contemporaries that he served in the Ottoman Army for a while. He was with General Bem until Bem's death in Aleppo in 1850, then emigrated to the United States.[284]

In America he worked as a porter at a hotel in Washington, D.C., as a coastal surveyor, and later as a draftsman at the patent office. This latter job was secured through his acquaintance with Joseph Holt, who was made postmaster general by President James Buchanan in 1857. Holt then had Schoepf transferred to the War Department.[285]

When the Civil War came, Holt arranged an interview for Schoepf with General Winfield Scott, who gave him a warm letter of recommendation: "I have had an interview with Mr. Schoepf. I have become so pleased with him that I am anxious he should be brought into the military service of the U.S. Mr. S is very intelligent, a scientific soldier, and evidently a most trustworthy man. I have no doubt that he would make an able and efficient brigadier-general. Respectfully submitted to the Secretary of War, Sept. 24, 1861, Winfield Scott."[286]

Scott's support secured him a brigadier-generalship on September 30, 1861. Most of the accounts describe him as a strict disciplinarian. Confederate General Felix K. Zollicoffer, after a series of successes against the Kentucky Home Guards, attacked his fortified position, called Wildcat Camp, on the hills of Rock Castle County, Kentucky, and was defeated on October 21, 1861. However, a few weeks later Schoepf retreated precipitately, by order of his superior officer, from London to Crab Orchard, which the Confederates called the 'Wildcat Stampede.'[287]

In early 1862, General George B. Crittenden hoped to crush Schoepf's force at Fishing Creek, or Mill Springs, but encountered General George H. Thomas's entire army, and suffered a disastrous defeat on January 19, 1862. General Schoepf's brigade led in the pursuit of the enemy to Monticello. On June 1, 1862, he went on sick leave due to the chronic enlargement of a testicle and deafness caused by neuralgia in the head. After his return he commanded a division under General Charles C. Gilbert at the battle of Perryville on October 8, 1862. In March 1863 he was examined again, and the commission found him in general good health, but had a large varicocele on the left side that caused considerable pain when sitting in saddle. He also felt pain in the right upper abdomen, accompanied by a cough, when on horseback. The commission declared him unfit for field service, but he was appointed commander of the prison at Fort Delaware, upon an island in the Delaware River opposite Delaware City, about 40 miles below Philadelphia, on April 14, 1863, and served in that capacity until January 1866.[288]

We have many accounts of him from these years. Numerous inmates kept diaries, many of which were published after the Civil War. Of course, some held him personally responsible for their sufferings, but the majority of the prisoners liked him. One described him as a "tall, rather good-looking man, with pleasant manners, [who] had been in the United States for a number of years, but spoke very broken English." Isaac Handy, another prisoner, wrote about Schoepf, "From all I can learn, he is a mere turnkey, who has no power or authority beyond the care of prisoners. He seems, however, to be a man of humane feelings, but coarse in manner and of variable temperament.... He was courteous, and I thought sympathetic. His tones were mild, and his address kind." Abram Fulkerson, Colonel of the 63rd Tennessee Infantry, even offered an explanation for why Schoepf commanded the prison, "He married a Virginia lady [Julia Bates Kelsey] who was said to be a Southern sympathizer, and on this account, possibly, the General's actions were closely watched." But he also concluded that "Fort Delaware was one of the best of Northern prisons." His superiors were of the same opinion, the inspection reports always found good general conditions. In September 1863, for instance, Charles H. Crane reported, "Gen. Schoepf appears to be very zealous and attentive in the discharge of his duties and gives all his time to a personal supervision of the wants of those under his charge and labors to improve their condition."

After the surrender of the Confederate troops at Appomattox on April 9, 1865, Schoepf agreed with President Lincoln that the U.S. should absorb the seceded states as soon as possible. He warned the Confederate prisoners-of-war in heavily-accented English: "Your confederacy is gone up and busted. De bottom it did fall de pot, an' you's better get out from under the rubbish. Dat's what I tink; Git out and take allegiance to de best government vat ever was." He paroled the officers, and they were allowed to move freely around on the island. They were finally released on July 25, 1865. Schoepf himself was discharged in January 1866.[289]

He returned to the patent office in Washington, D.C, and lived in Hyattsville, Maryland, with his wife and seven children. In the early 1880s he became unfit for work, and fell so seriously ill that he could not even get up from bed. He had been having stomach problems for about sixteen years of his life, and possibly his death was caused by cancer in his stomach. He passed away on May 10, 1886, in Hyattsville, Maryland. He is buried at the Congressional Cemetery in the federal capital.[290]

Schoney, Lazarus, M.D.

Dr. Schoney was born in Pest on October 18, 1838. According to his obituary he studied at the Kaiser Karl Ferdinand University in Prague and graduated in 1857. He went to the United States in 1860. He continued his studies in America as well and graduated from the University of Pennsylvania in 1862. Upon his graduation, he volunteered in the Union Army and served in the positions of assistant surgeon and contract surgeon from 1862 to 1865. Later he became chief contract surgeon and had his office at the Senate Chamber, and became acquainted with President Lincoln. He was employed at the Lincoln Hospital in the federal capital, but he did active field duty as well; for instance, he participated in the battle of Gettysburg.[291]

After the war, he went to Paris and Berlin to continue his studies, and after his return to America in 1868, he practiced medicine. He became professor of pathology and clinical microscopy at the New York Eclectic Medical College, was fellow of the New York Academy of Sciences, of the American Association for the Advancement of Science, and member of the American and New York State Medical Associations. He was one of the most prominent members of the New York Microscopical Society. He had a son, Emanuel, who was born in Washington, D.C., in 1863. Dr. Schoney died in New York on February 17, 1914.[292]

Semsey, Charles

Two excellent scholars carried out extensive research on Semsey. József Pozsonyi, director of the Andor Semsey Museum in Balmazújváros, studied the origins of the Semsey family, whereas Stephen Beszedits focused on Charles Semsey himself.[293]

Their work shows that he was born in Bártfa, Sáros County, in 1829. His family was one of the oldest noble families in the country, his father was a rich landowner and influential local politician.

Charles studied for the clergy, but the revolutionary wave of 1848–49 captivated him and he, like thousands of Hungary's finest youth, volunteered for the Hungarian Army. He took part in a number of engagements and by the end of the conflict rose to the rank of 1st lieutenant.[294]

He fled the Austrian retaliation which followed the collapse of the Hungarian cause and he wound up in the Ottoman Empire. He accepted the word of Austrian government emissaries who promised him and other refugees amnesty if they returned to Hungary. Instead of the promised amnesty, he was impressed into the Habsburg Imperial Army.

He managed to desert in Hamburg and escaped to London. He made use of the British governmental support financing the Hungarian refugees' transatlantic voyage, and on April 7, 1851, he left Liverpool for New York.

Once in the United States, Semsey had a really hard time trying to find employment. Without any qualification and fluency in English, he was hired for menial works only. He worked as a carver, and along with a fellow Hungarian, John Menyhart, was employed at Beniczky's daguerreotype studio in New York City, where he chose to stay despite all the hardships.[295]

In 1853 he saw an opportunity in joining the German Legion of mercenaries recruited by the British government to supplement the regular troops in the Crimean War. Semsey moved to Britain, but never saw action. He married Franziska Haubold, a German immigrant from Dresden, and their first child, a girl named after her mother, was born while still in London in 1858. The family then returned to New York where Semsey's son, Kálmán, was born in 1859, followed by three brothers and a sister.[296]

At the start of the Civil War, Charles Semsey volunteered in the Union Army. He was mustered into Company F, 20th New York Volunteer Infantry Regiment, as captain on May 3, 1861. On July 6, 1861, he resigned and later joined the all-German 45th New York Volunteers as major on October 7, 1861. Along with the regiment, he took part in several battles and engagements, but in June 1862 he resigned and was discharged on June 15, 1862.[297]

Back in civilian life, Semsey continued his previous profession and was involved in photography. Later, mainly due to his service in the Civil War, he was awarded a position with the U.S. Customs Service. He also worked for the immigration bureau of the Port of New York at Castle Garden and on Ellis Island, and eventually he became a member of the Board of Special Inquiry.[298]

Semsey was very actively involved in the life of the Hungarian-American community. He frequently published articles in the Hungarian-language newspaper, *Nemzetőr*. He was among the founders of the Hungarian Grant and Wilson Campaign Club at 26 Delancey Street. He was eager to participate in veterans' associations, too. He was elected president of the Veteran Association of the 45th Regiment New York Volunteers Infantry for the year 1882.[299]

Charles Semsey died on June 18, 1911, in New York City and was laid to rest at the Koltes Lot of Lutheran Cemetery.

Solyom, Louis

Although a scion of one of the oldest Hungarian families, he was born in Pienkowce, Poland in 1836. His father was Hungarian and his mother was of Polish origin. The family had an estate at Antalfa, and Solyom later named his own estate, close to Washington, D.C., Antalfa.

In 1842 he joined the Imperial Army, served in a Lichtenstein hussar regiment and served for eight years, including the period of the Hungarian war for independence. He contemplated joining Garibaldi in 1859, but the war was over by the time he could have reached Italy.[300]

He arrived in the United States in June 1861. He joined the Union Army as a lieutenant of the 31st New York Volunteer Infantry. He participated at the battle of Antietam, and was wounded. According to Vasváry, in May 1863 he escaped capture by swimming across the Rappahannock River. He was mustered out as 1st lieutenant in June 1863.[301]

After the Civil War, he worked as an accountant in New York City, and also at a second hand bookstore. In 1868 he was hired by the Library of Congress where he worked for the next 46 years! He had a special talent with languages: he was fluent in 20 languages and could make himself understood in a dozen more. He translated books from Turkish into English, and he even received an award from the Sultan in 1899.

His wife, Sallie, was from Maryland and they had four children. Louis Solyom died in Bethesda, Maryland, on April 23, 1913.[302]

Spelletich, Stephen

Son of Felix (Bódog) Spelletich, a prominent Hungarian politician of the age, and member of the Hungarian Parliament, Stephen was born in 1844. His father participated in the Hungarian freedom fight in 1848–49 and he had no other option but to escape after the surrender of the Hungarian forces. (He was even hanged by the Austrian authorities "in effigy.") He took his family to America, where he purchased a farm close to Davenport in Iowa called Hickory Grove. Compared to other émigrés from Hungary, they were relatively well off, as Nicholas Perczel concluded after his visit to them: "His [Spelletich's] house is a quite nice, one-storey brick building, which is very rare to see here, as most farm houses are log buildings. His land is about 430 acres, and he has a nice forest as well, which is very valuable as [it] is a rarity again."[303]

Stephen was barely 18 years old when the Civil War broke out, but he volunteered at once. He enlisted on April 24, 1861, in the 2nd Regiment Iowa Infantry as a private. He participated in a number of engagements, among the most notable was the capture of Fort Donelson (February 11–16, 1862). In this battle he distinguished himself so that he was commended in the official report of Maj. Gen. H.W. Halleck (according to Vasváry he shot sixteen rebels single-handedly):[304]

> Headquarters Dept. of Mississippi; St. Louis, April 1st 1862.
> Hon. J. B. Leake — Sir, With the approval of the Secretary of War I have directed to be presented to Stephen Spelletich, of Co. C. 2d Iowa Infantry, the rifle which he so heroically captured at the battle of Fort Donelson.
> Very respectfully your obedient servant,
> H. W. Halleck, Maj. Gen.[305]

Spelletich soon joined the 14th Missouri Cavalry and served there until the end of the Civil War. He remained in the military even after the end of the war, and took part in the fights against various Native American tribes. However, his health was damaged by the harsh conditions of military service, and he died in

1868. He is buried at Oakdale Cemetery in Davenport, Iowa. His family returned to Hungary with the exception of his brother, Michael, who stayed in Davenport and became a respected citizen: he was justice of peace and member of the school board. His descendants still live in and around Davenport.[306]

Stahel, Julius H.

For a detailed biography see Chapter Five, "The Triumvirate"

Szabad, Emeric

Szabad was born Frereych in 1822 and changed his name in 1848. Having completed his studies, he started working as a language teacher and he became very successful, authoring two textbooks within three years. He was also involved in journalism and got several articles published in magazines, among them the periodical *Életképek*.[307]

In 1848 he joined the Hungarian revolutionary army immediately, and he not only served in the armed forces, but was an official in the War Department, as well. He continued writing and authored a series of articles analyzing domestic and foreign political issues.

After all hope of Hungarian independence vanished, Szabad emigrated, first to Germany, then to London. He continued his literary career, contributed to the 8th edition of *Encyclopedia Britannica* and in the 1850s authored three volumes: one on Hungarian history, another on state policy of the modern times, and the third on the two Napoleons and England.[308]

In 1859 Szabad was attracted to Italy by the promise of a new freedom fight. He joined the Hungarian Legion in Garibaldi's army. He served in the rank of captain. He published a book in Italy as well on the events preceding and following the peace treaty of Villafranca in 1859.[309]

At the news of the outbreak of the Civil War, he crossed the Atlantic Ocean and soon joined the Union Army. Szabad joined fellow Hungarian émigrés Charles Zagonyi, Nicolai Dunka and Philip Figyelmessy, who served in General Frémont's Mountain Department. When Frémont was relieved from command in the summer of 1862, Szabad also left active service for a while. He made excellent use of this period and he wrote his first book in the United States: *Modern War: Its Theory and Practice* (1863). When he returned to service, he was assigned to the staff of General Daniel Sickles. On October 27, 1863, he was captured by Confederates while scouting near Licking Run, Virginia. He was held at the infamous Libby Prison until exchanged on March 15, 1864.

After his release it took him some time to recover, then he returned to active service to the 5th Army HQ under the command of Major General Gouverneur K. Warren. He performed meritous service, and was breveted major and lieutenant colonel of volunteers on March 13, 1865, then, for his gallant service in the battles around Petersburg, he rose to the rank of colonel-by-brevet of volunteers in March 26, 1865. He was severely wounded in the neck and right shoulder, which had permanent effects on him. He was mustered out on October 7, 1865.[310]

Returning to civilian life, Szabad was appointed assistant collector of customs at the port of Galveston, Texas. His war wounds caused him great pain, but he continued writing. He published a book on General Grant's presidency in French in 1868. He authored a series of letters on army management for the *New York Tribune*.[311]

According to the Census of 1880, Szabad lived in Laredo, Texas, and, although his occupation was not indicated, it is known he engaged in various businesses involving estate transactions. He died on March 13, 1894, at Boerne, Texas, of an unnamed "dangerous and alarming malady." A monument over his grave was erected only on August 14, 1987.[312]

Szabo, Ignatz

Virtually nothing is known about Szabó's life prior to his arrival in America. Based on Census data, he was born in 1834, although upon his enlistment in 1861 he was registered as being 29 years of age. Either way, he served in the Hungarian War of Independence as sergeant, being too young to be an officer.[313]

After the fall of the Hungarian cause, he fled to Turkey. He arrived in Britain in June 1851, then emigrated to America and joined the great number of Hungarians who decided not to stay in the East Coast, but moved to west. He wound up in New Buda along with the Rombauer brothers on December 16, 1851. Later he hoped to find better opportunities and moved to Ohio.[314]

At the commencement of the Civil War, he enlisted at Company E, 106th Ohio Infantry Volunteer Infantry Regiment, as 1st lieutenant on August 20, 1862. On December 7, 1864, he was promoted to captain and transferred to Company A. He was mustered out on June 29, 1865, in Nashville, Tennessee.[315]

After the war he returned to Montgomery, Ohio, and went back to farming. He died in 1875.[316]

Szabo, Joseph

Even less is known about Joseph Szabo than about his namesake, Ignatz Szabo. He was born in Hobály in 1817. A special report of the Hungarian emigrants in America, carried out for the use of the Austrian court, mentioned him living in New York City in 1852. In the Civil War he enlisted in Company I of the 39th New York Volunteer Infantry Regiment under the command of another Hungarian émigré, Frederick D'Utassy. He served as a private. His Civil War pension application was filed in 1911.[317]

Szegedy, Matthias

Szegedy was either born in 1825 or 1828. He probably participated in the Hungarian War of Liberation and was among the first to leave the country after the surrender of the Hungarian troops. He fled to Britain, but soon made up his mind to emigrate to the United States. He arrived in New York on July 3, 1850, onboard the vessel *Jamestown*.[318]

There is no trace of Szegedy in the archival sources in most of the 1850s. In 1860 he lived in St. Louis, Missouri, and was employed as fencing master. He was single.[319]

No wonder that he decided to join the ranks of the Union Army, and tried to make use of his military experience. He was commissioned on December 27, 1861, as first lieutenant of Company A, 1st Missouri Volunteer Cavalry. After a brief service, he resigned on February 28, 1862, for unknown reasons. No further details have come to the surface so far concerning his life in the post–Civil War era.[320]

Takats, Francis

There were two Hungarian soldiers in the American Civil War named Francis Takats. One served at the 39th New York Volunteer Infantry Regiment as captain, whereas the other has remained unnoticed up to now. The journal *Hazánk s a Külföld* published a series of four articles in 1867 which were based on this latter Takats's diary and his letters to the editor.[321]

According to these articles, Takats was born in Békéscsaba in 1840. In his hometown he learned the trade of locksmith, and later worked as a bookbinder. His adventurous spirit attracted him to Constantinople, where he worked as a bookbinder and waiter during the two years spent there. He considered joining the Hungarian Legion in Italy, but eventually decided to emigrate to the United States. He arrived in Boston on November 4, 1862. Within a couple of months he was in New Orleans, where he decided to join the Union Army. He enlisted in Company K of the 47th Massachusetts Infantry as corporal on December 10, 1862. He often complained both about the inexperienced officers and men in the regiment. He served through his nine-month term without ever being engaged in battles — he was discharged on July 4, 1863. Scarcely a week later, he joined the 1st Louisiana Cavalry regiment in which he claimed to have met another Hungarian serving there named Eisner (also Aisner) with a pseudonym.[322]

His baptism of fire took place at Franklin on October 3, 1863, but he fought his first big battle at the Caloaso river on November 9, 1863. The regiment spent the harsh winter close to New Town, and in March he was transferred to an arms factory in Franklin for a brief period, then he returned to his unit. On May 14, 1864, he took part in a real cavalry engagement at Morganza in which his friend Aisner was captured by the Confederates. On June 7, 1864, he was promoted to sergeant. In his diary he gives an interesting account of how he captured a Hungarian named Szabo serving in the Confederate Army. He spent the Christmas of 1864 in New Orleans, and in January 1865 his regiment was stationed close to Baton Rouge. In February he was court-martialed for murder, and the court sentenced him to death. Luckily, the real murderer was arrested and he escaped the gallows.[323]

The 1st Louisiana was then ordered to Alabama, where it joined General Sherman's Army. That is where the end of the Civil War found them. However, they were first ordered to Austin, Texas, and then to New Orleans. Takats was mustered out on December 20, 1865.

After the Civil War he opened a small grocery in New Orleans, and he lived there in 1867. Nothing more is known about his later years.[324]

Takats, Francis

According to his Civil War muster roll files, Takats was born in 1826. However, Hungarian sources claim that he was born in Székesfehérvár in 1823. He studied the trade of joiner and later enlisted in the Imperial Army. In 1847 he was a corporal in the 1st Imperial Hussar Regiment. He deserted and joined the Hungarian revolutionary army in the fall of 1848. He was mustered in as sergeant, but on February 22, 1849, he was promoted to lieutenant. At the end of the conflict he was stationed at the fortress of Komárom.[325]

After the end of the war, he escaped from the country. He emigrated to the United States in September 1851. He participated in organizing the 39th New York Volunteers, nicknamed Garibaldi Guard, and on May 28, 1861, he enlisted in Company G, under the command of Col. Frederick D'Utassy, another Hungarian emigrant. He served in the rank of captain and as adjutant paymaster.[326]

Starting in June 1861, however, there developed a disagreement between the two Hungarians over rations and pay. On July 8, 1861, Takats convinced two other captains and eight lieutenants of the regiment to sign a paper asking D'Utassy to resign, but the lieutenant colonel of the unit refused to present their petition to the colonel. Next day, two companies refused to drill, and when D'Utassy ordered Takats to give up his sword and go under arrest, he resisted and ordered his men to load and follow him. He marched his company to Washington, where they let themselves be arrested at the order of General Mansfield. They were imprisoned at the Treasury Building, and following the investigations, Takats was discharged on November 19, 1861.[327]

Apparently he was still alive in 1894, living in San Francisco.[328]

Tauszky, Rudolph, M.D.

Rudolph Tauszky, one of the Hungarian surgeons serving in the American Civil War, was born in Pest in 1833. He started his studies at the medical faculty of the University of Pest before the outbreak of the Hungarian War of Liberation. One of his professors was Dr. Ignác Semmelweis (1818–1865), who discovered the cause of puerperal, or childbed, fever, which very often proved to be fatal at the time, and introduced antisepsis into Hungarian medical practice. Semmelweis was on the staff of the St. Rókus Hospital in Pest between 1850 and 1856, and became professor of obstetrics at the University of Pest in 1855. In Europe he was one of the pioneers of creating antiseptic conditions at operations. Tauszky obtained his medical degree in 1861, then went to Italy and joined Garibaldi's Hungarian Legion as captain and staff physician.[329]

He was one of the foreigners to be attracted to the United States by the Civil War. He volunteered in the Union Army as 1st lieutenant and assistant surgeon of volunteers on September 24, 1863. He worked as a hospital surgeon, but also performed field duty. Later he applied for a position as a regimental surgeon; however, when he was offered one as an assistant surgeon at the 1st Colored Regiment, he immediately declined.[330]

He was honorably mustered out of service on July 27, 1865. He returned to

Europe and continued his studies specializing in women's diseases in various hospitals of Vienna, Austria. Upon his return to America, he joined the regular army for a brief period, then, in 1868, he settled down in New York City.[331]

His medical practice there proved to be very prosperous. Tauszky became a highly respected member of New York medical circles. He had a keen interest in the situation of the needy in New York, and as a member the city's board of health, he promoted sanitary reform. His pet project was a free warm bath system for the winter which would have been self-supporting. Although many prominent citizens supported the plan, it would have cost $200,000, and it eventually came to nothing.[332]

Tauszky was affiliated with the Mount Sinai Hospital, originally founded as Jews' hospital in 1852, the first Jewish institution of its kind in the United States, and was in charge of one of the gynecology clinics. Around 1880 he became interested in the field of mental illnesses and was soon acknowledged as an expert on insanity.[333]

In 1883 he married the barely 20-year-old Frances Rosenthal, who did not understand her husband's devotion to his profession. Their regular arguments and the death of Tauszky's father possibly all contributed to his deep depression. On January 3, 1885, he shot his wife and then attempted to commit suicide. Both survived. After a series of examinations Tauszky was declared insane and was to be confined at Bloomingdale Asylum. He stayed there for the rest of his life. He passed away on November 21, 1889.[334]

Tenner, Louis

Louis Tenner was probably born in 1832 or 1833 in Hungary. He emigrated to the United States after the end of the Hungarian War of Liberation, and all we know for sure is that he was in New York in 1852.[335]

What seems to be certain is that, like many Hungarian emigrants living in New York, Tenner enlisted at Company G of the 39th New York Volunteer Infantry on May 28, 1861. He served as a private and was discharged on July 26, 1861. A couple of months later he volunteered again, and was mustered in as captain of Company B, 7th New Jersey Infantry, on November 4, 1861. He resigned on April 15, 1862.[336]

After the Civil War he returned to New York and lived there as a worker. He was actively involved in the life of the Hungarian-American community, and in 1902, at the centenary celebrations of Kossuth's birth, the *New York Times* mentioned him as one of the three Hungarian Civil War veterans in New York City still alive. The exact date of his death has not been identified.[337]

Toplanyi, Alexander

Toplanyi was born in 1825. He took part in the Hungarian War of Independence: he joined the 4th Honvéd Battalion in Pozsony. He fought in the campaigns in Southern Hungary and rose to the rank of corporal. In October he was promoted to lieutenant and transferred to the 26th Honvéd Battalion in Eger. Another unit in which he served was the 43rd Honvéd Regiment. In May 1849 he was elevated to 1st lieutenant and was appointed to the staff of General Klapka. The end of the fights found him in the fortress of Komárom serving as captain.[338]

After the surrender of the Hungarian forces to the Autrian-Russian coalition forces, he left Hungary by making use of the safe-conduct granted by each defender of Komárom. He emigrated to the United States, where his name appears again in the sources at the outbreak of the Civil War.[339]

He enlisted at Company H, 5th New York Heavy Artillery, as a private, but he rose to the rank of 1st lieutenant by February 24, 1862. In April 1863 he was summoned in front of an examining board which concluded about him,

[Toplanyi is] totally deficient in Infantry tactics and considering the length of time he has been in service deficient in Artillery tactics. He knows little or nothing about guard duty and very little about the internal economy of a company. He is a foreigner but understands the English language exceedingly well. Nothing has appeared unfavorable to his character as a man of honor, or to his general habits of life; but he does not seem to have shown the disposition to learn his duties and his course has been meddlesome and troublesome. He is not qualified to hold the position of first lieutenant in the Service of the United States.[340]

Toplanyi refused to accept the decision of the board and asked for another examination. This second time he could answer all the questions, and Brigadier General Barry found him an excellent officer, "equal if not superior to any artillery officer." What is more, Col. William Birney proposed in his report: "It would gratify this command, both officers and men, to have him added to the list of our captains."[341]

Indeed, upon the recommendation of Colonel Birney, Toplanyi was elevated to the rank of captain of the 3rd Colored Infantry Regiment on August 21, 1863. However, in February 1865 he had to stand trial for assaulting one of his black soldiers. Pvt. John Banks testified that while he was on guard duty, Toplanyi, drunk, approached him and charged him with sleeping on the post. When he requested that witnesses be called, the Hungarian captain started beating him. Toplanyi explanation did not involve racist sentiments. Toplanyi said that he had felt insulted by the soldier's lack of discipline and morale. All his officers substantiated that Toplanyi rejected corporal punishment, and his superiors praised him as a disciplinarian. Brigadier General E. P. Scammon wrote to him, "[You managed to transform] a company of untaught Negroes into a highly disciplined and most efficient company of Artillery." This incident did reveal his heavy drinking. He had already had bouts with drinking in his former unit, and this seemed to be the gravest problem this time as well. The court found him guilty and dismissed him. His corps commander, Major Gen. Quincy A. Gillmore, intervened and Toplanyi managed to obtain a pardon and retain his reputation.[342]

After the Civil War, he settled down in New York City. He became actively involved in the life of the Hungarian community in the city: he was elected president of the Hungarian Grant and Wilson Campaign Club. In 1869 he married Leila Blydenburgh in Brooklyn, and the subsequent year their daughter, Leila Grace Toplanyi, was born. In 1884 he visited his home country and spent some time in Budapest.[343]

Toplanyi's post Civil War career was not void of scandals either. He worked in the position of marshal at Marine Court, and he was charged by a Dr. Wells with disorderly conduct in 1872. According to the charges, Toplanyi was performing a levy upon the doctor's furniture, but he threatened that he would shoot him if he had not surrendered his watch. He also removed pieces of medical equipment without authorization. During his trial it turned out that there were more numerous complaints of him for extorting illegal fees, disorderly conduct, and several instances of intoxication. His ex-brother-in-arms, William S. Andrews, recalled that he liked Toplanyi "for his fine education and family." However, he added, "His one fault was his weakness for liquor." On January 9, 1874, Mayor William F. Havemeyer removed him from office.[344]

Alexander Toplanyi died in 1886. His name is commemorated on the African American Civil War Memorial in Washington, D.C.[345]

Ujffy, John Henry

He was born on March 14, 1820. There are family stories that he fought for the Hungarian independence as an officer, in contrast to his father and brother, who supported the Austrian cause. After the fall of the Hungarian cause, he emigrated to the United States in 1850. He settled down in Fayette County in Texas. He married Ida Hermine Walz in 1855 and fathered 5 children. In 1857 the family purchased 320 acres in Bexar, Texas.[346]

They moved to La Grange and opened a pharmacy. He was a charter member of the Fayetteville Masonic Lodge. In January 1863 he enlisted for 3 months and was mustered in as 3rd sergeant of the 22nd Brigade, CSA, at La Grange and served in Columbus and Houston. His unattached company was undrilled, had no uniforms, and was armed with hunting rifles and shotguns. After the expiration of his term, he re-enlisted for 6 months as a private in the 1st Regiment Infantry, 22nd Brigade, Texas State Troops at Camp Columbus, TX.[347]

After the Civil War, he returned to Texas. In 1867 he contracted yellow fever. The exact date of his death is not known.

Vandor, Joseph

There are quite a few references to the early period of Vandor's life, but discrepancies abound. For instance, based on the Census of 1860, it can be inferred that he was born in 1824. Other sources claim that he was born in 1822 or 1823. Therefore, it is safe to conclude only that he was born in the early 1820s. *The Milwaukee Journal* wrote that his original name was Unteschield. His name probably derives from one of his father's estates, as he was the baron of Vándorhely.[348]

According to the *Wisconsin Patriot*, Joseph attended the Imperial Military Academy in Vienna and marched in the Imperial Army under Gen. Radetzky. When the Hungarian War of Liberation broke out in 1848 he joined the Hungarian Army. He served under General Bem and it was widely known in his later Civil War regiment that he had participated in 19 battles. In one of the battles he was severely wounded in the left breast and leg and he was confined in a Russian prison, but eventually managed to escape. (The *North American and United States Gazette* gave an account of his impressment into the Austrian Army as a private, and how he managed to desert on the Bohemian border.)[349]

He arrived in the United States in May 1850. Soon he started to study law under Chief Justice Parker in Cambridge, Massachusetts, and was admitted to the bar in 1854. The *Wisconsin Patriot* reported that about that time he was employed as an instructor at the Maryland Military Academy, and also in Richmond. Afterwards he moved to Wisconsin and started a legal practice in the city of Milwaukee. In 1857 he appeared as member of the law firm Corson and Vandor. His overall conduct in his profession earned him an excellent reputation. He became actively involved in the public life in Milwaukee. On August 2, 1857, he married Paulina Knoblesdorff.[350]

When the Civil War broke out, the best sign of Vandor's influence and popularity was that he was requested by Wisconsin Governor Alexander Randall to organize an infantry regiment and become its colonel. Vandor, who was recommended to the governor as "a brave man and a thorough disciplinarian," raised the 7th Wisconsin Infantry Regiment, which was mustered into service in August 1861 with him in command. He still had problems making himself understood in English, which caused several instances of misunderstandings during the early drills. Also, he was described as extremely stubborn, and showing little patience towards amateur soldiers. These traits may have led to the alienation of his officers, who drafted a letter and presented it to him asking for his resignation. Vandor was actually wounded not much later, and rumors suggest that one of his own dissatisfied soldiers shot him in the shoulder. Anyway, due to the effects of his wounds, and his immense unpopularity, he resigned his command.[351]

After his resignation, Abraham Lincoln appointed him U.S. consul to Tahiti in 1862. He served in this position for almost six years. Particularly in the first phase of his consulship, he was frequently criticized for not being effective enough in attracting business interests to Tahiti. His salary was $1,000, which was barely enough to support his family. In 1868 President Andrew Johnson recalled him, and he returned to the United States. With his wife and children, he settled in San Francisco, California, and started a legal practice. Besides his thriving practice as an attorney, he had a deep interest in culture and education; in 1870 he was one of the initiators of a public library in the city of San Francisco.[352]

His health constantly deteriorated due to his wounds suffered in the Civil War, and he gradually developed cancer. He died on May 7, 1873, in San Francisco and was buried at the city's National Cemetery.[353]

Varga, Alexander

He was one of at least 5 sons of Hungarian-born master saddle and harness maker Benjamin Varga and Magdelene Vida. According to James P. McGuire's excellent book *The Hungarian Texans*, Benjamin Varga had participated in the Hungarian War of Independence in 1848–49 (no data confirms this statement) and sought refuge in the United States after the surrender of the Hungarian Army. First he settled down in Iowa and later started a business enterprise as a saddler in San Antonio,

Texas. Having established himself in the United States, he sent for his sons living in Hungary in 1858 and they not only joined him, but worked in the saddlery as well.[354]

Alexander, who was born in 1836, was one of them. When the Civil War came, he volunteered in the 3rd Texas Infantry Regiment (also designated as Luckett's Regiment), yet no further information is available on his military service.[355]

After the war, he returned to San Antonio, founded his own harness and saddle company and opened a shop on Military Plaza. He married Natalie Kleabe from Prussia, and they had three sons: Howard, Alexander, Jr., and Leonel. After 1891 he managed the Lone Star Saddlery Company, which was taken over later by his son Leonel. Alexander died on September 24, 1921, and was buried in the San Antonio City Cemetery.[356]

Varga, John

The eldest son of Ben Varga, John was born in 1833. Like his brothers, he joined his father in San Antonio in 1858 and worked as a saddler in the family shop. At the commencement of the war, he joined the 3rd Texas Infantry Regiment and was mustered in as a private. In 1863–64 he worked at the ordnance depot in San Antonio as a saddler in 1863 and 1864. In 1865 he was treated for rheumatism in the Confederate General Hospital at Shreveport, Louisiana. After the defeat of the Confederacy, he was paroled on June 8, 1865.[357]

In 1866 he married Roselia Deák, who was a chambermaid from Transylvania, but his wife died soon, probably when giving birth to their first child. John Varga later married the German Katherine Keuppers. He remained a saddler and was also engaged in farming in San Saba County. On October 21, 1875, the *Galveston Daily News* reported that a John Varga was arrested because of murder and assault with the intent to murder; however, it is impossible to validate that this was indeed the very same person. In the 1890s he worked for C.J. Langholz in San Antonio. He died in San Antonio in 1915 and his body was buried at the local Confederate Cemetery.[358]

Varga, Joseph

Joseph Varga was one of the sons of Ben Varga. He was born in 1839 and emigrated to the United States at the age of 19. He also learned the trade of saddlery, but when the Civil War broke out, he followed the example of his brothers and volunteered in the Confederate Army. He was mustered in as a private on March 27, 1862, at Captain Maclin's Company of the 1st Light Artillery Regiment. The end of the war, however, found him serving as a sergeant at Company C, 8th Texas Field Battery.[359]

After the war he helped out in his father's shop, but in 1876 he opened his own saddlery. His saddlery and that of his brother Alexander's were on the opposite sides of the same street. He married a German woman and they had six children. Joseph was actively involved in the life of the local community: for instance, he served on the jury a number of times. He died in San Antonio in 1898. By then, his son, Ben, had entirely taken over the family business.[360]

Varga, Paul

Born in 1843, Paul was the youngest of the Varga brothers to serve in the Confederate Army. He volunteered for Captain D.H. Ragsdale's Company, Texas Mounted Volunteers, 5th Texas Cavalry, and was mustered in as a private. He took part in a number of engagements in New Mexico, including the battles of Glorietta and Peralta in 1862. He was captured by the Union troops at Santa Fe, where he was responsible for the Confederate wounded. He was later exchanged at Vicksburg, Mississippi. Upon returning to his unit, he became its saddler and remained in that position up to the end of the war.[361]

After the Civil War, he farmed in San Saba County, and in 1876 he owned a 160-acre farm. In 1888 he gave land to the Methodist Episcopal Church for the Richland Mission Church, which named its chapel and the cemetery after him. Paul Varga died on August 5, 1912.[362]

Vertessy, John

According to Tivadar Ács, Vertessy was born on December 25, 1825, in Csákvár. He participated in the Hungarian War of Independence and was promoted to lieutenant on June 29, 1849, while in the 91st Honvéd Battalion. After the collapse of the Hungarian cause, he was impressed into the Imperial Army as a private on October 31, 1849, but he managed to desert on September 1, 1850, in Tirol. He escaped to Britain and was involved in the activities of the Hungarian exiles in London. He was a cadet of the short-lived Hungarian Military Academy.[363]

Having received British governmental support financing the Hungarian émigrés' transatlantic voyage, Vertessy left Britain for New York onboard the vessel *Cornelius Grinnell* on April 2, 1852.[364]

All we know about his first eight years in the United States is that he worked as an assistant at a pharmacy and later he studied medicine and obtained a medical degree in Milwaukee, Wisconsin. He started his practice there first, then, at the end of the decade, he moved to Dayton, Ohio. The census data reveals that his parents, John and Theresa Vertessy, were living there, and his father was also a physician.[365]

When the Civil War broke out, he joined the Union Army. He was mustered in as captain of Company E, 106th Ohio Infantry Regiment, on August 11, 1862. He served throughout the war and was mustered out on June 29, 1865, in Nashville, Tennessee.[366]

After the war, he returned to his civil profession. He opened a pharmacy in Milwaukee, but, according to Ács, it went bankrupt. In 1880 he practiced medicine in Milwaukee. He never married. He died in Milwaukee on March 23, 1903, and was buried at Wood National Cemetery in Milwaukee.[367]

Vidor, Charles

Vidor was born in Buda-Pest on October 16, 1834. Some sources suggest that he studied for the priesthood, but it is more likely that he attended military school.

All that is certain is that he was among those who left Hungary after the collapse of the Hungarian freedom fight in 1848–49. He joined Ladislaus Újházy, probably the most prominent pioneers of the Kossuth emigration, and first he moved to Britain, then to the United States. His cabin mate onboard the *Mount Stuart Elphinstone* was another Hungarian exile, Eugene Kozlay, later also participant of the American Civil War. They set foot on American soil in New York on February 25, 1850. Unlike many Hungarians, including Újházy, who set out to establish a Hungarian colony in Iowa, Vidor stayed in New York City for at least 3 years. In the mid-1850s he lived in Galveston, a relatively small yet thriving community in Texas.[368]

In 1855 he was hired as a clerk by Lent Munson Hitchcock, a successful merchant and landowner, and he married Hitchcock's daughter Emily in 1858. Unfortunately, death cast its shadow on the family: both of their children died in infancy and Emily herself died in 1860 or 1861.[369]

When the Civil War approached, Vidor volunteered for the Galveston Lone Star Rifles, one of the most popular militia units in the state of Texas. He was mustered in on December 3, 1860, as 4th sergeant. Later this unit became part of the 1st Regiment Texas Infantry, and was assigned to Hood's Texas Brigade. In November 1862, Vidor was appointed clerk for the brigade and division quartermaster, while on February 9, 1864, he was promoted to the rank of captain in the Confederate Quartermaster Department. Eventually he was paroled at Greensboro, NC, on May 1, 1865.[370]

After the Civil War he became very actively involved in business and entered into a partnership at the firm of John Walston, Wells and Vidor, which lasted until 1885. A daily paper introduced them as "one of the oldest and best houses in the cotton factorage business in Galveston." Vidor was also charter member of the Galveston Cotton Exchange. And he was a founding member of the city's very first volunteer firefighting company organized in 1868.[371]

On January 23, 1866, he married the 16-year-old Anna Walter, and the couple had altogether 10 children, of whom five lived to see adulthood.

Vidor seemed fairly successful until his business partner, Clinton G. Wells, president of the Cotton Exchange, committed suicide on January 26, 1885. This event signaled the end of Walston, Wells and Vidor, which went bankrupt. Vidor changed careers and entered the insurance business as member of Hughes, Stowe and Co. in 1885 and this partnership lasted until 1901. Charles Vidor passed away on September 14, 1904.[372]

Vöneky, Louis

One of the least-known Hungarians who offered their arms to the cause of the Union, Louis Vöneky was born in 1830 in Ungvár. He claimed to have been a lieutenant at the 5th Radetzky Hussar Regiment, yet his name is nowhere to be found in the pre-1850 rosters.[373]

At the commencement of the Hungarian War of Liberation, Vöneky deserted and enlisted in the Hungarian Army as lieutenant. He was soon placed on General Bem's staff and ended the war with the rank of 1st lieutenant.

Like many other soldiers of the revolutionary army, he was impressed into the Imperial Army as private in 5th Hussar Regiment. When he was placed in the reserves at last, he immediately joined Garibaldi's Hungarian Legion in Italy. He was bitterly disappointed over the Peace Treaty of Villafranca in 1859, and he emigrated to the United States.[374]

Once in America, he settled down in St. Louis and got integrated into the German-speaking population of the city. In the Civil War, he joined the Union ranks relatively late: he became captain at 68th Colored Infantry Regiment in 1864, later major of the 51st Missouri Infantry Regiment. As a field officer of the latter unit, he had to face the lack of understanding between him and his subordinate officers. He attributed this to his outsider status of a foreigner in America: "I am so unfortunate as to be a German — a Dutchman; that I never do anything by halves and cannot conform myself to do business in a lackadaisical style, but follow up my purposes and duties without regard to persons or showing favor or affection to anyone."[375]

This latter regiment of his was organized solely for the period of reconstruction, and he felt that all of his actions and initiations were thwarted because of his being an immigrant. Eventually, he made up his mind and resigned.[376]

Being disappointed with America, he returned to Hungary after the Compromise of 1867. He took part in the activities of veteran associations. The exact date of his death is unknown, but he was still alive in 1890. His name is commemorated on the African American Civil War Memorial in Washington, D.C.[377]

Waagner, Gustave

Gustave Waagner was born on May 5, 1813, in Peterswald-Schönewald, Bohemia, in a German-speaking family. Between 1828 and 1830 he attended the academy in Vienna studying military engineering. Having obtained a degree as an engineer, he served two years in the Imperial Army as an artillery officer, then worked as an engineer in Pressburg. When the Hungarian War of Liberation started, he joined the revolutionary army and played a major role in the first stage of organizing the Hungarian war machine, particularly the artillery forces. On December 2, 1848, he obtained the rank of 1st lieutenant, and barely a week later he was made captain in the regular army. He even rose to the rank of major on March 8, 1849. He was the governmental supervisor of gunpowder production in Southern Hungary, and on June 27, 1849, he was appointed director of saltpeter production for the entire country.[378]

After the surrender of the Hungarian forces to the Austrian-Russian coalition, Waagner followed Kossuth and sought asylum in Turkey. The sources mention him in Viddin in Kossuth's closest circle, and in most of them he is referred to as Hungarian. He left the country with the Hungarian ex-governor onboard the steamer USS *Mississippi*. He arrived in New York on November 10, 1851. As one of the closest associates of Louis Kossuth, and probably the most experienced artillery officer among the Hungarians, he received a special task from him: Kossuth appointed him director of the ammunition factory established in Morningsville with the aim of producing war material for the new Hungarian freedom fight which they hoped would come soon. The factory was, however, soon closed down, along with the belt factory at Weaverton, under the directorship of Alexander Asboth.[379]

Practically nothing is known about Waagner in America in the rest of the 1850s. He offered his service to the Union Army in the Civil War, and he was mustered in as colonel under General B. McClellan. His first assignment was to go to Cairo, Illinois, and supervise the training of the green troops. McClellan was very pleased with Waagner's performance; he was particularly impressed by the fortifications that had been erected according to the plans of Waagner.[380]

Soon General Frémont, who had recently become commander of the Western Department, appointed Waagner chief of artillery at Cairo, in which position his direct superior was Gen. Ulysses S. Grant. Waagner was highly suspicious of the military capacities of American volunteers. "It is most astonishing" he told William Howard Russell, correspondent for the *Times* of London, "how ignorant they are; there is not one of these men who can trace a regular work. Of West Point I speak not, but of the people about here, and they will not learn of me — from me who know [sic]." Waagner carried out numerous reconnaissance missions around Cairo, and captured Belmont, Missouri, on September 2, 1861. He was soon transferred to St. Louis, Missouri, at Frémont's Departmental Headquarters. Grant could not but praise him, "Col. Waagner, Chief of Ordnance, left here this evening in pursuance of orders telegraphed to him. His energy and ability have been of great service to me, particularly in directing reconnaissance, and his loss from this post will be felt." However, when Frémont resigned, Waagner also found himself out of commission in the Western front. On March 5, 1862, he was appointed lieutenant colonel of the 2nd Heavy Artillery, and became colonel of the regiment just nine days later. He was mustered out on August 26, 1862.[381]

As far as his career subsequent to the Civil War is concerned, unfortunately not much has been discovered. It seems very likely that he was living in the National Home for Disabled Soldiers in Virginia in 1890 and he died on December 27, 1891. He was probably buried at Hampton National Cemetery in Virginia.[382]

Wadgymar, Arthur, M.D.

Wadgymar had one of the most adventurous careers among Hungarian Civil War participants. He was born probably in Debrecen on May 26, 1824. He attended high school in Pest, then studied medicine in Vienna (1839–1847). In 1848 he was a surgeon of the 35th Battalion. Later he moved to the Netherlands and became a surgeon in the Dutch Navy, serving between 1850–1852. According to L.E. Daniell, he participated in the Crimean War as well.[383]

James McGuire gives account of a strange story according to which Wadgymar and his father fell in love with the same ballerina, and the son finally killed his father in a duel. He mentions this event as the main reason for Wadgymar's leaving Hungary for the United States, and also the fact that his brother vowed to take revenge on him.[384]

In the mid–1850s he was practicing medicine in Louisville, Kentucky. He fell in love with a woman, but her parents opposed their marriage. Wadgymar, however, eloped with his love and they got married. This marriage, unfortunately, also ended tragically when his wife fell overboard on a steamer on the Ohio River and drowned. In 1858 he married Maria Theresa Drewes of Bredenborn, Prussia. Later they had to leave Louisville, because his revenge-minded brother was in hot pursuit. The family moved to St. Louis, Missouri. There were 11 children born of this marriage, but only four of them lived to be adults.

When the Civil War broke out, the Hungarian physician became 2nd lieutenant of ordnance in the Provisional Army of Tennessee, and he also worked with the C.S. Laboratory in Nashville. (There are some claims that he served as a surgeon at the Memphis South Artillery in Chattanooga, 1862–63.) In 1863–64 he was already living in Cairo, Illinois, where he advertised himself as "Physician, Surgeon and Accoucheur. Women and Children's Diseases on Specialty."[385]

After the Civil War he got back to his practice as physician in St. Louis, and he taught botany at a local pharmaceutical college. Later he even became professor of chemistry and botany at Humboldt Medical College, during 1866–67, and he published several articles in medical journals.

At a later stage of his life, he moved to Texas and this period was full of scandals. He acquired a young man's body to perform an autopsy, which was illegal at the time, and when he was about to get started, it turned out that the person was not dead, but in a deep coma. At the end of the 1870s, the *Galveston News* reported that Wadgymar had performed an amputation on a wounded Mexican person. Next day, the locals found the limb in the doctor's hog pen while the hogs were eating it. The writer of the article expressed the common sentiment of the citizens that Wadgymar deserved to be "tar and feathered," however, somehow he managed to escape punishment. But, of course, he had to move again. In 1882 he became first physician in Carrizo Springs, Texas.[386]

He published a report on the diseases of cattle and horses in Medina County in 1877, and another one on the agriculture of the same county for the United States Department of Agriculture. He also authored papers in medical journals, such as the one entitled "Trichina Spiralis, and its Origin and Development in Muscle, and the Disease Trichinosis," published in 1866–67 in the *St. Louis Medical Reporter*. Most sources mention that he had a keen interest in studying insects and plants in southwestern Texas. In 1899 both Dr. Wadgymar and his wife died of influenza.[387]

Weekey, Anthony

This younger brother of Sigismund Weekey, whose distinguished career in Australia earned him an entry in the Australian Dictionary of Biography, Anthony Weekey was born in 1831 or 1832, probably in Tokaj. Both of them were students at the college of Sárospatak, then Anthony continued his studies in Késmárk. He studied law in Pest and was preparing for his bar examination in Zemplén County when the Hungarian War of Liberation came in 1848. Similarly to his brother, he joined the Hungarian army. He volunteered for the 9th Battalion at Kassa. He was promoted to the rank of corporal in October 1848 and was transferred to the fortress of Komárom as lieutenant of the 98th Battalion on June 1, 1849.[388]

After the Austrian-Russian coalition crushed the Hungarian freedom fight, he had to leave the country. As a defender of the fort in Komárom, he was granted a safe conduct by the Austrian authorities. First he went to Hamburg, then on to Britain. István Kinizsi lists his name among the cadets of the Hungarian military school in London. Some time in 1850, he emigrated to the United States.[389]

Barely anything is known about his career in the United States in the 1850s. Vasváry mentions him as a civil engineer, but his name cannot be located elsewhere in the sources. He lived in New York, and he indicated his profession as lawyer in 1861, yet we have no information on whether he actually practiced law in the United States.[390]

At the start of the War Between the States, Weekey followed several fellow Hungarians, joined the 39th New York Infantry Regiment and was mustered in as 1st lieutenant on May 1, 1861. He rose relatively fast in the ranks: on July 15, 1861, he was made captain and was promoted to major on February 1, 1862. Along with his regiment, he performed defense duty in the vicinity of Washington, D.C., in the spring of 1862, and he contracted some disease, which turned out to be fatal. Anthony Weekey died on April 28, 1862, at Winchester, Virginia. His body rests in the Winchester National Cemetery.[391]

Xantus, John

Although John Xantus is by all means one of the best-known members of the Kossuth emigration, few are familiar with his brief and dubious participation in the Civil War.

Xantus was born in Csokonya on October 5, 1825. His father, Ignatz Xantus, was a solicitor, land agent, and a steward on the estate of Count Széchényi, one of the most influential noblemen in Hungary at the time. John attended the Benedictine high school in Győr, graduating in 1841, then he went to the Academy of Law in Győr. He served as vice-notary at Somogy County for three years. He took his bar exams in 1847, and returned to his home town.[392]

At the commencement of the Hungarian War of Liberation, Xantus joined the artillery as sergeant and was later transferred to the infantry with the rank of 1st lieutenant. Close to the end of the war, he was captured by the Austrians and imprisoned at Königgraetz. He was stripped of his rank and impressed into the Imperial Army as a private. Finally his influential parents managed to secure his release. John, however, was infected with the liberal ideas of the Reform Age, and was heard making patriotic declarations in Dresden, Saxony, and was arrested again. Much to his luck, he managed to escape this time, and he fled to the United States. On May 5, 1851, he sailed for America with only 7 dollars in his pocket.[393]

Xantus spent the next 13 years in the United States and gained fame studying natural history. His wrote numerous letters back home which could serve as excellent sources, however, he seems to have distorted the facts more often than not, particularly in the letters to his mother. He gave accounts of his wonderful progress while he was doing mostly menial jobs, and told tales of participation in exploring expeditions that never took place. In 1857 in his letter to István Prépost he was complaining, "Speaking 6 languages, playing a piano and being a good topographical draftsman, after all efforts I could never bring my existence higher up than to 25 dollars a month."[394]

Eventually, "in a moment of utmost despair and under circumstances completely beyond [his] control," as he described in a letter written to Spencer Fullerton Baird, renowned ornithologist, he joined the U.S. Army in 1855 as a private under the assumed name Louis Vesey. He served at Fort Riley, Kansas, where he met naturalist Dr. William Alexander Hammond, a future surgeon general of the Army, and became his assistant in collecting species. Together they collected some 2,000 birds and 200 mammals for the Smithsonian. (There is actually a reptile named after him: *Lizard Xantusia*, and some fishes, *Labrisomus xanti* and *Umbrina xanti*.) Hammond arranged that Xantus be transferred to the medical department at the grade of hospital steward, the equivalent of a senior sergeant, and he was finally discharged in January 1859. (A painting shows him in a full U.S. Navy officer's uniform, which is fake, as he never served in the navy. He himself had the painting made.) Hammond secured him an employment as tidal observer for the U.S. Coast Survey, and he participated in an expedition to Cape San Lucas.[395]

In 1861 Xantus returned to Hungary, where he was elected honorary president of Budapest Zoo, and became a member of the Hungarian Academy of Sciences, but all these brought no employment for him. Therefore, disappointed, he returned to the United States in June 1862.

By that time, the Civil War had been raging, and his friend Hammond became surgeon general. He secured Xantus the position of assistant surgeon general in the army on July 28, 1862, although he had no medical degree. In December 1862 he was appointed consul at Manzanillo in Mexico, although his consulship was really short lived: when he recognized Topaz, a rebel chief, the State Department recalled him and closed the consulate. Xantus became unemployed again, as Hammond himself was court-martialed and dismissed.[396]

Xantus returned to Europe, spending some time studying zoos in Belgium and Holland. In 1869–71 he led an expedition to Southeast-Asia collecting plants and animal species for Hungarian museums. Later he became curator of the ethnographic section of the Hungarian National Museum. He passed away on December 13, 1894.[397]

Zagonyi, Charles

For a detailed biography see, Chapter Five "The Triumvirate"

Zerdahelyi, Edward

In some sources, he is referred to as Charles Zerdahelyi. This reflects the uncertainties concerning his life and career. He was born in 1821 and was a pupil and friend of Franz Liszt. Vasváry claims that he joined the Hungarian revolutionary army in 1848–49 and served as a recruiting officer. Vasváry's *Lincoln's Hungarian Heroes* is the only source that states that Zerdahelyi was captured by the Austrians and imprisoned in Pest, Laibach and Olmütz for about two years.[398]

After his release, he left the country. In 1851 he spent some time in Weimar with his mentor, and Liszt had a very high opinion of him. "I am very happy about Zerdahelyi's exertion and diligence," he wrote, "and I will do my best to make sure that his stay in Weimar will prove to be fruitful for him." Liszt dedicated the 1st Hungarian Rhapsody to him. Zerdahelyi went to Britain, where he got involved in the infamous Baroness von Beck case. Mainly this was the reason why he decided to emigrate to the United States. He settled down in Boston, and soon became a celebrated member of the artistic elite. He gave a series of concerts, all with great success.[399]

It is not quite clear why he decided to take part in the American Civil War. He enlisted on July 30, 1862, in Company K of the 39th New York Volunteers as 2nd lieutenant. During the war, he regularly returned to Boston to lecture on military art and field service, apparently with great success. *The Boston Daily Advertiser* refers to him in this period as captain. According to Vasváry, he authored a book entitled *Military Field Service,* but there is no trace of this book in the catalogues.[400]

After the Civil War he moved to Philadelphia and worked as a music teacher. He died on August 16, 1906, in his home. He left a widow and a son.[401]

Zulavsky, Casimir

Casimir was born in 1841 or 1842, the second youngest son of Emilie Kossuth and Casimir Zulavksky, Sr. He was taken to America by his mother in 1852 and came of age exactly at the outbreak of the Civil War. He enrolled in Mound City, Kansas, on July 24, 1861. He first became adjutant of the 3rd Kansas Infantry and later transferred to the 10th Kansas Infantry.[402]

According to James McGuire, he got involved in the robbery of an express office in 1862 and was sentenced to Kansas State Prison, but this cannot be confirmed. On April 13, 1864 he volunteered for Company F, 25th New York Cavalry, as a private. He was mustered out on June 9, 1865, in Washington, D.C.[403]

Zulavsky, Emile

One of the four Zulavsky brothers, nephew of Louis Kossuth, Hungarian governor during the War of Liberation, Emile was born in Sátoraljaújhely, Zemplén County, in 1834. His father, Casimir Zulavsky, a "frivolous Pole," as one of his contemporaries labeled him, left his mother, Emilie Kossuth. Emile was still a student at the time of the Hungarian War of Liberation, so he stayed out of the conflict. Nevertheless, after the surrender of the revolutionary army, he joined his family and they emigrated. They went to Britain and finally made their way across the Atlantic to try their luck in America; they left Southampton for New York onboard the *Humboldt* on July 6, 1852. Overseas the family enjoyed the financial support of George L. Stearns and his "Hungarian Club," and they managed to purchase a small farm. However, they soon went bankrupt, and their estate was auctioned off. Emilie moved to Brooklyn, where she opened a restaurant, but her health became more and more fragile. She was probably tubercular, and she died on June 29, 1860.[404]

Emile tried a number of occupations but did not stick to any very long. In 1859 he went to Italy and joined Garibaldi's Hungarian troops only to see all their hopes of a new Hungarian freedom fight fade away with the Treaty of Villafranca. Disappointed, Emile returned to America and volunteered in the Union Army. He was mustered in as corporal and later sergeant major of the 82nd Colored Infantry Regiment, the unit in which his brother Ladislaus served. Having passed the necessary examination, he became 2nd lieutenant of the regiment.[405]

After the Civil War it was his "ardent wish to embrace military life as a permanent profession," as he put it in his letter written to President Andrew Johnson, but we do not know whether he managed to do so, as we have no information about the later phase of his life and career.[406]

Zulavsky, Ladislaus

Ladislaus was born in 1837 in Szürte, Ung County. He and his three brothers were still children at the time of the Hungarian freedom fight in 1848–49, and he was taken to America by his mother in 1852, after a short stay in Britain. It seems that Ladislaus continued his studies in America, and Károly László mentions him as an engineer in 1859. Based on an article published in *Leslie's Illustrated Newspaper*, it can be assumed that he was employed as inspector of pipelines at Brooklyn Waterworks. In 1860 his mother died of tuberculosis, and the grief-stricken young man followed his elder brother, Emile, and left New York on September 22, 1860. He joined the Hungarian Legion in Italy, Dániel Ihász, commander of the unit, wrote to Gyula Tanárky that Ladislaus did not seek exalted status since he could join the legion only at the rank of private, as he was a *supernumerativus* (supernumerary), similar to many other volunteers. Eventually he was mustered into the 1st Hungarian Cavalry, the same regiment where his brother, Emile served, and later he was appointed lieutenant on the staff of General Antal Vetter. In October he was mustered out and soon returned to the United States.[407]

In America he applied for a commission in the U.S. Colored troops, and his personality and military experience secured him a lieutenant colonelcy in the 82nd Colored Regiment at the age of just twenty-seven. Martin Öfele seems to be right when he argues that Ladislaus saw a parallel between the freedmen's struggle and that of the Hungarians in 1848–49.[408]

Although he was often mentioned as a soldier of proverbial heroism, organizing and drilling his new regiment gave Zulavsky difficulty. He emphasized the moral education of his men, but as far as military training was concerned, the regiment seemed to lag behind, and many blamed the Hungarian officer for this. Lt. Col. Isaac S. Bangs, for instance, thought that "Zulavsky especially lacked the persistent discipline required in such an organization as the USC." In December 1864 he faced court-martial for negligence of duty, because he had never instructed his regiment in battalion drill. Although Zulavsky himself often declared that he was not competent enough to command a regiment, the jury found him not guilty and confirmed his rank and position. Although his further Civil War service was not entirely devoid of criticism either, Zulavsky did a good job in leading the regiment. Brig. Gen. William A. Pile mentioned the 82nd in his report on the battle of Fort Blakely (April 9, 1865): "Although in reserve and consequently late in starting on the charge, preserved their regimental organization throughout, the officers exhibiting both skill and bravery."[409]

Zulavsky saw an important connection between the military service of blacks and the final victory of the Union troops, and he linked the victory over secession to the final triumph over the institution of slavery. Many excerpts from his speeches show that he did believe in the equality of the Negro race: "The eyes of the world are upon you," he exhorted his men, "to you the friends of your long oppressed race look for the proof of that manliness which they hold to be just as much your gift from Almighty God as that of any white man." Apparently he managed to cope with the problem of black soldiers occasionally attack white women. For Zulavsky, who represented the European style of code of honor for soldiers, felt these were personal insults. On one occasion he pointed out: "We are soldiers and not disperadoes [*sic*] and only men of that class will be guilty of insulting women especially when those poor women like these poor refugees, come to us of themselves asking for help and protection. Tis a crying shame that any one wearing a soldiers uniform, should so far forget himself, and the sacred cause he represents to be guilty of such attrocious brutality."[410] In punishing the atrocities, he made no distinction between blacks and whites.

Probably the best piece of evidence that he was an ardent supporter of the equality of blacks is his message to his soldiers right after the assassination of Abraham Lincoln: "The U.S. Colored Troops above all classes of men, must carry love and veneration of Mr. Lincoln's memory in their hearts. They owe freedom, justice, consideration, fame, and every other blessing they and their kindred enjoy to him above all other men. He has been the redeemer of the colored race in this country, and his name must be as sacred on their lips as that of mankind's Redeemer."[411]

After the Civil War, he played an important role in the life of the Hungarian-American community. He married Emma C. Norton, daughter of John Norton, a wealthy shipping merchant from New York, on November 7, 1866. Many Hungarian émigrés were invited to the ceremony, including Károly László. Something definitely went wrong with the marriage, as Ladislaus left the United States next year, and according to the Census of 1880, Emma was living in her parents' house, although still indicated as married. We do not have any further information on their lives; all we know is that Ladislaus died in 1884 in New York.[412]

Zulavsky, Sigismund

Sigismund, the youngest nephew of Louis Kossuth, was born in 1843 or 1845. He was the only son who stayed with their mother, Emilie, to the very end of her life in 1860. He had a very hard time not only emotionally, but financially as well. His problems were finally solved by his adoption by a New Hampshire family sympathetic to the Hungarian cause.[413]

When the Civil War came, he joined Company D of the 8th New Hampshire as a private on December 3, 1861. About two years later, he made up his mind to apply for a commission in the regiment of his brother, Ladislaus. He was found suitable for this and was transferred to the 82nd Colored Regiment in April 1863 with the rank of 2nd lieutenant.[414]

He contracted typhoid fever when his regiment was transferred to Louisiana and died at Port Hudson on September 16, 1863.

Appendix: Misspellings and Anglicized Versions of Hungarian Names in American Sources

Asboth, Alexander = Asbóth, Sándor
Barothy, Charles = Baróthy, Károly
Botsay, Alexander = Botsay, Sándor
Csermelyi, Joseph = Csermelyi, József
Debreczeny, Ignatz = Debreczenyi, Ignác
De Korponay, Gabriel = Korponay, Gábor
De Korponay, Stephen = Korponay, István
De Zeyk, Albert = Zeyk, Albert
Dobozy, Emeric = Dobozi, Imre
Dobozy, Peter Paul = Dobozi, Péter Pál
Dunka, Nicolai = Dunka, Miklós
D'Utassy, Anthony = Utassy, Antal
D'Utassy, Carl = Utassy, Károly
D'Utassy, Frederick George = Utassy, Frigyes György
Estvan, Bela = Estván, Béla (Heinrich, Peter)
Fejervary, Nicholas, Jr. = Fejérváry, Miklós, Jr.
Fekete (also: Feckete), Alexander = Fekete, Sándor
Fiala, John = Fiala, János
Figyelmessy, Philip = Figyelmessy, Fülöp
Finto, John = Finto (Finta?), János
Fornet, Cornelius = Fornet, Kornél
Gaal, Alexander = Gál, Sándor
Gallfy, Andrew = Gállfy (Gállik?), András
Gerster, Anton = Gerster, Antal
Grechenek, George = Grechenek, György
Grossinger, Charles = Grossinger, Károly
Haraszthy, Gaza = Haraszthy, Géza
Hillebrandt, Hugo = Hillebrandt, Hugó
Hollan, Hugo = Hollán, Hugó
Holmy, Johann Rudolph = Holmy (Halmy?), János Rudolf
Jekelfalussy, Alexander = Jekelfalussy, Sándor
Kappner, Ignatz = Kappner, Ignác
Kemenyffy, Joseph = Keményffy, József
Kiss, Anthony = Kiss, Antal
Knefler, Frederick = Knefler, Frigyes
Kovacs, Stephen = Kovács, István
Kovats, Augustus = Kováts, Gusztáv
Kozlay, Eugene = Kozlay, Jenő
Kune, Julian = Kuné, Gyula
Lang, Henry = Láng, Henrik
Langenfeld, Francis = Langenfeld, Ferenc
Langer, Ignatz = Langer (also Langner), Ignác
Lederer, Immanuel = Léderer, Emánuel
Lulley, Charles = Lülley, Károly
Lulley, Emanuel = Lülley, Emánuel (also Manó)
Majthenyi, Theodore = Majthényi, Tivadar
Menyhart, John = Menyhárt, János
Meszaros, Emeric = Mészáros, Imre

Mihalotzy, Geza = Mihalótzy (also Mihalóczy), Géza
Mundee, Charles = Mándy, Károly
Nagy, Alexander = Nagy, Sándor
Nemett, Joseph = Németh, József
Perczel, Nicholas = Perczel, Miklós
Pomutz, George = Pomutz (also Pomuţ), George (also Georghe)
Pulitzer, Joseph = Pulitzer, József
Radnich, Emeric = Radnich, Imre
Radnich, Stephen = Radnich, István
Rombauer, Robert = Rombauer, Róbert
Rozsafy, Matthias = Rózsafy (also Ruzicska), Mátyás
Schoepf, Albin = Schöpf (also Schöff), Albin
Schoney, Lazarus = Schöney, Lázár
Semsey, Charles = Semsey, Károly
Solyom, Louis = Sólyom, Lajos
Spelletich, Stephen = Spelletich, István
Stahel, Julius = Stahel (Számwald), Gyula
Szabad, Emeric = Szabad, Imre
Szabo, Ignatz = Szabó, Ignác
Szabo, Joseph = Szabó, József
Szegedy, Matthias = Szegedy, Mátyás
Takats, Francis = Takács, Ferenc
Tauszky, Rudolph = Tauszky, Rudolf
Tenner, Louis = Tenner, Lajos
Toplanyi, Alexander = Toplányi, Sándor
Ujffy, John Henry = Újffy, János Henrik
Vandor, Joseph = Vándor, József
Varga, Alexander = Varga, Sándor
Varga, John = Varga, János
Varga, Joseph = Varga, József
Varga, Paul = Varga, Pál
Vertessy, John = Vértessy, János
Vidor, Charles = Vidor, Károly
Vöneky, Louis = Vöneky (also Veneky), Louis
Waagner, Gustave = Wágner, Gusztáv
Weekey, Anthony = Wékey (also Vékey), Antal
Xantus, John = Xantus (also Xántus), János
Zagonyi (also Zagony), Charles = Zágonyi, Károly
Zerdahelyi, Edward = Szerdahelyi, Edward
Zulavsky, Casimir = Zsulavszky, Casimir
Zulavsky, Emile = Zsulavszky, Emil
Zulavsky, Ladislaus = Zsulavszky, László
Zulavsky, Sigismund = Zsulavszky, Zsigmond

Notes

Preface

1. Eugene Pivány, *Hungarians in the American Civil War*, (Cleveland, OH: Dongó, 1913); Edmund Vasváry, *Lincoln's Hungarian Heroes: The Participation of Hungarians in the American Civil War, 1861–65* (Washington, D.C., 1939); Ács Tivadar, *Magyarok az észak-amerikai polgárháborúban 1861–65* (Pannónia, Budapest, 1964).

2. Ella Lonn, *Foreigners in the Confederacy* (Chapel Hill: University of North Carolina Press, 1940); Ella Lonn, *Foreigners in the Union Army and Navy* (Baton Rouge: Louisiana State University Press, 1951); William Burton, *Melting Pot Soldiers: The Union's Ethnic Regiments* (New York: Fordham University Press, 1998); Dean B. Mahin, *Blessed Place of Freedom: Europeans in Civil War America* (Washington, D.C.: Brassey's, 2002); Martin Öfele, *German-speaking Officers in the U.S. Colored Troops, 1863–1867* (Gainesville: University Press of Florida, 2004).

3. Julianna Puskás, *Ties That Bind, Ties That Divide: One Hundred Years of Hungarian Experience in the United States* (New York and London: Holmes and Meier, 2000).

Introduction

1. "Kossuth in Prison, After His Last Battle," in *The United States Democratic Review* Vol. 26, Issue 139, (January 1850), 72.

2. Gábor Egressy, *Törökországi Naplója, 1849–50*. Budapest: Terebess Kiadó, 1997, http://www.terebess.hu/keletkultinfo/egressy.html.

3. István Deák, *The Lawful Revolution: Louis Kossuth and the Hungarians, 1848–1849*. London: Phoenix Press, 2001, 63–106.

4. Aladár Urbán, "A Lesson for the Old Continent: The Image of America in the Hungarian Revolution of 1848/49," *The New Hungarian Quarterly*, Vol. 17, No. 63, Autumn 1976, 85–96; Tibor Frank, "Through the Looking-glass: A Century of Self-reflecting Hungarian Images of the United States (1834–1941)," in Lehel Vadon, ed., *Multicultural Challenge in American Culture: Hemingway Centennial* (Eger: EKTF, 1999), 21–36. http://www.fulbright.hu/culture/worksp2/frank.htm.

5. Quote in Tivadar Ács, *Népek tavasza: Ismeretlen levelek, naplójegyzetek a magyar szabadságharc és emigráció korából* (Budapest: Altalanos Nyomda es Grafikai Intezet, 1943), 60. Author's translation.

6. *The Reminiscences of Carl Schurz* (New York: Doubleday, Page, 1909), Vol. I, 385; Stephen Beszedits, "The Nation's Guest: Kossuth in America" http://www.hccc.org/A2e/A20224a.shtml (accessed 8/8/08).

7. Cited in *New York Times*, December 6, 1851, 1.

8. Beszedits, "The Nation's Guest"; *The New York Times*, December 6, 1851, 1; for information about Kossuth's visit to America among others, see John H. Komlós, Louis Kossuth in America, 1851–1852 (Buffalo, N.Y.: East European Institute, 1973) and Tibor Frank, "Marketing Hungary: Kossuth and the Politics of Propaganda," in *Lajos Kossuth Sent Word*, edited by László Péter, Martyn Rady, and Peter Sherwood (London: Hungarian Cultural Center, 2003), 221–249.

9. Abraham Lincoln, "Resolutions in Behalf of Hungarian Freedom" (January 9, 1852) in Roy P. Basler, ed., *Collected Works of Abraham Lincoln* (New Brunswick, N.J.: Rutgers University Press, 1953–1955), II, 115–116.

10. Cited in *Letter to Louis Kossuth, Concerning Freedom and Slavery in the United States in Behalf of the American Anti-Slavery Society* (Boston: R.F. Wallcut, 1852), 110.
11. Frederick Douglass, *My Bondage and My Freedom* (New York: Miller, Orton and Mulligan, 1855), xxv.
12. Samuel C. Busey, *Immigration: Its Evils and Consequences* (New York, 1856), 47.
13. Busey, *Immigration*, 61.
14. *Letter to Louis Kossuth*, 6.
15. *The New York Times*, June 9, 1852, 2.

Chapter One

1. James McPherson, *Ordeal by Fire: The Civil War and the Reconstruction* (New York: Knopf, 1982), 82; for an excellent analysis of the image of America in Hungary up to 1848 see Géza Závodszky, *Az Amerika-motívum és a polgárosodó Magyarország: A kezdetektől 1848-ig* (Budapest: Korona Kiadó, 1997).
2. Mrs. Princz's letter written to her relatives in Hungary (1818), Vasváry Collection, Somogyi Library, Szeged, Hungary, R1, d, 31. Author's translation.
3. Cited in Kende, Géza. *Magyarok Amerikában: Az amerikai magyarság története, 1583–1926* (Cleveland: Szabadság, 1926), I, 42–43. Author's translation.
4. Lőrinc Tóth, "Ó és Uj Világ," *Athenaeum* (August 31, 1837), 273–280. Author's translation.
5. Cornelius Fornet, "Amerika rokonszenve a magyar szabadságharcz férfiai iránt," *Történelmi Lapok* (April 1, 1893), 69. Author's translation.
6. Sándor Farkas Bölöni, *Utazás Észak-Amerikában* (Cluj: Dácia, 1975), 326; Várdy, *Magyarok az Újvilágban*, 35; for a comparison of the two books consult Csaba Lévai, "A French Aristocrat and a Hungarian Nobleman in Jacksonian America: A Comparison of the Views of Alexis de Tocqueville and Sándor Farkas Bölöni" in *Global Encounters—European Identities* (eds. M. Harris, A. Agnarsdóttir, and Cs. Lévai) (Pisa: Plus-Pisa University Press, 2010), 247–258.
7. Ágoston Haraszty, *Utazás Éjszakamerikában* (Pest: G. Heckenast, 1844). For a study of the role Haraszty played in vine-culture in California, see Csaba Lévai, "Haraszthy Ágoston mint a 'kaliforniai szőlőkultúra atyja': vélemények és viták az újabb egyesült államokbeli szakirodalom tükrében" in István Orosz and Klára Papp (eds.), *Szőlőtermelés és borkereskedelem* (Debreceni Egyetem Történelmi Intézete, Debrecen, 2009), 249–268.
8. Miklós Kiss to Kossuth, on the transportation of Hungarians to the U.S. from Britain (March 26, 1852), London, in Dénes Jánossy, *A Kossuth emigráció Angliában és Amerikában, 1851–1852*, 2 vols. (Budapest: Magyar Történelmi Társulat, 1940), II, 709–711.
9. Lajos Dancs, *Töredékek tíz éves emigrationalis élményeimből* (Nagy-Szőllős: Székely Simon, 1890), 12.
10. Homer L. Calkin, "The Modern Ark: The Coming of the Foreigners," *The Palimpsest*, State Historical Society of Iowa (April, 1962), 182.
11. Eugene Kozlay, "Let you Emigrate," Kozlay Papers, Sándor Petőfi Museum of Literature, Budapest, under procession. Janet Kozlay called my attention to this piece of writing and shared it with me.
12. József Madarász, *Emlékirataim* (Budapest: Franklin-Társulat, 1883), 296. Author's translation.
13. Salamon Neumann, "Amerikai vázlatok," *Pesti Napló* (February 26, 1860). Author's translation.
14. Charles Loring Brace, *Hungary in 1851: With an Experience of the Austrian Police* (New York: Charles Scribner, 1852); in Hungarian: Charles Loring Brace, *Magyarország 1851-ben* (Csaba Lévai and István Kornél Vida, eds.) (Máriabesenyő-Gödöllő: Attraktor, 2006).
15. *The New York Times*, November 18, 1851, 4.
16. Pál Hajnik's report on Kossuth's incomes and expenditures in the U.S. (June 10, 1852), Washington, D.C., Jánossy, *Kossuth-emigráció*, II, 867; *New York Daily Times* (July 27, 1852), 4.
17. Cited by Stephen Beszedits, "The Nation's Guest: Kossuth in America," http://www.hccc.org/A2e/A20224a.shtml (accessed July 21, 2006); Howe to Kossuth (June 27, 1852) Jánossy, *Kossuth-emigráció*, II, 896–897.
18. Mrs. Eliot to Kossuth (May 5, 1852), Pittsburgh, PA; Jánossy, *Kossuth-emigráció*, II, 816–817.
19. Dancs, *Töredékek*, 28.
20. Lukács's letter published in *Pesti Napló* (December 24, 1850). Author's translation.
21. József Majthényi to his wife, Philadelphia, PA (August 14, 1851). Cited in Stephen Taba, "Hungarian Pioneers in America," *The Hungarian Quarterly*, Vol. 7, No. 1 (Spring 1941), 52.

Chapter Two

1. Popular saying in Latin among Hungarians at the time, meaning "There is no life outside Hungary, if there is, it is not real life."
2. Újházy to Pulszky (December 25, 1849), cited in Ács, *New Buda*, 107.
3. Dancs, *Töredékek*, 29.
4. Pulszky's letter to J. Neumann, Niagara Falls (May 25, 1852), quoted in Jánossy, *Kossuth-emigráció*, II, 462. *Otium cum dignitate* means leisure in dignity in Latin.
5. József Majthényi to his wife, Philadelphia, PA (August 14, 1851) in Taba, "Hungarian Pioneers," 52; Kinizsi, *Sánta Huszár*, 117.
6. Lázár Mészáros to Antal Mészáros, Brooklyn, NY (Sept. 5, 1853), cited in Szokoly, *Mészáros Lázár*, 32. Author's translation.
7. Robert Ernst, *Immigrant Life in New York City, 1825–1863* (Port Washington, NY: I.J. Friedman, 1949), 17; László, cited in Ács, *Magyar úttörők*, 13.
8. Ernst, *Immigrant Life*, 213.
9. Quoted in Ács, *New Buda*, 116; Majthényi wanted his wife and children, whom he had left behind, to join him in America.
10. Kinizsi, *Sánta Huszár*, 135.
11. Jánossy, *Kossuth-emigráció*, II, 698–699; Gábor Albert, ed., *Szemere Bertalan leveleskönyve, 1849–1865* (Balassi Kiadó: Budapest, 1999), 86.
12. Ács, *Kossuth papja*, 79.
13. Péter Bogáti, ed., Gedeon Ács, *Mihelyt gyertyámat eloltom. Bostoni jegyzetek, 1856–63* (Budapest: Gondolat kiadó, 1989), 10–12.
14. Ács, *Kossuth papja*, 79.
15. Várdy, *Magyarok az Újvilágban*, 95; for articles on Kornis's newspaper, see Stephen Béla Várdy, "A magyar Számüzöttek Lapja: Az első amerikai-magyar újság megszületése," *Amerikai Magyar Népszava/Szabadság* (April 2, 1999), 15–16; Stephen Béla Várdy, "Az első magyar újság és újságszerkesztő Amerikában," *Debreceni Szemle* (1999/4), 511–515; Ernst, *Immigrant Life*, 150–161; Kende, *Magyarok Amerikában*, I, 130.
16. Lajos Lukács, *A magyar politikai emigráció 1849–1867*. (Budapest: Kossuth könyvkiadó, 1984), 251–252.
17. *Chicago Press and Tribune*, June 25, 1859, 1.
18. Asbóth's letter to Hungarians, published in *Chicago Press and Tribune*, July 11, 1859, 1; *The New York Times*, July 8, 1859, 8; Klapka's proclamation published in *Chicago Press and Tribune*, July 2, 1859; Kossuth's letter to Hungarians appeared in *Chicago Press and Tribune*, June 25, 1859.
19. "Summer View of New Buda," *The New York Times*, November 19, 1851, 4.
20. Pál Liptay, "Uj-Buda (Amerikai Naplómból)," *Fővárosi Lapok*, January 24, 1877, and January 25, 1877.
21. István Cserépy, "Iparos Hazánkfia Észak-Amerikában," *Vasárnapi Újság* (1859/11): 127–128.
22. Újházy to Beöthy Ödön, published in *Pesti Napló*, December 14, 1850, cited in Ács, *New Buda*, 130.
23. Liptay, Pál, "Uj Buda (Amerikai Naplómból)," *Fővárosi Lapok*, January 24, 1877, and January 25, 1877.
24. Majthényi to his wife (December 4, 1851), in Ács, *New Buda*, 209; statistical data compiled from records of the Bureau of the Census, Record Group 29, Census of 1850 M432 and Census of 1860 M653, National Archives, Washington, D.C., Records of the Bureau of the Census, Record Group 29.
25. Rudolph J. Vecoli and Suzanne M. Sinke, eds., *A Century of European Migrations, 1830–1930* (Urbana: University of Illinois Press, 1991), 295.
26. Roderick E. Rombauer, *The History of a Life* (St. Louis: By author, 1903), 17.
27. John Xantus, *Travels in Southern California* (Wayne State University Press, Detroit, 1976), 94; Quoted in *Szabadság*, Cleveland, OH (1911/21); Ács, *Kossuth papja*, 115.
28. Ferenc Varga, "Bujdosásom története," *Szabadság*, Cleveland, OH (December 20, 1900); Dániel Kászonyi, *Magyarhon négy korszaka* (Budapest: Szépirodalmi Kiadó, 1977), 340–341. Author's translation.
29. Ladislaus Újházy to Mrs. Pulszky, Turin, Italy (September 1, 1860), quoted in Ács, *New Buda*, 279; *The New York Times*, December 6, 1851, 1; bill granting land to the refugees from Hungary, 31st Congress, 1st Session, 1851.
30. Ács, *Kossuth papja*, 137; Ács, *Kossuth papja*, p. 175; for this issue in detail, see István Kornél Vida, "The Concept of Citizenship and the Hungarian Immigrants in the United States in the 1850s: A

Case Study," in S.G. Ellis, G. Hálfdanarson, and A.K. Isaacs, eds., *Citizenship in Historical Perspective* (Pisa, Italy: Pisa University Press, 2006), 227–236.

31. The text of the pledge is quoted in several works written by Hungarian emigrants, for instance, Ács, *Magyar úttörők*, 24.

32. Brace, *Hungary in 1851*, 37, 136.

33. Joseph P. Ferrie, "Migration to the Frontier in Mid-nineteenth Century America: A Re-examination of Turner's Safety Valve," manuscript. http://eh.net/abstracts/archives.php?order=date&rev=.

34. David W. Galenson and Clayne L. Pope, "Economic and Geographic Mobility on the Farming Frontier: Evidence from Appanoose County, Iowa, 1850–1870," *Journal of Economic History*, 49, No. 3 (1989): 635–55.

Chapter Three

1. Perczel, *Naplóm*, II, 184–185.
2. Ács, *Kossuth papja*, 200.
3. Lengyel, *Americans*, 73; Vasváry, *Lincoln and the Hungarians*, 3; Ács, *Magyarok az észak-amerikai polgárháborúban*, 122.
4. *The New York Times*, May 3, 1861. The same article in *The New York Herald*, May 3, 1861, 8.
5. For details concerning these ethnic regiments, see Michael Bacarella, *Lincoln's Foreign Legion: The 39th New York Infantry, the Garibaldi Guard* (Shippensburg, PA: White Mane, 1996); Ray W. Burhop, *The Twenty-fourth Illinois Infantry Regiment: The Story of a Civil War Regiment* (Tampa, FL: Burhop, 2003).
6. Albert Ruttkay to Maj. Gen. N.P. Banks (May 30, 1865), service records, Albert Ruttkay, 1st Florida Cavalry, National Archives, Washington, D.C., RG 94.
7. Albert Ruttkay to Maj. Gen. N.P. Banks (May 30, 1865), service records, Albert Ruttkay, 1st Florida Cavalry, National Archives, Washington, D.C., RG 94; Madarász: *Emlékirataim*, 317–318.
8. Quoted in Stephen Beszedits, "Some Notes on the Life and Career of Major-General Julius Stahel, Insignia No. 1491 New York Commandery," 4; *Louisville Journal*, June 11, 1861, 2; Marquis Adolphe Chambrun, *Impressions of Lincoln and the Civil War: A Foreigner's Account* (NY: Random House, 1952), 64–65.
9. *Az Egyesült Északi-Amerikai Respublica had seregében levő Magyarokhoz intézett búcsú szava Újházi Lászlónak* (December 1, 1861) Nyomtatvány. OL, Kossuth Gyűjtemény. Emigr. Ir. (1861): 75.
10. *The New York Herald*, July 20, 1861, 5; Beszedits, *Libby Prison Diary*, 75; "Zagonyi's Testimony on February 24, 1862," *The War in the West* (Millwood, New York: Kraus Reprint, 1977), 190.
11. Mary Boykin Miller Chesnut, *Mary Chesnut's Civil War* (New Haven: Yale University Press, 1981), 207; quoted in Russell, *My Diary*, 341; James M. McPherson, *For Cause and Comrades: Why Men Fought in the Civil War* (New York: Oxford University Press, 1997), 5; Michael Egan, *The Flying, Gray-haired Yank* (Philadelphia: Edgewood, 1888), 251; Michael Loeffler, *Preussens und Sachsens Bezeihungen zu den USA Waehrends des Sessessionskrieges, 1860–65* (Berlin: Free University of Berlin, 1999), 180.
12. For the American consul's offer see *Figyelmessy's letter to his comrades*, Torino, Italy (November 9, 1861) OL, Türr Iratok, 71/a; Lukács, 256–257.
13. Éber to Türr (June 5, 1862) OL, Türr Iratok, 1434.
14. I have gained information on Kozlay's motivations for volunteering from my correspondence with Janet Kozlay; András Csillag, *Joseph Pulitzer és az amerikai sajtó* (Budapest, Osiris Kiadó, 2000), 29–30.
15. Quoted in Lonn, *Foreigners in the Confederacy*, 58; Béla Estván, *War Pictures from the South* (New York: D. Appleton, 1863), iii; *The New York Times*, July 19, 1863, 3.
16. William C. Harris, *Prison-Life in a Tobacco Warehouse at Richmond* (Philadelphia, PA: G.W. Childs, 1862), 87.
17. Sherman to Ellen Ewing Sherman (November 3, 1860, and December 5, 1860), in Brooks D. Simpson and Jean V. Berlin, eds. *Sherman's Civil War: Selected Correspondence of William T. Sherman, 1860–65* (Chapel Hill: University of North Carolina Press, 1999), 4 and 39.
18. *Journal of the Provisional Congress of the Confederate States of America* (Washington, D.C.: Government Printing Office, 1904–1905), I, 621; Mahin, *Blessed Place*, 63; Lonn, *Foreigners in the Confederacy*, 385.
19. *Daily Richmond Examiner*, February 5, 1864, 6.
20. William Watson, *Life in the Confederate Army: Being the Observations and Experiences of an*

Alien in the South During the American Civil War (New York: Scribner and Welford, 1888), 58–59; quoted in Beszedits, *Libby Prison Diary*, 75; *The Old Guard* Vol. 4, Issue 5 (May 1866), 306–307.

21. William H. Russell, *My Diary North and South* (New York: Harper and Bros., 1954), 234; *Deutsche in den Diensten der Konfoederation* (Technical University of Berlin, Germany) (http://www2.tu-berlin.de/presse/tui/95jan/deutsche.html); Mahin, *Blessed Place*, 67–69.

22. Lonn, *Foreigners in the Confederacy*, 387.

23. Watson, *Life in the Confederate Army*, 395; James M. McPherson to Civil War Newsgroup (August 16, 1996).

24. McPherson, *Cause and Comrades*. The fourteen major motivations are as follows, according to Professor McPherson: martial enthusiasm, discipline, leadership, comradeship, character, religion, defense of homeland, preservation of the union, liberty, slavery, vengeance, duty, glory, honor.

Chapter Four

1. Pivány, *Hungarians in the Civil War*, 5–6, Vasváry, *Lincoln and the Hungarians*, 1–2, Ács, *Magyarok az észak-amerikai polgárháborúban*, 22–23.

2. Mahin, *Blessed Place of Freedom*, 10; Irene M. Franck, *The German American Heritage* (New York: Facts on File, 1989), 109.

3. See Csillag, *Pulitzer*.

4. For information on the Union cavalry, consult Edward G. Longacre, *Lincoln's Cavalrymen: A History of the Mounted Forces of the Army of the Potomac* (Mechanicsburg, Pa.: Stackpole Books, 2000).

5. Anthony Tihamer Komjathy, *A Thousand Years of the Hungarian Art of War* (Toronto, CA: Rakoczi Foundation, 1982), 110.

6. *The New York Times*, May 24, 1861, 8; Also, *Harper's Weekly*, June 8, 1861, 359, 362.

7. Susan Lyons Hughes, "The Daughter of the Regiment: A Brief History of the Vivandieres and Cantinieres in the American Civil War," http://womenshistory.about.com/gi/dynamic/offsite.htm?site=http://www.ehistory.com/uscw/features/articles/0005/vivandieres.cfm (June 18, 2007).

8. For details, see D'Utassy in the Biographical Dictionary section of this book.

9. For information about the Civil War in Missouri, consult Carolyn M. Bartels, *The Civil War in Missouri, 1861–1865* (Independence, MO: Two Trails, 2003); also, Robert J. Rombauer, *The Union Cause in St. Louis in 1861: An Historical Sketch* (St. Louis: Press of Nixon-Jones, 1909).

10. Judy Yandoh, "Taking off the Kid Gloves," *America's Civil War* (March 1992), 46–54.

11. Samuel R. Curtis to Lincoln (October 12, 1861) *Collected Works*, IV, 549–550; Andrew Rolle, *John Charles Frémont: Character as Destiny* (University of Oklahoma Press, Norman, 1991), 196.

12. Stephen Beszedits, "Hungarians with General John C. Frémont in the American Civil War," *Vasváry Collection Newsletter* (2003/2) http://www.sk-szeged.hu/szolgaltatas/vasvary/newsletter/03dec/beszedits.html.

13. Samuel R. Curtis to Lincoln (October 12, 1861) *Collected Works*, IV, 550.

14. The English translation of the dispatch is as follows, "Please, communicate the following to the President of the United States — Your letter of the 10th August just received with contents had no battle — the enemy retreated to New Madrid I nevertheless expect an engagement very soon. A telegram just received from Cairo informs me that several steel plated war vessels left Memphis advancing on us. Their vessels being better than ours Cairo is endangered. Could not you get from a near arsenal sixteen gun carriages to suit 10 inch Dahlgren guns — The guns are here but the carriages are wanting — I was waiting in vain these ten days past the promised help from Washington though the enemy is moving rapidly."

15. For further details as well as the full-text version of the proclamation see http://www.longcamp.com/proc3.html (accessed on May 23, 2007).

16. Beszedits, "Hungarians with Frémont."

17. Julian Kuné, *Reminiscences of an Octogenarian Hungarian Exile* (Chicago: By author, 1911), 91; Mihalótzy's letter, Chicago Historical Society, Richard Yates Manuscript Collection, F38AS, C4C4 v. 2 No. 5, 133–136.

18. Due to the lack of reliable archival sources, these pieces of statistics are definitely not ones to draw conclusions from, particularly as the two Hungarians commissioned as colonels served for a brief period before they left the Confederate service for good.

Chapter Five

1. Pivány, *Hungarians in the American Civil War*, 15; Vasváry, *Lincoln and the Hungarians*, 2; Ács, *Magyarok az észak-amerikai polgárháborúban*, 68–69.
2. *The New York Times*, November 26, 1864.
3. For information on his pre–1848–49 career, consult Vasváry Collection A3/14, and Ferenc Fodor, *Magyar vízimérnökök* (Budapesti Műszaki Egyetem Központi Könyvtára, No. 8, 1957); István Ágoston, *A nemzet inzsellérei: vízimérnökök élete és munkássága, XVIII–XX. sz* (Szeged, 2001); Ács, *Kossuth papja*, 92; Beszedits, "Hungarians with Frémont."
4. *The New York Times* (September 3, 1861), 3.
5. For the medical file of Asboth, see Jack D. Welsh, M.D., *Medical Histories of Union Generals* (Kent, Ohio: Kent University Press, 1996).
6. John H. Eicher and David. J. Eicher, *Civil War High Commands* (Stanford University Press, Stanford, California, 2001), 108–109; for the involvement of German-speaking foreigners, including Hungarians in the colored regiments, see Öfele, *German-speaking Officers*; István Kornél Vida, "'A régóta elnyomottak barátai': Magyar katonák az észak-amerikai polgárháború néger ezredeiben" ("Long-time friends of the oppressed": Hungarian soldiers in the Colored Troops in the American Civil War") *Aetas* (2008/2): 68–82; William Watson Davis, *The Civil War and Reconstruction in Florida* (New York: Columbia University, 1913) quoted in Beszedits, *Hungarians*.
7. A.J. Bedford, Sergeant, 25th U.S. Colored Infantry, in Edwin S. Redkey, ed., *A Grand Army of Black Men* (New York: Cambridge University Press, 1992), 149; *Medical and Surgical History of the Civil War* (Wilmington, N.C.: Broadfoot, 1991), Vol. 8, 389.
8. *The New York Times*, November 26, 1864.
9. On the centennial of Asboth's death, the periodical *Szabadság* published a series of articles: Péter Halász, "Asbóth," in *Szabadság*, February 17, 1968; Edmund Vasváry, "Asbóth tábornok sírja," *Szabadság*, March 18, 1968; Edmund Vasváry, "Golyó a fejben," *Szabadság*, July 18, 1968.
10. For the genealogy of the Számwald family, see Döme Lugosi, *Szeged hős fiai az USA szabadságharcában* (Szeged, 1939); Beszedits, "Julius Stahel," 14.
11. Author's translation.
12. Julius H. Stahel Papers, Library of Congress. Washington, D.C.; Information taken from the letter of Zsigmond Kemény. *Irodalomtörténeti Közlemények* (1915), 360; *Herringshaw's Encyclopedia of American Biography in the Nineteenth Century* (Chicago, IL: American Publishers' Association, 1902), 880.
13. Beszedits, *Life of Julius Stahel*, 2.
14. Vasváry, *Lincoln and the Hungarians*, 4.
15. Robert K. Krick, *Conquering the Valley: Stonewall Jackson at Port Republic* (New York: William Morrow, 1996), 168; Francis F. Wayland, ed., "Frémont's Pursuit of Jackson in the Shenandoah Valley: The Journal of Col. Albert Tracy, (March–July 1862)," *The Virginia Magazine of History and Biography*, Vol. 70 (1962), 334.
16. Krick, *Stonewall Jackson*, 180.
17. Alexander Hamilton's letter written to H.W. Halleck (November 21, 1861) Julius H. Stahel Papers, Library of Congress, Washington, D.C., No. 6/2; George B. McClellan, *McClellan's Own Story* (New York: Webster, 1887), 139.
18. Beszedits, *Life of Julius Stahel*, 4.
19. Edward G. Longacre, *The Cavalry at Gettysburg* (London: Associated University Presses, 1986), 61; Adams McFadden Hays to Rachel McFadden (June 12, 1863) Centreville, VA, *Life and Letters of Alexander Hays* (Pittsburgh: privately published, 1919), 396.
20. Carl Sandburg, *Abraham Lincoln* (New York: Harcourt, Brace, 1954), 443.
21. Hunter's letter to Major Gen. Halleck (June 9, 1864), Julius H. Stahel Papers, Library of Congress, Washington, D.C., No. 19; Beszedits, *Life of Julius Stahel*, 7.
22. Welsh, *Medical Histories*, 316–317.
23. Sigel to Stahel (February 10, 1865), Julius H. Stahel Papers, Library of Congress, Washington, D.C.
24. Beszedits, *Life of Julius Stahel*, 8.
25. Henford Lennox Gordon, "Charge of Fremont's Body-guard."
26. Beszedits, *Hungarians in Civil War Missouri*. http://www.missouricivilwarmuseum.org/mo-hungarian.htm.
27. Ács, *Magyar úttörők*, 135.
28. Yandoh, "Kid Gloves," 46–54.

29. Zagonyi's testimony (February 24, 1862). In *The War in the West* (Millwood, N.Y.: Kraus Reprint Co., 1977) (hereafter cited as Zagonyi, *Testimony*), 190.
30. Jay Monaghan, *Civil War on the Western Border, 1854–1865* (Boston: Little, Brown, 1955), 183.
31. For the sequence of events of the charge, see Yandoh, "Kid Gloves"; William Edward Dorsheimer, "Frémont's 100 Days in Missouri," *Atlantic Monthly* (January 1862) (hereafter cited as Dorsheimer, "Frémont"), 251–258; Robert E. Miller, "Zagonyi," *Missouri Historical Review*, Vol. 76 (January 1982), 174–192.
32. Quoted in Yandoh, "Kid Gloves," 51.
33. Dorsheimer, "Frémont," 254.
34. J. Winston, *Cora O'Kane; or the Doom of the Rebel Guard* (Claremont, N.H.: Association of Disabled Soldiers, 1868), 80.
35. For Zagonyi's report, see OR, Series I, Vol. 3, Serial Vol. 3, 251–252; *Medical History*, 8, xxxviii.
36. Frank Moore, ed., *Rebellion Record* (New York: G.P. Putnam, 1862), III, 272.
37. *Littel's Living Age*, Vol. 73, Issue 935 (May 3, 1862): 230.
38. James A. Congdon, *Congdon's Cavalry Compendium* (Philadelphia: J.P. Lippincott, 1864), 4–5.
39. Zagonyi, *Testimony*, 189; Vasváry, *Lincoln and the Hungarians*, 3.
40. *Congressional Globe*, 28, U.S. 37th Congress, 2nd Session, Part 2 (March 7, 1862): 1118–1124; "Zagonyi's Charge with the Fremont Body-guard: A Picturesque Fol-de-rol," *Southern Historical Society Papers*, No. 3 (1887): 195–196; *The Sentinel*, May 29, 1898; *The Oregonian*, March 6, 1897.
41. Miller, "Zagonyi," 183; OR, Series 1, Vol. 3, 252–253; Yandoh, "Kid Gloves," 54.
42. Linda Allart, et al., eds., *The Journals and Miscellaneous Notebooks of Ralph Waldo Emerson* (Cambridge, MA.: Belknap Press, 1982), 15, 191–192.
43. *Lowell Daily Citizen and News*, September 15, 1865, 2.
44. Dancs, *Töredékek*, 69. Author's translation.
45. *Tuscumbia Osage Valley Sentinel*, February 24, 1871; Károly Rácz-Rónay to Sándor Márki, Hamburg (August 3, 1921); cited in Mária Kórász, "Az amerikai történetírás kezdetei," *Aetas* (1996/1), 129; *Marriage Registers, Extracts from Manhattan (1869–1880) and Brooklyn (1895–1897)* (Dept. of Health, Division of Vital Statistics, New York, 1870), Certificate 7289; John Maurath, an ardent researcher of the body-guard, reached the same conclusion.
46. Beszedits, *Hungarians in Missouri*; for information on the Zagonyi Park, visit http://www.richgros.com/Springfield_History/Sites_HTML/Zagonyi.html (January 12, 2008).
47. Quoted in Beszedits, "Julius Stahel," 4; "The German Brigadier," *Chicago Tribune*, October 21, 1861, 1.
48. Quoted in Vasváry, *Magyar Amerika*, 129.

Chapter Six

1. This chapter is the modified and extended version of my earlier discussion about the subject. See István Kornél Vida, "Magyar katonák a konföderáció hadseregében. Estván Béla szélhámos pályafutása" in Tibor Frank, ed., *Gyarmatokból Impérium: Magyar kutatók tanulmányai az amerikai történelemről* (Gondolat Kiadó: Budapest, 2007), 72–87.
2. Estván, *War Pictures*.
3. András Pogány, *Béla Estván: Hungarian Cavalry Colonel in the Confederate Army* (New York: Kossuth Foundation, 1961); quoted in Lonn, *Foreigners in the Confederacy*, 58.
4. Vasváry, *Lincoln and the Hungarians*, 30.
5. *Béla Estván* Pogány, 5. Pogány possibly gained this information from the Catalogue of the Library of Congress; *The Census of 1860*, Richmond, VA (National Archives, Washington, D.C., m-653); Pogány, *Béla Estván*, 4. He refers to the following book: Béla Kempelen, *Magyar nemes családok (Hungarian Noble Families)* (Budapest: Grill Károly Könyvkiadóvállalata, 1911); Béla Estván to Jefferson Davis (June 10, 1861) National Archives, Washington, D.C., Letters Received by the Confederate Secretary of War, RG 109, M-437, Reel 3, fl378.
6. Béla Estván to Jefferson Davis (June 10, 1861), National Archives, Washington, D.C., Letters Received by the Confederate Secretary of War, RG 109, M-437, Reel 3, fl378.
7. Vasváry Collection, Somogyi Library, Szeged, R1/E, 22.
8. The reason for this was the fact that Turkey had afforded asylum to the Hungarian political refugees who left Hungary after the defeat of the War of Independence by Austria and Russia. *The New York Times*, November 17, 1853, 4; See Dénes Jánossy, *Die Ungarische Emigration und der Krieg im Orient* (Budapest: Ostmitteleuropäische Bibliothek, 1939).

9. Hermann Schuricht, *History of the German Element in Virginia* (Baltimore, 1898–1900), 88–89; *The National Intelligencer*, May 24, 1854.

10. *The Census of 1860*, Richmond, VA (National Archives, Washington, D.C., M-653).

11. Lonn, *Foreigners in the Confederacy*, 175; Pogány, *Béla Estván*, 7.

12. *Chicora, the Original Name of Carolina; Chicora, the Indian name of Carolina*. Barhamville, South Carolina, 1861. Conf. Music 132, Rare Book, Manuscript, and Special Collections Library, Duke University, Durham, N.C.

13. Estván, *War Pictures*, iii.

14. National Archives, M-437, Letters Received by the Confederate Secretary of War, RG 109, Reel 3, f1378.

15. National Archives, M-437, Letters Received by the Confederate Secretary of War, RG 109, Reel 4, f475.

16. *The Standard*, June 29, 1872, 4.

17. *The New York Herald*, July 29, 1863; *The New York Times*, July 19, 1863, 3.

18. Letter of Henry T. Clark to J.P. Benjamin, Secretary of War (March 11, 1862), *OR*, Series IV, Vol. 1, 987.

19. For the firm, see L. Froehlich and B. Estvan, National Archives, M-346, Confederate Papers Relating to Citizens or Business Firms, Roll 287; *OR*, Series IV, Vol. 1, 987; *The Weekly Standard*, April 23, 1862, 3; for the firm's contracts with the Ordnance Office at Raleigh, see National Archives, M-346, Confederate Papers Relating to Citizens and Business Firms, RG109, Roll 327; Lonn, *Foreigners*, 333.

20. Estván, *War Pictures*, 175; Lonn, *Foreigners in the Confederacy*, 166; quoted in Lonn, *Foreigners in the Confederacy*, 33; Schuricht, *History*, II, 88–89; National Archives, M-1371: Registers and Indexes for Passport Applications, Roll 03, No. 8325.

21. *War Pictures from the South* was first published in Britain by Warner and Routledge in 1863. Under the same title in the United States it was published by D. Appleton in 1863, which was soon followed by the German translation under the title *Kriegsbilder aus Amerika: Von B. Estvan, oberst der cavalerie der Conföderirten armee* published in Leipzig by F.A. Brockhaus in 1864; *Daily Richmond Examiner*, February 5, 1864, 6; *The New York Times*, July 19, 1863, 3; *The North American Review* Vol. 97, Issue 201 (October 1863): 583–584.

22. Schuricht, *History*, II, 89.

23. Robert W. Frazer, "Maximilian's Propaganda Activities in the United States, 1865–1866," *Hispanic American Historical Review*, Vol. 24, No. 1 (February 1944), 4–5.

24. Arroyo to Castillo, October 24, 1865. Hausarchiv, Archiv Kaiser Maximilians von Mexiko, Karton 146, Arroyo, fol. 76. Library of Congress facsimiles from Austrian archives, hereafter cited as Arroyo, Hausarchiv; quoted in Frazer, "Maximilian," 19; *The New York Herald*, March 10, 1866, 4.

25. Estván to Fischer (January 12, 1867); Hausarchiv, Archiv Kaiser Maximilians von Mexiko, Karton 144, Berichte von B. Estvan aus New-York, fols. 685–687, hereafter cited as Estvan, Hausarchiv; Frazer, "Maximilian," 20–21.

26. Frazer, "Maximilian," 22.

27. Estván to Castillo (February 23, 1866), Estvan, Hausarchiv, Karton 144, fols. 629–631.

28. Frazer, "Maximilian," 24–25.

29. Frazer, "Maximilian," 27.

30. *The New York Times*, July 6, 1867, 4.

31. Estván to Cassius Marcellus Clay (December 13, 1867), Cassius Marcellus Papers Special Collection, Abraham Lincoln Library and Museum of the Lincoln Memorial University, Harrogate, Tennessee; Estván, B., *Der badische Entwurf einer Wertzuwachssteuer; eine kritische Studie* (Mannheim: J. Bensheimer, ca. 1911); Hardly any documents have been found so far which would reveal further details of Estván's life. There is a trace, however, which may serve as a starting point for additional research. In the database of WorldCat one can find a book written by — according the catalogue — B(éla) Estván; the work titled *Der badische Entwurf einer Wertzuwachssteuer; eine kritische Studie* (*The Draft of a Value Added Tax in Baden; A Criticial Study*) was published in Mannheim, Germany, around 1911. It is highly probable that there is some confusion about the author as — according to the catalogue of the Central Library of Mönchengladbach, Germany — the author of the work is a Dr. Heinrich Peter. This name is included in WorldCat as well, labeled as the person responsible for the publication. If it is taken into consideration that Estván would have been well over 80 by 1911, and no detail in the book refers to the writer, we have no reason to suspect that the author was Estván himself, especially as the book is of highly theoretical nature and to our knowledge the Hungarian had no economic qualification whatsoever. So, it is likely that there is a simple confusion of names here. There is one more thing, however, which would be interesting to track down. In 1872 a book titled *Harry Delaware; or, An American in Germany* was published

in New York, which was written by a Mathilde Estvan. It would be necessary to confirm whether she was in any kind of relationship with Béla or not; Mathilde Estvan, *Harry Delaware, or, An American in Germany* (New York: G.P. Putnam, 1872); for basic information on Mathilde Estvan, see John Foster Kirk, *A Supplement to Allibone's Critical Dictionary of English Literature* (Philadelphia: Lippincott, 1891), I, 562. Unfortunately, no details of her family background are given.

    32. Vasváry Collection, R1E, p. 22, R1, d, 25; Constant von Wurzbach, *Biographisches Lexikon des Kaiserthums Oesterreich: enthaltend die Lebensskizzen der denkwürdigen Personen, welche 1750 bis 1850 im Kaiserstaate und in seinen Kronländern gesetzt haben* (Vienna: Univ-Buchdruckerei [etc.], 1856–91), 24, 406.

    33. Béla Estván, "The Yankee Wounded" in *The Romance of the Civil War* (New York: Macmillan, 1903). The same article was re-published in *Skedaddle*, Vol. 1, Issue 2 (March 3, 2004): 1–3.

Chapter Seven

    1. This chapter is the modified and extended version of my earlier article. See, István Kornél Vida, "'A régóta elnyomottak barátai': Magyar katonák az észak-amerikai polgárháború néger ezredeiben," *Aetas*, 2008/2, 68–82.

    2. General Order No. 25, by Col. L.L. Zulavsky, HQ 82nd Regt. U.S. Infantry (Colored), Barrancas, FL (May 1, 1864), Document G-130, Freedom Archives, Freedmen and Southern Society Project, University of Maryland, College Park, MD.

    3. Tivadar Ács, for instance, concluded about the Hungarians' motivations in his *Magyarok az észak-amerikai polgárháborúban*: "Their blood was not shed for the unity of the North-American states, but for the cause of the liberation of slaves." Ács, *Magyarok az észak-amerikai polgárháborúban*, 122.

    4. Sándor Farkas Bölöni, *Napnyugati utazás: Napló* (Budapest: Helikon, 1984), 467–468.

    5. Madarász, *Emlékirataim,* 297.

    6. Madarász, *Emlékirataim,* 312–313.

    7. Újházy's letter to Ödön Beöthy, *Pesti Napló* (December 14, 1850), quoted in: Ács, *New Buda*, 130.

    8. For information about Brock see, Tom Blake, *Lauderdale County, Alabama: Largest Slaveholders from 1860 Slave Census Schedules*. http://freepages.genealogy.rootsweb.com/%7Eajac/allauderdale.htm; United States. Bureau of Land Management. *Alamaba Pre-1908 Homestead and Cash Entry Patent and Cadastral Survey Plat Index*. General Land Office Automated Records Project, 1996. No. 21163; Újházi's letter to his daughter, Klementin (January 10, 1856), Sír Mező, TX, Hungarian National Archives, Újházi Papers, Budapest, Hungary; Béla Széchenyi, *Amerikai utam* (Pest: G. Emich, 1863), 30–31 and 34–36. For an analysis of the book: Tibor Glant, "Fájdalmas küldetés: Gróf Széchenyi Béla amerikai útja 1862-ben," in Frank Tibor, ed., *Gyarmatokból impérium. Magyar kutatók tanulmányai az amerikai történelemről* (Budapest: Gondolat, 2007), 88–103.

    9. *Chicago Daily Tribune* (September 22, 1857).

    10. *Chicago Daily Tribune* (September 8, 1857); Dale E. Watts, "How Bloody was Bleeding Kansas? Political Killings in Kansas Territory," *A Journal of the Central Plains*, Vol. 18 (Summer 1995): 116–129.

    11. *Népszabadság*, March 11, 2006.

    12. Eugene Kozlay, "The Slave Market," Kozlay Papers, Courtesy of Janet Kozlay; the full text version of the novel is available on the Internet, as well as in the Making America Collection of Cornell University: http://cdl.library.cornell.edu/cgi-bin/moa/moa-cgi?notisid=AGD1642-0041-71.

    13. Here Kozlay referred to John Charles Frémont's Emancipation Proclamation; Kozlay Regimental Diary (July 14, 1862), Shenandoah Valley, Kozlay Papers, Courtesy of Janet Kozlay.

    14. Kozlay Papers (April 19, 1865), South Carolina. Courtesy of Janet Kozlay.

    15. Robert Singleton, "William Gilmore Simms, Woodlands, and the Freedmen's Bureau," *Mississippi Quarterly* (Winter 1996): 19–37.

    16. Öfele, *German-speaking Officers*, 28.

    17. Joseph T. Glatthaar, *Forged in Battle: The Civil War Alliance of Black Soldiers and White Officers* (New York: Meridian Books, 1990), 35.

    18. Glatthaar, *Forged in Battle*, 41.

    19. Glatthaar, *Forged in Battle*, 41.

    20. Rudolph Tauszky to Surgeon General, U.S. Army (August 31, 1863), Personal Papers, Tauszky, RG 94, National Archives, Washington, D.C. I am indebted to William Dobak for clearing up Dr. Tauszky's likely motivations.

    21. Öfele, *German-speaking Officers*, 126; Regimental Papers, 4th USC Heavy Artillery, RG 94, National Archives, Washington, D.C., Inspection Report by John Rush, Act. Med. Insp. (May 30, 1864).

22. Isaac S. Bangs, "The Ullmann Brigade," in *War Papers Read Before the Commandery of the State of Maine, Military Order of the Loyal Legion of the United States* (Portland, ME: Thurston Print, 1898), II, 290–310; Öfele, 189.

23. Military Order of the Loyal Legion of the United States, Commandery of the State of Missouri, in Memoriam Colonel Ignatz Kappner (St. Louis, MO, 1892); Col. I.G. Kappner, 1st Tennessee Heavy Artillery, commanding Fort Pickering, to Lt. Geo. A. Mason, acting assistant adjutant general, U.S. Colored Troops of Tennessee (March 4, 1864), Document G-9, Freedmen and Southern Society Project, University of Maryland, College Park, MD.

24. Findings of a board of examination (April 13, 1863), LR AGO V.S. 1863 M 767, RG 94, NA; Öfele, *German-speaking Officers*, 127.

25. Brig. Gen. E.P. Scammon to Alexander Toplanyi (December 7, 1879), pension file, Alexander S. Toplanyi, RG 15, NA.

26. Vöneky to Maj. H. Hannahs (June 28, 1865), service records, Louis Vöneky, 51st Missouri Infantry, RG 94, NA.

Chapter Eight

1. Ulysses S. Grant, *Personal Memoirs of U.S. Grant* (New York: C.L. Webster, 1885–86).

2. Figyelmessy emlékirata, *Magyarország*, June 10, 1914, 17; *Medical History of the Civil War*, p. 173; *Daily Whig Republican*, Quincy, Illinois, April 8, 1863, 3; *Medical History*, 9, 457.

3. *Historical Magazine*, Vol. 10, Number 4, April 1866; *Philadelphia Inquirer*, June 22, 1865.

4. Edmund Vasváry claimed that there was another Hungarian Congressional Medal recipient, Leopold Karpeles. However, the careful study of genealogical sources makes it clear that Karpeles was born in a Bohemian Jewish family in Prague and had no connections with Hungary. *Rhode Island Jewish Historical Notes*, Vol. 12, No. 1 (November 1995).

5. Xantus, *Travels*, 94.

6. *The United States and Hungary: Paths of Diplomacy, 1848–2006* (Washington, D.C.: U.S. Department of State, 2006), 20.

7. Abraham Lincoln to William H. Seward (January 3, 1865) Library of Congress, Abraham Lincoln Papers, Series I, General Correspondence, 1833–1916, http://memory.loc.gov/cgi-bin/query.

8. *Journal of the Executive Proceedings of the Senate of the United States of America, 1861–62* (hereafter cited as *JEP*) (January 6, 1862), 71; *Daily Evening Bulletin*, December 13, 1862; *JEP*, July 25, 1868, 359.

9. Farkas Újházy's letter to Francis Pulszky, Ancona, Italy (Feb. 16, 1862), quoted in Ács, *New Buda*, 309; "Zeyk Albert József," *Vasárnapi Újság*, July 19, 1885, 461–462.

10. *JEP*, March 3, 1869, 498.

11. Edgar Erskine Hume, *Ornithologists of the United States Army Medical Corps* Vol. I (Baltimore: John Hopkins Press, 1942), 511–512.

12. There are a number of controversies concerning Czapkay. He was a physician who participated as a surgeon in the Hungarian War of Liberation. He was attracted to California by the gold rush and became rich through real estate transactions; he was the owner of the so-called Hungarian Block in San Francisco. He founded a medical and surgical institute in the city, even the Philadelphia College of Medicine conferred upon him an honorary degree. At the same time, there were investigations against him, because he allegedly gave certain medicinal substances to patients to cause miscarriages. For information about him see, *Frank Leslie's Illustrated Newspaper*, October 23, 1858, 330; *Morning Oregonian*, August 6, 1862; *Daily Evening Bulletin*, San Francisco, CA, May 29, 1882.

13. Green Clay to Durando foreign minister (August 31, 1862), Archivio Storico del Ministero degli Affari Esteri, Note delle Legazioni, Stati Uniti, 1860–68, 13491/862 (Busta 784), Green Clay to Durando foreign minister (August 31, 1862).

14. Charles W. Marsh, *Recollections, 1837–1910* (Chicago: Farm Implement News Co., 1910), 144.

15. Allene Chapin, "Colonel Peter Paul Dobozy: Exile in the Ozarks," *West Plains Gazette* 21 (March–April 1983), 36–40.

16. Stephen Beszedits shared the manuscript of his article "The Life and Times of Charles Vidor: A Hungarian Immigrant in Galveston, Texas" with me.

17. Stephen Beszedits, "Frederick Knefler: Hungarian Patriot and American General," http://www.jewish-history.com/civilwar/knefler.html.

18. Vasváry, *Lincoln's Hungarian Heroes*, 5.

19. See "Historical Markers of Springfield and Greene County, Missouri, Marker No. 17, Zagonyi's Charge," http://thelibrary.springfield.missouri.org/lochist/historicalsites/17.cfm.

20. "Patriot Finally Comes Home: Hungarian Hero of Civil War is Buried in Arlington," *Washington Post*, October 24, 1990.

21. Szabad's books included: *Elméleti és gyakorlati angol nyelvtan magyar hangokkal kifejezett kiejtéssel* (1848); *English and Hungarian Dialogues for the Use of Travellers and Students* (1851); *Hungary Past and Present: Embracing its History from the Magyar Conquest to the Present Times* (Edinburgh: A & C Black, 1854); *The State Policy of Modern Europe, from the Beginning of the Sixteenth Century to the Present Time* (Longman, Brown, Green, Longmans and Roberts, 1857); *Two Napoleons and England: Two Pages of History* (London, 1858); *L'Europe avant et aprés la Paix de Villafranca* (Turin, 1859); and *Le Général Grant président de la république américaine par le colonel Éméric Szabad* (Paris, 1868).

22. Pál Békés, *Tévé-játék; New-Buda* (Budapest: Neoprológus, 2002).

23. Péter Bogáti, *Őrnagy úr, keressen magának ellenséget!* (Budapest: Móra kiadó, 1978); *Flamingók Új Budán* (Budapest: Kossuth Kiadó, 1978); *Édes Pólim* (Budapest: Móra Kiadó, 1979); *A mahagóni ember* (Budapest: Móra kiadó, 1986).

24. Gábor Bódy, dir., *Amerikai Anzix* (Balázs Béla Stúdió, 1975); The Béla Balázs Movie Studio was founded in 1959 and soon became the most important workshop of Hungarian experimental film. It made low budget movies, and without the pressure of actually showing the works; this made it possible to avoid communist censorship and allowed experimenting without any compromise.

25. For an excellent study exploring the cultural significance of the Civil War in general, see Will Kaufman, *The Civil War in American Culture* (Edinburgh: Edinburgh University Press, 2006).

Biographical Dictionary

1. Schuricht, *History*, II, 177; Robert E. L. Krick, *Staff Officers in Gray* (Chapel Hill: University of North Carolina Press, 2003), 59; National Archives, M237, Roll 75, No. 1161611.

2. Peter Egill Brownfeld, "The Civil War: A Crucible of Jewish Acculturation Issues,"(Fall 2000), http://www.acjna.org/acjna/articles_detail.aspx?id=42; "An Interesting Narrative: Statement of Col. Adolphus Adler," *The New York Times*, September 4, 1862, 2; Report of Brig. Gen. Henry A. Wise, C.S. Army, of skirmish July 16, and of action at Scarey Creek (July 19, 1861); OR, Chapter 9, Series I, Vol. 2, Serial No. 2, 289.

3. William C. Harris, *Prison-Life in a Tobacco Warehouse at Richmond* (Philadelphia, PA: G.W. Childs, 1862), 56.

4. *The Weekly Raleigh Register*, September 18, 1861, Issue 37, 1; Charles Lanman, ed., *Alfred Ely, Journal of Alfred Ely, a Prisoner of War in Richmond* (New York: Appleton, 1862), 139n.

5. *The New York Times*, September 4, 1862, 2.

6. Gábor Bona, *Tábornokok és törzstisztek a szabadságharcban 1848–49* (Budapest: Heraldika Kiadó, 2000), 195.

7. Anselm Albert service records, National Archives, M390 roll 1; Beszedits, *Hungarians in Missouri*.

8. Frémont's Report (June 12, 1862), OR, Series I, Vol. 12, Part 1, Reports, Serial No. 15, 26.

9. Quoted in Beszedits, *Hungarians in Missouri*.

10. Beszedits, *Hungarians in Missouri*.

11. Civil War Service Records File, Charles Barothy. National Archives, M547 Roll 1; "Lost Hungarian American Civil War Veteran," *Verhovayak Lapja*, February 14, 1941.

12. Vasváry, *Lincoln and the Hungarians*, 16; Marsh, *Recollections*, 144.

13. Leslie Konnyu, *Bettelheim, 1811–70: Trailblazer of Western Civilization* (Kansas: American Hungarian Review, 989), 37; *With Perry to Japan: A Memoir by William Heine* (Honolulu: University of Hawaii Press, 1990), 192; Gerald H. Anderson, ed., *Biographical Dictionary of Christian Missions* (New York: McMillan Reference, 1998), 59.

14. Bernard J.C. Bettelheim (November 11, 1845 to 1910), born onboard the *William Jardine*, an English sailing vessel bound from London to Loochoo Island, Japan (*Cemetery Records of Lin County, Missouri*, Vol. II.); Allan B. Cole, ed., *With Perry in Japan: The Diary of Edward Yorke McCauley* (Princeton: Princeton University Press, 1992), 72; Anderson, *Christian Missions*, 60; on the monument the following can be read about Bettelheim: "First a resident of Rin Kae Ji, later of Gokokuji for eight to nine years; translator of the Bible, interpretor to Perry, early teacher of Jenner's methods of vaccination and pioneer in Western civilization" (http://www.baxleystamps.com/litho/bettelheim_mon.shtml) (December 8, 2007); A.P. Jenkins, ed., *The Journal and Official Correspondence of Bernard Jean Bettelheim, 1845–54* (Naha: Okinawa-ken Kyoikuiinkai, 2005).

15. Anderson, *Christian Missions*, 349737.

16. Andrew B. Booth, *Records of Louisiana Confederate Soldiers and Confederate Commands*, 3 Vols. (New Orleans, LA, 1920), n.p.; Civil War Service Records, NA, M253, Roll 44.

17. Census of 1880, NA, T9, Roll 461, 355; New Orleans, LA Directories, 1890–91 (LA: L. Soards, 1890–91); *New Orleans Death Index, 1908–1917*, State of Louisiana, Secretary of State, Division of Archives, Records Management and History, Vital Records Indices, Baton Rouge, Vol. 159, 394.

18. Vasváry, *Lincoln and the Hungarians*, 35; Vasváry Collection, CsI/47; for a list of Hungarians, including Csermelyi, held captive in Ceuta, see *Daily National Intelligencer*, September 5, 1851.

19. For his service at 82nd Colored Infantry Regiment, see Öfele, *German-speaking Officers*, 131, 133.

20. Gábor Bona, *Hadnagyok és főhadnagyok az 1848/49. évi szabadságharcban* 3 vols. (Budapest: Heraldika Kiadó, 1998), I, 298; Zsigmond Mikár, *Honvéd Schematismus, vagyis az 1848/49-ki honvédseregből 1868-ban még életben volt főtiszteknek névkönyve* (Pest, 1869), 88.

21. Vasváry, *Lincoln and the Hungarians*, 15–16.

22. *Történelmi Lapok* (1894/7–8); Antal Czibula's novel *A nagy diktátor: Az ügysegéd naplója* (Szeged, 1928) is partly about his life.

23. National Archives, M237, Roll 54, No. 30136731; *The New York Herald*, May 28, 1844, and July 1, 1844; for Bayard's biography see http://stonewall.hut.ru/leaders/bayard.htm.

24. Helen J. Eldridge and James E. Eldridge, "History: Second Battle of Cimarron River, July 20th 1848," http://rootsweb.com/~modallas/Cimarron_480720.html/; for the story about "Gabriel's Barbecue" see, http://www.stjohnks.net/santafetrail/research/gabriels-barbeque.html (October 22, 2006).

25. Civil War Service Records, National Archives, M554, Roll 27; Samuel P. Bates, *History of the Pennsylvania Volunteers, 1861–65* (Harrisburg: B. Singerly, State Printer, 1868–1871); for Korponay's report on the skirmish at Point of Rocks, see OR, Series I, Vol. 5, Serial No. 5, 473; Korponay ordered back to his regiment: OR, Series II, Vol. 5, Prisoner of War, etc., Serial No. 118, 375.

26. Obituary: *Historical Magazine*, Vol. 10, Number 4, (April 1866).

27. Stephen Beszedits called my attention to Stephen De Korponay. For his Civil War service records, see *American Civil War Soldiers* (database online). (Provo, UT: Generations Network, 1999); for De Korponay's death notice, see *Philadelphia Inquirer*, June 22, 1865.

28. Gábor Bona, *Kossuth kapitányai* (Budapest: Zrínyi Kiadó, 1988), 671; Tivadar Ács, "Lincoln egyik magyar diplomatája," *Magyar Világ* (December 1965).

29. Jánossy, *Kossuth-emigráció*, II, 674; Károly László, *Napló-töredék* (Budapest: Franklin Társulat, 1887), 82; "Come to Hamilton County," *The Palimpsest* (August 1934): 275–286, 279 (Charles Aldrich, editor of the Hamilton *Freeman*, reprinted some "Notes on Webster City" written on Dec. 15, 1857, by the travelling correspondent of the *Dubuque Express and Herald*) (hereafter cited as "Hamilton County"); *Daily National Intelligencer*, March 13, 1857; *Report of the Superintendent of the Coast Survey* (Washington: Government Printing Office, 1861), 103; in 1860 he was employed for 40 days for a payment of $59.75. See, *Coast Survey: Persons and Pay of Employees, etc. Letter from the Secretary of the Treasury, Transmitting a List of the Number and Names of Persons Employed in the Coast Survey, &c.* December 24, 1860, Serial Set Vol. No. 1097, Session Vol. No. 6, 36th Congress, 2nd Session, H. Exec. Doc. 15.

30. Clerks and other persons employed in the Post Office Department, letter from the postmaster general transmitting a list of clerks and other persons employed in the Post Office Department, January 29, 1862, Serial Set Vol. No. 1129, Session Vol. No. 3, 37th Congress, 2nd Session, H. Exec. Doc. 42, 4–5; *Patent Office Report for the Year 1861*, Serial Set Vol. No. 1132, Session Vol. No. 5, 37th Congress, 2nd Session, H. Exec. Doc, 53 pt. 2, 68; John A. Kasson to A. Lincoln, September 5, 1861 (The Abraham Lincoln Papers, Series 2, Gen. Correspondence, 1858–1864, Library of Congress), http://memory.loc.gov/cgi-bin/query/r?ammem/mal:@field(DOCID+@lit(d4211200)).

31. Farkas Újházy's letter to Pulszky, Ancona (Feb. 16, 1863), cited in Ács, *New Buda*, 309. In this letter Újházy asked Pulszky, "Did not you meet an Albert Zeyk in Paris who was on his way to Italy? He has become a consul in Taranto. My father recommended him to Seward"; *Letter from the Secretary of State, in answer to a resolution of the Senate of the 10th instant, in relation to the number, names, and residences of all consuls and commercial agents appointed under the act of August 2, 1861.* January 13, 1862, Serial Set Vol. No. 1121, Session Vol. No. 4, 37th Congress, 2nd Session, S. Exec. Doc. 12, 4–5.

32. "Zeyk Albert József," *Vasárnapi Újság*, July 19, 1885, 461–462.

33. J.M Howell and H.C. Smith, *History of Decatur County, Iowa* (Chicago: S.J. Clarke Publishing Company, 1915), II, 370–371.

34. Ács, *New Buda*, 71; Howell, *Decatur County*, II, 372; for further information on his life, consult Vasváry Collection, D2, p. 38; for his Civil War career, see National Archives, M541 Roll 7; National Archives, Civil War Pension Files, Application No. 520651.

35. Lajos Lukács, *Az olaszországi Magyar Légió története es anyakönyvei, 1860–67* (Akadémiai Kiadó,

Budapest, 1986), 94; Census of 1910; Census Place: West Plains Ward 1, Howell, Missouri; Roll T624_784, 2a; Öfele, *German-speaking Officers*, 100–101;

36. Civil War Service Records: Peter Paul Dobozy, National Archives, M589 Roll 24; for the charges against him, see Lt. Col. Charles H. Adams to Cpt. T.H. Harris, assistant adjutant general, 16th Army Corps (December 19, 1863), Regimental Papers, 4th USC Heavy Artillery, RG 94, NA; Öfele, *German-speaking Officers*, 126.

37. Chapin, "Dobozy," 36–40; Census of 1870, NA, Roll T9_691, Family History Film: 1254691, page 456c; *South Central Missouri Genealogical Society Newsletter*, Vol. 19, No. 2 (April 2001); Peter P. Dobozy, Plaque Number A-10.

38. Vasváry Collection, D3, 42; Vasváry, *Lincoln and the Hungarians*, 7; "Figyelmessy ezredes emlékiratai," published serially in *Magyarország*, translated and edited by Géza Kacziány (hereafter cited as *Figyelmessy emlékiratai*) *Magyarország* (June 4, 1914), 17.

39. On his Civil War career, see OR, 1st Series, XII, pt. 1, 35; Francis B. Heitman, *Historical Register and Dictionary of the United States Army, 1789–1903*, 2 vols. (Washington, D.C.: Government Printing Office, 1903), I, 388, 339n.

40. Figyelmessy emlékiratai, *Magyarország*, June 10, 1914, 17; Krick, *Stonewall Jackson*, 193; Wayland, "Journal of Tracy," 339.

41. Michael Bacarella, *Lincoln's Foreign Legion: The 39th New York Infantry* (Shippensburg, PA: White Mane, 1997), 258, Appendix III.

42. F. Phisterer, *New York in the War of the Rebellion* (Lyon, 1912), 2200.

43. For his Civil War records, see NA, M551, Roll 41.

44. Bacarella, *Lincoln's Foreign Legion*, 259, Appendix III; Phisterer, *New York*, 2200; Catherine Catalfamo, "The Thorny Rose: The Americanization of an Urban, Immigrant, Working Class Regiment in the Civil War; A Social History of the 39th New York Volunteer Infantry." Ph.D. dissertation (Faculty of the Graduate School of the University of Texas, August 1989) http://www.dmna.state.ny.us/historic/reghist/.../39thInfThornyRoseTOC.htm (December 12, 2007), no pages indicated; Bona, *Hadnagyok*, I, 397–398; William Howard Russell wrote about him, "At dinner, Col. D'Utassy, of the Garibaldi Legion, who gives a curious account of his career, a Hungarian by birth went over from Austrian service...." Russell, *My Diary*, 580.

46. Catalfamo, "The Thorny Rose."

47. Catalfamo, "The Thorny Rose."

48. Cornelia McDonald, *A Diary: With Reminiscences of the War and Refugee Life in the Shenandoah Valley, 1860–1865* (Nashville: Cullom and Ghertner, 1934), 75.

49. For D'Utassy's report on the Harper's Ferry incident, see OR, Chapter 31, Series I, Vol. 19, Part 1, Reports, Serial No. 27, 580; Col. Daniel Cameron on D'Utassy. OR, Chapter 31, Series I, Vol. 19, Part 1, Reports, Serial No. 27, 636.

50. "The Col. D'Utassy Court Martial," *The New York Times*, March 23, 1863, 1.

51. Catalfamo, "The Thorny Rose"; D'Utassy request of pardon to Lincoln, Abraham Lincoln Papers, Series I, General Correspondence, 1833–1916 (January 22, 1864), www.memory.loc.gov/mss/mal/mal1/297/2974100/002.gif).

52. Catalfamo, "The Thorny Rose."

53. *The Democratic Standard*, May 20, 1892.

54. Marie E. Mayer, "Nicholas Fejervary," *The Palimpsest* (June 1928): 189–198; Census of 1860, NA, M653, Roll 340, 509; Harry E. Downer, *History of Davenport and Scott County, Iowa* (Chicago: S.J. Clarke, 1910), 685–710.

55. Mayer, "Fejervary," 195.

56. Vasváry, *Lincoln and the Hungarians*, 7; *Tombstone Records of Scott County, Iowa*, 163. Birth: 1846, Death: March 13, 1863, Cemetery: Oakdale, Davenport, IA; lot. 13 (http://iowagravestones.org).

57. Wilbur Norton, *Centennial History of Madison County, Illinois and Its People, 1812–1912* (Salem, MA: Higginson, 1998), 403–404;

58. Census of 1860, NA, M653, Roll 208, 693.

59. Beszedits, *Hungarians in Missouri*; Stephen Beszedits, "Dr. Rudolph Tauszky: A Hungarian Physician in the American Civil War," *Vasváry Collection Newsletter* (2003/1); Leslie Konnyu, "Eagles of Two Continents," *The American Hungarian Review* Vol. I, No. 3 (July 1963): 1.

60. *Bangor Daily Whig and Courier*, August 8, 1866; *Saturday Herald*, Decatur, IL, December 21, 1889, 8.

61. Beszedits, *Hungarians in Missouri*; Ács, *Számüzöttek*, 34–36; Bona, *Tábornokok*, 329.

62. Beszedits, *Hungarians in Missouri*; General Map of the United States and Their Territory Between the Mississippi and the Pacific Ocean (Kansas, Nebraska and Arizona) (Library of Congress,

Geography and Map Division, Washington, D.C., Call Number: G4050 1859 F5 RR 175); Census of 1880, NA, T9, MSF, Roll 78, Film 1254078, 81b.
  63. *JEP* (July 17, 1862), p. 423; *The New York Times*, September 3, 1861, 3.
  64. Frémont's Report (June 25, 1862), Mountain Dept., OR, Series I, Vol. 12, Part 1, Reports, Serial No. 15, 35.
  65. Census of 1870, NA, M593, Roll 811, Image 54; San Francisco, California, Directories, 1889–1891 (database online), (Provo, UT: Ancestry.com, 2000); Census of 1880, NA, T9, Roll 78, Film 1254078, page 81b; Pension File: Widow: Ida Fiala, January 4, 1912, No. 977.864.
  66. One of the most crucial sources concerning Figyelmessy's life is his memoirs which were translated and edited by Géza Kacziány and published in the daily paper *Magyarország* between April 5 and June 19 in 1914 (hereafter cited as Figyelmessy, "Memoirs"). Similarly to many other memoirs, one has to approach this one with reservations. Eugene Pivány allegedly said about him, "The old man is just like Münchausen." For the most excellent short biography of Figyelmessy, Stephen Beszedits, "The Life and Times of Philip Figyelmessy," *Vasváry Collection Newsletter* (2006/2).
  67. Bona, *Kossuth kapitányai*, 209.
  68. Lengyel, *Americans*, 81.
  69. Dániel Kászonyi, *Magyarhon négy korszaka* (Budapest: Szépirodalmi kiadó, 1977), 344; Lukács, *Magyar Légió*, 68–69, 74; on the Vetter incident see Jenő Koltay-Kastner, ed., *Tanárky Gyula naplója* (Budapest: Szépirodalmi Kiadó, 1961), 99, 259; Kászonyi, *Magyarhon*, 372; Beszedits, "Philip Figyelmessy."
  70. Vasváry, *Lincoln and the Hungarians*, 12; Bona, *Kossuth kapitányai*, 210; Frémont's report on the skirmish at Strasburg (June 12, 1862), OR, Series I, Vol. 12, Part 1, Reports, Serial No. 15, 650.
  71. Abraham Lincoln to William H. Seward (January 3, 1865) Library of Congress, Abraham Lincoln Papers, Series I, General Correspondence, 1833–1916, http://memory.loc.gov/cgi-bin/query.
  72. "Figyelmessy ezredes emlékiratai," *Magyarország*, June 17, 1914, 23.
  73. "Figyelmessy ezredes emlékiratai," *Magyarország*, June 17, 1914, 17.
  74. "Figyelmessy ezredes emlékiratai," *Magyarország*, June 19, 1914, 17–18.
  75. James P. McGuire, *The Hungarian Texans* (University of Texas, San Antonio, 1993), 134.
  76. Census of 1880, NA, T9 Roll 1291, 37; About Finta's purchasing a farm: *Texas General Land Office: Abstracts of all Original Texas Land Titles Comprising Grants and Locations* (Austin, TX, 19 —), Vol. 7, 304, File 1049.
  77. László Fornet, ed., *Fornet Kornél, 1848—as őrnagy, amerikai ezredes élete—The Life of G.C. Fornet Colonel of Lincoln's Army. Adatok az amerikai magyar emigráció életéhez* (Budapest, 1946) (hereafter cited as *The Life of Fornet*), 4–8; Beszedits, "Hungarians in Missouri."
  78. Bona, *Tábornokok*, 333.
  79. *The Life of Fornet*, 9; Ács, *New Buda*, 21; Cornelius Fornet—John Pragay, *The Hungarian Revolution* (New York: Putnam, 1850).
  80. Ács, New Buda, 21; *The New York Times*, October 4, 1852, 7.
  81. Lázár Mészáros to Antal Mészáros (July 24, 1854), in Szokoly, *Mészáros Lázár*, 67.
  82. For his Civil War career, see Civil War Service Records, NA, M550, Roll 8; Beszedits, *Hungarians in Missouri*; *The Life of Fornet*, 25; William S. Stryker, *Record of Officers and Men of New Jersey in the Civil War, 1861–1865* (Trenton, NJ: John L. Murphey, 1876), 761.
  83. Lengyel, *Americans*, 80; reference to him living in Hungary: Edmund Vasváry, "Három amerikai a Dunán," *Szabadság*, December 4, 1963, 1–5.
  84. It is very important not to confuse Alexander Gaal with his namesake, Sándor Gál (1817–1871), Hungarian general in the Hungarian War of Independence, who was actively involved in the Hungarian insurgent activities in Transylvania in the first couple of years after 1849, and was colonel of the Hungarian Legion, but never visited the United States and, of course, did not fight in the War of the Rebellion.
  85. Civil War Service Records, NA, M264, Roll 1.
  86. Census of 1870, NA, M593 Roll 527, 331; New Orleans, LA, Directories, 1890–91, New Orleans, LA: L. Soards, 1890–91; *New Orleans Death Indices, 1908–1917* (Ancestry.com, Provo, UT), Vol. 154, 488; Alexander Gaal, Chalmette National Cemetery, Section 136, Grave 12596.
  87. József Szinnyei, *Magyar Írók élete és munkái* (Budapest: Hornyánszky Viktor császári és királyi udvari Könyvnyomda, 1891–1914), III, 976–978; Dénes Balázs, ed., *Magyar utazók lexikona* (Budapest: Panoráma, 1993), 133; about Gállfy-Gállik in Australia, see Egon Kunz, *Magyarok Ausztráliában* (Budapest: Teleki László Alapítvány, 1997), 45.
  88. Whitelaw Reid, *Ohio in the War* (Cincinnati, Ohio: Moore, Wilstach and Baldwin, 1868), http://www.ohiocivilwar.com/58oh.html (December 12, 2007); about his release, see letter of Brig. Gen. John Adams, Provisional Army, C.S., to Major R.W. Memminger, assistant adjutant general (March 24, 1863), OR, Series II, Vol. 5, Prisoners of War, etc., Serial No. 118, 856.

89. *Official Roster of the Soldiers of the State of Ohio in the War of the Rebellion, 1861–66* (Cincinnati, OH: Wilstach, Baldwin, 1886), V, p. 167; Civil War Service Records, NA, M552, Roll 37.

90. Census of 1870, M593, Roll 782, 470; Szinnyei, *Magyar írók*, III, 979.

91. Bona, *Hadnagyok*, I, 462; Gerster's nephew, Dr. Árpád Gerster, also mentioned his uncle in his memoirs, "My father's youngest brother, Anthony, joined Gorgey's [sic] insurgent army in 1848." A.S. Gerster, *Recollections of a New York Surgeon* (New York: Paul B. Hoeber, 1917), 9.

92. Beszedits, *Hungarians in Missouri*; Hamilton Schuyler, *The Roeblings: A Century of Engineers, Bridge Builders and Industrialists; The Story of Three Generations of an Illustrious Family, 1831–1931* (New York: AMS Press, 1972).

93. For Gerster's service records see NA, M390 Roll 16; Pension Application File: NA, Johanne Gerster, No. 652.436, (1897); Cpt. Anton Gerster to Maj. Gen. Curtis, Fort Smith, Arkansas (April 9, 1864) OR, Series I, Vol. 34, Part III, Correspondence, Serial No. 63, 113; Cpt. Anton Gerster to Cpt. William Hoelcke, St. Louis, MO (Aug. 20, 1864), OR, Series I, Vol. 41, Part II, Correspondence, Serial No. 84, 806.

94. Gerster, *Recollections*, 148; Bona, *Hadnagyok*, I, 462.

95. According to Gábor Bona, he was born in 1826, but the muster roll in his Civil War Service Records indicates that he was born in 1825; Ács, *Magyar úttörők*, 28–29, Vasváry, *Lincoln and the Hungarians*, 3.

96. Bona, *Hadnagyok*, I, 489–490.

97. Perczel, *Naplóm*, I, 86.

98. "Grechenek," *New York Tribune*, April 22, 1852; "Grechenek will stay in U.S.," *Pittsburgh Gazette*, June 2, 1852; "Hamilton County," 279.

99. Vasváry, *Lincoln and the Hungarians*, 3; *Medical History*, XI, 173.

100. Bona, *Hadnagyok*, I, 496. Bona is probably wrong when he writes that Grossinger was born in 1831. There are numerous sources that disprove this.

101. Dancs, *Töredékek*, 90; Bona, *Hadnagyok*, I, 496.

102. Passenger Lists of Vessels Arriving at New York, NY, 1820–1897, NA, M237, Roll 102, No. 1068; Dancs, *Töredékek*, 29, 33.

103. *Universal Masonic Lodge Directory, 1860* (Leon Hyneman, 1860); Census of 1860, NA, M653, Roll 694, 562; *The New York Herald*, July 2, 1860.

104. Civil War Service Records, NA, M551, Roll 56; Brown, Henri Le Fevre, *History of the 3rd Regiment Excelsior Brigade, 72d New York Volunteer Infantry* (Jamestown, NY: Journal Print Co., 1902).

105. Civil War Pension Application Files, Charles Grossinger, Sarah Grossinger (widow), NA, No. 334 181 (1877).

106. Brian McGinty, *Strong Wine: The Life and Legend of Agoston Haraszthy* (Stanford: Stanford University Press, 1998), 38; Census of 1860, NA, M653, Roll 69, 659; Tivadar Ács writes in his *Magyarok az amerikai polgárháborúban* that Gaza was admitted to the naval academy but never finished it. He claims that the Hungarian joined the U.S. Army in 1848 and served for four years. However, based on the available sources, all these cannot be substantiated (Ács, *Magyarok az észak-amerikai polgárháborúban*, 39).

107. McGinty, *Life and Legend*, 387, 425; Civil War Service Records, NA, M551, Roll 59; Haraszthy was among the prisoner-of-war officers who wrote a letter to Maj. Gen Canby, commander of the Military Division of West Mississippi, calling his attention to their miserable condition and the fact that they were not exchanged while they had attempted to escape. February 11, 1865, OR, Series II, Vol. 8, Prisoners of War, Serial Number 121, 207.

108. For the information on the exact date of his death, see *Collections of the State Historical Society of Wisconsin*, Vol. 14 (Madison, WI: The Society, 1888–1931), 80–81.

109. Obituary, Hugo Hillebrandt. *The New York Times*, April 7, 1896, 5, and *New York Herald*, April 7, 1896, 5; for his testimony, see OR, Series I, Vol. 19, Part I, Reports, Serial No. 27.

110. Bacarella, *Lincoln's Foreign Legion*, 258; Civil War Service Records, NA, 636 Roll 19; for Hillebrandt's version of the Harper's Ferry incident, see OR, Series I, Vol. 19, Part I, Reports, Serial No. 27.

111. William F. Fox, *New York at Gettysburg* (Albany, 1900), I, 322.

112. Civil War Service Records, NA, 636, Roll 19; Pension Application Files: Hugo Hillebrandt: Claire Hillebrandt (widow), NA, Application No. 642.084; *JEP* (March 3, 1869), 498.

113. *Brooklyn Directory, 1888–89 and 1889–90* (Brooklyn, NY: Lain and Co., 1889, 1890); for his obituary, see *The New York Times*, April 7, 1896, 5.

114. Bona, *Kossuth kapitányai*, 265; Beszedits, *Hungarians in Missouri*.

115. Bona, *Kossuth kapitányai*, 265.

116. Adams County, Illinois, Marriages, 1851–1900. Records at Quincy, Ill., Family History Micro-Film Library: 1845384–1845385; Census of 1860, NA, M653, Roll 154, 94.

117. Civil War Service Records, NA, M390, Roll 22.
118. Beszedits, *Hungarians in Missouri*; Brigadier General J.M. Schofield to Col. J.C. Kelton (January 2, 1862), OR, Series II, Vol. 1, Prisoners of War, etc., Serial No. 114, 250.
119. Civil War Service Records, NA, M390, Roll 22; *Daily Whig Republican*, Quincy Illinois, April 8, 1863, 3.
120. McGuire, *Hungarian Texans*, 154; Census of 1850, M432, Roll 837, 422; Civil War Service Records, NA, M227, Roll 17.
121. Bona, *Hadnagyok*, II, 131.
122. Bona, *Hadnagyok*, II, 131, Civil War Service Records, NA, M539, Roll 45; some sources claim that he offered his resignation to his commander, Col. Géza Mihalótzy, when he learned that he was ordered to arrest and surrender all fugitive slaves in and around the regiment camp; however, he declined to accept the resignation. This piece of information needs confirmation in the future (Susan M. Papp, *Hungarian Americans and their Communities in Cleveland*. E-Book, 91). http://www.clevelandmemory.org/Hungarians/index.htm) (January 13, 2008).
123. *Edwards' Manitowoc Directory for 1868–1869: Village and County Record* (Manitowoc, WI: Richard N. Cote, 197–); Census of 1880, NA, T9_1434, Roll: 1255434, 165; *Manitowoc Herald*, May 23, 1923.
124. László, *Napló-töredék*, 30; Common Pleas Court, NY County (January 10, 1860), Vol. 252, Record No. 12.
125. László, *Napló-töredék*, 30.
126. Common Pleas Court, NY County (January 10, 1860) Vol. 252 Record No. 12. Soundex Index to Petitions for Naturalization filed in Federal, State, and Local Courts, NA, RG 85.
127. Civil War Service Records, NA, M551, Roll 73.
128. Civil War Service Records, NA, M390, Roll 25; for Kappner's appointment, see General Order No. 45, Memphis, TN (April 15, 1863), OR, Series III, Vol. 3, Union Correspondence, etc., Serial No. 124, 123.
129. Service Records of Volunteer Union Soldiers Who Served with U.S. Colored Troops, NA, M589 Roll 50; Öfele, *German-speaking Officers*, 130–131; Major General Q.A. Gillmore to Major General N.J.T. Dana (December 14, 1864), OR, Series I, Vol. 41, Part IV, Correspondence, Serial No. 86, 857; *In Memoriam Colonel Ignatz Kappner*. Military Order of the Loyal Legion of the United States, Commandery of the State of Missouri (St. Louis, MO, 1892); Kevin R. Hardwick, "'Your Old Father Abe Lincoln is Dead and Damned': Black Soldiers and the Memphis Race Riots of 1866," *Journal of Social History*, Vol. 27 (Fall 1993): 109–128.
130. *Decatur Morning Review*, October 21, 1891, 1.
131. Col. Ignatz G. Kappner, African-American Civil War Memorial, Plaque Number A-8.
132. Bona, *Tábornokok*, 433.
133. Tibor Ács, "A tudományegyetem hadi tanfolyama és a Pesti Egyetemi Légió, 1848–1849," *Hadtörténelmi Közlemények* (2000/3): 515.
134. Dancs, *Töredékek*, 91.
135. Bona, *Tábornokok*, 433.
136. Census of 1860, NA, M653, Roll 161, 829.
137. Civil War Service Records, NA, M551 Roll 77.
138. Civil War Service Records, NA, M550, Roll 13; Stryker, *Record of Officers*, 1394.
139. For an excellent biography on Knefler see Stephen Beszedits, "Frederick Knefler: Hungarian Patriot and American General," Jewish American History on the Net, http://www.jewish-history.com/civilwar/knefler.html; Another biography on him: Marla Hirsch, *Indiana's Great Jewish Civil War General: General Frederick Knefler (April 12, 1834–June 14, 1901)* (Indiana: M. Hirsch, 1979) typescript.
140. Beszedits, "Knefler," 3.
141. Hirsch, *Knefler*, 4.
142. For Knefler's Civil War career, see Civil War Service Records, NA, M540, Roll 42; W.H.H. Terrell, ed., *Indiana in the War of the Rebellion: Report of the Adjutant General* (Indiana Historical Society, 1960), 565, Appendix; Beszedits, "Knefler," 4–12; for the ominous 'note incident' at the battle of Shiloh consult Wiley Sword, *Shiloh: Bloody April* (New York: William Morrow, 1974), 219; Larry J. Daniel, *The Battle That Changed the Civil War: Shiloh* (New York: Simon and Schuster, 1997), 257; James Lee McDonough, *Shiloh: In Hell Before Night* (Knoxville: University of Tennessee Press, 1977), 157.
143. Beszedits, "Knefler," 14.
144. Report of Colonel George F. Dick (November 27, 1863) OR, Series I, Vol. 31, Part II, Reports, Serial No. 55, 307.

145. Recommendation for Promotion by Brigadier General Thomas J. Wood (January 8, 1865) OR, Series I, Vol. 45, Part II, Correspondence, Serial No. 94, 544.
146. Beszedits, "Knefler," 32; Knefler appointed pension agent: *The Daily Inter Ocean*, June 11, 1877, 6; On Knefler's funeral: *Sandusky Daily Star*, June 15, 1901.
147. Bona, *Tábornokok*, 458–459.
148. Gábor Egressy, *Egressy Gábor törökországi naplója. 1849–1850* (Pest: Kozma V., 1851), 128.
149. For the list of passengers transported from Turkey onboard the U.S steamer *Mississippi*, consult *The New York Times*, November 11, 1850; his employment by Genin was mentioned in several sources: Perczel, *Naplóm*, II, 99; Kinizsi, "*Sánta Huszár*," 115; Census of 1860, NA, M653, Roll 816, 817; Kovács was member of the Hungarian committee organized in 1859 with the task to prepare plans for the formation of an expeditionary unit to be sent to Italy. *The New York Times*, May 21, 1859, 5.
150. *New York Herald*, July 20, 1861, 5; Civil War Service Records, NA, M551, Roll 78; Beszedits, *Libby Prison Diary*.
151. *Regimental Journal of Col. Eugene A. Kozlay*. (Transcribed by Janet Kozlay), 58. http://www.dmna.state.ny.us/historic/reghist/civil/infantry/54thInf/54thInfKozlayJournal1.htm (September 21, 2007).
152. Kozlay, *Regimental Journal*, 34.
153. Civil War Service Records, NA, M551, Roll 78.
154. Census of 1880, NA, T9, Roll 873, 98; for his obituary see *The New York Times*, April 17, 1884.
155. A.T. Andreas, *History of Cook County, Illinois: From the Earliest Period to the Present Time* (Chicago, IL: A.T. Andreas, 1884), 762; Bona, *Hadnagyok*, II, 277.
156. Andreas, *Cook County*, 762; Ács, *New Buda*, 74.
157. Civil War Service Records, NA, M539, Roll 50; Pension Application File: Martha A. Kovats. NA, No. 351.759 (March 14, 1887); *JEP, March 4, 1867–November 30, 1867* (March 28, 1867), 130.
158. *Report of the Adjutant General of the State of Illinois* (Springfield, Baker, 1867), I, 488; Andreas, *Cook County*, 762; for his death notice see *The Daily Inter Ocean*, November 9, 1886, 8.
159. For some details on his life, see Janet Kozlay, "The writings of Eugene Kozlay: 19th-century Hungarian Emigré," *Vasváry Collection Newsletter* (2003/1); for an informative article on his life and career, see Zsuzsanna Ágnes Berényi, "Hazakerült egy '48-as evangélikus honvédtiszt hagyatéka," *Evangélikus Élet*, March 26, 2006, http://www.evelet.hu:8080/ujsagok/evelet/archivum/2006/13/051 (October 10, 2007).
160. Bona, *Hadnagyok*, II, 293.
161. Kozlay, "Eugene Kozlay"; I have gained much information about Kozlay from our correspondence with Janet Kozlay. I am very grateful for her devotion for preserving the memory of her ancestor and making the material available for the public; the full-text version of *Secrets of the Past* is available on the Internet as well: http://cdl.library.cornell.edu/cgi-bin/moa/moa-cgi?notisid=AGD1642-0041-71; some other works allegedly written by Kozlay include *The Treasuries of the Ruins, The Grandmother, The Two Sisters, We and They, The Two Idlers*; however, they have not been located so far.
162. For details of his Civil War career, consult Kozlay, *Regimental Journal*; Civil War Service Records, NA, M 551, Roll 78; lots of useful information can be found in Final Report on the Battlefield of Gettysburg (New York at Gettysburg) by the New York Monuments Commission for the Battlefields of Gettysburg and Chattanooga (Albany, NY: J.B. Lyon, 1902); Frederick Phisterer, ed., New York in the War of the Rebellion (Albany: J.B. Lyon, 1912); Fox, *New York at Gettysburg*, I, 402–405.
163. Kozlay, *Regimental Journal*, 65–74.
164. Kozlay, "Eugene Kozlay"; Berényi, "48-as honvédtiszt"; Census of 1880, NA, T9, Roll 843, 517.
165. Beszedits, *Hungarians in Missouri*; Kozlay's descendants, Janet and Douglas Kozlay made every effort to preserve the Kozlay material: they transcribed his regimental journal and saw to the translation of his German and Hungarian letters. These sources offer a unique insight into how an immigrant saw the United States at the time, as well as details about the life of his regiment during the Civil War. Janet and Doug Kozlay donated the entire Kozlay collection to the Petőfi Sándor Museum of Literature in Budapest and were awarded the *Pro Cultura Hungarica* decoration by the Hungarian Department of Culture on March 15, 2006 (*Népszabadság*, March 11, 2006).
166. Julian Kune, *Reminiscences of an Octogenarian Hungarian Exile* (Chicago: By the author, 1911).
167. Kune, *Reminiscences*, 1.
168. Kune, *Reminiscences*, 62–69.
169. Kune, *Reminiscences*, 70; "Julian Kune and the Chicago Historical Society," *Chicago History*, IL, (Spring 1949), 83–87 (hereafter cited as "Kune and CHS").

170. Kune, *Reminiscences*, 72–85; *Chicago Press and Tribune*, Cairo, Oct. 5, 1860; Vasváry, *Lincoln and the Hungarians*, 13; on his interview with Lincoln, see Kune, *Reminiscences*, 87.

171. Burhop, *Twenty Fourth Illinois*; information on Kuné, http://www.burhop.net/24illinois/thebookpage.htm; Civil War Service Records, NA, M539, Roll 50.

172. Burhop, *Twenty Fourth Illinois*.

173. Kune, *Reminiscences*, 115–124.

174. Census of 1880, NA, T9, Roll 186, 213; "Kune and CHS," 86–87; Kune, *Reminiscences*, 125–128.

175. For a short biography of Lang, see Miklós Mihály Nagy, *Magyar hadiutazók* (Budapest: Kornétás Kiadó, 2001), 23–31; *Vasárnapi Újság* (No. 7, 1876), 102; Civil War Service Records, NA, M551, Roll 80; Henrik Láng, "Egy magyar hadifogoly a confoederált államokban," *A Hon*, January 6, 1865, 2; *Vasárnapi Újság*, (No. 9, 1876), 135; *Vasárnapi Újság*, November 28, 1875, 762; Application Files for Civil War Pensions, NA, Application No. 666778.

176. Census of 1870, NA, M593, Roll: 203, p. 279; Chicago Voter Registration (Illinois State Archives, Roll 25, 1888 and 1892).

177. Beszedits, "Tauszky"; Ács, *Száműzöttek*, 229.

178. *Medical History*, XI, 349–350.

179. *Medical History*, Part III, Vol. II, Chapter 15, "Transportation of the Wounded: Ambulance Wagons."

180. *The New York Times*, August 22, 1917, 7; Loretto Dennis Szucs and Sandra Hargreaves, eds., *Research in Directories. The Guidebook of American Genealogy* by Gordon Lewis Remington (Salt Lake City, UT, 1997); Civil War Service Records, M551, Roll 81.

181. *The New York Times*, August 22, 1917; Emanuel Lederer to Augustin Daily, Augustin Daily Papers, Folger Shakespeare Library, Washington, D.C., Y.c. 4157 (1–8).

182. Stephen Beszedits, "Notable Hungarians of the Civil War," http://www.hccc.org/A2e/A20303c.shtml; Census of 1860, NA, M 653, Roll 102, 576.

183. Beszedits, "Notable Hungarians"; Perczel, *Naplóm*, I, 157.

184. László, *Napló-töredék*, 82.

185. *New York Herald*, July 20, 1861, 5; Beszedits, "Notable Hungarians"; Census of 1870, NA, M593, Roll 89, 142.

186. Beszedits, "Hungarians in Missouri"; Vasváry, *Lincoln and the Hungarians*, 6.

187. For references on Majthenyi's Civil War service, see OR, Series I, Vol. 40, Part III, Serial No. 82, 728; Civil War Service Records, NA, M540, Roll 46.

188. OR, Series I, Vol. 42, Part I, Serial No. 87, 215.

189. Beszedits, "Hungarians in Missouri."

190. Lillian May Wilson, "Some Hungarian Patriots in Iowa," *The Iowa Journal of History and Politics* (October 1913), 494.

191. Bona, *Hadnagyok*, II, 471.

192. Dancs, *Töredékek*, 29; László, *Napló-töredék*, 190.

193. Civil War Service Records, NA, M551, Roll 95; 45th New York Volunteers Regiment Muster Roll, http://www.enter.net/~alw/45th/images/45off.gif) (March 8, 2006).

194. Census of 1880, NA, T9, Roll 870, p. 332; *Directory of New York City, 1890* (Orem, UT: Ancestry, Inc., 1999); Bona, *Hadnagyok*, II, 472, Civil War Pension Application Files, NA, No. 1106335, Date: 1892.

195. Census of 1880, NA, T9, Roll 131, 421; Bona, *Kossuth kapitányai*, 408.

196. For the conditions of leaving Britain for America see, Miklós Kiss to Lajos Kossuth (March 26, 1852), London. Jánossy, *Kossuth emigráció*, II, 709–711. Loosey's Report of the list of the Hungarian Emigrants (June 23, 1852) to Buol (Bericht No. 638, Haute Police, Amerika, 1852, HHStA., Vienna); Kinizsi, "*Sánta Huszár*," 81, 120.

197. Beszedits, *Hungarians in Missouri*; for Mészáros's Civil War service records see, NA, M551, Roll 96; M 390, Roll 32; Report of Brig. Gen. Franz Sigel, Pea Ridge, AR (March 15, 1862), OR, Series I, Vol. 8, Serial No. 8, 209; for Burns and Mészáros see William S. Burns' Papers, William L. Clements Library, University of Michigan, Schoff Civil War Collection, Soldiers' Letters, Subject Index, 11–15.

198. Civil War Service Records, NA, M264, Roll 1.

199. U.S. Bureau of Land Management, Gen. Land Office Automated Records Project, Florida Land Records, Doc. No. 535, Statutory Reference: 12 Stat. 392; Census of 1880, NA, T9, Roll 131, 421.

200. Bona, *Kossuth kapitányai*, 411.

201. Kászonyi, *Magyarhon*, 291–292.

202. Loosey's Report of the List of the Hungarian Emigrants (June 23, 1852) to Buol (Bericht No. 638, Haute Police, Amerika, 1852, HHStA., Vienna).

Notes — Biographical Dictionary

203. The original of the letter is in the custody of Chicago Historical Society. Most of the seconday sources dealing with various aspects of Hungarian-American historical links, however, published a copy or the transcript of it: e.g. Lengyel, *Americans*, 74–75, about the letter, "Collector's Piece: Mihaloczy's Letter to Lincoln," *Chicago History*, Vol. II (Fall 1949), 134.

204. Burhop, *Twenty Fourth Illinois*.

205. Theodore J. Karamanski, "Civilians, Soldiers and the Sack of Athens, Alabama," *Illinois History Teacher*, Volume 4: 2, (1997): 48–55.

206. For the regimental history of the 24th Illinois, see 24th Illinois Regiment History, Adjutant General's Report, http://www.rootsweb.com/~ilcivilw/history/024.htm (February 10, 2007); for Mihalóczy's Civil War service records see NA, M539, Roll 61; Mihalótzy's report on an expedition led by him in the vicinity of Chattanooga: OR, Series I, Vol. 32, Part I, Reports, Serial No. 57, 103; Case No. 1320, *Medical History*, IX, 457; General Order by Brigadier General Whipple (June 29, 1864) OR, Series I, Vol. 32, Part III, Correspondence, Serial No. 59, 520.

207. Bona, *Hadnagyok*, II, 438–439; Census of 1860, NA, M653, Roll 350, 100; Census of 1870, NA, M593, Roll 131, 685.

208. William E. Connelley, *Standard History of Kansas and Kansans* (Chicago: Lewis, 1918), II, 909; *Leavenworth, Kansas Voter Registration, 1859* (Graden Debra, *Leavenworth Voters, 1859*) (Orem, UT: Ancestry, Inc., 1998), 96.

209. *American Civil War General Officers Historical Data Systems*. Kingston, MA; Civil War Pension Application Files, Charles Mundee, Alice Mundee. NA, File No. 325552.

210. OR, Series I, Vol. 46, Part I, Reports, Serial No. 95, 971.

211. Brvt. Major Gen. Getty to Major C.H. Whittelsey (April 20, 1865), OR, Series I, Vol. 46, Part I, Reports, Serial No. 95, 958.

212. Florida Census of 1870, NA, M593, Roll 685.

213. For an account of his death see *The Daily Gazette*, June 13, 1871.

214. Jánossy, *Kossuth emigráció*, II, 671–672.

215. Census of 1860, NA, M653, Roll 65, 289.

216. Civil War Service Records, NA, M533, Roll 5.

217. Bona, *Kossuth kapitányai*, 441; Beszedits, *Hungarians in Missouri*.

218. Bona, *Kossuth kapitányai*, 441; Perczel, *Naplóm*, II, 229.

219. Kinizsi, "*Sánta Huszár*," 56–57.

220. *New York Daily Times*, November 11, 1851, 1; *New York Daily Times*, May 21, 1852, 2.

221. Census of 1860, NA, M653, Roll 647, 247; Concerning Lina Nemett see Census of 1920, NA, T625, Roll 116, 6a; Missouri Birth and Death Record Database, Permanent Record of Deaths, Missouri State Archives, St. Louis, MO, Roll C10364.

222. Civil War Service Records, NA, M390, Roll 35; Beszedits, *Hungarians in Missouri*; Frederick H. Dyer, *A Compendium of the War of the Rebellion* (Des Moines, Iowa: Dyer, 1908), 1312; Nemett's report on the Pea Ridge Campaign, OR, Series I, Vol. 8, Serial No. 8, 245; Heitman, *Historical Register*, II, 132.

223. Perczel, *Naplóm*, II, 229; Census of 1880, NA, T9, Roll 192, 386; *The Daily Inter Ocean*, August 13, 1895, 8; Civil War Pension Application Files, Lina Nemett. NA, Application File No. 280554 (1881).

224. Perczel, *Naplóm*, I, 6; Beszedits, *Hungarians in Missouri*.

225. Bona, *Tábornokok*, 563–564.

226. *New York Daily Times*, November 11, 1851.

227. Perczel also wrote about his encounter with Sedgwick, Perczel, *Naplóm*, II, 120, 123; Sedgwick quoted in Beszedits, *Hungarians in Missouri*.

228. Perczel, *Naplóm*, II, 129, 161–162.

229. Beszedits, *Hungarians in Missouri*; Perczel, *Naplóm*, II, 168–182.

230. Perczel, *Naplóm*, II, 184–185.

231. *The History of Jefferson County, Iowa, 1879* (Chicago: Western Historical Co., 1879), 235.

232. Report of 2nd Lieutenant L.D. Immel, 1st Missouri Light Artillery, commanding 12th Wisconsin Battery. (September 20, 1862), OR, Series I, Vol. 17, Part I, Reports, Serial No. 24, 108; for Perczel's own report on the battle see, OR, Series I, Vol. 17, Part I, Reports, Serial No. 24, 109.

233. Beszedits, Hungarians in Missouri; Heitman, *Historical Register*, II, 136.

234. Bona, Tábornokok, 564.

235. Maria Berenyi, "A Romanian from Gyula: A Freedom Fighter for Hungary and an American General and Consul," *Transylvanian Review*, Vol. 7, No. 4, (Winter 1998): 133–139; Ladislaus Újházi to Ödön Beöthy, first published in *Pesti Napló* (November 27, 1850), cited in Perczel, *Naplóm*, II, 212; Pomutz to Pulszky (February 16, 1861), in Ács, *New-Buda*, 291–295.

236. Berenyi, "A Romanian," 133–134; Ács, *New Buda*, 15–16.
237. Wilson, "Hungarian Patriots," 502; quoted in Berenyi, "A Romanian," 135; Census of 1850, NA, M432, Roll 183, 329.
238. Civil War Service Records, NA, M541, Roll 21; *JEP* (February 13 to July 28, 1866), 790; Heitman, *Historical Register*, II, 137.
239. Homer L. Calkin, "Iowans in the State Department and in the Foreign Service," *The Palimpsest*, February 1956, 104.
240. *The American Romanian Orthodox Youth News* (September 2004).
241. For reliable biographies of Pulitzer, consult Denis Brian, *Pulitzer: A Life* (New York: J. Wiley, 2001) and Nancy Whitelaw, *Joseph Pulitzer and the New York World* (Greensboro, N.C.: Morgan Reynolds, 2000); I also made use of András Csillag's excellent biography in Hungarian, *Joseph Pulitzer és az amerikai sajtó*.
242. Csillag, *Pulitzer*, 26–28.
243. George S. Johns, "Joseph Pulitzer," *Missouri Historical Review* (1930–31/5), 203; Csillag, *Pulitzer*, 29–30.
244. "Joseph Pulitzer Dies Suddenly," *The New York Times*, October 30, 1911, 1.
245. Csillag, *Pulitzer*, 33–45.
246. Census of 1880, NA, T9, Roll 734, 392.
247. William Randolph Hearst, "Praise of Pulitzer as a Journalist," *The New York Times*, October 30, 1911.
248. There are several documents in the custody of the Vasváry Collection at Somogyi Library, Szeged, Hungary. Most of these pieces of information were collected by Spencer Radnich, a direct descendant of the family, and Stephen Beszedits, by whose courtesy the copies got into the possession of the collection. Mária Kórász from Vasváry Collection secured for me copies of the relevant documents; Bona, *Kossuth kapitányai*, 490.
249. Passenger Lists of Vessels Arriving at New York, NY, 1820–1897, NA, M 237, Roll 85, No. 3068579.
250. Census of 1850, NA, M432, Roll 29, 294; for an account of a Hungarian participants in the expedition, see Louis Schlesinger, "Personal Narrative of Louis Schlesinger," *United States Magazine and Democratic Review*, Part I (September 1852), 210–225; Part II (October 1852), 352–369; Part III (November–December 1852), 553–592; Emeric Radnich to Kossuth (May 2, 1852), Jánossy, *Kossuth emigráció*, II, 811–812; John Barringer's letter to Radnich was published in *The New York Daily Times* (June 15, 1853), 3.
251. *The New York Herald*, July 2, 1860; Ács, *Magyar úttörők*, 135.
252. I have been able to reconstruct this phase of Radnich's life through my regular correspondence with Stephen Beszedits.
253. Stephen Beszedits located the obituary in the public library in Leon (seat of Decatur County). It is quite likely that it was published in a Leon paper and written by Francis Varga (hereafter cited as "Radnich Obituary"); Ács, *New Buda*, 61.
254. Passenger Lists of Vessels Arriving at New York, NY, 1820–1897, NA, M237, Roll 86, No. 3106388; Census of 1850, NA, M432, Roll 29, 295.
255. "Radnich Obituary"; Civil War Pension Files, Application No. 1293899 (1902).
256. *Grave Stone Records of Decatur County, Iowa* (Des Moines, W.P.A., 1939), 110.
257. Civil War Service Records, NA, M390, Roll 41; M539, Roll 77; Beszedits, *Hungarians in Missouri*; William B. Bell's Report (August 24, 1864), OR, Series I, Vol. 39, Part I, Reports, Serial No. 77, 479; Rombauer appointed chief-of-artillery at Memphis, TN (February 11, 1865), OR, Series I, Vol. 48, Part I, Reports, Correspondence, Etc., Serial No. 101, 815; on his muster-out, see Memphis, TN (August 18, 1865), OR, Series I, Vol. 49, Part II, Correspondence, Etc. Serial No. 104, 1102.
258. Cyrus R. Truitt, *History of Novinger, Mo.* (Novinger, Missouri, 1972), 4.
259. Bona, *Hadnagyok*, III, 51.
260. Beszedits, *Hungarians in Missouri*; Ács, *New Buda*, 272.
261. Civil War Service Records, NA, M390, Roll 41; Heitman, *Historical Register*, II, 142; for his service at 5th Regiment City Guard see OR, Series I, Vol. 41, Part III, Correspondence, Serial No. 85, 657; Pension Application Files., NA, Application No. 1846169 (1906).
262. Beszedits, *Hungarians in Missouri*; Census of 1870, NA, M593, Roll 811, 442; Rombauer, *Union Cause*; Robert Rombauer, *Biographical Notes of Robert J. Rombauer, 1917* (St. Louis, Mo.: R.J. Rombauer, 1922).
263. For his marriage records, consult *St. Louis Genealogical Society, St. Louis Marriage Index, 1804–1876* (St. Louis, MO: St. Louis Gen. Society, 1999), VIII, 249; Bellefontaine Cemetery, St. Louis, MO,

Notes — Biographical Dictionary 233

Plot: Block 24, Lot 2524. Accessible on the Internet along with photos of his gravestone: http://www.find agrave.com/cgi-bin/fg.cgi?page=gr&GRid=18217 (October 20, 2007).

264. Beszedits, *Hungarians in Missouri*; the major source for Roderick Rombauer's life is his autobiography: Rombauer, *History of a Life*.

265. Béla Forgáts, "Rombauer Tivadar, az 1848–49. évi szabadságharc fegyvergyári igazgatója és a Rimamurány-Salgótarjáni Vasmű Rt. Alapítója," *Bányászati és Kohászati Lapok*, June 1, 1940, 177–182.

266. Ács, *New Buda*, 62; Rombauer, *History of a Life*, 15–17.

267. Rombauer, *History of a Life*, 19; Beszedits, *Hungarians in Missouri*.

268. Beszedits, *Hungarians in Missouri*; Rombauer, *History of a Life*, 20–21; for his Civil War service records see NA, M390, Roll 41.

269. Beszedits, *Hungarians in Missouri*; *Harvard University Directory, 1913* (Harvard University Press, Harvard Alumni Association: Boston, MA, 1913); Rombauer, *History of a Life*, 142.

270. Arthur Paul Moser, Directory of Towns, Villages and Hamlets, Past and Present, of Butler County, Missouri (S.I.: s.n., 1975), 36.

271. Beszedits, *Hungarians in Missouri*; Lists of Vessels Arriving at New York, NY, 1820–1897, NA, M237, Reel 104, List 1307 (September 6, 1851), Vessel: *Copernicus*.

272. Civil War Service Records, NA, M390, Roll 41; M264, Roll 1; for his promotion see General Order No. 37, April 13, 1865, OR, Series I, Vol. 49, Part II, Correspondence, Etc. Serial No. 104, 354.

273. Beszedits, *Hungarians in Missouri*; Rombauer, *History of a Life*, 142.

274. For biographical notes see Perczel, *Naplóm*, I, 165; József Szinnyei, Sr. *Id. Szinnyei József komáromi histórái* (Szüpex: Tatabánya, 1997), 195–201 (hereafter cited as Szinnyei, *Komárom*).

275. Vasváry, *Lincoln and the Hungarians*, 14.

276. Kinizsi, "Sánta Huszár," 108; Vasváry, *Magyar Amerika*, 122–124.

277. Civil War Service Records, NA, M507, Roll 10.

278. Szinnyei, *Komárom*, 200; Census of 1880, NA, T9, Roll 123, 460.

279. Vasváry, *Lincoln*, 14; Szinnyei, *Komárom*, 201; János Vadona, *Az öt világrészből* (Budapest: Hornyánszky V. Könyvny, 1893), 256.

280. Bona, *Hadnagyok*, II, 72.

281. McGuire, *Hungarian Texans*, 161–162; Heitman, *Historical Register*, II, 143; Civil War Pension Application Files, NA, No. 588.502 (1899).

282. *Houston Directory 1882–1895* (Houston, TX: Morrison and Fourmy, 1894), n.p.

283. Brian Temple, *The Union Prison at Fort Delaware* (Jefferson, NC: McFarland, 2002), 32; Census of 1880, NA, T9, Roll 513, 28.

284. Lengyel, *Americans*, 77–79.

285. Temple, *Fort Delaware*, 32.

286. Chaille-Long, Col., *My Life in Four Continents* (London: Hutchinson, 1912), 9.

287. Chaille-Long, *My Life*, 10n.

288. For his appointment see OR, Series I, Vol. 25, Part II, Correspondence, Etc. Serial No. 40, 211.

289. J.G. DeRoulac Hamilton, "The Prison Experiences of Randolph Shotwell," *The North Carolina Historical Review* (July 1925), 345–346; Isaac W.K. Handy, *United States Bonds: A Journal of Current Events During an Inprisonment of Fifteen Months at Fort Delaware* (Baltimore: Turnbull Brothers, 1874), 28; "'The Prison Experience of a Confederate Soldier' by Abram Fulkerson, Late Col. 63rd Tennessee Infantry, Army of Northern Virginia," *Southern Historical Society Papers* (Vol. 22), 129; Crane's report quoted in Temple, *Fort Delaware*, 46; Ibid., 144.

290. Congressional Cemetery, Washington, D.C.: Range 84, Site 108.

291. For biographical information on Schoney consult his obituary: *The New York Times*, February 19, 1914, 9.

292. Beszedits, "Tauszky"; *Medical History*, IX, 159; for information about Schoney's Civil War career, consult Civil War Pension Application Files, NA, No. 1027.898 (1914); Census of 1880, NA, Roll 896, 45; Schoney as member of the New York Microscopical Society: *The New York Times*, February 4, 1882, 2.

293. Stephen Beszedits's article is the definite source to turn to for information on Semsey: "Charles Semsey: Hungarian Patriot, Union Soldier, and Ellis Island Official," *Vasváry Collection Newsletter* (2004/1).

294. Beszedits, "Semsey"; Bona, *Hadnagyok*, II, 135–136.

295. Ács, *Kossuth papja*, 184.

296. Beszedits, "Semsey"; Census of 1860, NA, M653, Roll 798, 994.

297. Heitman, *Historical Register*, II, 145; Civil War Service Records, NA, M551, Roll 126.

298. Census of 1880, NA, T9, Roll 879, 17.

299. *The New York Times* (September 30, 1872), 1; *The New York Times* (September 23, 1880), 5.
300. Vasváry, *Magyar Amerika*, 148.
301. Civil War Service Records, NA, M551, Roll 133; Civil War Pension Application Files, NA, No. 351622, (1880).
302. Eugene Pivány, "Sólyom C. Lajos emléke, 1836–1913," *Budapesti Hírlap*, April 8, 1914; Vasváry, *Magyar Amerika*, 149–150; Census of 1880, NA, T9 Roll 512, 408.
303. Vasváry, *Lincoln and the Hungarians*, 5; Perczel, *Naplóm*, II, 162, 241; Ács, *New Buda*, 61; Spelletich's letter to Kossuth (June 8, 1852); Jánossy, *Kossuth emigráció*, II, 913–914.
304. Civil War Service Records, NA, M541, Roll 25; Vasváry, *Lincoln*, 5.
305. Quoted in *Davenport Daily Gazette*, April 14, 1862.
306. Civil War Service Records, NA, M390, Roll 45; Stephen Spelletich, Oakdale Cemetery, Davenport, No Dates, Lot 130, add. 13. *Tombstone Records Adm. Graves Registration Project* (Washington, D.C., n.p.), 737.
307. Beszedits, *Libby Prison Diary*; Tibor Frank, "Marx egy anonim forrása," in Tibor Frank, *Marx és Kossuth* (Budapest: Magvető kiadó, 1985), 107–127; Emeric Szabad, *Elméleti és gyakorlati angol nyelvtan magyar hangokkal kifejezett kiejtéssel* (1848) and *English and Hungarian Dialogues for the Use of Travellers and Students* (1851).
308. Emeric Szabad, *Hungary Past and Present: Embracing its History from the Magyar Conquest to the Present Times* (Edinburgh: A & C Black, 1854); *The State Policy of Modern Europe, from the Beginning of the Sixteenth Century to the Present Time* (Longman, Brown, Green, Longmans and Roberts, 1857); *Two Napoleons and England: Two Pages of History* (London, 1858).
309. *L'Europe avant et aprés la Paix de Villafranca* (Turin, 1859); on his service in the Hungarian Legion, see Lukács, *Magyar Légió*, 68–69.
310. Civil War Pension Application Files, NA, No. 119.305 (1886); Beszedits, *Libby Prison Diary*, 68–72.
311. Emeric Szabad, *Le Général Grant président de la république américaine par le colonel Éméric Szabad* (Paris, 1868).
312. Census of 1880, NA, T9, Roll 1332, 320; Texas General Land Office, Abstracts of All Original Land Titles Comprising Grants and Locations, Austin, TX, 19 —, File 16986 (May 26, 1886), Vol. 36, Patent 127; Beszedits, *Libby Prison Diary*, 73.
313. Census of 1870 (http://www.ancestry.com) (February 10, 2007).
314. Kinizsi, "*Sánta Huszár*," 79; Ács, *New Buda*, 62.
315. Civil War Service Records, NA, M552, Roll 107.
316. Census of 1870 (http://www.ancestry.com) (December 11, 2007); U.S. Veterans' Gravesites, 1775–2006 (http://www.ancestry.com) (December 11, 2007).
317. Civil War Service Records, NA, M551, Roll 138; Civil War Pension Application Files, NA, No. 1 702.883 (1911); Loosey's report of the list of the Hungarian emigrants—June 23, 1852, to Buol (Bericht No. 638, Haute Police, Amerika, 1852, HHStA., Wien), cited in Jánossy, *Kossuth emigráció*, II, 956–963.
318. Passenger Lists of Vessels Arriving at New York, NY, 1820–1897, NA, M237, Roll 90, No. 14304175;
319. Census of 1860, NA, M653, Roll 652, 461.
320. *Annual Report of the Adjutant General of Missouri* (December 31, 1863), NA, M82, UA 43, 338.
321. "Egy magyar iparos Törökországban s Amerikában," *Hazánk s a Külföld*, April 4, 1867, 214–216; April 11, 1867, 234–236; April 18, 1867, 247–251 and April 25, 1867, 267–268 (hereafter cited as "Magyar Iparos").
322. "Magyar iparos," I, 215–216; II, 234–236; Civil War Service Records, NA, M544, Roll 39.
323. "Magyar iparos," III, 248–251; Civil War Service Records, NA, M387, Roll 4.
324. "Magyar iparos," IV, 234.
325. Bona, *Kossuth kapitányai*, 313.
326. Civil War Service Records, NA, M; Catalfamo, "The Thorny Rose," no pages indicated.
327. Takats to D'Utassy (June 15, 1861), D'Utassy Papers, New York Historical Society, New York; about Takats's role in the mutiny, see *New York Herald*, July 16, 1861, 2; *The Washington Star*, July 9, 1861.
328. *Történelmi Lapok* (1894), 200.
329. The definite biography to turn to is Stephen Beszedits's "Dr. Rudolph Tauszky: A Hungarian Physician in the American Civil War" published in *Vasváry Collection Newsletter* (2003/1).
330. Rudolph Tauszky to the surgeon general, U.S. Army (August 31, 1863), Personal Papers, Tauszky, RG 94, National Archives.

331. Beszedits, "Tauszky."
332. *The New York Times*, November 24, 1884, 2.
333. Beszedits, "Tauszky."
334. Tauszky's shooting was widely covered in the New York papers: "Dr. Tauszky's Two Shots," *The New York Times*, January 5, 1885, 8; His insanity: *The New York Times*, January 23, 1885, 8, and *The New York Times*, January 25, 1885, 4; for his obituary see *The New York Times*, November 24, 1884, 2.
335. Census of 1870, NA, M593, Roll 791, 308; Ács, *Észak-amerikai polgárháború*, 49.
336. Civil War Service Records, NA, M550, Roll 23; Stryker, *Record of Officers*, 309.
337. *The New York Times*, September 19, 1902, 9.
338. Bona, *Kossuth kapitányai*, 610.
339. József Szinnyei, *Komárom 1848/49-ben: Napló-jegyzetek* (Budapest: Aigner Lajos, 1887), 318.
340. Civil War Service Records, NA, M551, Roll 141; Findings of a board of examination (April 13, 1863), LR AGO V.S. 1863, NA, RG 94, M767.
341. Öfele, *German-speaking Officers*, 127.
342. Civil War Service Records, NA, M589, Roll 87; Öfele, *German-speaking Officers*, 127; Brig. Gen. E.P. Scammon to Alexander Toplanyi (December 7, 1879), Pension File, Alexander S. Toplanyi, NA, RG 15.
343. Information on marriage and his child derives from *Genealogy of a Stanton family from New York City* (www.Stanton-IIc.com) (March 12, 2007); *The New York Times*, September 30, 1872, 1; *St. Louis Globe-Democrat*, June 12, 1884.
344. *The New York Times*, December 2, 1873, 2; *The New York Times*, December 13, 1873, 5; *The New York Times*, January 10, 1874, 8; *The New York Times*, January 7, 1894, 10.
345. African American Civil War Memorial, Alexander S. Toplanyi, Plaque A-9.
346. McGuire, *Hungarian Texans*, 146; Texas Land Title Abstracts, Certificate No. 697 (www.ancestry.com) (April 1, 2006).
347. Civil War Service Records, NA, M227, Roll 37.
348. *The Milwaukee Journal*, October 24, 1891, 11; *History of Fresno County, CA* (Historic Records Co., 1919, Los Angeles, CA), Vol. 2, 1311–1312.
349. *Wisconsin Patriot*, September 21, 1861; *North American and United States Gazette*, May 9, 1850.
350. *North American and United States Gazette*, May 9, 1850; *Wisconsin Patriot*, September 21, 1861; *The Milwaukee Journal*, October 24, 1891, 11.
351. Civil War Service Records, NA, M559, Roll 31; "The Stubborn Colonel," *The Union Standard*, Vol. 11, No. 9 (October 2003), 7; Pension Application Files, NA, Application No. 225 543 (1876); about the hearsay on the attempt to murder him, consult Vasváry Collection, V1a/22.
352. *JEP* (January 6, 1862), 71; *Daily Evening Bulletin*, December 13, 1862; *JEP* (July 25, 1868), 359.
353. *Daily Evening Bulletin*, May 9, 1873; San Francisco National Cemetery, Section OSA, Row 69, Site 8.
354. McGuire, *Hungarian Texans*, 121.
355. McGuire, *Hungarian Texans*, 123.
356. Alexander Varga, Census of 1870, NA, M593, Roll 1575, 168; Census of 1880, NA, T9, Roll 1291, Film: 1255291, 583; *San Antonio City Directory, 1891, 1892–94* (San Antonio: Jules A. Appler, 1891, 1892).
357. McGuire, *Hungarian Texans*, 122.
358. *Galveston Daily News*, October 21, 1875.
359. McGuire, *Hungarian Texans*, 123.
360. Census of 1870, NA, M593, Roll 1575, 260; Census of 1880, NA, T9, Roll 1291, Film: 12555291, 83b; On him serving on jury, see *The Galveston Daily News*, January 21, 1892.
361. McGuire, *Hungarian Texans*, 124; Confederate Soldiers Civil War Service Records, NA, M227, Roll 37.
362. Census of 1870, NA, M593, Roll 1575, 119; McGuire, *Hungarian Texans*, 124.
363. Ács, *Magyarok az észak-amerikai polgárháborúban*, 104; Bona, *Hadnagyok*, III, 457; Kinizsi, "*Sánta huszár*," 108.
364. Jánossy, *Kossuth emigráció*, II, 671–672.
365. Census of 1860, NA, M653, Roll 1015, 36 and 49.
366. For Vertessy's Civil War service records see NA, M552, Roll 112; Henry A. and Kate B. Ford, *History of Hamilton County* (Cleveland, OH: L.A. Williams, 1881); for Vertessy's career consult Chapter 11, "Military History of Hamilton County."

367. Ács, *Magyarok az észak-amerikai polgárháborúban*, 105; Census of 1880, NA, T9, Roll 1436, 400; Wood National Cemetery, Milwaukee, WI, Plot 13 167.

368. Stephen Beszedits shared the text of his unpublished excellent biography of Charles Vidor, "The Life and Times of Charles Vidor"; McGuire, *Hungarian Texans*, 135.

369. Beszedits, "Vidor," 3.

370. Civil War Service Records, NA, M227, Roll 37; General and Staff Officers, C.S.A., NA, M818, Roll 24; Vidor gained a special mention in Maj. Gen. Carter L. Stevenson's report of the campaign in Tennessee at the end of 1864: OR, Series I. Vol. 45. Part I, Reports, Correspondence, Etc., Serial No. 93, 698.

371. McGuire, *Hungarian Texans*, 135.

372. *Morrison and Fourmy's General Directory of the City of Galveston, 1888–1889, 1890–1891* (Galveston, TX: Morrison and Fourmy Co., 1891), 209; Beszedits, "Vidor," 5–6.

373. Bona, *Hadnagyok*, III, 491.

374. Bona, *Hadnagyok*, III, 491.

375. For Voneky's service records in the Civil War see NA, M390, Roll 50, and M589, Roll 89; *Annual Report of the Adjutant General of Missouri for the Year Ending December 31, 1865* (Jefferson City: Emory S. Foster, 1866), 580–581; Louis Voneky to Maj. H. Hannahs (June 28, 1865), Service Records, Louis Voneky, 51st Missouri Infantry, NA, RG 94.

376. Öfele, *German-speaking Officers*, 227.

377. Bona, *Hadnagyok*, III, 491; Louis Voneky, African American Civil War Memorial, Plaque C-78.

378. For an excellent brief biography of Waagner, consult Beszedits, *Hungarians in Missouri*; Bona, *Tábornokok*, 710; Kinizsi, "Sánta huszár," 182; Ács, *Magyarok az észak-amerikai polgárháborúban*, 19.

379. *The New York Times*, November 11, 1850; Jánossy, *Kossuth emigráció*, II, 702–703.

380. Beszedits, *Hungarians in Missouri*; Heitman, *Historical Register*, II, 157.

381. Russell, *My Diary*, 341; for Waagner's report of the expedition on Belmont, consult OR, Series I, Vol. III, Serial No. 3, 152; John Y. Simon, ed., *The Papers of Ulysses S. Grant*, 24 volumes (Carbondale and Edwardsville: Southern Illinois University Press, 1969), 295.

382. Ronald V. Jackson, Accelerated Indexing Systems, Comp., VA Census, 1800–1900 (Provo, UT, Ancestry.com, 1999–), 234; Hampton National Cemetery, Hampton City, Virginia, Plot 6562, Cemetery Road at Marshall Avenue (U.S. Veterans Affairs National Cemetery Administration).

383. McGuire, *Hungarian Texans*, 164.

384. McGuire, *Hungarian Texans*, 164; L.E. Daniell, *Types of Successful Men of Texas* (Austin, Texas: Von Boeckmann, 1890), 241.

385. *Cairo Business Minor and City Directory for 1864–65*.

386. McGuire, *Hungarian Texans*, 164; *The Galveston Daily News*, April 13, 1878.

387. W.S. Geiser, "Notes on Some Workers of Texas Entomology," *Southwestern Historical Quarterly*, Vol. 49, No. 4, http://www.tsha.utexas.edu/publications/journals/shq/online/v049/n4/contrib_DIVL8774.html (June 21, 2008); Arthur Wadgymar, "Trichina spiralis, and its origin and development in muscle, and the disease trichinosis," *St. Louis Medical Reporter* (1866–67/1), 97–109.

388. Bona, *Hadnagyok*, III, 446.

389. Kinizsi, "Sánta huszár," 108.

390. Vasváry, *Lincoln and the Hungarians*, 9.

391. Civil War Service Records, NA, M551, Roll 148; Winchester National Cemetery, Lot No. 16.

392. For details of Xantus's life see the introduction to both John Xantus, *Letters from North America* (Wayne State University Press, Detroit, 1975) and Xantus, *Travels*.

393. Bona, *Hadnagyok*, III, 497; Jánossy, *Kossuth emigráció*, II, 673.

394. Xantus, *Letters*, 18.

395. Sándor Mocsány, "In Memory of János Xantus," *Hungarian Academy of Sciences* (1899/9), 234–235; Xantus, *Letters*, 18.

396. Edgar Erskine Hume, *Ornithologists of the United States Army Medical Corps* (Baltimore: John Hopkins Press, 1942), I, 511–512.

397. For an excellent overview of Xantus's career in Hungarian consult the Xantus exhibition site of the Somogyi Library in Szeged: http://www.sk-szeged.hu/kiallitas/xantus (January 21, 2008).

398. Vasváry, *Lincoln's Hungarian Heroes*, 165; Bence Szabolcsi and Aladár Tóth, eds., *Zenei Lexikon* (Budapest: Zeneműkiadó, 1965), III, 703.

399. Franz Liszt to Joachim Raff (January 6, 1851), Mária Eckhardt, ed., *Liszt válogatott levelei (1824–1861)* (Zeneműkiadó: Budapest, 1989), 137.

400. Beszedits, "Notable Hungarians"; *Boston Daily Advertiser*, February 9, 1863.

401. Vasváry, *Lincoln's Hungarian Heroes*, 165.
402. Ács, Magyarok az *észak-amerikai polgárháborúban*, 81; McGuire, *Hungarian Texans*, 161.
403. Civil War Service Records, NA, M542, Roll 10.
404. Ács, *Magyarok az észak-amerikai polgárháborúban*, 80–81; Jánossy, *Kossuth emigráció*, II, 674; Kinizsi, "*Sánta Huszár*," 135.
405. Öfele, *German-speaking Officers*, 97.
406. Emile Zulavsky to Andrew Johnson (January 10, 1866), Service Records, Emile Zulavsky, 82nd USC Inf., NA, RG 94.
407. Jánossy, *Kossuth emigráció*, II, 674; László, *Napló-töredék*, 136; *Frank Leslie's Illustrated Newspaper*, May 14, 1859, 376; Ihász to Tanárky, Torino, Italy (July 8, 1860), quoted in Koltay-Kastner, *Tanárky*, 351; Lukács, *Magyar Légió*, 70.
408. Civil War Service Records, NA, M589, Roll 98; Öfele, *German-speaking Officers*, 136.
409. Bangs, *The Ullmann Brigade*, II, 290–310, 296; Ladislaus L. Zulavsky, NA, RG 153, M1669; Öfele, *German-speaking Officers*, 189.
410. Öfele, *German-speaking Officers*, xi; General Order No. 25, by Col. L.L. Zulavsky, HQ 82nd Regt. U.S. Infantry (Colored), Barrancas, FL (May 1, 1864), Document G-130, Freedom Archives, Freedmen and Southern Society Project, University of Maryland, College Park, MD.
411. General Order No. 12 (May 18, 1865), OR, Series 1, Vol. 49, 2, 833f.
412. László, *Napló-töredék*, 193.
413. Vasváry, *Lincoln and the Hungarians*, 9.
414. Öfele, *German-speaking Officers*, 97.

Bibliography

Manuscripts
Abraham Lincoln Library and Museum of the Lincoln Memorial University, Special Collection, Harrogate, TN
    Cassius Marcellus Papers
Chicago Historical Society, Chicago, IL
    Richard Yates Manuscript Collection
Duke University, Rare Book, Manuscript, and Special Collections Library, Durham, NC
    Estván, Béla, Papers
Folger Shakespeare Library, Washington, D.C.
    Augustin Daily Papers
Hausarchiv, Vienna, Austria
    Archiv Kaiser Maximilians von Mexiko
Library of Congress Manuscript Division, Washington, D.C.
    Abraham Lincoln Papers
    Geography and Map Division
    Julius H. Stahel Papers
Magyar Országos Levéltár, Budapest, Hungary
    Ács Tivadar Papers, R328
    Asbóth Sándor Papers, R171
    Dancs Lajos Papers, R 21
    Kossuth Emigration Papers, R111
    Kossuth Lajos Papers, R90–92
    Számwald Gyula Papers, R170
National Archives, Washington, D.C.
    Records of the Veteran Administration, Record Group 15
        Civil War Pension Files
    Records of the Bureau of the Census, Record Group 29
        Census of 1850 M432
        Census of 1860 M653
        Census of 1870 M593
    Records of the U.S. Customs Service, Record Group 36
        Passenger Arrival Lists, M334
    Records of the Immigration and Naturalization Service, Record Group 85
    Records of the Adjutant General's Office, 1780s–1917, Record Group 94
        Compiled Military Records
        Personal Papers, Medical Officers and Physicians
        Regular Army Enlistment Papers
        Roster of Officers of United States Colored Troops, 1863–65, Dept. of Virginia and North Carolina
    Records of the Office of the Judge Advocate General (Army), Record Group 153
        Proceedings of General Courts-Martial

Petőfi Irodalmi Múzeum, Jenő Kozlay Papers, Budapest, Hungary
University of Maryland, College Park
Freedmen and Southern Society Project Archives (FSSP)
Vasváry Collection, Somogyi Library, Szeged, Hungary

Published Primary Sources

Ács, Tivadar. *A száműzöttek. Fiala János emlékiratai.* Budapest: Hungária, 1943.
———. *Magyar úttörők az Újvilágban. László Károly 1850-67: évi naplójegyzetei a Kossuth-emigráció amerikai életéből.* Budapest: Láthatár Kiadó, 1942.
Allart, Linda, et al., eds. *The Journals and Miscellaneous Notebooks of Ralph Waldo Emerson.* Cambridge, MA.: Belknap Press, 1982.
Angle, Paul M., and E.S. Miers. *Tragic Years 1860-65.* New York: Da Capo Press, 1992.
Basler, Roy P., ed. *Collected Works of Abraham Lincoln.* New Brunswick, NJ: Rutgers University Press, 1953-1955.
Berlin, Ira, Joseph P. Reidy, and Leslie S. Rowland, eds. *The Black Military Experience.* Series 2 of *Freedom: A Documentary History of Emancipation, 1861-1867.* New York: Cambridge University Press, 1982.
Beszedits, Stephen, ed. *The Libby Prison Diary by Colonel Emeric Szabad.* Toronto: B&L Information Services, 1999.
Bogáti, Péter, ed. *Ács, Gedeon. Mihelyt gyertyámat eloltom. Bostoni jegyzetek, 1856-63.* Budapest: Gondolat kiadó, 1989.
Bölöni, Sándor Farkas. *Utazás Észak-Amerikában.* Kolozsvár: Dácia, 1975.
Booth, Andrew B. *Records of Louisiana Confederate Soldiers and Confederate Commands.* 3 vols. New Orleans, LA, 1920.
Brace, Charles Loring. *Hungary in 1851: With an Experience of the Austrian Police.* New York: Charles Scribner, 1852.
Chaille-Long, Col. *My Life in Four Continents.* 2 vols. London: Hutchinson, 1912.
Chambrun, Adolphe Marquis. *Impressions of Lincoln and the Civil War: A Foreigner's Account.* New York: Random House, 1952.
Chesnut, Mary Boykin Miller. *Mary Chesnut's Civil War.* New Haven, CT: Yale University Press, 1981.
Child, Lydia M. *Letters of Lydia Maria Child.* Edited by John G. Whittier. Boston: Houghton Mifflin, 1883.
Cole, Allan B., ed. *With Perry in Japan. The Diary of Edward Yorke McCauley.* Princeton, NJ: Princeton University Press, 1992.
Congdon, James A. (Major, 12th Pennsylvania Cavalry). *Congdon's Cavalry Compendium.* Philadelphia: J.P. Lippincott, 1864.
Coulter, Merton E. *Travels in the Confederate States.* Norman: University of Oklahoma Press, 1948.
Crabtree, Beth G., and James W. Patton, eds. *"Journal of a Secesh Lady:" The Diary of Catherine Ann Devereux Edmondston, 1860-66.* Raleigh: Division of Archives and History, North Carolina Department of Cultural Resources, 1979.
Crist, Lynda Lasswell, and Mary S. Dix, eds. *The Papers of Jefferson Davis.* Vol. 7, 1861. Baton Rouge and London: Louisiana State University Press, 1992.
Dancs, Lajos. *Töredékek tíz éves emigrationalis élményeimből.* Nagy-Szőllős: Székely Simon kiadása, 1890.
DeRoulac Hamilton, J.G. "The Prison Experiences of Randolph Shotwell," *The North Carolina Historical Review* II (July 1925): 345-346.
"Diary of Captain Robert E. Park, Twelfth Alabama Regiment." *Southern Historical Society Papers* (January 1877): 43-46.
Dickinson, Henry Clay. *Diary of Cpt. Henry C. Dickinson.* Denver, CO: Press of Williamson, Haffner Co., 1913.
Eckhardt, Mária, ed. *Liszt válogatott levelei (1824-1861).* Zeneműkiadó: Budapest, 1989.
Egressy, Gábor. *Egressy Gábor törökországi naplója. 1849-1850.* Pest: Kozma V., 1851.
Ely, Alfred. *Journal of Alfred Ely, a Prisoner of War in Richmond.* Edited by Charles Lanman. New York: Appleton, 1862.
Estván, Béla. *War Pictures from the South.* New York: Appleton, 1863.

Filby, William P., and Mary K. Meyer, eds. *Passenger and Immigration Lists Index*. Detroit, MI: Gale Research, 1981.
Fleming, George T., ed. *Life and Letters of Alexander Hays*. Pittsburgh, PA: Privately published, 1919.
Fremont, Elizabeth Benton. *Recollections of Elisabeth Benton Fremont*. Compiled by I.T. Martin. New York: Frederick H. Hitchcock, 1912.
Gábor, Albert, ed. *Szemere Bertalan leveleskönyve, 1849–1865*. Budapest: Balassi Kiadó, 1999.
Garibaldi, Giuseppi. *Garibaldi's Memoirs*. Edited by Elpis Melena. Sarasota, FL: International Institute of Garibaldian Studies, 1981.
Garrison, William Lloyd. *Letter to Louis Kossuth, Concerning Freedom and Slavery in the United States in Behalf of the American Anti-Slavery Society*. Boston: R.F. Wallcut, 1852.
Gerster, A.S. *Recollections of a New York Surgeon*. New York: Paul B. Hoeber, 1917.
Glazier, Ira A., and William P. Filby, eds. *Germans to America.*. Wilmington, DE: Scholarly Resources, 1988.
Graff, Henry F., ed. *Bluejackets with Perry in Japan*. New York: New York Public Library, 1952.
Grant, Ulysses S. *Personal Memoirs and Selected Letters of Ulysses S. Grant*. New York: Library of America, 1990.
———. *Personal Memoirs of U.S. Grant*. New York: C.L. Webster, 1885–86.
Grave Stone Records of Decatur County, Iowa. Des Moines, IA: W.P.A., 1939.
Hamilton, DeRoulac J.G. "The Prison Experiences of Randolph Shotwell." *The North Carolina Historical Review* II (July 1925): 147–161.
Hamilton, J.G., et al., eds. *The Papers of Randolph Abbott Shotwell*. 3 vols. Raleigh: North Carolina Historical Commission, 1931.
Handy, Isaac W.K. *United States Bonds: A Journal of Current Events During an Imprisonment of Fifteen Months at Fort Delaware*. Baltimore, MD: Turnbull Brothers, 1874.
Haraszty, Ágoston. *Utazás Éjszakamerikában*. Pest: G. Heckenast, 1844.
Harris, William C. *Prison-Life in a Tobacco Warehouse at Richmond*. Philadelphia: G.W. Childs, 1862.
Heine, William. *With Perry to Japan: A Memoir by William Heine*. Honolulu: University of Hawaii Press, 1990.
Herr, Pamela, and Mary Lee Spence, eds. *The Letters of Jessie Benton Fremont*. Urbana and Chicago: University of Illinois Press, 1993.
Hewett Janet B., ed. *The Roster of Confederate Soldiers, 1861–65*. 16 vols. Wilmington, NC: Broadfoot, 1995–96.
Irwin, Ray W., ed. "Missouri in Crisis: The Journal of Captain Albert Tracy, 1861." *Missouri Historical Review* 51 (1956–1957): 270–283.
Jenkins, A.P., ed. *The Journal and Official Correspondence of Bernard Jean Bettelheim, 1845–54*. Naha: Okinawa-ken KyÉikuiinkai, 2005.
The Joint Committee on the Conduct of the War. 3 vols. Washington, D.C.: Government Printing Office, 1863.
Journal of the Congress of the Confederate States of America, 1861–65. U.S. Serial Set, 4610 to 4616. Washington, D.C.: Government Printing Office, 1904–05.
Journal of the Executive Proceedings of the Senate of the United States (February 13 to July 28, 1866).
Kamphoefner, Walter D., et al., eds. *News from the Land of Freedom*. Ithaca, NY: Cornell University Press, 1991.
Kinizsi, István. *A " "Sánta huszár" naplója*. Marosvásárhely: Impress Kiadó, 1999.
Knefler, Frederick. *To the Honorable, the Committee on Pension of the Senate and the House of Representatives of the United States*. Indianapolis, IN: Imprint, 1878.
Koltay-Kastner, Jenő, ed. *Tanárky Gyula naplója*. Budapest: Szépirodalmi Kiadó, 1961.
Kompolthy, Tivadar. *Amerikában. Elbeszélések s rajzok az amerikai életből*. Veszprém: Szent István Könyvnyomda, 1885.
Kónya, László. "Zágonyi Károly, s springfieldi hős kiadatlan jelentései a győztes csatájáról" In *Forradalom és szabadságharc a Felső-Tisza vidéken*, 71–77. Nyíregyháza, 1998.
Kuné, Julian. *Reminiscences of an Octogenarian Hungarian Exile*. Chicago: By the author, 1911.
Labádi, Károly, ed. *Ács, Gedeon. Meg vagyok én búval rakva*. Újvidék: Forum, 1992.
László Károly. *Napló-töredék*. Budapest: Franklin Társulat, 1887.
Lévai, Csaba and István Kornél Vida, eds. *Charles Loring Brace, Magyarország 1851-ben*. Máriabesenyő-Gödöllő: Attraktor, 2006.
Madarász József. *Emlékirataim, 1831–1881*. Budapest: Franklin Társulat, 1883.
Marsh, Charles W. *Recollections, 1837–1910*. Chicago: Farm Implement News Co., 1910.

McClellan, George B. *McClellan's Own Story*. New York: Webster, 1887.
McDonald, Cornelia. *A Diary: With Reminiscences of the War and Refugee Life in the Shenandoah Valley, 1860–1865*. Nashville, TN: Cullom and Ghertner, 1935.
Merrell, William Howard. *Five Months in Rebeldom, or, Notes from the Diary of a Bull Run Prisoner, at Richmond*. Rochester, NY: Adams and Dabney, 1862.
Moore, Frank, ed. *Rebellion Record*. New York: G.P. Putnam, 1862.
Mosby, John S. *The Memoirs of Col. John S. Mosby*. Edited by Charles Wells Russell. Boston: Little, Brown, 1917.
Neumann, Salamon. "Amerikai vázlatok" *Pesti Napló*, February 26, 1860.
New Orleans, LA Directories, 1890–91. New Orleans, LA: L. Soards, 1890–91.
Official Roster of the Soldiers of the State of Ohio in the War of the Rebellion, 1861–66. Cincinnati, OH: Wilstach, Baldwin, 1886.
Paulus, Margaret B. *Papers of Gen. Robert Huston Milroy*. 4 vols. N.a., 1965.
Perczel, Miklós. *Naplóm az emigrációból*. 2 vols. Budapest: Tankönyvkiadó, 1977.
Pickard, John B., ed. *The Letters of John Greenleaf Whittier*. 3 vols. Cambridge, MA: Belknap Press of Harvard University, 1975.
"The Prison Experience of a Confederate Soldier' by Abram Fulkerson, Late Col. 63rd Tennessee Infantry, Army of Northern Virginia." *Southern Historical Society Papers* 22 (January–December, 1894): 127–146.
Pulszky, Ferenc: *Életem és korom*. Budapest: Franklin Társulat, 1884.
Report of the Adjutant General of the State of Illinois. Springfield, IL: Baker and Co., 1867.
Rombauer, Roderick E. *The History of a Life*. St. Louis, MO: By author, 1903.
Russell, William Howard. *My Diary North and South*. New York: Harper and Bros., 1954.
Schlesinger, Louis. "Personal Narrative of Louis Schlesinger." *United States Magazine and Democratic Review*. Part 1. (September 1852): 210–225; Part 2 (October 1852): 352–369; Part 3 (November–December 1852): 553–592.
Sears, Stephen W., ed. *The Civil War Papers of George B. McClellan. Selected Correspondence, 1860–65*. New York: Ticknor and Fields, 1989.
Shuffler, Henderson, ed. *The Adventures of a Prisoner of War, 1863–64*. Austin: University of Texas Press, 1964.
Simon, John Y., ed. *The Papers of Ulysses S. Grant*. 24 vols. Carbondale and Edwardsville: Southern Illinois University Press, 1969.
Simpson, Brooks D., and Jean V. Berlin, eds. *Sherman's Civil War: Selected Correspondence of William T. Sherman, 1860–65*. Chapel Hill: University of North Carolina Press, 1999.
St. Louis Genealogical Society: St. Louis Marriage Index, 1804–1876. St. Louis, MO: St. Louis Genealogical Society, 1999.
Stryker, William S. *Record of Officers and Men of New Jersey in the Civil War, 1861–1865*. Trenton, NJ: John L. Murphey, 1867.
Széchenyi, Béla. *Amerikai utam*. Pest: G. Emich, 1863.
Szinnyei, József. *Id. Szinnyei József komáromi históriái*. Tatabánya: Szüpex, 1997.
———. *Komárom 1848/49-ben: Napló-jegyzetek*. Budapest: Aigner Lajos, 1887.
Szokoly, Viktor, ed. *Mészáros Lázár külföldi levelei és életirata*. Pest: Ráth Mór, 1867.
Terrell, W.H.H., ed. *Indiana in the War of the Rebellion. Report of the Adjutant General*. Indianapolis, IN: Indiana Historical Society, 1960.
Tóth, Lőrinc. "Ó és Uj Világ." *Athenaeum* (August 31, 1837): 273–280.
Turnley, Parmenas Taylor. *Reminiscences of Parmenas Taylor Turnley*. Chicago: Donohue and Henneberry, 1892.
Vadona, János. *Az öt világrészből*. Budapest: Hornyánszky V. Könyvnyomda, 1893.
Wallace, Lew. *An Autobiography*. 2 vols. New York: Harper and Bros., 1906.
The War of the Rebellion. A Compilation of the Official Records of the Union and Confederate Armies. Washington, D.C.: Government Printing Office, 1880–1901.
War Papers Read Before the Commandery of the State of Maine, Military Order of the Loyal Legion of the United States. Portland, ME: Thurston Print, 1898.
Wass, Samu, gr. *Kilencz év egy száműzött életéből*. Pest, Ráth Mór, 1861–62.
Watson, William. *Life in the Confederate Army: Being the Observations and Experiences of an Alien in the South During the American Civil War*. New York: Scribner and Welford, 1888.
Wayland, Francis F., ed. "Frémont's Pursuit of Jackson in the Shenandoah Valley: The Journal of Col. Albert Tracy, March–July, 1862." *The Virginia Magazine of History and Biography* 70 (1962).

Winston, J. *Cora O'Kane; or the Doom of the Rebel Guard.* Claremont, NH: Association of Disabled Soldiers, 1868.
Xántus János levelei Éjszak-Amerikából. Pest: Laufer and Stolp, 1858.
Xantus, John. *Letters from North America.* Detroit, MI: Wayne State University Press, 1975.

Electronic Sources

Collected Works of Abraham Lincoln. Edited by Roy P. Basler. New Brunswick, NJ: Rutgers University Press, 1953–1955. http://quod.lib.umich.edu/l/lincoln/.

Newspapers and Periodicals

Athenaeum
Bangor (ME) Daily Whig and Courier
Chicago Daily Tribune
Chicago Press and Tribune
Congressional Globe
Daily Evening Bulletin (San Francisco, CA)
The Daily Inter Ocean (Chicago, IL)
Daily National Intelligencer (Washington, D.C.)
Daily Richmond (VA) Examiner
Daily Whig and Republican (Quincy, IL)
Davenport (IA) Daily Gazette
Decatur (IL) Morning Review
Fővárosi Lapok (Budapest)
Frank Leslie's Illustrated Newspaper
Harper's Weekly
Hazánk s a Külföld (Pest-Buda)
Littel's Living Age
Louisville Journal
Magyarország (Pest-Buda)
Morning Oregonian (Portland, OR)
Népszabadság (Budapest)
New York Herald
New York Times
New York Tribune
North American and United States Gazette
The North American Review
The Old Guard
The Oregonian (Portland, OR)
Pesti Napló (Pest-Buda)
Philadelphia Inquirer
Pittsburgh Gazette
Sandusky (OH) Daily Star
Saturday Herald (Decatur, IL)
The Sentinel (Tuscumbia, MO)
Történelmi Lapok (Budapest)
Tuscumbia Osage Valley (MO) Sentinel
United States Magazine and Democratic Review
Vasárnapi Újság (Budapest)
Washington Post
Washington Star
Wisconsin Patriot
The Weekly Raleigh (NC) Register

Secondary Sources

Ács, Tibor. "A tudományegyetem hadi tanfolyama és a Pesti Egyetemi Légió, 1848–1849." *Hadtörténelmi Közlemények* (2000/3): 501–540.
Ács, Tivadar. *Akik elvándoroltak*. Budapest: Kapisztrán Nyomda, 1942.
_____. *Kossuth papja: Ács Gedeon*. Vác: Kapisztrán Nyomda, 1940.
_____. *Magyarok az észak-amerikai polgárháborúban 1861–65*. Budapest: Pannónia, 1964.
_____. *Magyarok idegenben*. Budapest: Magyar Téka, 1941.
_____. *New Buda*. Budapest, 1941.
Agárdi, Ferenc. "A Hungarian General in Lincoln's Service." *The New Hungarian Quarterly* (April–June 1963).
Ágoston, István. *A nemzet inzsellérei: vízimérnökök élete és munkássága, XVIII–XX. sz*. Szeged, 2001.
Aladár, György. "Xantus János." *Földrajzi Közlemények* (1894): 377–381.
Áldor, Imre. *Vázlatok a magyar emigráció életéből*. Pest, 1870.
Anderle, Ádám. "A 48-as magyar emigráció és Narciso Lopez 1851-es kubai expedíciója," *Századok* (1973/3): 687–709.
Anderson, Galusha. *The Story of a Border City During the Civil War*. Boston: Little, Brown, 1908.
Anderson, Gerald H., ed. *Biographical Dictionary of Christian Missions*. New York: McMillan Reference, 1998.
Andreas, A.T. *History of Cook County, Illinois: From the Earliest Period to the Present Time*. Chicago: A.T. Andreas, 1884.
"Az észak-amerikai polgárháború magyar katonái." In *Magyarország Hadtörténete*. Edited by Ervin Liptai. Vol. I. Budapest: Zrínyi Katonai Kiadó, 1984.
"B. István's War Pictures from the South." *The North American Review* 201 (October 1863): 583–584.
Bacarella, Michael. *Lincoln's Foreign Legion: The 39th New York Infantry*. Shippensburg, PA: White Mane, 1997.
Bakó, Elemér. "Zágonyi Károly." *Új Tükör* (May 1989): 19.
Balogh, Béla. "Zágonyi Károly emlékezete." *Romániai Magyar Szó*, August 5, 2000.
Bartels, Carolyn M. *The Civil War in Missouri, 1861–1865*. Independence, MO: Two Trails, 2003.
Barton, William E. *Lincoln at Gettysburg*. Indianapolis: Bobbs-Merrill, 1930.
Bates, Samuel P. *History of the Pennsylvania Volunteers, 1861–65*. Harrisburg: B. Singerly, 1868–1871.
Battles and Leaders of the Civil War. Edited by R.U. Johnson and C.C. Buel. 4 vols. New York: Century, 1887.
Békés, Pál. *Tévé-játék; New-Buda*. Budapest: Neoprológus, 2002.
Berenyi, Maria. "A Romanian from Gyula: A Freedom Fighter for Hungary and an American General and Consul." *Transylvanian Review* (Winter 1998): 133–139.
Beszedits, Stephen. "Charles Semsey: Hungarian Patriot, Union Soldier, and Ellis Island Official." *Vasváry Collection Newsletter* (2004/1).
_____. "Dr. Rudolph Tauszky: A Hungarian Physician in the American Civil War." *Vasváry Collection Newsletter* (2003/1).
_____. "Frederick Knefler: Hungarian Patriot and American General." http://www.jewishhistory.com/civilwar/knefler.html.
_____. "Hungarians with General John C. Frémont in the American Civil War." *Vasváry Collection Newsletter* (2003/2). http://www.sk-szeged.hu/szolgaltatas/vasvary/newsletter/03dec/beszedits.html.
_____. "The Life and Times of Philip Figyelmessy." *Vasváry Collection Newsletter* (2006/2). http://www.sk-szeged.hu/szolgaltatas/vasvary/newsletter/06dec/figyelmessy.html.
_____. "Some Notes on the Life and Career of Major-General Julius Stahel. Insignia No. 1491, New York Commandery." http://suvcw.org/mollus/art018.pdf.
Bigelow, John, Jr. *The Campaign of Chancellorsville*. New Haven, CT: Yale University Press, 1910.
Blackwell, Samuel M., Jr. *In the First Line of Battle: The 12th Illinois Cavalry in the Civil War*. Dekalb: Northern Illinois University Press, 2002.
Bogáti, Péter. "A Kossuth-emigráció." *Magyarország* 32 (1976).
_____. *A mahagóni ember*. Budapest: Móra könyvkiadó, 1986.
_____. *Édes Pólim*. Budapest: Móra Könyvkiadó, 1979.
_____. *Flamingók Új-Budán*. Budapest: Kossuth Könyvkiadó, 1979.
_____. *Örnagy úr, keressen magának ellenséget!* Budapest: Móra Ferenc Könyvkiadó, 1978.

Bona, Gábor. *Hadnagyok és főhadnagyok az 1848/49. évi szabadságharcban.* 3 vols. Budapest: Heraldika kiadó, 1998.
_____. *Kossuth Lajos kapitányai.* Budapest: Zrínyi kiadó, 1988.
_____. *Tábornokok és törzstisztek a szabadságharcban 1848–49.* Budapest: Heraldika kiadó, 2000.
Brian, Denis. *Pulitzer: A Life.* New York: J. Wiley, 2001.
Briggs, John E. "The Enlistment of Iowa Troops During the Civil War." *The Iowa Journal of History and Politics* (July 1917): 323–392.
Bright, Eric W. "'Nothing to Fear from the Influence of Foreigners': The Patriotism of Richmond's German-Americans During the Civil War." Master's thesis. Virginia Polytechnic Institute and State University, 1999.
Brockett, Livius Pierpont. *The Camp, the Battlefield and the Hospital: Lights and Shadows of the Great Rebellion.* Boston, MA: New England Publishing, 1866.
Bromwell, William J. *History of the Immigration to the United States.* New York: Redfield, 1856.
Bruncken, Ernest. *German Political Refugees in the U.S. During the Period from 1815–60.* Chicago: Deutsch-Amerikanische Gesichtsblatter, 1904.
Burhop, Ray W. *The Twenty-fourth Illinois Infantry Regiment: The Story of a Civil War Regiment.* Tampa, FL: Burhop Associates, 2003.
Burton, William L. *Melting Pot Soldiers.* New York: Fordham University Press, 1998.
Calkin, Homer L. "Iowans in the State Department and in the Foreign Service." *The Palimpsest* (February 1956): 65–116.
_____. "The Modern Ark: The Coming of the Foreigners." *The Palimpsest* (April 1962): 149–199.
Catalfamo, Catherine. "The Thorny Rose: The Americanization of an Urban, Immigrant, Working Class Regiment in the Civil War; A Social History of the 39th New York Volunteer Infantry." Ph.D. dissertation. Faculty of the Graduate School of the University of Texas, August 1989.
A Century of European Migrations, 1830–1930. Edited by Rudolph J. Vecoli and Suzanne M. Sinke. Urbana: University of Illinois Press, 1991.
Chaffin, Tom. *Fatal Glory: Narciso Lopez and the Final Clandenstine U.S. War Against Cuba.* Charlottesville: University Press of Virginia, 1996.
Chapin, Allene. "Colonel Peter Paul Dobozy: Exile in the Ozarks." *West Plains Gazette* 21 (March-April 1983): 36–40.
Collections of the State Historical Society of Wisconsin. Vol. 14. Madison, WI: The Society, 1888–1931.
"Collector's Piece: Mihaloczy's Letter to Lincoln." *Chicago History* (Fall 1949): 133–136.
Colletta, John P. *They Came in Ships: A Guide to Finding Your Immigrant Ancestor's Arrival Record.* Salt Lake City, UT: Ancestry, 2002.
"Come to Hamilton County." *The Palimpsest* (August 1934): 275–286.
Connelley, William E. *Standard History of Kansas and Kansans.* Chicago: Lewis, 1918.
Cooling, Benjamin Franklin. *Symbol, Sword and Shield: Defending Washington During the Civil War.* Hamden, CT: Archon Books, 1975.
Csillag, András. "A pétervári főkonzul." *Magyar Nemzet* (January 12, 1979): 9.
_____. "Az 'új hírlapírás' mestere: Emlékezés Pulitzer Józsefre." *Kapu* (1997/6–7): 101–104.
_____. *Joseph Pulitzer és az amerikai sajtó.* Budapest: Osiris Kiadó, 2000.
Czibula, Antal. *A nagy diktátor: Az ügysegéd naplója.* Szeged, 1928.
Daniel, Larry J. *The Battle That Changed the Civil War: Shiloh.* New York: Simon and Schuster, 1997.
Daniell, L.E. *Types of Successful Men of Texas.* Austin, Texas: Von Boeckmann, 1890.
Davis, William Watson. *The Civil War and Reconstruction in Florida.* New York: Columbia University, 1913.
Deák, István. *The Lawful Revolution: Louis Kossuth and the Hungarians, 1848–1849.* New York: Columbia University Press, 1979.
Denney, Robert E. *Civil War Prisoners and Escapes: A Day-by-Day Chronicle.* New York: Sterling, 1993.
Dictionary of American Immigration History. Edited by Francesco Cordasco. Metuchen, NJ: Scarecrow Press, 1990.
Dodd, Donald B., ed. *Historical Statistics of the States of the United States: Two Centuries of the Census, 1790–1990.* Westport, CN: Greenwood Press, 1993.
Dojcsák, Győző. *A kanadai Esterházy története.* Budapest: Magvető Kiadó, 1981.
_____. *Amerikai magyar történetek.* Budapest: Ifjúsági Lap-és Könyvkiadó, 1985.
Dorsheimer, William Edward. "Frémont's 100 Days in Missouri." *Atlantic Monthly* (January–March, 1862).

Dublin, Thomas, ed. *Immigrant Voices: New Lives in America, 1773-1986.* Urbana: University of Illinois Press, 1993.
Dunlevy, James A., and Henry A. Gemery. "Economic Opportunities and the Responses of 'Old' and 'New' Migrants to the United States." *Journal of Economic History* (December 1978): 901-917.
Dwight, Theodore. *The Life of General Garibaldi.* New York: A.S. Barnes, 1877.
Dyer, Frederick H. *A Compendium of the War of the Rebellion.* Des Moines, IA: Dyer, 1908.
Egan, Michael. *The Flying, Gray-Haired Yank.* Philadelphia: Edgewood, 1888.
"Egy magyar iparos Törökországban s Amerikában." *Hazánk s a Külföld* (April 4, 1867): 214-216; (April 11, 1867): 234-236; (April 18, 1867): 247-251; (April 25, 1867): 267-268.
Eicher, John H., and David. J. Eicher. *Civil War High Commands.* Stanford, Calif.: Stanford University Press, 2001.
Ernst, Robert. *Immigrant Life in New York City, 1825-1863.* Port Washington, NY: I.J. Friedman, 1949.
István, Béla. "The Yankee Wounded." *Skedaddle* (March 3, 2004): 1-3.
István, Mathilde. *Harry Delaware, or, An American in Germany.* New York: Putnam and Sons, 1872.
Farkas, Zoltán. "Hungarian City and County Names in the United States." *Names* (June 1971): 141-143.
Feleky, Károly. "Világos után. Prágay János meghalt Kubáért." *Világ* (February 21, 1923): 3-4.
Ferrie, Joseph P. "Migration to the Frontier in Mid-nineteenth Century America: A Re-examination of Turner's Safety Valve." Manuscript. http://eh.net/abstracts/archives.php?order=date&rev=.
_____. *Yankeys Now: Immigrants in the Antebellum United States, 1840-60.* New York: Oxford University Press, 1999.
Forgáts, Béla. "Rombauer Tivadar, az 1848-49. évi szabadságharc fegyvergyári igazgatója és a Rimamurány-Salgótarjáni Vasmű Rt. Alapítója." *Bányászati és Kohászati Lapok* (June 1, 1940): 177-182.
Fornet, Cornelius, and John Prágay. *The Hungarian Revolution.* New York: Putnam, 1850.
Fornet, Kornél. "Amerika rokonszenve a magyar szabadságharcz férfiai iránt." *Történelmi Lapok* (April 1, 1893): 68-69 and (May 1, 1893): 91-92.
Fornet, László, ed. *Fornet Kornél, 1848, as őrnagy, amerikai ezredes élete—The Life of G.C. Fornet Colonel of Lincoln's Army. Adatok az amerikai magyar emigráció életéhez.* Budapest, 1946.
Fox, William F. *New York at Gettysburg.* 2 vols. Albany, NY: J.B. Lyon, 1900.
Franck, Irene M. *The German American Heritage.* New York: Facts on File, 1989.
Frank, Tibor. *Ethnicity, Propaganda, Myth-Making: Studies on Hungarian Connections to Britain and America 1848-1945.* Budapest: Akadémiai Kiadó, 1999.
_____. "Marketing Hungary: Kossuth and the Politics of Propaganda." In *Lajos Kossuth Sent Word*, edited by László Péter, Martyn Rady, and Peter Sherwood, 221-249. London: Hungarian Cultural Center, 2003.
_____. "Marx egy anonim forrása." In Tibor Frank, *Marx és Kossuth*, 107-127. Budapest: Magvető kiadó, 1985.
_____. "'Through the Looking Glass': A Century of Self-reflecting Hungarian Images of the United States, 1834-1941" In *Multicultural Challenge in American Culture*, edited by Lehel Vadon, 21-36. Eger: EKTF, 1999.
_____. "Waiting to Return: The Hungarian Exile Community in England, 1848-1867." In *Exiles from European Revolutions: Refugees in Mid-Victorian England*, edited by Sabine Freytag, 121-134. New York: Berghahn Books, 2003.
Frazer, Robert W. "Maximilian's Propaganda Activities in the United States, 1865-1866." *Hispanic American Historical Review* 24 (February 1944): 4-29.
Freitag, Sabine. *Friedrich Hecker. Biographie eines Republikaners.* Stuttgart: Franz Steiner Verlag, 1998.
Fremont, Jessie Benton. *The Story of the Guard: A Chronicle of the War.* Boston: Ticknor and Fields, 1863.
Gál, István. "Amerika képe Széchenyi írásaiban." *Filológiai Közlöny* (1972/1-2): 32-46.
Galenson, David W., and Clayne L. Pope. "Economic and Geographic Mobility on the Farming Frontier: Evidence from Appanoose County, Iowa, 1850-1870." *Journal of Economic History* 49 (3) (1989): 635-55.
Gellén, József. "Colonel Prágay's Unknown Letter to American Statesmen." *Hungarian Studies in English* 11 (1977): 149-153.
Gereben, István. "Asbóth Sándor, nagyotmondó hős." *Kapu* (November 1995): 83-84.
Gibbs, Joseph. *Three Years in the Bloody Eleventh.* University Park: Pennsylvania State University Press, 2002.

Glant, Tibor. "Fájdalmas küldetés: Gróf Széchenyi Béla amerikai útja 1862-ben." In Tibor Frank, ed., *Gyarmatokból impérium. Magyar kutatók tanulmányai az amerikai történelemről*. Budapest: Gondolat, 2007, 88–103.
Glatthaar, Joseph T. *Forged in Battle: The Civil War Alliance of Black Soldiers and White Officers*. New York: Meridian Books, 1990.
Gould, Benjamin A. *Investigations in the Military and Anthropological Statistics of American Soldiers*. New York: Pub. for U.S. Sanitary Commission, by Hurd and Houghton, 1869.
Gould, J.D. "European Inter-continental Emigration: The Road Home; Return Migration from the U.S.A." *The Journal of European Economic History* (Spring 1980): 44–111.
Gracza, Rezsoe, and Margaret Gracza. *The Hungarians in America*. Minneapolis, MN: Lerner, 1969.
Green, Nancy L. "The Comparative Method and Poststructural Structuralism: New Perspectives for Migration Studies." *Journal of American Ethnic History*, 13, 4 (Summer 1994): 3–22.
Grimsley, Mark. "The Social Dimensions of the U.S. Civil War." *The Newsletter of Foreign Policy Research Institute*. Vol. 12, No. 13 (June 2007). http://www.fpri.org/footnotes/ 1213.200706.grimsley.socialdimensionscivilwar.html.
Guide to Genealogical Research in the National Archives. Washington, D.C.: National Archives Trust Fund Board, 1985.
Hajnal, István. *A Kossuth-Emigráció Törökországban*. Budapest: Magyar Történelmi Társulat, 1927.
Halász, Imre. "Magyarok az amerikai szabadságharcban." *Nyugat* (1914/2).
Hale, Laura Virginia. *Four Valiant Years in the Lower Shenandoah Valley, 1861–65*. Strasbourg, VA: Shenandoah Publishing House, 1968.
Hardwick, Kevin R. "'Your Old Father Abe Lincoln is Dead and Damned': Black Soldiers and the Memphis Race Riots of 1866." *Journal of Social History* 27 (Fall 1993): 109–128.
Heitman, Francis B. *Historical Register and Dictionary of the United States Army, 1789–1903*. 2 vols. Washington, D.C.: Government Printing Office, 1903.
Hennessy, John J. *Return to Bull Run: The Campaign and Battle of Second Manassas*. New York: Simon and Schuster, 1993.
Hermann, Róbert. "Görgei emlékiratai és a Kossuth-emigráció." *Aetas* (1996/2–3): 40–66.
Herringshaw's Encyclopedia of American Biography in the Nineteenth Century. Chicago: American Publishers' Association, 1902.
Hicken, Victor. *Illinois in the Civil War*. Chicago: University of Illinois Press, 1991.
Hirsch, Marla. "Indiana's Great Jewish Civil War General: Gen. Frederick Knefler" (April 12, 1834, to June 14, 1901) typescript.
Historical Statistics of the United States: Colonial Times to 1970. Washington, D.C.: U.S. Bureau of the Census, 1975.
History of Chicago. Edited by John Moses and Joseph Kirkland. 2 vols. Chicago: Munsell, 1895.
The History of Jefferson County, Iowa, 1879. Chicago: Western Historical Co., 1879.
Holcombe, R.I., ed. *History of Greene County, Missouri*. St. Louis: Western Historical Co., 1883.
Howell, J.M., and H.C. Smith. *History of Decatur County, Iowa*. Chicago: S.J.Clarke, 1915.
Hume, Edgar Erskine. *Ornithologists of the United States Army Medical Corps*. Baltimore: John Hopkins Press, 1942.
"An Interesting Narrative: Statement of Col. Adolphus Adler." *The New York Times*, September 4, 1862: 2.
Jánossy Dénes. *A Kossuth emigráció Angliában és Amerikában, 1851–1852*. 2 vols. Budapest: Magyar Történelmi Társulat, 1940.
_____. *Die Ungarische Emigration und der Krieg im Orient*. Budapest: Ostmitteleuropäische Bibliothek, 1939.
Japan Opened: Compiled Chiefly from the Narrative of the American Expedition to Japan in the Years 1852/53/54. London: Religious Tract Society, 1861.
Jeffrey, William H. *Richmond Prisons, 1861–62*. St. Johnbury: Republican Press, 1893.
Johns, George S. "Joseph Pulitzer." *Missouri Historical Review* (1930–31/5): 201–206.
Johnston, William Preston. "Zagonyi's Charge with Fremont's Body-guard: A Picturesque Fol-de-rol." *Southern Historical Society Papers* 3, 195–196.
Jones, Virgil Carrington. *Ranger Mosby*. McLean, Va: EPM, 1972.
Joslyn, Mauriel P., ed. *Immortal Captives. The Story of 600 Confederate Officers*. Shippensburg, PA: White Mane, 1996.
Journal of the Congress of the Confederate States of America, 1861–65. U.S. Serial Set, 4610 to 4616. Washington, D.C.: Government Printing Office, 1904–05.

"Julian Kune and the Chicago Historical Society." *Chicago History* (Spring 1949): 83–87.
Kacziány, Géza. *A magyar mémoire irodalom 1848-tól 1914-ig.* Budapest: Lantos, 1917.
Karamanski, Theodore J. "Civilians, Soldiers and the Sack of Athens, Alabama." *Illinois History Teacher* Vol. 4: 2 (1997): 48–55.
Kászonyi, Dániel. *Magyarhon négy korszaka.* Budapest: Szépirodalmi Kiadó, 1977.
Katona, Anna. "Hungarian Travelogues on Pre–Civil War America." *Hungarian Studies in English* (1971): 51–94.
———. "Nineteenth-Century Hungarian Travelogues on the Post–Civil War U.S." *Hungarian Studies in English* (1973): 35–52.
Kaufman, Will. *The Civil War in American Culture.* Edinburgh: Edinburgh University Press, 2006.
Kaufmann, Wilhelm. *Die Deutschen im Amerikanischen Bürgerkriege.* München and Berlin: R. Oldenburg, 1911.
Kempelen, Béla. *Magyar nemes családok.* Budapest: Grill Károly Könyvkiadóvállalata, 1911.
Kende, Géza. *Magyarok Amerikában: Az amerikai magyarság története, 1583–1926.* Cleveland: Szabadság, 1926.
Kerr, George H. *Okinawa. The History of an Island People.* Boston: Tuttle, 2000.
Kirk, John Foster. *A Supplement to Allibone's Critical Dictionary of English Literature.* Vol. I. Philadelphia: Lippincott, 1891.
Kirkland, Frazar. *The Pictorial Book of Anecdotes and Incidents of the War of the Rebellion.* Hartford, CT: Hartford, 1866.
Komjáthy, Anthony Tihamer. *A Thousand Years of the Hungarian Art of War.* Toronto: Rákóczi Foundation, 1982.
Komlós, John H. *Louis Kossuth in America, 1851–1852.* Buffalo, N.Y.: East European Institute, 1973.
Konnyu, Leslie. *Bettelheim, 1811–70. Trailblazer of Western Civilization.* Kansas: American Hungarian Review, 1989.
———. *Eagles of Two Continents: The American Hungarian Review* Vol. I, No. 3 (July 1963).
———. *John Xantus, Hungarian Geographer in America (1851–64)* Köln: American Hungarian Publisher, 1965.
Kórász, Mária. "Az amerikai magyar történetírás kezdetei: Rácz Rónay Károly levelei." *Aetas* (1996/1): 119–138.
Kozlay, Janet. "The Writings of Eugene Kozlay: 19th-Century Hungarian Émigré." *Vasváry Collection Newsletter* 29 (2003/1) http://www.sk-szeged.hu/szolgaltatas/vasvary/newsletter603jun/kozlay.html.
Kretzoi, Miklósné. "Az amerikai polgárháború a magyar sajtóban 1861–65 között." *Századok* (1974/3): 680–698.
Krick, Robert E.L. *Staff Officers in Gray.* Chapel Hill: University of North Carolina Press, 2003.
Krick, Robert K. *Conquering the Valley: Stonewall Jackson at Port Republic.* New York: William Morrow, 1996.
Kunz, Egon. *Magyarok Ausztráliában.* Budapest: Teleki László Alapítvány, 1997.
L. Gál, Éva. *Újházi László. A szabadságharc utolsó kormánybiztosa.* Budapest: Akadémiai Kiadó, 1971.
László-Bencsik, Sándor. *Nagy magyarok idegenben.* Budapest: Móra Könyvkiadó, 1971.
Lengyel, Emil. *Americans from Hungary.* New York: Lippincott, 1948.
Lévai, Csaba. "Bölöni Farkas Sándor koncepciója a nemzetről és a nemzeti nyelvről." *Debreceni Szemle* (1996/2): 195–201.
———. "A French Aristocrat and a Hungarian Nobleman in Jacksonian America: A Comparison of the Views of Alexis de Tocqueville and Sándor Farkas Bölöni" in *Global Encounters-European Identities.* (Eds. M. Harris, A. Agnarsdóttir, and Cs. Lévai) Pisa: Plus-Pisa University Press, 201, 247–258.
Lewis, Virgil A. *The Soldiery of West Virginia.* Baltimore: Genealogical Publishing Co., 1967.
Life of Gen. Narciso Lopez by a Filibustero. New York: Dewitt and Davenport, 1851.
Linder, Bill R. *How to Trace Your Family History: A Basic Guide to Genealogy.* New York: Everest House, 1980.
List of Synonyms of Organizations in the Volunteer Service of the United States During the Years 1861, 62, 63, 64 and 65. Washington, D.C.: Government Printing Office, 1885.
Loeffler, Michael. *Preussens und Sachsens Bezeihungen zu den USA Waehrends des Sessessionskrieges, 1860–65.* Berlin: Free University of Berlin, 1999.
Longacre, Edward G. *The Cavalry at Gettysburg.* London: Associated University Presses, 1986.
———. *Lincoln's Cavalrymen. A History of the Mounted Forces of the Army of the Potomac.* Mechanicsburg, PA: Stackpole Books, 2000.

Lonn, Ella. *Foreigners in the Confederacy.* Chapel Hill: University of North Carolina Press, 1940.
_____. *Foreigners in the Union Army and Navy.* Baton Rouge: Louisiana State University Press, 1951.
Lowenthal, David. *George Perkins Marsh: Prophet of Conservation.* Seattle: University of Washington Press, 2000.
Lugosi, Döme. *Szeged hős fiai az USA szabadságharcában.* Szeged: Szegedi Új Nemzedék Lapvállalat R.-T. nyomása és kiadása, 1939.
Lukács, Lajos. "A missouri hadműveletek magyar vonatkozásai. Frémont tábornok és a magyar emigránsok 1861-62-ben." *Hadtörténelmi Közlemények* (1994/1): 76-90.
_____. *A magyar Garibaldisták útja.* Budapest: Kossuth Könyvkiadó, 1971.
_____. *A magyar politikai emigráció 1849-1867.* Budapest: Kossuth könyvkiadó, 1984.
_____. *Az olaszországi Magyar Légió története es anyakönyvei, 1860-67.* Budapest: Akadémiai Kiadó, 1986.
Luvaas, Jany. *The Military Legacy of the Civil War: The European Inheritance.* Chicago: University of Chicago Press, 1959.
Magyar Emigráns Irodalom Lexikona. Edited by Csaba Nagy. Budapest: Petőfi Irodalmi Múzeum, 1990-1992.
Magyar írók élete es munkái. Ed. Gulyás, Pál. Budapest: Magyar kőnyvtárosok és levéltárosok Egyesülete, 1941.
Magyar utazók lexikona. Ed. Balázs, Dénes. Budapest: Panoráma, 1993.
Mahin, Dean B. *The Blessed Place of Freedom: Europeans in Civil War America.* Washington, D.C.: Brassey's, 2002.
Márki, Sándor. "Amerika s a magyarság." *Földrajzi Közlemények* (March 1893): 49-94.
Marraro, Howard R. "Lincoln's Italian Volunteers from New York." In *New York History.* Vol. 24 (January 1943): 56-67.
Martin, Samuel J. *"Kill-Cavalry:" Sherman's Merchant of Terror.* London: Associated University Presses, 1996.
Massachusetts in the Army and Navy During the War of 1861-1865. Edited by T.W. Higginson. Vol. 2. Boston: Wright and Potter, 1896.
Mayer, Marie E. "Nicholas Fejervary." *The Palimpsest* (June 1928): 189-198.
McDonough, James Lee. *Shiloh: In Hell Before Night.* Knoxville: University of Tennessee Press, 1977.
McElroy, John. *The Struggle for Missouri.* Washington, D.C.: National Tribune Co., 1909.
McGinty, Brian. *Strong Wine: The Life and Legend of Agoston Haraszthy.* Palo Alto, CA: Stanford University Press, 1998.
McGuire, James P. *The Hungarian Texans.* San Antonio: University of Texas, 1993.
McPherson, James M. *For Cause and Comrades: Why Men Fought in the Civil War.* New York: Oxford University Press, 1997.
McPherson, James P. *Ordeal by Fire: The Civil War and Reconstruction.* New York: McGraw and Hill, 1982.
Medical and Surgical History of the Civil War. Wilmington, N.C.: Broadfoot, 1991.
Merényi, Gábor. "A springfieldi halálroham." *Honismeret* (1986/6): 44-45.
Merényi-Metzger, Gábor. "Családtörténeti és életrajzi adatok Zágonyi Károlyról." *Korunk* (April 2003).
_____. "Egy vers az amerikai polgárháborúból." *Korunk* (September 2001).
Merrill, Catharine. *The Soldier of Indiana in the War for the Union.* Indianapolis, IN: Merrill, 1869.
Mészáros, Erzsébet. "Modesty and Wordly Wisdom: George Washington in Hungarian Periodicals between 1776 and 1840." In *Americana and Hungarica,* edited by Char-lotte Kretzoi, 19-28. Budapest: Department of English, L. Eötvös University, 1989.
Mikár, Zsigmond. *Honvéd Schematismus, vagy is az 1848/49-ki honvédseregből 1868-ban még életben volt főtiszteknek névkönyve.* Pest, 1869.
Miller, Robert E. "Zagonyi."*Missouri Historical Review* 76 (January 1982): 174-192.
Mitchell, Joseph B. *The Badge of Gallantry.* New York: Macmillan, 1968.
Mitták, Ferenc. *Hadvezérek, hősök, katonák a magyar történelemben.* Debrecen: Tóth Kiadó, 1998.
Mocsány, Sándor. "In Memory of János Xantus." *Hungarian Academy of Sciences* (1899/9): 234-235.
Monaghan, Jay. *Civil War on the Western Border: 1854-1865.* Boston: Little, Brown, 1955.
Moser, Arthur Paul. *Directory of Towns, Villages and Hamlets, Past and Present, of Butler County, Missouri.* S.l.: s.n., 1975.
Nadel, Stanley. *Little Germany: Ethnicity, Religion, and Class in New York City, 1845-80.* Urbana: University of Illinois Press, 1990.

Nagy, Miklós Mihály. *Magyar hadiutazók*. Budapest: Kornétás Kiadó, 2001.
Norton, Wilbur. *Centennial History of Madison County, Illinois and Its People, 1812–1912*. Salem, MA: Higginson, 1998.
Öfele, Martin. *German-speaking Officers in the U.S. Colored Troops, 1863–1867*. Gainesville: University Press of Florida, 2004.
Papp, Susan M. *Hungarian Americans and their Communities in Cleveland*. E-book.
Peterson, Robert L., and Hudson, John A. "Foreign Recruitment for Union Forces." *Civil War History* 7 (1961): 176–189.
Phisterer, F. *New York in the War of the Rebellion*. Lyon, 1912.
Pivány, Eugene. *Hungarians in the American Civil War*. Cleveland, OH: Dongó, 1913.
———. *Magyar-amerikai történelmi kapcsolatok. A Columbus előtti időktől az amerikai polgárháború befejezéséig*. Budapest: Királyi Magyar Egyetemi Nyomda, 1926.
———. "Sólyom C. Lajos emléke, 1836–1913." *Budapesti Hírlap*, April 8, 1914.
Pogány, András H. *Béla Estván: Hungarian Cavalry Colonel in the Confederate Army*. New York: Kossuth Foundation, 1961.
Pulszky, Francis, and Theresa Pulszky. *White, Red and Black. Sketches of American Society in the U.S.* 2 vols. New York: Redfield, 1853.
Puskás, Julianna. *From Hungary to the United States, 1880–1940*. Budapest: Akadémiai Kiadó, 1982.
———. "Hungarian Overseas Migration: A Microanalysis," in *A Century of European Migrations, 1830–1930*. Edited by Rudolph J. Vecoli and Suzanne M. Sinke, 221–239. Urbana: University of Illinois Press, 1991.
———. *Kivándorló Magyarok az Egyesült Államokban, 1880–1940*. Budapest: Akadémiai Kiadó, 1982.
———. *Ties that Bind, Ties that Divide*. New York: Holmes and Meier, 2000.
Rácz-Rónay, Károly. "Az amerikai magyar telepek története II. St. Louis." *Külföldi Magyarság* (1922/6): 2.
———. "Az amerikai magyar telepek története III. New Orleans." *Külföldi Magyarság* (1922/7): 2.
———. "Az amerikai magyar telepek története IV. New Buda." *Külföldi Magyarság* (1922/8): 8–9.
———. "Az amerikai magyar telepek története V. Philadelphia." *Külföldi Magyarság* (1922/10): 2.
———. "Az amerikai magyar telepek története VI. Haraszthyfalva." *Külföldi Magyarság* (1922/11): 2.
———. "Az amerikai magyar telepek története VII. Chicago." *Külföldi Magyarság* (1922/13): 2.
———. "Az amerikai magyar telepek története VIII. Az első külföldi magyar dalárda." *Külföldi Magyarság* (1922/14): 2.
———. "Az amerikai magyar telepek története IX. Bridgeport." *Külföldi Magyarság* (1922/19): 2.
———. "Az amerikai magyar telepek története X. Cleveland." *Külföldi Magyarság* (1923/2): 2.
———. "Az amerikai magyarság bölcsőkora I. A New York-i magyar telep." *Külföldi Magyarság* (1921/15): 2–3.
Rácz, István:" "Attempts to Curb Hungarian Emigration to the United States Before 1914." *Hungarian Studies in English* 7 (1973): 5–33.
———:" "Emigration from Hungary to the U.S.A." *Magyar Történeti Tanulmányok* 10 (1973): 117–154.
Redkey, Edwin S., ed. *A Grand Army of Black Man*. New York: Cambridge University Press, 1992.
Reid, Whitelaw. *Ohio in the War*. Cincinnati, OH: Moore, Wilstach and Baldwin, 1868.
Robertson, James I. *Soldiers Blue and Gray*. Columbia, SC: University of South Carolina Press, 1988.
Rolle, Andrew. *John Charles Frémont: Character as Destiny*. Norman: University of Oklahoma Press, 1991.
Rombauer, Robert J. *The Contest: A Military Treatise*. St. Louis, MO, 1863.
———. *The Union Cause in St. Louis in 1861: An Historical Sketch*. St. Louis: Press of Nixon-Jones Print Co., 1909.
Rombauerné, Hogel Emília. "Egy magyar nő élete az emigrációban." *Budapesti Szemle* (1913): 286–298.
Rosengarten, Joseph George. *The German Soldier in the Wars of the United States*. Philadelphia: Lippincott, 1890.
Sajti, Károly. "Zágonyi Károly." *Új Tükör*, July 23, 1989.
Sandburg, Carl. *Abraham Lincoln*. New York: Harcourt, Brace, 1954.
Schantz, Hans Gregory. "John Charles Frémont: Explorer, Politician, Man of Principle." *Reality Magazine* Vol. 1, No. 9 (May 1993): 6–10.
Schuricht, Herrmann. *History of the German Element in Virginia*. Baltimore: Theo. Kroh and Sons, 1898–1900.
Schuyler, Hamilton. *The Roeblings: A Century of Engineers, Bridge Builders and Industrialists; The Story of Three Generations of an Illustrious Family, 1831–1931*. New York: AMS Press, 1972.

Sears, Stephen W. *George B. McClellan: The Young Napoleon*. New York: Ticknor and Fields, 1988.
Shea, William L., and Earl J. Hess. *Pea Ridge: Civil War Campaign in the West*. Chapel Hill: University of North Carolina Press, 1992.
Singleton, Robert. "William Gilmore Simms, Woodlands, and the Freedmen's Bureau." *Mississippi Quarterly* (Winter 1996): 19-37.
Sisa, Stephen. *America's Amazing Hungarians*. Huddleston, Va.: Published by the author, 1987.
Smith, William E. "The Blairs and Fremont." *Missouri Historical Review* 23 (1928-1929): 217-226.
Souders, D.A. *The Magyars in America*. New York: George H. Doran, 1969.
Spencer, James, ed. *Civil War Generals: Categorical Listings and a Biographical Directory*. New York: Greenwood Press, 1986.
Starr, Stephen Z. "Cold Steel: The Saber and the Union Cavalry." *Civil War History* 11 (1965): 142-159.
Stephen Beszedits. "The Life and Times of Charles Vidor." Typescript.
Supka, Géza. "Pomutz Gyuri, az amerikai polgárháború magyar generálisa." *Magyar Hírlap*, December 2, 1934.
Sword, Wiley. *Shiloh: Bloody April*. New York: William Morrow, 1974.
Szabad, Emeric. *Hungary Past and Present: Embracing its History from the Magyar Conquest to the Present Times*. Edinburgh: A & C Black, 1854.
_____. *L'Europe avant et aprés la Paix de Villafranca*. Turin, 1859.
_____. *The State Policy of Modern Europe, from the Beginning of the Sixteenth Century to the Present Time*. Longman, Brown, Green, Longmans and Roberts, 1857.
Szabad, György. "Kossuth and the Political System of the United States of America." *Studia Historica Academiae Scientiarum Hungaricae* 106 (1975), 5-31.
Szeplaki, Joseph, ed. *The Hungarians in America, 1583-1974*. Dobbs Ferry, NY: Oceana, 1975.
Szinnyei, József. *Magyar Írók élete és munkái*. Budapest: Hornyánszky Viktor császári és királyi udvari Könyvnyomda, 1891-1914.
Szucs, Loretto Dennis, and Sandra Hargreaves, eds. *Research in Directories. The Guidebook of American Genealogy*. Salt Lake City, UT: Ancestry, 1997.
Szuhay-Havas, Ervin. *Kék-szürke tragédia*. Budapest: Gondolat Kiadó, 1966.
Taba, Stephen. "Hungarian Pioneers in America." *The Hungarian Quarterly* 7 (Spring 1941): 47-55.
Tabori, Paul. *The Anatomy of Exile*. London: Harrap, 1972.
Tap, Bruce. *Over Lincoln's Shoulder: The Committee on the Conduct of the War*. Kansas: University Press, 1998.
Taylor, Philip. *The Distant Magnet: European Emigration to the USA*. New York: Harper and Row, 1971.
Temple, Brian. *The Union Prison at Fort Delaware*. Jefferson, NC: McFarland, 2002.
Third Reunion of the Society of the Army of the Cumberland. Cincinnati, OH: Robert Clarke, 1870.
Thomas, William G., and Alice E. Carter, eds. *The Civil War on the Web*. Wilmington, DE: SR Books, 2001.
Treichel, Charles. "Major Zagoni's Horse Guard." In *Personal Recollections of the War of the Rebellion*: Military Order of the Loyal Legion, Vol. 3, 240-246. New York, 1907.
Truitt, Cyrus R. *History of Novinger, Mo.* Novinger, Missouri, 1972.
The United States and Hungary: Paths of Diplomacy, 1848-2006. Washington, D.C.: U.S. Department of State, 2006.
Urbán, Aladár. "A Lesson for the Old Continent: The Image of America in the Hungarian Revolution of 1848/49." *The New Hungarian Quarterly* 17 (1976), 85-96.
_____. "Széchenyi és a reformkor Amerika-képe." In *Nemzeti és társadalmi átalakulás a XIX. században Magyarországon. Tanulmányok Szabad György 70. születésnapjára*, edited by István Orosz, Ferenc Pölöskei, Tamás Dobszay, 119-127. Budapest: Korona, 1994.
Várdy, Béla, and Várdy Huszár Ágnes. *Újvilági küzdelmek. Az amerikai magyarság élete és az óhaza*. Budapest: Mundus Magyar Egyetemi Kiadó, 2005.
Várdy, Stephen Béla. "Az első magyar újság és újságszerkesztő Amerikában." *Debreceni Szemle* (1999/4): 511-515.
_____. *The Hungarian Americans*. Boston: Twayne, 1985.
_____. "A magyar Száműzöttek Lapja: Az első amerikai-magyar újság megszületése." *Amerikai Magyar Népszava/Szabadság* (April 2, 1999): 15-16.
Várdy, Stephen Béla. *Magyarok az Újvilágban. Az Észak-amerikai Magyarság Rendhagyó Története*. Budapest: Magyar Nyelv és Kultúra Nemzetközi Társasága, 2000.
Vári, András. "Fenyegetések földje. Amerika a 19. század második felében — magyar szemmel." *Korall* (November 2006): 153-184.

Vasváry, Edmund. *Lincoln and the Hungarians.* Pittsburgh, PA: William Penn Fraternal Association, 1963–1964.
_____. *Lincoln's Hungarian Heroes. The Participation of Hungarians in the Civil War, 1861–65.* Washington, D.C., 1939.
_____. *Magyar Amerika.* Szeged: Somogyi Könyvtár, 1988.
Vecoli, Rudolph J. "Contadini in Chicago: A Critique of the 'Uprooted.'" *Journal of American History,* 51, 3 (December 1964): 404–416.
_____, and Suzanne M. Sinke, eds. *A Century of European Migrations, 1830–1930.* Urbana: University of Illinois Press, 1991.
Vida, István Kornél. "All Quiet for Forty Years: The Hungarian Participation in the American Civil War, A Historiographical Essay," in *Europe and the World in European Historiography.* Edited by Csaba Lévai, 231–241. Pisa, Italy: Pisa University Press, 2006.
_____. "'American and Un-American Immigration': European Otherness in the Context of Old and New Immigration in the United States" in *Global Encounters — European Identities.* (Eds. M. Harris, A. Agnarsdóttir, and Cs. Lévai) (Pisa: Plus-Pisa University Press, 2010.), pp. 119–125.
_____. "The Concept of Citizenship and the Hungarian Immigrants in the United States in the 1850s: A Case Study," in *Citizenship in Historical Perspective.* Edited by S.G. Ellis, G. Hálfdanarson, and A.K. Isaacs, 227–236. Pisa, Italy: Pisa University Press, 2006.
_____. *Doing Away with Myths: A New Look at the Participation of Hungarians in the American Civil War.* National Students' Conference Paper. Debrecen, 2001.
_____. "International Fraud or Southern Hero?: Col. Estván Béla, Hungarian (?) Cavalry Officer in the Confederate Army" in *Vasváry Collection Newsletter* (2007/2) http://www.sk-szeged.hu/szolgaltatas/vasvary/newsletter/07dec/estvan.html.
_____. "Két nemzet határán: a Kossuth-emigráció és az állampolgárság amerikai megítélése a XIX. század derekán," in *Nemzet és Állam a XIX-XX. században.* Edited by Erzsébet Bodnár and Gábor Demeter. Debrecen, 2006.
_____. "Magyar katonák a Konföderáció hadseregében. Estván Béla szélhámos pályafutása," in *Gyarmatokból Impérium: Magyar kutatók tanulmányai az amerikai történelemről.* Edited by Tibor Frank, 72–87. Budapest: Gondolat Kiadó, 2007.
Wadgymar, Arthur. "Trichina Spiralis, and its Origin and Development in Muscle, and the Disease Trichinosis." *St. Louis Medical Reporter* (1866–67/1): 97–109.
The War in the West. Millwood, New York: Kraus Reprint, 1977.
Warner, Ezra J. *Generals in Blue.* Louisiana University Press, 1964.
Warring, G.E. *The Garibaldi Guard.* New York: Liber Scriptorum, 1893.
Wasserman, Fred. *Ellis Island: An Illustrated History of the Immigrant Experience.* New York: MacMillan, 1991.
Watts, Dale E. "How Bloody Was Bleeding Kansas? Political Killings in Kansas Territory." *A Journal of the Central Plains* 18 (2) (Summer 1995): 116–129.
Welsh, Jack D., M.D. *Medical Histories of Union Generals.* Kent, OH: Kent University Press, 1996.
Whitelaw, Nancy. *Joseph Pulitzer and the New York World.* Greensboro, N.C.: Morgan Reynolds, 2000.
Wilson, Lillian May. "Some Hungarian Patriots in Iowa." *The Iowa Journal of History and Politics* (October 1913): 479–516.
Wittke, Carl. "Lincoln's Hungarian Heroes." *The Mississippi Historical Review* 26 (June 1939 to March 1940): 422.
_____. *Refugees of Revolution: The German Forty-eighters in America.* Philadelphia, PA: University of Pennsylvania Press, 1952.
Wolf, Simon. *The American Jew as Patriot, Soldier and Citizen.* Boston: Gregg Press, 1972.
Wurzbach, Constant von. *Biographisches Lexikon des Kaiserthums Oesterreich : Enthaltend die Lebensskizzen der denkwürdigen Personen, welche 1750 bis 1850 im Kaiserstaate und in seinen Kronländern gesetzt haben.* Vienna: Univ-Buchdruckerei [etc.], 1856–91.
Xantus, John. *Travels in Southern California.* Detroit: Wayne State University Press, 1976.
Yandoh, Judy. "Taking off the Kid Gloves." *America's Civil War* (March 1992): 46–53.
Závodszky, Géza. *Az Amerika-motívum és a polgárosodó Magyarország: A kezdetektől 1848-ig.* Budapest: Korona Kiadó, 1997.
Zenei Lexikon. Edited by Bence Szabolcsi and Aladár Tóth. Budapest: Zeneműkiadó, 1965.
Zucker, A.E. *The Forty-eighters: Political Refugees of the German Revolution of 1848.* New York: Columbia University Press, 1950.

Index

abolitionism 10, 12–14, 52, 56, 61, 110, 112, 114; *see also* slavery
Ács, Gedeon 30, 34, 35, 44, 45, 51, 137
Ács, Tivadar 1, 51, 63, 64, 75, 79, 100, 147, 163, 201
Adler, Adolphus 58, 59, 77, 106, 133–134
African American Civil War Memorial 118–119, 141, 158, 198, 203
Albert, Anselm 72, 74, 134–135
American Torso (film) 130
Antietam, Maryland, battle of 150, 191
Arroyo, Luis de 107–108
Asboth, Alexander 31, 34, 36, 51, 52, 55, 72–74, 75, 79, 80–83, 96–98, 99, 115, 117, 118, 121, 123, 127, 137, 140, 163, 185, 187, 204

Baróthy, Charles 125, 135–136
Batthyány, Lajos 7
Beecher, Henry Ward 10, 176
Beecher, James Chaplin 114
Békés, Pál 129, 130
Bem, József 8, 89, 134, 135, 146, 155, 182, 187, 198, 202
Bennett, James Gordon 107
Beöthy, Ödön 40
Beszedits, Stephen 9, 72, 129, 182, 189
Bettelheim, Bernard 128, 136
Blair, Frank 96
Blenker, Louis 70, 84–86
Bódy, Gábor 130
Bogáti, Péter 130
Boker, George Henry 94
Bölöni, Farkas Sándor 19–20, 111
Bona, Gábor 142, 153, 157, 158, 161, 163, 171, 173, 181
Borg, Louis 107
Botsay, Alexander 136–137
Brace, Charles Loring 26, 45
Brown, John 103
Buchanan, James 71, 187

Catalfamo, Catherine 143–144
Chambrun, Adolphe 54

Channing, William Ellery 12
Chesnut, Mary Boykin Miller 55
Chicago: Hungarians in 40, 41, 74–75
Clay, Cassius Marcellus 109
colored regiments: Hungarians in 115–119, 137, 140, 157–158, 187, 195, 197, 203, 209–210; *see also* slavery
Confederate States of America: aversion to foreigners 58–60, 106; Hungarians in 33, 40–41, 100–109
Congdon, James A. 95
Congressional Medal of Honor: Hungarian recipient 83, 87, 98, 121, 127
Copway, George 10
Crimean War 21, 36, 72, 102, 138, 142, 148, 177, 190, 204
Cserépy, István 38
Csermelyi, Joseph 117, 119, 137
Cuba 137, 162, 181
Curtis, Samuel R. 72
Czapkay, Lajos 124, 224

Damburghy, Ede 150
Damjanich, János 176
Dancs, Lajos 23, 28, 29, 34, 35, 97, 153, 158, 170
Davenport, Iowa: Hungarians in 75, 126, 129, 134, 145
Davis, Jefferson 54, 58, 59, 101, 103–104, 181
Davis, William Watson 81
Debreczeny, Ignatz 122, 137
Declaration of Independence, of Hungary 7
Degollado, Mariano 107
De Korpinay, Gabriel 121, 138
De Korponay, Stephen 138
De Zeyk, Albert 73, 124, 139–140, 152
diplomatic service, U.S.: Hungarians in 54, 56, 87, 123–125, 140, 148–149, 155, 179, 199, 207
Doane, Sidney A. 44
Dobozy, Emeric 140
Dobozy, Peter Paul 115–116, 126, 140–141
Douglass, Frederick 12

253

Dred Scott Decision 45, 57
Duff, James 60
Dunka, Nicolai 56, 120, 140, 148, 192
D'Utassy, Anthony 141–142
D'Utassy, Carl 142
D'Utassy, Frederick George 68–69, 142–145, 155, 159, 168, 193, 195

Éber, Nándor 56
Ely, Alfred 134
Emerson, Ralph Waldo 97
Emich, Gusztáv 83
Estván, Béla (Heinrich, Peter) 27, 57–59, 77, 100–109, 129, see also *War Pictures from the South*

Fejérváry, Nicholas, Jr. 121, 126, 145
Fekete, Alexander 146
Ferrie, Joseph P. 47
Fiala, John 31, 72, 74, 130, 146–147, 167
Figyelmessy, Philip 56, 121, 123, 141, 147–149, 192
Fillmore, Millard 9
Finto, John 149
Fish, Hamilton 26
Fornet, Cornelius 19, 20, 122, 149–151
Francis Joseph I 7
Frazer, Robert W. 58, 107
Frémont, John Charles 55, 57, 70–74, 80–81, 85, 88, 89–90, 92–94, 95, 96, 97, 98, 120, 124, 135, 139, 141, 144, 147, 148, 150, 170, 171, 183, 185, 192, 204
Frémont Bodyguard 72, 74, 90–97
Froehlich, Louis 105

Gaal, Alexander 151
Galenson, David W. 49
Gallfy(Gallik), Andrew 151
Galveston, Texas 77, 126, 129, 156, 193, 200, 202, 205
Garibaldi, Giuseppe 56, 125, 133, 155, 191, 192, 195, 203, 208
Garibaldi Guard, 39th New York Volunteers 68, 70, 76, 142, 143, 155, 159, 195
Garrison, William Lloyd 12
Genin, John N. 161
German-Americans: Hungarians' connections with 2, 10, 38, 53–54, 68, 70, 71, 74–75, 84, 98
Gerster, Anton 31, 38, 71, 152
Gettysburg, battle of 70, 86, 136, 155, 161, 164, 189
Gordon, Henford Lennox 88
Görgei, Artúr 6–7, 86
Gorszky, Xavér 35
Grant, Ulysses S. 120, 160, 183, 193, 204
Great Britain: and Kossuth emigrants 9–10, 18, 22–23
Grechenek, George 120, 139, 152–153

Greeley, Horace 108
Grossinger, Charles 153, 171
Guyon, Richárd 84, 161
Gy, Károly 18

Hajnik, Pál 27
Hamilton, Alexander 86
Hammond, William Alexander 207
Haraszthy, Ágoston 20, 154
Haraszthy, Gaza 154
Harris, William 58
Haynau, Julius Freiherr von 7
Hays, Alexander 86
Hearst, William Randolph 181
Hecker, Friedrich 2, 75, 166, 172
Hillebrandt, Hugo 70, 124, 154–155
Hollan, Hugo 120, 155–156, 171
Holmy, Johann Rudolph 156
Hungarian-American: assimilation 3, 57, 114, 121, 180; associations 34, 35–36, 74, 88; church 34–35; employment patterns 18, 30–31, 43, 49, 55, 125; female immigration 41–43; homesickness 23, 43–44, 184; language problems 26, 38, 56, 115, 166; motivations for enlistment 50–62, 89, 107–108, 114, 187; naturalization 44–45, 59, 121, 157, 163, 178, 181; real estate property of 46–47; settlements in the U.S. 33–34, 40–41; see also New Buda
Hungarian Legion (Italy) 22, 36, 37, 56, 123, 140, 141, 142, 148, 151, 192, 194, 203, 209
Hunter, David 87, 95

Ihász, Dániel 148, 152, 209

Jackson, Claiborne F. 71
Jekelfalussy, Alexander 75, 156–157
Johnson, Andrew 70, 87, 106, 123, 124, 155, 179, 199, 209
Johnston, William Preston 96

Kaiser, Ferenc 112
Kalapsza, János 34, 89, 152
Kansas-Nebraska Act 45, 57
Kappner, Ignatz 116, 157–158
Kászonyi, Dániel 44, 148, 172
Kelemen, Attila 52, 162
Kemenyffy, Joseph 122, 158
Kende, Géza 36
Kinizsi, István 30, 34, 89, 152, 171, 206
Kiss, Anthony 159
Kiss, Miklós 22–23
Klapka, György 36–37, 56, 197
Klauzál, Gábor 184
Knapp, Shepherd 37
Knefler, Frederick 76, 121, 126, 159–160
Komjáthy, Tihamér Antal 68
Kornis, Károly 35
Kossuth, Lajos 2, 17, 20, 21, 23, 28, 29, 34, 36, 44, 52, 53, 80, 81, 101, 103, 104, 116, 120, 129,

130, 136, 140, 146, 147, 148, 149, 150, 152, 153, 154, 157, 165, 169, 170, 175, 176, 177, 179, 181, 182, 186, 187, 196, 203, 208, 210; Governor 7–8; Hungarian colony in the U.S. 37–38; Hungarian reform movement 5–6; internment 8–9; lecturing tour 9–13, 18, 26, 27
Koszta, Martin 112, 129
Kovacs, Stephen 52, 70, 161–162
Kovats, Augustus 75, 162–163, 172
Kozlay, Eugene 23–25, 56–57, 70, 112–114, 121, 161–164, 202
Kozlay, Janet 57
Kune, Julian 36, 75, 129, 164–166, 167, 172

Lang, Henry 166
Langenfeld, Francis 75, 167
Langer, Ignatz 122, 167–168
László, Károly 31, 89, 130, 139, 152, 157, 169, 170, 182, 209, 210
Lederer, Immanuel 168–169
Lee, Robert E. 63, 104, 120
Lengyel, Emil 51
Lincoln, Abraham 12, 51, 53, 71, 72, 73, 74, 75, 86, 87, 94, 95, 96, 98, 106, 123, 124, 139, 140, 144, 165, 172, 180, 188, 189, 199, 210
Lincoln Riflemen, 24th Illinois Volunteers 52, 75, 129, 157, 163, 165, 166, 172
Liptay, Pál 40
Liszt, Franz 207–208
London 18, 22, 36, 109, 148, 153, 162, 171–172, 174, 180, 186, 188, 190, 201, 204, 206
Longfellow, Samuel W. 165
Longstreet, James 103
Lonn, Ella 2, 57, 101, 103, 105
Lopez, Narciso 117, 137, 162, 181
Lukács, Sándor 28
Lulley, Charles 169
Lulley, Emanuel 52, 169
Lyon, Nathaniel 71, 90, 124

Mack, Joseph 147, 186
Madarász, József 25, 53, 111
Magyar Száműzöttek Lapja (newspaper) 35–36
Mahin, Dean B. 2, 63, 64
Majthényi, József 28, 30, 33, 42, 169
Majthenyi, Theodore 93, 122, 169–170
Marianna, Florida, battle of 81, 121
Márki, Sándor 98
Maximilian I 109, 180
McClellan, George B. 56, 75, 86, 102, 166, 172, 204
McGuire, James 199, 204, 208
McPherson, James M. 55, 61
Menyhart, John 170–171, 190
Mészáros, Emeric 171
Mészáros, Lázár 30, 35–36, 150
Mexico 60, 106–108, 124, 180, 207
Mihalotzy, Géza 75, 120, 163, 165, 166, 167, 171–173

Miller, Robert E. 96–97
USS *Mississippi* 9, 52, 80, 136, 161, 169, 175, 176, 203
Molitor, Géza 150
Monaghan, Jay 90
Mosby, John Singleton 86, 88
Mundee, Charles 121, 173–174

Nagy, Alexander 174–175
Napoleon III 106
nativism 13, 58–59, 60, 72, 86, 118, 133, 172, 202
Nemett, József 175
Nevins, Alan 72
New Buda, Iowa 37–38, 40–41, 44, 48, 130, 140, 161, 162, 169, 178, 182, 184, 193; *see also* Hungarian-American settlements
New Buda (play) 129
New Orleans: Hungarians in 13, 26, 33, 40–41, 113, 136, 146, 151, 163, 194
New York: Hungarians in 19, 23, 26, 27, 28, 31, 32, 33, 36, 37, 41, 52, 68–69, 70
Nicholas I 7

Öfele, Martin 2, 114, 157, 209
Olmsted, Frederick Law 31, 80

Paskevich, Ivan Fyodorovich 7
Pea Ridge, Arkansas, battle of 81, 82, 171, 175
Perczel, Mór 134, 176
Perczel, Nicholas 50, 76, 122, 176–177, 191
Petőfi, Sándor 83–84
Piedmont, West Virginia, battle of 87, 121, 127
Pivány, Eugene 1, 51, 63, 64, 79, 100
Pleasonton, Alfred 86
Pogány, András H. 100–101, 103
Pomutz, George 123, 127–128, 177–179
Pope, Clayne L. 49
Pope, John 72, 86
Pozsonyi, József 189
Pragay, John 20, 150, 181
Princz, Gáspárné 18
Pulitzer, Joseph 22, 57, 67, 125, 158, 166, 179–181
Pulszky, Ferenc 29–130, 124, 166, 172, 178, 183

Rácz-Rónay, Károly 40–41, 84, 98, 102
Radnich, Emeric 76, 122, 181–182
Radnich, Stephen 76, 182–183
return migration 121–122
Roebling, John Augustus 31, 152
Rombauer, Raphael 71, 73, 78, 125, 183
Rombauer, Robert 71, 78, 126, 129, 183–184
Rombauer, Roderick 43, 71, 78, 129, 184–185
Rombauer, Roland 71, 78, 185–186
Roosevelt, Franklin Delano 99, 127
Rozsafy, Matthias 186
Russell, William Howard 60, 204
Ruttkay, Albert 53, 81, 118, 119, 187

St. Louis: Hungarians in 41, 71
San Antonio, Texas 60, 77, 126, 149, 199–201
San Francisco 41, 98, 124, 147, 195, 199
Sárpy, György 148
Schoepf, Albin 121, 187–189
Schofield, John 156–157
Schoney, Lazarus 125, 189
Schoolcraft, Henry Rowe 169
Schuricht, Hermann 102, 105–106
Schurz, Carl 2, 9, 53–54
Schwarzenberg, Felix 8
Schweiger, Amanda 89
Scott, Winfield 187–188
Semmelweis, Ignác 195
Semsey, Charles 189–190
Seward, William Henry 27, 44, 123, 124, 140, 148
Sherman, William Tecumseh 58, 96, 194
Sigel, Franz 53–54, 86–87
slavery: Hungarians' approach to 45, 61, 110–114; *see also* abolitionism; colored regiments
Solyom, Louis 125, 190–191
Spelletich, Stephen 191–192
Springfield, Missouri, battle of 73, 79, 88, 90–97, 122, 127, 170
Stahel, Julius H. 53, 70, 79, 83–88, 97–99, 121, 123, 127, 141, 148, 149
Stanton, Edwin M. 53
Stowe, Harriet Beecher 112, 114, 176
Sturgis, Samuel D. 72
Szabad, Emeric 54–55, 59, 129, 162, 192–193
Szabo, Ignatz 193
Szabo, Joseph 193
Széchenyi, Béla 112
Széchenyi, István 19, 206
Szegedy, Matthias 193–194
Szekula, Jenő 149
Szemere, Bertalan 34
Szépréthy, Adél 150

Takats, Francis (captain) 69, 195
Takats, Francis (sergeant) 194
Tauszky, Rudolph 115, 125, 195–196
Taylor, Zachary 7, 26
Tenner, Louis 196
Thomas, Lorenzo 115
Thoult, István 89
Tocqueville, Alexis de 20
Toplanyi, Alexander 117–118, 119, 196–198
Tóth, Lőrinc 19
Török Lajos 34
Train, George Francis 108
travelogues 19–20, 26, 111
Türr, István 56

Ujffy, John 198
Újházy, László 20, 23, 26, 27, 28, 29, 37, 38, 40, 43, 44, 48, 54, 55, 111, 112, 124, 125, 130, 140, 178, 181, 202
Uznay, István 150

Vallas, Anthony 58
Vandor, Joseph 124, 198–199
Vardy, Stephen Bela 20
Varga, Alexander 199–200
Varga, Benjamin 60, 77, 126, 199–200
Varga, Ferenc 44
Varga, John 200
Varga, Joseph 200
Varga, Paul 201
Vasvary, Edmund 1–3, 51, 64, 75, 79, 96, 99, 100, 101, 109, 124, 127, 137, 138, 186, 191, 206, 207, 208
Vertessy, John 201
Vetter, Antal 35, 148, 209
Vidor, Charles 126, 129, 201–202
Világos: Hungarian forces surrender at 7, 101
Villafranca, Peace of 22, 37, 56, 192, 203, 208
Vöneky, Louis 118, 202–203
Vörösmarty, Mihály 176

Waagner, Gustave 34, 55, 73, 183, 203–204
Wadgymar, Arthur 125, 204–205
Walker, Leroy P. 104
Wallace, Lew 159–160
War Pictures from the South 57, 100–102, 104–106, 109, 129; *see also* Estván, Béla
Wass, Samu 150
Watson, William 59, 61
Weekey, Anthony 70, 120, 205–206
Wesselényi, Miklós 20
Whittier, John Greenleaf 74
Wise, Henry A. 104, 133–134

Xantus, John 43, 122, 124, 178, 206–207

Yandoh, Judy 97

Zagonyi, Charles 34, 54, 72–74, 79, 88–99, 122, 127, 129, 130, 148, 153, 170–171, 192
Zerdahelyi, Edward 207–208
Zulavsky, Casimir 78, 208
Zulavsky, Emile 78, 81, 118, 119, 208–209
Zulavsky, Emilie Kossuth 153, 182
Zulavsky, Ladislaus 78, 81, 116, 118, 119, 141, 209–210
Zulavsky, Sigismund 78, 118, 120, 210

www.ingramcontent.com/pod-product-compliance
Ingram Content Group UK Ltd.
Pitfield, Milton Keynes, MK11 3LW, UK
UKHW041933140426
5217IPUK00014B/452

Well-Being as Value Fulfillment

How We Can Help Each Other to Live Well

Valerie Tiberius

OXFORD
UNIVERSITY PRESS

Great Clarendon Street, Oxford, OX2 6DP,
United Kingdom

Oxford University Press is a department of the University of Oxford.
It furthers the University's objective of excellence in research, scholarship,
and education by publishing worldwide. Oxford is a registered trade mark of
Oxford University Press in the UK and in certain other countries

© Valerie Tiberius 2018

The moral rights of the author have been asserted

First published 2018
First published in paperback 2020

All rights reserved. No part of this publication may be reproduced, stored in
a retrieval system, or transmitted, in any form or by any means, without the
prior permission in writing of Oxford University Press, or as expressly permitted
by law, by licence or under terms agreed with the appropriate reprographics
rights organization. Enquiries concerning reproduction outside the scope of the
above should be sent to the Rights Department, Oxford University Press, at the
address above

You must not circulate this work in any other form
and you must impose this same condition on any acquirer

Published in the United States of America by Oxford University Press
198 Madison Avenue, New York, NY 10016, United States of America

British Library Cataloguing in Publication Data
Data available

Library of Congress Cataloging in Publication Data
Data available

ISBN 978-0-19-880949-4 (Hbk.)
ISBN 978-0-19-289468-7 (Pbk.)

Links to third party websites are provided by Oxford in good faith and
for information only. Oxford disclaims any responsibility for the materials
contained in any third party website referenced in this work.

To my parents, Merike Lugus and Richard Tiberius

Preface

I have been thinking about well-being for many years. I started to want to write this book when I realized that my last book (*The Reflective Life*) was not exactly about well-being, even though that's what I thought it would be about when I started writing it. In that book I ended up distinguishing the topic of well-being from my topic there: what it is to live a good life from your own point of view. I am now extending some of the ideas that I developed in previous work to the topic of well-being. In order to do this, I have had to move away from the first person point of view and talk about how we assess the well-being of others. My aim here has been to do this without sacrificing the intimate relationship between well-being and the person whose well-being it is. This new focus has allowed me to move from questions about how to live one's own life to questions about how to help other people. How friends can help each other and what kinds of qualities it makes sense for friends to cultivate in order to be helpful are topics that I take up in the second half of the book.

My thinking about the topic of well-being has been greatly influenced by the work of psychologists on well-being and happiness. I appreciate this work and the contribution these researchers are making to the field and to society. I firmly believe that questions about the nature of well-being and how to improve people's lives are questions that can only be answered by putting together the contributions from different fields. For these reasons, I did not write this book only for philosophers; rather, I set out to write a book that has something to say to psychologists and philosophers. Indeed, I hope that any person with an interest in the topic will be able to get something out of the book, but that may represent too much optimism about my skills as a writer.

Writing for a broader audience (or at least attempting to) may result in a final product that disappoints everyone in different ways.

There is a lot less discussion of the literature and of particular objections than philosophers will expect, and not much engagement with the method of counter-exampling beloved by philosophers. I was advised by a wise (and patient) editor, Peter Momtchiloff, that people do not find it interesting to read detailed discussions about the dialectic in another field (and readers who want to avoid this type of discussion altogether should skip Section 1.4). Psychologists might be surprised to find very little discussion of data and experiments. This is a theoretical work that is informed by empirical research, but it is not primarily about psychological research. I have tried to steer the right path between competing interests, but I may have erred in one direction or another. I ask for the reader's patience and hope that the overall picture presented here will be worth it.

There are a number of people I would like to thank for their help in thinking about the ideas that have turned into this book. Very special thanks are due to Mike Bishop and Paul Bloomfield who provided detailed, generous, and constructive feedback on the manuscript, as well as needed encouragement at crucial moments. Gwen Bradford also provided challenging and extremely helpful comments on the manuscript. I hope to have done some justice to this feedback. Justin Ivory read the manuscript with care and provided excellent research assistance in the last stretches of writing. Colin DeYoung also deserves special thanks for keeping me on track empirically, and for putting up with all sorts of questions about psychology to which he invariably supplied comprehensible answers at the drop of a hat. I'm very grateful to Stephen Setterberg and Lauren Kuykendall for providing helpful perspectives from psychotherapy and psychology. For helpful comments and discussions of parts of the book I am grateful to Mark Alfano, Ben Bradley, Ruth Chang, Juliette Cherbuliez, Susan Dwyer, Alicia Hall, Jennifer Hawkins, Dan Haybron, Chris Heathwood, Geoffrey Hellman, Claire Horisk, Justin Kuster, Hallie Liberto, Eden Lin, Andrew Mills, Jason Raibley, Peter Railton, Wayne Riggs, David Shoemaker, Karen Stohr, Sharon Street, Kiry Tiberius, and Paula Tiberius. I would also like to thank audiences at the University of Connecticut, the University of Edinburgh, the University of Maryland, the University of Michigan, Tulane University, the University of Twente, the University of Virginia, and my own department at the University of Minnesota. I am grateful to the audience at an invited session at the Central APA in New Orleans and to the Princeton Ethics Network. Connie Rosati has been particularly encouraging as I developed my value fulfillment theory and particularly helpful in discussions that delved into metaethics.

I am very grateful for a year-long fellowship from the National Endowment for the Humanities, which made room for some sustained work on the manuscript at an early stage, and to the John Templeton Foundation for funding two projects that contributed indirectly to this book. I am also grateful to Judy Grandbois, Pam Groscost, and Anita Wallace; there is no way I could have completed a book while department chair were it not for such a terrifically reliable staff. Because this book is partly about friendship, I'm very aware of how much I have learned from my friends, and I'm thankful for their presence in my life; I have certainly learned more from my friends about what it is to be a good friend than I have by reading philosophy. In particular, I want to single out my amazing sister Paula, from whom I have learned so much about friendship both by observing her with her own friends and by experiencing her friendship myself. And, last but not least, as always, I am tremendously grateful for the unwavering support and editorial talents of my husband, J. D. Walker. I could not write anything good without him.

A Note about Pronouns

Because there is no inclusive third person singular pronoun in English, I have used "they" and "their" as gender neutral, *singular* pronouns. So, when I talk about "a person" or "an individual", I will use "they", as in, for example, "a person's well-being should not be something they find alien". I realize that this will make some people cringe, but times they are a changin' and language changes with them. As I write in 2018, I'm betting that we will eventually all become accustomed to this. (My undergraduate students are already entirely used to it, and I am trying to overcome my own inclination to cringe when I hear them use "they" and "their" in this way!) I also frequently use the pronouns "we" and "us" when I want to talk about people in general with whom I have certain things in common. I recognize that this "we" does not include everybody, but I do think it includes most people. I don't really think there's an alternative to starting out by talking about "us" when we do ethics; I think that ethics is always built on a foundation of common concerns. So, my use of "we" is as much a philosophical stance as a grammatical one. I should make clear that I do not mean to imply that people who do not share central ethical concerns with me are not persons, nor that they do not have well-being. My theory may not apply to them, that's all.

Contents

1. Introduction — 1
   1.1. Maxine, Sander, and Jules — 4
   1.2. The Focus on Friendship — 8
   1.3. The Focus on Values and the Value Fulfillment Theory in a Nutshell — 10
   1.4. Why this Theory? — 17
2. The Value Fulfillment Theory of Well-Being — 34
   2.1. Main Features of the Value Fulfillment Theory — 34
   2.2. What are Values? — 37
   2.3. The Value-Fulfilled Life and the Long-Term Perspective — 46
   2.4. Can Ultimate Values be Improved? — 55
   2.5. Value Fulfillment Theory: Subjective or Objective? — 61
   2.6. Conclusion — 65
3. What is Value Fulfillment? — 66
   3.1. What is Value Fulfillment for a Single Value? — 69
   3.2. What is Value Fulfillment for Multiple Values? — 76
   3.3. Values and Virtues — 86
   3.4. Adaptive Values — 94
   3.5. Conclusion — 96
4. Assessing Well-Being: Value Fulfillment Theory in Practice — 98
   4.1. Friendship and Helping — 100
   4.2. Friends are not Other Selves — 105
   4.3. Informational and Interpersonal Challenges — 114
   4.4. When Does it Make Sense to Discount, Ignore, or Try to Change People's Values? — 122
   4.5. Beyond Friendship — 133
   4.6. Conclusion — 138
5. Being a Good Friend — 140
   5.1. Good Friends — 140
   5.2. Perspective-Taking and Its Challenges — 144
   5.3. Humility in Friendship — 155

5.4. How Open-Minded Should We Be about Our Values?	165
5.5. Friendship and Moral Decency	170
5.6. Conclusion	173
6. Conclusion	174
Notes	181
Bibliography	197
Index	211

1

Introduction

Meditation is supposed to be good for you. So are regular exercise, having a strong network of friends, and feeling grateful for what you have. Having children, it turns out, will not help you in the happiness department and nor will making more money beyond a certain point. Sleeping more is good for you and long commutes are bad. You'll be better off if you have an optimistic outlook and a sense of purpose and if you spend more time at 13.9 degrees Celsius (57 degrees Fahrenheit) (Tsutsui 2013). Advice about how to be happy and achieve well-being is everywhere.[1]

Happiness and well-being are very important to people, but few people take all the advice that has been given. People have not ceased to have children, they continue to live in cities where they have unavoidable commutes, they fill their lives with activities that prevent them from getting enough sleep and they fail to meditate, exercise, or count their blessings. There are lots of reasons for this, of course: it's hard to make major changes, there are other considerations in life besides one's own well-being, and not everyone has heard the advice. But there is another reason, too, which is that we all have different ideas about what happiness is and how to get it. So even if we hear the advice, we're not necessarily going to believe it. Unlike the advice to floss your teeth to avoid gum disease, which we know we should take even if we're too lazy, we're often not sure that advice about how to be happy will make our lives better in the way that matters to us. Psychological studies, after all, generate advice based on what works on average, and not all of us are (or at least think we are) average!

The point here is that happiness or well-being is *personal*. Well-being is something good, but it is a special kind of good: it is the good *for* a person.[2] The fact that well-being is personal creates some troubles for anyone who wants to promote it for other people. To see this, let me ask you to think about the last time you believed you knew what was good for someone else, say, a friend or family member, or someone you read a story about in the news. If you're an oldest sibling like me (and for many others too), you have probably experienced frustration when you've tried to tell others what would be good for them to do. Just as people don't listen to the advice they get from journalists reporting on happiness research, so too they don't listen to big sisters, partners, parents, or friends. If well-being is personal, then it's probably not simply that these people are stubbornly resisting our excellent advice; rather, it's that well-being is not the kind of thing that others (like meddling older sisters and psychological experts) can determine for us.

This can make it hard to help people. Add to this the fact that when we do aim to help people, we almost always have other interests. We want the people we love to continue to love us back, we want our friends to continue to enjoy our company and be fun for us to spend time with, and we want people in our community to be law-abiding and nice. Sometimes these other interests conflict with helping people. For example, it might be best for your drinking buddy who actually has a serious problem with alcohol to join Alcoholic Anonymous and become sober, even though this will mean a change to your friendship in ways that might not be very fun for you. More often, though, these other interests are not so much in direct conflict with helping others, but they do influence what looks to us like the best way of helping.

The problem of how to help is the focal point of this book. To get a better grip on the problem, let's start with what we know. First, sometimes it's easy to see what would help improve someone's well-being. Say that you do have a friend who is an addict and there is a program he could go to that would be very likely to lead to recovery. Helping the friend choose to complete this program would be a great improvement to his well-being, because recovering from drug addiction would make so many things in his life—work, family relationships, physical health—go better. It is obvious that parents whose lives are too financially insecure to provide for their children can be helped by improving their financial situation. Elderly people living in assisted living facilities can be helped by ensuring that they have as much autonomy as possible and some things to do that are meaningful for them. For people who do not have access to clean drinking water, enough food, shelter, or medical care for themselves and their families, it is clear that getting these things would improve their lives. Not that it's always easy to know *how* to get these things to them—that's a different question. What's not difficult in these cases is knowing the kind of things that would help if they could be done.[3]

Second, when it's not easy to help, this can be for a variety of reasons. I've already mentioned conflicts between your interest in helping to improve a person's well-being and other interests you may have (some selfish, some not). Such conflicts create epistemic problems for helping: it's difficult to know what things are like from someone else's point of view and, therefore, difficult to know how to help them. Sometimes this is because we have other interests that prevent us from knowing, but sometimes it's the result of failures of communication, limited imagination or sympathy, or just the degree of difference in what things are like for us and for them. There are also practical problems that make it difficult to help. Even if we could be fairly sure that we know what is good for another person, helping to move that person along the right path may be annoying, condescending, manipulative, or coercive. Your addict friend may not see that it is in his interest to go to rehab and your pushing might end up just alienating you from him.

You might think that the answer here is to help in the obvious ways and otherwise butt out. I think the first part of this answer is on target: we should help people in obvious ways. Much work has been done by moral philosophers to argue for fairly demanding obligations to help people who are vastly worse off than those of us who are likely to read these philosophical arguments (for example, Ashford 2007, 2011; Singer 1972; Unger 1996). Even if we disagree about just how demanding these obligations are, it's hard to deny that we ought to do more than we do. But there's a problem with the second half of the answer, which is that close relationships with friends and family are just the kinds of relationships that make us want to help each other. Friends—and let's think of that category broadly so that it includes family members and romantic partners—are people we care about for their own sake. What else is it to care about someone for their own sake but to want their lives to go well? And if their lives are not going well, it's just a natural part of friendship to want to help. Butting out of your friend's life may sometimes be the best thing to do, but when it is it's because that is the best way to help (or because the friend does not actually need help), not because you've ceased to have any concern for helping. When we do stop being concerned about how to help our friends when they need help, this usually means that something has gone wrong with the friendship.

So, one thing we know is that it can sometimes be difficult to help our friends. This is a problem that gives rise to ethical thinking. It's not a purely strategic problem about how to get from point A to point B, because often we don't even know what "point B" is. When helping is difficult, it's not just because we don't know how to get there, but also because we don't know where to go. The theory of well-being defended in this book—the value fulfillment theory—is a solution to this problem.

1.1 Maxine, Sander, and Jules

Before we proceed to more abstract theoretical discussions of well-being, I want to start with a few examples of the "not easy" cases that demonstrate some of the complexities involved in helping friends. These cases will serve to illustrate the problem that the value fulfillment theory is meant to solve, and it will be useful to return to them at various points along the way.

Maxine has always wanted children. She has tried everything but cannot get pregnant. She has already tried some expensive fertility treatments and is now considering the very expensive, potentially heartbreaking option of surrogacy. Her partner is supportive, but doesn't feel the same need for children. Maxine is quite certain about the importance of being a mother and has always held that it's crucial for children to be biologically related to their parents—it is this certainty that has propelled her to take the steps she has already taken. She has always valued family more than anything and her heart melts at the thought of seeing the child that she and her beloved partner would produce. But now she is considering putting herself further into debt and opening up the possibility of yet more disappointment. Friends and doctors are urging her to think about adoption or not having children at all. She's also not sure what she thinks about the ethics of surrogacy; she and her partner think that they would have to allow the surrogate to have some connection to the child she carried, but they're uncertain how this would work. At the same time, she cannot imagine a life that does not include being a parent.

Would Maxine be better off adopting? Would she be better off embracing the role of "favorite aunt" to her nieces and nephews? Is surrogacy the best option for her? How much should she consider the financial burden? How much do her partner's interests matter? These are difficult and multifaceted questions. Women in Maxine's circumstances often turn to their friends to talk through these topics, and these friends can be more or less helpful. There will be much more to say about helpful friends later in the book, but it seems likely that friends who push their own agenda without regard for what Maxine really cares about are less helpful than friends who listen. The main point for now is that if you were Maxine's friend, helping her is complicated: it isn't obvious what to do or say.

Sander is a gay man who is also a member of the Church of Latter Day Saints, which does not accept homosexuality. Sander wants to have romantic relationships with men, but he is also deeply committed to his faith and has a personal connection with God that sustains him. His commitment to the Church gives meaning to his life and also binds him to what he takes to be a community of loving, like-minded people. He does not think the Church doctrine about homosexuality is correct, but he also doesn't think they will come around to the right view in his lifetime. Sander has thought about leaving the Church to make it easier to live as a gay man, but has been drawn back to it. Instead of leaving the Church, Sander participates in a Mormon LGBT advocacy group, and blogs about being gay in the Mormon Church. Sander is a fictionalized case, but there are many real people who experience a conflict between their religious faith and other aspects of their personalities (Swartz 2011). One very eloquent example is John Gustave-Wrathall, a gay man and member of the Church of the Latter Day Saints, who writes about the struggle between his sexual and religious identities:

> ...the Spirit spoke to me with a clarity and power I had never before experienced in my life, telling me that it was time for me to come back to the Church. I wept, I cursed, I tried to deny it. But in the end, I realized that I wanted the peace that came from following that prompting more than I wanted a life free from contradiction and conflict.
> (John Gustave-Wrathall, "Pillars of My Faith", Aug. 2014, http://affirmation.org/pillars-faith/)

Sander (like the real person just quoted) decides to live with the conflict, but it isn't easy. He's not permitted in the Temple, some other members of the Church shun him, and the friends he meets who are more accepting of his sexual orientation do not understand the importance of the Church in his life.

Would Sander be better off finding a different, more accepting Church? Should he continue to be friends with fellow Mormons who don't accept this important aspect of his life? If he does stay with the Mormons, is it good for him to devote his time to reforming the Church, even if he thinks this is hopeless? If you were Sander's friend and you were aware of this conflict, you might want to help. Perhaps you would want to bring him to your more accepting Church, or try to convince him to abandon faith entirely (if you're a philosopher, perhaps by telling him about the problem of evil), or join his fight to change the Mormon Church. Again, the point for now is that it's not easy to know how to help Sander.

Finally, Jules (a character from Meg Wolitzer's novel, *The Interestings*) is an aspiring actor, living in New York City and waitressing to make ends meet. She has been taking acting lessons and going to auditions since graduating from college with a degree in psychology. She is now approaching 30 and uncertain about whether to continue. As Wolitzer describes her situation:

During the day when she could, Jules went to open-call theater auditions, and only once received a callback, but still she kept going to them.

Her friends were too nice to suggest that she might think about an alternative field. Parents were the ones who handed you law school admission test study guides unprompted, and when you responded with revulsion or rage, they defensively said, "But I just wanted you to have something to fall back on." The world of law was filled with the fallen, but theater wasn't. No one ever "fell back" onto theater. You had to really, really want it...

"I should quit," Jules said [to her best friend Ash].

"No, you shouldn't. You're too good."

"No, I'm not."

Ash always encouraged Jules, despite the truth.   (Wolitzer 2014, pp. 55–6)

In the novel, it's clear that Jules' struggle is affecting her well-being. But again, it's not easy to know how to help. Is her friend's unconditional support of her artistic ambitions good for Jules? Would she be better off finding a new way to fulfill her need for creativity? How much should financial considerations play a role in how we think about what's good for Jules? If Ash had the resources to help financially (which she does, in the novel), would that kind of help be good for Jules in the long term?

One thing that the examples of Maxine, Sander, and Jules have in common is that their situations raise concerns for the people who care about them. Their situations are ones that tend to make loved ones wonder what they can do to help. If these examples don't sound familiar to you, try to think of someone whose well-being you have been concerned about in your own life. Reflecting on these examples, we can see that when we are concerned about a loved one it is because we think that something is not going well in the person's life. This could be because the friend is (psychologically) unhappy or suffering (as in the case of Maxine), or because the friend has made a choice that seems to us to reduce his well-being (as in the case of Sander), or because the friend is taking a course of action now that will lead to bad consequences for her in the future (as in the case of Jules). In each case, though based on different kinds of evidence, we make a judgment that our friends' lives are taking a blow, whether in the immediate term or in the anticipated future.

In all of these cases, judgments about what is good for someone else are difficult to make: there are many relevant factors and it isn't obvious how they should be weighed or put together. My emphasis on the difficulties should not be taken to support pessimism about helping other people; I think caution (not pessimism) is the right attitude to take. One might think that the need for caution is too obvious to be mentioned, but I'm not so sure. First, there has been a lot of attention paid recently to how little we really know about ourselves and what makes us happy (Doris 2015; Haybron 2008b; Wilson 2002) and it is sometimes implied that we know others *much better* than we know ourselves. I agree that we lack self-knowledge, but I think we shouldn't infer from this that we know our friends a whole lot better.[4] Second, at least in my experience, people often fail to exercise caution when they "help", and they end up being overbearing, judgmental, paternalistic, or just plain unhelpful. We'll talk much more about these pitfalls in later chapters.

1.2 The Focus on Friendship

My focus on helping friends achieve well-being, illustrated by the three examples in the previous section, requires some explanation. Why start here? The ultimate answer is that I think normative ethical theories—theories that aim not just to describe but to prescribe—are best thought of as tools for answering the practical, ethical questions we confront in living our lives.[5] Ethical theories are for solving practical problems that raise questions about what is good or bad, better or worse, worth doing or important to avoid. To construct an ethical theory, on this way of thinking, we start by identifying the problem we want to solve and the practical questions we want to answer.[6] From here the goal for ethical theory is to provide a framework that justifies answers to these questions. When it comes to well-being, the relevant questions are about what it is for a person's life to go better or worse *for them*, and how to improve people's lives *for their own sakes*. (Theories of well-being are ethical theories, then, but they may not exhaust ethics, because there may be ethical questions that do not have to do with well-being.[7])

But one still might ask: Why *this* problem—Why focus on helping friends and family members who are having a tough time? People with whom I've discussed the book as I've been writing it have asked this question in various forms that boil down to two main concerns: First, why start here when we should get our own house in order before helping others? And, second, why start here when it's relatively rare for friends to have the sorts of problems that raise these challenges and require this kind of help?

On the first point, I don't disagree. As I mentioned in the preface, much of my previous work has been focused on getting one's own house in order. But getting one's own house in order is a lifelong project, so it would be unwise to put off thinking about our friends until we have achieved perfection. It's also worth noting that thinking about how to be a helpful friend will shape how we aim to get ourselves in order. For example, I argue later in the book that we ought to cultivate habits of humility about how much we can understand what it's like to be someone else.

The second point about the rarity of relevant cases has a two-part answer. First, I'm not sure how rare these kinds of cases are, at least when it comes to romantic relationships, family relationships, and friendships between women. Certainly, the particular circumstances of Maxine, Sander, and Jules are uncommon, but challenges that have to do with "family planning" (whether to marry, whether to have kids, whether to have another kid) and career management (whether to get additional education, whether to move away from family for a job, whether to retrain) are very common. Further, it is very common for people to talk about these problems with their families, their romantic partners, and (at least) their female friends. On this last point, it is interesting to me that the people who have raised this concern have all been men who have said more or less the same thing: "I just play/watch football/baseball and drink beer/eat pizza with my friends; I don't have friends who need this kind of help". Of course, I have talked to other men who deny this stereotype of male friendship, but there may be some truth in it; and so there may be some people for whom the experience of feeling the need to help friends with their struggles is indeed rare. (I'll return to the topic of gender and friendship in Chapter 5.)

The second part of the answer to the rarity point is that even if these occasions are rare, we can learn something about well-being from thinking about them. In his book *Welfare and Rational Care*, Stephen Darwall (2002) argues that there is a conceptual connection between well-being and care for another person (the kind of care we have for friends). As he puts it, "what it is for something to be good for someone is for it to be something that is rational (makes sense, is warranted or justified) to desire for him insofar as one cares about him" (pp. 8–9). Whether or not we agree with Darwall that well-being should be *defined* in terms of rational care, we can agree that there is an intimate connection between the two ideas.[8] Caring for another person must involve wanting what is best for them. If we accept this, then it makes a lot of sense to think about well-being through the lens of the problem of how to help friends. This problem focuses our attention in the right place: on the very kind of value that well-being is supposed to be.

1.3 The Focus on Values and the Value Fulfillment Theory in a Nutshell

Now I'm going to make a rather bold claim that will take the rest of the book to fully explain and defend. I believe that if these are the parameters of our problem, then when we think about how to improve well-being, we ought to focus on people's values.[9] To understand this bold claim, we first need to know what values are. Intuitively, values are things we care about, things that are important to us, things we organize and plan our lives around. This intuitive notion is more or less what I mean by a value: *values* are the projects, activities, relationships, and ideals that we value, and to *value* something in the fullest sense is to have a relatively stable pattern of emotional, motivational, and cognitive dispositions or tendencies toward what is valued. For example, to value your collection of antique teapots is to tend to feel joy when you contemplate them and sad when one breaks; to tend to be motivated to protect them from damage and to buy new additions when they appear; and to consider your teapots in your practical deliberation (say, about how to ship your possessions when you move). Different values call for different emotional, motivational, and cognitive dispositions, but fully *appropriate* values include all three components.

There will be much more to say later about what I mean by "appropriate". For now, the rough idea will suffice: values are more appropriate when they integrate our emotions, desires, and judgments and are less appropriate when they pull our emotions, desires, and judgments in different directions. Most values are somewhere on a continuum of appropriateness: they are neither perfectly appropriate nor disastrously inappropriate. For example, valuing playing the piano is more appropriate for Yuja who both enjoys it and believes that it is a worthwhile use of her time than it is for Juri who thinks it is important but hates to play. In Juri's case, it may be a difficult task to figure out whether he should find a way to enjoy the piano, or whether he should try to talk himself out of the idea that it's good for him to play. Many different considerations are relevant: Would a different piano repertoire be more fun? Does he really love the flute? Is the thought that playing is important just a residual imperative from an authoritarian music teacher? Whether we should say that Juri *values* playing the piano, despite the fact that he lacks one dimension of valuing, is also a question that admits of different answers depending on the context; there are no bright lines here, and this will turn out to be OK.

Values, then, are complex psychological states that carry their own standards for improvement along the dimension of appropriateness. They also carry their own standards of success. You can fulfill, actualize, or promote your values to various degrees and in better or worse ways. Your teapots may all shatter into a thousand pieces, your collection might be shown to include mass-produced fakes, or you may suddenly find them a silly waste of time. Yuja may play terribly, she may find no time to practice, or she may stop enjoying the music. (It should be said that the real pianist, Yuja Wang, does not seem to have these problems.) In this way values are like preferences or goals. (Indeed, psychologists may well think of "goals" or "personal projects" as the more natural term for what I am calling "values".[10] I've chosen to stick with the word "value" because I want the category to be as broad as possible, and "goal" conveys a kind of intentional pursuit with a definite endpoint that I don't think always fits; for example, it's odd to think of one's marriage or a great friendship as a goal, but these things are very important values.) These standards of success or fulfillment may be subjective (for example, continuing to enjoy the music is a subjective standard of success), and they need not be explicit. A reflective person could articulate these standards in response to a question like "What is it that you value about playing the piano?", but this isn't necessary. People who have values in the sense I'm talking about have some notion of what it takes for their values to flourish or fail, even if that notion is implicit.

Finally, because we have multiple values that compete and cooperate in various ways, *systems* of values can be more or less suited for fulfillment over time. This provides yet another way to assess our values—we can ask how well they work together. For example, the person who values a collection of antique teapots *and* a nomadic lifestyle—couch surfing with nothing but a backpack to carry their possessions from place to place—doesn't have a set of values that are conducive to mutual fulfillment over time. Teapots in backpacks is a recipe for tears.

With this explanation of values in hand, we can ask why we should focus on them. The short explanation for the focus on values is that when we help people, we are pulled in two directions: we want to do something that they can see as helpful (that is, something that won't seem manipulative or alienating to the person we're trying to help), but we also have our own standards for what counts as good things to do and we do not want to pander to people who seem to us to have crazy ideas about what's good for them. Values are the right thing to focus on because they are fundamental to people's own perspectives on what makes their lives worth living and yet they also afford standards of improvement that allow the helper to reach beyond the person's limited current perspective. I will call the view that will unfold *the value fulfillment theory* of well-being.[11] To see the virtues of this theory we will need to understand more about what values are, how they are related to each other, how we can succeed or fail in terms of them, how we can focus on them, and how values allow us to reach beyond the immediate perspective of the person we're trying to help. These are the questions that will occupy us for the rest of the book.

For now, we have enough to state the basic idea: Well-being consists in the fulfillment of an appropriate set of values over a lifetime. In a little more detail, we can say that well-being is served by the successful pursuit of a relatively stable set of values that are emotionally, motivationally, and cognitively suited to the person. In a sound bite: well-being is a life rich in value fulfillment. Or at least we can say that this is a good way to think about well-being when our aim is to help people.[12]

To get an overview of how the value fulfillment theory works, let's consider how the idea of value fulfillment allows us to think about the happiness advice with which I began. (Note that "happiness" from here on should be taken in the "good feelings" sense, not the broader sense in which happiness is the same as well-being.) Consider commuting times. Research indicates that long commutes decrease people's happiness without any compensating benefits; long commutes make us unhappy and the stress doesn't pay off (Stutzer and Frey 2008). What should we do with this information? We first need to think about the practical context. Is there anything we can do about our commute? Could we change jobs, move, or switch to a different form of transportation that is less stressful and alienating? If you have a specialized job in a large urban area, there might not be much you can do. But even if there is something we can do, many of the changes we can make are costly so we need to think about whether it would be worth it. To figure this out, if we take a value fulfillment approach, we next need to ask what values are affected. Studies of the causes and correlates of happiness typically measure life satisfaction or positive affect (positive emotions and feelings). According to the value fulfillment theory, neither life satisfaction nor positive affect is equivalent to well-being, but both are likely to be a part of well-being since they are widely valued. Most of us do value our own psychological happiness (feeling good and feeling good about how our lives are going) and so the effect of commuting on these values is relevant to our well-being. Happiness isn't the only thing we value, though. Most commuters (and others) also value meaningful work and achievement in their careers, and these must also be taken into account. If we probe a little deeper, we can see that other values might be affected by this decision. Moving closer to work might mean less money for valued leisure activities; taking public transportation might mean more time for valued leisure activities such as reading or knitting.

The value fulfillment theory does not give us an easy way to calculate what is good for a person, nor does it give us a list of goods people *must* achieve in order to live well. It does, however, give us a sensible way to think about how people's lives could go better. It directs us to think about all the values that are in play, and it also directs us to think about the long term: How will these choices influence how much value fulfillment we can achieve over all, throughout the course of our lives? For example, when we sacrifice health for the sake of other values (say, we move for a job to a neighborhood that contains no good places to walk or bike), this affects how much value fulfillment we can expect over time because health is a prerequisite for the long-term pursuit of so many of our values. In short, the theory recommends we focus on how to live a life rich in value fulfillment, a life in which we find some things to be important to us and we succeed in terms of these values over the long term.

Of course, our current values and standards are not always ideal. We sometimes want things we are ashamed of wanting, love things we think are bad for us, and think things are good for us when we have no passion for them. We have ideas about what it means to succeed in terms of our values that are better and worse: sometimes we hold ourselves to impossible standards, sometimes our standards are so vague we don't know when we're succeeding. We are often prevented from achieving greater value fulfillment by normal human limitations: we can be incredibly short-sighted, we ignore or downplay the probabilities of change or failure, we exaggerate our own skills, and we get very attached to things that aren't working and then fool ourselves into thinking that they are. The goal of an overall value-fulfilled life—a life rich in the fulfillment of appropriate values according to standards of success that make sense for us—allows us to go beyond a person's limited subjective perspective in our thinking about how a person could be doing better. Moreover, this overarching goal gives us a way to think about how people's lives could go better without imposing external standards and abandoning the subjective point of view altogether: the ultimate standard for what values are appropriate is still the person whose values they are.

Does the value fulfillment theory say the right things about what we seem to know about how people's lives can go better or worse? As I mentioned above, it isn't hard to see that some questions about how to make life go better for people are easily answered. But other questions about how to make life go better for people are complex and difficult. What if Maxine were less certain about being a mother, and what if she were a lawyer who just made partner in a small firm? Would having children improve her life? Would it be good for Sander to come out to his very strict Mormon parents? If you were Jules' friend, do you help by telling her that you really doubt she'll ever be a successful actress, or by supporting her efforts?

The value fulfillment theory explains why the easy questions about making life go better for people are easy, and the hard questions hard. It makes easy questions (relatively) easy, because there are basic values that are shared by just about everyone (such as relationships, happiness, and meaningful work) and because there are necessary conditions for the successful pursuit of any values (such as health, having one's material needs met, and possessing sufficient liberty). How does the value fulfillment theory make the difficult questions difficult in the right way? When we think about what's good for a person in terms of value fulfillment we are led to think about what kinds of projects and goals are worthwhile for a person in their circumstances, how larger projects can be translated into specific goals they can act on, and which projects and goals fit together in a way that will allow the person to live a life that does them justice. These are just the right things to be thinking about. For example, whether having children is good for a new law partner depends on how motherhood will suit her as a person, how it fits into her life and how it will contribute to her ability to continue to pursue valuable projects over time. For a number of aspiring parents these days, it might also become relevant to think about how the value of being a parent can be realized if the normal route to parenthood isn't working. Would adoption or surrogacy result in a relationship with a child that would fulfill the value of parenthood? Is there a point at which further extraordinary means should be abandoned, because the values that one took to be most important can be modified in some way? When it comes to understanding how best to realize the near universal basic values (relationships, happiness, meaningful work) in a particular life, or how to fit more specific values into that life, there are many difficult questions. Moreover, the value fulfillment theory makes sense of the epistemic problems we encounter when we try to figure out what is good for other people. We often don't understand these deep features of people's psychological lives, and it is very difficult to make accurate predictions about how things will change and how these changes will affect the realization of our values.

The value fulfillment theory directs us to think about our values: what they are, how they suit us, how they can be variously interpreted and realized, and how they fit together over the long term. It tells us that a good life for a person, a life with well-being, is a life rich in value fulfillment, and a life rich in value fulfillment is a life in which we successfully pursue or realize appropriate values over time. For difficult questions—like the question of whether to adopt a child—this makes figuring out what is good for a person complex. For easier questions—like the question of whether to save for retirement—figuring out what to do or how to help someone does not require such intricate deliberations. This is as it should be and so I think it is an advantage of the value fulfillment theory that it respects this fact about life.

1.4 Why this Theory?

In the remainder of this book, I will explain the value fulfillment theory in more detail and show how it can be applied. You might reasonably wonder, before bothering to read the rest of the book, why you should consider *this* theory as opposed to a different one? How does this theory compare to other available theories and what's the argument that this theory is the correct one? (If you're not wondering, about this, as I mentioned in the preface, this would be a good section to skip.)

A standard way of proceeding in ethics is to argue that one theory is the correct one by showing that it gives the right verdicts about every imaginable case, or at least that it gives the right verdicts about more cases than any competitor. I'm not going to do this. Why not? My own view is that testing ethical theories for correctness by examining their implications for complex and unrealistic counterexamples is not the best use of our time.[13] It would take a really long time to consider all the fancy examples philosophers have come up with and at the end of the day we are likely to end up with camps divided by their intuitions about these cases anyway. Instead, I think we should identify the problem we are trying to solve (such as the problem of how to help each other) and look for an approach to that problem that makes sense, given our commitments and concerns. We should think about our aims (such as helping others and being happy ourselves) and our commitments (to the importance of happiness and autonomy, for example), and we should evaluate our theory by how well it helps to guide us, given these starting points. Constructing an ethical theory, I believe, is more like designing a method for solving problems than it is like discovering values or principles that it is someone else's job to apply.

This approach to ethics means that the argument for the theory I'm proposing is really the rest of the book. It will take that long to try to show that the theory is a reasonable and helpful guide to a practical problem. That said, it is worth situating the value fulfillment theory of well-being in the array of well-being theories and indicating some advantages it has over others before we get started. In philosophy, theories of well-being have often been divided into three camps: hedonism, desire satisfaction, and objective theories.[14] Hedonism identifies well-being with pleasure and the absence of pain and it is most compatible with psychological theories of subjective well-being that focus on positive affect or pleasant experience.[15] Desire satisfaction theories identify well-being with the satisfaction of desires or preferences, often informed or rational preferences.[16] These theories don't really have a match in the psychological research, but they predominate in standard economics where preferences have been favored over good feelings. Objective theories include objective list theories that posit lists of goods (like knowledge, friendship, and health) and eudaimonist or perfectionist theories that take well-being to be the fulfillment of our nature.[17] There are eudaimonist theories in psychology, too, that tend to emphasize satisfying central human needs (such as the need for relatedness or autonomy) and subjective feelings beyond pleasure such as feelings of meaning or worthwhileness.[18] Life satisfaction theories (left out of the above triad) are popular in psychology and at least one central figure in philosophy defends the view that well-being consists in "authentic life satisfaction".[19] Finally, these days, hybrid theories of well-being are recognized and favored by many.[20] These are theories that identify well-being with some objective goods (as objective list and eudaimonist theories do) but also recognize that for these goods to count as good *for us* we must respond positively to them (say, by desiring or enjoying them).[21] They are considered hybrid theories because they combine elements of objective and subjective theories.

You may now understand why a thorough comparison between my value fulfillment theory and all the other available alternatives is unappealing. We would do nothing else! But there are some general things to say that will motivate further consideration of the value fulfillment theory. First, to avoid a battle of intuitions about cases, let's start with what successful theories of well-being should look like: What are the criteria of success for well-being theories in philosophy? There are basically three. First, these theories should be adequate to our ordinary understanding and use of the concept; as Sumner puts it, they should be *descriptively adequate*.[22] This means, in part, that a theory of well-being should capture (or at least not be at odds with) as many as possible of our ordinary judgments about who has well-being and who doesn't. For example, someone who is lonely and chronically in pain should not turn out to have well-being (other things equal), and someone who enjoys good health, close friendships, and various interesting activities should not turn out to lack well-being (other things equal). Descriptive adequacy, in this sense, tends to be the criterion that preoccupies philosophers and it is the criterion that gives rise to the counter-exampling methodology. If I can come up with a case—the case of Bob, let's say—that elicits the judgment "Bob lacks well-being", and your theory does not have the result that Bob lacks well-being, this is a problem for your theory. Well-being theories should not be out of whack with our ordinary judgments, but this isn't the only criterion to consider.

Second, well-being theories should be adequate to explain the value of well-being and why we have good reason to pursue it or why we have good reason to follow the recommendations of the theory; in other words, the theory should be *normatively adequate*.[23] Normative adequacy is not a criterion that psychologists who study well-being usually acknowledge. Indeed, psychologists tend to eschew claims about the *value* of well-being on purpose: they are scientists studying an empirical phenomenon, not preachers or gurus making pronouncements about how people should live. Many philosophers, however, take "well-being" to be a "thick concept"—that is, a concept that is used both to describe the state of a person and also to prescribe, recommend, or praise.[24] I am one of these philosophers: I think that a good comprehensive theory of well-being should explain what's good about it and why people have good reasons to pursue it. In their research, psychologists may not be able to operationalize a concept that has this normative dimension, but I think they will be better served by a theory that does have this dimension, even if they need to focus on the descriptive side of the theory in their research.[25]

Normative adequacy matters to philosophers because many of us see our work on well-being and happiness as part of a long philosophical tradition that aims to answer ethical questions about the nature of a good life for a person. Psychologists have a different tradition, but I would wager that many of them (in their heart of hearts) take themselves to be studying things that are importantly related to what is good for people. Psychological research doesn't aim at defining what is good for people, but it does make assumptions about it. A theory of well-being that doesn't have any explanation for why well-being is a good thing would be lacking from either perspective.

Third, well-being theories should be compatible with our best understanding of how the world works; that is, well-being theories should be *empirically adequate*. Just as psychology makes assumptions about what is good for people, philosophers make assumptions about what people are actually like. The criterion of empirical adequacy demands that insofar as philosophical theories make empirical assumptions, or generate prescriptions that rely on empirical assumptions, those assumptions are well founded. Often, in the domain of well-being, the relevant empirical assumptions are assumptions about our psychology. For example, Aristotelian eudaimonist theories assume that virtues are real components of personality that can be cultivated through modeling and habituation. If John Doris (2002) is correct that the traditional virtues do not map onto real psychological entities, such theories have a problem.[26] Philosophical theories of well-being may also make empirical assumptions about measurement. A person who defends a theory of well-being as the good to be promoted by morally right action assumes that well-being can be compared across time and across different individuals. Such comparisons are needed for the possibility of rational decisions between actions with different outcomes. These assumptions do not demand perfect or easy measures, but they do require some capacity to make rough estimates of how much well-being would result from different choices.

If these are the criteria of success for a theory of well-being, why favor the value fulfillment theory? Again, let me remind the reader that I can't do justice to the enormous literature on theories of well-being in this introduction, and that my main point in this book is to paint a relatively detailed portrait of a theory worth considering.[27] I do not intend these critical remarks to be knock-down objections; rather, they are meant to explain why I think it's worth considering value fulfillment. With that disclaimer in mind, let's start with hedonism.

Hedonism tells us that pleasure and the absence of pain are the only goods. This view has problems with both descriptive adequacy and normative adequacy. A much discussed case that makes this point is Nozick's "Experience Machine" thought experiment (1974). In it, we are to imagine trying to choose between our normal life and a life hooked up to a very sophisticated virtual reality machine that would absolutely guarantee us a life with (on balance) more pleasure than the life we would otherwise have. Nozick takes the case to show that people care about other things than pleasure, such as knowledge of the real world and real relationships with other people; in other words, we might say, people's ordinary judgments about well-being track other goods besides pleasure, and this means that hedonism is not descriptively adequate.[28] Maybe we shouldn't put too much weight on science fiction cases, but we don't have to. Consider a different, serious (and possibly upsetting) kind of example. In some cases, victims of sexual abuse experience pleasure from the abusive behavior: the body reacts independently of the mind. Victims who have these experiences are profoundly confused and often deeply ashamed. Do we think these pleasures are in any way good for the victim? Granted, it is difficult to bracket moral questions and to focus on well-being here, but I don't think it's impossible. With that qualification in mind, my answer to the question is "not at all!" I think they make things worse. I think it would be really awful to say that despite the pleasure's not being wanted, the victim is better off (at least in one respect) having experienced pleasure with the abuse than they would be if they had experienced the abuse without pleasure, which is what hedonists will have to say about such a case. When I presented this case at a conference on well-being, this is just what several hedonists did say, which caused many others in the audience to say "yuck, so much for hedonism"; the die-hard hedonists dug in their heels, but for some, this implication of hedonism was a deal killer. My point in mentioning the reactions of the audience at the conference is to point out that hedonism does not fit the ordinary judgments of many people who seem to think that only certain kinds of pleasures, or pleasures in a certain context, are good for people. The case also seems to cause trouble for the normative adequacy of hedonism, because of the gap between certain pleasures and any claims about what is good or what we have reason to do.

What about life satisfaction? Dan Haybron (2011) has argued that the problem with life satisfaction is that it comes too cheap and for the wrong reasons. People can be satisfied with very little in their lives because they don't know that it could be any better, because they're trying to cultivate gratitude for spiritual reasons, or because they're just resigned. Life satisfaction depends on our perspective, Haybron argues, in a way that well-being should not. This creates problems for the descriptive adequacy of the life satisfaction theory. Life satisfaction theory fails to account for ordinary judgments that people are doing poorly when they are living in terrible circumstances regardless of whether those same people assess their lives as satisfying.[29] Haybron gives the example of Pop Bickham who spent nearly half his life in a Louisiana penitentiary, including fourteen years on death row, and who was finally released from prison in part because of information that came to light about the injustice of his conviction. Bickham, it seems, was very satisfied with his life. Should we say that Bickham achieved well-being? That the life he lived was a good life for him? This is really not clear. Many people will think that Bickham's life could have been much better—regardless of his assessment of it—had he not been wrongly imprisoned. As with hedonism, life satisfaction suffers some descriptive *in*adequacy, which also creates problems for normative adequacy: skepticism about the importance of life satisfaction for a good human life creates skepticism about whether it is what we ought to pursue.

Eudaimonist theories and objective list theories—theories that include objective values, things that are good for people independently of their psychological attitudes—do better than hedonism or life satisfactionism when it comes to descriptive adequacy in some ways. At least such theories can explain why Pop Bickham and the person hooked up to the experience machine are missing something crucial to well-being even if they are satisfied with or pleased by their lives. For instance, they may be missing the objective goods of knowledge, relationships, or autonomy. But these theories have other problems. For one thing, they require some heavy philosophical lifting, because they rely on a defense of some form of objectivism about values. For another thing, even if objective values can be defended, it's not clear that they would be the right kind of thing to play a primary role in a theory of well-being. To get off the ground, eudaimonism and objective list theory require a defense of the idea that there are goods whose value is independent of individual human psychology *and* whose value contributes to the well-being of a particular person. Whether such defenses are possible is something that divides philosophers quite profoundly, and I am definitely on the skeptical side of this divide. I suspect that nothing I could say here would convince anyone on the other side to join me, so I'll confine myself to three points that are, again, designed to clear space for considering the value fulfillment theory.

First, psychologists tend to be highly skeptical of the very idea that there are values that transcend individual human psychology (Tiberius 2016). For this reason, they should be interested in a theory, like the value fulfillment theory, that does not presuppose objective values. Second, even if you're optimistic about defending claims about objective prudential values, you may still realize the challenges and find it interesting to see what can be done without them. Third, and most importantly, even if you think there are objective *moral* values, you may be skeptical about objective *prudential* values. In other words, even if you're willing to accept that there are *moral* goods and evils that transcend individual human psychology, you may find it plausible that the values that make an individual's life go well *for them* must have something to do with that person's psychological attitudes. Many philosophers have made basically this point in favor of theories that define well-being by reference to the individual's own point of view. L. W. Sumner (1996) puts it this way: the "relativization of prudential evaluation to the proprietor of the life in question is one of the deepest features of the language of welfare". And Peter Railton (2003) tells us that a conception of the good for a person that didn't engage their own subjective point of view would be an "intolerably alienated" conception of well-being (p. 47). (The need to explain the special connection to the subject is also sometimes called the "resonance constraint": a person's well-being ought to "resonate" with them.) Both of these philosophers think that the best way to explain the "subject relativity" of our concept of well-being is with a theory that defines well-being in terms of subjective attitudes (life satisfaction for Sumner, and desire for Railton).[30] Objective theories have more difficulty capturing the "relativization of prudential evaluation to the proprietor of the life in question" and avoiding the possibility of alienation between the person and her own good.

Sumner takes his point about the subject relativity of the concept of well-being to be a point about descriptive adequacy. Well-being (but not other kinds of value) just is the kind of value that has a special connection to the individual who possesses it. The potential gap that objective theories create between a person and their well-being also creates a problem for normative adequacy. An objective theory that says something is good for a person, even though that person doesn't like or want it, invites us to wonder why the person would have good reason to follow the recommendations of the theory.[31]

Finally, what about desire satisfaction theories? The value fulfillment theory is most similar to desire satisfaction theories. Both theories take the good for a person to be defined, basically, by success in terms of their own aims. The theories share the basic assumption that when we think about well-being, we should start with the point of view of the creature whose well-being it is, and they share the further idea that the most important aspect of someone's point of view is what matters to them. Theories that have this basic structure (focused, broadly speaking, on a person's aims) fill an important role very well. When we want to help other people, their well-being is our ultimate target. Notice that when we want to help other people we don't always know or agree on what things are objectively good for people, and attempting to promote other people's good by procuring the things we believe are good for them is a risky thing to do. We might be incorrect about what things are objectively good for others, our help might be disrespectful or paternalistic, our efforts may interfere with the other person's autonomy, or the things we are sure are good for others may be so abstract that thinking about helping in this way isn't actually very helpful. We need a sense of "good for"—a sense of "well-being"—that provides a goal or target for helping others who may be quite different from us, when we don't know what things are objectively good, or at least not in enough detail for the knowledge to be of much use.

I think the value fulfillment theory fills this role very well, even better than desire satisfaction theories. Why better? Theories of this kind also share a common problem, the most serious problem for subjective theories of well-being, which is that it sure seems like we can want or value things that don't turn out to be good for us. We might call this "the problem of defective desires".[32] Value fulfillment and desire satisfaction theories take very seriously the person's aims, but our aims can be defective in ways that lead us to misery. We can want or value things due to an impoverished upbringing (for example, Ian who does not want an education, because his family thinks education corrupts) and we can want or value things because we're grossly misinformed (for example, Mona who values making as much money as possible, because she incorrectly believes that this will make her feel contented). Subjective theories might be in some trouble if they are stuck saying that we will achieve well-being if we get whatever we happen to desire or value right now.

Defenders of desire satisfactionism rule out the satisfaction of "defective desires" as contributing to our well-being by adding some restrictions on which desires count. Desire satisfactionism can insist, first of all, that we focus on *ultimate* desires, rather than *instrumental* desires (Heathwood 2005). Mona who values making tons of money doesn't want the money for its own sake; after all, she wants money because she thinks it will make her feel happy. If we focus on Mona's ultimate desires, desire satisfaction theory does not entail that making lots of money is good for Mona. This move does not allow desire satisfactionism to criticize people's ultimate desires, however. To go further, some defenders of desire satisfactionism have argued that all of our desires (including the ultimate desires) must be fully informed for their satisfaction to count toward our well-being. Such theories are often called *idealized* desire satisfaction theories or "full information theory".[33] To take an example from this literature, consider Lonnie who is lost in the desert craving a comforting glass of milk, which would actually make him sicker. Peter Railton (1986), defending an informed desire theory, argues that what's good for Lonnie is to satisfy the desires that his fully informed self would want him to have, namely (in this case) a desire for clear fluid.[34]

I think these theories are on the right track, and the value fulfillment theory also recognizes that sometimes our values are in need of improvement by our very own lights. Nevertheless, the criterion of full information has turned out to create a lot of problems. Philosophers have argued that a truly *fully* informed version of ourselves would not be a version of ourselves at all.[35] Indeed, this omniscient creature would be so different from us that its advice to us would be quite alien. The value fulfillment theory is similar to informed desire theories in acknowledging that by our own lights, our values are sometimes in need of improvement. But it doesn't take "being fully informed" as the standard. In the previous section I said a little bit about the standards for improvement according to the value fulfillment theory—our values should be emotionally, motivationally, and cognitively suited to us, and capable of fulfillment over the course of a lifetime—and these ideas will be elaborated in the chapters to come.[36]

The picture that emerges will show that the value fulfillment theory can make good sense of the ways in which people's values are open to criticism, even from the point of view of their own well-being. This picture also helps to address a different problem for subjective theories. Richard Kraut has argued that the problem with subjective theories of well-being (like desire satisfactionism) is that they don't give us the right kind of guidance. Subjective theories, according to Kraut, hold that "your current goals fix the standpoint from which your life should be evaluated"; there are no external or objective standards for a good life (1979, p. 186). Because of this, subjectivism "says so little about how we should lead our lives: it tells us that if we want to be happy we should make up our minds about what we value most, and this is of little help to those who are uncertain about what kind of life to lead" (1979, p. 192).[37] Notice that Kraut says that subjectivism takes your *current* goals to be the standards for how your life is going. Neither desire satisfactionism nor value fulfillment theory needs to say this. Instead, both theories can say that it is total satisfaction or fulfillment over the course of a life that determines how well your life goes (Heathwood 2005). This creates an opportunity for guidance already, because our current values might not be sustainable— pursuing what you value or desire most right now might lead to less fulfillment overall. Value fulfillment theory, I will try to show, can take us even farther, because of the standards for appropriate values.

So far I have ignored the third criterion for a successful theory of well-being, that the theory's assumptions should be empirically adequate. Most theories of well-being assume, at least implicitly, that the thing they call well-being can be measured and compared, both intra-personally over time and inter-personally. If we're proposing prescriptive theories, we need to be able to determine how things are, how they could be better, and whether improvements occur. The value fulfillment theory makes measurement and comparisons of levels of well-being more complicated than, say, hedonism. But it does not make it impossible to measure and compare. The value fulfillment theory lends itself to empirical investigation in a few different ways.

First, we can measure the degree to which people fulfill common human values such as health, relationships, financial security, and psychological happiness. The methods psychologists already use to measure subjective well-being (scales that ask people to self-report their levels of life satisfaction or positive feelings, for example) are well tested and do track things that people care about.[38] In addition, there are good measures of many other psychological states that are valued: lack of stress, the sense of worthwhileness, feelings of purpose, meaning, mastery, and autonomy.[39] Second, there are objective measures of people's success in terms of common human values that are part of an appropriate set of values for just about anyone. For example, suicide rates tell us something about how people, in general, are doing in terms of mental health, and employment rates give us some information about how people are doing in terms of work, another common and appropriate value.

Finally, we can ask people about their values and find out how well they are doing at achieving them. One way to do this that I have been exploring with some psychologist colleagues is with a method called Personal Projects Analysis (Little 2015). Personal projects are "extended sets of personally salient action in context" (Little, Salmela-Aro, and Phillips 2007, p. 25). They are, in other words, very much like values. Included in many people's personal projects are many of the values that comprise a value-fulfilled life for most people: improving health, being happier, becoming more virtuous (being nicer, more diligent, more compassionate toward others), learning new things, and being a good friend. Personal projects analysis elicits participants' important personal projects and then asks them to rate their projects in various ways, including how each project helps or hinders the others. This approach allows us to focus on the values that are actually important to the individual, rather than starting with assumptions about common human values. Use of this approach for studying well-being as value fulfillment is promising and worth exploring (Bedford-Petersen et al. 2018).

Of course, these various methods do not measure *appropriate* values. They couldn't. Appropriate values are the values we can grow into if our developmental path is a good one, and you can't measure what should happen or what would be better than what is. This just is the gap between the empirical *is* and the normative *ought*. Nevertheless, I don't think we're at a complete loss here, because we can make reasonable assumptions about the kinds of values that are appropriate for most people. Indeed, the common human values that I mentioned above—mental and physical health, psychological happiness, and relationships—are highly likely to be included in a system of appropriate values for almost anyone. In part this is because these values are so abstract that there are many different ways for individual people to instantiate them in their lives in ways that suit them emotionally, motivationally, and cognitively.

The value fulfillment approach doesn't lend itself to simplistic operationalization, but it does have other advantages for psychologists. The value fulfillment approach offers an underlying, unifying explanation for using the multiple measures that psychologists have at their disposal. It makes sense to use subjective measures to assess how people feel about their lives in a variety of ways *and* objective measures of how they are succeeding in various terms because people have various values and various ways of understanding what it means to fulfill them. The value fulfillment theory explains why we should care about how we feel *and* about how we are actually doing. Additionally, the value fulfillment theory assumes a model of human agency that will be familiar to social scientists. Human beings are highly social, goal-directed creatures who learn from experience; not a jarring picture from the point of view of science (DeYoung 2015). That is all the value fulfillment theory needs to assume; there is no need for special powers of practical reason, special insight into objective moral facts, or a special biological nature that is itself imbued with value. The value fulfillment theory may not have an advantage over hedonism and preference satisfactionism on the criterion of empirical adequacy, but it has nothing to be embarrassed about.

I began this section with the question, "What is the argument that this theory is the correct one?" I want to end the section with reasons to care about value fulfillment even if this isn't the right theory. One thing about hedonism and most objective theories is that the goods they propose are very general. According to hedonism, we should go for pleasure, and according to objective theories we should go for such things as achievement, friendship, and knowledge. But what kind of pleasure? Physical or psychological? Tranquil or exciting? The pleasure taken in exercising our higher capacities (as John Stuart Mill suggested in *Utilitarianism*) or any old pleasure? What kind of achievement? Difficult achievement (as Gwen Bradford 2015 suggests)? Achievements in sports, or art, or philosophy? What about friendship? Should we go for intimate friendship with one or two people? A large network of many friends? Knowing that these things—pleasure, achievement, friendship—are good for us does not get us very far in terms of knowing just what to do or what to aim for in our lives. (Psychologists may be tempted to think they can answer these questions with data about life satisfaction or affect balance, but this would be an answer only if we have already determined that life satisfaction or positive affect is the most important value).

To get more specific guidance, I think we have to pay at least some attention to a person's values. The list of possible achievements, for example, is vast, even if we restrict it to morally permissible, genuine achievements that use important human capacities. Narrowing the possibilities by attending to the person's values means that the person will tend to be motivated to do what it takes to achieve in that particular way, and pleased with the result.[40] It's hard to imagine how else we would decide among the myriad possibilities. Similarly for pleasure itself: if hedonism is true and pleasure is the good, a person still needs to determine which pleasant things to do, and aiming at the most pleasure does not seem to be the best way of getting it. Henry Sidgwick ([1907] 1962, p. 48) called this the "fundamental paradox of hedonism, that if the impulse towards pleasure is too predominant it will defeat its own aim...to get pleasure we cannot aim directly at it". Instead, we need to have goals that bring pleasure in their pursuit and achievement. Paying attention to values removes the paradox: we pursue pleasure by pursuing what matters to us. This would not mean that *only* valued pleasures are good, nor would it mean that pursuing painful values is good—that would no longer be hedonism—but it does mean that there is a reason to think about people's values, even for a hedonist, when making specific recommendations about what to do to increase a person's well-being.

It is open to people from many different theoretical backgrounds to see the advantages of the general value fulfillment approach even if they do not see it as the correct theory of well-being. Adherents to other theories can, instead, see the argument of this book as a set of guidelines about how to help people under conditions of uncertainty, and they can substitute their own deep theoretical explanation of these guidelines for mine. Fans of desire satisfaction theory should like the fact that it pays attention to subjective states and the perspectives of individual people (rather than imposing objective values from an external point of view as some objective theories do). Aristotelian eudaimonists should find something to love in the value fulfillment theory because valuing and putting together sustainable sets of values is a fundamentally human activity that uses our practical reasoning skills and that can be done well or badly. Objective list theories and hybrid theories of well-being (according to which well-being is constituted by the *enjoyable* pursuit of objective values) should find something to like here, too, since many of the values that are most important to people and that will be discussed in this book (like friendship) are on everyone's list of objective values. (Of course, any theory that presupposes objective values will have different criteria for what counts as an appropriate value from the ones that I defend. Nevertheless, there will be a lot of overlap in practical recommendations.)

Some psychologists who study well-being will be in the same boat as philosophers who defend alternative theories of well-being. But many other psychologists shy away from endorsing or assuming a theory of well-being per se. They operationalize technical notions of "subjective well-being" (Diener 1984) or "psychological well-being" (Ryff 1989) so that they can observe and measure what is observable and measurable, but they do not claim to have answered ethical questions about the good life for a human being. I can only guess at psychologists' deep motivations, but I think they take this stand for one of two reasons. Sometimes, they just realize that it's not their business to theorize about an evaluative notion like the human good; they study what they can study using their methods. But sometimes, I think psychologists assume a specific value theory implicitly, namely, a subjective theory according to which if people want something, then it's good for them and they have reason to pursue it (Tiberius 2017). My main evidence for this hypothesis is conversations I've had with psychologists who, when I ask annoying questions about why certain items are on the list of components of well-being, will tell me that those items are there because people want or value them. If this kind of subjectivism is the background assumption for at least some psychologists, then they should be interested in the value fulfillment theory, which is (if I do say so myself) a sophisticated form of subjective theory that makes room for standards of improvement from the status quo. To see how a subjective theory like the value fulfillment theory can be used to defend prescriptive conclusions about how we ought to treat each other, should be of interest to psychologists grappling with how to reconcile their descriptive scientific research with their often prescriptive popular work.

Most of what I will say in this book, then, is relevant to the application of any theory (implicit or explicit, philosophical or psychological) that takes the successful pursuit of central human values to be essential to living well. My hope is that readers with commitments to other such theories of well-being will find that our disagreements about the underlying principle that unifies these values into a single theory, or about the ultimate explanation for what makes something valued good for a person, are less important than what we have in common.

· · ·

In this introduction I have tried to give a sense of what the value fulfillment theory is about and why it is worth considering. In the next two chapters I'll describe the theory in much more detail. Chapter 2 elaborates on the general features of the theory that I've highlighted in this introduction. Chapter 3 focuses on the nature of fulfillment for the complex systems of values that human beings tend to have. In Chapters 4 and 5 I'll turn to applying the theory to the practical problem of how to help people. Chapter 4 is about the challenges we face when we aim to help others, particularly our friends. Chapter 5 discusses what it is to be a good and helpful friend, given these challenges and the value fulfillment theory of well-being.

2

The Value Fulfillment Theory of Well-Being

2.1 Main Features of the Value Fulfillment Theory

According to the value fulfillment theory, our lives go well to the extent that we pursue, and fulfill or realize, our appropriate values. In short, we live well when we succeed in terms of what matters to us emotionally, reflectively, and over the long term.[1] This includes achieving certain states of affairs (such as career goals) and also maintaining the positive emotional orientation that comprises valuing something. If your values include your own enjoyment, relationships with family and friends, accomplishing something in your career, and contributing to certain morally worthwhile projects, then your life goes well for you insofar as you have good relationships and career success, make a moral contribution, and enjoy what you're doing, as long as these continue to be the things you care about. (These are common values for human beings, but if you have different values, and those values are appropriate for you, your well-being will look different—more on these differences later.)

Your life goes badly to the degree that you live a life that has little value fulfillment. This can happen because you find no value in anything, because what you disvalue comes to pass, because your values are thwarted by external obstacles, or because your values are difficult to fulfill together over time. This last problem can be caused by values that are in conflict with each other, or values that do not suit you.

(This is a very rough description of "ill-being"—more deserves to be said, but a full theory of ill-being according to the value fulfillment theory would require a book of its own. I will say a little more about it in Section 3.2.) People who are significantly depressed and whose affective capacities are dampened do not fare well (according to the value fulfillment theory), because they have trouble finding value in their projects and relationships. People who suffer material deprivation or loss of loved ones do not fare well because their values are threatened by the world. People who have values that create obstacles to health, happiness, or psychological harmony, do not fare well because they have values that conflict with other values that are (in most cases) essential to a set of values that can be fulfilled successfully over time.

There are, then, three main parts of the value fulfillment theory: values, fulfillment, and time. We'll discuss each of these components in more detail shortly, but let's start with an overview that goes a little deeper than the one I provided in the introduction. First, to value something in the fullest sense is to have a relatively stable pattern of emotions and desires with respect to it and to take these attitudes to give you reasons for action and (for the most important values) standards for evaluating how your life is going. If you value your job, then you will want to do well at it and to have time for it; you will be disposed to enjoy what you do, to feel proud when you get promoted, and disappointed when you don't do your best work; when you reflect on how your life is going you will tend to think about how you are doing in your work as relevant to this question and you'll tend to take your job into account when you're making plans for the future. Valuing, therefore, has an affective, a conative, and a cognitive dimension—it involves our emotions, our desires, and our judgment—and values are the objects of these valuing attitudes.[2] Because values have these dimensions, our values themselves can be more or less appropriate for us; that is, they can be more or less suited to our emotions and desires, and more or less aligned with our judgments about what's good.[3] Appropriate values are the objects of relatively sustainable and integrated emotions, desires, and judgments.

What it is for a value to be fulfilled and what it means to say that one life has more value fulfillment than another are obviously very important for the theory I'm proposing. Values, like desires, bring with them standards of success, and living up to these standards is the essence of value fulfillment. In the example above, it's easy to see how valuing one's job entails standards of success or fulfillment: whatever counts as doing well at your job fulfills that value. But standards for values are not always obvious. Some values—such as the value of honesty or integrity—are such that we succeed in their terms by having the right attitudes or being a certain kind of person. Nevertheless, there are standards for values in the sense that there are ways of responding appropriately or inappropriately given the nature of what is valued (Anderson 1995). Moreover, most values encompass standards that are objective in the sense that whether or not we fulfill them is not a matter of whether we believe we are fulfilling them. There is something to meeting the standards that our values impose that goes beyond our subjective experience. In this respect, value fulfillment is similar to preference satisfaction: you may fail to get what you want without knowing it (say, if you are seriously deluded), and you may fail to fulfill your values, though you believe otherwise. Finally, if we are going to achieve what matters to us, it is not only success in terms of what is valued that matters, but also the valuing attitudes themselves. We require some stability in our valuing attitudes if we are going to succeed by the standards we think are important. (Of course, there is such a thing as too much stability: how much stability is required, and when change is recommended, are difficult practical questions, as we will see in later chapters.) Value fulfillment, then, requires succeeding by the standards of that value while continuing to think that these standards are important to how well your life goes.

Assessing *overall* value fulfillment requires attending to the relationships between values and their development over time. People typically have numerous values of different kinds and degrees of importance. We value some things largely as a means to others (for example, you might value running marathons as a means to the values of health and fitness). We value some things as specific expressions of other more abstract things (for example, you might value playing the piano *as a way of* valuing music). Some values are more important to us than others and some values have a more central role in the whole system. Further, values develop. Our basic values probably don't change much, but we do change how we understand their fulfillment and how they are prioritized. These considerations must be taken into account when we evaluate overall value fulfillment and we ask whether choosing one path over another promises more overall value fulfillment.

We can now proceed to fill in the details. The remainder of this chapter will focus on what values are, how they can be improved, and why we should consider them over time. In Chapter 3 we'll turn to fulfillment.

2.2 What are Values?

Values are defined in various ways for different purposes. Because we are looking for a characterization of values that can play a central role in a theory that captures the special relationship of well-being to the subject (the way in which well-being is supposed to be good *for* the person), we will do best to understand values by reference to the activity of valuing. What can we say about the activity of valuing?

First, intuitively, to value something is to care about it in a particular way, and to care about something is to have particular feelings and desires with respect to it.[4] Other things equal, we are motivated to pursue or promote the values to which we are committed and we are disposed to react emotionally when these values are helped or threatened. For example, a mother who values being a parent wants to spend time with her child and is relatively robustly disposed to enjoy that time. She is disposed to feel proud when her child tells her she's a great mom, to be ashamed when she forgets to pick her child up from school, and so on.[5]

Second, to value something, and not merely to prefer it or like it, is to judge that it is the kind of thing that is good in some way. To put the point in terms that are common in philosophy, we take our values to generate *reasons* for us (reasons to respond in certain ways and not others), and to be the sort of thing we should consider in our planning and evaluation of how our lives are going.[6] Our exemplary mother takes her being a parent to justify certain decisions and plans she makes for her life, including decisions that require sacrificing other things she wants. She takes 'being a good parent' to be highly relevant to how well her life is going. The particular standards we have for how to value something in a fitting way are influenced by cultural expectations and norms, and by the emotions that are included in our valuing attitudes. For example, someone who values being a parent is likely to think that attending to her child's needs is a standard for valuing parenthood in a fitting way; if you habitually don't notice your child's needs, you are failing to value parenthood (and your child). We'll talk more about these standards when we talk about value *fulfillment*. For now, the important point is that when we *value* something as opposed to merely wanting it, we take it to give us reasons that are relevant to how we shape our lives. We might put the point this way: Appropriate values are "reflectively endorsed" (though the word "reflectively" should not be taken to imply anything too extravagant or intellectual).[7]

These observations about valuing lead to a view according to which valuing is a complex pattern of attitudes; it includes emotion, desire, and judgment. This is not the standard view in philosophy. Philosophers who write about valuing tend to fall into two camps: those who take valuing to be equivalent to desiring (Lewis 2000; Railton 2003); and those who take it to be equivalent to believing or judging that something is valuable (Dorsey 2012; Korsgaard 1996; Smith 1995). There may be reasons for wanting a more streamlined characterization of valuing when it comes to articulating a metaethical position, but for our purposes, these simpler characterizations are unnecessary and inadequate. Values that harmonize our emotions, desires, and judgments are a better focus for a theory of well-being, because we do better at meeting our aims when our emotions, desires, and judgments are more integrated.[8] Conflict creates obstacles to success. Anyone who has tried to start an exercise program or change their diet has likely had the experience of recalcitrant desires and emotions in conflict with judgments about what to do. As we all know, such conflicts make it more difficult to succeed. Recalcitrant *judgments* are also possible—think of the person raised in the Church of the Nazarene, who loves dancing and wants to dance professionally more than anything else, but who can't shake the belief that dancing is sinful.

This multifaceted understanding of values also helps to make sense of the way we tend to talk about values. We tend to be less confident in attributing values to people who lack the affective *or* the cognitive dimension of valuing and more confident saying that a person values something when they have both components in a relatively stable way. For example, which man more clearly *values* his marriage: the one who loves his wife, but believes he should have been a priest and never have married, or the one who both loves his wife and believes his marriage to be a good thing? Which person more obviously counts as *valuing* music? The woman who plays the piano because she believes it is good for her or the woman who believes it is good for her and loves it? It seems to me the compelling answer in both cases is the second option. When the person's emotions and judgments track together in favor of something, there's nothing to make us skeptical about whether they *value* that thing. Making a judgment about the goodness of something or having an emotional attachment to it are each evidence for valuing, but valuing—in the sense best suited for the value fulfillment theory—includes both.[9]

Values in which desire, emotion, and judgment are perfectly harmonized may not be the norm—we do live with a lot of conflict—but that's OK for the purpose of thinking about how to improve people's lives. Values that integrate our desires, emotions, and judgments are an ideal to aspire to. When we talk about a person's actual values we will have to make a judgment call about how much the person's attitudes represent valuing. There are practical reasons to take people's word for it by just allowing them to tell us what they value, but this needn't prevent us from noticing that what they say they value does not line up well with what they actually want, like, or approve. As we'll see, lack of integration leaves room for improvement.

Values, then, in the specialized sense required by the value fulfillment theory, are patterns of relatively robust desires and emotions that we endorse as giving us reasons relevant to planning and evaluating our lives.[10] I mean to be very inclusive about what counts: people can value activities, relationships, other creatures (human or otherwise), character traits, goals, ideals, principles, and so on, and so all of these things can count as values. I'll also talk about "instrumental values" (things we value as a means to other values) and "ultimate values" (things we value at least in part for their own sakes); instrumental values can contribute to well-being, though their contribution will depend on the value of the end to which they are a means.

There is one more important feature of values to discuss, which has to do with how they work together. Values form systems of mutual reinforcement and integration that help or hinder their fulfillment. Some values will be more "core" than others in the sense that they are used more often in explanations of the importance of other values. For example, the value of (psychological) happiness is likely to be a core value for many because it will be appealed to in explaining what is important about other values such as sports, hobbies, and friendships. I do not assume that values occupy a rigid hierarchy (though they may for some people); rather, values are more likely to be arranged in a web of mutual support with some values more centrally located than others. Notice that some values are purely instrumental (the value of money is usually like this), which means that these things are valued only as a means to something else. Many things are valued partly for their own sakes and partly as a means to something else. A good friendship, for example, may be valued for itself and also because it brings happiness. Even ultimate values can vary in degrees of centrality; happiness may explain the value of more instrumental values than, say, a particular friendship though both are valued (in part) for their own sakes. Further, the means–end relationship is not the only way in which values are related to each other. For instance, some values are expressions of other, more abstractly described values. A person who values music may value playing the piano as a *way* of valuing music. In this case playing the piano is valued intrinsically, not as a means to appreciating music; the piano player does not value a distinct musical good that is caused by playing the piano.

Now, we sometimes say that we value something when we care about it, but don't have terribly robust judgments about its value for us, and we sometimes say we value things when our emotions are not quite aligned. Further, especially when taken together, our values can be unsustainable, impossible to fulfill together over time. Value fulfillment is imperiled by serious conflict among core values, poor connections between instrumental and ultimate values, or dysfunctional ways of interpreting the standards of success for our values. There are ways that values can fall short of the rather ideal picture I've described; actual values vary in appropriateness, and not all of the values people claim to have will exhibit this kind of psychological harmony. We can say, then, that *appropriate* values are (1) suited to our desires and emotions, (2) reflectively endorsed, and (3) capable of being fulfilled together over time. In other words, as I put it in the previous chapter, appropriate values are the objects of relatively sustainable and integrated emotions, desires, and judgments.

Three qualifications are in order. First, I mentioned that there are ultimate values and instrumental values. We value some things (like friendship, health, and meaningful work) for their own sakes and others (money, healthcare, and a college diploma) as a means to something more ultimate. I don't think the line between ultimate and instrumental values is always a bright one for people. Do you value physical health for its own sake or for its contribution to your ability to do everything you want to do? It's hard to say, and people surely differ about this. One reason it can be hard to say is that values can be mixed. Health may be something we value both for its own sake and as a means to other things. Another reason it's hard to say is that we don't have ready vocabularies for explaining why we value something for its own sake, which makes us reach for some further, more ultimate value. As we'll see as we go along, I don't think it matters very much where the line is drawn. It does matter that some goals we have are so clearly instrumental that it starts to strain the notion of "value" to call them values. For example, I aim to floss my teeth regularly to avoid gum disease, and ultimately for the sake of my physical health. It would be odd to say that I *value* flossing my teeth (even though it is something about which I have stable desires and judgments that figure into my planning!); it's just too trivial. When this happens, I think it's more natural to talk about desiring the means to a more ultimate value, and that's what I'll do.

Second, people have moral values. Most of us value being a basically morally decent person, and failing to be morally decent would be a failure to thrive from our own point of view. Moral commitments like these are easy to mesh with the value fulfillment theory of well-being; we fare well when we fulfill a variety of values, including moral ones. But not all moral commitments are like this; sometimes moral values seem to be at odds with well-being. This leads to a well-known problem for the value fulfillment theory and theories like it (desire satisfactionism, for instance). This is the problem of self-sacrifice, which is that if well-being is getting what we want or value, it seems that it is conceptually impossible to sacrifice our own interests for the sake of a moral goal that we also want or value (Overvold 1980). In other words, the worry is that the value fulfillment theory rules out moral sacrifice by definition, and this seems wrong. For example, consider Dahlia, who cares, more than anything, about saving other people from the devastating effects of climate change. Dahlia therefore decides to devote her life to lobbying the U.S. government to approve stronger fossil fuel regulations, and she throws herself into this work with an intensity that leaves no room for anything else. It could seem that as long as Dahlia is successful in terms of this goal, her life is going well according to the value fulfillment theory even if she herself regards her choices as sacrificing her own good for the sake of others.

Moral sacrifice may be psychologically difficult, but it shouldn't be made conceptually impossible by a theory of well-being. Fortunately, the value fulfillment theory is not saddled with this result. Recall that what matters to well-being as value fulfillment is the overall amount of fulfillment of values that are emotionally, motivationally, and cognitively suited to the person. So, one thing we can say is that Dahlia may be sacrificing more value fulfillment of this kind over the long run if the stress of her work shortens her life or leaves her burned out, exhausted, and unable to attain much value fulfillment in the second half of her life.[11] A person who literally sacrifices her life for a moral cause is naturally described in this way: even if that person values the moral cause and nothing else, she sacrifices her own well-being by forgoing all future value fulfillment. Similarly, if Dahlia forgoes having children and spending time with friends, and if the work she does for climate justice ends up not succeeding terribly well, she may eventually relinquish greater value fulfillment over the long term even though working for climate justice is what she values most at this moment.

But what if these "ifs" aren't true of Dahlia? What if she is psychologically organized in such a way that she would not gain greater value fulfillment by pursuing a life with a greater diversity of values? What if she's just the rather unusual, slightly obsessive sort of person for whom the addition of fun, friendship, and time spent with her family, would not increase her overall value fulfillment? The value fulfillment theory implies that *this* Dahlia would not sacrifice her own well-being by devoting herself to the moral cause. But now this doesn't seem like such a bad result. If Dahlia continues to enjoy her work and doesn't come to value things that are incompatible with her choices, then it is not so unintuitive to say that she is doing what is best for her. As Heathwood (2011) says in his defense of desire satisfactionism against the problem of self-sacrifice, the claim that Dahlia is sacrificing well-being for a moral cause "appears rather question-begging". Just because Dahlia "isn't acting with herself, or with her own best interests in mind, and is instead acting benevolently for others, we cannot conclude that she must therefore fail to be doing what is in her best interests" (p. 35).

There's one more thing to say about moral values, which is that not all moral ideals are values in the sense relevant to the value fulfillment theory. As I said above, the relevant values for well-being are endorsed as the kind of thing we should consider in our planning and evaluation of how our lives are going. Not all of our moral ideals are so directly practical: we see the moral importance of ending injustice, but we don't think it translates into a full-time job for us. Personally, I'm deeply committed to the wrongness of slavery and torture, but these commitments do not come into play in my life as a philosophy professor very often (except maybe in my choice of topics to discuss in ethics classes). (Of course, these commitments *could become* be more directly relevant to how I live my life; things could take a turn for the much worse and then everyone would be called upon to prioritize these commitments in action.) So, moral ideals and commitments are not always values in the sense that is relevant to well-being as value fulfillment. This point does not help much with the problem of self-sacrifice, though, because moral ideals that are not taken to be practical will not be ones that people make sacrifices for in the first place. Still, it is worth noting that not everything that might fall under the label "value" is a value in the sense relevant to the value fulfillment theory.

The third qualification is that people also disvalue. Often there are positive correlates to our disvalues. I hate meanness and pettiness, but these negative attitudes are part of valuing kindness and generosity. Part of what it is to value kindness and generosity, in other words, is to be disposed to negative emotions toward the vices that express their absence. Sometimes our disvalues are instrumental to things we value. I disvalue military museums and naval history. I am very consistently disposed to avoid them, to feel bored and miserable when I'm exposed to them, and to take them not to contribute to a good life for me. In this case, I disvalue these things because I regard them as a hindrance to things I value intrinsically (my happiness, for instance). There are also things we disvalue for their own sakes, as it were. Pain, for instance, is something most people are disposed to abhor, desire not to experience, and take to be a relevant consideration in planning and decision-making.[12]

Values, in the sense relevant to the value fulfillment theory, are complex psychological states that come in degrees (some may be more emotionally entrenched than others, for example). Many of our actual values, especially our basic, core values, are appropriate: they involve our desires and emotions, we use them to plan and deliberate, and they are part of sustainable systems of values. That said, the values we have are not *necessarily* appropriate and there are some things we should value even if we don't claim to.[13] For example, it follows from what I've said that health and happiness are appropriate values for most people, even though it isn't necessarily the case that people would put these at the top of their list if you asked them to enumerate their values. It may be that people wouldn't mention health and happiness if asked because they are taking them for granted at the moment. Nevertheless, emotional dispositions, desires, and tendencies to take health and happiness in account in your decision-making contribute significantly to a stable system of values that can be fulfilled over time. I'll say more about the ways in which values can be assessed as better or worse in the next section, and even more in the next chapter.

With this account of values in hand, we can return to the question I posed in the previous chapter: If we are contemplating a theory of well-being that starts with the agent's own point of view, why focus on values rather than desires, say, or life satisfaction? My answer is that values just are the part of a person's own point of view that they take to determine how well their life goes. People identify themselves in terms of their values more readily than they do in terms of their desires, and values are of particular importance to people from their own point of view. Further, because values are complex psychological patterns, they are better able to explain the various ways in which we can go wrong when it comes to well-being.[14] We sometimes challenge or change our view about what is good for us in the light of judgments about what is worth valuing. For instance, a person (like Maxine from Chapter 1) who discovers she cannot conceive a child might reconsider how important biological connection is to the real value of being a mother and she might decide that it would be best for her to adopt. We also challenge judgments about what is good for us on the basis of our emotional responses: we may realize just how much something matters to us because we notice that we feel bad when it is taken away from us, or elated when it comes back into our lives (Stocker 1990). When this happens we learn from our feelings that there are things about our well-being of which we were not aware. Because values have these different dimensions, they are well suited to explain how both types of change constitute improvements to our views about what is good for us.

In short, values embody our own view of what's worth seeking in a way that mere preferences or life satisfaction judgments do not, and this gives the theory an advantage (over these other theories) in accommodating the sense in which well-being is supposed to be something good.[15]

2.3 The Value-Fulfilled Life and the Long-Term Perspective

Well-being, I have said, is the fulfillment of appropriate values over time; it is a *life* rich in value fulfillment. This makes it seem like the value fulfillment theory privileges the long term and discounts what we might call "momentary well-being". This isn't quite accurate, though, because a life cannot be rich in value fulfillment without its having many moments in which values are being fulfilled. Still, the value fulfillment theory does have us evaluate choices in the moment with an eye to how they will contribute to the whole.

To some extent the focus on values makes this "whole life" or "overall" perspective inevitable, because values are not typically the kinds of things we can fulfill in the moment, nor the kind of thing we can weigh by looking at them in isolation. One can satisfy a desire for gustatory pleasure in an instant, but people who *value* gustatory pleasure must organize their lives so that they have opportunities for it that fit with the other things they do. Of course, what happens in the moment is important to many values too: you won't fulfill the value of gustatory pleasure if you turn down every opportunity to eat something tasty in the moment. The point is that attention to the long term, and to the overall shape of a life, is built into a theory that focuses on values. For example, my Uncle Paul is an avid bird-watcher who keeps a list of birds and travels all over the U.S. at the drop of a hat to see a new bird that has been spotted somewhere. If you focus on individual moments of Paul's bird-watching—moments in which he sees or doesn't see a particular rare bird, buys a plane ticket, cleans his binoculars—it seems like a decent hobby, but there are a lot of costs (frustration when the rare bird gets away, airport security lines, and so on) that might come close to outweighing the benefits. But if you see birding in the context of his life as a whole, you begin to see what's so great about it for Paul. The value of a rare bird sighting for Paul is not exhausted by the experience (as it would be for a person like me who knows nothing about birds and has no list); the sighting has value beyond the momentary experience because of the larger context of Paul's extended pursuit, which is shaped by the accumulation of knowledge about birds over time and the achievement of increasingly difficult goals (seeing rarer birds) over time.

But is the "whole life" perspective a good thing? I think so. Indeed, I think it is part of our ordinary way of thinking about well-being, particularly in the context of thinking about how to improve people's lives. Start with the observation that things that seem good for us in the short term may not be good for us when seen from the long-term perspective (the point of view of overall well-being). This is true for many different theories of well-being. A second martini now may be good for me in the next twenty minutes, because of the pleasure it brings, but it may cause enough pain tomorrow that it isn't good for me when we take a longer-term perspective. Similarly, satisfying my desire for cake with buttercream frosting is good for me now, but not good for me in the long term if I am supposed to be on a low cholesterol diet. Value fulfillment also produces these disparities: I may value a friendship that provides short-term fun but isn't good for me in the long term because the friend is bad for my self-esteem; I may value a career path that pays well enough for me to enjoy short-term benefits, but that doesn't suit me very well and won't be fulfilling in the long term. In both cases, pursuing what I value now is good for me now, but not good for my life as a whole. These are simple and under-described examples, but I think the phenomenon should be familiar enough. Things are parallel in the context of helping others where we tend to think about people's *lives* going well or badly, better, or worse. We would not think it terribly helpful to give a person one great moment that ruins the rest of their life.

I do not mean to deny that it can be sensible to talk about doing well in the moment, and it is important that the value fulfillment theory allows for this. Well-being at a particular time is appropriate value fulfillment at that time. But notice that the focus on *appropriate* values builds in some future orientation, because better integration (among our values and among the psychological states that comprise them) makes these values easier to fulfill over time. So, even when we evaluate well-being in the moment, we have one eye on the future. I think this is appropriate when it comes to helping people, though precisely how we divide our attention between momentary and overall well-being will depend on the context.

For the value fulfillment theory, overall well-being consists in total value fulfillment: the ultimate goal is a life as rich in value fulfillment as it could be. This raises some questions. How should we think about the value-fulfilled life, the life "as rich in value fulfillment as it could be"? Is there only one such life per person? What if a person does something that forever prevents them from achieving *that* life? Is such a person doomed to a sub-optimal life? I think we should think about the value-fulfilled life (from now on, my shorthand for "a life as rich in appropriate value fulfillment as it could be") in the following way. For any person at a time there is a set of values (or a few different sets) and standards of fulfillment for those values such that, were those values to be fulfilled according to those standards, that person would get the most value fulfillment overall.[16] There may be more than one best set of values because value fulfillment is not fine-grained. You can trade a bit of this for a bit of that and not affect your total very much. You can lower your standards of success in one domain and raise them in another, and come out even in terms of value fulfillment. This means that it's very unlikely that there will be a unique set of values and one best (richest) life for each person at a time. Further, the life richest in value fulfillment for a person will change with time, as the person's circumstances, values, and standards of success evolve. This makes sense, and it reflects the fact that we would give quite different advice to the same person at age 20, 40, and 60. Finally, improvements are steps that take a person closer to the richest life (or one of the lives richest in value fulfillment). We may not know with certainty what these steps are, but we can make reasonable judgments about what brings a person closer to more value fulfillment by following the standards of improvement discussed earlier (integration of emotion, desire, and judgment, plus sustainability over time).[17]

The idea that what counts as a value-fulfilled life for a person will change as that person develops will raise some eyebrows. My reason for thinking of things this way is that the value fulfillment theory is a practical theory, aimed at giving guidance about how to make improvements to a person's well-being. If the value-fulfilled life is an unchanging ideal that could become completely unattainable from a person's current position, then the theory isn't much use. There is a problem with my way of thinking, however, which is that the idea of what is "available" to a person is vague. But I don't think this problem is as serious as it would be if we were so adaptable that we could value almost anything in any way. (Though the powers of adaptation we do have create a serious problem that I consider in its own section, 3.4.) For most of us (as I've said before), our development, personalities, and environments constrain us to value fairly typical things. That said, I think we do have to tolerate some vagueness about what we could come to value and in what ways (this will be explained further later in this chapter). There is vagueness here because we simply can't know with certainty all the possibilities that are open to us in terms of what we value and how we understand the fulfillment of these values. But this uncertainty is an unavoidable feature of life.

Some readers might find this explanation of the value-fulfilled life disappointingly imprecise. One way to try to remove the imprecision would be to adopt the *rational life plan view* according to which well-being is evaluated in a top-down manner rather than constructed out of bits of momentary fulfillment. On this way of thinking, the good for a person is to live a life in accordance with the plan that they would want their life to take were they to deliberate about it rationally. As John Rawls (1971, p. 408) elaborates the idea, "[t]he rational plan for a person determines his good" and a person's plan of life is rational if and only if: "(1) It is one of the plans that is consistent with the principles of rational choice when these are applied to all the relevant features of his situation, and (2) it is that plan among those meeting this condition which would be chosen by him with full deliberative rationality, that is, with full awareness of the relevant facts and after a careful consideration of the consequences". In other words, the best life plan is the one you would choose if you knew what you were doing. You are doing well at a particular moment if you are doing something that contributes to this plan.

According to the rational life plan view, then, the value of a part of a life is determined by its relationship to the whole; the bits cannot be assessed first and added up because we do not know how much each bit is worth without looking at the entire life. The rational life plan view adds precision, because it gives us a principle to identify the best life for each person. But there are some reasons to worry about the idea that value-fulfilled lives are just the lives we would choose if we were fully rational. First, there are good reasons to be suspicious that rational choice—choice made "with full awareness of the relevant facts and after a careful consideration of the consequences"—will by itself guarantee a life rich in value fulfillment. This suspicion is fueled by research showing that careful consideration of our reasons does not always lead us to make good choices.[18] In the context of the value fulfillment theory, we can imagine this happening because values are comprised partly of emotional dispositions, and these emotions might be at odds with where reason leads us. Most people know someone who thinks extremely clearly and thoroughly, and yet who isn't really in touch with their feelings and therefore sometimes makes poor choices. Second, any choice you make among rational life plans will have to be made on the basis of the values that you have at the moment you choose. How else could you choose which life is better? But if that's the case, then the rational life plan view requires that we specify a particular point in time at which you have a determinate set of values to form the basis for choice. And then we need to know how to identify the standpoint from which a person is to make this rational choice of life plan.[19] If I were to have chosen a plan for my life at the age of 21, it would have looked very different from the plan I would choose now. *Now*, things have already gone the way they've gone and some of the things that would have been in my 21-year-old self's plan are now ruled out of any plan that could make sense for me going forward. Moreover, I've learned things about myself that make it the case that some of the values highlighted by my 21-year-old plan would now be quite unsuited to me. Which standpoint should be privileged? Privileging any particular age—21, 30, 47, 85?—seems arbitrary.

According to the value fulfillment theory, the best life for a person is the one with the most value fulfillment and this is a broad and shifting target. It is a broad target because there is almost always more than one way for a person to live a value-fulfilled life. There are different ways of fulfilling our most basic, core values (like friendship, meaningful work, and felt happiness), different standards of success we can hold these values to, and different ways of prioritizing them that might lead to value-fulfilled lives that are different but equal. It's a shifting target, because the point of view from which "most" is defined depends on the possibilities that are open to the person at the time. If you are wishing the best life for a baby in their crib,[20] there will be many possibilities for how the baby's life could go that haven't been closed off by steps they have already taken. If you're asking how an adult friend could improve their life, the target will be narrower, because the first few decades of living will have shaped what is possible for them. The target also shifts as our values change in degrees of appropriateness: some values become better for us as we find ways of pursuing them compatibly with other important values, while other values may become less appropriate as it becomes clear that they cannot change to accommodate our other concerns. (I'll say more about degrees of appropriateness at the beginning of Chapter 3.)

The idea that there's not a single, unique best life for each person is intuitive, but it could also create a big problem. If there are a number of lives that are equally good, how can we identify a path forward? How do we know how to make things better if we don't know precisely where we're going?

To solve this problem we need to distinguish between two questions. One question is ontological; it has to do with what is the case: If there is more than one way to live a value-fulfilled life for a person, is there a fact of the matter about how that person should proceed? Is the idea of a value-fulfilled life determinate enough to give us any guidance? The answer to this question had better be "yes", and I think that it is. There would be real trouble here if there were an infinite number of value-fulfilled lives for each person, or if value-fulfilled lives were so different from each other that mutually inconsistent courses of action constantly turned out to be equally good. But this is not how things are for us humans. People tend to care about certain things very deeply, they have fairly stable personalities, and they face consistent challenges. While it is true that a life in which I had two children and didn't learn to sing probably would have resembled a value-fulfilled life just as much as my actual life (in which I have two dogs and take singing lessons), the life in which I became a Catholic nun or a hermit, given my personality, would not contain much fulfillment of appropriate values for me. While there may be many, many various lives in which I have *some* values and pursue them, the set of lives in which I successfully pursue emotionally, motivationally, and cognitively appropriate values together over the long term is likely to be much smaller and more homogeneous.

My claim that there is a fact of the matter about the most value-fulfilled life available to a person, and therefore a fact of the matter about how that person could improve their situation, will raise further questions (at least for those who are curious about metaethics). First, if there are facts about value-fulfilled lives, does that mean that I have succeeded in reducing the normative notion of well-being to natural, psychological facts about what people value? Whether I have done this or not depends on what you think about the norms of appropriateness for values. If you think the idea of an appropriate value can be spelled out without using any value terms, then—yes!—I have bridged the gap between facts and values. But I don't think I have done this. I think that, ultimately, the norms of appropriateness cannot be fully articulated and applied without using more evaluative judgments to do so.[21] For example, when we ask whether a combination of values can be pursued together over time we will need to think about an "acceptable" degree of conflict and a "reasonable" sacrifice, and what counts as "acceptable" or "reasonable" is not something that can be determined empirically.

The other question raised by the imprecise target is epistemological; it has to do with what we can know: Can we have reasonable beliefs about what to do if we cannot identify (even in principle) a unique goal for each person? This question will be the topic of Chapter 4 where we begin to put the value fulfillment theory to work. There, we'll ask how we should go about forming beliefs, making choices, and devising plans about what to do for other people (and ourselves) given our limited knowledge. So, I'll ask the reader to trust me that there is an answer to this question (though not a quick one) for now.

One might have a more specific concern about the value-fulfilled life. Doesn't privileging the long term create problems for taking the subjective perspective seriously? What about those who want to live hard and die young, or those who are willing to sacrifice the long term for the sake of something important now? There are people who value high-risk activities in the fullest sense. Of course, we all value things that include some risk to our longevity; just driving a car to get to work involves some risk. But then there are those who seem to have a greater discount rate for the future than the rest of us do—for example, free rock-climbers and other extreme sports enthusiasts, astronauts, and journalists who cover conflict in dangerous parts of the world. If our guiding theory of well-being privileges the overall value-fulfilled life, then won't such people be living worse lives despite the fact that they are doing what they love to do? Wouldn't taking such risks always be bad for a person?

These worries are overblown. The value fulfillment theory tells us that we should pay attention to the shape of a whole life when we aim to help people, but this does not mean "the longer the better" and it doesn't mean that short-term gains are never worth the risk of a long-term sacrifice. The contribution of individual choices to the whole is relevant to their evaluation, but what counts as a good whole is partly determined by the values that a person has. Staying alive for an extra ten years would not be worth it for most of us if we had to sacrifice our loved ones in order to do it. The difference between most of us and the risk-tolerant climber or journalist is in what we value, what we would not be willing to sacrifice, and how these values are prioritized. Further, some people value risk itself, or they value dramatic peaks and valleys in their experiences. These values also figure into what counts as a life that has the most value fulfillment, and a good deal of variability in future-orientation can be accommodated by including them. Once we acknowledge this, we can see that many of the examples we might have in mind as problems for the value fulfillment theory are not really problems. For people who value risk-taking, or spontaneity, or novelty, appropriately and relatively steadily, these values are some of their standards for how to live.

Now, if I am cautious, unspontaneous, and afraid of novelty, then it will be difficult for me to help people who live by the motto "live hard, die young!" or "no risk, no reward". It is difficult to know how to help someone whose values are different from our own, in part because when we don't share values (or we don't prioritize them in the same way) we may not know how to weigh competing values appropriately for that person. If you are the kind of person whose life would be completely impoverished by giving up mountain climbing, and I simply cannot understand this, then I'm unlikely to be very good at helping you achieve a value-fulfilled life. The relative weight of some values against threats to our long-term survival is just one example of the way in which there can be large individual variation in the shape that a value-fulfilled life takes for different people. We'll talk more about this problem and these kinds of cases in Chapters 4 and 5.

One might also object that this emphasis on the long term leaves out people who will not, as a matter of fact, have long lives. What is good for a person who is going to die at 25 is likely to be quite different from what is good for a person who will live to be 83. The value fulfillment theory does not deny this. What counts as a person's whole life is however long that person actually lives. As far as the ontological question goes (the question about what the value-fulfilled life *is* for the person), it will be determined by the amount of time they have. The real problem here is epistemic. If we knew how long each person's life would be, we could plan accordingly and think about what values they can best fulfill in the time they have. The thing is, though, that we don't usually know this with much certainty at all. We will make mistakes, then, in assessing people's well-being, but these mistakes are inevitable given the limits of our knowledge. We can err on the side of giving the future too much weight, assuming we'll live to be 120 and sacrificing too much for our future selves. Or, we can err by putting too much weight on the possibility of disaster, living for the moment since tomorrow we may die! There is surely a range in the happy medium, but that range will move with more information (e.g., about terminal illnesses or giant meteors heading for the earth).

Privileging the long term makes sense of the practical perspective we have when we think about well-being. It fits with the kind of helpfulness we hope for in friendship, and with the nature of the values most of us have. Thinking about the long-term perspective introduces greater uncertainty, because we don't know the future, but this is a problem in life, not a problem with the value fulfillment theory.

2.4 Can Ultimate Values be Improved?

With the notion of a value-fulfilled life in hand, we can now return to the question of how our values can be improved. What critical perspective do we have on our actual values, according to the value fulfillment theory?

When we ask whether a person's values contribute to a value-fulfilled life overall, we are, at least in part, appealing to instrumental rationality. The norm of instrumental reason—take the necessary and available means to your end, or give up pursuit of it—is used frequently to evaluate people's values, desires, or goals. For example, Peggy values having a partner with whom to share her life, and as a means to this valued end she desires to go to speed dating events in her town. If she hates speed dating and hasn't found a single suitable partner after many attempts, her instrumental desires can be criticized on the grounds that their satisfaction would not actually bring about the ends they are supposed to serve. If speed dating is a bad way for Peggy to find love, then the satisfaction of Peggy's desire to continue going to these events would not be good for her.

Criticisms of instrumental desires can take us pretty far in assessing well-being. The anorexia sufferer's desire for excessive weight loss is not an efficient means to feeling in control; the miser's desire for piles of money is not a good means to being loved; and the tyrant's desire for power over others is not a means to happiness. Such criticisms are available to the value fulfillment theory. Often our basic values are pretty good, but we are taking inappropriate means to them. We make friends (good thing) with people who threaten our self-respect (bad means).

We might wonder whether the value fulfillment theory gives us more than this. Does the value fulfillment theory allow us to critically evaluate the things we value for themselves? Does it allow us, in the words of a friend of mine, to ask whether our ladder is up against the right wall? I think it does, not by imposing objective standards to which our values must measure up, but by way of the idea of *appropriate values* that I've been describing.

Consider some examples of values people have to one degree or other that intuitively seem bad for us. Some people value being thin, being loved by everyone, being perfect, wielding power over other people, being rich and famous, or being "the best". Often, people value these things instrumentally—as a means to happiness or security, say. But some people do value these things for their own sakes; that is, their attitudes toward thinness, power, or the like are stable, long-standing, and resistant to evidence that these values are not a means to something else they care about. Nevertheless, many people find these values questionable as constituents of well-being. When we confront people whose lives seem to be governed by the pursuit of money, fame, or power for its own sake we are inclined to ask whether money, fame, or power really deserve the position of ultimate values. Does the value fulfillment theory allow us to ask this question?

We can ask this question by applying our instrumental standard to the whole pattern of values our friend has. Even if being universally liked (or being "the best", or having great power) is an ultimate value, we can ask whether having that value contributes to or frustrates the fulfillment of other values and, therefore, whether its pursuit has a negative effect on overall value fulfillment. If pursuing this value would create less value fulfillment over time, if it would mean a life that is farther from the life richest in value fulfillment, then this is a value one is better off without.[22] This way of looking at things still doesn't allow us to say that caring so much about being universally loved is just a mistake, whatever its effects on the pursuit of other values. Does the value fulfillment theory give us more to say?

There are other questions we can ask about our values if we follow the value fulfillment theory. These questions will vary with the context (more about this later), but they will include some versions of the following:

- Is this value appropriate to the person? Does it integrate emotion, desire, and judgment?
- Can the value in question really be fulfilled over time at all? Does the person have even an implicit standard for what would count as succeeding? (Status is a notoriously elusive value.)
- Is the value in question (perfection, money, power) really a stand-in for something else (say, friendship, achievement, or acceptance)? And if it is, would the person be better off in terms of value fulfillment if they could learn to construe the latter values in a different way?
- Are there values that the person does not have at the moment but that might be very important for a value-fulfilled life (such as the

value of integrity or self-acceptance) that will be frustrated by the attempt to fulfill the value in question?

Again, these questions do not allow us to say that a value is defective, period, as opposed to its being defective in virtue of the person's psychology, their other values, and the kind of life they are capable of living. But they do take us a fair way past simple questions about means to ends.

According to the value fulfillment theory, valuing being liked, famous, thin, powerful, and so on, should be assessed in terms of the role of these values in an ongoing system. If that role is uniformly negative, then there is nothing good about fulfilling those values. It is worth pointing out that *any* value can be subjected to this scrutiny, not just those values that are commonly condemned. I think that money, power, fame, and perfection are values that are more likely to have a largely negative effect on most people's systems of values than are the values of family, health, and meaningful work. But this is a contingent claim and individual results may vary. Here, as elsewhere, I'm talking to and about most people.

We can improve ultimate values, then, by appeal to other values in the system or by appeal to the overarching goal of a life as rich in value fulfillment as could be. Are these the only ways our values could be improved? Couldn't it be that sometimes more radical improvement would be good for a person? Philosophical research on "transformative experience" suggests this might be the case. A transformative experience is one that we cannot know what it's like to have without having already had it. Further, according to some philosophers, it is an experience we cannot choose to have on the basis of the values we have now. For example, Laurie Paul (2014) argues that when we confront the option of a transformative experience we cannot use our current values to assess whether we would be better off having the experience, because we cannot know what it will be like to be the transformed person. Paul gives the example of having children. The experience of "gestating, producing, and becoming attached to that child" is epistemically transformative because the experience changes what you know about what it is like to have a child (pp. 77–8).

If there are genuinely transformative experiences, does that show that we need other ways of thinking about how to improve our values besides the ones that the value fulfillment theory admits? You might think so. After all, as discussed in the previous section, the idea of a value-fulfilled life is tied to the person whose life it is; it is not defined as a life that *would* work for a radically transformed person.

Ultimately, however, I agree with Ruth Chang that these epistemically transformative experiences do not provide an insurmountable challenge to the view that we improve our future values based on our current values or our current selves.[23] Chang (2015) argues, first, that not many experiences are truly epistemically transformative, because few experiences engage basic capacities that we have not experienced engaging before. Having children, for instance, involves basic human sensory, emotional, and rational capacities. It employs these capacities in new ways, but it does not represent something that has absolutely no connection to previous experiences, and we can narrow the gap by exercising our imaginations and talking to others who know more than we do. Second, Chang argues that the subjective experience of having a child (or of any potentially transformative experience) is not the only basis we have for choosing to have it or not. We can also choose based on objective considerations: "having a child will objectively enrich your life in significant ways, be instrumental in bringing a valuable human life into the world, help create in the world a loving family bond between you and your spouse, etc. On the basis of these objective values of the experience, you can know that the experience of having a child will be better than, say, the experience of being skinned alive" (Chang 2015, pp. 256–7). For my purposes, the point here is that even if a person does not know exactly what the subjective experience of having a child would be like, she can know enough about the value of having children to make a reasonable judgment about whether a value-fulfilled life for her would include being a parent. This is not to say that this assessment would be easy to make, nor that the person couldn't make a mistake; it is just that we don't require an additional criterion for the improvement of values.

But we're not done yet. In her discussion of transformative experiences, Chang introduces a different kind of case—the case of "choice-based transformative choices". When you make this kind of choice, "you change who you are by the very making of a choice, not by some experience or event downstream from your choice" (p. 239). This kind of choice is possible when we are choosing between options that are "on a par", that is, where one option is not better than the other, but they are also not equal in value. It may be difficult to grasp what is meant by "on a par" if it doesn't mean "equal". The intuitive idea, it seems to me, is that two options are on a par when they have different kinds of value that aren't on the same scale. Many choices in life seem to be like this. Decisions about whether to maintain long-distance friendships or concentrate on the friends who live nearby, to pursue a clinical practice or focus on research, to be a parent or to put more energy into your career, and so on, are often decisions where neither option is better overall than the other—things can work out well, though differently, either way. Why not say that these options are actually equal in value? Well, Chang points out that if a pair of options were truly equivalent in value, then if you added a tiny bit of goodness to one, it would make it *better*. But this isn't how we think about options like the ones I've just mentioned. If I see being a parent and not being a parent as on a par, and you tell me that I can be a parent and have an extra piece of cheesecake (certainly a good thing as far as I'm concerned), will that make the life in which I'm a parent better? This seems wrong. It would also seem wrong to flip a coin to decide—but if the options were truly equal in value, this would be a rational strategy. The message is that there isn't a single scale on which to weigh the value of these different lives that could establish that they weigh the same amount. Nevertheless, Chang does not think on-a-par options are incomparable, if that means that we cannot choose between them. We can, and when we do so we create reasons for ourselves and determine the kind of person that we will become.

Chang's idea that options can be on a par is compelling (though it is also controversial in philosophy: Andreou 2015; Williams 2016). Does it create problems for the value fulfillment theory? If options can be on a par, and if we change who we are by choosing between such options, there would be greater indeterminacy about what counts as a value-fulfilled life for a person. After all, if value-fulfilled lives are anchored to the person and the person is in flux, then the life that is best for a person—the target—will also be in flux. Notice, however, that the flux isn't (typically) *radical*. For one thing, our personalities are usually stable enough that radical transformations in our appropriate values are unlikely (Briley and Tucker-Drob 2014; Ferguson 2010). When options are on a par, by definition, one is not better than another. The life in which I'm a parent is not going to be on a par with the life in which I become an axe murderer or a hermit. Also, the flux does not mean we cannot make decisions or take action. What does the value fulfillment theory say we should do about options that seem to be on a par? We should think about our values and the various ways in which our lives could move closer to a life very rich in value fulfillment. We should make sure they really are on par and that we're not just missing something, and we should consider whether there's some third option that's better than the two that are on a par. Then we should choose. If the options really are on a par (and there's no option better than both), then we'll do well whichever way we go.

2.5 Value Fulfillment Theory: Subjective or Objective?

Discussions of well-being in philosophy often divide theories of well-being into two camps: subjective theories and objective theories. According to one way of drawing this distinction, subjective theories say that whether or not something contributes to a person's well-being always depends on that person's attitudes (Sumner 1996). A person must like (or be disposed to like under certain conditions), want, value, or have some other subjective response to any candidate component of well-being for it to be good for them. Objective theories, on the other hand, deny this. These theories say that something could be good for a person even if they don't like, want, or value it (or have any other subjective response toward the thing). The value fulfillment theory says that something could be valuable for a person who doesn't currently value that thing, because it could be that a certain value (for example, health or self-respect) is needed for that person to live a value-fulfilled life. But the value fulfillment theory still holds that if the person could not ever value this thing—if it could never be one of their values in any improved version of their life—then it is not good for that person. In this way, the value fulfillment theory preserves the grain of truth in subjectivism that for something to be good *for me* it has to be something that I can see as good for me.

The fact that the value fulfillment theory posits an ideal that is independent of a particular person's subjective responses—that is, the value-fulfilled life—might make it seem like an objective theory. Indeed, the value fulfillment theory has in common with objective theories that it does make room for a critical perspective on a person's actual values. We have this critical perspective because there are norms for the improvement of a person's values that reach beyond that person's current psychological states. First, the goal of living a value-fulfilled life imposes a standard of sustainability on a person's values. For example, a person who values partying with hard drugs and lots of alcohol is not doing as well as they could if these values are going to cause an early death and the forfeiture of many other things they would come to value more. Second, the social context in which we pursue many of our values imposes constraints on the standards for what counts as fulfilling a value. For example, someone who values being a father cannot simply make up what it is to succeed in terms of this value. An impatient and neglectful father is not doing well at being a father. I'll say more about these standards for what counts as fulfilling a value in the next chapter. For now the important point is that the value fulfillment theory does not simply take a person's actual values as a given; rather, it allows for the possibility that a person would be better off making changes to their values.

This does not make the value fulfillment theory an objective theory, however, in an important sense. The value fulfillment theory says that a fruitful way to think about well-being, in the context of helping other people, is to think about what is good for people as anchored by their values and guided by the ways in which their values could be improved. The theory rejects the idea that certain things are good for people entirely independently of how they feel about them or could come to feel about them. In this respect (an important respect, I think) the value fulfillment theory is not an objective theory.

Moreover, the value fulfillment theory does not constrain which values can be part of a value-fulfilled life in the way that an objective theory would. For example, the value fulfillment theory implies (in contrast to objective theories) that it is at least possible for a Mafioso with a stable set of values that fit his personality to achieve well-being even though his values are morally questionable. (Though the value fulfillment theory certainly doesn't imply that it's easy for the immoral person to achieve well-being.) This implication—that someone could achieve well-being by pursuing morally bad goals, or satisfying morally bad desires—is usually thought to be a serious problem for subjective theories. I think the problem is a problem with the world: what's good for one isn't always good for all. And if this is a problem with the world, I think we're better off facing it squarely than trying to define it out of existence. (This topic will come up again in Section 5.2 where we'll consider whether being a helpful friend requires you to help a friend pursue values that you find morally objectionable. To anticipate, I think the answer is "definitely not". My point here is just that this implication about the possibility of a happy villain reveals the subjective commitments of the value fulfillment theory.)

To my mind the most plausible candidate for an objective value is, somewhat paradoxically, psychological happiness. Dan Haybron argues that well-being consists in the fulfillment of a person's individual nature, which in turn requires emotional fulfillment in the form of happiness, and rational fulfillment in the form of the successful pursuit of values (Haybron 2008a). Happiness, according to Haybron's theory, is a favorable emotional condition, which includes three types of positive emotional state: endorsement, engagement, and attunement (2008b). Obviously these are subjective psychological states, but Haybron takes them to be good for people independently of their own choices or attitudes toward these psychological states. To put it quickly: You don't have to want to be happy for happiness to be good for you. I think it is extremely plausible that these positive emotional states are good for everyone, so why not say that emotional happiness is an objective value? First, notice that the distinction between subjectivism and objectivism starts to break down here, when it comes to the value of emotional happiness. This is because to value something is partly to be disposed to have certain kinds of positive emotions, and, therefore, the positive emotional states that constitute your happiness are going to be interwoven with your values. For example, feelings of engagement or flow when you play basketball are one component of valuing basketball. The feelings of attunement you feel when you are in nature are part of what it is to value nature. Because of this overlap, value fulfillment will naturally and inevitably coincide with the pursuit of emotional happiness. So, I don't think much is to be gained from treating emotional happiness as the sole objective value. Second, when there are choices to be made—for example, the choice of how to prioritize the different emotional components of happiness, or how to compare happiness to other ultimate values—I maintain that what determines which path is best for a person depends on how that person is able to integrate their emotions, desires, and judgments.[24]

I am a subjectivist at heart, though the value fulfillment theory has moved away from any simple form of subjectivism. That said, allow me to repeat a point from the introduction, which is that thinking about how value fulfillment works is not just for subjectivists. Any theory of well-being should recognize the importance of successfully doing things that matter to us, and understanding how to help the people we care about to do so as well. Readers who think there are objective prudential values can think of the value-fulfilled lives posited by the value fulfillment theory as constrained by these objective facts.

2.6 Conclusion

We are looking for a theory of well-being that addresses our practical concern for helping people to improve their lives. We need an understanding of well-being that does not make well-being something alien to the people we're trying to help, but that also gives us some legitimate grounds for questioning a person's current perspective on what is good for them when it seems very much at odds with what we think is good for them. I hope this chapter has established how the value fulfillment theory promises to do this. It defines well-being in terms of a person's individual psychology, namely, that person's values. But it also allows for the possibility that a person's values are in need of improvement or transformation (thus allowing for the possibility of error) and provides standards for improvement that preserve the close tie between well-being and the subject.

To recap, the value fulfillment theory says that well-being is the fulfillment of appropriate values over a lifetime. Appropriate values integrate our emotions, desires, and judgments about what makes our lives go well and what we have reason to do. Fully appropriate values are also ones that we can pursue and achieve together over time. Appropriate values, then, are (1) suited to our desires and emotions, (2) reflectively endorsed, and (3) capable of being fulfilled together over time.

Of course, as we have already observed, these guidelines leave room for many different ways of living a life in which you value and enjoy good friendships, meaningful work, pleasurable experiences, and so on. There are, in other words, many different shapes that the value-fulfilled life can take and if our theory is going to guide us in how to help people it will also have to direct our thinking about the details. This leads us directly to the application of the value fulfillment theory, which is the subject of the rest of the book.

3

What is Value Fulfillment?

The value fulfillment theory says that well-being consists in the fulfillment of appropriate values over the course of a life. We have so far been working with a rough understanding of what it means for a value to be fulfilled—we attain a goal, cultivate a relationship, inhabit a way of being, uphold an ideal, and so on. How does this rough idea of fulfillment get put into practice?

As soon as we start thinking about which values to fulfill and how to go about it, we see that our simple way of formulating the theory is problematic. "Well-being is the fulfillment of appropriate values over time" is problematic because of the fact that—as we saw in the previous chapter—people's values typically exist on a continuum of appropriateness. Because our emotions, desires, and judgments are not perfectly harmonious, there will be many things we value that are not fully or perfectly appropriate. Further, it would be odd to say that the only fulfillment that adds to your well-being is the fulfillment of a perfectly integrated value. This would imply that the person who is somewhat conflicted about their love of cheesy romantic comedies does not benefit at all from watching *The Proposal* for the twenty-seventh time. Maybe no one could ever benefit from watching the sizzling chemistry between Sandra Bullock and Ryan Reynolds twenty-seven times, but there is a serious problem here. If it is true that many of our values are not perfectly integrated (and it does seem to be true), then we cannot identify well-being with the fulfillment of perfectly integrated values—doing so would make well-being nearly impossible.

To solve this problem we need to acknowledge some subtleties that are glossed over by the slogan "well-being is the fulfillment of appropriate values over time". First, appropriateness comes in degrees and much of what we are doing when we think about how to improve our lives is trying to inch our values toward greater appropriateness. Completely inappropriate values would be projects, relationships, and ideals that do not motivate us, that leave us emotionally cold, and that we could not successfully pursue over time even if we tried. Completely inappropriate values, then, are not going to get onto our radar. Mostly what we've got, and what we will think about when we're thinking about our well-being, are values that are at varying degrees of appropriateness, and our task is to think about how to make the system of values better for us. This may involve jettisoning values that are on the "less appropriate" end of the spectrum, but there is no bright line between values that are appropriate enough and values that are too inappropriate to keep even in a modified form.

Second, whether a particular choice or course of action contributes to a person's well-being is determined by the role it plays in value fulfillment over time, and values that are not perfectly appropriate can nevertheless make positive contributions. One reason for this is that specific choices are often made with respect to our more core, ultimate values (such things as relationships, meaningful work, and psychological happiness) that do tend to be well integrated and more appropriate. For example, Christophe's well-being may be improved by watching a new rom-com, even if he is self-critical about his enjoyment of this low-brow form of entertainment, because he does entirely appropriately value joyful experiences and these movies (given his low-brow emotions) are the best means to the kind of experience he seeks. Decisions about how to improve our lives will often be decisions about how better to fulfill these core values. In such cases, success in terms of a value that isn't perfectly integrated into a person's personality nevertheless contributes to their well-being because it is a good means to achieving an ultimate value that is an appropriate value. In other words, it is total value fulfillment that matters, and given all the constraints we are under (from our own personalities and from our environments) some values that are not the absolute best fit for us will nevertheless make a sufficient contribution to total value fulfillment.

When we aim to improve our overall value fulfillment, in some cases the question is whether one specific value is the best means to a more ultimate value, but the question might also be about how to understand what it means to succeed in terms of the ultimate value. Much of what we're doing when we think about how to improve our lives is thinking about how to interpret and understand our values and what it means to succeed in terms of them. Christophe, a film scholar, may think about whether the value of intellectual integrity requires that he not enjoy formulaic movies starring Ryan Reynolds or Sandra Bullock. Or he may think about whether valuing enjoyment means being less self-critical in general. Depending on his answers to these questions, his interpretations of the values of intellectual integrity and personal enjoyment will take different shapes, and his valuing romantic comedies will become a more or less appropriate way for him to seek enjoyment. The more he sees this form of entertainment as at odds with his other core values, feels ashamed of his enjoyment, and wishes he didn't like it, the less appropriate this value is and the less it contributes to well-being. The more he sees this form of entertainment as a harmless pleasure, feels embarrassed by his intellectual pretentions, and wants to be rid of them so he can enjoy the latest fluff with impunity, the more this value is appropriate and the more it can contribute to his well-being. When we look at value fulfillment over time, we can see that values that are not perfectly appropriate at one time may become more appropriate as the person reflects on how to resolve the conflict among her feelings, desires, judgments, and other values. This is another way that imperfect values can contribute to total value fulfillment over time.

These complexities about the appropriateness of values mean that the more accurate slogan for the value fulfillment theory would be something like this: "Greater well-being consists in the fulfillment of more appropriate values over time". I'm going to stick with my original, catchier slogan, and trust us to remember that there is a spectrum of appropriateness and that values do not have to be perfectly appropriate in order to contribute to a life rich in value fulfillment. An important implication of these subtleties (discussed briefly in

Section 2.1) is that ill-being should not be understood as the fulfillment of inappropriate values. This is either too broad (if it includes any value that isn't perfectly appropriate) or too narrow (if it includes only values that are perfectly inappropriate). Ill-being, we should say, consists in a life that has little fulfillment of values that are somewhat, albeit imperfectly, appropriate. Again, a life may have little such value fulfillment because the person does not value anything (due to depression or deprivation), or because their values are frustrated by the world, or because the person's values are in conflict with each other or with other features of the person in ways that make it difficult to fulfill them.

In order to apply the value fulfillment theory, we need to understand how we get from a general idea of a life replete with realizations of things that matter to us to specific judgments about which choices would make a person's life go better or worse. There are two aspects to the application of the theory. First, there is the content: What should we actually think about when we aim to help someone gain more well-being? Second, there is the process: How should we go about thinking about these things and what obstacles are there to doing a good job? The answer to the first question is that we should think about what it means to fulfill our values. When we do this, we will see that for most values, fulfillment isn't a simple matter of checking to see whether you "have it". Rather, value fulfillment for our most important values depends on the standards of success we have for these values and this makes things significantly more complicated. Exploring these complexities will be the business of this chapter; we'll turn to questions about the process in Chapter 4.

3.1 What is Value Fulfillment for a Single Value?

The first thing to notice is that values, like goals and desires, bring with them standards for success and living up to these standards is part of value fulfillment. As I discussed above, we take our values to give us reasons to do certain things and to respond in certain ways; our values create norms or standards for us. These standards need not be (and usually aren't) explicitly defined or endorsed; they are just the norms that make up a person's sense of what it means to succeed in terms of, or live up to, something they value. Some of these standards are subjective: whether they are met or not is entirely a matter of our own experience. For example, for me, part of the value of singing is that I enjoy it. When singing is joyless I am not fulfilling the value that it has for me and whether or not I enjoy it is determined by me and my psychological states. (I could *enjoy* singing, even if I were in an experience machine.) Having certain experiences is an important standard of success for many of our values: we care about enjoying our leisure pursuits, we want to feel a sense of meaning from our work, the pleasure we get from our friendships matters to us, and so on. But most values encompass some standards that are objective in the sense that whether or not we fulfill them is not merely a matter of our experience. I would also like to learn to be a better singer, one who doesn't make others run away, and whether I succeed according to that standard depends on other people. This is not a standard I could meet lying in the experience machine where I would not actually be interacting with other people.[1] (Of course, in the experience machine I could *believe* that I'm a good singer, but that's not the same as actually being one.) There is, then, something to meeting at least some of the standards that our values impose that goes beyond our subjective experience. In this respect, value fulfillment is similar to preference satisfaction: you may fail to fulfill your values, though you believe otherwise just as you may fail to get what you want without knowing it (say, if you are grossly deluded or in an experience machine).[2]

The distinction between subjective and objective standards is different from another important distinction between personal and "inter-subjective" standards. To see this second distinction consider the value that athletic activities have for the people who enjoy them. For many such activities, part of what we enjoy about them is competing with others, improving our abilities, and honing our skills.

For people who care about these features of sports, there are standards of performance that we conform to in order to see our sport as contributing to life going well, despite the fact that most of us are not elite athletes. Call these our personal standards; personal standards are our own standards of success that we do not take to define success for others. Personal standards are contrasted to inter-subjective standards that define success for groups of people. There are standards of true excellence in sports that are inter-subjective—the standard set by the Olympic athlete, for example. Our personal standards may be lower than the inter-subjective standards of success, because they take into account a reasonable assessment of our abilities and circumstances (recommended for aging athletes), or they may be higher than the inter-subjective standards of success because we are willing to demand more of ourselves than we do of others. Notice that a personal standard might be perfectly objective in the sense that whether or not you have met the standard is not determined by your subjective experience alone. One of the standards aging athletes might endorse is to maintain their ability to run a marathon in under five hours, knowing that they are at an age where most people's pace declines. Running a marathon in under five hours isn't the inter-subjective standard for good long-distance running. Nevertheless, it is a matter of fact (beyond the runner's experience) whether they run the marathon in under five hours.

Personal standards can be objective in the sense that it is not up to you whether you've met them. There is another way in which they are not simply "made up". Because so many of the activities and practices we value are shared activities, you can bend the standards for what kind of participation contributes to your life going well only so much. To take an obvious example, if you value being a good friend, you don't get to make up what counts as a good friend—you're not a good friend if none of your friends think you are. Or think about sports again. Since running is a fairly solitary sport, it might be an example in which the standards you accept are indeed highly tailored to you, but other sports and many practices are not like this. Team sports like baseball are such that you do not get to invent your own standards for what counts as participating in a way that's worthwhile.[3] Your standards can sink so low or be so idiosyncratic that you don't even count as playing anymore, or you can hold yourself to such a high standard that you become overly competitive, a bad team player, or a bad sport. These are contingent facts about activities and practices we tend to value. It's possible that someone who is self-centered enough could care about perfecting his throwing skill without worrying about whether he throws to the right person and gets the opposing team out. But this person would be highly unusual and the way he values baseball is not likely to be sustainable: he's bound to get kicked off the team at some point.

The fact that our values often impose objective standards means that you are not likely to be an infallible source of information about how well your life is going. You might be mistaken about how well you are fulfilling certain of your values. You may lack information about the degree to which your life is on the path toward greater value fulfillment—on the assumption that you, like most people, value something other than your own experiences. It's possible, then, for you to be wrong about how good your life is. To be sure, people do also have subjective standards for the achievement of values, and here subjective experience is highly relevant to determining whether the standard has been met. For example, like me with my singing, you might value playing the violin in part because you enjoy it, and if that's so, your subjective experience is key to whether you are achieving what you value. (Though even here you may not be infallible. If we can be wrong about our own emotions, then we can be mistaken in our assessments of how well we are doing, even subjectively. Haybron (2008b) argues that we can even be mistaken about how happy we are.)

Our standards for value fulfillment can be subjective or objective (met by having a subjective experience or by actually attaining something in the world), personal or inter-subjective (authoritative just for us, or for a group). Which are the *best* standards to have? Naturally, according to the value fulfillment theory, the best standards are the ones that contribute to a life rich in value fulfillment. Now, as I've already suggested, we can't just go changing our standards willy-nilly.

Some of our values are deeply socially enmeshed and we cannot change what it means to succeed in them without many other people changing with us. Sometimes it is our own fundamental convictions that prevent us from altering our standards. Nevertheless, there are cases—the aging athlete described above, for example—where it does make sense to change our standards. What cases are these?

To answer this question, let's think more about why we might sometimes want to change our standards for the sake of value fulfillment. It isn't to make value fulfillment easier: lowering our standards to the point where they're already met might result in a reduction of stress, but it doesn't by itself secure value fulfillment if it requires us to lower our standards for the sake of something other than the value in question. Sometimes it is reasonable to lower our standards: if experience teaches you that you'll never learn to speak Chinese without an accent, it might be appropriate to think about success in terms of being able to communicate well enough to be understood by taxi drivers and waiters. But for many of our values, what counts as success is intrinsic to the value itself or reinforced by others and so we cannot lower our standards in any old way and expect a value-fulfilled life. You do not speak Chinese at all if no Chinese speaker can understand the simplest thing you are trying to say. The values themselves and the social context in which we pursue them impose limits on what our standards can be, but there is room for interpretation within these limits.

The primary reason to change our standards is so that we can continue to fulfill all of our appropriate values over time. The problem with simply lowering our standards for the sake of meeting them more easily is that this doesn't obviously constitute a way of continuing to value what we value; rather, it is a way of sacrificing what we value for the sake of something else (like a reduction in stress). But there are ways to change our standards that respect the values we have rather than sacrifice them for ease. When there are such ways, the need to sustain our values over time together with our changing circumstances can make it sensible to change our standards. Standards for fitness and physical accomplishment can adapt to our aging bodies. Standards for career success can be modified as the shape of our careers change. Standards for hobbies can change as our lives take more definite shape and we acknowledge how much time we actually have for these activities. When it is possible, without sacrificing the essence of what we value, we need to change how we understand success in a way that allows us to achieve the fulfillment of our values in the long run.

When we find we are falling short of fulfilling one of our values, we have several options. We can admit failure and abandon the value entirely. We can reject the standards we have taken to count as success and replace them with other standards. Or, we can modify the standards that we have had. The first option is difficult, maybe even impossible, particularly for core values like friendship, health, and meaningful work, though it may be a good option for values like status or wealth (see the discussion of how ultimate values can be improved in Section 2.4). In the remainder of the chapter, I'll focus on the second and third options: replace or modify.

In some cases, changing our standards will mean adjusting them to fit our limitations. For example, consider the fact that the vast majority of us are going to engage in activities in which we have no hope of being among the best in the world or excelling according to the inter-subjective standards for true excellence. If our personal standards are just the inter-subjective standards of excellence—in no way modified or tailored to our abilities—most of us are in trouble. The aging athlete who holds himself to the standard of the Olympian is bound to be frustrated and to find the pursuit of what he values unsatisfying. It's desirable (and possible) to recognize what counts as the best performance and also to recognize that your participation in this sport can excel in other terms (improving relative to your age and ability, being a good sport, having fun, and so on).

In other cases, adjusting our standards may mean making them more specific. A new physician may see herself as fulfilling the value of her medical career if she cares about her patients and keeps up with the latest research. A seasoned physician is likely to have much more specific standards of success that are tailored to her medical specialty, the challenges she has faced with particular patients, and so on. An 18-year-old college student may value "being musical" and may fulfill this value by taking a class in music appreciation, trying to learn some different instruments, or joining a band. At 58, this same person is likely to think of the value of music in different ways; he may think that the contribution of music to his life depends on his participation in a choir and making an effort to listen to the music his children enjoy. At 18 and 58 music is an appropriate value, but the standards for what counts as fulfilling it are different.

There are changes we can sensibly make to how we understand our values and what it means to fulfill them, but we should also acknowledge the real constraints we are under. There are, as I've already discussed, the expectations of other people who are integral to the fulfillment of our values in one way or another. How your partner thinks about a good marriage, how your family thinks about parenting, how your teammates thinking about teamwork, and so on, are real constraints. The values inherent to marriage, parenting, and team sports are values we achieve together with other people. We can't change the standards of success by individual fiat. Further, we sometimes have standards of success that are in competition with each other. For example, a young professor who values her career as a scientist may think that to fulfill this value she must mentor undergraduate and graduate students, and publish at least three papers per year in top journals. These standards are difficult to meet individually, and meeting them both is even more demanding. Our young professor needs to look for ways to reduce the conflict without sacrificing the value of being a good scientist, but we shouldn't pretend that this is a simple task.

The standards we have considered so far give us some guidance when we aim to help people. One way that we can help people is to enable them to see how well (or poorly) they are meeting their own standards. This is what we do when we point out to a friend that they are spending so much time at work that they are neglecting their children even though they claim that attentive parenting is a primary value. We can also help by showing a friend that their standards are unreasonable and in need of modification. But before we turn our attention to the practical context, we need to discuss the complexities introduced by the fact that we have many values.

3.2 What is Value Fulfillment for Multiple Values?

How do values get put together? First, some of our goals or ends are more important to us than others: they figure more centrally in our planning, they have greater stability, or they are more deeply emotionally entrenched. For example, parents typically take the welfare of their children and being a good parent to be centrally important values that could not be given up for anything else. For such parents, the value of parenthood is more important or stronger than any other value and it therefore has a large role in the assessment of how the parent's life is going overall.

Second, some values help to produce the fulfillment of other values, while some values make success in other areas more difficult. For example, health contributes to many other values by keeping you fit enough to partake in work, hobbies, helping others, and so on. Some values have only instrumental importance; their value is limited to what they procure in other terms. Nevertheless, some purely instrumental goals can be genuinely valued. For many people, I suspect money is like this. If they are really forced to think about why they want money, they will admit that it is because of other purposes it serves; nevertheless, they have stable positive emotional responses toward making money and making money figures centrally in planning and assessing how life is going. So, instrumental values count in overall value fulfillment, but we do need to make sure that we don't ultimately give them independent weight if they aren't important to people except insofar as they bring about something else.

Notice that one goal might have instrumental value with respect to another goal, even though the first goal is not *pursued* by the person as a means to the second. We need not value our health for the sake of being able to do our hobbies in order for health to benefit the pursuit of our hobbies. Indeed, some values, which we could call "resultant values", are such that they are brought about by the pursuit of other things that are valued for their own sakes. Meaning, balance, and enjoyment (at least in some of their incarnations) are like this. We achieve meaning in our lives when we pursue worthwhile things for their own sake. We achieve balance when we succeed in pursuing a variety of worthwhile ends. Enjoyment comes about as a result of engagement in an activity that is pursued for its own sake. Relationships between resultant values and the intrinsic values on which they rely are important to overall value fulfillment because the former augment the importance of the latter. (By "intrinsic value" I mean that which is valued for its own sake. I'm ignoring some fine distinctions here for ease of expression.)

Strength of commitment and degree of intrinsic worth are two obvious ways in which some values matter more to judgments about overall value fulfillment. There are also some less obvious considerations that are relevant to such judgments. A third important point about how values get put together is that some values are related as the abstract to the specific.[4] For example, a person might value music and also value singing opera and listening to recordings of opera music. Performing and appreciating opera isn't a means to music, because music is not an independent end brought about by the pursuit of opera. Rather, for someone who values both, opera is a *way of expressing* the value of music, and the means to both values include buying tickets to opera performances and listening to opera on the radio. The distinction between abstract and specific values is relevant to overall value fulfillment because abstract values can be specified in ways that are more or less conducive to value fulfillment over a lifetime, and because the significance of specific values can be augmented by the importance of the abstract value they specify. For example, Jules (the struggling actor from Chapter 1) would probably be better off valuing "creativity" or "having a creative outlet" than valuing "dramatic performance" or "acting". If she has the former value, she can choose to find new ways to express it when she learns that her talent for acting is not conducive to success. Moreover, in some cases the person who values "creativity" and finds ways to express it is better off than the person who just values her specific artistic hobby. If for some reason you could not engage in this hobby anymore and understanding your hobby as part of a larger good allows you to find something else that would fill this role, then the *pattern* of achievable values (though not necessarily the specific values that fill out the pattern) would be more stable over time.[5]

Fourth, some values constrain others insofar as the standards they impose on action make it impossible to pursue other values in certain ways. Moral values tend to constrain the pursuit of other values: for example, you cannot easily value being an honest person if you cheat your way to the top of your profession (Tiberius 2005). Constraining values are relevant to overall value fulfillment because they can decrease the importance of other values that tend to require violating constraints. Constraining values also reveal ways in which some goals contribute more to overall value fulfillment because they are easily pursued within these constraints. Importantly, constraining values may rule some pursuits out of court so that they have no weight in overall value fulfillment at all. For example, a commitment to being there for your aging parents might rule out working for the Foreign Service even if that is something you really want to do. Constraining values might function independently of strength—they can function as principles or background intentions that impose limits even if we aren't actively motivated by them as much as we are by other values.

Finally, there are relationships of justification between values that are relevant to overall value fulfillment. Ultimate values serve to justify what we pursue as means, abstract values such as art or knowledge often serve as a justification for specific pursuits, and resultant values like meaning may help to justify the pursuit of the multiple values that give rise to them. This is important because values in the fullest sense are patterns of response that we take to give us reasons that we ought to heed. Having justification for our values that knits them together contributes to their stability and reduces conflict. This is particularly true for people who are reflective and tend to question frequently what they're doing and why, but even people who aren't that prone to reflection are sometimes prompted to wonder and then stability and long-term value fulfillment are served by having an answer. Of course, we do not always have a worked-out, articulate justification for what we value, but when such relationships exist they are important to the stability of the total package of values over time. The example of creativity and a specific creative hobby discussed above provides one illustration of this.

An important lesson we can learn from the complexity of our values is that the best overall life is not necessarily promoted by fulfilling a single value to a greater degree at the expense of fulfilling others to a smaller degree. This is because of the ways in which values are related to each other in a whole life. So called "work/life balance" affords what is probably the most familiar example of competing but indispensable values. Many people, particularly in North American culture, find that the two values of work and family often conflict with each other because of the amount of time they each demand. You might think that the value fulfillment theory implies that those of us who experience this conflict would be better off quitting our jobs to devote more time to our families, or not having a family in the first place so that we can focus on our careers. That this would be an unfortunate implication for a theory of well-being is something we can see by thinking about the question, "What would you give up?" If you are like me, the thought that it's difficult to have a career and strong relationships with family and friends at the same time does not give any weight to one of these options over the other. Indeed, it seems to me that giving up one for the sake of another would make my life much worse. Fortunately, the value fulfillment theory does not imply that we should make such a sacrifice.

Why not? First, if work and family are really both important to most people, pursuing the two together may result in greater value fulfillment overall despite the conflict between them. For one thing, there are coping strategies for dealing with conflicts, but the complete loss of a core value will leave a big hole that may be difficult to bear. Also, it may be very difficult to make great strides in one if the other were entirely abandoned, because of diminishing returns (working all the time often does not lead to progress and our families can drive us crazy if we have nothing else to attend to).

Second, values that compete with each other for our time and attention may nevertheless be mutually supporting. For example, one of the things that sustains my work as a teacher is that my family and friends value education and help confirm the value of this path for me. Most of the musicians I know have the value of their music reinforced by friends and family who themselves value music and who provide a community of appreciation, support, and sometimes even collaboration. Work and family are implicated in many of our other values, too, in ways that make it more likely that abandoning one of these values is not best. Health is likely to be affected by working all the time and by not developing close personal relationships, enjoyment is likely to decrease for those who spend all their time in one way, many of our leisure activities are social, many of our work activities are sources of self-esteem, and so on.

Third, and relatedly, a larger set of interrelated values puts us in a better position to respond constructively to changes in our circumstances. For those of us who are not asocial, world-altering geniuses, putting all our eggs in one basket—counting on work to sustain us without any help—is not a good strategy. This point is clear in cases in which one of our values becomes impossible to fulfill. If your marriage fails, or you get fired from the job you love, or you trash your knees and can't ski anymore, you're better off if you have other values. In these cases, having multiple values gives you something else to turn to. (I do not mean to say that our values are interchangeable. There are some losses from which we never fully recover, and change is often difficult and painful. Nevertheless, the point is that we are better off when we have other values to turn to than we would otherwise be.) The metaphor of a web of values might be helpful here. If you think of values as forming a web that supports each individual value as well as the various practices that fulfill them, then the idea is that a web of just one very thick strand is less helpful than a web with several reasonably sturdy strands.

Further, the importance of having a larger set of values is not just about spreading out the risk. Our values create a narrative that helps to make sense of, or to justify, changing our standards over time. And changing our standards for what counts as fulfillment (as we discussed at the end of Section 3.1) is often extremely important to overall value fulfillment. For example, you may identify as an athlete in your youth, and think of athletic success in terms of continuous improvement, competing with the best, and breaking records. As you age, unless you are an extremely unusual specimen, you either have to give up some of these standards or give up your sport. Other values can provide a rationale for modifying your standards. If you value your health, it would be better to change your standards than to give up sports altogether. If you value friendships with teammates or running buddies, it is again better to change your standards than to give up completely. Also, for the sake of friends and teammates, it's better to modify your standards than to become a cranky malcontent because you continue to hold yourself to the standard of a 20-year-old Olympian. These other values recommend new standards like having fun, helping teammates achieve their best, developing new skills to compensate for the loss of quickness, and so on.

Meaningful work affords another example of this phenomenon. In your thirties and forties, you may find your career incredibly exciting and thrive on thoughts about how you're going to change your field, revolutionize your company, break through the glass ceiling, or invent life-altering technologies. These are not unreasonable standards to have for a talented person in the early stage of their career when good fortune is unknown and talent is untested. But then in your fifties and sixties you begin to gain perspective on what kind of contribution is reasonable to expect of a single person, and a clearer view of what the obstacles are to success by these grand standards. This perspective might make you lose motivation and you may contemplate quitting or changing careers entirely (or, in true "mid-life crisis" mode, you may think about buying a red convertible or buying a beachfront bar in Costa Rica). But many people can't afford to quit their career, and many are doing worthwhile work (work that they value) despite these unsettling feelings. At this point your other values help you to justify modifying your standards. For example, if working long hours creates stress and takes you away from family members who need more attention (young children or aging parents), then the values of health, happiness, and family recommend thinking about your work in a different way. You may think about success in your career as determined by the valuable end to which you and others have made modest contributions. You may move from thinking about climbing the ladder to thinking about how you have helped pave the way for others, or made a difference to your team. Notice that even someone who succeeds according to the most ambitious standards of success is likely to need to make changes as they age. If you did change your field, win the Nobel Prize, invent the Internet, what then? Once you've accomplished what you wanted to accomplish and you wonder what else there is you need other values.

In the two cases I've just described (sports and career), if you have nothing else to draw on, you'll have a harder time recalibrating what matters in your life. As our circumstances change, having a range of values in our life will give us the flexibility to change our standards of success in ways that make sense. It is worth pointing out that this aspect of the value fulfillment theory helps solve a problem for subjective theories of well-being, which has to do with one way that our values (or desires) can seem to be "defective". The best example for our purposes here is John Rawls' (1971, p. 432) example of the man who cares about nothing except spending his life counting blades of grass. The thought here is that this man has trivial or silly values the fulfillment of which does not make his life go well. It seems really implausible to say that the grass-counter is achieving well-being. The value fulfillment theory cannot rule out the possibility of a person who is incapable of valuing anything else. However, given what I've just said about the importance of multiple values, the successful grass-counter would have to be an extremely lucky and atypical person for his life to count as going well for him. The grass-counter would have to be someone who not only does not value anything else, but also someone for whom no other life would have greater value fulfillment over time than the one in which he counts blades of grass. He would, then, have to be such that he will never develop in ways that will make him tire of counting grass and never have any experiences that cause him to find counting grass boring or pointless. It seems to me that such a person would be so limited that it is no longer implausible to say that the life spent counting blades of grass is good for him.

I've been singing the praises of having a diverse set of values, but you might be wondering: "Doesn't having many values open us up to the possibility of more unfulfilled values?" Picture Denise the dentist who decides to take up golf and watercolor painting once her dental practice is moving along swimmingly. She turns out to be an acceptable golfer, but she has no sense of color so her paintings are a disappointing mess. Wouldn't Denise be better off sticking with her career and not taking on all these new opportunities for failure? Doesn't taking on new values that you then fail to fulfill bring ill-being? It certainly could, and spreading yourself too thin isn't a recipe for a life rich in value fulfillment. (Returning to the metaphor of the web, a web made of many, many very weak strands isn't very reliable either.) But whether it does or not will depend on why she takes on these new values, and what ultimate values they are serving. Not every unsuccessful project or failed attempt at something counts as the kind of decrease in value fulfillment that constitutes ill-being. When new projects are adopted to serve ultimate values like enjoyment, friendship, and health, failing by the standards of these projects does not necessarily constitute a threat to overall value fulfillment. For example, if Denise tries out watercolor painting in order to alleviate boredom, to meet new people, or to improve her health, being a bad painter need not mean a reduction in value fulfillment. If she is truly a bad painter, she is unlikely to come to value painting for its own sake, and she may not stick with it very long, but it may still serve the ultimate values it was meant to serve.

What would be bad for Denise is if she stuck with painting, even though she's better at golf, ceased to get any enjoyment out of painting, began to think of it as valuable for its own sake, and to think of herself as a failed painter. What diminishes well-being (or increases ill-being) is failure of a certain kind: failures that frustrate our ultimate values, failures that we cannot interpret as contributing to other values (in the way that one might think about being a bad painter as doing something just for fun that has no point or purpose).

So, there are a number of reasons why the value fulfillment theory would not recommend dogged pursuit of a single value. As I pointed out about the grass-counter, this is not to say that no one who is single-mindedly in pursuit of one value could possibly achieve well-being. There might be people for whom this is the best kind of life, but such people are likely to be unusual. It's possible that a person who is a genius at a particular kind of work (perhaps a scientist who will make a revolutionary discovery), who has little need for reinforcement or social support, and who is fortunate enough to enjoy rather stable circumstances, could live a perfectly good life (rich in value fulfillment) without much else in their life besides work. But the existence of such exceptions doesn't give the rest of us a reason to become workaholics, if we're not like this genius scientist in relevant ways.

A value-fulfilled life, then, is not a life of dogged pursuit of a single goal (though it might be so for certain rare individuals). Value-fulfilled lives for most of us embrace some tension between values. Tension comes in degrees, however, and when tension veers into incompatibility, it is not conducive to well-being. On one end of the spectrum, we have the tension between values that is exemplified by the work/life balance problem. These values are in tension because we have limited time and energy, but it isn't impossible to include both in the same narrative about how your life will go well. To the contrary, there are often ways in which these values are mutually supporting, even while they compete for your time: you work more efficiently when you take time to relax with friends, your family may care about whether your career is going well, and so on. On the other end of the spectrum we have outright incompatibility. This occurs when we have values that cannot practically be pursued together (for example, being an astronaut and being a stay-at-home parent) or when one of the things we value weakens our commitment to something else we value (by casting doubt on our reasons for it or by undermining our emotional attachment to it). This kind of conflict does make it difficult to live a value-fulfilled life.

Sander from Chapter 1 provides an example of the second kind of case: the case in which the conflicting values cast doubt on each other. Sander's religious faith is in conflict with his sexual orientation and his prospects for a happy romantic life. This is not merely a competition for time, because the tenets of his religion say that his having a happy romantic life would be morally bad. According to the value fulfillment theory, this kind of conflict—where our values undermine each other—is bad for Sander. What to do? For those of us who don't have any religious commitments, it seems obvious that he would be better off giving up the faith. But those of us who don't share the faith also don't see what he would sacrifice: what he sees as his main access to a profound relationship with God and the foundation for a meaningful life. For those who share Sander's faith, it might seem obvious that he should give up the possibility of a fulfilling romantic relationship. Some gay evangelicals do take this option; they marry opposite sex partners and treat their homosexuality as a challenge to test their faith (Swartz 2011). But it's not obvious that this option makes for a life with more overall value fulfillment either.

The fact that incompatibility of values is bad for us does not necessarily mean that the only way forward is to eliminate one of the incompatible values. Another possibility (though it's not available to everyone, to be sure[6]) is to change the standards of success to reduce the conflict. For example, John Gustave-Wrathall, the real person who inspired my example of Sander, married his male partner, helped to create a community of LGBT Mormons, and contributes to the cause of reforming the Church. It seems to me that he has also, through the LGBT community and his own writing, found a way to interpret the Church's rejection of him that does not undermine his own sense of worth.[7] Instead of thinking that to honor the value of his faith he must accept everything that the Mormon Church says, he takes the Church to be in need of reform, which allows him to continue valuing his faith without sacrificing his marriage. For Gustave-Wrathall, the conflict between two ultimate values has created new valuable projects that help him to make sense of the conflict. These new values and the new relationships he forges with people in this community will contribute to the overall value fulfillment he achieves.

When we pay attention to the complex relationships among values, we will also see that sometimes there are values that a person doesn't have currently but would be better off having, or values they currently have that ought to occupy a more central place in their system of values. For example, most of us would do better if we valued our health and took some pains to secure it, since good physical health is conducive to the pursuit of many other values. Indeed, most of us do care about our health to some degree and take the facts about what is healthy to be reasons for us to change our behavior. This is not to say that health is an objective value in the sense that the explanation of its value transcends the person's perspective. Rather, health is a value that strengthens most people's system of values and allows them to fulfill the values that they have. For a different example of someone who should have different values, we can return to Jules (the insufficiently talented aspiring actor from Chapter 1). Jules would be better off valuing a different career path. Ultimately, she does recognize that her talents in psychology and her ability to help people with their problems could lead her to a more successful career as a therapist. At the time when she is still going to auditions, given her other values, we can say about her that she would be better off valuing something other than being an actress.

When we pay attention to the way in which values form patterns of mutual reinforcement (or mutual frustration) we can see how the overarching goal of a value-fulfilled life allows us to evaluate ends, not just means to ends.[8] We can also see that the standards of success that we have for our values provide another opportunity for improvements that will lead to greater value fulfillment.

3.3 Values and Virtues

Traditionally, many philosophers have thought that there is a close connection between well-being and virtue. The idea is that virtues—these days often conceived as characteristics that are other-regarding or socially beneficial—are good for the virtuous person himself or herself. Aristotle, for example, argued that virtuous activity is the essence of a good human life; acting with justice, courage, temperance, and wisdom, according to Aristotle is not a *means* to achieving happiness, rather it is just what it is to live a flourishing human life (Aristotle 1999). Positive psychology, influenced by Aristotle, also celebrates the relationship between flourishing and virtue. There are a number of studies that aim to show an instrumental link between virtuous actions and subjective well-being, and positive psychologists have written about the virtues themselves (Peterson and Seligman 2004; Tiberius 2013b). One might wonder how the value fulfillment theory accommodates virtue and the idea that virtue is essential to well-being.

The short answer is that the value fulfillment theory can easily explain why virtue is good for people who value it, or for people whose other values (like friendship or parenthood) require virtues in some way. Because it anchors well-being to the individual person's perspective, however, it cannot accommodate the Aristotelian idea that the traditional virtues are constitutive of, or absolutely necessary for, well-being. As discussed in Section 2.5, there could be a person with appropriate values (recall: values that integrate emotion, desire, and judgment, and form a system that can be successfully pursued over time) who is not served by the traditional virtues. Such a person may still have *moral* reasons to cultivate virtues, but they would not have prudential (well-being-based) reasons to do so. Now it is possible that certain virtues are good for everyone, according to the value fulfillment theory, simply because of the nature of value fulfillment. Persistence and temperance, for example, seem to be required for the fulfillment of any values over time; a certain kind of courage may also be needed.[9] But the value fulfillment theory can't say that the other-regarding virtues (justice, compassion, and kindness, for example) are absolutely necessary for every person's well-being, no matter what the person is like. It is really these other-regarding virtues that make people worry about subjective theories of well-being like mine, so I will focus on these in the remainder of this section.

Before we can explore a longer answer to the question, I'll need to say something about what I mean by "virtue". First, in my own thinking about virtue, I am influenced by Hume who understood the conception very broadly. Virtues, according to Hume, are those qualities that are useful or agreeable to the self or others (1739, pp. 587–91). So, fairness and kindness are virtues, and so are perseverance and a sense of humor. To put it simply, virtues are the traits that are conducive to a person's own well-being or the well-being of others. Second, I'm mindful of the recent controversy about the existence of character traits that reliably produce behavior in a variety of contexts (Adams 1999; Doris 2002; Harman 1999; Kamtekar 2004; Merritt 2000; Miller 2003). I've been persuaded by personality psychologists that there is enough stability in our character traits that it makes sense to talk about virtues (Fleeson 2001; Jayawickreme et al. 2014), though I agree with the critics that virtues that entirely overcome the influence of the situational circumstances all the time are extremely unlikely. I do think we can make ourselves behave better in more situations, by adopting strategies and policies for coping with predictable situational factors, and that some people more frequently behave well in more circumstances than others. People can reasonably hope to make themselves more virtuous in some respects, even if there's no hope for the kind of virtue that would have satisfied Aristotle. (I don't intend this paragraph to settle the debate between virtue skeptics and their opponents; committed virtue skeptics are not my audience here, because if you are a virtue skeptic, you won't care about whether a theory of well-being has the right relationship to virtue anyway.)

Now, what do the social or other-regarding virtues have to do with our values and personal projects? First of all, many people value virtues such as honesty, kindness, compassion, and fairness. Such people want to be honest, kind, and so on, feel guilty when they fail, pleased when they succeed, and take these ways of being in the world to be important standards for how they are doing in life. That makes for a rather short answer to the question, but it's not unimportant.

There is more to be said here that doesn't rely on quite such a direct relationship between virtues and values. Some of the standards of achievement for typical personal projects give us non-instrumental reasons to develop virtues. In the case of friendship, we can see this by attending to the fact that an intimate or deep friendship is a relationship of mutual caring: friends care about each other for each other's sake. Caring about someone for their own sake might itself be considered a virtue, or we might think that other, more specific virtues comprise caring, such as empathy, kindness, generosity, and helpfulness. The important point is that the reason that a person who values friendship has to be empathetic, kind, generous, or helpful, at least with their friends, is that what matters to them is a relationship with others that is characterized, in part, by the possession of these virtues. In other words, caring, helpfulness, and the like are partly constitutive of the value of friendship. So, the point is not that caring is a means to friendship (though it may be that too); rather, the point is that to have the kind of friendships that make your life good is to be a caring person. Being a certain kind of person is part of what is valuable about friendship to most of us. If caring were merely a means to friendship, we could do just as well by faking it, or by finding a work-around, such as paying for friends. This may sound rather self-focused: be caring so that you'll fulfill the value of friendship and live a good life! But this way of thinking of it misses what it is to be caring. You just aren't caring unless you are actually concerned for someone else for his or her own sake. So, while I am arguing that being a caring friend benefits you (if you value friendship), I am also saying that if you are caring you will not think only of your own benefit. You just aren't a caring friend unless you attend to something beyond your own benefit, namely the benefit of your friend. We can have self-interested reasons to develop genuinely other-regarding virtues.

These observations about what many people value about friendship do not compete with the fact that there are also plenty of self-interested desires we have with respect to our friends and friendship, and that many purely instrumental reasons arise from friendship. I may help a friend pack up her apartment partly because I want her to help me move my piano the following weekend. I may remember birthdays in part so that others remember mine. But this isn't all there is to valuing friendship, particularly for those of us who see the quality of our friendships as a measure of how well our lives are going. Consider what people think about toward the end of life, reflecting on how they lived. One hears that people take comfort from thinking "I was a good friend" (or a good father, daughter, husband, aunt). It's now almost a cliché to point out that people nearer to death do not reflect on how much money or how many possessions they accumulated during their life, but that instead they regret not spending more time with their loved ones.[10] Often, what's regretted is not being there for the people you loved, that is, not being a good enough friend (or parent, or spouse). Of course, the relationship between the reflective end-of-life perspective and how well your life goes while you're living it is not simple, which is why it's important to note that these other-regarding aspects of our values, which tend to come to the fore when we're engaged in reflection, are not the only thing that's relevant to well-being (the pleasure of friendship is important too).

You might think that if caring for friends for their own sakes is an inherent standard of friendship, and if I happen to be a rather selfish person who isn't terribly good at caring about others, there are two options for me: I could become better at caring, but I could, alternatively, adopt a different standard for successful friendship. Perhaps "selfish me" could assess my friendships entirely on the basis of how much fun they are. My deliberations and plans will be directed at grabbing opportunities for doing fun things with my friends and avoiding un-fun things, such as helping them pack up their apartments or letting them talk about their marital problems. When I think about how my life is going I can think about the fun to un-fun ratio and feel good about my life so long as that ratio favors fun. In other words, one might object that the connection between virtue and well-being according to the value fulfillment theory is far too contingent: if our values require us to cultivate qualities we don't like, then we can simply change our values.[11]

This is not as easy as it sounds, however, because success in this endeavor depends on other people, most of whom probably do think that caring about the interests of a friend is a key part of friendship. Moreover, even aside from the expectations of our friends, if we have been brought up in a culture that identifies friendships (not to mention romantic partnerships or parental relationships) as caring relationships, then we cannot simply change the value of friendship to "fun-only". There are strong cultural reinforcements of these standards for friendship and overcoming them to replace them with something else may be nearly impossible. People who do not demonstrate genuine concern for their friends, but who treat them as mere sources of fun, are often labeled "users", "jerks", or "assholes", and although a jerk doesn't always get their due, allowing yourself to be a jerk in order to avoid the other-regarding standards of friendship is probably not a winning strategy.[12]

Of course, it has to be admitted that there are jerks and that, therefore, there are people who find it perfectly possible to reject the other-regarding standards of friendship. Indeed, there are some people who will never be moved by the standards of friendship promoted by their community. Again, it is *possible* for a jerk to achieve well-being according to the value fulfillment theory. If well-being is defined, ultimately, in reference to the values of individual subjects, and if there are individual differences with respect to the value of friendship (and jerkiness), then we have to admit that there are no claims we can make about good lives for individuals that are truly universal. That said, we need to ask what the existence of jerks means for the rest of us. First of all, jerks are not always satisfied with how their lives are going. It is one thing to reject the norms or your culture and another to resist all influence of those standards in how you assess your own life. (The person who is entirely unmoved by the relationship norms of the people around him may be more of a psychopath than a jerk.) Second, to become a satisfied jerk if you're not one already requires exceptional powers of resistance to the influence of others, or a massive amount of self-deception. It is a costly option, because of our sympathetic nature and the pervasive influence of other people on our self-conceptions. This influence is recognized now by social scientists as "social contagion" on obesity, divorce, and smoking, for example (Christakis and Fowler 2009). It was also recognized by Hume (1739) in the eighteenth century:

> A man will be mortified, if you tell him he has a stinking breath; though it is evidently no annoyance to himself. Our fancy easily changes its situation; and either surveying ourselves as we appear to others, or considering others as they feel themselves, we enter, by that means, into sentiments, which no way belong to us, and in which nothing but sympathy is able to interest us. And this sympathy we sometimes carry so far, as even to be displeased with a quality commodious to us, merely because it displeases others, and makes us disagreeable in their eyes; though perhaps we never can have any interest in rendering ourselves agreeable to them. (*Treatise* III.III.i)

For most of us, social creatures who feel a profound need to be understood by others (particularly our friends), the standards we use to assess how well we are doing with respect to our values are not entirely discretionary.

Friendship is one obvious example of the kind of value that has the features I just mentioned: non-discretionary standards of success that give us non-instrumental reasons to develop virtues. Family roles, which share features with friendships, provide an even more obvious example: a person who values being a parent, or a son or daughter, does not get to make up what counts as being a good one. Further, many of the requirements of being a good parent involve virtues such as compassion, understanding, patience, and consistency. But there are other kinds of examples that fit this description to some degree. Role-defined personal projects such as being a good doctor, nurse, teacher, or scientist seem to have virtues that are associated so strongly with success that they give rise to non-instrumental reasons to develop these virtues. While you can be a scientist without being open-minded, objective, and diligent, you can't really be a good scientist without these intellectual virtues. To be a good nurse is, in part, to care about the health of your patients and to be honest with them about their care. For nurses who value nursing as part of what makes their lives go well—those who think of nursing as a calling, perhaps—there is no further end toward which cultivating these virtues is a means; rather, being a compassionate, honest, and skilled nurse *is* the goal.

Other personal projects that fit the relevant profile are community-based. These are projects that depend on one's identity as a member of a group. The best example is probably religious communities and the project of being a good Christian/Muslim/Jew (etc.). Cultivating faith, hope, and charity are not rightly thought of as tools for getting the good result of being a good Christian; rather, these virtues define what it is to be a good Christian. Moreover, it's obvious in the case of religious communities and their associated values that the standards are not entirely up to us to decide. We can (sometimes) decide which religious community to belong to, but the choice is among different packages of pre-existing norms and standards. A person who changes churches does not typically make up their own religion (and people who do are usually thought of as cult leaders). Religious communities are not the only ones that provide an identity for members that is partly constituted by virtues. Many clubs and groups organized around common interests have unwritten (or sometimes written) codes that define good membership and often these codes invoke virtues such as honesty, duty, fairness, and courage. This is not to say that community-based standards cannot be changed. Again, consider Sander who belongs to an advocacy group that aims to change the norms of the Church of the Latter Day Saints. Notice, though, that Sander cannot change these norms by dint of his own will; rather, change (if it comes) will likely take the form of a process by which members of the Church consider the importance of the qualities they see as virtues and question whether there are some Church norms (such as intolerance of homosexuality) that are incompatible with these virtues. While a community is undergoing this kind of change, it may be difficult to say how well or how poorly a person is doing at living up to the community's values. This may be the case with Sander, and it is what we would expect when the standards for fulfilling our values are not entirely up to us.

The connection between our values and virtues is an important one, given the context of how to help others. One of the challenges we face is that we want to help people live lives that they see as better, but we also cannot help the fact that we don't want to help them become impossible for the rest of us to live with. Ideally, we'd like to help people in ways that also make them more pleasant, kinder, and so on. If, as I've argued, many of our most important values require other-regarding virtues to achieve, this isn't an unrealistic goal. But acknowledging this general interest in social harmony and the role of culture in upholding interpersonal standards for value fulfillment reveals a deep problem for the value fulfillment theory, which we'll consider in the next section.

3.4 Adaptive Values

Our interest in social harmony can impede our ability to see when our community norms need changing. Social harmony is often served by social conformity, and conformity isn't good for people who are different from the herd. If we really care about other people, we should want them to live better lives and to develop the virtues that are necessary for doing so, but we should also be on guard that we don't promote "virtues" or values that are convenient for us and harmful to them. I think this is still a realistic goal if we are willing to cultivate some humility about our own understanding of what's good for others, as we'll see in Chapter 4. So, this isn't the deep problem.

The deep problem stems from the fact that social norms don't just begin to operate on fully formed adults who were allowed to develop their values in whatever way best suited them. Social norms influence the development of our values from the word go. Further, social norms are not always benign; indeed they can be downright nefarious. Hence the problem of "adaptive preferences", or, I might say, the problem of adaptive values. L. W. Sumner (1996), one of the most influential defenders of subjectivism about well-being, acknowledges that the problem of adaptation to oppression is the most serious problem for any subjective theory of well-being. Briefly, the problem is this: it appears that people's subjective states—their desires, satisfactions, or values—sometimes adapt to oppressive circumstances so that they want, like, or value states of affairs that serve the interests of others, but are bad for them.¹³ For example, women living in an oppressive patriarchal society may be raised to value being devoted wives who have no options outside of the home; they may reject their own rights to vote, to get an education, or to drive a car, as incompatible with their values. Plausibly, these women's values are not good *for them*. But how can a subjective theory of well-being make sense of this? If there are no standards for well-being that transcend the individual's psychology, what grounds do we have for saying that oppression is bad for the people who adapt to it? In other words, it seems that according to subjective theories, being a slave doesn't detract from your well-being if you want to continue being a slave. This is a problem. What can the value fulfillment theory say about this?

The first thing to say is that the value fulfillment theory does have the resources to say that there are values that are bad for people. So, it has the resources to say that adaptive values can be bad for the person who has them. This will be true of values that prevent greater value fulfillment over time either because they conflict with more appropriate values, or because they threaten values that are prerequisites for value fulfillment in the long term. For example, values that tend toward ill health, unhappiness, or loss of security, conflict with other pervasive and stable values. Some cases of adaptation to oppression are like this. For example, imagine a person who rejects educational opportunities because she values a traditional role for women, and who is therefore unable to find a job that will allow her to feed her children. Assuming her children are very important to her, in such a case, the value fulfillment theory can say that valuing her traditional role is not best for her in the long run. Of course, not all adaptive values are like this; there are people for whom their oppression is so internalized (and their circumstances so accommodating) that it isn't true that they would have greater value fulfillment with different values. In such cases, it will become less obvious that the person's values are bad for her, which means that the pressure on the value fulfillment theory of well-being to accommodate that idea is reduced. Nevertheless, it will be helpful to look at other ways of tackling the problem.

The second response we can make to the problem of adaptive values relies on ideas about justice. Policies that shape people's values and preferences ought to be constructed to allow all citizens of a state to thrive. This means that as a matter of justice, policy should not perpetuate oppression if some proportion of the oppressed reject their role and the values that go along with it. History has surely shown that there are always victims of oppression who do not like it, who do not value the subordinate role they have been given, and who buck against the constraints that are imposed on what they may choose to do. Just institutions, laws, and policies must take such people into account. Further, just institutions that are concerned to promote the well-being of citizens must also take into account those for whom adaptive values prevent greater value fulfillment over the long term (because they conflict with other values or their prerequisites, as discussed above). What this means is that even if it is true that *some* oppressed people do not suffer a loss of well-being due to their adaptive values, we still have well-being-based reasons to combat oppression.

Finally, it is worth noting there may also be moral reasons to combat oppression that do not derive from well-being: principled reasons for equal treatment or respect for persons, for instance. Appeal to these moral values does not allow us to say that oppression is bad *for* the oppressed person (bad for their well-being), but it would allow us to explain why oppression is to be resisted even if well-being is ultimately subjective.

3.5 Conclusion

Overall value fulfillment is a complex function of individual values, the standards they impose, their strengths, and the various ways in which they are related to each other over time. I began the book with the observation that helpful friends want to help in a way that will seem helpful, but that doesn't pander to seriously misguided ideas. To do this, I said, we should focus on a person's values, since values are both tied to a person's own sense of what a good life is for them and open to criticism and improvement. We now have a more complete picture of this critical perspective. We can add to what I said at the beginning of the chapter, putting it this way: appropriate values are (1) suited to our desires and emotions, (2) reflectively endorsed, and (3) interpreted with standards of success that enable them to be fulfilled together over time.

The application of these three criteria will require sensitive interpretation and the balancing of competing interests. For example, in many cases very general values (like the value of friendship) are stable across time, but to remain viable these values need to be realized in different ways as a person's circumstances change. This will not be a simple process, but it will make us attentive to the right kinds of considerations. In the remainder of the book, we'll talk more about how to apply and balance these norms in order to help our friends.

4

Assessing Well-Being
Value Fulfillment Theory in Practice

When we think of well-being as value fulfillment, we see that being helpful to another person requires paying attention to their values with a critical eye to how overall fulfillment can be improved. Of course, this quick statement hides a whole lot of complexity. In this chapter and the next, we'll dive into this complexity to try to characterize how to be a helpful friend (and maybe even a good person).

Summarizing where we are so far, and putting together the discussion of appropriate values (from Chapter 2) with the discussion of the fulfillment of values (from Chapter 3), we see that we can assess how a life is going and consider how we might help by asking these questions:

1. What does the person value, how are these values understood, and how are they prioritized?
2. Given a person's values, their relative strengths, and standards for success, how well is the person doing at fulfilling them, or succeeding in terms of them? Is the person taking effective means to their ultimate values and, if not, are there other available means to these values?
3. To what extent are these values appropriate (do they integrate desires, emotions, and judgment?) Are there some values the person would be better off without?
4. To what extent are the standards of success associated with the person's values conducive to living a value-fulfilled life? Could some values be reinterpreted with different standards of success?

5. Are there values that the person should have but doesn't? (Values they could adopt that would make their life richer in value fulfillment?)

Taken together, these questions tell us about the degree to which a person's values and her ways of fulfilling them are likely to produce a life rich in value fulfillment, and about the ways in which this could be improved.

These questions are difficult ones, and our strategies for answering them (as well as our prospects) may vary depending on our relationship to the person we are trying to help. To answer these questions about large groups of people we don't know, the best we can do is to make informed judgments based on information about people in general. We would need to know what typical human values are, how people tend to define success in terms of them, what particular plans or projects conduce to this success on average, what psychologically tenable options there are for changing these values or their associated standards (either rejecting them completely or redefining them), and what kinds of commitments tend to foster value fulfillment over time.

We will return to the question of helping people we don't know later, but now, as I explained in the introduction to this book, our main focus will be on helping friends (defined broadly to include close family relations and romantic partners). This is for two reasons. First, helping strangers who are in dire need raises different questions (about the scope of moral obligation and the effectiveness of various forms of aid) that have been addressed very well by others (see the beginning of Chapter 1 for some references). Second, friendship is a central value for almost everyone and caring about our friends' well-being is central to friendship. The focus on friendship, therefore, allows us to investigate a less studied aspect of the question of how to be helpful to others, while at the same time exploring how we can make our own lives more successful by the standards of our own values. To live well, according to the value fulfillment theory, we should uphold the values that suit us and contribute to a system of values we can achieve over time; since friendship is a value most of us have, and since succeeding in terms of friendship means, in part, being helpful to our friends, learning how to help our friends will help us live better lives too.

4.1 Friendship and Helping

Philosophical accounts of friendship tend to highlight three features of this relationship: caring, intimacy, and shared experiences (Helm 2013). Caring is the feature most central to the discussion of promoting well-being. We care about our friends in the sense that we care about their well-being for their sake, not just because we'll be happier if they are doing well. There is controversy among philosophers about what kind of intimacy is characteristic of friendship. Some argue that this intimacy consists in telling each other things that they don't tell others (Thomas 1987), and others argue that intimacy is much more demanding, requiring that friends actually share values (Cocking and Kennett 1998).

For our purposes, there's no need to take sides on such philosophical controversies about friendship. I suspect there are many individual and cultural differences about what counts as friendship, and besides, I mean to *include* other kinds of relationships (romantic and familial) that philosophers analyzing friendship usually want to distinguish. Nevertheless, it's worth addressing the question of shared values among friends. If friendship ruled out differences in values, the application of the value fulfillment theory to the problem of helping friends would be considerably simpler. The project of figuring out how to help a friend would be just like the project of figuring out what to do for yourself—not an easy project, to be sure, but not complicated by disagreement about the goal. It may be that the best, most enduring friendships include significant agreement about what matters in life, especially at the level of abstract, core values, but (as we'll see in this chapter) this is not enough to ensure that we always agree with our friends about how our lives could go better. Disagreements about how to understand our core values, how to think about their fulfillment, and how to prioritize them—disagreements that often only surface in conversation—create conflict that must be managed.

So, I will be talking about relationships in which we care about our friend's well-being for their own sake and we share some core values but may also have disagreements, especially over the standards for value fulfillment. Are there other features of friendship that are important to acknowledge in the background? As I said, I think it's better to avoid taking sides on matters of controversy so that more people can recognize the kind of friendship featured here, but there is one other feature of friendships that seems important in this context, which is that most friends have a concern for the health of the relationship itself; friends tend to care about *continuing* to be friends. A person who values a friendship with another person is likely to want to avoid doing things that will jeopardize the friendship. A concern for the endurance of a friendship may be other-regarding: you see that your friendship is good for your friend and want it to continue for their sake. Concern for the friendship itself can motivate us to take care not to be condescending or judgmental. But when the concern is entirely self-regarding it may actually conflict with concern for the friend's well-being. When purely self-interested, this concern for the friendship (rather than the friend) can motivate unhelpful behavior. For example, you may be inclined to talk a friend out of moving across the country (away from you) for a job despite the fact that the job would be really good for them. This concern isn't always a good thing, then, but I do think it is part of many friendships and it is worth acknowledging because of its potential influence on helping.

In addition to a concern for our friend's well-being and a concern for the friendship itself, respect for a friend's autonomy is an important component of friendship for most of us. There does seem to be a general presumption (probably stronger in Western cultures) that each of us is the author of our own life; we should each make our own choices and decide on our own values, even if someone else could do a better job. In other words, most of us value our own autonomy, and consider mutual respect for autonomy to be necessary for a good friendship.[1] The concern about autonomy might have different sources. It may ultimately reduce to a concern about well-being if, for example, you think that people do better when they make their own choices and learn from their mistakes. It may reduce to the concern for the endurance of the friendship, say, if you think that friends are annoyed by too much interference or that the toll it would take on you to run someone else's life would be too much. Or, finally, you may think of the concern for autonomy as a moral constraint on friendship.[2] Given the different kinds of reasons for thinking that respect for friends' autonomy is important, I suspect it is a common norm. (Though there will be variation, especially when we're talking about romantic or family relationships.) As we go in this chapter, we'll explore some of these reasons with examples.

If we are concerned not to interfere with our friend's choices, and we care about the continuation of the relationship, the easiest cases for helping are ones in which our friend knows what they value, and we both agree that these values are fairly appropriate. In such cases, we can help by aiding or supporting our friend in the fulfillment of their appropriate values in ways that are compatible with those values and with respecting the friend as the author of their own life. One thing we can do is to *remind* our friends of their values. A considerable obstacle to living a value-fulfilled life is a lack of agreement between what is important to us and what we actually do. This kind of conflict was the subject of my book *The Reflective Life* in which I talked about this problem from the first person point of view. I value my friends and family and don't care much about responding to emails, but I spend so much time responding to email that I don't have time for my loved ones (to take a purely hypothetical example). Examples like this abound in life. People focus on the most pressing deadline or the loudest demand, even if these are not aligned with their values. We can be helpful to our friends by reminding them what they care about when they seem to be ignoring it for the sake of something comparatively trivial. We can help them gain perspective.

Another way to help in these relatively easy cases is by providing material support for the pursuit of values. It is often not very difficult to figure out the kind of thing that would be helpful. In general, friends with new babies are helped by bringing food or offering to do errands. A friend with a broken leg will be helped by shoveling the snow from their sidewalk. Of course, it's not always easy to know exactly what to do. Say you have a friend who is moving to a new state to take a new job. You both think this is the right move, and you want to help. Do you pack dishes? Offer to babysit so that your friend can pack them? Offer to put the old, ugly dishes on eBay? Arrange a going-away party? Buy a present? In practice, questions about exactly how to help when there is broad agreement about values can be important to think about, but they aren't *philosophically* very interesting questions. There isn't going to be a general answer to "food or errands?". The answers to these questions are going to be highly context dependent and the best initial strategy is probably to ask your friend how you can help.

For the purposes of this book, I'm going to focus on trickier cases: cases in which our friends seem to have values that are unlikely to lead to a value-fulfilled life, or they have standards of fulfillment or plans for how to fulfill their values that are not conducive to a value-fulfilled life. What is theoretically interesting about these trickier cases is that they shed light on the main problem for subjective theories like the value fulfillment theory. As I discussed in Section 1.4, theories that start with the person's point of view as defined by their aims need to find a way to explain how a person's current aims can be defective, that is, not conducive to well-being. Now that we have reviewed a number of examples of how people's lives can be off track it may be easier to see why this is a problem. It turns out that it's quite common to find people whose values, standards of fulfillment, or priorities are not leading them to anything that resembles much of a good life. This puts a large burden of proof on theories that tie well-being to the person's own point of view: such theories (including mine) need to explain how a person's own point of view can be open to criticism even though it is ultimately the anchor for well-being. The value fulfillment theory does this by giving center stage to the fulfillment of *appropriate* values *over time*, which provides a standard we can use to evaluate a person's current values. (This standard—a life rich in value fulfillment—is the basis for the five questions that opened this chapter.) The focus on friends whose value systems are off track allows us to see how this evaluation works in practice.

Our focus, then, will be mainly on cases in which friends are facing obstacles to their well-being. I will talk about the challenges we face when we want to help our friends, and in this chapter and the next chapter I make some recommendations about how to be a helpful friend in such cases. As I have discussed my work with other philosophers, I have had mixed reactions to this focus. Some people have said that they just don't have friendships in which they need to think about how to help each other improve their lives. Others have said that the kinds of struggles I talk about—to understand what one values, to figure out how best to achieve it without sacrificing too much of something else of value, to cope with conflicts among values—are rare and not a normal topic of conversation among friends. Interestingly, these comments have only come from men, and there is empirical evidence that men have fewer close, supportive friends in whom they can confide (Carbery and Buhrmester 1998).[3] My experience is that all of my female friends (and many of my male friends) struggle in these ways (though fortunately not all the time and not all at once), and talk to each other with the aim of helping. Just in the last five years, I have had friends who are dealing with difficulties conceiving a child, disagreements with spouses about parenting, disputes with siblings about how to care for aging parents, extra-marital affairs, unemployment, career changes, life-altering illness, and the death of loved ones. These events have a profound impact on people's well-being, and they invite consideration of what is important to us and how to make things better.

Now, if it's true that the experiences I have had are rare for men, it may be that the remainder of the book will be primarily of interest to women. I suppose I could live with that. But there is also solid evidence that close or caring friendships have benefits for people in terms of health, subjective well-being (feeling satisfied with your life, which is important to many of us) and reduced psychological distress (Requena 2011; Umberson et al. 1996; van der Horst and Coffé

2012[4]). Perhaps, then, people who do not recognize the kinds of relationships I'm talking about would do well to try to cultivate some of them for their own well-being. (I'll say more about the reasons to value caring friendships in Chapter 5.) Finally, I think we can learn something about how the value fulfillment theory answers the practical question of how to increase well-being from these examples. This is true even for people who don't currently have a pressing need for guidance in this domain.

4.2 Friends are not Other Selves

It is difficult to figure out what is good for oneself. After all, we don't know the future, whether it's our friend's future or our own. We are all too frequently mistaken about what kind of change we're capable of, deceived about what's important to us, and generally lacking in self-knowledge. But in your own case, you are always constrained by the perspective that you have, the values you endorse, the standards that you have taken on. If we can think of the self as metaphorically divided into the beneficiary and the adviser, the adviser never has a truly independent perspective: the values, standards, and personality of the adviser are the same as the beneficiary's even when the adviser recommends trying new things.

This is not how we are with respect to our friends. Even if there is significant overlap between us and our friends, we have our own perspectives—our own specific values, standards, goals, personalities, and tendencies—that we bring to the table when we aim to help someone. This means there is a gap between us and them and this gap is the source of all sorts of ways that helping can go wrong. Not understanding another person's perspective—what that person values, how they understand their own goals and what would count as achieving them, what they believe about their prospects for success—means that we may "help" in ways that are unhelpful because they do not take into account what the person cares most about and what changes the person is actually able (or unable) to make. Such help can offend, alienate, or decrease trust; it can also be just plain unhelpful or even downright harmful. Sometimes "help" ruins friendships because the fact that one person sees a certain course of action as helpful reveals a profound lack of understanding. To take a rather obvious case, consider a friend of Sander (the out, gay Mormon from the first chapter) who wants to help his lonely pal by introducing him to some lovely single Mormon women. Since Sander has made clear that he values both his gay identity and his relationship to the Church, this "help" conveys either a serious lack of attention, or serious prejudice, and Sander is likely to be appropriately insulted or hurt. Some people try to help by accepting a friend's point of view unquestioningly, with no critical perspective on the status quo and no imagination about what else could be. Sometimes help like this amounts to enabling, in which we "help" by encouraging and facilitating behaviors that are not sustainable in the long term or not compatible with other values our friend has.

The fact that we have different perspectives from our friends creates both risk and opportunity: on the one hand, we may fail to understand what things are like for our friends, but on the other hand we may be able to see how things could be better for them in ways that they cannot. Think of helping to improve someone's well-being as analogous to helping them to navigate to a specific destination, say, home. Your friend Goldie is lost in the woods and you have a GPS and a map, but you can only communicate by cell phone, because you're not in the same place. (For some reason, Goldie doesn't have GPS or a map; you'll have to imagine that your friend is a Luddite with a flip phone and no data.) In order to help Goldie get where she wants to go, you'll need to know a lot more about where she is and which way she's pointed. You can easily go wrong, since you're not in her position, but you have information that she needs. Of course, it's also difficult to get *yourself* out of the woods when you're lost; indeed, it might be impossible. My point is not that there are no challenges to improving your own life; rather, the point is that the challenges to helping others are different.

The situation is made worse by the fact that we rarely know with great certainty where "home" is for our friends. The kinds of complex human problems that call for support from friends are rarely ones that have simple answers. We can make the navigation metaphor more apt if we elaborate the story so that we're unsure of exactly where Goldie is trying to get (we only know the general direction), but we can see some important landmarks (cliffs, quicksand, which way the sun is setting) some of which she can't see from where she is. In other words, to unpack the metaphor, though we can see some obvious ways of going wrong (drug addiction, life of crime, clinical depression), we don't have a detailed picture of what the life richest in value fulfillment would be for our friend. Indeed, in some cases we may flat out disagree with our friends about their destination. For example, among women of a certain age (that is, still able to change their minds) who choose not to have children it is not uncommon to be told that a life without children could not possibly be a good life. This represents a deep disagreement about the destination, which is essentially a disagreement about what a value-fulfilled life is.

Perhaps this seems melodramatic and you are thinking that we have a lot more in common with people than all that. It is true that we have much in common with each other, particularly our friends, but I think we often underestimate the importance of the differences that there are. We have already seen a number of examples of these differences, and there are more. As someone who is highly risk averse, I do not understand people who take on serious risks to life and limb for their jobs or avocations. When presented with a friend who has had a serious rock climbing accident, my immediate inclination would be to help by talking them out of any more silly climbing plans. But, as you know if you know people with a passion for these sorts of activities, this is usually a way to get the rock climber to stop talking to you about their interests, not a way to help. People who have a deep and profound desire to have children have trouble understanding those who don't want children, and many of us in the latter category have been frustrated (and even offended) by our friends' attempts to talk us into being the first kind of person.

Similarly, people like Maxine (from the first chapter of this book) who are willing to spend tens of thousands of dollars to have biologically related children are sometimes hurt by friends who suggest adoption as if that were an easy solution.

There are at least four kinds of differences between us and our friends when it comes to values. First, there are differences in our ultimate values (what we value for its own sake). A friendship between an atheist and a devoutly religious person is one example: the value of faith to the religious person is a value that the atheist just doesn't have and may find it difficult to understand. In my experience talking with people about gay Mormons and gay evangelical Christians, I have found that my liberal audiences react with something like disgust to the idea that a person like John Gustave-Wrathall could be better off staying with the Mormon Church than leaving it. I must confess that when I first read Mimi Swartz's (2011) article on gay evangelicals and their therapists I was aghast that any mental health professional would sanction the suppression of sexual identity for the sake of religious faith. Having been raised an atheist, it's very difficult for me to understand how one's faith could be such an important part of one's identity. But for many people of faith, their religious commitments are crucial to how they see themselves and to what they value. Consider the words of one Christian author and priest, Henri J. M. Nouwen (1994): "To the degree that we embrace the truth that our identity is not rooted in our success, power, or popularity, but in God's infinite love, to that degree can we let go of our need to judge" (p. 71). And then, "We have to keep asking ourselves: 'What does it all mean? What is God trying to tell us? How are we called to live in the midst of all this?' Without such questions our lives become numb and flat" (p. 84). For Nouwen and those like him, faith in God sustains commitments to other people and a sense of the very meaning in life. My point is not that religious commitments can't be questioned, and I'm definitely not saying that it could never be better for a gay person of faith to switch to a Church that accepts him for what he is. Rather, my point is just that such struggles are evidence of a difference in ultimate values between non-religious and religious friends.

The value of being a parent might be another example of a difference in ultimate values. Parents experience a profound shift in perspective when their children are born; they suddenly value another person more than anything else in the world and think of their own good as fundamentally tied to the good of this other little human being. People who choose not to be parents do not value being a good parent for its own sake, and some non-parents can be quite dense about the commitments that their parent friends have taken on and why.

Of course, most non-parents do have other loving human relationships they can use to understand a person who values being a parent.[5] This raises the question of whether there is really a difference in ultimate values here, or just a difference in the particular instantiation of a more abstract value that parents and non-parents have in common. Most people (parents or not) value close personal relationships and family in general, and some specific relationships (to children, partners, friends, and so on). Perhaps valuing being a parent is just an instance of the more abstract value of "family relationships" and valuing your child is just one specific instance of valuing a loved one. Indeed, it may be that all apparent disagreements about ultimate values can always be reduced to some other kind of difference. It seems to me that different people see this differently, and there is no payoff to insisting on one answer or the other.[6] It makes little practical difference whether someone thinks that valuing being a parent is ultimately an expression of a more abstract value, or not. After all, it's not as if the mother or father who values their relationship with their child as an ultimate end can be helped when that relationship is challenged by telling them that there are other relationships they could have that may go better.

The second way in which friends' values can differ is in terms of how they are prioritized. Even people who agree on the basics about what matters may differ over what is worth sacrificing for what. As a self-confessed risk averse person, when I read about the lives of war reporters, I cringe and wonder whether these people are abnormally brave or just insane. Take for example the photojournalist Lynsey

Addario who writes about being captured by soldiers in Libya with three of her colleagues. As they sit in the small cell she observes:

> There was nothing to do but sleep and talk, mostly about the pain we were causing our spouses... I had imposed unspeakable worry on my husband... on more occasions than I could count. And Anthony and Steve [two of her colleagues] each had infants at home. Yet as guilty as we felt, and as terrified as we were, only Steve sounded convinced by his own declaration that he would no longer cover war. Each one of us knew that this work was an intrinsic part of who we were: It was what we believed in; it governed our lives.
>
> (Addario 2015)

Addario had a baby the following year and continues her work in dangerous places. One of the colleagues with whom she was captured died in Syria, another (Steve) no longer covers war, and the third continues as a war photographer.

I do not think that I have different ultimate values from Addario and her colleagues, but I find it very difficult to understand their choices. I care about peace and justice, I think good reporting is vitally important, and I value my own work, which I find meaningful and sustaining. I imagine that these are the same values that drive Addario and her colleagues to do the kind of work they do. They may also have more of an interest in risk for the sake of the excitement of it, but I'm not entirely immune to the value of excitement either. Addario also clearly values her family and wants to be responsible to them; I'm sure she also values her own life and would prefer to live, work, and love her family for a long time. What's different, it seems to me, is the priority we give to these different values. There's a way in which it is true of Addario and of me that we would both like to live as long a life as possible. But what counts as possible is constrained by other things we value. If the only way for me to extend my life were to participate in genocide, I like to think that I would refuse: when I'm thinking clearly, I believe that the value of being a minimally morally decent person outweighs the value of a longer life for me. But if my job demanded even a moderate risk to my own life (and, I have to confess, even if my work were as important as the work done by Addario), I would quit and find something else to do. Not so for

Addario who thinks that the value of the work she does and the value to her of doing it outweighs some moderate risks to her life and her other values (including her family).[7] This way of putting it surely over-simplifies to some degree. I doubt that Addario would endorse this simple calculation as I've presented it. Leaving the details aside, however, my point is that there are important differences between people (and potentially between friends) that have to do with how values are prioritized.

The third way in which friends' values can differ is in terms of what counts as living up to or succeeding in terms of the value in question. In other words, people can have different standards of success for value fulfillment. Sometimes we have the same basic values as our friend under one level of description, but the value means something different to each of us once you try to spell out or interpret what its fulfillment would consist in and by what means it can be appropriately pursued. For a simple example, we can return to sports (discussed also in Section 3.2). Two long distance runners may both value athleticism, but one thinks that to be an athlete—to succeed in terms of this value—is to be competitive, to win races, to improve their time from race to race, while the other thinks that to be an athlete is to participate in a running club and finish a few races a year at whatever pace they can manage. These two athletes have different standards for their valued activity. In general, people can differ in terms of how high a standard they hold themselves to, and also in the kinds of standards they accept (inter-subjective or personal, subjective or objective, as discussed in Section 3.1).

My imaginary friend Audrey presents a more complicated example of differences about the standards for fulfillment.[8] Audrey is similar to Jules (the character from Meg Wolitzer's novel discussed in Chapter 1) in that as a young woman she wanted to be an artist (a painter in Audrey's case), and struggled to "make it", not because of a lack of talent but because it takes a lot of luck for even very talented artists to make a living in our society. For some years, Audrey's parents supported her painting career in the view that art should be better supported than it is and children should be encouraged to follow their passions. Eventually, Audrey didn't want to accept her parents' financial support and she put together a life in which she teaches some classes, helps paint sets at a local theater, and still has time to paint and show her work. She chooses not to look for a full-time teaching job or to move into management of the theater (something for which she also has some natural talent), because these paths would mean giving up the life of an artist. According to Audrey, some of her most supportive friends and family members have the view that she didn't "make it" as an artist, so she is now making ends meet by cobbling together jobs that are not her passion. But this is not how Audrey sees her life at all. For Audrey, the fact that she is able to paint, that she is free to take on new projects as she chooses, that people think of her when there is work to be done that uses her creative skills, that she is part of a community of people for whom making art is their work, means that she is living the life of an artist. It isn't the most financially secure life in the world, but her lifestyle is one she values tremendously.

The reason I think that the difference between Audrey and her friends has to do with her standards for value fulfillment is that Audrey's friends also value art and being artistic. These are people who support arts organizations and make time for creative hobbies in their own busy lives. But they do not interpret what it is to value art in the way that Audrey does: for them, "being self-scheduled and identifying as an artist in a community of artists" is not part of what it is to value art. For Audrey, what counts as valuing art and being artistic means something different from what it means to her friends, even though under some description they value the same thing. It might appear that this is really another example of a difference in ultimate values: Audrey values *being an artist* (a way of life), while her friends value *art* (a product or activity). There is probably some truth in this, and sometimes it's difficult to tell whether we have a case of different ultimate values or similar values with different standards (and it may be both). But I think there is a good reason to understand some cases as ones in which what's really different is what the standards are for what counts as fulfilling our values. The reason is that when we think about how to attain our values or how to help our friends attain theirs, values and goals are often unspecified so that it isn't clear what counts as valuing whatever it is, or what would count as succeeding by its standards. We start with the idea that "I want to be an artist" or "I love art", but these ideas do not come already broken down into goals, sub-goals, and standards of success. We don't know what they really mean even to ourselves until we start thinking, choosing, and reacting to our successes and failures. The importance of understanding that we can have differences in interpretation like these is that discovering what the things we value mean to us, discovering what counts as success for us or our friends, is an important task that we can do better together if we acknowledge that we are doing it together. In other words, acknowledging the interpretative project alerts us to the fact that the values we seem to have in common, and describe in the same way, do not always recommend the same course of action for everyone.

I suspect that differences in the interpretation or specification of widely shared very general values is actually the focus of many conversations between friends who are trying to understand each other. For one thing, it's natural to start with something shared and move from there. Two friends who both agree that being a good parent is ultimately valuable, might disagree about divorce, for example. One thinks "I want to be a good parent and divorce isn't compatible with that; it's too hard on the kids", and the other thinks "I want to be a good parent, but I'm not sure the best way to be a good parent is to stay married to a person I'm not in love with anymore". Further, people differ rather a lot in terms of their ability to articulate and define their values, and one of the services friends can provide is to help each other refine their cares and concerns so that they can be properly acknowledged and put into action. If I'm right about this, it's going to be very important for us to acknowledge that while we all value "family", or "health", or "security", our friend may interpret these values in ways that are different enough from our own that different courses of action are recommended for each of us.

The last kind of difference I'll discuss has to do with what means we take to our valued ends. Differences about the most efficient means to an end (if that's really what they are) are not differences in evaluative perspective; rather, they are typically differences in information. To take a simple example, my free-climbing friend and I might have more or less the same value system when it comes to life and risk, but different beliefs about the risks involved. If he thinks his risk of falling off a cliff and dying is much smaller than I think it is, he may think free climbing is an acceptable means to thrill and excitement while I do not, even though we would agree about the wisdom (or idiocy) of free climbing if we agreed about the facts. Disagreements about the facts of whether some action actually constitutes a good means to a given end can be difficult to navigate, too, but usually there is a brighter and easier path to resolving the disagreement than there is in cases where there are differences in the values (or their associated standards) themselves. This is not always the case, however, because sometimes what looks like a simple difference of opinion about the best means to a given end is really something else. Sometimes different choices about the best means to an end reveal that there are also different additional values, or that those values are prioritized differently. For example, Audrey the painter may willfully underestimate the degree to which financial insecurity will cause her anxiety, or her disapproving friend may exaggerate the degree to which the misery of feeling like a sell-out can be assuaged by a steady salary.

Navigating these gaps between how we see things and how our friends see things is a fundamental challenge to knowing how to be helpful. In the next section we'll consider two different contributors to this challenge: one that has to do with all the information we need and the other that has to do with our relationship to the person we are trying to help.

4.3 Informational and Interpersonal Challenges

The complexity of value fulfillment and the fact that well-being is identified with value fulfillment over time create challenges for our ability to assess well-being when we need some specific guidance about which steps will bring a person closer to a life rich in value fulfillment. Typically, when we set about trying to ascertain how we could benefit someone, we need to decide what's wrong with how things are going for them now and what would make them better off. To do this with an eye to well-being as defined by the value fulfillment theory seems to require knowledge of which values are the most appropriate for them and of all the ways in which these values could be interpreted and pursued to bring the greatest fulfillment. This is daunting.

One challenge to assessing well-being, then, is a kind of informational challenge: we just do not have enough information or processing power to know what lives are truly best for anyone (including ourselves), given the number of variables and the ways they change over time. Fortunately, there are many assumptions we can reasonably make and many strategies we can use to lighten the load. Many of the values people have are socially sanctioned, highly stable, and abstract enough that how they are fulfilled is open to interpretation. For example: health, pleasure, close family ties, friendship, comfort, security, and achievement. These values are quite likely to be a part of any of the best lives a person could live (though particular means to them will vary) and therefore they form an excellent basis for well-being assessments. We can also assume that values that are related to other values in fundamental ways—as necessary conditions for their pursuit (such as health), or as a justification for other values (such as psychological happiness)—will be stable and emotionally sustained over the long term. A useful strategy, then, in assessing well-being and making judgments about how to benefit people, is to pay attention to the basic values that are likely to be part of any value-fulfilled life.

Furthermore, we can improve our epistemic situation. Some of the information we lack can be acquired. Recall from earlier in this chapter the basic questions we can ask about how a person's life is going and how it could go better (here repeated in abbreviated form):

1. What are the person's values?
2. How well is the person doing at fulfilling them, or succeeding in terms of them?

3. To what extent are these values appropriate, and are there some values the person would be better off without?
4. To what extent are the standards of success associated with the person's values conducive to living a value-fulfilled life and could some standards be modified?
5. Are there other values that could be adopted that would bring the person's life closer to a value-fulfilled life?

Given these questions, at least three types of information are relevant. First of all, information about the person whose well-being is being assessed is obviously important. It would be good to know about the person's psychological dispositions and skills. Knowing something about their personality would be helpful; a person who is more flexible and open-minded is more likely to be able to change their ways, for example. Second, information about human psychology in general and how human beings can change is also helpful insofar as it would allow us to supplement the information we have about the individual to make informed predictions about how things are likely to go for them in the future. Finally, information about values, how they can be fulfilled, and how they help or hinder each other over time is important.

One of the crucial ways of gaining information about our friends and their values is by having a conversation with them. For the most part, it isn't that people have perfect information about their own values and so we find out about someone else by asking them directly. Rather, by talking with our friends we hear what they worry about, what themes they return to, what goals are on their mind, and we can make inferences about what they are like and what really matters to them. (I think it should be clear that I take "talking with" to include listening!) We can also learn about tensions and conflict among their values and in their dispositions with respect to their values. I'm sure many academics have had the experience of talking to undergraduate students whose judgments about what major they ought to be interested in conflict with their passions. In talking with such students, we can learn that accounting, or biology, isn't an appropriate value for them even if they don't see this themselves.

By talking with our friends we do find out more about them, but there are other important things we accomplish. We make them feel supported just by listening, and in doing so we contribute to the fulfillment of the value of friendship for both of us. To put it more colloquially, by talking with our friends we show them that they have friends they can count on, which they are likely to think is part of a good life. We also help them figure out the answer to questions about their values for themselves. This is crucially important, because most of the steps that could be taken toward better value fulfillment are steps that must be taken by the person whose life it is. For example, if your friend doesn't arrive at a clearer grasp of how their unrealistic standards of success are hindering their own value fulfillment, they aren't likely to do anything to change.

The first step in being a helpful friend, then, is often just to talk. For friends whose lives are already on a good path, this may be all that's required of the helpful friend. For friends who need to change something in order to get on a better path, talking is normally still the first step. The thing about talking that most people will have noticed is that we're not always on the same page as the people we are talking to. We have different background information, we make different assumptions, we interpret things in different ways, and—crucially for our topic, as discussed in the last section—we may have different values and different ideas about the nature of a value-fulfilled life. This means that we would always do well to exercise some humility about what we know when we talk to other people, and humility will be a central topic of Chapter 5. For now, I want to introduce a different kind of challenge, the interpersonal challenge, which also arises because of our differences, and which is also (as we will see) ameliorated by humility. The interpersonal challenge is the difficulty in navigating the differences between you and your friend without doing more harm than good.

Let's start with the most significant kind of difference in order to illustrate the most dramatic form of the interpersonal challenge. In some cases, talking with and observing our friend will lead us to believe that the friend's values are really dysfunctional. What do we do when we have good grounds for thinking that someone's life isn't going very well because they have very inappropriate values, values that are really at odds with a life rich in value fulfillment? What do we do when it seems clear to us that some of our friend's current values are not conducive to a value-fulfilled life? One possibility is that we're just incorrect. According to the value fulfillment theory, appropriate values (the ones that contribute to a value-fulfilled life) are ultimately anchored in the person whose life it is, and (as we just discussed) we can certainly be wrong about what people are really like. But let's put aside the epistemic challenge and imagine that we have the best possible evidence that our friend's values are at odds with their emotions, desires, or judgment, or that they are unlikely to be successfully pursued over time. Under these conditions, may we discount or ignore a person's inappropriate values for the sake of helping them?

In practice, there are often reasons *not* to discount inappropriate values. As anyone who has tried to tell a friend (or worse, a sibling) how to live their life knows, thinking you know better is a dangerous business in friendship. Why is that? One reason is epistemic (you might not know what you're talking about), but that's not the whole story. Even if you are correct about what's good for someone else, there are many reasons to respect each other's autonomous judgment. Intervening in someone's life on behalf of values that you think would be more appropriate for them introduces costs in value fulfillment terms: ruptures to the bonds of friendship, pain, and dissatisfaction. Most of us have had friends who pursue romantic relationships that are bad for them, but it is rarely a good idea to take drastic measures to prevent our friends from making dating mistakes. A friend who criticizes our choices too much is not one we are likely to confide in or turn to for help when things turn out badly. Finally, there are moral reasons to respect friends' autonomous choices even if we have good evidence that the choices are not best for them. For all these reasons, the fact that a person's values could be better for them does not automatically license us to ignore their actual values in the usual case.

It does seem, though, that there are some contexts in which it makes sense to discount a person's inappropriate values in practice, such as when these values are so dysfunctional that they do not have any of these connections to other values and rewards, and when the risk of violating the norms of friendship or the requirements of morality is minimal. For example, a friend who is putting herself and her children at risk by staying in an abusive relationship probably needs to stop valuing this relationship (if she does) in order to live a life in which she can fulfill her other central values. (I say that she *may* need to adjust her values, because values are not necessarily the issue here. The more likely case is that she wants to leave, but doesn't have the resources or ability to do so safely. She may also have incorrect factual beliefs such as the belief that the abuse is her fault. Often inappropriate values and false beliefs are intertwined because the harmful values are sustained by the false beliefs.) In this case, continuing to value the relationship with the abusive partner is at odds with other things she values and with values (like mental and physical health) that are conducive to a value-fulfilled life by her own lights. It might indeed be a duty of friendship to try to intervene in some way or another in this friend's situation. To take a less dire example, a student who asks for guidance from a teacher might be well served by advice that recommends changing goals.[9]

So, there are circumstances in which it makes sense for us to work around a person's own view about what's good for them in our efforts to improve their well-being. But as we've already observed, this is tricky and what it makes sense to do depends on more variables than just the facts about well-being; hence the interpersonal challenge. To see some of these variables, consider the example of Harry, a character similar to Jules, the aspiring actor from *The Interestings* discussed in previous chapters. Harry values artistic expression and wants to write the great American novel. Harry is not a brilliant writer, though he's good enough that he has received some accolades over the many years he has been at it. Harry's commitment to the writer's life has now become a strain on his family, because of how little money it earns him. Because of his devotion to writing, Harry is not considering quitting, but he is seeing a therapist for stress. As Harry's friend, it might be appropriate to suggest that he would be better off channeling his talents into a more lucrative direction, or finding a paying job and keeping up his writing on the side. He needs your support and encouragement and you can support him with stories of successful artists who have had to keep full-time jobs. You may not be in a position to question the value Harry places on writing, however. On the other hand, Harry's therapist whose relationship is not going to be jeopardized by asking pointed questions, and who is trained to counsel people about their goals, is in a good position to encourage Harry to question the value of writing for him. It might be that Harry really values having a creative outlet and there are other ways to conceive of creativity besides writing the great American novel. It might be that Harry wants fame and can be made to see that the means to his goal are inappropriate, given his talents. Or, it might be that Harry loves the process of writing, in which case he doesn't need to write the great American novel to be happy, he just needs to find some time for writing. It's not that a friend could not be in the position to figure these things out with Harry, but many friends will not be.

Notice that knowledge by itself does not solve the interpersonal challenge. Harry's friend might know what is good for Harry as well as the therapist does, yet it may still be a bad idea for the friend (but not for the therapist) to help Harry by challenging his values directly. Moreover, it might be a bad idea to proceed in this way even for the therapist if Harry doesn't want this kind of advice. The interpersonal challenge is affected by the levels of trust and intimacy, and also by the type of relationship between the beneficiary and assessor. Trusting that the person trying to help you has your best interests at heart makes some room for honesty about what might be wrong with a person's life, but trust isn't really sufficient. A certain level of intimacy (mutual affection and understanding) also seems to be required among friends; without it, advice about how to live one's life better might be taken to be nosy or condescending. If the person advising has a professional relationship to the beneficiary (such as the relationship of a therapist to a patient), less intimacy is required in part because there is more trust and more presumed knowledge. The kind of intimacy found in marriages or romantic partnerships allows for judgments that a person's values are inappropriate in part because so much is shared that there are dramatic effects of one person's life on the other. Certain friendships have sufficient trust and enough shared experiences that such friends are also free to give advice based on how they imagine things could be different.

The interpersonal challenge, then, is to navigate between our own evaluative perspective and the perspective of the friend, knowing that there are things we don't understand about what it is like to be them and that there are yet things they can't see from where they stand. If our aim is to help someone who is not on the best path, we need (ideally) to think about what changes would benefit our friend in the long term, to recognize when we don't agree, and to be able to communicate these ideas in a constructive way. We need to do all this without causing collateral damage to the relationship or to the beneficiary, and without violating the friend's autonomy. The informational challenge is therefore part of the problem: we often do not know enough about our friends to be able to make reasonable assessments. But, as I've said, there is more to the interpersonal challenge than a possible lack of knowledge. You can make things worse for your friend even if you are right about what is good for them, and this means that if you think your friend is screwing up their life, you need to tread carefully. When a person *asks* for help (as they typically do in the context of therapy), the value of autonomy is in less danger and the threats to the continuation of the friendship are reduced. And when a person gets help from a trusted, insightful, and considerate friend, they can be brought to see the value of the other perspective without it seeming threatening or obnoxious.

The first step toward solving the epistemic challenge, I said, is to talk, to have a conversation, and by talking to learn more about what we don't know. Talking also helps to address the interpersonal challenge. It is by talking with our friends that we can learn how we differ (rather than blundering in and assuming they think like we do) and what sorts of help they are open to. By talking, we may also end up giving advice, providing support, imagining options, or asking helpful questions. Sometimes, though, talking together doesn't lead anywhere helpful. Eventually, if our friend doesn't take our suggestions, rejects all the options we propose, and seems wedded to their dysfunctional, life-ruining values, we may wonder about helping in ways that are less polite. Must our conversations respect our friends' values? And when conversation doesn't work, is there more we can or should do?

4.4 When Does it Make Sense to Discount, Ignore, or Try to Change People's Values?

The interpersonal challenge is not confined to cases of conflicts about values. It can be challenging to help friends even when our values are very similar. Nevertheless, I'm going to continue focusing on such cases because I think that understanding the norms that govern the most difficult situation will help guide us in less difficult situations. In this section we'll pin down the norms that govern what to do when we disagree with our friends about what is good for them. This can happen in conversation, but it is when conversation runs out that the really tough questions arise.

I have been talking in a familiar way about when it might "make sense" to discount people's actual values in practice and about the problems that may result from doing so. It is worth pausing to ask what sense of "make sense" I have in mind. I am not thinking of what it makes sense to do in the sense of what is rational or most conducive to the truth, but rather what it makes sense to do in light of the goal of promoting well-being. This is why the problems I have focused on have to do with effects on well-being: both giving bad, misinformed advice and giving good advice that jeopardizes valuable relationships can affect people's well-being. So, we are asking under what conditions a potential benefactor is in a position to discount, ignore, or attempt to change a person's actual values for the sake of that person's well-being. In other words, under what conditions can this be done without too much risk of reducing value fulfillment for either friend?

Many of the considerations that are relevant to this question depend on details of the situation about which we cannot generalize, so the purpose here will not be to advance a set of rules for promoting well-being; rather, the goal in this section is to indicate what the variables are, what we should look out for, and what criteria we should apply when faced with a decision about whether we ought to second guess someone's own assessment about what's good for them.

Drawing on the examples discussed above, we can see that there are three conditions that are particularly important in determining whether it makes sense for a person to discount, ignore, or override a friend's actual values in assessing or trying to improve their well-being. It makes sense (that is, the benefits are likely to outweigh the risks to well-being) to discount, ignore, or try to change people's actual values in our assessments of their well-being when: (a) the beneficiary's values are not good for her, that is, not capable of being pursued together over time to a degree that will frustrate efforts to live a life that is rich in value fulfillment, (b) there is a way that the beneficiary could change their values to a more appropriate set, and (c) the relationship between the helper and the beneficiary is such that discounting will not result in greater harm (to the relationship or to the people in it). Further, in the background for all three conditions is the helper's epistemic position, which is also relevant to the practical decision about whether to intervene in some way. The more knowledge you have about the beneficiary's values, their capacity for change, and your relationship with them, the better positioned you are to know whether it would make sense to discount their values.

The first condition (a) was the topic of Sections 2.3 and 2.4. Essentially, values are bad for a person to the degree to which they prevent them from living a value-fulfilled life. Notice that there are important distinctions to be made between "not good for", "bad for", and "harmful"; surely "harmful" is worse than "not good for", for example. But for current purposes, we are interested in the broad category of values that are not conducive to a life rich in value fulfillment. The question of just *how* unconducive the values are is just what is at issue in figuring out whether it makes sense to intervene. Regarding the second condition (b), whether or not a person is able to make changes along a dimension that would improve their prospect of living a value-fulfilled life is certainly a difficult question; indeed, it may be one that few of us who are not professional therapists have the right skills to answer. Nevertheless, it is clear what is being asked: Can the person change, or are they too stuck in their ways, too limited, too constrained by external conditions?

The third condition (c) is more difficult, and little has been said about it so far. What kinds of relationships make this sort of helping more helpful than harmful? Recall the kinds of harms that can be done: feelings of insult, condescension, disrespect, the violation of respect for autonomy, damage to the relationship itself, and removal of needed support. I suggest that there are four important variables. We have already observed that intimacy and trust make a difference to whether someone will benefit from help that rejects their current values. Making changes to our values is difficult, so we need to have some reasonable prospect that a proposed change would be good for us before we'll put in the effort. Advice from a person who understands and likes us (intimacy) and whom we trust to care about how well our lives are going is, prima facie, better than information from someone who knows us less well or whom we suspect of having ulterior motives. Intimacy and trust vary with type of friendship, though not always in a completely obvious way. Sometimes spouses do not know each other very well even though they spend a lot of time together, and family members who ought to have our best interests at heart can have their own agendas. Moreover, trust and intimacy can come apart. For example, a jealous romantic partner may understand and love you, but may be so blinded by their own fear of loss that they are not to be trusted to see what's good for you.

A third important variable (in addition to intimacy and trust) is the extent to which the friends' lives are intertwined. One thing that might make it more acceptable for a husband or wife to criticize the spouse's actual values is that the two of them have to live together and share each other's burdens to a greater extent than most friends. If we think back to our initial examples from the introduction, Maxine's partner is in a position to challenge her commitment to parenting only a biologically related child because the partner will be co-parenting the child and sharing the emotional and financial costs.

A fourth important variable is the skill that the friend has in communicating challenging information.[10] Unfortunately, it's likely that all of us have experienced a friend trying to help in clumsy or insensitive ways. We can imagine a frustrated friend of Jules (the aspiring but insufficiently talented actress), who is less kind (but more honest) than her friend Ash, suggesting that she "Grow up and stop being so impractical". If Jules isn't ready to hear the message put so frankly, it may not be helpful. On the other hand, if Jules is ready to face the music, a friend who beats around the bush so much that the truth just gets lost is also not very helpful.

No one of these four variables is sufficient to determine whether a relationship can withstand one person helping by discounting the values of the other. You might have an intimate relationship with someone in the sense that you have a long history together and know each other to the core, but without trust such a friend's suggestions about how we could better our lives are not helpful. Think of acrimoniously divorced partners who might know each other better than anyone else in the world, but who are in no position to give advice because there is no presumption that each cares about the other's well-being any more. Trust without intimacy (or at least relevant knowledge) is also not sufficient, because a trusted person who doesn't know you very well can't make good assessments about how you would be better off. For example, many of us have parents who value our welfare more than anything else, but are not well positioned to help us live better lives because they still see us as the children we once were. Trust and intimacy without skill are also problematic: someone who wants to help and knows enough about you to have a useful perspective, but who doesn't have enough sensitivity to communicate that perspective in a way you can accept isn't in the best position to help you overcome your dysfunctional values. Finally, mutual dependence weighs against shortcomings with respect to the other factors, because the cost of sticking with the status quo is shared between the helper and the beneficiary. Notice that we can't count on a particular type of relationship to be one that warrants helping in this way. Some parents are more accepting of their children's independence than others, some best friends are better at perspective taking than others, and so on.

So far we have been talking about well-being assessments that are used in giving people advice, and we have seen that there are significant constraints on who may discount a person's actual values and in what context. Well-being assessments can also be used as a basis for more intrusive actions than advice-giving. We can act for the sake of a friend in a way that interferes with the pursuit of their actual values in a much more direct way than advising against these values. Is this ever a good thing to do? That is, according to the value fulfillment theory, could it ever benefit a person to do something that actually frustrates that person's pursuit of their own values?

One important difference between advice and direct action is that when you give advice, the friend can decide whether or not to take it and in doing so they can decide whether they will try to change in the way that the advice requires. On the other hand, if you try to help someone by directly changing their values to more appropriate ones, you cannot be sure that the person will cooperate in maintaining the new values. If the action you take in order to change the person's values is permanent brain alteration or something like that, this might not matter. But if the action is something like physically removing them from a bad marriage, burning their 5,000-page manuscript, or breaking their violin on the rocks, there will be no benefit if the friend's attitudes do not also change. If the friend returns to the bad spouse, rewrites the terrible novel, or buys another violin, nothing will change except that you will now be seen as untrustworthy or worse.

If we are going to attempt to change our friends' values more actively than just by giving advice, we have to have reason to believe that our actions will create some lasting beneficial change. This raises the bar for the conditions under which it makes sense to go against a friend's actual values. Even with that high bar, I think there are cases in which it makes sense to do more than give advice. There are at least four strategies worth discussing. I'll take these four in increasing order of severity.

First, you can get your friend to try something new with the intention of causing them to shift their values to this new thing by giving them extrinsic reasons to do it such as "do it for me" or "here's some money to do it". For example, imagine your friend Marco is dead set on running marathons even though his knees are shot and his doctor recommends against running. Perhaps he comes from a long line of marathon runners and running has really become part of his identity. You might realize that he'd be better off changing sports now, while he's in his thirties, than waiting until he completely trashes his joints and it's more difficult for him to take up something new. But Marco is stubborn. Without trying to get him to think about changing, you might just encourage him to try your (knee-friendly) sport with you, just for the sake of spending time with you, or making you happy. To take a weightier example, perhaps you are friends with someone like Sander whose Church rejects his sexual identity. Perhaps your friend is struggling with the conflict unsuccessfully since his commitment to his faith is very strong. One thing you could do as a perceptive friend is to invite the friend to your (more accepting and open) Church where he might find faith that doesn't conflict with his identity. The idea here is that you would get him to go, not by persuading him that he needs to abandon the Church, but by telling him that you'd like him to share that part of your life.

This method for trying to change a friend's values is fairly unproblematic, it seems, because it doesn't violate the friend's autonomy, at least on the assumption that your intentions are good (not manipulative or shaming, say) and the proffered options are really proffered as *options*. ("If you don't come with me to my church, I'll kill myself" is coercive and would not be a true case of providing an option.) Sharing our own good practices with friends is a normal friendly thing to do, even if we don't have any concern about how well the friend is faring. In the best cases of this method for helping, the friend ends up choosing to make improvements on the basis of the evidence you provided them.

Second, you can remove or refuse support for the value that you think ought to be changed. We often support our friends and families in their projects in more or less direct ways. Parents and spouses often give direct financial support. Friends typically support in other ways (helping with childcare, talking through plans, and so on). Another way we can act for the sake of someone's well-being against their current values, then, is to cut off these forms of support for a project we think is bad for the person. Removing support could be harmful (other things equal), but it might still be justified. If you really think your friend is ruining their life, refusing to support them in ruinous activity is a good way of communicating your view without removing all support and terminating the friendship. (Removing support can be done with or without communicating to the person *why* you are cutting off support; which is better for encouraging a change depends on the details, but I suspect in most cases it will be more effective to tell the person your reasons for withdrawing support.)

Third, you could get your friend to try something new by tricking or manipulating them. Imagine a more ruthless friend of Jules who forges a letter from a casting agent recommending that she look for a different form of employment. Or a friend of Maxine's who sends uninvited pictures of adoptable infants and exaggerated information about the risks of surrogacy. There may sometimes be cases in which it makes sense to manipulate a person, though such situations will be unusual. It's not often the case that we are so certain about what is good for another person that we are justified in undermining their choices in these blatantly disrespectful ways. There may be some such cases, however. For example, you might think it would be justified to trick a friend who has become brainwashed by a cult into leaving the cult's premises so that you can get him deprogrammed. But the situation would have to be fairly dire for the benefit of the manipulation to outweigh the reasons to respect the friend's own capacity for choice.

Finally, you can take drastic measures such as forced physical relocation or medical help. If the brainwashed cult member isn't fooled by the trick, and depending on what kind of cult it is, it may make sense to physically remove him from the premises and force him to succumb to deprogramming. Similarly for drug addicted friends. Parents sometimes remove their kids from their surroundings and force them into clinics to break the addiction, and this seems justified by the severe consequences to well-being (by the lights of any theory, really, but certainly according to the value fulfillment theory) that drug addiction carries. Unless dire consequences are likely, however, resorting to force would be very difficult to justify.

The case of the cult raises some interesting questions about personal identity. If your friend Cuthbert joined a cult and then became a different person whose emotions, desires, and judgments about what he has reason to do were fairly well aligned with being a cult member, how could it be good for this new person to remove him from the cult? This case may seem far-fetched, but analogous cases arise in biomedical ethics that are not so far-fetched. Is someone who has lost significant chunks of memory the same person as they were when they created a living will? And if not, is abiding by that will good for the person who exists now? What about a person whose personality has changed due to brain damage: Does it benefit that person to help them pursue the values they had before their personality changed? These are very tricky questions and I cannot even try to solve the problem of personal identity here. But I can say a few things that are relevant to the practical question of how to help our friends and to show how the value fulfillment theory approaches such cases.

First, although the value fulfillment theory does have a bias toward the long term (as discussed in Section 2.3), it is focused on the well-being of the person who exists now. The value fulfillment theory takes well-being to be a feature of a whole life and it urges us to attend to the way that a person's values can be developed over time, but this does not mean that the past person's values have authority over the present person's values. What this means for cases of dramatic and enduring change is that it is the current person whose value fulfillment we should focus on. When there is a break in personal development, typically, greater value fulfillment overall will be achieved by attending to the values of the new person rather than by continuing to focus on the values of the previous person (in ways that will thwart the values of the new person). I am, therefore, in agreement with Jennifer Hawkins (2014) who argues that when we are thinking about the well-being of a person with dementia, what matters is the psychological states of the dementia sufferer, not the psychological states of the person they used to be.

Of course such cases are difficult. We don't always know whether the change is temporary or lasting. In the case of Cuthbert, we may not know whether the old Cuthbert is "still there", or whether the brainwashing has permanently altered his values. This is just a dramatic example of the information problem discussed earlier in this chapter. Such cases are also tremendously interpersonally difficult and there are often many parties competing for the right to determine what to do for someone who has (or is perceived to have) lost the capacity to decide for themselves.

Fortunately, we are not entirely without guidance in these difficult cases. The second point to make about these cases of radical change is that such change very often happens over time and certain basic values persist though they manifest themselves in different ways. Millicent loses her memory, but she still values family; it's just that now the way for her to succeed in terms of this value is to sit with her loved ones and feel a sense of familiarity and comfort. Cuthbert joins a cult but he still loves music and dancing—it's just that now he does it with a tambourine and purple robes. Continuity in values makes it possible for us to help our friends even if some things about them have changed dramatically.

Third, some things are bad for almost everyone, no matter what has changed about them. This is true even for the value fulfillment theory, because human beings are generally better at pursuing our own goals or fulfilling our own values over the long term when we are physically and mentally healthy and we do not have unresolvable conflicts among these values. Even if your friend Cuthbert has become a very different person after joining a cult, participation in the cult may be bad for him in terms of his prospects for a value-fulfilled life if it involves harmful rituals (such as suicide) or choices (such as renouncing his family or handing over all his income to the cult leader) that cut off options that might be valued in the future. So, according to the value fulfillment theory, there are some forms of help that are very likely to be helpful however much our friend changes after a drastic experience.

To summarize this section so far, it makes sense (i.e., the likely benefits outweigh the risks to well-being) to discount, ignore, or try to change people's actual values in our assessments of, and efforts to promote, their well-being when: (a) the beneficiary's values are not conducive to a value-fulfilled life, (b) there is a way that the beneficiary could change so as to change their values to a more appropriate set, and (c) the relationship between the helper and the beneficiary (assessed in terms of trust, intimacy, mutual dependence, and skill) is such that discounting will not result in more harm (to the relationship or to the person being helped). We can now add that how well these criteria are met is a matter of degree and the more intrusive the intervention, the higher the standard and the more certain we must be about our own perspective. Notice that how we respond to our friend's values may influence what is possible for them. For example, changing a career path to something that suits you better may be something that is only possible for you if you have friends who point the way and support you. In this way, the informational and interpersonal challenges are dynamically related: our actions and capacities as friends can change the facts about how our friends are capable of developing.

We can now return to our friends whose circumstances are not so dire. I promised that thinking about the dramatic cases of friends who are truly screwing up their lives would help to think about the more typical cases (of friends who are screwing up their lives in a very moderate way). Helpfulness here too starts by paying attention to the friend's values with a critical eye to how overall fulfillment can be improved, and similar informational and interpersonal obstacles exist in these cases. The main difference is that, for friends who have the ordinary kinds of problems that most of us have, the stakes are lower and so the first condition for serious intervention will rarely be met. As we have discussed in previous chapters, appropriateness of values comes in degrees. There will be cases in which a person has values that are at odds with emotion, desire, or judgment, or are not capable of being pursued together over time, to a degree that will frustrate any efforts to live a life that is rich in value fulfillment. But ordinary problems seem unlikely to reduce the possibility of living a value-fulfilled life in a dramatic way, given that there are a number of paths to value fulfillment. Manipulation or physical force are rather desperate means of trying to help someone; the risks are unlikely to be outweighed in cases in which a friend is slightly unhappy in their career, holding themselves to somewhat unreasonable standards for their leisure pursuits, or the like.

Less intrusive means of intervention are often appropriate in less dire circumstances, however. Exactly what kind and in what circumstances depends on the variables we have discussed for the more dire circumstances. It makes sense to offer advice to someone who isn't thriving, who wants your help and thinks change is possible. It makes sense to try to talk a close friend into trying something new for your sake, if you can see they are struggling but neither of you is sure whether change is possible. Getting friends to try new things—or old things in a new way—is a good strategy for these less dire cases for a variety of reasons. It may help the friend to see a new way to think about succeeding in terms of their values that puts them on a better path to value fulfillment. It may also be a gesture of support that helps to solidify your friendship, which is itself one of the values you both hold dear. For example, think again of Marco the marathon runner whose knee has now degenerated to the point at which he will be simply unable to pursue this favorite activity. Thinking about what other values are connected to running, and what else might fill that role in his life, you might research forms of exercise that people with knee injuries can do and suggest that the two of you try one of these activities together. Or, say you have a friend whose standards are so high that she's constantly frustrated by not meeting them in an activity that you share. Perhaps you are able to model a different way of thinking about what success means by focusing on the joy of the activity itself and how fortunate you are to be able to do it.

Helping friends in this way can also benefit us. Observing how a friend suffers due to unachievable standards of success can make us think more explicitly about our own standards and how they are helping or hindering a value-fulfilled life. Watching a friend suffer because they are prioritizing a project that brings them little joy can make us think about our own emotional connection to the things we spend our time doing. There will be more to say about what it is to be a good friend (in typical and non-typical cases) in Chapter 5.

4.5 Beyond Friendship

The focus of this book is helping in the context of friendship and we will return to friendship in the next chapter. But I think it would be useful to think a little bit about how the value fulfillment theory extends to other contexts. I do not think that a theory of well-being has to solve every problem we have, but it would be disappointing if a theory of well-being that is meant to guide helping behavior in one context were completely insufficient for thinking about helping in other contexts. It would require a different book to fully apply the value fulfillment theory to questions about how to help strangers, or animals, or infants, but we would at least like to see that this way of thinking about well-being is not at odds with how we ought to think about well-being in other contexts. Can the value fulfillment theory be extended beyond the context of friendship? I think it can.

When it comes to helping people we don't know, as we might do through aid policy, volunteer work, or contributions to non-profits, I think the value fulfillment theory does have some action guiding recommendations. First, we should have some humility about what we can know about other people's lives. (The importance of humility given the complexity of what we need to know in order to help people was discussed briefly in Section 4.3 and it will be an important topic of the next chapter.) That said, we should not let the difficulty of helping other people paralyze us so that we end up doing nothing, because even with our limited knowledge, we can see that there are ways of helping that we can be relatively certain will contribute to the well-being of strangers. So, second, we should focus on helping others to secure the necessary conditions for maintaining commitments to values and pursuing a value-fulfilled life. This recommendation is not out of line with well-established views about how to improve global well-being that emphasize the need to focus on primary goods or basic human capabilities that are required for functioning (Nussbaum 2001; Rawls 1971). According to these views, rather than promoting a specific way of life or particular substantive goods, our focus should be on ensuring that people have what they need to function well in the pursuit of their own values or projects. The capabilities approach, for example, holds that "freedom to achieve well-being is of primary moral importance, and . . . freedom to achieve well-being is to be understood in terms of people's capabilities, that is, their real opportunities to do and be what they have reason to value" (Robeyns 2011). Now, Nussbaum's theory is not a subjectivist theory; it posits an objective notion of human flourishing that is inspired by Aristotle. The value fulfillment theory does not posit objectively good lives; rather, it defines value-fulfilled lives, ultimately, in terms of the individual's psychology. However, this difference does not matter much in practice when we're thinking about helping large numbers of strangers. When this is our practical problem we have to make assumptions about probable values and the necessary means for pursuing them. The capabilities approach could guide us in our thinking about which values are important to most people, and therefore what forms of aid would be genuinely helpful.[11]

The value fulfillment theory is not merely compatible with compelling views in the development literature. I think it also helps to illuminate a question about the state's promotion of well-being, namely, whether the state must always defer to people's preferences or whether the state is sometimes permitted to promote the well-being of its citizens in ways that contravene their preferences.[12] This is the question we just considered with respect to friends—when does it make sense to discount, ignore, or try to change people's values?—now applied to governments and citizens rather than friends. In our discussion of friends, we distinguished advising from more direct action that might be taken on the basis of well-being assessments. When it comes to the state, we can distinguish between policies that recommend without coercing and coercively paternalistic policies. Could the state ever be justified in discounting people's actual values?

Analogizing between friends and the state, the best case for discounting actual values would be a case in which the state is in a good epistemic position to know that citizens' current values are harmful in ways that could be changed, there is an action the state could take that promotes new values without violating its own laws or commitments to its citizens, and the relationship between citizen and state is such that citizens have some reason to trust that the state has their interests in view (at least with respect to the policies in question). One example of a state action that might be thought to meet these criteria is fast food regulation and the promotion of healthy choices through the creation of public parks with bike paths and so on. Here the state may deem that people's willingness to spend money on high-calorie, low-nutrition food does not represent their best set of values, which would include health and longevity. Similarly, the state might deem that people's apparent interest in sitting on the couch watching TV rather than moving does not represent the values that would be best for them. On the assumption that the state's creating parks and regulating fast food (e.g., by requiring restaurants to post nutritional information) does not jeopardize the citizens' trust, and that the policies do not decrease well-being by unduly burdening citizens, this could be an acceptable form of discounting, according to the value fulfillment theory.

Whether other forms of state action are permissible will depend on the details. As with the case of friends, as the intrusiveness of the policy intervention increases, so does the risk of negative effects on well-being and, therefore, the requirements for acceptable interventions become more stringent. Further, in the context of state action, of course, we cannot focus solely on promoting well-being as we did in the case of friendship. What the state is actually permitted to do will depend on your views about the legitimacy of political authority. My point here is simply that *if* it were legitimate for the state to promote citizens' welfare, the value fulfillment theory points to plausible examples.

So far we have focused entirely on typical adult human beings—peers, if not friends. The value fulfillment theory takes typically functioning adult human beings as its standard subjects. But many creatures who differ from this norm in various ways are also well-being subjects. This could seem like a problem for the view: it would be at least odd if well-being for other kinds of subjects were completely different from well-being for typical human adults.[13] In particular, since children develop into adults, it would be very strange indeed if there were a different conception of well-being for each. I don't think there is a real problem here.

An ethical theory like the value fulfillment theory can be described at different levels of generality, and there is a general description of the value fulfillment theory that has very broad application. This is because the deep motivation for the value fulfillment theory, the animating core of the theory, is an idea about what it is to have a good life that applies to any goal-directed creature.[14] That is, to live well is to have goals or values that suit you and to succeed in terms of these goals. The basic insight of the value fulfillment theory, in other words, is the same basic insight that fuels desire satisfaction theories and interest satisfaction theories, and these theories do well at capturing an intuitive sense of well-being for animals and other creatures who are not typical adult human beings.[15] Valuing or having a goal may be psychologically simpler for a simple creature; dogs do not make judgments about their reasons for pursuing their values, for instance, so there will be no cognitive component of valuing for them. There will also be significant differences in *what* is valued, depending on the sophistication of the creature in question; dogs care about treats and slow squirrels, for example, not training for difficult physical challenges or reading philosophy. But despite these differences, the basic insight is the same: what is good for a creature is to achieve what matters to it.

Seen at this level of general description, the value fulfillment theory does not seem at odds with compelling ideas about what's good for animals. For example, one of my dogs loves belly rubs, seeks them out, and takes great pleasure in them; my other dog has little interest in this form of affection and far prefers small bits of cheese. The core of the value fulfillment theory allows us to explain why belly rubs are good for Sugar, but not for Olive. To help Sugar or Olive, I don't need to think much about how sustainable their values are over the long term, how they might change what they value to suit their circumstances, or how much I can presume to know about what they care about. Their values (or, more accurately, their desires and cares) are fairly obvious and simple enough that they will be able to continue to achieve them for the duration of their lives (with my help). Notice that not all non-human animals are like this, and one of the lessons we might learn from the value fulfillment theory is that we can make things worse for animals when we assume that we know how things are for them.[16]

Of course, the value fulfillment theory that I have described in this book is designed to help us help other adult human beings in the context of friendship. So, what the value fulfillment theory does is to recognize that typical adult human beings are complex creatures and that it is worth saying something in particular about *our* well-being that makes it different from the well-being of other creatures. One could make too much of this distinction and define human well-being as something entirely different in kind from the well-being of other creatures. But one can also make too little of it by ignoring the ways in which our being self-reflective creatures with complex emotional lives changes the game.

Children raise different questions, because they are developing into adults and do not yet have systems of values that we can help them to realize. Because the value fulfillment theory posits a value-fulfilled life as a goal, it does have plausible implications for thinking about the well-being of children. Given this ideal, and children's developmental trajectory, the thing to do if we are concerned about a child's well-being is to help ensure that children can develop into adults who have relatively stable value commitments that suit their personalities and circumstances and that can be achieved over the long term. That is, in addition to attending to the child's current cares and concerns, we should also attend to the necessary conditions for developing a fitting and sustainable set of values. Saying exactly what these necessary conditions are would require some expertise about child development that I do not possess, but there are a few obvious things to say.[17] Basically, the value fulfillment theory supports the idea that children should be encouraged to find pursuits that suit their physical and psychological dispositions and that conduce to the necessary conditions for value fulfillment generally, such as (psychological) happiness and physical health. The ideal of a value-fulfilled life does not lead us to think in terms of maximizing a single kind of satisfaction, but rather in terms of putting together the many things that are important to people and that will be important to children as they develop. Beyond this, there are many possibilities. Does it make sense to encourage reflective moments during which children think about how well they are doing with respect to the things they care about? (I know some parents who perform gratitude exercises with their children at the end of the day that take this form.) Does it make sense to discuss with children what are reasonable standards for success in terms of the values they have? There are many questions to answer about how to help children develop into adults who will live value-fulfilled lives. The point here is that the value fulfillment theory is not left empty-handed when it comes to discussions of the well-being of children.

4.6 Conclusion

We care about our friends' well-being and generally want to help them if we can. We may deem that there isn't any respectful and effective way to help, or we may decide we don't have the time, but we are usually motivated to help the people we care about, and doing this well (or at least not doing it badly) will help us with our own well-being. In this section we have seen that there are a lot of challenges to helping well: we don't know enough, we aren't skilled enough, our friends aren't open to the kind of help we can provide, or we just don't have the resources. Identifying these obstacles does provide some guidance about how to be a more helpful friend: we should listen to what friends have to say, we should be supportive and patient, we should respect the limits of our own abilities to be helpful, and we should consider the situation carefully before we help in a way that would be intrusive. To improve along any of these dimensions requires that we acknowledge that we aren't perfect, that we don't know everything about what things are like for our friends, and that we may not know what's good for other people. And this leads us to the importance of a certain kind of humility, which will be a major focus of the next chapter.

5

Being a Good Friend

5.1 Good Friends

Throughout this book, our background practical problem has been the problem of how to help others in complex situations, particularly our friends and loved ones. The value fulfillment theory aims to help us by telling us what to attend to in our friends' lives (their values, circumstances, and potential for change) and in ourselves (our values, skills, and limitations). I hope readers now have a sense of how this is supposed to be helpful, and how the value fulfillment theory is therefore a good tool for these purposes. In this chapter we'll continue the practical application of the theory to articulate more fully what kind of friend it makes sense to be.

One reason to focus on the value of friendship, as I've said before, is that it is a very popular value (especially if we include family and romantic relationships, as I've meant to do). Another reason is that it is a social or other-involving value that sheds some light on an ancient philosophical problem about the relationship between morality and self-interest. Because friendship is, for most people, part of an appropriate set of values, helping our friends actually helps us too. At least this is true insofar as the kinds of relationships we value are ones in which we care about each other for each other's sake. In other words, when being a good, helpful, caring friend is part of what is valued about friendship, helping friends improves our own well-being at the same time as it helps them. This is a good thing. It demonstrates that there may be less of a gap between self-interest and the interests of others than we sometimes tend to think. It also provides a model for how we can make arguments for being better (nicer, more helpful) people that are anchored in claims about individual well-being.

Friendship is a particularly important value to consider, then, because it is a widely shared value that can move us toward better other-regarding behavior. To see this, consider that the value of friendship is tied to various other values: a person who values *friendship* typically values particular relationships with other people, the well-being of these friends, and being a good friend to others. For many of us, these other values are constitutive of the somewhat abstract value of friendship. These values bring with them standards of success: to be a good friend one must care about and be available to one's friends, and each particular relationship has its own specific standard for what counts as fulfillment (bowling together, remembering birthdays, monthly phone calls, and so forth). Let's focus on the value of being a good friend, since it's easy to see the disparity here between what one values and what one actually achieves. Most people with a little bit of self-awareness are aware that they are not perfect friends. Someone for whom being a good friend is a value that determines how well their life is going has a personal interest in being a better friend. And, on the assumption that there are some aspects of "being a better friend" that compete with other things they want in the moment, the value of being a better friend can motivate a project of self-improvement or the cultivation of virtue.

Now, we might wonder how *much* the value of friendship reduces the gap between self-interest and the interests of others. The answer to this question depends, for one thing, on how many people value the kind of friendship we've been discussing—let's call them "caring friendships"—and how much those people value it. So far I've been talking about norms of friendship that involve caring about others for their own sake, wanting to help your friends, and so on. I've proceeded as if this is how everyone conceives of friendship, but maybe this isn't the case. Consider Aristotle's distinction between the three different types of friendship: friendships of pleasure, of utility, and of virtue (Aristotle 1999). Today, we might call these three types "drinking buddies", "contacts", and "real friends". Then and now, there do seem to be different kinds of friendship. For some people, the value of friendship is not at all constituted by the value of being a good friend. For such people, one succeeds in terms of this value if one has people around with whom to have some fun or get ahead in business.

What can we say in favor of caring friendship? Is there an argument to be made that even those who do not value friendship of this kind ought to do so? We have seen that there are sometimes values that a person does not have but ought to have as part of a sustainable set of values, and a person who aspires to live a value-fulfilled life has self-regarding reasons to cultivate such values. Is this the case with caring friendships? There is some reason to think so.

First, there are instrumental reasons to value caring friendships. As I have already mentioned (at the beginning of Chapter 4) there is strong evidence for the benefits of close relationships in terms of health, subjective well-being, and reduced psychological distress. Further, it is part of the human condition that we experience loss as we age—loss of people we love, loss of our own abilities and powers, and so on. Friends who are with us for the fun of it are not likely to be there for us when we are in the midst of suffering a loss. Yet the times when we are suffering are precisely when we need friends the most: to help us cope in practical ways or to make sure we don't sink into despair. Caring friends are motivated to stick around when you're down, because they care about your well-being. Of course there are cases in which one person (call him Andy) cares about another (call her Bea) for her own sake, even though Bea just regards Andy as a source of amusement, but such one-sided caring friendships are not easy to find and maintain. The very one-sidedness of the friendship may make Andy seem rather pathetic to Bea and a poor choice for a friend. And, it's often true that when someone like Andy detects that someone like Bea is only in it for number one, he'll look elsewhere.

Caring friendships may also have better effects on other common values such as psychological happiness. Psychologist Barbara Fredrickson has argued that positive emotions such as love, joy, and gratitude—emotions that are integral to caring friendships—produce lasting effects on our life satisfaction and continued positive feelings (Fredrickson 2001). Her theory is called the "Broaden and Build Theory of Positive Emotions", because it holds that positive emotions broaden the options that come to our minds when we're called upon to make a choice (our "thought-action repertoires"), which in turn builds the resources that we have to respond to future choices. "Resources" include physical resources (like health) and psychological resources (like "the urge to savor and integrate recent events and experiences creating a new sense of self and a new world view") (Fredrickson 1998, p. 306).

Because of the far-reaching effects of positive emotions on our way of seeing the world and our options, positive emotions, including those that are part of caring friendship, seem to contribute to success in any of our goals and projects. Caring friendships are, therefore, a component of what Fredrickson calls an "upward spiral" and the philosopher Michael Bishop calls a "positive causal network". A positive causal network is the opposite of a vicious cycle: it is a cluster of properties "made up of an agent's feelings, emotions, attitudes, behaviors, traits and accomplishments" that consists of relatively more of these states that feel good, bring about good feelings, or bring about what is valued (Bishop 2015, pp. 40–1).

If caring friendships are part of a network that builds on itself to make us more likely to achieve our goals or fulfill our values, it begins to look like the reasons to favor caring friendships are not merely instrumental. If Fredrickson and Bishop are correct about the kinds of creatures we are—creatures who are better able to succeed in terms of what we value when we experience positive emotions that are integral to relationships—then valuing relationships like this is something that inherently suits us. Most of us human beings are naturally social and sympathetic; we like to share experiences with each other, we need support, we suffer loneliness. When we care about others for their own sakes, then, we are engaging in an activity that suits us psychologically, which makes it something highly likely to be part of a value-fulfilled life, and therefore an appropriate thing to value in the long term. The value of caring friendships isn't likely to be overturned by experience or reflection. Indeed, it usually seems that the more experience we have, the more we realize that we need close friends in our lives.

So, there are reasons to value caring friendships—instrumental reasons that have to do with our other values, and non-instrumental reasons that have to do with the nature of friendship and how it fits us. I'm not claiming that these reasons are reasons for absolutely everyone. I don't think there is any argument that will persuade uncaring, selfish people, or reclusive loners to value friendship in this way.[1] But most of us are not uncaring or reclusive, and this kind of friendship is a value that has deep roots and wide appeal. The fact that we can't persuade an uncaring, selfish jerk to change does not make these values any less a part of the best lives to which most of us can aspire.

5.2 Perspective-Taking and Its Challenges

There are reasons for valuing caring friendships, and most of us already do. So, how should we do it? What does it mean to be a helpful friend? We already have some idea: a helpful friend helps the other to achieve greater value fulfillment by paying attention to the friend's values, noticing ways in which overall fulfillment could be improved, and finding ways to help create these improvements without doing more harm than good. As we've seen, though, the various differences between us and them presents some serious obstacles to being helpful in this way.

In Section 4.1, we looked at some examples of gaps between our own evaluative perspectives and understanding of ourselves and our circumstances, on the one hand, and the perspectives and understandings of our friends, on the other. You may find it incomprehensible that your gay friend would look for a way to stay with his homophobic Church, while he takes the very worthwhileness of his life to depend on his faith and religious community. You may think of Audrey as a failed painter, while she thinks of herself as a successful artist, given the different ways the two of you think about the goal of "being an artist". I may think of Lynsey Addario, the photojournalist, as putting too much importance on her work, while she sees her dangerous work as a mission or a calling and cannot imagine life without it. These are representative cases of differences in ultimate values, what they mean to us, or how they are prioritized.

We also saw how these gaps between us can matter to helping. If I don't understand what you value, it will be difficult for me to see what a value-fulfilled life is for you and how to help you achieve it. If the difficulty in helping friends is the possible gap between us, the solution would seem to be trying to close the gap. This observation might lead us to think that empathy or perspective-taking is the key to being a good friend. Much has been written about empathy and not everyone agrees on how to define it or how it differs from sympathy and compassion.[2] These debates don't really matter for our purposes here, so I'm just going to stipulate that I'm talking about empathy in the sense that at least includes actively taking another creature's perspective. Here I am following Lori Gruen whose book on empathetic engagement with animals presents a very compelling picture of what she calls "entangled empathy", defined like this:

A type of caring perception focused on attending to another's experience of wellbeing. An experiential process involving a blend of emotion and cognition in which we recognize we are in relationships with others and are called upon to be responsive and responsible in these relationships by attending to another's needs, interests, desires, vulnerabilities, hopes, and sensitivities.
(Gruen 2015, p. 3)

Many psychologists who study empathy agree that empathy has an affective component (the feeling side of empathy) and a cognitive component that comprises an active attempt to see things from another's point of view (Decety and Cowell 2014; Zaki and Ochsner 2012). I emphasize the perspective-taking side of empathy in my discussion here, because I think this focus points to some interesting conclusions about how to be a good friend.

Unfortunately, we're not very good at taking other people's perspectives. One of the main barriers to accurate perspective-taking is a kind of self-focus or "egocentric bias" that encourages us to think that other people's shoes feel much the same as our own. This is the bias that is responsible for the fact that most people tend to think they are above average drivers and, indeed, above average at doing all sorts of things from teaching to using a computer mouse (Kruger 1999; Svenson 1981). Egocentric bias also leads us to make inaccurate judgments about other people's perspectives. According to Nicholas Epley and Eugene Caruso (2008, p. 303), two psychologists who have studied perspective-taking, "When given no explicit instructions about how to adopt another's perspective, people appear to start by using themselves as a default or a guide." Epley and Caruso (2008, p. 298) also tell us that there are three main barriers to accurate perspective-taking: "activating the ability, adjusting an egocentric default, and accessing accurate information about others". They do not point out, though it seems true, that egocentric bias is likely to discourage us from engaging our perspective-taking capacities in the first place. Why make an effort to see things from another's point of view when you're pretty sure your assumptions are right at the start?

There is a good deal of evidence for this egocentric bias. Some of it comes from research done by psychologists like the ones mentioned above. For example, Van Boven and George Lowenstein asked participants to predict the feelings of three hikers in the backcountry wilderness of Alaska who were forced to forego food for several days (Van Boven and Loewenstein 2003). They predicted that people's assessments of the degree to which the hikers would be hungry, thirsty, or cold would be influenced by their own feelings of hunger, thirst, and cold. Sure enough, their prediction was borne out. Participants who were thirstier (due to a bout of vigorous exercise and the promise of water later) projected their thirst onto the hikers and were much more likely to say that the hikers would regret not bringing water. In another study featuring the same unfortunate hikers, Van Boven and Loewenstein examined whether people try to predict what others are feeling by attending to their own feelings. This also proved to be true, at least according to the participants' self-reports. Seventy-nine percent of the participants "explicitly referred to mentally trading places with the hikers and imagining how they would feel in their situation" and "participants' rating of how much they relied on trading places was very close to the high end of the scale" (Van Boven and Loewenstein 2003, p. 1162).

None of this should surprise us. One of the main metaphors we use to talk about taking another's perspectives encourages this way of thinking: when you are told to "put yourself in someone else's shoes" you are instructed to think of what it would be like to be *you* in different circumstances, rather than thinking of what it would be like to be someone else in those circumstances.[3] If you think about it, we learn to take others' perspectives by thinking about how *we* (with all of our idiosyncrasies) would feel in the other person's situation. For anyone who has a sister or brother, the injunction to think about how you would feel if someone did to you what you just did to your sibling must seem painfully familiar. The advice is also encoded in The Golden Rule, one of the most recognizable moral rules we have: Do unto others as you would have them do unto you. In other words, think about how you would like to be treated and do likewise to others. I don't mean to suggest that we should stop teaching children to think about how they would feel if someone took their favorite toy; these thoughts often lead us in the right direction. But when the questions we're trying to answer become more complicated, thinking about how we would feel is not always enough.

Of course, most of the psychological research on perspective-taking and egocentric bias does not concern friends. Maybe we are better at seeing things from the perspectives of our friends. Maybe, but on the other hand it seems to me we're not *that* much better at it when it comes to friends. We do know more about our friends than we know about strangers, but we also have greater motivations to distort the truth when it comes to friends that we have when it comes to strangers.[4] We want friends to be like us in important respects: we want to understand them and to be affirmed by their understanding of us. This is due to our sympathetic nature and the way in which our self-conception is shaped and sustained by the people in our inner circle (something we discussed in Section 3.3). One reason it is difficult to admit that a friend's values are different from our own is that this difference puts pressure on us to justify the values that we have. It's easier to think that our way of looking at things is the right way if we do not have to confront dissent, and dissent from strangers can be dismissed more easily than dissent from people we love. Further, differences between friends can cause problems for the friendship itself. Acknowledging that your friend's conception of good parenting, say, is so different from yours that it reveals a basic disagreement about what it is to be a good person may weaken the friendship and drive you apart. It can be easier to ignore the deep disagreements and to assume that the differences in parenting style you witness are merely about what are the best means to the same goal. When it comes to friends there is more at stake in the realization that they value other things or see things in a very different way.

We have already considered quite a few relevant examples of differences in perspective, but it's worth introducing a few more to underscore how the difficulties of perspective-taking extend to friendship. Examples of this kind of deep evaluative difference between friends are often personal and involved, and the cases I provide will have to be simplified; nevertheless, I think they illustrate some important points and I think they may be common enough that everyone reading along can bring to mind their own real case to compare. First, think about divorce. Sometimes divorces proceed amicably between two very reasonable people who have mutually decided that both of their lives will go better if they are no longer married to each other. Often this is not the case, though, and divorce is fueled by and produces more misunderstanding and animosity. I have known several couples who fall into the second camp of unhappy people and one thing that stands out about couples like this is how profound the gap seems to be between their perceptions about basic things. I have had divorcing parties report the same event to me in such different ways that I would never guess they were talking about the exact same point in space and time. For example, one sees the other's sexual infidelity as the thing that undid their relationship, the ultimate betrayal, motivated by selfish drives; the other sees the same infidelity as the inevitable (and in itself not that significant) result of a long process of emotional distancing on the part of the other. This is not necessarily a case of a difference in evaluative perspective, but it is a case of two people who are not able to see things from each other's point of view because of the emotional entrenchment of certain attitudes toward the other. Because divorce can be so painful for people, in this case, the barrier to perspective-taking is more likely to be self-protection than ordinary egoistic bias. In a way, the divorcing spouses cannot afford to see things from the other's point of view if doing so means acknowledging their own responsibility for their problems. These observations about divorce probably seem familiar. My point in making them here is to emphasize the ways in which *knowing* another person well does not necessarily render us good at taking up their point of view.

Second, think of people who have decided to cut someone significant out of their lives (a close relative, say). I have known a number of people who have completely broken ties with a parent, a sibling, or an old friend, in ways that have shocked their inner circles. For those of us who have good relationships with our family members, it can be difficult to understand what could compel someone to cease all communication with their sister, for example. For those who have not experienced toxic family relationships, it's hard to imagine what it would be like to find, for example, that someone in your family so upsets your sense of yourself and your happiness that you cannot bring yourself to speak to them. For those of us who have fairly decent and like-minded people in our families, it's hard to image what it would be like to find, for example, that brother Brad is stealing from you to buy drugs, or that Mom has joined the American Nazi Party. These different experiences form a barrier to perspective-taking that is fortified by our cultural norms surrounding the importance of biological family relationships.

The above example also illustrates the way that our own experience with the world shapes our values and sometimes blinds us to the fact that others, due to different experiences, may see these values in a different way. Perhaps Joan's friend Shaun—who grew up in a very happy family with supportive parents and who never had any reason to think much about the value of family—simply thinks that family is very important and cannot understand how Joan could stop talking to her father even if he wrecks her self-esteem. Surely, Shaun thinks, at Joan's age, armed with therapy, she can now withstand the assault on her sense of self and buck up! But given the way Joan has developed, she may not value 'family' per se, at all. She may have thought about the particular kind of relationships that are worth her attention and care, and the one with her father does not fit the bill. Or, she may value family very much and think that the standards of fulfillment for this value do not require continuing a relationship that harms another of her values (her self-respect).

Surely not having shared experiences can make it difficult to take another person's perspective, but this doesn't mean that sharing similar experiences always makes it easy. This may be particularly true of tragic experiences that are processed in different ways by different people. Consider this moving passage by Nicholas Wolterstorff about the death of his son, Eric:

> The son of a friend—same age as Eric—died a few weeks before Eric. The friend's son committed suicide. The pain of his life was so intense that he took the life that gave the pain. I thought for a time that such a death must be easier to bear than the death of one with zest for life. He wanted to die. When I talked to the father, I saw that I was wrong.
>
> Death is the great leveler, so our writers have always told us. Of course they are right. But they have neglected to mention the uniqueness of each death—and the solitude of suffering which accompanies that uniqueness. We say, "I know how you are feeling." But we don't.
>
> (Wolterstorff 1987, pp. 24–5)[5]

Tragedies call out for helpfulness from friends, but they also seem to be a place where it's easy to go wrong when we assume we understand what other people need. You may assume that a friend wants to hear comforting words, because you think that's what you would want, but your friend may just want you to listen to them rail against the world without saying anything. Here again we see the importance of conversation with our friends to find out what matters to them and, therefore, what we can do to be helpful. In the case of tragic experiences that we have not shared, the listening part of conversation is particularly important.

Until now I have focused mainly on differences in evaluative perspectives—differences in our ultimate values, how we understand and interpret them, and what steps we think we ought to take to fulfill them—because these differences are particularly salient to thinking about how to help each other according to the value fulfillment theory. But there is another very important kind of difference that is relevant to how we help each other, which is also affected by egocentric bias. These are differences in limitations and capacities to change. Some people are more flexible than others and have a greater capacity to give up something that isn't working for them. Some are more cautious and reluctant to change. Some changes might be simply impossible for some people but not for others. These differences in limitations are difficult to recognize, in part because we aren't usually very aware of our own abilities, which makes it easier to assume everyone else is just the same. For example, for my father, eliminating an unhealthy food from his diet is easy. Butter has too much saturated fat, so he switched to margarine. Margarine turned out to have too much trans-fat, so he switched to olive oil. When oatmeal was thought to prevent heart disease, he started eating lots of oatmeal. When it turned out that drinking black tea with dinner was reducing his iron absorption, he stopped drinking black tea with dinner (even though he loves tea). My father is not a foodie. To exaggerate only slightly, he eats for health, not for taste (though he does have a weakness for pecan pie). Obviously, most other people have far more difficulty making change to their diets. For someone like my father, it can be difficult to understand why other people can't just stop eating junk food when they know it's bad for them. In general, when something is easy for you it can be difficult to see just how hard it might be for someone else. Further, when we think of cases where the changes to be made are deep changes to emotionally entrenched values, we can see how differences about capacities to change are highly relevant to our ability to be helpful to our friends. If you think that your friend should be able to do without his homophobic Church, it will be difficult for you to be helpful if he is a long way from being able to do that.

It's important, then, to understand our friends' limitations and capacity to change. But this is a place where egocentric bias seems very natural. It's difficult to tell from observation what a person is truly capable of in changing circumstances—we may overestimate or underestimate—and so we fill in the gaps with our own inner experience.

Egocentric bias is a strong force, but it's not the only possible barrier to understanding other people. Other biases can pull at us in different ways. Racial, ethnic, and gender prejudices are by definition distortions of what other people are like. To "prejudge" a person based on skin color, gender, or sexual orientation, for example, is to assume you know what that person is like based on your schema for people "like that". Prejudices are a barrier to understanding other people because they almost always continue to influence how we see other people even in the face of appearances that contradict our schemas. We also have cultural prejudices that lead us to make assumptions about the values of people in general, including those who share our demographics. Shaun's rather uncritical assigning of absolute value to family relationships is reinforced by a common cultural narrative that makes it easy for him to think that everyone must value family relationships in the same way.

The point about prejudiced schemas leads to another, very practical, barrier to accurate perspective-taking, which is that we simply don't always have the time to think about how things *really* are for other people. Schemas are time-saving devices that allow us to sort the world automatically without having to figure out from scratch each new person we meet, how they're likely to behave, and so on. We just can't make the effort for every one of our friends and family members to correct all the assumptions we've made and investigate the evidence thoroughly.

My point in providing so many examples—and I hope some of them will sound familiar to you—is to help us overcome the idea that it's not that hard to figure out what it's really like for other people we know. I think most of us have a lot invested in thinking that we're at least pretty good at this. Our sense of ourselves as good friends, good partners, good siblings, and so on, requires that we not see ourselves as egomaniacs projecting ourselves onto everyone else. I certainly don't think we are all lazy egomaniacs, but I do think that we can be better than we are at understanding what things are like for others, and that if we value friendship, we ought to try. There are cases where the differences between us and them are so great that we really can't make much progress at all in understanding what things are like for them (cases of serious trauma are often like this). But, first, we don't know that the situation we're in is like this until we try, and, second, we're better off knowing that we don't understand than blithely assuming that we do when we don't.

Fortunately, there is evidence that we can get better at perspective-taking in a way that corrects our egocentric bias. One strategy that seems to work is getting feedback from the target of your perspective-taking that corrects your inaccurate assumptions. According to psychologists William Ickes (1997, p. 299) and colleagues, "It appears that empathic understanding is a trainable skill, and that through the provision of immediate, target-generated feedback a 'generalized' or global improvement in this skill can be obtained." The research supporting this claim was done in a clinically relevant context, with the ultimate goal of determining whether therapists can be taught to better understand their patients (Marangoni et al. 1995). In these studies, participants watched videotapes depicting volunteers who were discussing an ongoing problem together with a psychotherapist. Participants were asked to watch these videos and to report what each volunteer was actually thinking or feeling at various stopping points on the tape. In the experimental "Feedback" condition, after the tape stopped to allow the participant to record their observations, the volunteer's own report about what they were feeling and thinking was displayed on the screen. In the experimental condition, then, the participant could read the volunteer's report and compare it with their own notes about the volunteer. In the control condition no feedback from the volunteer was provided to the participants. Apparently, this kind of feedback works: it made the participants better able to understand what the person was feeling (compared to those who did not receive feedback), and—more remarkably—feedback from one volunteer made the participants better at perceiving the feelings expressed by the other volunteers.

The trouble with the feedback strategy is that it's pretty difficult to get this kind of training for those of us who are not preparing to become therapists. Since we can't count on someone volunteering to help us, we have to actively seek feedback about how well we do at seeing things from their perspective, and this brings us to another point about improving our perspective-taking skills: motivation counts. Apparently, people can be effectively incentivized with money to be more accurate in their assessments of how other people feel, which caused the authors of one study to remark, "When all else fails, if you find yourself faced with someone who just cannot seem to understand your point of view, it might be worthwhile to offer him or her a dollar" (Klein and Hodges 2001, p. 729). This is tongue in cheek, of course, and it's likely that offering your friend a dollar to try harder to understand you would have some undesirable consequences. But the point about motivation is important: we can do better when we are motivated to try to do better.[6]

Fortunately again, there are other forms of motivation besides money. As friends, we are already motivated by concern for our friends for their own sake. And indeed, other research has shown that caring about others' welfare makes us better at empathizing with them.[7] Now, this research shows that we are more likely to *try* to understand the other person if we care about them, not that we are more likely to succeed in understanding them. To be motivated to succeed and to acquire feedback, we have to entertain the possibility that we may have it wrong. Enter humility.

5.3 Humility in Friendship

I think one of the most important virtues for being a helpful friend is a kind of humility. Humility has been a problematic virtue, historically, insofar as it has been associated (particularly in the Christian tradition) with self-abasement, a low opinion of oneself, and feelings of unworthiness.[8] Being self-abasing or undervaluing yourself won't make you a better friend and this isn't the kind of humility that is recommended by the value fulfillment theory. To rescue humility as a moral virtue from its associations with self-abnegation, philosopher Thomas Nadelhoffer, psychologist Jen Wright, and colleagues defend the "decentering" conception of humility. According to them:

> [H]umility does not require us to hold ourselves in low regard, but rather it merely requires us not to be *enamored with* ourselves. Like previous views, this account involves a "reduction" of the self—but here it involves a "decentering" rather than a "decreasing". We cease to experience ourselves as centers of our own universe, recognizing that there is more out there to think about, and to *care* about, than ourselves. On this view, being humble doesn't require us to hold ourselves in low regard (or in a lower regard than is merited). Instead, humility merely requires us to avoid thinking too highly of ourselves. (Nadelhoffer et al. 2017, p. 10)

This seems an important way of conceiving of humility given our purposes.[9] Moreover, if we do tend toward *self*-centeredness, decentering may be exactly what is required. David Foster Wallace (2009) described our natural self-centeredness as the deep (and utterly wrong) "belief that I am the absolute center of the universe, the realest, most vivid and important person in existence". Many good things about friendship are made difficult to achieve if one of the friends clings to the belief that they are the center of it all. (Notice that you need not think you're great to be self-focused; some very insecure people think about themselves a lot.)

De-centeredness is an aspect of a virtue that I have called "perspective" (Tiberius 2008). A person who has perspective sees what really matters, and is able to bring their feelings, thoughts, and actions in line with their appropriate values. In other words, a person with perspective responds to the world in proportion to what merits a response.[10] For example, you might advise someone who is absolutely distraught because their favorite brand of tea has been discontinued, that they really need to get some perspective. People with perspective don't sweat the small stuff, they don't cry over spilled milk, but they do respond when important things are thriving or threatened. The kind of perspective that is key to humility has to do with our responses to our own point of view. A person who lacks perspective in this domain gives their own outlook exaggerated importance, while a person who has perspective understands that theirs is just one point of view among many. To be decentered, then, is to have perspective on the significance of your own beliefs, values, and experience.

De-centeredness is crucial, but there is more to the kind of humility we need to help us with various epistemic biases and limitations. For more we can turn to philosophical work on *intellectual humility*.[11] Here we find the helpful idea of "owning our limitations", especially our limitations concerning what we know and how we learn. Owning our limitations means taking responsibility for them; in more detail, owning our limitations means having "a dispositional profile that includes cognitive, behavioral, motivational, and affective responses to an awareness of one's limitations" (Whitcomb et al. 2017, p. 518).[12] People who own their limitations realize that they have them (cognitive response); are not overbearing and judgmental (behavioral responses); are disposed to improve their information and reasoning (motivational response); and disposed to feel disappointed in themselves if they do become overbearing or pigheaded (affective response). Putting these ideas together, the key to humility in friendship is that we shouldn't be full of ourselves, we shouldn't think we know everything, and we should be willing to take steps to improve.

The kind of humility we need in friendship (from here on, just "humility"), then, has two mutually reinforcing elements:

- De-centeredness (not being self-absorbed, perspective on the importance of one's own point of view).
- Owning of (taking responsibility for) one's limitations.

Owning our limitations is of particular importance to our ability to see things from a friend's point of view. We need to recognize that we don't know everything and that our capacity for understanding someone else's perspective is limited by our imagination, experience, and biases, our assumptions, and our own entrenched set of values. Responding appropriately to what we know about what we don't know (that is "owning") means (at least) not assuming that you know what's best for others, being open to other new sources of information, and having forbearance with respect to any inclination to be "judgy" or domineering. Yet, epistemic humility (humility about what we know) is not enough for a good friend, because a good friend must care about the other, which requires the decentering of our attention and concern. Further, in the context of helping friends, it's not just our epistemic limitations that are important to recognize. We would also do well to acknowledge and own our limitations with respect to various other capacities, for example, our capacities to make sacrifices for others, to convey information sensitively, to think creatively about alternative options, or to think practically about how to get things done.

Humility is part moral virtue (it requires that we not be self-centered and that we acknowledge and own our general limitations) and part intellectual virtue (it requires that we own limitations with respect to understanding how things are for our friends). We can see how the two elements of humility support each other. If you're not thinking about yourself all the time, you are more likely to see how things look from someone else's perspective and, therefore, more likely to realize that your perspective is limited and to care that it is. In turn, owning your limitations (acknowledging them, being concerned about them, and being prepared to correct them), encourages us to explore alternative perspectives with an open mind in a way that thwarts self-absorption.

The properly humble friend, then, is inclined to be less self-focused, less self-satisfied, less certain about her own powers of observation, and disposed to question her assumptions about what other people are like and what they ought to do. Humble friends do not assume that they know what things are like for others. Crucially, they are not high-handed or domineering, both because they know they may not have the right picture *and* because they see that even if they do have the right picture it's not their job to live other people's lives for them.[13]

Humility helps by motivating you to care about how things are for others and by lowering the barriers created by thinking that everything revolves around you. Humility isn't all we need to be helpful friends, of course. Ideally, a helpful friend needs genuine concern for the friend's welfare, respect for the friend's autonomy, empathy or perspective-taking ability, knowledge of human psychology, sensitivity, and skill in communicating difficult information. But I think humility has a special importance. First, this is because we're less likely to try to improve if we don't acknowledge our own limitations. Second, having humility about what we can't do and what we don't know will mitigate the bad effects of our other shortcomings. If you lack sensitivity and you know it, you'll be less likely to say something stupid in your effort to be comforting. If you know that you have trouble understanding people who don't share your faith, you will be less likely to alienate your non-religious friends by insisting that they join your Church. Having humility will make us less likely to blurt, barge in, or take over in disrespectful or annoying ways.

It might help to see the importance of humility more clearly if we think about the capacity for friendship of those who lack this virtue. If we think of humility in friendship as a mean between two extremes, on one side we would have the (relatively underpopulated) domain of limitless approval and the complete absence of any willingness to make judgments about anything that others do.[14] Such a person may not have too much confidence in their own beliefs about what it's like for someone else, but also doesn't really have the right disposition to examine their own assumptions; indeed, this uncritical person is quite satisfied with the assumption that things are exactly as the other person says they are. The person who abdicates judgment really believes "I have no idea what it's like to be you and could never presume to make any suggestions about what you should do". I don't know many people like this in real life, but we can see what would be undesirable about such a friend. If I really am going to do something stupid—something I would recognize as stupid eventually—I would like a friend to take a stand on the stupidity of my plan and stop me. Moreover, sometimes this lack of judgment is really a lack of engagement that does not befit a good friend. In such cases the extreme reluctance to think you know something about what another person's life is like comes from an unwillingness to try to imagine, which itself (in its worst form) comes from a lack of concern. This is no longer an excess of qualities relevant to humility; rather, it is its own vice (indifference or unconcern) that can motivate and reinforce being limitlessly approving. It's easier to approve of someone's stupid plans when you don't really care what happens to them.

On the other side, consider those who are strongly disposed to judge and act confidently on their judgments—bossy know-it-alls and condemnatory, fault-finding critics. Such people don't sound like ideal friends, yet it seems to me that tendencies in this direction are fairly common. There's a character in Jane Austen's novel *Emma* who perfectly represents this vice. Here is Mrs. Elton, explaining how to help her less fortunate friend Jane Fairfax, by preventing her from walking to the post office:

"Oh! do not tell *me*. You really are a very sad girl, and do not know how to take care of yourself.—To the post-office indeed! Mrs. Weston, did you ever hear the like? You and I must positively exert our authority"..."Oh! she *shall not* do such a thing again. We will not allow her to do such a thing again:"—and nodding significantly—"there must be some arrangement made, there must indeed."   (Austen 2008, p. 231)

Jane responds by insisting that she wants to walk, but Mrs. Elton simply insists: "My dear Jane, say no more about it. The thing is determined..." Mrs. Elton "helps" in more significant ways too. Ultimately, Mrs. Elton forges ahead and procures a position for Jane Fairfax, completely oblivious to the fact that Jane has been waiting to announce her engagement to Frank Churchill (a well-heeled young man whose mother had to die before he could go public with his intentions toward Jane). Mrs. Elton is a perfect example of the lack of humility needed for friendship, because she is entirely focused on her own priorities and completely oblivious to her lack of information about Jane.

In my experience, there are more Mrs. Eltons than there are those who lack virtuous humility because they aren't willing to judge at all. Maybe your experience of the distribution of people across this spectrum of judginess is different from mine, but the point is that neither of these extremes makes for a friend who will be well positioned to help you when you need help. The first will let you do whatever you want and the second will do what they want without waiting to find out if that's good for you. To get it just right, a friend needs to be willing to judge but only on the basis of good information when it's available. With a lack of self-absorption and ownership of their limitations, friends with humility are more likely to avoid these problems. Not thinking we are the center of the universe will facilitate the concern we need to have for our friends; it will provide motivation to be genuinely helpful and to consider our limitations. Owning our limitations will dispose us to find the information we lack and to exercise forbearance with respect to being high-handed or domineering.

If we care about our friends, we should be concerned to develop our own humility. But now you will be wondering whether we *can* become less self-absorbed, less inclined to judge, less disposed to assume we know how it is for others, less centered on our own perspectives. Humility was supposed to help us with our limited capacity to take another person's point of view, but what if we are just as limited in our capacity to develop humility?

There is not an abundance of evidence in psychology about the cultivation of humility. Positive psychologists have developed and tested various interventions designed to increase happiness in ways that seem to make people more virtuous. For example, expressing gratitude and performing kind or altruistic acts are thought to have a moderate effect on life satisfaction and positive affect.[15] But I only know of one attempt to create a "humility intervention", consisting in a humility workbook in which participants spend about seven hours answering open-ended questions and providing examples on the following themes:

(a) *Pick* a time when you weren't humble; (b) *Remember* the place of your abilities and achievements within the big picture; (c) *Open* yourself and be adaptable; (d) *Value* all things to lower self-focus; (e) *Examine* your limitations and commit to a humble lifestyle. (Lavelock et al. 2014, p. 103) [The list of themes creates the acronym "PROVE", hence the workbook is called the "PROVE humility workbook"].

The psychologists who conducted this study did find that completing the humility workbook raised participants' scores on the Modesty/Humility subscale of the Values in Action Strengths Inventory (Peterson and Seligman 2004). Moreover, this scale and the PROVE workbook do (at least in part) target the kind of humility that is of interest to us here, because they both emphasize the decentering of the self and the recognition of the limitations of one's own perspective. However, this is just one study conducted on just seventy participants, mainly women from one geographic location. Much more work would need to be done for us to be sure that this kind of intervention works and much more would need to be done to show that it works for everyone.

Of course, we don't have any great evidence that we *cannot* cultivate humility either, and it might be something that we ought to try to do insofar as we care about being a good friend even if we aren't sure of our chances of being successful. Now, making the effort would be a waste of time if it's only the achievement of perfect humility that could make us better friends. If we think that a good friend must have a robust disposition never to respond in any circumstances with quick judgment and self-satisfaction, none of us is likely to become a good friend. But this sets the bar too high. Lesser (and more likely) achievements will still make us better friends.[16] In particular, the *intention* to be more humble is itself likely to be good for friendship, insofar as the intention to cultivate greater humility introduces new policies or habits that affect how we behave toward our friends over time. We will be better friends if we adopt some humility-inducing habits that counter our detrimental tendencies, even if we don't achieve the full-blooded virtue of humility. For example, we can plan to reflect on conversations with friends after the fact and ask ourselves whether we understand their priorities, whether we are assuming they care about the same things we do, and whether we shut them down with condescension or disapproval. These habits do not need to work in a single moment. Usually, the kinds of troubles that require our attention and care are long-term problems that we will revisit with our friends many times. There is a process to being a better, more helpful friend, and that includes imperfect immediate responses, later reflection, recalibration, and more conversation.

To illustrate the point, once again consider Jules, the aspiring but frustrated actress from Chapter 1 whose friend Ash does not want to talk with her about other career options. Perhaps Ash assumes that Jules is like her and would choose an artistic life over any other path, no matter the sacrifices. Perhaps Ash, having grown up in a wealthy family, doesn't really understand the stress Jules experiences living paycheck to paycheck. Ash can't suddenly make it the case that she understands Jules' point of view perfectly, nor can she transform herself into a person who always appreciates what she doesn't know. What she can do, however, is to ask herself to consider the possibility that her experiences make her see things differently from the way Jules sees things. She can say to herself: What if I'm getting this wrong? She doesn't have to reflect on these questions in the moment, because in the context of friendship there are many moments that extend over time. (Of course, there isn't *always* time for navigating the tricky waters of perspective or point of view; sometimes friends need immediate help. In such cases, often what counts as helpful is more obvious anyway: if your friend's car breaks down and their kids are stranded at the daycare, picking up the kids is what you should do and it doesn't matter much if you and your friend have different perspectives on parenting.)

There is some evidence that supports my idea that we ought to try to cultivate humility by changing our habits of thought; we don't have to rely entirely on the point that there's no proof to the contrary. There is, for example, evidence (though not an overwhelming amount) for the effectiveness of general reflective strategies, similar to the strategies I've suggested for humility, against cognitive biases such as confirmation bias. Confirmation bias is the tendency to seek out evidence in favor of what you believe (confirming evidence) and to ignore evidence against what you believe (Nickerson 1998). Some research has been done on "debiasing" techniques and this research suggests that reflective habits such as imagining different points of view, considering competing arguments, and taking more time to make a decision help to overcome confirmation bias and other self-centered biases (Lilienfeld, Ammirati, and Landfield 2009). In research on education there is a large body of research that shows the benefits of meta-cognitive strategies—strategies that involve thinking about how you ought to think through a problem—for various cognitive skills such as memory and understanding (Bransford et al. 2000; Kruger and Dunning 1999; Willingham 2008). Making it a habit to reflect on the fact that you might not know how your friend sees things is a meta-cognitive strategy: it requires you to interrupt and challenge your automatic patterns of attention and inference, and in doing so it may help to reduce egocentric bias.

In this section I have focused almost entirely on the helping friend rather than the one who is helped. If we turn to the beneficiary, we can see that there are some implications of what I've said so far about helping for what it is to be a good friend on the receiving end of help. Given the problem of perspective-taking that has been our focus, there are things that friends who want help can do to be better at living up to the value they place on friendship. They can help their friend understand what it's like to be them. They can appreciate friends who are trying. They can themselves be open to the possibility that they are mistaken about what would be good for them, and that their friend might actually know better. Indeed there are times when our friends have expertise from which we could benefit if we would listen and be open to the possibility that we don't know everything about what is best for us.

These suggestions are a bit tricky, however. Putting the burden of understanding on the friend in need of help seems unfair, particularly when the reason that the helping friend doesn't understand has to do with biases or prejudices. Expecting a friend to appreciate your help when the help is insensitive or just not helpful also doesn't seem fair. In general, it's not easy to be in need of help—both because of the problem that creates the need and because many people don't like to be dependent on others—and it seems like we shouldn't make the situation of someone who is in need of our help worse by putting these other demands of friendship on them. So, we perhaps shouldn't hold our friends to a high standard when they are in need of our help; nevertheless, it is part of being a good friend to be able to receive help from your friends when you need it.

I have also focused, throughout the book, on cases in which our friends are having real problems that require significant help. This might lead to the impression that the virtues of friendship I have been recommending are only needed for people who are particularly gung ho about helping or who have particularly silly friends. Let's pause to bring the discussion down to earth a little bit and focus again on the easier cases (also discussed in Chapter 4). Caring friends spend time together and share their lives with each other. We may sometimes discuss our serious problems with our friends, but to a large degree the way in which we help each other is just by being around, generally supportive, and willing to listen. A friend who is going through a necessary and relatively amicable divorce might just want to hang out, have a beer, and not think about the fact that they're getting divorced. A friend who is temporarily dissatisfied with their job may just want to go for a walk and not talk about work. Notice, though, that empathy, perspective taking, and humility are very useful for these rather mundane situations too. Overbearing, condemnatory people who think they always know what's best are not the people I choose to spend time with when I have even a very minor need of support. Further, empathy, perspective taking, and humility are useful for the good times too: when we have a better understanding of what matters to our friends (or at least an awareness that we need to ask), we will have a better idea of what accomplishments are worth praising and what outcomes are worth celebrating.

5.4 How Open-Minded Should We Be about Our Values?

Can there be too much humility? The two main components of humility—de-centeredness and owning of our limitations—are already described as good states to be in, in that they avoid various excesses and deficiencies (overbearingness, lack of concern for others, abdication of judgment). But there is one specific feature of this kind of humility that we should explore in more detail, which is the openness to others' perspectives that is implied by taking ownership of our limitations. If we respond appropriately to the limitations of our capacity to understand what it's like for someone else, we will be inclined to try to be open to finding out more and to being sympathetic to what we hear.[17] But you might think there are some things we should not be open-minded about. After all, being open-minded about—and therefore unwilling to criticize—a friend's dysfunctional values or unhealthy choices can be bad for the friend's well-being. There are times we really need to hear that we're on the wrong track according to the people who love us. Intuitively, we shouldn't be open-minded about a friend's suicidal tendencies, love of an abusive partner, or commitment to heroin. Where do we draw the line between the different values we understand and accept and the different values we condemn or criticize? And what justifies these distinctions? One way to try to answer these questions would be to appeal to a moral theory that tells us which values are non-negotiable. This would be a good strategy, but I haven't defended a moral theory in this book and I don't want to rely on one now. So, I'm going to give an answer that relies on what I have already said about well-being as value fulfillment and the psychology of values.

The first thing we can say is that the goal of a value-fulfilled life imposes some constraints on which values are negotiable. If we are genuinely concerned about a friend's capacity to live a value-fulfilled life, self-destructive values (like a love of heroin) are not ones we need to accept. This doesn't mean that we should not have humility about our ability to understand what it is like to be someone with a heroin addiction—it's likely to be quite difficult for those of us with no similar experience to understand this; rather, it means that we do not need to withhold our judgment that the addiction isn't good for the person who has it.

This is not the whole of the story, however. It also seems intuitive to say that we should not be open-minded about the values that we take to be basic requirements of decent people: we should not be non-judgmental about a friend's admiration for the Nazis, for example. What can we say about moral differences that is compatible with the value fulfillment theory? As we discussed in Section 2.5, a value-fulfilled life could be a morally bad life—that's a possibility, though not a likely one for most people. This is one of the consequences (a cost, you might say) of taking a subjectivist stance on well-being: if the individual is the ultimate arbiter of what is good for her, then the possibility of a life that is bad for other people but nevertheless good for the person who lives it cannot be ruled out. I think the benefits of being a subjectivist in this sense are worth the costs, and I think this in part because the costs are not as high as they seem. In particular, the value fulfillment theory can make sense of the idea that we do not have to help our friends pursue their immoral values, and the idea that we are permitted to be judgmental about friends' values that we find beyond the pale.

How? First, we can employ the same strategy we use to explain why we can be critical of a friend's *self*-destructive values. For most people, it's hard to live a value-fulfilled life if you're a Mafioso or a genocide enthusiast. It will be hard to make friends, hard to pursue your passions unhindered, hard to avoid a short life span, and so on. Given the kinds of social, mutually dependent creatures we are, life with anti-social values is no picnic.[18] So, we can be intolerant of morally retrograde values for the same reasons we can be intolerant of a love of heroin or a commitment to an abusive relationship.

There is a second way that the value fulfillment theory can make sense of why we do not have to be tolerant of a friend's abhorrent values. When I was in college, there were a number of my women friends for whom being pro-choice was a litmus test for potential long-term boyfriends. You could go out for an evening with someone who was pro-life, but you weren't going to marry him. I'm sure other people had other litmus tests (sometimes religious faith is one), but the idea that "you couldn't be married to someone who..." is probably familiar to many readers. What's going on here? Looking back, I'm certain it was not calculated prudential reasoning: "He may get me pregnant and I may want an abortion, so I'd better not pair up with him!" No, that wasn't it. Rather, I believe the thought was that a man who was against letting a woman make this decision for herself had importantly different values from the women with the litmus test. I don't recall my college friends being terribly precise about what these different values were, but they had to do with autonomy and the role of women in society. The point is that there are some values that are so important to us, so central to our sense of what matters, that we cannot stay friends with people who reject them. In cases like these, open-minded acceptance isn't an option, because accepting the friend's values requires a sacrifice of something that is worth more to you than the friendship. Your options are to abandon the friend, or to try to change them by challenging the value you oppose. Here, what makes it acceptable to be intolerant or judgmental about the values you find abhorrent is the demands that your own values make on you. Certain moral values (respect, fairness, basic kindness, for example) tend to be like this: their inherent standards of fulfillment require that we not tolerate others' disregard of them.

Which values are like this? Which values demand that we not tolerate uncritically their absence in other people? Is it all and only moral values? I don't think so. I'm a vegetarian for moral reasons, but I'm friends with many carnivores. Which values are so important that they are worth sacrificing a friendship for depends on many things including what those values imply about the rest of the person's character (her trustworthiness, for example), the explanation for the difference, and the history of the friendship. The line is not simply drawn at the boundary of the moral and the non-moral (though it may be for some people). People think differently about which values are moral values in the first place and if you define your moral values as those that are requirements for basic human coexistence, then you're likely to think that anyone who doesn't share your moral values is not a good candidate for a friend. But if you think of morality broadly in a way that encompasses all other-regarding norms, then you'll be less likely to think that a moral difference excludes someone as a friend. No one wants to be friends with a murderous thief, but many of us are willing to be friends with those who disagree with us about how much money we should give to charity. The important point for our purposes is that the value fulfillment theory allows for these differences and does not require people to sacrifice or disavow the values that are most dear to them for the sake of being a good friend. At the same time, we can observe that sometimes our moral values are parochial and confining and having a bit of humility about them wouldn't be a bad thing for us. Both these points are compatible with the implications of the value fulfillment theory for how to be a good friend.

From this discussion of differences in values, we can see that the value fulfillment theory helps to explain why friendships between people who have profoundly different values can be so difficult. It can happen that our conception of a value-fulfilled life is so different from our friend's that we can see no way to help them that looks like help to both of us. Such cases—for example, a case in which Sander and his homophobic friend do not share a conception of a value-fulfilled life that includes being openly gay—are very difficult for friends and sometimes result in the dissolution of the friendship. The value fulfillment theory makes sense of this: part of what it is to be a true friend is to care about your friend's well-being and to want to help him or her. If the two of you do not share enough values in common, you will be unable to help in ways that are tolerable to both of you, and this is itself intolerable. Not only does it make it impossible for you to act as a caring friend, it also forces you to acknowledge that your friend sees you as screwing up your own life in a profound way, which presents a rather serious obstacle to mutual respect.

This discussion of profound differences between conceptions of a good life will make some readers think that what really matters in these cases is "who's right?" If the homophobic friend is wrong about whether a value-fulfilled life can include living with a gay partner, then shouldn't that friend defer to Sander's better conception of a good life? Aren't the limits of open-mindedness set at the truth about what is valuable? This is certainly one way to think about it and I am deeply committed to thinking that Sander's homophobic friend is wrong about what matters in life. But I have opted to talk about well-being and benefit without presuming that there are objective values to draw on, and the current discussion provides an opportunity to think about why this lack of objective values doesn't leave us empty-handed.

Furthermore, in the practical context of figuring out how to help a friend, how does it help us to know that we need not exercise open-mindedness when we're *right* about what's valuable? How do we know when we're right? We make better or worse judgments about what's valuable in life by consulting experience and our other values, thinking about the short- and long-term implications of taking this thing to be valuable or not, and considering other possibilities with an open mind. This kind of reflection results in more or less confidence, but it does not result in a discovery of "rightness" that is independent of that confidence.[19] My suggestion is that we should be more open-minded about the things we're less confident of, where our degree of confidence is responsive to the relevant considerations regarding how a particular value fits into a value-fulfilled life. But if we think about it, what else could we do? Of course, there will be people—like Sander's homophobic friend—who draw lines in the wrong places: the deeply homophobic friend will not be open-minded about his anti-gay values and will not be willing to help Sander reconcile his faith with his sexual orientation. Similarly, a friend with deeply anti-church values may not be open-minded about the value of faith, and will not be likely to help Sander with his goal of reconciliation either. But closed-minded friends are not going to be helped by philosophical arguments about what the right values are.

This section has mainly focused on making room for the idea that we do not always have to be open-minded about another person's values. But we should recall the context here: good friends need to try to see things from the point of view of the friend they are trying to help, and this is made difficult by self-centeredness, self-satisfaction, and closed-mindedness. It's important to explain why a theory of well-being does not imply that we must tolerate terrible values in our friends, but tolerance of terrible values is not (for most of us) the main temptation. That said, there may be exceptions. There may be some people for whom the real danger is excessive open-mindedness and acceptance due to cowardice or an obsessive need to please. Sometimes friends are so invested in being supportive that they fail to challenge each other when they really should. Women may be particularly at risk for this, because we are encouraged to be pleasant and sympathetic. Being sympathetic, pleasant, and uncritical when our friends are almost certainly ruining their lives is not a way to be a good friend. Granted, the need for a less pleasant, more critical response from a friend has to be balanced with other considerations such as the capacity for the needy friend to change and the likely effects of criticism on a supportive friendship. But if things are really dire, the risk may be worth it. Fear of rocking the boat or an obsessive need to make people happy in the short term are not good reasons for refusing to critically assess a friend's values.

Humility, then, is a virtue of a friend when it functions together with respect, compassion, and genuine concern for the friend's well-being. These other virtues constrain when one ought to be open-minded about and accepting of a friend's different values. The dispositions involved in humility are also constrained by our own values and their relative importance.

5.5 Friendship and Moral Decency

Stepping back now, and thinking about the person who values friendship, we can see how well-being as value fulfillment engages people's self-interested motivations and their more altruistic interests at the same time. Because the value of friendship involves other people and cannot be fulfilled without attending to the concerns of others, the aspiration to fulfill this value taps two sources of motivation for the same goal. So, the fact that our values reach out beyond our psychological states means that in aspiring to live value-full lives we have reasons to uphold standards in a way that might lead to self-improvement or transformation. Further, in aspiring to achieve value-full lives over the long term, we may have reasons to modify our old values, adopt certain new values (or new specifications of abstract values) that we didn't have before, which might also lead to self-improvement or transformation.

One transformation that is suggested by the cultivation of humility has to do with humility's scope. I argued in the previous section that we have reasons to adopt strategies for humility toward our friends. But now I think we can see that there is a case for humility with a broader scope. Notice that in addition to being good friends, most of us care about being morally decent people. Few of us care about being moral superstars, but we also don't want to be jerks. If we think about our relationships to other members of our moral community as analogous to friendship, we can see the importance of humility for being a morally decent person. Consider that one important moral concern is the welfare of our fellow creatures and that making others' lives better means making their lives better in a way that is sensitive to their point of view. If these things are true, then in order to be morally decent people we should have some humility about what things are like for other people.[20] As we learn about the importance of humility in friendship, we may come to see that being morally decent also requires a certain amount of humility. In other words, we may begin by valuing humility as a part of friendship and come to think of it as a virtue with much wider purpose in a way that transforms how we think about what it is to be a morally decent person. Here we can see the way in which our values can change over time as we reflect on what they mean and what they demand from us.

One way in which greater humility can make us better moral agents is by making us less quick to assume that we know what it is like to be a member of a group that is treated badly, thereby improving our ability to help (or at least not harm) such groups of people. To make the point dramatically, consider the fact that many colonizers thought that they were improving the lives of the people in the colonies by bringing them "culture" or by "civilizing" them in ways that completely disrespected the values and perspectives of the colonized. There isn't much humility in the history of colonialism, at least on the part of the colonizers.[21] I'm not naïve enough to think that character development is the solution to oppression! But we do see an extreme lack of humility in some of the worst examples of immoral agency and so we might hope that greater humility would be a moral improvement. Notice, again, that we do not need a highly stable disposition that produces reliably humble behavior and attitudes across all contexts (though it would be nice to have that). Rather, it would help just to have a policy of asking sincerely how well we understand the point of view of other people. If this would be a moral improvement, then for many of us, the path toward greater value fulfillment is also the path to better moral agency, because the changes required to fulfill the value of friendship are changes that stand to make us better moral agents as well.

It's worth saying that other values can also lead us to change our habits and to transform ourselves for the better. Take psychological happiness—something most people value—as an example. If the happiness intervention studies are correct, and if we value our own happiness, then we ought to cultivate habits of expressing gratitude and kindness (Lyubomirsky 2008). Fully realizing the value of happiness could have the effect of highlighting the value that others contribute to our lives, making us more aware of the value of kindness, and so on, which will, in turn, change the system of values that we have. Someone could begin a gratitude exercise because they want to feel happier, learn from the exercise to reflect on the nice things that people have done for them, and then come to give more weight to the value of close relationships.

Many projects we take on require patience, perseverance, and courage to pursue well; many other projects require working cooperatively with others in ways that require some compassion and generosity. Many normal human values cannot be successfully realized without attending to the interests and concerns of other people, because almost any project that is worth doing requires a teacher, an audience, an apprentice, a team, or a co-worker. Because our values reach beyond us and compel us to meet their standards, the goal of a value-fulfilled life creates room for high aspirations for human improvement.

5.6 Conclusion

When we want to help others, we should attend to their point of view. There are a number of barriers to understanding or grasping someone else's perspective on their life, their values, circumstances, and options. We can and do make mistakes about what people really care about, how they understand or conceptualize what they care about, how they understand their options, what counts as success for them, which things matter more in life than others, and how they understand the facts about risk, rewards, and opportunities. Egocentric bias inclines us to think that other people see things exactly as we do, but this just isn't true. In this chapter I've argued that cultivating habits that make us less self-centered and more aware of our limitations is a good way to try to overcome some of the biggest barriers we face as friends who want to help. This is good for us insofar as we value friendship as part of what it is to live a good life for ourselves. Of course, becoming better at helping is also better for those we aim to help.

6

Conclusion

In the first part of this book, I argued that when we want to benefit another person—to do something for his or her own sake—we ought to pay attention to that person's values. The values that the person has at the moment are important but not decisive, because these values might not be the ones that the person can best fulfill together over time. When we aim to help people we should attend to the goal of a life rich in value fulfillment that is shaped by the value system of the individual we aim to help. The goal of a value-fulfilled life that is responsive to the individual's values, and to the facts about how these values could change, is the right anchor for our judgments about well-being, because it provides both an intimate connection to the person and a way of identifying improvements. Judgments about what would be an improvement are again tied to the person, but in practice they are also inevitably informed by the perspective of the person trying to help.

A major theme of this book has been that people's systems of values are complex and involve many interrelationships among various values and standards of fulfillment. It can be really hard to figure out how to make these systems better. The second part of the book focused on how friends can (and can't) help. A life rich in value fulfillment is not a clear and vivid destination like a painted target, or Disneyland. Rather, we fill in the details as we reflect on our lives, our values, our circumstances, and our options, often together with people who care about us and our point of view, but who also bring their own understanding of what matters to the conversation. As merely human friends, we can't avoid bringing our own values to the conversation, but we can be more helpful in this process if we have some humility about this. We should acknowledge that we do not tend to be very good at grasping the intricacies of other people's value systems and we are frequently just ignorant of the facts that are relevant to how another person's life could be improved.

I have not provided any simple rules for how to help people, nor have I presented a formula for ascertaining whether a life is going well or badly. So, in the end, there are no easy answers for Maxine, Sander, or Jules. Simple solutions are not possible, because of the complexity of the systems of values that they (like most people) have. Our deepest values are not interchangeable and there's no single "uber-value" we can convert everything to in order to decide what to do. We need to try to fit these ultimate values together as best we can by adjusting how we prioritize them, the means we take to them, and how we understand success in terms of them, in ways that are sustainable. This is challenging, and it's made even more challenging by the fact that our environments are also changing. On the plus side, there are some values that are anchors for most of us: the value of friendship is one of these; the values of health and happiness are others. When we help people to attain greater value fulfillment we are not starting from nothing; friends in need of help come to us with a system of values already in place and a range of alterations they are capable of making. With this background, we do our best. The process of figuring out how to create a life with greater value fulfillment is as difficult as it needs to be.

As I've articulated it, the value fulfillment theory avoids making assumptions about values or standards that we *must* have. The constraints on what counts as a value-fulfilled life that I've discussed here derive, ultimately, from the individual—from the facts about them and their circumstances and how they can change. I hope I've shown that this is not a pernicious form of individualism. For most of us, our central values encompass other people in profound ways and it is our social circumstances that are the most salient. Indeed, I've argued that good friends can help each other figure out what to value and how. They can do this by illuminating conflicts in a friend's system of values, pointing out ways that those values could be better pursued, and by using their own point of view to help envision a value-fulfilled life that is within reach for their friend. There are no objective standards for value external to the individual, but the individual is enmeshed in a web of relationships with other people and communities.

I've avoided making these assumptions about external standards in part because of a concern to speak to social scientists and value skeptics, and in part because of my basic Humean philosophical temperament. The only argument I have provided against such standards is the implicit argument that we can get along pretty well without them, and I don't expect this argument to convince those who disagree with me for their own philosophical reasons. For this reason, it's worth pointing out once more that much of what I've said about helping people is compatible with there being more objective standards for the values that make human life go well. If you think that pleasure, knowledge, and achievement are goods that must be part of any well-lived life, and you want to help your friend live a better life, you will still need to know how your friend thinks about these values, what standards they take to determine success, what else they value, how their values fit together, and how they can change. If your friend has profoundly different values from you, you will need to know how to help them see the value of what you think is important and this will mean trying to see things from their perspective.

Although I have avoided making assumptions about what values a person *must* have, or what standards they must adhere to on pain of irrationality or guaranteed misery, I have certainly said a lot of things about what people should do. You should develop values that you can pursue together over time, you should help your friends figure out how they can develop values they can pursue together over time, and you should have some humility about what you can know about other people. I think you should almost certainly value emotional happiness, health, friendship, and meaningful work. Strictly speaking, my "shoulds" are aimed at people with whom I share certain values that ground these imperatives, but I do think that audience is fairly large. So, you might wonder, who am I to tell you what to do? At the risk of seeming defensive, I'll close with some thoughts about this question.

Who is a philosopher to tell other people what to do? This is a question I have grappled with professionally in part because of my interest in how philosophical thinking fits into the larger context of research on well-being, happiness, and the good human life, and in part because in our current cultural moment there are many who think that psychologists are the real experts on these topics. Of course, philosophers have been writing about happiness, well-being, and virtue far longer than psychology has been a discipline, but perhaps this is just a very long-running mistake. To frame the question in philosophical terms, it is a question about the legitimacy of first-order normative (or prescriptive) ethics. What sense can be made of the long-standing project in philosophical ethics of recommending courses of action for others to take?

On certain views about what ethics is, it isn't too difficult to see why prescriptive ethics is a legitimate project. If we think that ethical properties are special properties that cannot be discovered by scientific study, but that can be revealed by careful philosophical reflection, then it makes sense that philosophers would be specially positioned to figure out what these properties are and which actions have them. Alternatively, if we think that ethical truths are derived from rational principles, philosophers who study the nature of reason also have an obvious role to play.

But if ethics is not about discovering special, non-natural properties or discerning principles of reason, if instead ethics has to fit into the ordinary natural world that is studied by scientists, then what business do philosophers have telling people what to do? The short answer to this question is that philosophy in the sense I'm talking about (the kind of philosophy I've tried to do in this book) is just inevitable for anyone who cares about anything and wants to know what to think, feel, or do about it. Discovering the facts about the world does not get us out of doing ethics. It might seem as if it does. Sam Harris (2010) has argued that we don't need ethics anymore because we now have science that can tell us what makes people happy. But this approach doesn't replace ethics with science; it makes a huge ethical assumption (that happiness is the one and only appropriate goal of human life) and uses science to draw conclusions from it. Why start with that assumption in the first place? I think it's not a bad assumption, but it's certainly not one that has universal consensus, particularly if we specify that happiness is something entirely subjective. If we try to avoid reflecting on what is worthwhile and what that means, we'll just end up making philosophical assumptions about it anyway.

What kind of reflection is in order? In ethics, the answer is: Reflection on what matters and what to do about it. When we begin to reflect in this way, we have no other choice but to start with our values and go from there. We are guided by a multitude of norms and values and our deliberation can go better or worse depending on how well these norms and values are interpreted, acknowledged, put together, and applied. Philosophy helps us to think through how to interpret, compare, and apply the various norms that bear on our choices, including our choices of which values to prioritize. The standard for success here is not accuracy, but instead making sense to your audience and solving a practical problem that requires a choice to be made. What needs to be done is to identify the values and standards that are at stake—which may include epistemic norms against self-deception and in favor of open-mindedness—and to figure out what these norms jointly imply for choice and action. Philosophers, then, can make a "proposal", in Philip Kitcher's (2011) words, for how we ought to proceed in our ethical lives: how we ought to reason together to figure out what's best to do.

To say that the standard of success for practical philosophy is not accuracy is not to say that anything goes, or that "it's all relative". There are better and worse proposals and better and worse ways of following them.[1] In this book I have made a proposal for how it makes sense to think about helping each other, especially our friends, to live better lives.[2] Obviously, it isn't just professional philosophers who can make such proposals, but I think making such proposals is just what practical philosophy is (whether the person who is doing it is a novelist, historian, pastor, or philosopher). Further, it may be that philosophers have some skills that make us good "proposers". If philosophers are good at anything, we are good at making distinctions among different values and thinking about what is entailed by the application of a set of norms. That is what we are trained to do, and these skills are useful for making coherent proposals that are designed to guide people to the relevant norms and questions.

David Hume analogized practical philosophy (or practical morality, as he called it) to the art of painting; practical philosophy succeeds when it creates something beautiful that moves the viewer. Natural philosophy—Hume's project—is like anatomy; it succeeds when the body is accurately described. But Hume also thought that the painter should learn from the anatomist:

An anatomist, however, is admirably fitted to give advice to a painter; and 'tis even impracticable to excel in the latter art, without the assistance of the former. We must have an exact knowledge of the parts, their situation and connexion, before we can design with any elegance or correctness. And thus the most abstract speculations concerning human nature, however cold and unentertaining, become subservient to *practical morality*; and may render this latter science more correct in its precepts, and more persuasive in its exhortations. (Hume 1739, p. 395)

Drawing on Hume's analogy, I would say that normative or prescriptive ethics is like painting insofar as the resulting product is intended to be compelling or moving and is informed but not determined by the "cold and unentertaining" facts about the subject matter. What's missing from the metaphor of painting is that a painting is completed by the painter and intended to be regarded and appreciated by the viewer, but not touched or altered. Kitcher's idea that the philosopher makes a proposal is better in this regard, because proposals are entertained, engaged, and sometimes negotiated. Another metaphor that I have found illuminating is the metaphor of recipes and cooking. A recipe contains a list of ingredients and a set of instructions for how to put them together, but a good cook will tweak the ingredients and the instructions to suit their own circumstances. Practical philosophy creates recipes for living and for thinking about how to live better, but the recipe can't be followed unreflectively. You have to use judgment to figure out how to apply the suggestions to your own case, just as a chef has to use judgment to follow the recipe that says "add salt and pepper to taste". The point of this metaphor is not that philosophers are expert cooks; many of us do not cook well at all (even metaphorically). Rather, the point is that philosophers may have skills that enable us to write good recipes that will then be adopted and adapted by others.

In this book I have tried to create a recipe for a good human life and good human friendships that can guide our choices about how to live and how to help each other. You can't follow my "recipe" without asking questions about what your values are, how they differ from other people's values, what you know or don't know about other people's situations, and so on. Still, the recipe provides guidance because it directs your attention to a certain set of ingredients—the ingredients we need for creating our own feast. Scientific studies about well-being also provide guidance, but of a different kind. Scientific studies can tell you how many blessings to count if you want a bit more life-satisfaction, how meditation will reduce your stress, or what kind of exercise will improve your mood. These may be important things to know. When we want to feel satisfied with our lives, reduce stress, and improve our mood, this science is exactly what we need. But no scientific study is going to tell us whether feeling satisfied is a *good* goal to have, whether reducing stress is worth sacrificing something else we value (such as demanding and meaningful work), or whether a better mood is more important than whatever else we could do with the time it takes to improve it. To answer these questions, we need to think about our values, how they fit together, and what they mean to us—which is just the kind of ethical reflection that my recipe puts on the table. If we take Hume's point seriously, science and philosophy need to work together on the ethical topics that are so important to human life. The role of the sciences is to tell us what human beings are like. The role of the ethicist is to use that information to create a compelling vision of what we could be.

Notes

Chapter 1

1. There are many popular books written by psychologists about how to be happy, such as Gilbert 2006; Lyubomirsky 2008; and Seligman 2004. And the online advice is piling up. See, for example, Mayo Clinic, "How to be Happy: Tips for Cultivating Contentment", May 2015, http://www.mayoclinic.org/healthy-lifestyle/stress-management/in-depth/how-to-be-happy/art-20045714; WikiHow, "How to be Happy Always", June 2017, http://www.wikihow.com/Be-Happy-Always; Beth Cooper, Aug. 2013, "10 Simple, Science-Backed Ways to Be Happier Today", https://www.fastcompany.com/3015486/how-to-be-a-success-at-everything/10-simple-science-backed-ways-to-be-happier-today.
2. From this point on, I will use the word "well-being" rather than the word "happiness". As much as some authors (Annas 1995; Bloomfield 2014) have tried to vindicate the word "happiness" to talk about a general goal in a human life, I think those who use the word to refer to positive feelings (rather than the broader notion of the prudential good) are winning the day.
3. These difficulties are sometimes exaggerated by those of us who want to rationalize not doing anything. The Life You Can Save (https://www.thelifeyoucansave.org) and Effective Altruism (https://www.effectivealtruism.org) are good sources of information.
4. Simine Vazire 2010 has done some very interesting work on the comparisons between self-knowledge and knowledge of others. She has found that there are regular differences in the kinds of things we know better about ourselves than others, and vice versa.
5. Philosophers distinguish between first order, normative theories and *metaethical* theories. The former aim to answer questions about what is good/bad, right/wrong, virtuous/vicious; the latter focus on questions about normative language (e.g., how do words like "good" and "right" convey the force they seem to convey?) or about the status of normative claims (e.g., are claims such as "giving money to charity is the right thing to do" true or false in the way that ordinary empirical claims are true or false?). Many philosophers also distinguish between ethics and morality. Ethics is the broadest field that encompasses the most general questions

about how to live one's life; morality is more narrowly concerned with duties, particularly the duties we owe to others. This book defends one *normative* theory about a particular domain within ethics.

6. This makes me a *constructivist* about ethics, and it puts me in opposition to philosophers who think that ethics is about something else, such as identifying objective values. For a more detailed discussion of constructivism about well-being, see my 2017.
7. Philosophers who think that well-being is the *only* value, and that all of ethics and morality should be organized around it, are often called "welfarists"; welfarists are the inheritors of utilitarianism. This is a prominent but not uncontroversial position in philosophy. For general discussion, see Crisp 2016 and Keller 2009b.
8. My project is different from Darwall's: I am not offering an analysis of the concept of well-being. As will become clear to those familiar with Darwall's book, I also don't agree with Darwall about the right normative theory. Darwall favors an Aristotelian view according to which welfare (or well-being) consists in appreciatively engaging in objectively valuable activities.
9. Cheshire Calhoun's (2015) treatment of the meaning of life is very sympathetic to my account of well-being. I regret that her 2018 book, *Doing Valuable Time: The Present, the Future, and Meaningful Living*, was not available in time for me to take account of it here.
10. Thanks to Lauren Kuykendall for pointing this out. According to her, in organizational psychology, the term "value" would be reserved for something more abstract or ideal.
11. Jason Raibley 2010, 2013 also defends a value fulfillment theory of well-being. His view and mine have much in common and I have benefitted tremendously from reading his work.
12. Anna Alexandrova 2013, 2017 has argued that there is little hope (or need) for a *comprehensive* theory of well-being that serves every purpose (from geriatric medicine, to public policy, to everyday questions about how to help friends). For those who share her skepticism, my project could be seen as a response to her challenge for more "mid-level" theories that are sensitive to considerations of the kind of creature whose well-being we are interested in, the nature of the inquirer, and the circumstances of the inquiry (Alexandrova 2017, pp. 51–2).
13. I do think that, in the end, the theory one constructs should end up having reasonable implications for all sorts of cases. But I don't think testing against possible counterexamples is where we should start and I believe that too much philosophical energy is expended on this kind of testing.

14. This three-part taxonomy was proposed by Parfit 1984.
15. The two main philosophical defenders of hedonism about well-being are Roger Crisp and Fred Feldman (Crisp 2006a, 2006b; Feldman 2004, 2010). These two have recently been joined by Ben Bramble 2016. In psychology, Ed Diener (Diener 1984 and Diener, Scollon, and Lucas 2003) takes positive affect (with low negative affect) to be one of three constituents of subjective well-being (life satisfaction and domain satisfaction are the other two). In behavioral economics, Daniel Kahneman 2003 takes what he calls "objective happiness" to be central to well-being. Objective happiness is defined in terms of "instant utility", which is determined by the degree to which a person is pleased or distressed by their current experience.
16. In philosophy, see Angner 2011; Brandt 1979; Griffin 1986; Heathwood 2006; Railton 1986. In economics, see Harsanyi 1977. For a general discussion of the view, see Heathwood 2016.
17. For objective list theories, see Arneson 1999, Finnis 2011. Eudaimonist theories inspired by Aristotle take well-being to consist in the fulfillment of our species nature (Badhwar 2014; Besser-Jones 2014; Bloomfield 2014). A different form of eudaimonism takes well-being to consist in the fulfillment of our individual nature (Haybron 2008a, 2008b). It may be more standard in the philosophical literature to use "perfectionism" to refer to nature fulfillment theories of well-being (Bradford 2016). I am following Haybron in using terminology that will be more familiar to psychologists. Note that the main proponent of perfectionism, Thomas Hurka 1993, defends it as a theory of intrinsic value, not a theory of well-being.
18. For eudaimonism in psychology, see Ryan and Deci 2001; Waterman 2013.
19. See Sumner 1996. Tiberius and Plakias 2010 defend a version of life satisfaction theory. (My own view has changed since this publication.) As mentioned in footnote 15, one of the founders of life satisfaction research in psychology defines subjective well-being in terms of overall life satisfaction, satisfaction in important areas or "domains" of life, and positive affect. See Diener 2000; Diener, Scollon, and Lucas 2003.
20. For example, Adams 1999; Fletcher 2013; Kraut 1994.
21. For an excellent overview of hybrid theories, see Woodard 2016.
22. In his very influential book, *Welfare, Happiness, and Ethics*, L. W. Sumner 1996 identified descriptive and normative adequacy as the two criteria of success for theories of well-being. I am basically in agreement with Sumner, though my interpretation of "normative adequacy" is broader and I have added a third criterion.

23. I have learned that the term "normative" has different meanings in different fields. "Normative" is the word philosophers use to describe judgments that give us justifying reasons to do things (or in the case of epistemic normativity, to believe things). Normative judgments (about what *should* be) are typically opposed to descriptive judgments (about what *is* the case). "Normative" in philosophy (unlike in psychology) does not have to do with what is typical or statistically normal. Note that Sumner, who introduced this terminology, takes normative adequacy to require that the resulting theory is adequate to playing a particular role in moral theory such as welfarism (the view that the right action is to maximize welfare for all). I don't disagree, but moral theory is not my main concern here.
24. Bernard Williams 1985 coined the phrase "thick concept". For more on well-being as a thick concept see my 2013a.
25. For more on the division of labor between philosophers and psychologists see my 2017.
26. There is a sizeable literature on this critique of virtue ethics. See Section 3.3 for more discussion and references.
27. For those wanting an entrée into this enormous literature, I recommend the following: Crisp 2016; Fletcher 2016a, 2016b; my 2015.
28. Hedonists have responded in different ways, but they haven't given up (Crisp 2006b; Feldman 2004; Silverstein 2000).
29. The main philosopher who defends a life satisfaction theory of well-being, L. W. Sumner 1996, argues that life satisfaction only constitutes well-being if it is informed and autonomous. This may solve the problem Haybron raises, but it also creates the new problem of articulating and defending the additional criteria. I myself have argued that a modified version of life satisfaction theory may succeed, though I've now come to think the value fulfillment theory is superior to what I called "the value based life satisfaction theory" (Tiberius and Hall 2010; Tiberius and Plakias 2010).
30. These same philosophers often think that our subjective point of view isn't perfect as it is, and I agree with this. As I said above, because the value fulfillment theory identifies well-being with a life rich in the fulfillment of *appropriate* values, it does allow us to go beyond the subjective perspective. This raises some important questions that we'll take up in the next chapter (Sections 2.3 and 2.4).
31. This point about normative adequacy raises complex issues about the kinds of reasons that a theory of well-being ought to provide. For a defense of a sympathetic view about the kinds of reasons well-being provides, see Rosati 1996. For an opposing view, see Sarch 2011. I won't

belabor this here, because I think the debate about well-being-based reasons ultimately turns on very large questions in ethical theory and metaethics about which there is reasonable disagreement. Reasons for defenders of objective theories to read the rest of the book anyway follow in the text.

32. The problem of adaptive preferences is one specific type of this problem. In a nutshell, the problem is that subjective attitudes can adapt to oppression and deprivation, which means that a subjective theory of well-being can have the implication that a person who has never had the opportunity to develop desires for more is doing quite well. This is troubling if it leads us to conclude that nothing needs to change for people who are oppressed. For more discussion of adaptation and value fulfillment see Section 3.5. For general discussion of the problem, see Sen 1987 and Sumner 1996.

33. Versions of "idealized desire satisfactionism" have been defended by Brandt 1979; Griffin 1986; Railton 1986; Sidgwick [1907] 1962; Sobel 2009.

34. Note that this problem in particular could be solved by the distinction between ultimate and instrumental desires, since Lonnie's ultimate desire is surely to feel better. Full-information theories solve the problem in a different way that at least allows for the possibility that someone could have a defective ultimate desire.

35. For a taste of the criticisms of informed desire theory, see Rosati 1995; Sobel 1994; my 1997; Velleman 1988.

36. Someone might argue that value fulfillment theory is, ultimately, a species of desire satisfactionism. I think that the role of emotion and judgment in valuing, and in the appropriateness of values, make the two theories importantly different, but I don't think this is an important matter to settle. If the value fulfillment theory is a version of desire satisfactionism, then this is true only at a very high level of abstraction.

37. I find it interesting that this objection to subjectivism has received a lot less attention than the various problems of defective desires. My hunch is that this is due to philosophers' preoccupation with articulating the boundaries of concepts rather than attending to how philosophy can help us live our lives. The latter was the preoccupation of the Ancient philosophers—perhaps it's not a coincidence that Kraut is a specialist in Ancient philosophy.

38. On the psychological methods see, for example, Diener, Inglehart, and Tay 2013; Keyes, Shmotkin, and Ryff 2002. For the claim that people do value life satisfaction, domain satisfaction, and positive affect, see Diener 2000.

39. For example, Cohen, Kamarck, and Mermelstein 1994; Ryff 1989; Steger et al. 2006.
40. For a very helpful discussion of Aristotle's view about the importance of pleasure to the activities that comprise the human good, see Kraut 1979.

Chapter 2

1. I use different verbs to talk about the fulfillment of values: we fulfill, realize, achieve, or succeed in terms of our values. This is intentional; as we'll see, what counts as value fulfillment (and therefore which verb is appropriate) depends on the value and how it is understood by the person whose value it is.
2. To those familiar with debates in metaethics, the terms "cognitive" and "judgment" will raise questions about the status of the normative judgments involved in valuing; for an overview of the relevant debate, see van Roojen 2016. The value fulfillment theory is not a metaethical theory; it is intended to be neutral about how best to understand the semantics and the psychology of normative judgments.
3. Connie Rosati argues that fittingness is the defining feature of the property of the personal good: something that is good for a person *fits* her (Rosati 2006). Rosati is developing a metaethical theory of well-being, so she and I put the notion of 'fit' to somewhat different uses, but I have been influenced by her work here.
4. For an illuminating discussion of caring, see Jaworska 2007.
5. Notice that these affective patterns are likely to include dispositions to experience some negative emotions (such as shame) when the value in question is at risk.
6. I want to leave open that these judgments about reasons could be given an expressivist interpretation, though I'm not assuming this here. For a defense of expressivist semantics about reason judgments, see Gibbard 1992. See also footnote 2.
7. The language of "reflective endorsement" is often associated with Kantian theories according to which reflection leads us to acknowledge that we are bound by reason to value our rational nature, or to follow certain rational principles. I don't follow this Kantian path, but I like the language of reflective endorsement because it suggests thinking things through and making a commitment on the basis of reasons. I explore what counts as reflection in detail in my 2008.

8. There is some evidence for this in the research on personal projects, which I mentioned in Chapter 1. According to this research, personal projects that include both affective and cognitive components are more likely to be successful and also more likely to promote happiness (life satisfaction and positive affect), which is a core value for most people (Little, Salmela-Aro, and Phillips 2007).
9. This is true for normal adult human beings, anyway. If we want to talk about the values of animals or humans with diminished cognitive capacities, we should focus on their affective and motivational orientation. (And in some such cases it may make more sense to talk about their cares, concerns, or attachments.) More about such cases in Section 4.5.
10. For more on this account of valuing and values, see my 2000, 2008. The precise way I have delineated the features of values has changed over the years, but the basic pictures of values as involving emotions, desires, and judgments that form relatively stable patterns has remained the same. For sympathetic treatments, see Anderson 1995; Raibley 2010; Schmuck and Sheldon 2001.
11. This is roughly Chris Heathwood's 2011 solution to the problem on behalf of desire satisfactionism.
12. Intrinsic disvalues, often partly constituted by aversion, may have a special role to play in ill-being. On the distinct importance of aversion, see Arpaly and Schroeder 2013.
13. In my 2008, I argued that life satisfaction and self-direction are two values that are presupposed by anyone who is committed to living a life that is good from her own point of view. I'm still convinced by this argument, but I don't count on it here.
14. In philosophical terminology we could say that the focus on values helps explain the normativity of well-being.
15. Notice that many of the unintuitive implications of desire theories stem from the fact that we do not take all of our desires to give us reasons that justify action. But values just are those patterns of attitudes that we take to be reason-giving, so a value-based theory of well-being will not have this problem. Also, note that Sumner understands life satisfaction as comprising an affective and a cognitive response, unlike psychologists who think of life satisfaction as a global cognitive appraisal (Diener, Scollon, and Lucas 2003). This may put Sumner's view on better footing with respect to this point.
16. I take value fulfillment to be additive (Bradley 2009), which means that overall value fulfillment is determined by adding up individual moments or components of value fulfillment. An alternative to this is the *holistic*

paradigm-resemblance view defended by Jason Raibley 2012. According to this holistic approach, momentary bits of well-being (individual moments of value fulfillment) contribute to overall well-being insofar as they make for greater resemblance to a paradigmatically well-lived life. A person achieves well-being to the degree that she resembles the paradigm of the flourishing agent and, as Raibley (2010, p. 596) puts it, "[i]n order to resemble this paradigm, a person must (a) have values, as opposed to mere desires or enjoyments, (b) actively realize these values, and (c) maintain the physical and psychological attributes that are the causal basis for the disposition to succeed". I am tempted by Raibley's holism and I have learned a tremendous amount from his work, but I think that the notion of a paradigm introduces unnecessary complexity to an already fairly complex theory.

17. Note that the goal of a value-fulfilled life (the life, or set of lives, richest in value fulfillment) is an aspirational goal, an ideal. We can live very well without achieving the greatest value fulfillment.
18. See Haidt 2006; Haybron 2008b; Wilson 2002. I have discussed this research in detail in my 2008 and 2013.
19. This is one of the reasons Raibley 2012 rejects the rational life plan view.
20. On the "crib test", as Fred Feldman has called it, see Feldman 2010. See Kraut 1979 for a different perspective on a similar thought experiment.
21. I gravitate toward a *constructivist* construal of these norms, rather than a *reductive* construal. See my 2012, 2017.
22. Actual desire satisfaction theories can say the same thing about ultimate desires. An ultimate desire is defective, for desire satisfactionism, if it will prevent more satisfaction in the future than it will produce now; it is not intrinsically defective (Heathwood 2005).
23. Chang has a different target. She aims to show that epistemically transformative experiences do not undermine standard approaches to rational choice according to which we choose rationally on the basis of the value of the options. But her arguments work well for my purposes, too.
24. Proving that this is the best way to think about the value of happiness would take us deep into metaethics, which would be quite a diversion. The divide between subjectivism and objectivism about value in metaethics is deep and long-standing, and I don't think it really matters for the conversation about happiness and well-being. Ultimately, it's difficult to imagine a person for whom their own happiness is not an appropriate value, especially when we see that the emotional states that comprise happiness are themselves valuing attitudes.

Chapter 3

1. The experience machine thought experiment was discussed in Section 1.4. Basically, the experience machine is a very advanced virtual reality program, and the thought experiment is designed to get us to see that there are some things we value other than our own experiences.
2. Does the value fulfillment theory accept the experience requirement (Griffin 1986) as a necessary condition on well-being, then? I think that in most cases, given what values are and how people regard their fulfillment, value fulfillment is experienced. But there might be some values for some people that are not understood in this way. Think of parents who value the happiness of their children and who sincerely claim that their own lives would be worse for them if their children suffered, whether or not they (the parents) ever knew about the suffering. In such cases, well-being would be affected though experience would not be. I don't want to rule out this possibility, so I will remain agnostic about the experience requirement (which says that nothing that isn't experienced by you could possibly affect your well-being).
3. These standards sustain what Alasdair MacIntyre 1984 called the "goods inherent to a practice".
4. For similar views about ends and goals, see Carver and Scheier 1998 on abstract goals, Richardson 1990 on the specification of ends, and Schmidtz 1994 on "maieutic ends" ("an end whose content consists of having other ends or desires", p. 9).
5. I am not arguing that this is *necessarily* the case. If the more abstract, general value to which your particular hobbies are contributing is in conflict with too many other important things, it might be that you would be better off without it.
6. Perhaps unsurprisingly, the cases I have read about in which gay members of extremely conservative religions live successfully without leaving their churches have almost all been cases of people with relative privilege: they tend to be white men who have some supportive friends or family. Not everyone has these privileges or the resources that come with them and this can make a tremendous difference to what paths are available for a person. We'll talk about such differences again in Chapter 4.
7. I do not mean to downplay the difficulty of taking this path, nor do I mean to ignore the harm that churches can do to LGBTQ people. I have learned a lot from Dawne Moon and Theresa Tobin about the harm that churches sometimes do to members of the LGBTQ community through the mechanism of shame. See their paper "Sunsets and Solidarity" in

Hypatia (2018). For an eye-opening discussion of the views of transgender people about their treatment by the Mormon Church, see Sumerau, Cragun, and Mathers 2016.

8. Putting it this way may make it seem like we're really still talking about instrumental reasoning about the means to a value-fulfilled life. I don't think that's an illuminating way to describe what's happening. Most people, I suspect, would balk at the claim that they value their relationships and careers *as a means to* a value-fulfilled life. A life in which you have strong friendships and a satisfying career just is a value-fulfilled life; these values are constitutive of the life, not a means to a separate valuable end. That said, not much hangs on whether this kind of evaluation is ultimately classified as instrumental reasoning: it is still a kind of evaluation that goes beyond what we standardly think of as instrumental. See Section 2.4 for more on this topic.
9. I argued in *The Reflective Life* (2008) that a certain kind of reflective wisdom (comprising perspective, attentional flexibility, and realistic optimism) is essential for anyone who wants to live a good life from their own point of view
10. A cliché that has some truth to it; see Ware 2012.
11. Notice that sometimes this might actually be a good thing. If you knew that majoring in economics would make you callous or uncooperative (which it might—see Frank, Gilovich, and Regan 1993), this might be a reason to do something else.
12. "Asshole" (not "jerk") is really the perfect word here, but I'm reluctant to use it too frequently in print. For examples of less reluctant philosophers, see Aaron James' 2012 book *Assholes: A Theory*, and Harry Frankfurt's 2005 trailblazing example, *On Bullshit*.
13. My understanding of oppression has been shaped by Marilyn Frye's 1983 essay "Oppression". Frye defines structural oppression as "a system of interrelated barriers and forces which reduce, immobilize and mold people who belong to a certain group, and effect their subordination to another group (individually to individuals of the other group, and as a group, to that group)" (p. 33).

Chapter 4

1. I do not mean to assume that autonomy has absolute value. Rather, I am taking autonomy to be something that people value and respect in their relationships.

2. This would be the Kantian way of looking at it: when we aim to help someone who seems to be making bad choices we are pulled in one direction by sympathy and in the opposite direction by the moral emotion of respect. For an excellent discussion of the limitations of the Kantian picture, see Stohr 2009.
3. There are interesting differences between men and women on questions about friendship in the MIDUS (Midlife in the United States) data—a very well-regarded, nationally representative dataset. Women are less likely to report that they *never* ask a friend or relative for help or advice with a personal problem (11% for women, 17.6% for men), and less likely to say that friends never ask them for help or advice (6.9% for women, 9.2% for men). Notice that these numbers mean that *most* men and women do ask friends for help or advice, at least sometimes. More than half of women say that they open up to friends "a lot", while less than a third of men do. The majority of women (60%) say they rely on friends for help with problems "a lot", while slightly under half of men say so (48.8%). (National Survey of Midlife Development in the United States (MIDUS 3), 2013–14, Aggregate Data. Analysis ran on 2017-06-19 (09:50 PM EDT) using SDA 3.5: Tables. Thanks to Lauren Kuykendall for the analysis.)
4. Interestingly, van der Host and Coffé 2012 found that receiving help from friends was negatively correlated with subjective well-being, but they think this might be because it isn't pleasant to *need* help: "it may be positive to have friends who are willing and able to help you, but not to actually need their help". Their study did not allow them to distinguish this factor.
5. How much it is possible to understand what it is like to be a parent is a matter of philosophical controversy. See Chang 2015 and Paul 2014. I discuss transformative choices in Section 2.4.
6. In philosophy, this difference is represented in the debate between monists and pluralists about value (Mason 2015). The fact that philosophers don't agree about whether there is one ultimate value or many leads me to think that these are abiding differences.
7. One might argue that the difference between Addario and me is a simple difference in our beliefs about risk. Knowing myself as I do, I maintain that even if Addario and I had the same beliefs about the risks, I would make different choices than she does, because we have different priorities.
8. Audrey is an amalgam of several real people I know, with a name chosen to protect the innocent.

9. The fact that good advice can take this form may also have metaethical implications. Eric Wiland 2003 argues that this feature of advice giving—that we sometimes advise people to acquire motivations that they do not currently have—creates problems for certain advisor-based models of practical reason.
10. Talking about skills will make some readers think of virtues, because virtues are often thought of as skills (Annas 2011). Indeed, we do need virtues to be good at giving advice: we need courage to tell people what they don't want to hear, we need compassion and tact to tell it in the right way, and we need the wisdom to be able to discern which situations call for honesty and which for compassionate bending of the truth. Because I'm not defending a virtue theory in this book, I thought it would be better to describe the conditions for intervention without relying on claims about virtues. Nevertheless, I'm happy to admit that what I've said could be recast in terms of the virtues requisite for helping.
11. See my 2007 for a discussion of how subjective and objective theories may both be correct, but about different questions.
12. There is, of course, the prior question of whether the state is permitted to promote well-being at all. I think the answer to this question is yes, once the relevant qualifications and distinctions are made. There is a long theoretical tradition according to which the point of the state is to ensure the well-being of citizens, and the open questions are about *how* this is best accomplished. Some argue that the best way to promote citizens' well-being is by leaving them free to pursue their own conceptions of it. For more discussion, see Haybron and Tiberius 2015.
13. Eden Lin 2017 argues that the case of infants' well-being presents a particular problem for subjective theories such as the value fulfillment theory. If a theory of well-being is false for newborn infants, he argues, we ought to reject it. There are aspects of the value fulfillment theory that do not apply to infants: infants do not have integrated patterns of psychological attitudes that form complex patterns, so they cannot be helped in the ways that we help our adult friends as I discuss in this book. But, as I'll argue in this section, a life rich in value fulfillment is a target that is a sensible one for infants (though the infants themselves won't aim at it!). Lin (2018) also argues for invariabilism, which is the view that the same theory of well-being is true of every welfare subject. The argument here turns on thinking that a theory of well-being must make sense of certain counterfactual claims about well-being such as the claim "were Fido the dog capable of philosophical contemplation, he would benefit from it". Lin says, "Why insist that [the dog] Fido's actual nature

determines what he would benefit from in far-out counterfactual scenarios in which he has a very different nature?" (p. 12). Lin and I have fundamentally different views about the nature and purpose of ethical theories. Because I think ethical theories are designed to solve our practical problems, I'm not much concerned about achieving the kind of generality that would cover such counterfactuals. Ultimately, however, if Lin is correct that the concept of "well-being" *must* be general in this way, then my response would be to use a different concept. Rather than change the view I am defending, I would change what I call it—perhaps it would be the value fulfillment theory of "the good for most adult humans".

14. It does not apply to sentient creatures who are not goal-directed, but this does not entail that such creatures have no moral standing. If there are any such beings, what the value fulfillment theory could say is that although such creatures are not well-being subjects they can be made happy or unhappy and their happiness or unhappiness could be morally important.
15. Preference or desire satisfaction theories of well-being say that what is good for us is the satisfaction of our preferences (sometimes our informed preferences or the preferences that an informed version of ourselves would want us to have). Such theories are popular in philosophy and dominate in economics. See Brandt 1979; Griffin 1986; Harsanyi 1977; Heathwood 2006; Railton 1986. These theories are discussed in more detail in Chapter 1.
16. For a sympathetic discussion of our relationships with animals that emphasizes the importance of empathizing with other creatures, see Gruen 2015.
17. See Raghavan and Alexandrova 2015 for a theory of well-being developed specifically for the case of children. I am sympathetic to their approach.

Chapter 5

1. Nor does an argument have to convince everyone for it to be a good argument. My point here is that the value fulfillment theory does not have the resources to say that *anyone* who does not value caring friendship is making a mistake. Therefore, the reasons for valuing such relationships are reasons for *most of us*. Some will doubtless find this to be a cost of the value fulfillment theory. I think this it is just a

consequence of thinking that well-being has to have a special connection to the person whose well-being it is. See Sections 1.4 and 2.5 for more on this topic.

2. There have also been some recent forceful attacks against empathy as a *moral* motive. Critics may be right that empathy is an inadequate moral motive because of its partiality, but partiality is not a problem in the context of friendship, so I won't discuss the criticism here. If you're interested in what the empathy critics have to say, see Bloom 2014 and Prinz 2011.

3. Lori Gruen (2015, p. 66) humorously objects to this way of thinking about empathizing with animals, because "other animals don't wear shoes!"

4. Interestingly, some philosophers argue that friendship requires a certain kind of epistemic *in*accuracy—an "interpretive charity" that inclines us to have more positive beliefs about our friends' actions and character than are strictly warranted by the evidence (the quoted phrase is from Stroud 2006, p. 507; see also Keller 2004a). If this is a feature of friendship, it may make seeing things from the friend's point of view even more difficult (if we see them through rose-colored glasses, they will look rosy). The perspective-taking that I am recommending is not necessarily incompatible with this bias, however, because the bias need not extend to facts about the person's values that will enable us to be helpful to her.

5. Thanks to Karen Stohr for the reference.

6. The kind of motivation referred to here is motivation to engage in behaviors that will improve your epistemic position. It must be distinguished from "motivated reasoning", which usually refers to reasoning that is biased by a desire to reach a certain conclusion or to reduce cognitive dissonance, and which usually worsens your epistemic position (see Kunda 1990).

7. In a number of experiments, psychologist Daniel Batson and his colleagues (2007, pp. 72–3) showed that the "manipulation of valuing (low, high) had a strong, clear effect; participants reported considerably more empathy for the [target] whose welfare they valued. Nor could this effect be attributed to differences in perceived fairness (deservingness)."

8. For an excellent discussion of the history of the concept, see Nadelhoffer et al. 2017. Nadelhoffer and his colleagues also discuss their work on the ordinary folk-concept of humility and they make a good case for thinking that our current conception of humility is closer to their decentering view than to the old-fashioned self-abasement view.

9. I take the same position on theorizing about virtues that I do on theorizing about well-being, which I mentioned in Section 1.2. We should aim to explicate normative concepts for certain purposes; we should hope that there are unifying features at a certain level of abstraction across different contexts, but we should start with our problems and work from there.
10. "Merit" here is not intended to invoke mind-independent standards; rather, merited responses are based on the value that are appropriate for individual agents, as discussed in Chapter 2.
11. Philosophical accounts of humility sometimes define it as a moral virtue and sometimes an intellectual or epistemic virtue. For accounts of humility as a moral virtue, see Driver 2001; Snow 1995; Tangney 2009. For intellectual humility, see Hazlett 2012; Roberts and Wood 2007.
12. Whitcomb et al. separate awareness and owning into two different components of humility. This makes sense, but since awareness is implied by owning (you can't take responsibility for something you're not aware of), I favor the simpler, two-part account below.
13. Although he doesn't use the word "humility", William James' essay "On a Certain Blindness in Human Beings" contains a beautiful plea for this kind of humility. The blindness referred to in the title is our blindness to the experience of others, which, James says, "absolutely forbids us to be forward in pronouncing on the meaninglessness of forms of existence other than our own; and it commands us to tolerate, respect, and indulge those whom we see harmlessly interested and happy in their own ways, however unintelligible these may be to us" (James 1900, pp. 45–6). Thanks to Justin Ivory for drawing my attention to this wonderful essay.
14. Humility in general terms is often thought to be the mean between servility and arrogance (Whitcomb et al. 2017). In the context of friendship, I think the extreme is this abdication of judgment about the friend (rather than the abdication of one's own autonomy that is characteristic of servility).
15. Sonja Lyubomirsky has been one of the most active psychologists in making the case for happiness interventions. See Lyubomirsky 2008; Sin and Lyubomirsky 2009. For a meta-analysis of happiness interventions, see Bolier et al. 2013.
16. These lesser achievements may not count as virtue, if virtues are thought of as stable, cross-situationally reliable traits. There is a large literature on whether virtue requires cross-situational reliability. See, for a start, Doris 2002; Merritt 2000; Miller 2013. This topic is also briefly discussed in Section 3.3.

17. Open-mindedness may be a distinct virtue, but I think some portion of it is required by owning our limitations. Some philosophers think that, in the intellectual domain at least, open-mindedness and humility are more or less the same (Riggs 2010).
18. This doesn't make it impossible, of course, and for someone who cannot change, living anti-socially or even immorally may still be for their own good. For those who defend objective theories of well-being, this is the big bullet that subjective theories like mine have to bite.
19. This remark is a bit cheeky and opens a huge philosophical debate about the reality of moral properties. This isn't the place to argue about this and I think even a die-hard moral realist could accept the position that from the point of view of one friend confronting another, the best one can do is reflect and decide on the basis of what seems most sound. For an excellent introduction to the realism debates in metaethics, see Van Roojen 2015.
20. Our humility should perhaps also extend to the other animals. Lori Gruen 2015 has some beautifully described examples of how entangled empathy will improve our treatment of non-human animals.
21. While I do think that most people tend to think they know more about what it's like for someone else than they do, it's also true that this tendency varies with one's group membership. Oppressed people, for example, are likely to be better at taking the point of view of the oppressor than the other way around, because their success in life may depend on their learning this skill (Collins 1986; Wylie 2003).

Chapter 6

1. In saying this, readers familiar with the options in metaethics will see that the underlying metaethics of my own view is basically constructivist. I have defended versions of constructivism in my 2012 and 2017.
2. More philosophers, including Kitcher, have been concerned with proposals for how to organize our political lives together. I think there is some overlap between how we should treat fellow citizens and how we should treat friends (see Section 4.4), but—as I hope to have shown in this book—the case of friendship is different enough that it warrants special attention.

Bibliography

Adams, R. M. (1999), *Finite and Infinite Goods: A Framework for Ethics*. New York: Oxford University Press.

Addario, L. (2015), "What Can a Pregnant Photojournalist Cover? Everything", *The New York Times Magazine*, February 1, https://www.nytimes.com/2015/02/01/magazine/what-can-a-pregnant-photojournalist-cover-everything.html?ref=magazine.

Alexandrova, A. (2013), "Doing Well in the Circumstances", *Journal of Moral Philosophy*, 10(3): 307–28.

Alexandrova, A. (2017), *A Philosophy for the Science of Well-Being*. New York: Oxford University Press.

Anderson, E. (1995), *Value in Ethics and Economics*. Cambridge, MA: Harvard University Press.

Andreou, C. (2015), "Parity, Comparability, and Choice", *The Journal of Philosophy*, 112(1): 5–22.

Angner, E. (2011), "Are Subjective Measures of Well-Being 'Direct'?", *Australasian Journal of Philosophy*, 89(1): 115–30.

Annas, J. (1995), *The Morality of Happiness*. New York: Oxford University Press.

Annas, J. (2011), *Intelligent Virtue*. New York: Oxford University Press.

Antony, L. M. (2000), "Natures and Norms", *Ethics*, 111(1): 8–36.

Aristotle (1999), *Nicomachean Ethics*, trans. T. Irwin. Indianapolis, IN: Hackett.

Arneson, R. J. (1999), "Human Flourishing versus Desire Satisfaction", *Social Philosophy and Policy*, 16(1): 113–42.

Arpaly, N. and Schroeder, T. (1999), "Praise, Blame and the Whole Self", *Philosophical Studies*, 93(2): 161–88.

Arpaly, N. and Schroeder, T. (2013), *In Praise of Desire*. New York: Oxford University Press.

Ashford, E. (2007), "The Duties Imposed by the Human Right to Basic Necessities", in T. Pogge (ed.), *Freedom From Poverty as a Human Right: Who Owes What to the Very Poor?* New York: Oxford University Press: 183–218.

Ashford, E. (2011), "Obligations of Justice and Beneficence to Aid the Severely Poor", in P. Illingworth, T. Pogge, and L. Wenar (eds.), *Giving Well: The Ethics of Philanthropy*. New York: Oxford University Press: 129–55.

Austen, J. (2008), *Emma*. New York: Oxford University Press.
Badhwar, N. K. (2014), *Well-Being: Happiness in a Worthwhile Life*. New York: Oxford University Press.
Batson, D. C., Eklund, J. H., Chermok, V. L., Hoyt, J. L., and Ortiz, B. G. (2007), "An Additional Antecedent of Empathic Concern: Valuing the Welfare of the Person in Need", *Journal of Personality and Social Psychology*, 93(1): 65–74.
Bedford-Petersen, C., DeYoung, C. G., Tiberius, V., and Syed, M. (2018), "Integrating Philosophical and Psychological Approaches to Well-Being: The Role of Success in Personal Projects", *Journal of Moral Education*, https://doi.org/10. 1080/03057240.2018.1463203.
Besser-Jones, L. (2014), *Eudaimonic Ethics: The Philosophy and Psychology of Living Well*. New York: Routledge.
Bishop, M. (2015), *The Good Life: Unifying the Philosophy and Psychology of Well-Being*. New York: Oxford University Press.
Blackburn, S. (1984), *Spreading the Word: Groundings in the Philosophy of Language*. Oxford: Clarendon Press.
Bloom, P. (2014), "Against Empathy", *Boston Review*, http://bostonreview.net/forum/paul-bloom-against-empathy.
Bloomfield, P. (2014), *The Virtues of Happiness: A Theory of the Good Life*. New York: Oxford University Press.
Bok, D. C. (2010), *The Politics of Happiness: What Government Can Learn From the New Research on Well-Being*. Princeton, NJ: Princeton University Press.
Bolier, L., Haverman, M., Westerhof, G. J., Riper, H., Smit, F., and Bohlmeijer, E. (2013), "Positive Psychology Interventions: A Meta-Analysis of Randomized Controlled Studies", *BMC Public Health*, 13(1): 119–38.
Bradford, G. (2015), *Achievement*. New York: Oxford University Press.
Bradford, G. (2016), "Perfectionism", in G. Fletcher (ed.) *Routledge Handbook of Well-Being*. Oxford and New York: Routledge: 124–34.
Bradley, B. (2009), *Well-Being and Death*. New York: Oxford University Press.
Bramble, B. (2016), "A New Defense of Hedonism about Well-Being", *Ergo*, 3(4): 85–112.
Brandt, R. B. (1979), *A Theory of the Good and the Right*. New York: Oxford University Press.
Bransford, J. D., Brown, A. L., Cocking, R. R., and Educational Resources Information Center (2000), *How People Learn: Brain, Mind, Experience, and School*. Washington, DC: National Academy Press.
Briley, D. A. and Tucker-Drob, E. M. (2014), "Genetic and Environmental Continuity in Personality Development: A Meta-Analysis", *Psychological Bulletin*, 140(5): 1303–31.

Brown, B. (2012), *The Power of Vulnerability: Teachings on Authenticity, Connection, & Courage.* Louisville, CO: Sounds True.
Calhoun, C. (2015), "Geographies of Meaningful Living", *Journal of Applied Philosophy*, 32(1): 15–34.
Calhoun, C. (2018), *Doing Valuable Time: The Present, the Future, and Meaningful Living.* Oxford: Oxford University Press.
Carbery, J. and Buhrmester, D. (1998), "Friendship and Need Fulfillment During Three Phases of Young Adulthood", *Journal of Social and Personal Relationships*, 15(3): 393–409.
Carver, C. and Scheier, M. (1998), *On the Self-Regulation of Behavior.* Cambridge and New York: Cambridge University Press.
Chang, R. (2005), "Parity, Interval Value, and Choice", *Ethics* 115(2): 331–50.
Chang, R. (2015), "Transformative Choices", *Res Philosophica*, 92(2): 237–82.
Christakis, N. A. and Fowler, J. H. (2009), *Connected: The Surprising Power of Our Social Networks and How They Shape Our Lives.* New York: Little, Brown.
Cocking, D. and Kennett, J. (1998), "Friendship and the Self", *Ethics*, 108(3): 502–27.
Cohen, S., Kamarck, T., and Mermelstein, R. (1994), Perceived Stress Scale: Measuring Stress: A Guide for Health and Social Scientists, http://mindgarden.com/documents/PerceivedStressScale.pdf.
Collins, P. H. (1986), "Learning from the Outsider Within: The Sociological Significance of Black Feminist Thought", *Social Problems* 33(6): s14–s32.
Crisp, R. (2006a), *Reasons and the Good.* New York: Oxford University Press.
Crisp, R. (2006b), "Hedonism Reconsidered", *Philosophy and Phenomenological Research*, 73(3): 619–45.
Crisp, R. (2016), "Well-Being", *The Stanford Encyclopedia of Philosophy* (Summer 2016 Edition), ed. Edward N. Zalta, https://plato.stanford.edu/archives/sum2016/entries/well-being/.
Darwall, S. (2002), *Welfare and Rational Care.* Princeton, NJ: Princeton University Press.
Decety, J. and Cowell, J. M. (2014), "Friends or Foes: Is Empathy Necessary for Moral Behavior?", *Perspectives on Psychological Science*, 9(5): 525–37.
DeYoung, C. G. (2015), "Cybernetic Big Five Theory", *Journal of Research in Personality*, 56: 33–58.
Diener, E. (1984), "Subjective Well-Being", *Psychological Bulletin* 95(3): 542–75.
Diener, E. (2000), "Subjective Well-Being: The Science of Happiness and a Proposal for a National Index", *American Psychologist*, 55(1): 34.

Diener, E. (2009), *Well-Being for Public Policy*. New York: Oxford University Press.

Diener, E., Inglehart, R., and Tay, L. (2013), "Theory and Validity of Life Satisfaction Scales", *Social Indicators Research*, 112(3): 497–527.

Diener, E., Scollon, C. N., and Lucas, R. E. (2003), "The Evolving Concept of Subjective Well-Being: The Multifaceted Nature of Happiness", *Advances in Cell Aging and Gerontology*, 15: 187–219.

Doris, J. M. (2002), *Lack of Character: Personality and Moral Behavior*. Cambridge and New York: Cambridge University Press.

Doris, J. M. (2015), *Talking to Our Selves: Reflection, Ignorance, and Agency*. Oxford: Oxford University Press.

Dorsey, D. (2012), "Subjectivism Without Desire", *The Philosophical Review*, 121(3): 407–42.

Driver, J. (2001), *Uneasy Virtue*. New York: Cambridge University Press.

Epley, N. and Caruso, E. M. (2008), "Perspective Taking: Misstepping Into Others' Shoes", in K. D. Markman, W. M. P. Klein, and J. A. Suhr (eds.), *Handbook of Imagination and Mental Simulation*. New York: Psychology Press: 295–309.

Feldman, F. (2004), *Pleasure and the Good Life: Concerning the Nature, Varieties and Plausibility of Hedonism*. New York: Oxford University Press.

Feldman, F. (2010), *What is This Thing Called Happiness?* Oxford: Oxford University Press.

Ferguson, C. J. (2010), "A Meta-Analysis of Normal and Disordered Personality across the Lifespan", *Journal of Personality and Social Psychology*, 98(4): 659–67.

Finnis, J. (2011), *Natural Law and Natural Rights*. New York: Oxford University Press.

Fleeson, W. (2001), "Toward a Structure-and Process-Integrated View of Personality: Traits as Density Distributions of States", *Journal of Personality and Social Psychology*, 80(6): 1011–27.

Fletcher, G. (2009), "Rejecting Well-Being Invariabilism", *Philosophical Papers*, 38(1): 21–34.

Fletcher, G. (2013), "A Fresh Start for the Objective-List Theory of Well-Being", *Utilitas*, 25(2): 206–20.

Fletcher, G. (ed.) (2016a), *Routledge Handbook of Well-Being*. Oxford and New York: Routledge.

Fletcher, G. (2016b), *The Philosophy of Well-Being: An Introduction*. Oxford and New York: Routledge.

Frank, R. H., Gilovich, T., and Regan, D. T. (1993), "Does Studying Economics Inhibit Cooperation?", *The Journal of Economic Perspectives*, 7(2): 159–71.

Frankfurt, H. G. (2005), *On Bullshit*. Princeton, NJ: Princeton University Press.
Fredrickson, B. L. (1998), "What Good Are Positive Emotions?", *Review of General Psychology: Journal of Division 1, of the American Psychological Association*, 2(3): 300–19.
Fredrickson, B. L. (2001), "The Role of Positive Emotions in Positive Psychology: The Broaden-and-Build Theory of Positive Emotions", *American Psychologist*, 56(3): 218–26.
Frye, M. (1983), *The Politics of Reality: Essays in Feminist Theory*. Berkeley, CA: Crossing Press.
Gibbard, A. (1992), *Wise Choices, Apt Feelings: A Theory of Normative Judgment*. Cambridge, MA: Harvard University Press.
Gilbert, D. (2006), *Stumbling on Happiness*. New York: Alfred A. Knopf.
Griffin, J. (1986), *Well-Being: Its Meaning, Measurement, and Moral Importance*. Oxford: Clarendon Press.
Gruen, L. (2015), *Entangled Empathy: An Alternative Ethic for Our Relationships with Animals*. New York: Lantern Books.
Haidt, J. (2006), *The Happiness Hypothesis: Finding Modern Truth in Ancient Wisdom*. New York: Basic Books.
Harman, G. (1999), "Moral Philosophy Meets Social Psychology: Virtue Ethics and the Fundamental Attribution Error", *Proceedings of the Aristotelian Society*, 99: 315–31.
Harris, S. (2010), *The Moral Landscape: How Science Can Determine Human Values*. New York: Free Press.
Harsanyi, J. C. (1977), "Morality and the Theory of Rational Behavior", *Social Research*, 44(4): 623–56.
Hausman, D. M. (2012), *Preference, Value, Choice, and Welfare*. New York: Cambridge University Press.
Hawkins, J. (2014), "Well-Being, Time, and Dementia", *Ethics*, 124(3): 507–42.
Haybron, D. and Tiberius, V. (2015), "Well-Being Policy: What Standard of Well-Being?" *Journal of the American Philosophical Association*, 1(4): 712–33.
Haybron, D. M. (2007), "Life Satisfaction, Ethical Reflection, and the Science of Happiness", *Journal of Happiness Studies*, 8(1): 99–138.
Haybron, D. M. (2008a), "Happiness, the Self and Human Flourishing", *Utilitas*, 20(1): 21–49.
Haybron, D. M. (2008b), *The Pursuit of Unhappiness: The Elusive Psychology of Well-Being*. New York: Oxford University Press.
Haybron, D. M. (2011), "Taking the Satisfaction (and the Life) Out of Life Satisfaction", *Philosophical Explorations*, 14(3): 249–62.

Hazlett, A. (2012), "Higher-Order Epistemic Attitudes and Intellectual Humility", *Episteme*, 9(3): 205–23.
Heathwood, C. (2005), "The Problem of Defective Desires", *Australasian Journal of Philosophy*, 83(4): 487–504.
Heathwood, C. (2006), "Desire Satisfactionism and Hedonism", *Philosophical Studies*, 128(3): 539–63.
Heathwood, C. (2007), "The Reduction of Sensory Pleasure to Desire", *Philosophical Studies*, 133(1): 23–44.
Heathwood, C. (2011), "Preferentism and Self-Sacrifice", *Pacific Philosophical Quarterly*, 92(1): 18–38.
Heathwood, C. (2016), "Desire-Fulfillment Theory", in G. Fletcher (ed.), *The Routledge Handbook of Philosophy of Well-Being*. Oxford and New York: Routledge: 135–47.
Helm, B. (2013), "Friendship", *The Stanford Encyclopedia of Philosophy* (Fall 2013 Edition), ed. Edward N. Zalta, https://plato.stanford.edu/archives/fall2013/entries/friendship/.
Hume, D. (1739), *A Treatise of Human Nature*, ed. D. R. Norton and M. J. Norton. New York: Oxford University Press.
Hurka, T. (1993), *Perfectionism*. Oxford: Oxford University Press.
Ickes, W. J. (ed.) (1997), *Empathic Accuracy*. New York: Guilford Press.
Izard, C. E. (2013), *Human Emotions*. New York: Springer Science & Business Media.
James, A. (2012), *Assholes: A Theory*. New York: Anchor.
James, W. (1900), "On a Certain Blindness in Human Beings", in W. James, *On Some of Life's Ideals: On a Certain Blindness in Human Beings, What Makes a Life Significant*. New York: Henry Holt and Company: 3–46.
Jaworska, A. (2007), "Caring and Internality", *Philosophy and Phenomenological Research*, 74(3): 529–68.
Jayawickreme, E., Meindl, P., Helzer, E. G., Furr, R. M., and Fleeson, W. (2014), "Virtuous States and Virtuous Traits: How the Empirical Evidence Regarding the Existence of Broad Traits Saves Virtue Ethics from the Situationist Critique", *Theory and Research in Education*, 12(3): 283–308.
Kagan, S. (1992), "The Limits of Well-Being", *Social Philosophy and Policy*, 9(2): 169–89.
Kahneman, D. (2003), "Objective Happiness", in D. Kahneman, E. Diener, and N. Schwarz (eds.), *Well-Being: Foundations of Hedonic Psychology*. New York: Russell Sage Foundation: 3–25.
Kamtekar, R. (2004), "Situationism and Virtue Ethics on the Content of Our Character", *Ethics*, 114(3): 458–91.

Keller, S. (2004a), "Friendship and Belief", *Philosophical Papers*, 33(3): 329–51.
Keller, S. (2004b), "Welfare and the Achievement of Goals", *Philosophical Studies*, 121(1): 27–41.
Keller, S. (2009a), "Welfare as Success", *Noûs*, 43(4): 656–83.
Keller, S. (2009b), "Welfarism", *Philosophy Compass*, 4(1): 82–95.
Keyes, C. L., Shmotkin, D., and Ryff, C. D. (2002), "Optimizing Well-Being: The Empirical Encounter of Two Traditions", *Journal of Personality and Social Psychology*, 82(6): 1007–22.
Kitcher, P. (2011), *The Ethical Project*. Cambridge, MA: Harvard University Press.
Klein, K. J. K. and Hodges, S. D. (2001), "Gender Differences, Motivation, and Empathic Accuracy: When It Pays to Understand", *Personality and Social Psychology Bulletin*, 27(6): 720–30.
Korsgaard, C. M. (1996), *The Sources of Normativity*. New York: Cambridge University Press.
Kraut, R. (1979), "Two Conceptions of Happiness", *The Philosophical Review*, 88(2): 167–97.
Kraut, R. (1994), "Desire and the Human Good", *Proceedings and Addresses of the American Philosophical Association*, 68(2): 39–54.
Kraut, R. (2006), "How to Justify Ethical Propositions: Aristotle's Method", in R. Kraut (ed.), *The Blackwell Guide to Aristotle's Nicomachean Ethics*. Oxford: Blackwell Publishing: 76–95.
Kraut, R. (2009), *What is Good and Why: The Ethics of Well-Being*. Cambridge, MA: Harvard University Press.
Kruger, J. (1999), "Lake Wobegon Be Gone! The 'Below-Average Effect' and the Egocentric Nature of Comparative Ability Judgments", *Journal of Personality and Social Psychology*, 77(2): 221–32.
Kruger, J. and Dunning, D. (1999), "Unskilled and Unaware of It: How Difficulties in Recognizing One's Own Incompetence Lead to Inflated Self-Assessments", *Journal of Personality and Social Psychology*, 77(6): 1121–34.
Kunda, Z. (1990), "The Case for Motivated Reasoning", *Psychological Bulletin* 108(3): 480–98.
Lavelock, C. R., Worthington, E. L., Davis, D. E., Griffin, B. J., Reid, C. A., Hook, J. N., and Van Tongeren, D. R. (2014), "The Quiet Virtue Speaks: An Intervention to Promote Humility", *Journal of Psychology and Theology*, 42(1): 99–110.
Layard, R. (2005), *Happiness: Lessons Form a New Science*. London: Penguin Books.

Lewis, D. (2000), "Dispositional Theories of Value", in *Papers in Ethics and Social Philosophy*, Cambridge: Cambridge University Press: 68–94.
Lilienfeld, S. O., Ammirati, R., and Landfield, K. (2009), "Giving Debiasing Away: Can Psychological Research on Correcting Cognitive Errors Promote Human Welfare?", *Perspectives on Psychological Science*, 4(4): 390–8.
Lin, E. (2017), "Against Welfare Subjectivism", *Noûs*, 51(2): 354–77.
Lin, E. (2018), "Welfare Invariabilism", *Ethics*, 128(2): 320–45.
Little, B. R. (2015), "The Integrative Challenge in Personality Science: Personal Projects as Units of Analysis", *Journal of Research in Personality*, 56: 93–101.
Little, B. R., Salmela-Aro, K. E., and Phillips, S. D. (2007), *Personal Project Pursuit: Goals, Action, and Human Flourishing*. Mahwah, NJ: Lawrence Erlbaum.
Lyubomirsky, S. (2008), *The How of Happiness: A Scientific Approach to Getting the Life You Want*. New York: Penguin.
MacIntyre, A. (1984), *After Virtue: A Study in Moral Theory*. Notre Dame, IN: University of Notre Dame Press.
Marangoni, C., Garcia, S., Ickes, W., and Teng, G. (1995), "Empathic Accuracy in a Clinically Relevant Setting", *Journal of Personality and Social Psychology*, 68(5): 854–69.
Mason, E. (2015), "Value Pluralism", *The Stanford Encyclopedia of Philosophy* (Summer 2015 Edition), ed. Edward N. Zalta, https://plato.stanford.edu/archives/sum2015/entries/value-pluralism/.
Merritt, M. (2000), "Virtue Ethics and Situationist Personality Psychology", *Ethical Theory and Moral Practice*, 3(4): 365–83.
Miller, C. (2003), "Social Psychology and Virtue Ethics", *The Journal of Ethics*, 7(4): 365–92.
Miller, C. (2013), *Moral Character: An Empirical Theory*. Oxford: Oxford University Press.
Moon, D., Tobin, T. W., (2018), "Sunsets and Solidarity: Overcoming Sacramental Shame in Conservative Christian Churches to Forge a Queer Vision of Love and Justice", *Hypatia*. Early view at https://doi.org/10.1111/hypa.12413
Nadelhoffer, T., Wright, J. C., Echols, M., Perini, T., and Venezia, K. (2017), "Some Varieties of Humility Worth Wanting", *Journal of Moral Philosophy*, http://philosophycommons.typepad.com/files/varieties-of-humility.pdf.
Nickerson, R. S. (1998), "Confirmation Bias: A Ubiquitous Phenomenon in Many Guises", *Review of General Psychology*, 2(2): 175–220.
Nouwen, H. J. M. (1994), *Here and Now: Living in the Spirit*. New York: The Crossroad Publishing Company.
Nozick, R. (1974), *Anarchy, State, and Utopia*. Malden, MA: Basic Books.

Nussbaum, M. C. (1992), "Human Functioning and Social Justice in Defense of Aristotelian Essentialism", *Political Theory*, 20(2): 202–46.

Nussbaum, M. C. (2001), *Women and Human Development: The Capabilities Approach*. Cambridge: Cambridge University Press.

Overvold, M. C. (1980), "Self-Interest and the Concept of Self-Sacrifice", *Canadian Journal of Philosophy*, 10(1): 105–18.

Parfit, D. (1984), *Reasons and Persons*. Oxford: Oxford University Press.

Paul, L. A. (2014), *Transformative Experience*. New York: Oxford University Press.

Peterson, C. and Seligman, M. E. P. (2004), *Character Strengths and Virtues: A Handbook and Classification*. New York: Oxford University Press.

Prinz, J. (2011), "Against Empathy", *The Southern Journal of Philosophy*, 49(s1): 214–33.

Raghavan, R. and Alexandrova, A. (2015), "Toward a Theory of Child Well-Being", *Social Indicators Research*, 121(3): 887–902.

Raibley, J. R. (2010), "Well-Being and the Priority of Values", *Social Theory and Practice*, 36(4): 593–620.

Raibley, J. R. (2012), "Welfare over Time and the Case for Holism", *Philosophical Papers*, 41(2): 239–65.

Raibley, J. R. (2013), "Values, Agency, and Welfare", *Philosophical Topics*, 41(1): 187–214.

Railton, P. (1986), "Moral Realism", *The Philosophical Review*, 95(2): 163–207.

Railton, P. (2003), "Facts and Values", in *Facts, Values, and Norms*. Cambridge: Cambridge University Press: 43–68.

Rawls, J. (1971), *A Theory of Justice*. Cambridge, MA: Harvard University Press.

Requena, F. (2011), "Welfare Systems, Support Networks and Subjective Well-Being Among Retired Persons", *Social Indicators Research*, 99(3): 511–29.

Richardson, H. (1990), "Specifying Norms as a Way to Resolve Concrete Ethical Problems", *Philosophy and Public Affairs*, 19(4): 279–310.

Riggs, W. (2010), "Open-Mindedness", *Metaphilosophy*, 41(1–2): 172–88.

Roberts, R. and Wood, J. (2007), *Intellectual Virtues: An Essay in Regulative Epistemology*. New York: Oxford University Press.

Robeyns, I. (2011), "The Capability Approach", in *The Stanford Encyclopedia of Philosophy* (Summer 2011 Edition), ed. Edward N. Zalta, http://plato.stanford.edu/archives/sum2011/entries/capability-approach/.

Rosati, C. S. (1995), "Persons, Perspectives, and Full Information Accounts of the Good", *Ethics*, 105(2): 296–325.

Rosati, C. S. (1996), "Internalism and the Good for a Person", *Ethics*, 106(2): 297–326.

Rosati, C. S. (2006), "Personal Good", in T. Horgan and M. Timmons (eds.), *Metaethics after Moore*. New York: Oxford University Press: 107–32.

Ryan, R. M. and Deci, E. L. (2001), "On Happiness and Human Potentials: A Review of Research on Hedonic and Eudaimonic Well-Being", *Annual Review of Psychology*, 52(1): 141–66.

Ryff, C. D. (1989), "Happiness is Everything, or Is It? Explorations on the Meaning of Psychological Well-Being", *Journal of Personality and Social Psychology*, 57(6), 1069–81.

Sarch, A. (2011), "Internalism About a Person's Good: Don't Believe It", *Philosophical Studies*, 154(2): 161–84.

Scanlon, T. M. (1998), *What We Owe to Each Other*. Cambridge, MA: The Belknap Press of Harvard University Press.

Schmidtz, D. (1994), "Choosing Ends", *Ethics*, 104(2): 226–51.

Schmuck, P. E. and Sheldon, K. M. (eds.) (2001), *Life Goals and Well-Being: Towards a Positive Psychology of Human Striving*. Kirkland, WA: Hogrefe & Huber.

Schroeder, M. A. (2007), *Slaves of the Passions*. New York: Oxford University Press.

Seligman, M. E. (2004), *Authentic Happiness: Using the New Positive Psychology to Realize Your Potential for Lasting Fulfillment*. New York: Simon & Schuster.

Sen, A. K. (1987), *On Ethics and Economics*. Oxford: Blackwell Publishing.

Sidgwick, H. ([1907] 1962), *The Methods of Ethics*, 7th edn. Chicago, IL: University of Chicago Press.

Silverstein, M. (2000), "In Defense of Happiness: A Response to the Experience Machine", *Social Theory and Practice*, 26(2): 279–300.

Sin, N. L. and Lyubomirsky, S. (2009), "Enhancing Well-Being and Alleviating Depressive Symptoms with Positive Psychology Interventions: A Practice-Friendly Meta-Analysis", *Journal of Clinical Psychology*, 65(5): 467–87.

Singer, P. (1972), "Famine, Affluence, and Morality", *Philosophy and Public Affairs*, 1(3): 229–43.

Smith, M. (1995), *The Moral Problem*. Oxford: Blackwell Publishing.

Snow, N. E. (1995), "Humility", *The Journal of Value Inquiry*, 29(2): 203–16.

Sobel, D. (1994), "Full Information Accounts of Well-Being", *Ethics*, 104(4): 784–810.

Sobel, D. (2009), "Subjectivism and Idealization", *Ethics*, 119(2): 336–52.

Steger, M. F., Frazier, P., Oishi, S., and Kaler, M. (2006), "The Meaning in Life Questionnaire: Assessing the Presence of and Search for Meaning in Life", *Journal of Counseling Psychology*, 53: 80–93.

Steger, M. F. and Kashdan, T. B. (2013), "The Unbearable Lightness of Meaning: Well-Being and Unstable Meaning in Life", *The Journal of Positive Psychology*, 8(2): 103–15.

Stocker, M. (1990), *Plural and Conflicting Values*. Oxford: Clarendon Press.

Stohr, K. (2009), "Minding Others' Business", *Pacific Philosophical Quarterly*, 90(1): 116–39.

Stroud, S. (2006), "Epistemic Partiality in Friendship", *Ethics*, 116(3): 498–524.

Stutzer, A. and Frey, B. S. (2008), "Stress That Doesn't Pay: The Commuting Paradox", *The Scandinavian Journal of Economics*, 110(2): 339–66.

Sumerau, J. E., Cragun, R. T., and Mathers, L. A. (2016), "Contemporary Religion and the Cisgendering of Reality", *Social Currents*, 3(3): 293–311.

Sumner, L. W. (1995), "The Subjectivity of Welfare", *Ethics*, 105(4): 764–90.

Sumner, L. W. (1996), *Welfare, Happiness, and Ethics*. Oxford: Clarendon Press.

Svenson, O. (1981), "Are We All Less Risky and More Skillful than Our Fellow Drivers?", *Acta Psychologica*, 47(2): 143–8.

Swartz, M. (2011), "Living the Good Lie", *The New York Times Magazine*, June 19, http://www.nytimes.com/2011/06/19/magazine/therapists-who-help-people-stay-in-the-closet.html?mcubz=1.

Tangney, J. P. (2009), "Humility", in S. J. Lopez and C. R. Snyder (eds.), *Oxford Handbook of Positive Psychology*. New York: Oxford University Press: 483–90.

Thomas, L. (1987), "Friendship", *Synthese*, 72(2): 217–36.

Tiberius, V. (1997), "Full Information and Ideal Deliberation", *Journal of Value Inquiry*, 31(3): 329–38.

Tiberius, V. (2000), "Humean Heroism: Value Commitments and the Source of Normativity", *Pacific Philosophical Quarterly*, 81(4): 426–46.

Tiberius, V. (2005), "Value Commitments and the Balanced Life", *Utilitas*, 17(1): 24–45.

Tiberius, V. (2006), "Well-Being: Psychological Research for Philosophers", *Philosophy Compass*, 1(5): 493–505.

Tiberius, V. (2007), "Substance and Procedure in Theories of Prudential Value", *Australasian Journal of Philosophy*, 85(3): 373–91.

Tiberius, V. (2008), *The Reflective Life: Living Wisely with Our Limits*. New York: Oxford University Press.

Tiberius, V. (2012), "Constructivism and Wise Judgment", in J. Lenman and Y. Shemmer (eds.), *Constructivism in Practical Philosophy*. Oxford: Oxford University Press: 195–212.

Tiberius, V. (2013a), "Well-Being, Wisdom, and Thick Theorizing: On the Division of Labor Between Moral Philosophy and Positive Psychology", in S. Kirchin (ed.), *Thick Concepts*. Oxford: Oxford University Press: 217–33.

Tiberius, V. (2013b), "Why Be Moral? Can the Psychological Literature on Well-Being Shed Any Light?", *Res Philosophica*, 90(3): 347–64.

Tiberius, V. (2014), *Moral Psychology: A Contemporary Introduction*. Oxford and New York: Routledge.

Tiberius, V. (2015), "Prudential Value", in I. Hirose and J. Olson (eds.), *The Oxford Handbook of Value Theory*. New York: Oxford University Press: 158–74.

Tiberius, V. (2016), "The Future of Eudaimonic Well-Being: Subjectivism, Objectivism and the Lump Under the Carpet", in J. Vittersø (ed.), *Handbook of Eudaimonic Well-Being*. Basel: Springer International: 565–9.

Tiberius, V. (2017), "Does Virtue Make Us Happy?: A New Theory for an Old Problem", in W. Sinnott-Armstrong and C. Miller (eds.), *Moral Psychology Volume 5: Virtue and Happiness*. Cambridge, MA: A Bradford Book (The MIT Press): 547–78.

Tiberius, V. and Hall, A. (2010), "Normative Theory and Psychological Research: Hedonism, Eudaimonism, and Why It Matters", *The Journal of Positive Psychology*, 5(3): 212–25.

Tiberius, V. and Plakias, A. (2010), "Well-Being", in J. Doris (ed.), *The Moral Psychology Handbook*. Oxford: Oxford University Press: 402–32.

Tsutsui, Y. (2013), "Weather and Individual Happiness", *Weather, Climate, and Society*, 5(1): 70–82.

Umberson, D., Chen, M. D., House, J. S., Hopkins, K., and Slaten, E. (1996), "The Effect of Social Relationships on Psychological Well-Being: Are Men and Women Really so Different?", *American Sociological Review*, 61(5): 837–57.

Unger, P. (1996), *Living High and Letting Die*. New York: Oxford University Press.

Van Boven, L. and Loewenstein, G. (2003), "Social Projection of Transient Drive States", *Personality and Social Psychology Bulletin*, 29(9): 1159–68.

Van der Horst, M. and Coffé, H. (2012), "How Friendship Network Characteristics Influence Subjective Well-Being", *Social Indicators Research*, 107(3): 509–29.

Van Roojen, M. (2015), *Metaethics: A Contemporary Introduction*. New York: Routledge.

Van Roojen, M. (2016), "Moral Cognitivism vs. Non-Cognitivism", *The Stanford Encyclopedia of Philosophy* (Winter 2016 Edition), ed. Edward N. Zalta, https://plato.stanford.edu/archives/win2016/entries/moral-cognitivism/.

Vazire, S. (2010), "Who Knows What about a Person? The Self–Other Knowledge Asymmetry (SOKA) Model", *Journal of Personality and Social Psychology*, 98(2): 281–300.

Velleman, J. D. (1988), "Brandt's Definition of 'Good'", *The Philosophical Review*, 97(3): 353–71.

Ware, B. (2012), *The Top Five Regrets of the Dying: A Life Transformed by the Dearly Departing*. Carlsbad, CA and New York: Hay House.

Wallace, D. F. (2009), *This is Water: Some Thoughts, Delivered on a Significant Occasion, about Living a Compassionate Life*. New York: Little, Brown.

Waterman, A. S. (ed.) (2013), *The Best Within Us: Positive Psychology Perspectives on Eudaimonia*. Washington, DC: American Psychological Association.

Whitcomb, D., Battaly, H., Baehr, J., and Howard-Snyder, D. (2017), "Intellectual Humility: Owning Our Limitations", *Philosophy and Phenomenological Research*, 94(3): 509–39.

Wiland, E. (2003), "Some Advice for Moral Psychologists", *Pacific Philosophical Quarterly*, 84(3): 299–310.

Williams, B. (1985), *Ethics and the Limits of Philosophy*. Cambridge, MA: Harvard University Press.

Williams, J. R. G. (2016), "Indeterminacy, Angst and Conflicting Values", *Ratio*, 29(4): 412–33.

Willingham, D. T. (2008), "Critical Thinking: Why Is It so Hard to Teach?", *Arts Education Policy Review*, 109(4): 21–32.

Wilson, T. D. (2002), *Strangers to Ourselves: Discovering the Adaptive Unconscious*. Cambridge, MA: Harvard University Press.

Wolitzer, M. (2014), *The Interestings*. London: Vintage.

Wolterstorff, N. (1987), *Lament for a Son*. Grand Rapids, MI: Eerdmans.

Woodard, C. (2016), "Hybrid Theories", in G. Fletcher (ed.), *The Routledge Handbook of Philosophy of Well-Being*. Oxford and New York: Routledge: 161–74.

Wylie, A. (2003), "Why Standpoint Matters", in R. Figueroa and S. Harding (eds.), *Science and Other Cultures: Issues in Philosophies of Science and Technology*. New York and London: Routledge: 26–48.

Zaki, J. and Ochsner, K. N. (2012), "The Neuroscience of Empathy: Progress, Pitfalls and Promise", *Nature Neuroscience*, 15(5): 675–80.

Index

adaptive preferences 25, 94–6, 185n32
Addario, Lynsey 109–11, 144–5, 191n7
aging 71–4, 78, 104
Alexandrova, Anna 13, 182n12, 193n17
alienation 24
animals (non-human) 136–7
anti-social values 63, 165–6, 196n18
appropriateness
  continuum of 11, 66
  degrees of 51–2, 67–8, 131–2
  of values 41, 48, 56, 67, 97
Aristotle 87–8, 134, 141, 183n17, 186n40
Ash 7, 125, 162
aspiration 171, 173, 188n17
assessments 72, 115, 121, 123, 125–6, 131, 135
assholes 91, 190n12
atheism 108
Audrey (artist) 111–12, 114, 144, 191n8
Austen, Jane 159–60
autonomy 101–2, 190n1, 195n14

balance *see* work/life balance
Bickham, Pop 22–3
bird watching 47
Bishop, Michael 143
Bob 19
Boven, Van 146–7
Brad 149
Broaden and Build Theory (Fredrickson) 143

Calhoun, Cheshire 10, 182n9
capacity for change 105, 116, 123, 151–2, 170
caring 10, 57, 89–91, 99–100, 104–5, 140–5, 154, 164
Caruso, Eugene 146
Chang, Ruth 59–60, 188n23
children 59, 95, 107, 126, 129, 136–8
Christophe 67–8

Church of Latter Day Saints 5–6, 85, 93, 106, 108, 189–90nn6,7
Church of the Nazarene 39
closed-mindedness 169–70
compassion 87–8, 92, 145, 170, 173, 192n10
confirmation bias 163
conflict 2–3, 6, 34–5, 38–9, 66–9, 79, 85, 95–6, 122
constructivism 8, 182n6, 188n21, 196n1
crib test 51, 188n20
culture 79, 91, 94, 172
Cuthbert 129–30

Dahlia 42–3
Darwall, Stephen 10, 182n8
dementia 130
Denise (the dentist) 83
desire
  defective 25, 132
  instrumental and ultimate 26, 56–7
  satisfaction 18, 24–7, 29, 31, 42–3, 45, 94, 136, 188n22
discretionary (and non-discretionary) standards 92
disvalues 34, 44, 187n12
divorce 148–9
Doris, John 8, 20, 88, 195n16

egocentric bias 145–6, 152–3
Emma (Austen) 159–60
empathy 145, 154, 158, 194nn2,7
empirical adequacy 20, 29
enjoyment 34, 67–8, 77, 80, 83
Epley, Nicholas 146
ethics x, 8–9, 17–18, 177, 181n5, 182n7
eudaimonism 18, 20, 23, 31
'Experience Machine' thought experiment (Nozick) 21, 23, 70, 189n1

faith 5–6, 85, 93, 108, 127, 144, 158, 169
family 4, 110–11

feedback strategy 153–4
fittingness 2, 38
Fredrickson, Barbara 142–3
friendship
 and autonomy 18, 23, 25, 101, 127, 158
 caring 8–10, 100, 138–9, 143–4
 differing values 105–14, 116–17
 good 140–4, 194–5n1
 governing norms 122–33
 helping friends 99–105, 135, 191nn2–3
 and humility 155–70
 interpersonal challenges 117–22
 and moral decency 170–3
 perspective-taking, challenges 144–54, 194n4
 standards of 91–2
full information theory *see* informed desire theory

Golden Rule, The 147
Goldie 106–7
grass-counter (Rawls) 82, 84
gratitude 22, 138, 142, 160, 172
Gruen, Lori 145, 147, 171, 193n16, 194n3, 196n20
Gustave-Wrathall, John 6, 85–6, 108

happiness
 emotional state theory of 63–4
 and eudaimonia 18, 20, 23, 31
 good feelings sense 13, 18, 143
 means to 56, 172
 as a value 14, 15, 29, 35, 40, 45, 51, 63–4, 115, 138, 172, 175
 value of 172
 and well-being 2, 14, 45, 181n2
Harris, Sam 177
Harry 119–20
Hawkins, Jennifer 130
Haybron, Dan 8, 22, 63–4, 72, 183n17, 184n29, 188n18, 192n12
Heathwood, C. 26, 27, 43, 183n16, 187n11, 188n22, 193n15
hedonism 18, 21–3, 29–30, 183n15, 184n28
helping
 in dire circumstances 2–4, 9, 48, 99
 easiest & easier cases 2, 5, 8–9, 25, 48, 100–5
 in friendship 99–105, 135, 191nn2–3

Hume, D. 88, 92, 176, 179–80
humility
 as de-centering 155–7, 161, 194n8
 epistemic or intellectual 156–7, 195nn11–12
 and moral decency 170–2
 and owning our limitations 156–60
 and perspective 155–6
 scope 133, 171–2, 175, 195n14, 196nn20–1
 as self-abasement 155
 too much 165–70
hybrid theories 18, 31, 183n21

Ickes, William 153
idealized desire satisfaction *see* informed desire theory
ill-being 35, 69, 83, 187n12
inappropriate values 67, 69, 118–19
informed desire theory 26, 185nn34–5
integration (psychological) 39–40, 48–9
 of valuing attitudes 40, 48
interpretation (of values) 41, 68, 73, 113, 115

James, William 158, 195n13
Joan 150
judginess 160
Jules (from The Interestings) 6–9, 15, 77, 86, 111, 119, 125, 128, 162, 175
Juri 11

Kitcher, Philip 178, 179, 196n2
Kraut, Richard 27, 183n20, 185n37, 186n40, 188n20
Kuykendall, Lauren 12, 182n10, 191n3

life satisfaction 14, 18, 22–3, 28, 30, 160, 183nn15,19, 184n29, 185n38, 187nn8,13,15
Lin, Eden 136, 192–3n13
Lonnie 26, 185n34
Lowenstein, George 146–7
Lyubomirsky, Sonja 160, 172, 181n1, 195n15

Marco 127, 132
Maxine 4–7, 9, 15, 45, 108, 125, 128, 175
meta-cognitive strategies 163
mid-life crisis 81
Millicent 130

INDEX   213

momentary well-being 46
  compared to overall well-being 47–8
Mona 25–6
morality 96, 118, 168, 170–2, 196n19
Mormon Church *see* Church of Latter Day Saints
motivation 11–13, 154, 170, 194n6

Nadelhoffer, Thomas 155, 194n8
normative adequacy 19–24, 183–4nn22–3, 184–5n31
normativity/normative ethics *see* prescriptive ethics
Nouwen, Henri J. M. 108
Nussbaum's theory 134

objective theories 18, 23–4, 31, 61–4
obligation 3, 99
Olive (dog) 137
open-mindedness 165, 196n17
oppression 94–6, 185n32, 190n13
overall well-being 47–8
owning limitations 156–7, 160, 165

painter and anatomist 179
paradigm resemblance 187–8n16
parenthood 38, 58–9, 75–6, 109, 189n2, 191nn5–6
Paul 47
Paul, Laurie 58
Peggy 56
personal identity 129
personal projects 12, 28, 187n8
Personal Projects Analysis 28
perspective taking 126, 144–54, 158, 164, 194n4
positive causal network 143
positive emotions, positive affect 14, 18, 30, 34, 64, 142–3, 160, 183n15, 185n38, 187n8
positive psychology 87
preference satisfaction *see* desire satisfaction
preferences, adaptive 25, 94–6, 185n32
prejudice 152
prescriptive ethics 27, 177, 179
problems for subjectivism
  the no guidance problem (Kraut) 27
  the problem of adaptive preferences/ values 25, 94–6
  the problem of defective desires 25–6

Raibley, Jason 13, 182n11, 187n10, 188nn16,19
Railton, Peter 24, 26, 28, 183n16, 185n33, 193n15
rational life plans 49–51, 188n19
Rawls, John 50, 82, 134
recipes (metaphor of) 179–80
reflection 78, 90, 162, 178, 186n7
reflective endorsement 38, 97, 186n7
Reflective Life, The (Tiberius) vii, 102, 190n9
religion 93, 108
resonance constraint 24
resources 143
risk, risk aversion 53–4, 107, 109, 191n7
rock climbing 107

Sander 5–7, 9, 15, 85, 93, 106, 127, 168, 169, 175
schemas 152
self-centeredness 155, 170
self-improvement (transformation) 141, 171
self-satisfaction 170
shame 14, 21, 37, 68, 189–90n7
Shaun 150, 152
Sidgwick, Henry 30, 185n33
social harmony 94
standards (for value fulfilment) 69–76
  lowering of 73–5
  objective vs. subjective 74, 189n3
  personal vs. inter-subjective 70–3
state action 135
strangers 99, 133–4, 147–8
subjective theories 24, 27, 31–2, 61–4, 82, 94–5, 185n37
Sugar (dog) 137
Sumner, L. W. 19, 24, 61, 94, 183nn19,22, 184nn23,29, 185n32, 187n15
Swartz, Mimi 6, 85, 108

talking to friends 116–17, 121–2
therapists 108, 120–1, 124, 153–4
transformative choices 60, 191n5
transformative experience 58–9

value based life satisfaction 184n29
value fulfillment 13–15, 66–97
  complexity of 114, 175
  as an ideal 1–2, 52–5

value fulfillment (*cont.*)
    for multiple values 76–86
    for a single value 69–76, 189n2
value fulfillment theory
    adaptive values 94–6
    anchored in the person 118
    and anti-social values 165–6, 196n18
    assumptions 175–6
    conclusions 65, 96–7, 138–9
    and friends 140–1
    improvement 55–61
    introduction 4, 10–18, 21, 24–31, 34, 182n13, 184n30, 185nn36,38
    main features of 34–46, 129, 186nn1–2
    multiple values 76–86, 189–90nn5–7,8
    nature of 37–46, 66–9, 186–7nn3,5,7–10,13–15
    other contexts 133–8, 192–3nn12–15
    in practice 98–100
    subjective/objective 61–4, 70, 94
    value-fulfilled life 46–55, 187–8nn16–17
    values and virtues 86–94, 190nn9,11
values 10–17, 40, 57
    adaptive 94–6
    cognitive component 11, 38, 136, 145
    disvalues 34, 44, 187n12
    emotional dispositions 45, 50
    ignoring/changing 122–33
    motivational component 11, 26, 29, 43, 52, 156
    stability 36, 76, 78–9, 88
Vazire, Simine 8, 181n4
virtue 20, 86–94, 125, 161, 192n10, 195n16

war reporters 109
Welfare and Rational Care (Darwall) 10
well-being theories
    assessments 72, 115, 121, 123, 125–6, 126, 131, 135
    comparing 20–1, 115–22
    Desire Satisfaction Theory 26, 31
    eudaimonism 18, 20, 23, 31
    hedonism 18, 21–3, 29–30, 183n15, 184n28
    hybrid theories 18, 31
    objective theories 18, 23–4, 31, 61–4
    subjective theories 24, 27, 31–2, 61–4, 82, 94–5, 185n37
    value fulfillment theory *see* value fulfillment theory
whole life perspective 46–7
Wolitzer, Meg 6–7, 111
Wolterstorff, Eric 150
Wolterstorff, Nicholas 150
work/life balance 79, 84
Wright, Jen 155

Yuja 11–12

www.ingramcontent.com/pod-product-compliance
Ingram Content Group UK Ltd.
Pitfield, Milton Keynes, MK11 3LW, UK
UKHW021325180426
11947UKWH00017B/1439